The WPA Guide to

TENNESSEE

Reissued by
the University of Tennessee Press
in Celebration of
Tennessee's "Homecoming '86"

The WPA Guide to
TENNESSEE

Compiled and Written by the Federal Writers' Project
of the Work Projects Administration
for the State of Tennessee

With a New Introduction by
Jerrold Hirsch
and a Foreword by
Wilma Dykeman

THE UNIVERSITY OF TENNESSEE PRESS

Manufactured in the United States of America.

First published in December 1939 by Viking Press.

The paper used in this book meets the minimum requirements
of the American National Standard for Permanence of Paper
for Printed Library Materials, Z39.48-1984.
Binding materials have been chosen for durability.

Library of Congress Cataloging-in-Publication Data

Tennessee, a guide to the state.
The WPA guide to Tennessee.

Reprint. Originally published: Tennessee, a guide to the state. New York : Viking Press, 1939.
Includes index.
1. Tennessee. 2. Tennessee—Description and travel—Guide-books. I. Federal Writers' Project (Tenn.)
II. Title.
F436.T47 1986 917.68'0452 85-31507
ISBN 0-87049-383-3 (alk. paper)
ISBN 0-87049-384-1 (pbk. : alk. paper)

The WPA Guide to TENNESSEE

Foreword by Wilma Dykeman, vii
New Introduction by Jerrold Hirsch, xi
The WPA Guide to Tennessee, facsimile, lix

Foreword by Wilma Dykeman

Its formal title was *Tennessee. A Guide to the State. Compiled and Written by the Federal Writers' Project of the Work Projects Administration for the State of Tennessee.* We—James Stokely and I—called it "the WPA state guide." When we traveled across the country, we took along "WPA guides" to other states. None of these—and all were of exceptionally high quality—ever proved more thoroughly researched or more readable than our green-backed, bookmarked, underscored *Tennessee.* Now, as the state celebrates a year-long Homecoming, reappearance of this valuable volume is especially appropriate and welcome.

Are you a Tennessean whose enjoyment of the smoky blue eastern mountains, rolling mid-state bluegrass meadows, or bluffs and bottomlands of the mighty Mississippi is deepened by a sense of your homeland's rich natural heritage? Turn to page 15 and let your imagination roam free: "When Boone and Scaggs hunted in Tennessee, great herds of bison grazed in the river bottoms; elk and Virginia deer ranged through the forests and canebrakes; black bears were plentiful everywhere; and wolves, panthers, and lynxes followed the trails of the hoofed animals. Beaver colonies built their dams and mud houses in some of the smaller streams and there were vast flocks of birds and game fowl. So rich in game was the region that parties of Iroquois from the Great Lakes and Choctaw from the Gulf Coast, as well as Cherokee from the Great Smokies and Chickasaw from the Mississippi bottoms, came here for months of summer hunting. Tennessee was the Land of Peaceful Hunting, a neutral ground where ancient tribal hatreds were temporarily forgotten."

Or are you unfamiliar with Tennessee's past, surprised perhaps to learn of plagues and disasters such as devastating floods that once ravaged the state? Read on page 212: "The Mississippi flood of January–February 1937 imposed upon Memphis the huge task of providing for an estimated 50,000 to 60,000 refugees. Bewildered sharecroppers, fisherfolk, and river-town people from Mississippi, Arkansas, and Tennessee—most of them suffering from hunger and exposure—poured into Memphis by train, truck, rescue boat, and 'footback.' . . . The 'rivergees' sang:

Down at the Fairgrounds on my knees,
Prayin' to the Lord to give me ease—
Lord, Lord, I got them high-water blues!"

Are you an old-timer or TV-weary newcomer who relishes reminders of storytellers who once enlivened long winter evenings or drowsy summer afternoons? You will be at home on page 141: "In every locality are men and women, Negroes and whites, who are oral libraries for neighborhood history and gossip. . . . They will tell of famous railroad wrecks, the teething troubles of children dead these many years, and they will grow eloquent on Bryan's last stand at Dayton. And from the mountains of East Tennessee to the Mississippi lowgrounds they will tell you the eerie tales of Old Kate, the Bell Witch of Robertson County, who tormented John Bell to his grave and cowed Andrew Jackson. There are stories of ghosts and badmen, of lovers, family feuds, and political killings—all true folk tales, edited and garnished by thousands of tellings."

Do your family roots run back to farm days when the famous Tennessee mule filled a role no machine can replace? Description, on page 274, will evoke the scene in Columbia on every first Monday in April when "Mule Day" welcomed "the largest street mule market in the world."

Do strange tid-bits of fact or fancy intrigue you? Try this on for size: in case you thought all victims of scalping died on the spot, meet on page 286 Dr. Patrick Vance who discovered in 1776 a method of treating scalped persons. With "a flat-pointed, straight awl" he bored a number of holes around the skull, which he found "thick and somewhat difficult to penetrate." The scalped head cured slowly, "generally taking two years."

Are you a seeker after romance? Go on page 370 to Rock Castle, "one of the first stone houses erected west of the southern Alleghenies," on land "granted to Daniel Smith as a Revolutionary War bonus." Smith served as Territorial Governor and later as U.S. Senator. "Samuel Donnelson, Andrew Jackson's law partner and brother-in-law, wished to marry Polly, the only daughter of General Smith. The lovers planned to elope. Jackson assisted Donelson in preparing a rope ladder, by means of which Polly escaped from a second-story window, and he also waited with horses until Polly and Donelson arrived. That night the marriage was performed at Jackson's home, Hunter's Hill."

Are you a visitor sometimes vexed or surprised by the paradoxes of a lively people? Add to your list the story, page 295, of "one of the first periodicals in the United States exclusively devoted to the freeing of slaves" as contradiction to Tennessee's joining with the Confederate slave states in the Civil War during which, page 57, "some of the bloodiest battles of the war were fought on Tennessee soil." Or the paradox of pacifist Alvin C. York becoming one of the most decorated soldiers of World War I.

A wealth of factual information supports the lively anecdotal style in which this book is written. Complex political intrigues and sectional controversies are summarized clearly and succinctly. Geographic contrasts and famous personalities are rendered more memorable as we follow the sixteen minutely outlined tours that are the heart of the guide. With wit and insight each tour opens fresh acquaintance with Tennessee along the miles from one border to the next. We are prepared for the tours by seventeen informative chapters developing various aspects of the state's history and growth. These are followed by specific portraits of the seven largest cities. The sixteen tours, followed by a final description of the Great Smoky Mountains National Park, touch every corner of the state.

A question remains. What of the fact that this is a book researched and written in the 1930s, published in 1939? The world of not quite fifty years later seems altered in ways that suggest centuries rather than decades of change. Auschwitz, Hiroshima, Vietnam, Watergate, rock-and-roll, tv, computers' bytes, and walks on the moon have opened new perspectives of inner and outer space.

But *Tennessee,* like the state for which it provides a guide, continues to capture our attention and hold our interest. Some of the facts and travel routes set forth here are outdated. Relations between Tennessee's two major races (Negro is a term frequently used in these pages) and between the sexes have undergone major upheaval and reexamination. Faces of villages and cities, farms and countryside have changed. But much of the basic character and the history that has shaped Tennessee and all its people is captured in these pages, authentic and appealing as the ancient ballads, the lonesome blues and spirituals, the country music that has reached around the world.

The Preface to the first edition stated: "The writers have aimed not only to supply visitors from outside the State with information that may increase their interest, but also to give Tennesseans a ready source through which their understanding of their native territory may be deepened and enriched."

They succeeded in their aim, not only for their time but for this present time of Homecoming. Visitors and natives alike can welcome this delightful companion in their celebration of Tennessee Homecoming '86.

New Introduction by Jerrold Hirsch

REDISCOVERING TENNESSEE
ROADS BACK HOME AND INTO THE FUTURE

Yesterday's Guide and Today's Traveler

An introduction to a reprint of a Federal Writers' Project state guidebook has to acknowledge fundamental questions readers now bring to these volumes: Why reprint a guidebook that is almost a half century old? Can a guidebook that tried to address Americans in the waning years of the Great Depression still speak to us with authority?

Travelers who choose to see if the Tennessee guide can help them explore the state will find their own answers to these questions. Some visiting the state for the first time may wonder whether the guide can give them insight into the vast transformations that have occurred since it was published. Those turning to the guide while revisiting the state, or a section of the state they once lived in, may dip into the guide to see if it can help them compare what they remember with what they see during their homecoming. Some Tennesseans will recognize the guide's descriptions of their home towns; others might not. "Part of the fun" in reading the guides, Archie Hobson maintains, "was seeing what they had chosen in your town; it was not likely to be the obvious 'tourist attraction.'"[1] Some are bound to be disappointed by omissions of things they thought important. The question is whether the revelations outweigh the disappointments. All will wonder whether this guide can still point out the "sights." It may help you reconsider what a sight is. The contrast between the guide's verbal images of places and the contemporary scene can prove arresting and thought provoking.

Enduring Qualities

One reason so many FWP state guidebooks are being reprinted is simply that their encyclopedic inclusiveness is unrivaled. Federal Writers located throughout the United States provided material on places that other guidebooks do not acknowledge even exist. That is as true today as it was in the thirties. And it is the reason anyone in the thirties interested in American culture paid attention to the publication of the American Guide

Series. Thus Bernard DeVoto referred to the guides as an "educational force and even a patriotic force, an honorable addition to our awareness of ourselves and of our country." Before, tourists had "only Socony and local barkers to rely on," and those sources were as thin then as they are now. In the pages of the *New Republic,* Lewis Mumford called the guides "the first attempt . . . to make the country itself worthily known to Americans." The guides, he thought, contributed to the detailed knowledge of American life that would provide the basis for a revived national art and to the regional understanding necessary for a sound future. The guides could put Americans in touch with themselves. The books were addressed to every American. Thus Mumford maintained, "these guidebooks are the finest contribution to American patriotism that has been made in our generation."[2]

Those who have attempted to revise the guides have tried to make them conform to more typical tourist literature, to emphasize entertainment and consumption, while the earlier guide writers had stressed seeing, reflection, and learning. Such revisions pare away historical and economic analysis, seemingly on the grounds that these things are not part of tourism. They avoid supposedly embarrassing matters and anything that might suggest criticism or arouse controversy. In such a volume separate essays on "The Working Man" (pp. 81–90), the "Tennessee Valley Authority" (pp. 98–103), and the "Negroes in Tennessee" (pp. 104–10) would disappear. The tourist would be given much less, if any, information about the White Caps, a vigilante group, who, modeling themselves after the Ku Klux Klan, were active in the 1890s (p. 338); about the war between the Tennessee Coal, Iron, and Railroad Company, and mine workers over the use of convict laborers (pp. 85, 336); about "members of the Amalgamated Clothing . . . locked out of the Washington Shirt Company factory [in La Follette] on May 1, 1937"; and about "the Union, cooperating with the Highlander Folk School (*see Tour 16*). In the Federal Writers' Project (FWP) approach to travel, these are some of the things travelers are asked to think about as they tour Sevierville, Coal Creek and Briceville, and La Follette.

Social commentary and economic analysis are as much a part of an FWP guide as the quaint, the odd, and famous shrines. Take Tour 15 from the state border at Albany, Kentucky through Jamestown, and ending at Valdeau, "three miles from the heart of Chattanooga," and this guide will give you a capsule social and economic history of recent developments in the area—circa the late thirties (pp. 496–97). Much of the value of these guides is linked to their tone, the mood they create—a mood which is not a part of our time. Those who have tried to revise the guides have not been able to match the research that went into the earlier volumes and thus have damaged the mood, the ability of the guides, a thirties artifact, to speak from their time to a new generation about what they called rediscovering America.

Culture on Relief

Tennessee: A Guide to the State, a volume in the American Guide Series, was written by workers on the FWP, which was part of the New Deal's Works Progress Administration (WPA). For most project employees writing guidebooks was relief work. WPA's goal of providing meaningful work for the unemployed rather than the much maligned "dole" was extended to writers.[3]

In truth few FWP employees were "writers." Instead, there were many unemployed school teachers, librarians, typists, insurance sales people, and former executives. A job with the FWP was superior to the dole, but it was still relief; many people longed for a "real" job. Some project workers stood "around leaning on their typewriters"; others were malcontents and neurotics. Unpredictable cutbacks in funding often led to severe reductions in employment. Buffeted by the ill winds of the time, unsure of their place in human affairs and never knowing when their next paychecks would be their last, most field workers still kept on sending in the material they gathered from previously unexamined records, from local informants, from their knowledge of the area they wrote about. Often the manuscripts they submitted were only semiliterate and had to be rewritten by the few "real" writers on the project. A few, like James Aswell of the Tennessee project, told a story of going to work for a local newspaper after high school, then the "Depression hit—newspapers let youngsters go—I among them. . . . Run of bad luck, got on Writers Project, put to filing cards. Quit FWP when petition for chance to write instead of filing cards denied." He was later rehired in a non-relief position and eventually became state editor of the Tennessee project. More typical was Nellie Gray Toler, unemployed but a skilled stenographer who sent in her material from Paris, Tennessee.[4]

William McDaniel, the director of the Tennessee Writers' Project, remarked of one relief worker, "her greatest attribute is that she is one of the people. She shares their views, religion, and mode of living, and through that gets . . . the essence of their community life." Given the social mores of the times, most Tennessee Federal Writers had a limited perspective that included only a part of the community. Few blacks worked on the Tennessee or any other Southern state project. With the exception of Virginia, Louisiana, and Florida, which had special black units, the few black writers on the FWP in Southern states worked alone, and none occupied a supervisory position except on the Negro units.[5]

The FWP was organized somewhat on the model of a large metropolitan newspaper with its reporters, desk men and women, and editors. Reports from local field workers went to district supervisors and then to the state FWP office before being sent to Washington editors. Thus the FWP brought together, within a national framework, individuals from all points on a local-cosmopolitan continuum for the purpose of writing books about the United States. National FWP officials took pride in a method that they asserted "allows definite local color and feeling to penetrate into the guides." They argued that this was possible because "the material has actually been collected locally, on the spot by Guide workers who are native to the location and catch its real spirit."[6]

A Format for the Rediscovery of America

The Tennessee guide follows the general format of the American Guide Series. It is divided into three sections: general essays, descriptions of Tennessee's major cities, and automobile tours. The essays provide an overview, a survey of such topics as the contemporary scene, climate, geography, history, industry, agriculture, racial groups, labor, folklore, literature, and architecture. In the opening essay, "Cross Section of a Threefold State," the reader is reminded of what is still a persistent fact in Tennessee life: "East, Middle, and West Tennessee . . . in many ways are like separate states" (p. 3). These essays serve as both introduction and summary, an invitation to explore and a preview of what the traveler would find. The aim of the city descriptions is to provide a brief characterization of the city's contemporary functions, its physical environment, and history.

The federal writers and their critics, however, have always insisted that the heart of the guides is the automobile tours. *Tennessee: A State Guide* offers sixteen tours, not counting side tours and a special section on the Great Smoky Mountains. At first glance these may seem the most outdated aspect of the guide. Look for Interstate 40 in vain. Keep in mind that the roadbeds for still existing routes have been shifted over the intervening years.

And yet it is in the tours that one finds the routes that take the traveler from one section to another, across the French Broad River, across Stone's River at Burr's Landing; one notes that "between Dixon and Camden the clay-and-gravel road banks slant evenly back from the concrete as though sliced off with a knife," until between Brownsville and Memphis one finds "the dark Hatchie River bottoms and the level cotton lands of the Loosahatchie and Wolf Rivers" (p. 453). Along the way the reader learns about such things as what crops were grown in various sections of this route, where the alleged moonshine capital of the world was, how the moonshiners signaled each other that the "revenooers" were coming (p. 432), what life at an early frontier post was like (p. 452), how Burr's Landing and Aaron Burr are connected (p. 450), and where Indian mounds can be found (p. 454).

This tour, like the others, tells of the ordinary doings of the famous and the extraordinary doings of the ordinary. The Dandridge County Court has the marriage bond of David Crockett and Polly Finley and the record of an earlier license issued to Crockett and Margaret Elder and "returned unused" (p. 434); in the Huntingdon Courthouse a record book "saved" from two courthouse fires "shows that Crockett was paid a bounty here for wolf skins" (p. 459); the connection between the McSpadden House, Samuel McSpadden, Andrew Jackson, and the battle of New Orleans is explained (p. 434). The Archibald Roane Monument provides an occasion to recount an incident in the feud between Jackson and John Sevier. Because a FWP field worker had an eye for the significant detail, we get a quote from an official legislative report of a case in which Sevier is accused of fraudulent land dealings (p. 436). A few miles down the road the site of a "near" duel between Sevier and Jackson gives the tour writer a chance to offer the reader rather extraordinary details to relish (p. 437). A capsule biography of Jackson is offered when the tour reaches the Hermitage (pp. 448–50). It may, however, be the details of Jackson as gambler, horseracer, and duelist that will appear as the freshest and most interesting (pp. 450–51).

One does not have to be famous to have one's extraordinary doings commemorated in the guidebook accounts of American history and life. The old Mabry place provides an occasion for a vignette of antebellum life and this detail of war-related passions: "A quarrel between two Union soldiers ended in the murder of one in spite of Mrs. Mabry's attempt to save the man's life by locking him in the lower front room" (p. 436). The Fur Craft Shop of J. W. Hickey and several roadside stands he operates are located near Mammy's Creek. Hickey's skills as a trapper and curer of hides are described and related to local traditions (pp. 439–40).

The FWP guides focused on the daily and seasonal round of communal life in their portrait of America: turn to the Tennessee guide's description of the slaves who made the bricks for the Thomas J. Page House (p. 436); the sorghum making along the roadsides around Camden (p. 458); the foot washing and communion service at Hollow Rock Primitive Baptist Church near Bruceton (p. 459); the Brunswick stew suppers, the shopping crowds downtown on Saturday, and the Taylor Tabernacle Revival in the area of Brownsville and Haywood County (p. 462). The utopian dreamers at Ruskin and Nashoba are also part of this tour's portrait (pp. 455–57, 463–64). So too is a description of the industry and economic life of such cities as Lebanon (p. 446). Confronting a myriad of facts about American places with a sense of wonder, national FWP officials thought that the tourist following the automobile tours would find no American places and landscapes uninteresting.

A Changing Tennessee Scene, Enduring Questions, and the Tennessee Guide

So much has changed that thoughtful readers picking up this book will ask why they should consult it and how they can use it. Tennessee state historian Wilma Dykeman tells us that Fanny Wright often said, "Ask why."[7] If you are not quite sure who Fanny Wright was, what connection she had with Tennessee, or how she fits into this Tennessee guide, you can begin to find out by turning to pages 219 and 463–64 of this volume. The authors of the Tennessee guide never intended to give definitive answers but only to offer a starting point, a place to begin for those who wished to explore the state, to follow the guidebook tours by car or only as armchair travelers. Part of the answer to the guide's continuing value is that it is a starting point with special qualities that point directions that can be found nowhere else.

There are certainly more extensive and probing studies available of Fanny Wright and her Nashoba experiment, but none asks you to ponder these matters as you cross the Tennessee landscape. Surprisingly, the guide does not take you to the actual site of Nashoba, now in a subdivision of Germantown, a wealthy Memphis suburb. But try following Tour 12 going east on U.S. 70 until the highway "crosses Wolf River, 217 *m.*, not far north of the former NASHOBA, a plantation established in 1827 by Frances Wright (1795–1852)" (p. 463). Today when you arrive at that point on U.S. 70 there is a busy intersection, gasoline stations, several fast food *places,* and—practically lost in this ubiquitous modern urban scene—a historical marker about Frances Wright. The effect can be—should be—jarring. It requires an imaginative leap to make a connection between this scene and the attempt at Nashoba to address questions about the meaning of freedom, equality, citizenship, and the place of blacks in America—questions which Wright knew that a nation that prided itself on its "democratic" society and manners would have to address.[8] It is a leap worth making. It was the kind of jump from the seen to the unseen that Federal Writers constantly presented travelers as they sought to help them identify the places they were passing through and to help inhabitants strengthen their sense of possessing a place in the landscape.

For the Federal Writers everything in the environment could potentially be included in automobile tours to serve as symbols recalling past experience and creating shared information for both traveler and resident, a sense of familiarity with a place. The guide also recounts the efforts of Tennesseans to define, to create a sense of place, to embrace it:

> On March 25, 1901, Ripley's first charter of Jan. 17, 1838, was repealed; when on April 3, 1901, a new charter was granted, the corporate limits were outlined: . . . "thence north 85 degrees, east to a black gum marked with a cross and with a misletoe in the top, and with a blue bird sitting on a limb, which is a short distance east of Ed Johnson's horse lot. . . ." (p. 422)

The guidebooks tried to make buildings and other objects part of the landscape in which they were located. They linked facts of significance to objects. The object—house, inn, jail, cemetery, church, factory—offered the occasion to introduce the traveler to the economic, social, and cultural history of a place. If the information was *interesting* enough it could be offered even though the object with which it was associated was no longer present. The odd fact, the legend, the career of local figures or of national figures in their local aspects are not trivia in the context of these tours. Take Tour 16: cross the Wolf River, go through Byrdstown past Starpoint, take a right at State 53, and you come to the birthplace of Cordell Hull, who long before he became secretary of state in the Franklin Roosevelt administration was a shy youth noted locally "for two accomplishments—his ability to pilot log rafts safely down the river, and his skill in debate" (p. 507).

Material reality transports travelers into another world; makes them ponder the juxtaposition of past and present. Following the tours the travelers can view the built environment not only as evidence of the present but, like an archeologist, as the revelation of successive phases of a civilization:

> HARRIMAN, 64.5 *m.* (792 alt., 4,488 pop.), is a neat and prosperous city surrounded by beautiful rolling hills. The town is the trade center of a fertile farming region; its interests center primarily about large hosiery and woolen mills.
>
> In 1845 Col. R. K. Byrd bought large holdings and established a plantation here . . . . Nearly fifty years later the East Tennessee Land Company bought 10,00 acres of his land, planning a city that would have a population of 50,000 . . . the first 574 lots were sold at an auction conducted by the president of the land company, Gen. Clinton D. Fisk, who in 1888 had been a candidate for the Presidency on the Prohibition Party ticket. . . . The Women's Christian Temperance Union had much to do with the early life of the place, which was named for Gen. Walter Harriman, a former Governor of New Hampshire, and incorporated on Feb. 7, 1891. (p. 362)

"Every effort," national FWP director Henry Alsberg told state FWP officials, "should be made to make the traveler feel when he is traveling this or that highway that he is covering historic ground." It was, he thought, ground both travelers and inhabitants could share. A major theme in all the guides was that residents as well as outsiders needed to become better acquainted with their homes and the landscape in which they were located. The *Kansas City Star* supported the FWP on the grounds that "it is surprising how little the average resident of Kansas City knows of the background of his community."[9] Tennessee Federal Writers were less blunt but made the same point: "[they] aimed not only to supply visitors from outside the state with information that may increase their interest, but also to give Tennesseans a ready source through which their understanding of their native territory may be deepened and enriched" (p. vii).

The guides tried to create a sense that the places tourists passed through were part of a distinctive landscape. Alert travelers following Tour 14 from the Kentucky line to Nashville would learn that they were not the first people to pass this way. A lengthy quote from Colonel Valentine Sevier's letter to his brother General John Sevier concerning an Indian attack on November 11, 1794 reminds the traveler that others have been here before him: "Dear Brother: The news from this place is desperate with me. . . . my station was attacked by about forty Indians. . . . They also killed Ann King and her son James, and scalped my daughter Rebecca. I hope she will recover. . . . Such a scene no man ever witnessed before. Nothing but screams and the roaring of guns, and no man to assist me for some time" (p. 493). The guide writers give James Weir an opportunity to reach across the chasm of time and describe a street scene in Knoxville on a County Court Day in 1798: "I saw men jesting, singing, swearing; women yelling from doorways" (p. 235). By offering travelers and inhabitants references to past experiences associated with a specific spot, to a place that though it had changed over time continued to exist, these tours can make readers conscious, that Americans too, occupy a point in time, as well as space.

Still, replete with fascinating material as it is, can the Tennessee guide serve as a reference work, a ready source of pertinent information today? When this guide was published, 62 percent of Tennessee's people made their living on the farm; today less than 6 percent do. Mechanization has transformed farming. The average farm is four times the size of the farms the Tennessee guide writers knew. And Tennessee farms are actually much larger than that since many farmers increase the size of the land they farm by renting. This makes it economically feasible for them to use large scale equipment. The guide appeared at a time when almost one in five Tennessee farmers were sharecroppers. Almost half did not own their own farms. The census no longer asks questions about sharecroppers. The landscape of rural life has been transformed.[10] A photograph of cotton pickers, like the ones on pages 83 and 418, are now historic documents. Agricultural poverty has not disappeared, but the self-sufficiency the guide describes is more a part of some utopian's ideal society than a current reality. Gone are such communities as those around Mountain City or Pleasant Hill where the guide tells us mountain families walk or ride muleback to town, ready to pay in kind—green beans, pokes of popcorn, buckets of sorghum—or to swap—eggs, chicken, butter—for "store-boughten" delicacies because "cash money" is scarce (pp. 316, 466).

In ways the Federal Writers could not foresee, the transformation in agriculture led to urban changes that make the guide's descriptions of Tennessee's cities not merely out of date, but also written from a perspective that seems to bear little relation to the cities we know. The boundaries of today's Memphis are not those of yesterday and will hardly be those of tomorrow. Suburbanization was a long-term trend that did not capture the interest of the Federal Writers; we can hardly fail to notice it. The populations of Tennessee cities like Memphis and Knoxville have grown in recent years largely by annexing unincorporated towns; otherwise, suburban growth would have far outpaced the city's. Only decisions about political and administrative boundaries hid this fact. The Tennessee guide's city walking tours centered around downtown areas seem part of a lost urban heritage.[11]

And perhaps the "sights" in this seemingly transformed Tennessee are now totally different. Certainly, there are tourist attractions that did not exist in the thirties. At the least every local tourist bureau and chamber of commerce thinks everyone needs to visit them. Events in the intervening years have also created a host of new sights. You cannot find in this guide where Graceland is, the Country Music Museum, Oak Ridge, or the Lorraine Hotel. And it could be argued that Elvis Presely, Roy Acuff, the Manhattan Project part of the building of the atomic bomb, and the assassination of Martin Luther King, Jr. have done more to change life in Tennessee and the United States, than say, the ins and outs of Washington politics. And if there were another Federal Writers' Project that could really revise the Tennessee guide, all of this would deserve as much attention as Andrew Jackson, John Sevier, and J.W. Hickley receive.

Inherited Questions: Understanding the Tennessee Guide

The Tennessee guide is rich enough to be informative and fun for anyone who gives it a chance, but it can be more than that. For the guide to still speak to us, to have some authority, to guide us in our travels today, it is necessary to think about what the New Deal officials who directed the FWP were hoping to accomplish and the issues facing Tennesseans in the late thirties. For the challenges they faced, the questions they were trying to answer are in many ways now ours.

American Identity, Cultural Pluralism, and Romantic Nationalism

Not only were writers in the 1930s trying to rediscover America as so many commentators then and since have pointed out, they were also trying to redefine America. The work of the FWP was part of this effort. The studies published by the project tried to broaden the definition of who and what was American. They addressed inherited questions about the nature of American identity, nationality, and culture.[12]

American identity and nationality have always been problematic. The classic answer that St. John de Crevecoeur offered almost two hundred years ago to his famous query, "What then is this new man the American?" was based on the assumption that the American was "either a European or a descendent of a European." The passage of time has not made the answer any clearer; it has only shown the inadequacy of previous answers. Thus, historian Robert Wiebe observes that "each generation [of Americans] has to rediscover America, for its meaning has been a problem that could neither be ignored nor resolved." And time and again Wiebe finds that "try as they might most Americans stopped short of encompassing the nation. . . . Each generation passed to the next an open question of who really belonged to American society." The FWP tried to rediscover America, to encompass the nation, and to provide grounds for unity. In the American Guide Series (and it is helpful to think of the Tennessee guide as only a chapter in this larger work), guidebooks to every state in the union and to numerous cities, counties, and geographic areas, the FWP tried to provide the nation with a "road map for the cultural rediscovery of America."[13]

National FWP officials developed programs that they thought would make a significant contribution to American culture. In both idealistic and practical terms they contemplated the relationship between government and culture, and ultimately between culture and democracy. These programs were developed in the context of national depression, New Deal recovery programs, and the growing crisis in international affairs—the rise of the Fascist powers. They were infused with the idea that a rediscovery, an acknowledgment, and finally a celebration of the nation's cultural pluralism offered a basis for national integration that was inclusive, not exclusive, and democratic, not coercive, a form of unity based on cultural understanding, not merely the administrative ties of a large bureaucracy. Cultural pluralism complemented New Deal programs that attempted to address the problems of farmers, industrial workers, blacks, and ethnic groups. The FWP's American Guide Series tried to contribute to this goal by documenting American diversity. Other FWP programs probed deeper. By giving ordinary Southerners, ex-slaves, members of ethnic groups, urban workers an opportunity to speak directly to their fellow citizens, to share their life histories (what we would today call oral history) the FWP intended to reopen social, cultural, and historical issues that had been covered over with clichés. [14]

In trying to understand the thirties, one student of the subject argues that "no fact is more significant than the general and even popular 'discovery' of the concept of culture"; culture not in the traditional view as the achievement of great thinkers and artists of the past—what Matthew Arnold had called "the sum total of the best that had been said and thought in the world"—but in the anthropological sense, as a group's shared values and way of life. From this point of view American culture was not a European import, but something Americans had always possessed, only they had overlooked it. Now they sought to rediscover it. What they discovered was a pluralistic American culture. The guidebooks contributed to this rediscovery. [15]

FWP officials rejected the common notion that the United States lacked an indigenous folk culture because there was as yet no American race or nation, though they echoed romantic nineteenth-century ideas that knowledge of the cultural creativity of the "people" would provide the basis for great national achievements in the high arts. What the FWP helped discover was a pluralistic American culture, not the culture of Anglo-Saxon Americanism or the culture of an emerging American race. They did not use nationality, race, and culture as interchangeable terms. In discussing American culture, FWP officials used such phrases as "composite America," "the Negro as American," and "introducing America to Americans." They thought the study of the experience and cultural expressions of ordinary Americans could provide the basis for a revitalized national culture. [16]

National FWP officials were, however, pluralists as well as romantic nationalists. They insisted all groups had to be included in the national portrait they were trying to paint. It was their cosmopolitanism that made a romantic cultural pluralism possible. While they valued particular cultural differences, they thought that the parochialisms that made it difficult for individuals of different religions, classes, and races to understand, accept, and appreciate each other could be overcome. They took the cosmopolitan belief that it is necessary to transcend all parochialisms in order to be able to draw on the experience of a multiplicity of groups and thus to achieve a fuller human experience, and they translated it into national terms. As they looked at it, for Americans of different regional or ethnic backgrounds to be interested in each other as fellow citizens was a form of cosmopolitanism.[17]

Cultural nationalism has often been exclusive, reactionary, illiberal, and racist. The pluralist version of cultural nationalism, however, turns diversity into a virtue and celebrates it as a source of national vitality. The creation of an atmosphere in which cultural pluralism could develop was a triumph of New Deal nationalism. Conscious of developments in other countries, FWP officials saw a choice between an inclusive national community that recognized and encouraged differences, cultural pluralism, and an exclusive community that sought unity through the suppression of racial and cultural differences, totalitarianism. FWP officials valued *both* pluralism and unity. They thought mutual cultural understanding could provide a basis for national integration that provided a transcendent feeling of being part of more than a large bureaucratic society. New Deal officials intended for the government to play an increasing role in guiding and promoting both economic and cultural integration.[18]

The Washington editorial staff looked at the guides as an educational venture. They would provide "a new and valuable textbook," a "handy reference guide to America," which would serve as both tourist guide and "a social history of the country." Education in this vision was helping the nation develop its awareness and understanding of its own culture. It would enable Americans to take a good look at themselves in all their diversity and to see themselves in places and people who, while different from them, were also fellow Americans. Such an education, national FWP officials thought, would help create a cultural integration that could overcome the fragmentation of modern life without demanding everybody be the same or by excluding those who were different.[19]

Creating A FWP Guidebook

How were such goals to be achieved? The state director of the Minnesota FWP remembered initially "being completely baffled by the tendency of all federal editors to regard us as inhabiting a region romantically different from any other in the country." She eventually concluded that "this romanticism of the Washington editorial mind, disconcerting as it often was, is probably responsible for most of the best writing in all the guides." Katherine Kellock, national FWP tours editor, recalled that field workers were forced to dig to find the "minor differences among towns superficially much alike." State FWP offices that submitted manuscripts to the national office labeling some places dull or uninteresting had the material returned with specific suggestions for further research. National FWP officials proceeded on the romantic assumption that "hardly any place in America is wholly uninteresting."[20]

Alsberg talked about creating guides to America that could be sold in "tea-houses" and "up-to-date" gasoline stations. By playing on the multiple meanings of the word guide in determining the purpose of the American Guide Series, FWP officials sounded themes that would resonate with the interests of the diverse audience they sought. In search of an audience that would help justify the expenditure of public funds on the writing of guidebooks, FWP officials defined a guidebook whose encyclopedic aspects promised something of interest for virtually everyone—if you are not interested in the Tennessee guide's essay on TVA you might be interested in the essay on "Sports and Recreation," or Indians, or geology, or tours that take you to Indian mounds, or that recount the doings of Andrew Jackson, or describe tobacco growing. The list is endless. They aimed to make the work of "value to historians, scientists, teachers, and their students." At the same time the traditional tourist function of guidebooks was always kept in mind. And yet, FWP officials repeatedly insisted the American Guide Series would be "far more than a tourist enterprise." They claimed that in both scope and content the FWP guidebooks would be unprecedented: "No previous guidebooks were concerned with the historical, social, and economic backgrounds of the places they described."[21]

Celebrating American Diversity

FWP officials viewed the guides as a declaration of America's cultural maturity and independence from Europe. "Every other civilized country," national FWP director Henry Alsberg pointed out, "possesses a substantial guidebook." By awakening "the interest of people in their own cities and reveal[ing] to them the sights which they have been missing" the guides would show Americans there was as much to see and discover at home as in Europe. On this point there has been constant uncertainty, accompanied by frequent declarations of cultural independence and maturity, such as Ralph Waldo Emerson's "American Scholar," and Van Wyck Brooks's "America's Coming of Age." The Federal Writers' Project offered yet another such declaration. Yet for every Emerson and Whitman celebrating a new land presenting the individual a chance to develop an original relationship to the universe there has been a Henry James and a Van Wyck Brooks to lament the lack of institutions and traditions. FWP programs were a response to a felt need for a unifying tradition. National FWP officials assumed that a celebration of the nation's cultural pluralism, knowledge of the experience of ordinary American's, and a cosmopolitan attitude toward the country's diversity could fill the functions of a unifying tradition.[22]

FWP officials knew there were many Americans who felt that "every place I saw [on vacation in the United States] was just like every other place. All the houses were built the same way. All the people wore the same kind of clothes and drove the same kind of automobiles. When you see one place you see them all." They had an answer: "This man has seen nothing because he has gone about with no appreciation of what his country has to interest travellers." The truth was that "scattered throughout the American states are hundreds of communities which possess distinctive, scenic, historic, cultural, or economic features and which are known to only small groups of people." Without a guidebook "a man may traverse the Oregon Trail and see nothing under his feet but dirt."[23]

Although the guides were not put together solely with tourists in mind, the reader as tourist became the controlling symbol that dominated decisions about gathering and organizing material and the style in which it should be presented. The Federal Writers, however, did not condescend to the reader. The format, materials, and style made demands on the tourist-reader they envisioned—too many for the casual tourist. Rather, their tourist-readers had to want to explore and rediscover their country, to broaden their sense of the national community.

The essays, national FWP officials advised local writers, should summarize general tendencies and provide a historical background "with cross-references to specific manifestations in localities." Thus the Tennessee guide essay on history when it discusses the founding of the Ku Klux Klan at Pulaski in Giles County has a paraenthetical reference to Tour 7 (p. 58). The manifestation was the concrete example for the generalization; an example that could be visualized "localized and attached to the spot, tour, or city where they belong." One set of instructions pointed out that "strangers to your State would not be so much interested in the size of the peach crop as *where* it is grown; what are the things to see; picking, processing, etc.—the *story* of peaches."[24] One good example of this technique is the Tennessee guide's description of Mule Day in Columbia—read it and know something about the story of Tennessee farming (pp. 274–75).

It was not that difficult a task, according to national FWP officials. It did, however, require imagination: "Mention any of the great American industries or staple crops and the imagination is at once stimulated to picture places and people at work; lumberjacks in Oregon, Minnesota, Maine . . . beat workers in Colorado, steel workers and coal miners in Pennsylvania, and the like" and the description in this volume of the way "tobacco dominates the scene as it dominates the economic life of the section" between the Kentucky line and Nashville (p. 391). This went beyond the call for graphic tour copy, the "vivid picture," to encourage local FWP workers and guide readers to see ordinary Americans at work, as the stuff of romance, as heroes.[25]

Cultural nationalism was also promoted on practical economic grounds. Travel, FWP officials constantly emphasized, had a commercial dimension. Alsberg argued that by making Americans aware of "what there is to see right here at home," the guides could "bring back part of the six hundred million dollars spent in average years by Americans on travel outside this country." As a New Deal relief program the FWP had little choice but to point out ways in which their agency could contribute to economic recovery. Despite their willingness to sound commercial themes, national FWP officials were determined to keep the guidebooks from becoming simply promotional material. FWP editors in the Washington office eliminated such superlatives as largest, best, greatest, and prettiest from guidebook drafts submitted by state FWP offices. The rule of thumb, they advised local Federal Writers, was as much as possible to avoid words ending in "est." They demanded accurate observation and pertinent details rather than florid expressions and flowery hyperbole. They wanted a style that would help the traveler see and reflect. And unlike much of today's tourist "literature" the Tennessee guide and the other volumes in the series rarely enthuse or boast.[26]

The FWP manuals that guided the work of local project workers called for essays that would create a picture of ordinary life, past and present. Sometimes, as in the Tennessee history essay, the writer becomes a storyteller, the transmitter of tales: "The old Wilderness Road and Avery's Trace were congested with 'movers' during the summer months—great topheavy Conestoga wagons drawn by oxen, broad-tired farm wagons piled high with household goods, and crude sledges with runners of hickory or oak; befrilled gentlemen astride blooded horses, rawboned farmers on hairy plow-nags . . ." (p. 48). Such narrative passages elicited from reviewers talk about the guides as an epic tale recounting an American saga.

A New Deal View of American History and Art

In the guides there was an easy blending of an affirmation of diversity as a source of cultural vitality and traditional American ideas of progress—cultural and economic history as the unfinished story of American growth. For example, in this volume the essays on industry and agriculture end with lists pointing to accomplishments and progress: "On the whole, there is a wide diversification of activities, as shown by the U.S. Census of Manufactures for 1935" (p. 73). The social ills produced by the Depression and the social conflicts and costs associated with change recede from view. It is the New Deal of recovery, not reform that is stressed, or to put it another way, New Deal reforms are endorsed because they, like industrialism, promise material progress, not because they promise to remedy social injustice and promote equality. Despite the Depression, the New Deal had restored faith that America's material progress would continue. In the Tennessee guide this faith was closely linked to high hopes that the TVA would transform life in the region.

The guidebook essays offered a view of both American history and art that dealt with the past as a source of reassurance about the future but significantly only to a very limited extent with the present. They all followed an historical approach, whether concerned with such topics as transportation or architecture. Such an approach followed from the romantic nationalist assumptions FWP officials held.

As romantic nationalists, who were also pluralists, Washington editors insisted on a broad panoramic-like display of past endeavors that focused on ordinary Americans in all their ethnic, racial, occupational, and regional diversity. This, they hoped, would contribute to the creation of an inclusive democratic community. Artists would have a key role to play in attaining the fulfillment of this vision. In creating an art that was accessible, available, and meaningful to ordinary Americans, an art that reflected American diversity, artists would help create such a community. This could only be accomplished if artists were familiar with the forms of expression that had grown out of the past experience of the American people, if working with that knowledge they could give expression to the nature and meaning of their lives, and if they could substitute for alienation and isolation an organic relationship to their community like that FWP officials assumed existed in the past. Virtually all the essays in the guidebooks embody a vision of the relationship between past experience and the development of a culture, between experience and expression. It was a New Deal view of American history that, while it provided only limited analysis, did develop a hopeful myth that mixed traditional American themes with New Deal pluralism and reform in an effort to achieve a new basis for national unity.[27]

By deliberately not drawing a line between high culture and folk culture the essays on the arts could begin with those forms or art closest to the experience of ordinary Americans in the past, and offer them as the basis for a tradition. They argued that if present-day artists were to draw on this tradition, they, like its creators, would no longer be isolated from their community; they would succeed in creating an accessible and socially relevant art. At the same time, these essays hailed the growth of artistic institutions that could make all forms of cultural expression accessible to ordinary Americans. Thus high culture was no longer to be restricted to a privileged elite. Educational institutions would foster a new appreciation for art by encouraging everyone to participate in and learn about the creative experience. These essays cited the other New Deal WPA arts projects as both signs of and contributors to these developments[28] (see, for example, the list of the Federal Art Project's activities in Tennessee on page 170).

The guidebook essays on the arts make an effort to broadly define their subject. Thus the essay in the Tennessee guide on writers claims that the literature of the early settlers is found in the written forms with which they transacted the business of their everyday lives. This material is valuable, for "these trail-clearers, fort-builders, and Indian-fighters" have left "the framework of their collective biography" in these writings (p. 145). A broad definition of literature made it possible to assert that the United States had an indigenous literature independent of Europe. With a literary past rooted in the experience of ordinary people, the future held the promise of a great literary flowering.

Overall the guidebook essays on architecture were markedly superior in style and content to the other essays on the arts. The architectural manual instructed Federal Writers in the basic tenets of a modern functional approach. Architectural history was not to be thought of as simply a succession of styles; for "style is a matter of conception; not a means of treatment. It was only an analysis of form, structure, and purpose that made it possible to 'place' a building stylistically." Washington editors objected to a sensibility that would not call a building architecture unless it could identify a traditional high-culture historical style. From that perspective, neither the vernacular Southern dog-trot, a Sullivan skyscraper, public construction such as a TVA dam, nor a housing project were architecture. Rejecting such an approach the guides had architectural essays like the Tennessee one which dealt with all of the above except the Sullivan skyscraper.[29]

In all the guide essays on the arts there is a marked tendency to oversimplify the relationship between art and environment and to both assume and demand that the arts simply mirror the external social life of the majority. Such an approach short-changes ideas. Difficult material conditions is the stock explanation of the failure of early settlers to create art in the traditional forms of high culture. Little is said about their attitudes toward art. The possibility of artists as questioners, let alone as adversaries of their culture, is hardly present. The intellectual world of artists and the ideas embodied in their work receive little attention.[30]

Tradition, Place, and the FWP Guides

Beyond offering a vision of the past and the future, everything in the guides also functioned to create a sense of place. More than the essays, the tours were the key to this. Discussion of FWP publications among FWP officials and in the press proceeded on the assumption that knowledge of the United States, its diverse people and regions, would paradoxically create both a cosmopolitan feeling and a sense of primordial, inherited and unquestioned, family-like ties. They offered a way of rediscovering and celebrating a diverse landscape, a way of creating a consciousness of the United States that could feel at home in a diverse land—a consciousness that could fulfill the role of a unifying tradition. They were a way of looking at, approaching, and finally infusing the landscape with emotional and symbolic content. Knowledge of a variety of American places was offered as a way of making the abstraction America into a symbolic place. Identity and place became two sides of the same coin. Travelers were to know who they were by knowing where they were.

National FWP officials and critics saw the tours as a helpful response to the problematic nature of American nationality, identity, and culture, and to the complex question of the place of tradition in the modern world. Both concerns were voiced in a newspaper reporter's description of what she thought the Federal Writers were learning about America. Mary Hornaday conceded that "the history of American settlements is brief compared with those in other parts of the world." Nevertheless, she was convinced that the FWP's initial plans for a single national guide would produce a work that "will prove to its readers that it is not too soon for them to have customs, personages and landmarks distinguishing them from their neighbors." She also saw it as providing a counterweight to ubiquitous modern developments: "Chain stores and gasoline filling stations may give the impression that all American towns are alike, but writers of the American Guide have discovered that down underneath every settlement has an individuality all its own."[31]

The guides offered their readers a sense of place as well as identity, for in these guides American identity was closely tied to creating a feeling of definition and possession about the diverse places that constituted the nation. The tours were often appreciated for the way they juxtaposed diverse facts. One critic saw in the tours "the profuse disorder of nature and life, the dadaist jumble of the daily newspaper." Again one discovers a paradox that highlights the tension between modernity and tradition and the effort of FWP officials to cope with the conflict. On the one hand, the guidebook tours did parallel the arbitrary juxtaposition of materials that the Dadaists offered as art. Dadaism conveyed the idea that context and place had been destroyed by modern life. Yet using a method that resembled Dadaism, Federal Writers tried to create a sense of distinguishable places. Perhaps only in recent times would a juxtaposition of facts linked only with regard to place, but by no theme or thesis, seem a way of asserting the importance of place and tradition in a changing world.[32]

While many saw the automobile as a modern force contributing to the destruction of a sense of place, Federal Writers intended to make it possible for the imagined tourist-reader to tour different places, to identify them, to feel a sense of possession regarding them, and to orient his identity around his awareness of American diversity. Modern forms of transportation that seemed to threaten all sense of place and tradition could in the FWP's guide to America be used as a vehicle for discovery and exploration.

An FWP Invitation to See America

If Americans "really" wanted to know their country, they would, according to FWP officials, have to become "familiar with the [nation's] great resources of scenery, recreation, its history, its industry, its cities, and *infinitely varied landscape*" (emphasis added). The Tennessee guide acknowledges that "the Tennessee that the tourist knows, with its standard highways and hotdog stands, its industrial areas, cities, and hustling chambers of commerce—all smoothly integrated in surface America—is much like the tourist's Maine or Ohio" (p. 134) but insists that is only the surface, an appearance. FWP officials acknowledged that modern life made it possible "to jump from New York to San Francisco in about sixteen hours" but nevertheless did not think that the speed with which Americans could now cover space had to destroy a traditional sense of place and meaning if the traveler remembered that such phenomena as transcontinental flight did "not mean there is nothing to see in the thousands of miles you have skipped." If Americans stopped and looked they would see "we are a nation of infinite variety, of various races, historic developments, religious observances, and even of language and dialect."[33]

Ironically, during the Great Depression, the FWP guides invited Americans to travel. Everyone was invited. This was not an aristocratic grand tour, a finishing school for an elite. The invitation was democratic in theory though phrased in middle class terms. The FWP asked Americans, either literally or imaginatively to step outside their daily routine, to leave their places in the spatial, social, and class structure of their nation—to travel. They could share the excitement of the explorers' sense of new discoveries with the tourists' certainty of knowing exactly where they were.

Anthropologists studying tourism have described the individual leaving the ordinary workaday world to vacation as engaging in the modern world's equivalent of the more traditional alternation of profane and sacred days. And some of the FWP rhetoric about travel places the proposed tours in the tradition of religious pilgrimage. But while traditional pilgrimages drew individuals out of their diverse places in the social world into a community focusing on symbols of unity, the guidebook tours emphasized social differentiation. What is seemingly being worshipped (or in more secular terms explored, studied, honored) is society itself, not anything transcendent. From this perspective Federal Writers hardly differed from totem-makers, who without being fully aware of it, were constructing ways for their society to worship itself.[34]

Still, the FWP journey through America involved more than self-worship. The guides invited Americans to travel not only for the opportunity to live temporarily outside their ordinary world, but also for the chance to develop a sense of community with people different from themselves, people who might appear foreign and strange but who were fellow Americans. This emphasis on community paradoxically sought both to preserve differences and to transcend them.

The Cultural Politics of Landscape Images

Actual landscapes, cultural geographers have demonstrated, are often idealized and made into symbols. Donald Meinig has shown that Main Street America is one such symbol. In the idealized version of the community represented by this symbol the people are predominantly white Anglo-Saxon Protestants. This, despite the fact, that as Meinig points out "a panorama of the landscape of most towns in the Middle West . . . would reveal several other groups," Irish-Catholic laborers, Poor Whites, blacks, and "new industries full of 'foreigners.'" In this case, he concludes, "the symbol did not encompass the actual diversity of its landscape reference." The gap between symbol and fact was eventually seen as a gross distortion of reality. As Meinig observes, a large body of American literature reflects the revolt against Main Street as an inadequate symbol of American community. Although Main Street still has evocative power, Meinig's evidence indicates that its greatest appeal was roughly in the period from 1890 to 1930. In their own way, the FWP guidebooks were part of the American literature that sought to discredit the Main Street symbol, for the FWP embraced all American landscapes as symbolizing aspects of the nation. In sharp contrast to an idealized Main Street that excluded many non-WASP Americans, national FWP officials worked to create guidebooks reflecting an ethnically and regionally diverse America. While the Main Street symbol embodied the view that basic American virtues were found only in the dominant WASP groups, the FWP guides did not equate American virtues, American identity, with any one group.[35]

The pages of the Southern guides are full of contrasting images of the Old and New South used as a metaphor for tradition and change, buttressed with an insistence that the presence of blacks in their traditional roles is a sign that despite dramatic changes white Southerners are still loyal to Southern traditions. A Texas guide tour assures readers that "the old customs of the golden age of cotton survive," since Negroes can be seen "spending their days chopping and picking cotton," and that while the tenant houses of these blacks constitute a "squalid scene" their "usually smiling faces lend cheer."[36] This is much less true of the Tennessee guide, though the folklore essay claims that "the humorous philosophy which often underlies his life brightens for [the Negro] circumstances that would be unrelieved bleakness for the whites" (p. 139). A sense that an agrarian way of life will be displaced by industrialization permeates the guide.

In the tours blacks are treated as a part of the landscape, as heroes in the Cherokee War, as slaves who helped build a society, as part of the battle between pro- and anti-slavery Tennesseans, as sharecroppers, and as prominent contemporary leaders. By merely mentioning in the city descriptions that Negro "houses [in Chattanooga] range from well-kept bungalows, duplexes and small tenement houses in Churchville . . . to the ramshackle shelters of South Chattanooga and Tannery Flats" (p. 252), that some of Knoxville's black population "are professional men" while the majority are "common laborers or are in domestic service" (p. 234), the guide attacks views of Negro Tennesseeans that denies the complexity of the black community.

Nevertheless, the Tennessee guide views the state's black community from a distance, from the outside. It is this that helps account for the patronizing tone in seemingly straightforward factual descriptive material. Follow Tours 10 and 13 and learn "that the Negroes in this part of West Tennessee believe in the presence of 'topas,' animals that can be conjured into persons by those having witch powers. Negresses trace their 'miseries' to the baleful activities of such 'conjure' men" (pp. 413–14). The quotation marks around topas, miseries, and conjured indicate how odd but interesting such beliefs seemed to the writer and how strange he thought they would seem to his audience. Such descriptions do not explain how beliefs, behaviors, and institutions function in a culture. That would require taking into account the perspective of those who lived the life being described.

The strong point of all the FWP guides was their portrait of the visible diversity of America. The guidebook format did not lend itself to the examination of the daily life of any group. There was room for mentioning details about the life of a group but not for studying them. Thus the Federal Writer discussing "the people of the Cumberland Mountains" in Tour 15 creates the same type of distance between himself and the people he is writing about that exists in some of the guides' descriptions of Negro life. That space makes possible a patronizing tone: "their singing is high-pitched and sometimes harsh; the women sing in abnormally high registers" (p. 504). The descriptive words reflect the outsiders point of view.[37]

Tourism and Inherited Modes of Perception

An emphasis on the old-fashioned, the uncommon, the unfamiliar as tourist sights characterized part of the guide's tone, part of the effort to capture the atmosphere of other ways of living, different environments, and past times. This aspect of the guides in some ways did not demand much of the tourist. A portrait of America as quaint and picturesque offered a charming and agreeable experience. When the guides used the word "dramatic," it usually meant only that the "sight" being discussed demanded one's attention—for the moment. Used in this way, the drama had little to do with values and ways of life in conflict, with tragedy. At the same time, the traveler then and now is required to come to terms with the fact that in the Tennessee guide, like the other volumes in the series, the usual distancing factor in tourist literature, the sense of us and them was diminished, did not ultimately exist, for both were Americans. The idea of shared nationality permeated the books. National FWP officials pushed state workers to present differences as an integral, not a peripheral part of American life.

Both American writers of the late nineteenth century and Federal Writers of the thirties searched for local color. For the most part, the earlier group wrote nostalgically and patronizingly about regional and ethnic differences. They welcomed nationalizing and homogenizing tendencies that they thought could not be resisted. For them, what they saw as different, peculiar groups with strange ways were vanishing remnants of the past. National FWP officials, however, encouraged local FWP workers to seek out diversity with the goal of celebrating it as a sign of American vitality, as a counterweight to the standardizing forces of modern American culture. Thus the guides reassured one reviewer that though the American countryside and towns had, in his opinion, lost much of their unique flavor "ours is still a richer land than we ourselves sometimes suspect."[38]

In writing guidebooks FWP officials did not escape inherited modes of perception associated with tourism. The tours embodied aspects of the picturesque emphasis on the exotic, quaint, and outlandish. The superficial delight in such material makes it possible for the tourist to observe those different from himself in a patronizing manner and to see even poverty as picturesque. The Tennessee guide, like other volumes in the series, was of two minds about poverty. Tour 15, for example, discusses the economic problems of the area the traveler is passing through. Tour 5 offers a discussion of the handicraft revival as a means of promoting "the welfare of the mountain people." The tour writer explains why "the results of the movement have been far less satisfactory than those who started it had hoped" (p. 340). But Federal Writers also knew their readers were tourists, who would be as interested in knowing that at Tennga "for miles on both sides of the road are displays of homemade bedspreads, mats, rugs, beach coats, and other articles" (p. 355), as they would be in learning that such work provided a "relatively low" income. The celebration of diversity in the guide shades into a collection of picturesque sights. Charles Dickens much earlier offered an insight into the moral dangers of celebrating the picturesque. While traveling in Italy he wrote to a friend, "I am afraid the conventional idea of the picturesque is associated with such misery and degradation that a new picturesque will have to be established as the world goes onward."[39]

The FWP guidebooks strove for a new picturesque, while not completely shedding the old. They encouraged educated middle-class Americans to travel or contemplate travel, both because America was colorful and because they needed to broaden their vision of the country, of who they as Americans were. In the first instance they visualized the world in the old picturesque way. In the latter they were creating a new picturesque pluralism. Through an emphasis on the local and the particular, the idiosyncratic and the anecdotal, the FWP guides incorporated material that reflected regional diversity, local folkways, and ethnic pluralism.

As the guide series progressed, national FWP officials contemplated programs that the FWP could undertake that would let the Federal Writers explore aspects of American life more deeply than the guide format allowed. To a degree, national FWP director Henry Alsberg conceded, travel guides could not help but be superficial. Nevertheless they would become the source of controversy.[40]

Myth and History in the FWP Guidebooks

The American Guide Series neither constitutes the "critical portrait" of the nation that some have seen in them, nor were they merely, as one historian claims, part of an effort to "cope with the very real terrors of the present by rejoicing in the apparent serenity of the past." Using the Tennessee guide as evidence it is possible to find examples to support the "critical portrait" thesis: descriptions of sharecropping; an account of the war between the Tennessee Coal, Iron, and Railway Company and miners (pp. 85, 336); the "Night Rider trouble," which "formed a dark chapter in Robertson County history" (p. 395); details about strikes in Elizabethton's textile mills in 1929 (p. 86) and Wilder's coal mines in 1932 (pp. 86, 499); a photograph of a Memphis slum (p. 213). All of this was unusual material for tourist literature. Nevertheless while one can find "critical" facts in the guidebooks, the overriding context is celebratory.[41]

The guidebook tours abandon the historian's traditional task of constructing a meaningful explanation of past events. From an historian's point of view, the tours' vast array of facts constitutes a failure to distinguish the significant from the trivial, the central from the marginal, or to seek to establish the relationship between the facts. Only the place and landscape connects these facts as the tour jumps from an item associated with one period to that associated with another without indicating any relationship. Few causal relationships are noted, let alone explored.

By jumping from one period to another, from items separated by decades, often centuries, the tours give the impression that nothing happened in a place between the items noted. Such an approach makes it impossible to analyze the conflicts that underlay the social and economic transformations that the guides view as progress. Even when the tours pass through areas in economic decline there is no clear sense of how different groups or classes were affected by this. No effort is made to distinguish whether some gained or lost more than others. The traveler could not discover from the tours that change had ever been an ordeal. Economic and social revolutions took little toll; they simply produced progress.

The FWP guidebooks interpreted the nation's landscape so as to create a monument to America's cultural pluralism. They provided no definite answers to who and what was American, but they did insist that any answer would have to be broadly inclusive. At the same time they sacrificed any attempt to critically assess where the nation had been and where it was going. FWP officials never tried to determine what would hold this pluralistic nation together. They assumed that an acknowledgment that the United States was a diverse nation was a necessary starting point. What, however, were the underlying values that could bind Americans together? Project officials envisioned a diverse and inclusive national community, but they never confronted the question of whether all the parts were compatible. Were all aspects of various regional and ethnic cultures valuable? Which were not?

To the extent that national FWP officials used a romantic nationalist and pluralist approach to try to unite Americans while ignoring conflicts that divided them, they created a mythical view of the nation. An ideological view of America would have stressed conflict, sought to understand the interests of a particular social group, and to change its circumstances. In the inclusive American community the guidebook essays and tours worked to create in the act of portraying it, there was an inherently paradoxical attempt to both preserve and celebrate differences, while at the same time seeking to transcend them in a sense of shared nationality. In modern societies one of the functions of social myths is to unite individuals and groups with different interests. Such myths embody visions of the society's past and hopes for a utopian future. They do not indicate how a change from present circumstances to a better future can be achieved. That would be divisive. Thus to a large degree the American guidebook series is mythic. In part, it was this that made the guidebooks acceptable to the official private and public cultural and political institutions that lent them their authority as consultants and sponsors.[42]

The guidebook essays offer a mythic view of the arts in America that promises a resolution of the problems that national FWP officials perceived in the relationship between the artist and his people. Once, in their view, art and artists had been organically bound to the community. It could be that way again in the future, not, however, by seeking to go backward. The changes in economic and social relationships brought about in the course of the development of a modern society, or progress as the guidebooks preferred to call it, were not to be repudiated. The FWP offered no program beyond advocating that contemporary artists study the folk arts. Programs were potentially divisive. The unstated and unexamined question was whether a revitalized American culture could be created without fundamental political and social change.

The guides do not offer an explicit analysis of the past with a goal of revealing how the present can be transformed into a better future. They play down conflict and do not focus on the interests of specific groups at the expense of others. Yet both their form and content gave them qualities that kept them from being totally mythic. They might better be thought of as having dynamic qualities that keep them moving back and forth between two poles labeled myth and ideology, leaving much to the determination of the individual reader. National FWP officials, however, perceived that to encourage Americans to see as fellow citizens others that in the past had been excluded from their definition of the nation was to help change the future.

The Politics of Cultural Pluralism

The fight for the idea of America as a pluralistic nation was linked to the liberal-reformist politics of the 1930s. To defenders of exclusive definitions of America it was a threatening and radical idea about national identity. Narrow and exclusive definitions of who and what was American had buttressed the status quo in the 1920s. The twenties had witnessed a decade of fundamental cleavage between rural and urban Americans, fundamentalists and non-fundamentalists, and nativists and minorities. In the most extreme manifestations of these divisions, there was an attempt to seek cultural unity by crusading for "one hundred per cent Americanism," by regarding all nonconformists and minorities as the source of American problems, as outside the dominant definition of the national community.[43]

A cultural program that challenged such definitions was inherently reformist. An inclusive community as national FWP officials envisioned it, was not supposed to buttress social consensus, but to give weight to the claims of such scorned groups as black Americans. Thus to treat American identity and nationality as fluid was to challenge the status quo. And in the thirties Texas Representative Martin Dies and a majority of the House Un-American Activities Committee (HUAC) viewed such ideas as a radical attack on the status quo. For Dies and his supporters the FWP guidebook's mere mention of the history of labor and Negro Americans was unpatriotically promoting disunity. For them American identity was already defined, it was not unfinished, in the process of becoming. Dies wrote longingly of the period when "the racial unity of the United States was still intact," that time before "the great alien invasion of the United States took place"—the immigration from southern and eastern Europe. From this point of view, the ideas behind FWP guides that appear innocuous and non-controversial to later historians constituted a deep challenge to some Americans at the time. HUAC rhetoric about communism was a mode of discourse for voicing a rejection of the cultural as well as the political values of the New Deal.[44]

Yet by the 1950s pluralism was compatible with a conservative outlook. Democratic shibboleths were easily celebrated while the realities of class and racial differences that actually violated democratic principles were ignored. In wartime it had been useful to celebrate diversity and democratic institutions in a way that downplayed conflicting interests and tried to arouse primordial loyalties. When the American Guide Series was completed, President Roosevelt issued a special statement in honor of national guide week in November 1941. The President claimed that the guides showed that an integrated nation and national identity were compatible with "the variants in local patterns of living and regional development." It was a faith that assumed Americans could understand and accept cultural differences as part of their national identity.[45]

In post-war America pluralism embodied a vision that celebrated consensus, while either denying or ignoring existing inequalities. In contrast to the 1950s version of pluralism as consensus, national FWP officials as egalitarians and as cultural relativists had envisioned an inclusive community, one that cherished provincial cultures while advocating a cosmopolitan outlook, as part of a larger program of reform.

Tennesseans in Transition

Agriculture and Industry in Tennessee: Yesterday and Today

Tennessee guide writers thought they could discern the future that lay just over the horizon. Tennesseans, they insisted, were the products of a rural culture that had grown out of a struggle with the land; but Tennesseans stood on the edge of a new future. "The transition period has already begun" (p. 81), the guide's authors declared. In many ways they were right. It was a transition that they perceived would involve changes in ways of life and ways of making a living, in agriculture and industry, on the farm and in the city, and perhaps in race relations. And the New Deal, especially TVA, they thought was at the heart of the transition.

If the guide had been published only a couple of years later the tone would have been different. What the guide writers had seen as the future, they might have viewed as the new reality. In many ways the Second World

War did more to inaugurate major changes in Tennessee life than the New Deal did. It took Tennesseans both figuratively and literally out into a larger world. The Federal Writers did not have to address the question of whether the new realities fulfilled their dreams. It would help us to try to answer that question. And that also brings us back to the question of whether the guide and the vision that created it can still help us understand life in Tennessee. In many ways the transformations that have occurred in Tennessee since the guide was written make the issues they addressed all the more urgent. These issues centered around the meaning of place and tradition, identity and community, in an increasingly interrelated and diverse modern economy and culture. Changes occurring in Tennessee farming in the thirties and in the balance in the state between an agrarian and industrial way of life called attention to questions that those of us who think we live on the other side of the transition forget are still unanswered, still need to be addressed.

The New Deal succeeded in raising and stabilizing farm commodity prices by controlling farm output, and thus in the long run tipping the balance in Tennessee toward an industrial way of life. Guaranteed an income for not planting traditional crops, Southern farmers were able to experiment with new crops and labor saving machines. World War II increased demand for agricultural products and brought improvement in Tennessee's agricultural economy. At the same time the trend to further mechanization continued. Farm population in Tennessee declined from over a million and a quarter in 1940 to less than a million by the end of the war, while production increased. And this has remained the overall trend.[46]

The Tennessee guide offers an optimistic view of New Deal efforts to aid displaced farmers. Model communities set up by the Farm Security Administration are viewed as trend setters. We know they were not. At the rate the FSA and its successor the FHA helped farm tenants become owners between 1937 and 1947 one historian calculated it would take the government "nearly 400 years to make [all of the South's remaining tenant farmers] owners." Instead, these farmers went to the cities. New Deal farm policies that helped stabilize commodity prices also resulted in driving tenant farmers and sharecroppers off the land. Unwilling to share crop reduction payments with their tenants many farm landlords evicted them. In many cases, they and their children and their children's children have become an unskilled, chronically unemployed urban underclass. They traded subsistence farming for subsistence welfare, or a farm landlord for a welfare official.[47] The guide writers believed in the stated dreams behind slum clearance plans. Visit, for example, such public housing projects as Lauderdale Courts and Dixie Homes (the first was originally built for whites, the latter for blacks), listed in the guides as points of interest for Memphis, and compare the hopes of the past with the realities of the present.

Everywhere the guide writers thought they saw TVA helping to transform life for the better. It was, they thought, "one of the most important chapters in the history of Tennessee" (pp. 61–62). Transcending state boundaries, "it has become the proving ground for one of the most comprehensive social experiments in America" (p. 62). Planning promised to transform life in the Great Valley of the Tennessee River. Cheap power would help industry expand. Rural electrification would improve living conditions. TVA agents would introduce the benefits of scientific farming. They foresaw a valley "which flood waters and wasteful farming were turning into a desert," transformed "into a land of plenty where industry, agriculture, and *human values* may take their place in a balanced economy" (emphasis added, p. 62). TVA would be but the first of a series of such regional authorities that would substitute "order and design for haphazard, unplanned, and unintegrated development." Instead, it was the last.

In retrospect it is clear that TVA was most successful as a dam building, fertilizer producing, and power generating organization, although Roosevelt from the beginning insisted that TVA was not "initiated or organized for the purpose of selling electricity." TVA in the President's view was "a social experiment," that would help "forgotten Americans"—"as an incident to that it is necessary to build some dams." It is clear that Muscle Shoals nitrate plants were developed and that the Tennessee River and its tributaries were brought under control and their power potential harnessed.[48]

But what of Roosevelt's vision, which the Tennessee guide shared? Today, one scholar refers to the continuing "halo effect" of Roosevelt's "rhetoric" about what is essentially another power company. TVA was going to set a model for a combination of expertise and grass roots participation. A more jaundiced view sees "fifty years of grass roots bureaucracy." TVA has been criticized by both environmentalists and consumers.[49]

There is no denying the tremendous changes TVA has helped bring to the region. Over 95 percent of the people living in the Norris Basin in 1933 had no electricity. Indoor toilets were equally rare. Fire places were the most common form of heating. All of this TVA changed—forever. Older forms of community life disappeared beneath the flood waters of change. War-time demand and TVA's power facilities and improvements in river transportation fueled industrial growth that continues. TVA has succeeded in aiding economic development. The disappointments center around the gap between the social vision behind it and present realities. The Tennessee guide declared that in Norris, the new experimental city created by TVA, "a new standard for rural existence is being set" (p. 166). In less than a decade after that was written, Norris had become a TVA suburb. Per capita income today in the Norris Basin counties is among the lowest in Tennessee, and only in recent years has the outward flow of migration from this area been reversed. To address the regional socio-economic problems of the area would have required planning that the TVA abandoned. Progress has not solved the traditional social problems of the area, nor significantly altered its social structure.[50]

Transition and Tennessee Negroes

In this time of transition the guide saw that the state's blacks, like white Tennesseans, were "in active ferment, struggling for survival and status" (p. 108). The emphasis in the American Guide Series, national FWP Negro Affairs editor Sterling Brown maintained, was on "the history of the Negro in America, not as a separate entity. . . . the Negro has been an integral part of American life, however grudgingly received, a participant quite as much as a contributor." Slavery and segregation had not prevented participation. From the viewpoint of national FWP officials the problem with the contributions approach was that it divorced the individual from his group cultural context and totally accepted the measure of value offered by the dominant culture. Following the participation approach the Tennessee guide points out that "as laborer and as artisan, the Negro has been a significant factor in the development of agriculture and in the building of cities" (p. 107). Prominent Negroes are seen in relationship to the group. The development of black religious, educational, and economic institutions are noted. Black Tennesseans have achieved this despite legal barriers, economic hurdles, and prejudices against which they have struggled. The future was promising. This 1939 guide claimed the "dominance in the State as a whole of the disposition toward encouraging such development" (p. 110). By the standards of the time, this is a liberal southern view of race relations. Legal and social barriers to black advancement are alluded to, not discussed. Nowhere is segregation directly mentioned. Implicitly, it is treated as a system within which there can be progress. No note of protest is sounded. Few Americans in the thirties foresaw that in the near future the caste system would be directly challenged and dismantled by black Tennesseans and other Americans who viewed it as the primary barrier to blacks achieving the rights of full citizenship. Clinton, Nashville, Somerville, Memphis, and numerous Tennessee cities became the sights of a grass-roots civil rights movement that raised fundamental questions about race and class relations and the meaning of freedom, equality, and citizenship in America.[51]

Tradition and Change in Tennessee

The very changes that have done so much to transform Tennessee since *Tennessee: A State Guide* was published have paradoxically made this volume all the more meaningful. If Tennesseans in the thirties thought they were living in a period of transition, today's Tennesseans have enough experience with modern life to know that such a feeling is one of the characteristics of modernity. Yesterday's major industrial employer in many areas of Tennessee is today's declining industry. Tennesseans once went to Detroit to work in the automobile plants. Today, they can stay and work in Smyrna for a Japanese automobile company. There will soon be a General Motors plant in Spring Hill—some local farmers think it will ruin agriculture in the area. Both plants, some have claimed, will establish new models of industrial employee-employer relationships. What the guide saw as a transition in which "the sons and daughters of the small farmers, forced by circumstances to tend machines, are now writing the history of labor in Tennessee" (p. 90) has not yet been completed.

If all the benefits of "progress" that the guide writers envisioned have not arrived, much of what they described as traditional has persisted in ways they did not foresee and that are not always recognized or acknowledged today. True, progress has transformed the landscape of our everyday lives into freeways, suburbs, and shopping centers—a world that appears far removed from the guidebook's Tennessee. But that is because interstate highways and bypasses whiz us by that which reminds us of our past and the ways in which it is alive in a more diverse and idiosyncratic present than we usually acknowledge. Already in 1939 the Tennessee guide recognized that highways created an image of an homogenized "surface America" (p. 139). Tennesseans were living "in an age when the country has largely become one vast interlocked economic system" (p. 74). The guide predicted that natural resources and cheap power "seem destined within the next few decades to sweep Tennessee into the mainstream of industrialism" (p. 81). And while sunbelt growth boosterism cannot disguise persistent economic disparities—Tennessee was 44th in per capita income in 1979—the gap has been closing. Once the transmission power line was the symbol of the end of isolation, then the TV station, today the satellite dish beside the dog trot house in the mountain cove. It is often assumed that the disappearance of isolated communities, the closing of the economic gap between different parts of the country, means the United States is becoming a homogenized culture. The Tennessee guide argued that was not true in 1939, and it can help us discover that almost a half-century later it still is not true. Underlying the American Guide Series was the rather different assumption that national integration and diversity were compatible.

The Tennessee guide claimed that despite the growth of industrialism "urban areas are dominated by the traditions of farm life. With few exceptions, the cities largely retain the flavor of country towns" (p. 3). It may startle those who focus on the visible changes to learn that almost a half-century after the Tennessee guide was published, historian David Goldfield, surveying Southern cities, past and present, thinks there are no exceptions: "In a region covered with tradition, the agrarian character of urbanization is probably one of the oldest. . . . Rural values dominated southern cities because rural people inhabited southern cities."[52]

Today more than in the thirties, Tennesseans, rural and urban, are aware of and in contact with a diverse world; our lives take place within a variety of communities and many of these are not defined by place but by choice. These informal communities overlap with more formal bureaucratic types of organization that once did not so deeply touch intimate aspects of community life. Once place names like Mammy's Creek defined the boundaries of a community (p. 439). Today knowledge of place names can contribute to creating a sense of place and identity that was once taken for granted.

Pluralism and Tradition

FWP officials feared totalitarian attempts to achieve unity and wholeness by eliminating those who were different and rejected attempts to establish a cultural hierarchy valuing some groups in a community above others. We have seen the murderous results of what they feared. We have reason to be interested in what they saw as an alternative. Totalitarian societies by trying forcibly to restore a sense of wholeness, a world with one folk, one Reich, one Führer, could only offer the allusion of restoring community to a fragmented nation. Living in a pluralist world while maintaining some sense of being part of a place and tradition is an even more formidable challenge today than it was yesterday.

Awareness of a multiplicity of traditions has reached unprecedented proportions, and the recognition of pluralist diversity has become unavoidable. Not only are we all more knowledgeable about diversity, but we come into more contact with it. In unprecedented numbers non-Southerners are moving to Tennessee, some from such far away places as Vietnam, and many Tennesseans who went away to other regions have returned home—all bring knowledge of other ways of life. Some have seen this as helping to create a homogenized nation—a development many have loathed. In the thirties this "threat" was associated with industrialism, and some Tennesseans were prominent among those who made this argument (see the discussion of the Nashville Agrarians on pp. 151–52).

Perhaps of all Americans in the thirties, white Southerners found it hardest to attach positive value to the reality of American cultural pluralism. In 1934 when T. S. Eliot told a University of Virginia audience that the South being "farther away from New York," and being "less industrialized and less invaded by foreign races," had a better chance "for a re-establishment of a native culture" than even New England, he assumed he had a sympathetic audience for what was not a unique view of tradition and modernity. Tradition, Eliot maintained, could only thrive among a stable and homogeneous population, for "where two or more cultures exist in the same place they are likely either to be fiercely self-conscious or both to become adulterate." In the interaction between cultures, he saw only the possibility of an intense struggle to maintain identity or the corruption and debasement of culture. In contrast, national FWP officials did not use words like adulterate with their implication that there was a choice only between purity and impurity. For them, diversity offered hope of cultural renewal. A different view of tradition, culture, and industrialism and urbanism was at the heart of their attempt to rediscover America through guidebooks, folklore studies, and oral histories.[53]

Late nineteenth-century anthropologists developed an evolutionary view of culture that continues to be echoed in popular thought—a view that national FWP officials tried to combat. These anthropologists saw culture as a series of stages in a progressive human development. They never referred to cultures, for in their view there was only one culture and different groups could be located on an evolutionary ladder—savages and barbarians abroad at the bottom, the folk at home next, and at the top of this hierarchy people like themselves. Groups at the bottom of this ladder they thought might be able with education to move up; however, some groups, in this view were permanently relegated to the bottom rungs because of their genetic make-up. Folklore was the survival of materials from an earlier stage; with progress it would disappear. In this discussion folklore and tradition were easily equated. For the cultural evolutionists folklore meant traditions which they did not respect, which they saw as outmoded by progress. For those who shared these assumptions but not the belief in progress, modern culture was largely an example of decayed remnants of the past. Industrialization and urbanization destroyed the agrarian myths that had given life meaning and wholeness. Pluralism was chaotic fragmentation, creating, especially in modern cities, a feeling of homelessness. Early twentieth-century sociologists lent support to this point of view in works that argued that urbanization and industrialization stripped individuals of their traditional cultural heritage. National FWP officials intended their programs to play a role in creating an alternative view. The Tennessee guide can still help in that task.[54]

If folklore is defined as cultural survivals from either an earlier and inferior state of cultural development or as material that was brought from elsewhere—that had "ceased to have any direct and organic connection with actual life," that survived only among rural and isolated groups separated from the mainstream of American life, and that was gradually dying out—it has no relevance to the future of American culture. Working from a different set of assumptions, the FWP offered guides to diverse American traditions. National FWP officials saw diverse American cultural groups in a state of transition, adapting old ways to new circumstances and fitting new ways to old patterns.[55]

B. A. Botkin, national FWP folklore editor, disagreed with those who thought there were no folk in America and with those who felt threatened by American diversity. "There is," he maintained, "not one folk group [in America] but many folk groups—as many as there are regional cultures or racial or occupational groups within a region." In the modern world, Botkin claimed, not only geography but the social structure itself produces the isolation and separation out of which comes a folklore of the educated as well as the uneducated, an urban as well as a rural folklore. Folklore was not disappearing, it was something still being created, in the city as well as in the country, in the factory as well as in the fields. Cultural contact between diverse groups, as well as isolation, could generate new folklore, as "the folk group adapts itself to its environment and change." In the interaction between diverse groups Botkin saw not cultural decay but the possibility of creating a new unity that allowed for differences.[56]

The Tennessee guide tours can provide an introduction to Tennessee folk traditions, a way to begin thinking about tradition and modernity in Tennessee. From Walt Whitman's songs of the road to Charles Kuralt's televised reports, the road has always had a powerful cultural and historical resonance for Americans. It has served as a metaphor for discovery and a symbol of unity. FWP guidebooks also use streets and highways to create a sense of place and a feeling that we in the modern world can also create a sense of home by using shared public places such as roads as a way to explore our diverse traditions, to rediscover who we are.

Like Walt Whitman, the Federal Writers found an American epic in the doings of ordinary as well as great men, and in the present as well as the past. By placing himself at the center of his poem Whitman treated himself and America as each engaged in a process of self-realization. It was not an epic that celebrated past heroic deeds and that accepted and justified present social arrangements but instead a new epic of becoming. Out of his experience Whitman sought to create a new personality for a democratic age—"tallying, the momentous spirit and facts of its immediate day"—and thus guide others in discovering their possibilities. Unlike Whitman's *Leaves of Grass* there is no self at the center of the FWP tour expressing and fusing private lyric and public epic. Still the guides do invite an exploration of the open road, do invite Americans to place themselves in the center of the guide automobile tours and to realize and celebrate a pluralistic culture still in the process of becoming and thus to know themselves in a new way. The Tennessee guide lets them know that they are the inheritors of traditions of sorghum making, Brunswick stew suppers, barbecues, canning, the making of lye soap, church and family homecomings, dinner on the grounds, cunjur lore, shape note singing, play parties, "jump-up songs," mule days, the blues on Beale Street, "the free for all preachings," at city wharf in Nashville.[57]

What can the reader or traveler do with information about Tennessee places and traditions? How much of this is alive in today's Tennessee? As one tries today to follow any of the tours in this volume the question arises, "Are the decaying tenant houses—examples of the double pen, the dog trot, and the shotgun—weathered barns, the old tobacco sheds, and on rare occasions the mule you see merely the remnants of a culture that has disappeared? Perhaps travelers would do better to focus their attention on the mobile homes, the brick houses, the TV satellite dishes, the appearance of country clubs and golf courses even in some of the state's poorest counties, the strip architecture on the outskirts of cities—characterized by neon signs and national franchises—all seemingly disconnected from any local tradition. The answer involves seeing traditions as fluid and changing rather than as static.

The fluid change characteristic of the modern world makes viewing life as a process of becoming a necessity. Individuals and groups in Tennessee have been making choices so as to play an active role in making their history. People do not progress in lock-step through stages such as provincial to cosmopolitan, agrarian type to industrial worker, shedding their older selves in the process. The visible remnants of past ways of life that dot the rural landscape and the towns and cities of Tennessee are not the "real"

Tennessee, as some would have it, covered over by a thin layer of the symbols of contemporary American life. They are not even remnants, for the traditions of the past are alive and interacting with the realities of the present to create the possibilities of the future. The men and women who knew how to make ties and lye soap are still alive and influencing the culture in which their college-graduate children pursue their professional careers. Computer programmers know the lore of their work community—stories of famous hackers, the endless loop, and proverbial wisdom using computers as metaphor. But this is only one of the communities in which their lives take place. They may also attend decoration day services at the churches in which they grew up.

American diversity and the process of cultural interaction allows room for creative individual and group responses to new realities; pluralism makes for complex identities. In the modern world no one is actually at either end of the folk-nonfolk continuum. And since total movement toward either absolute end of the scale is not possible, why not try to consciously make the most of being between these two poles as Tennesseans have been doing? Talk with a Tennessee woman who still uses her sadiron. Of course she will explain that she does not heat it up on the fire place; she now uses her electric stove for that. A country fiddler tape records lessons for local young people learning the tradition he is passing on. Today you can find people along the Tennessee River who attended annual singing conventions in the 1920s and 1930s (p. 486) and who still get together with their children, and their children's children, to spend Sunday afternoons singing. They are links in a living tradition. You can talk with women who learned how to can from their mothers. Today their freezers make it possible for them to can more than ever. Ask a Memphian barbecuing in his backyard how he learned to barbecue, and he will probably tell you that "you don't learn that, you just pick it up." He may explain that he doesn't do it the same way his mother did, but then after reflection he may declare, "it's the same thing in a new way."

Building an identity out of one's relationship to American diversity can constitute an individualism that is far different from mere egoism. The emphasis in American travel literature has been more on the individual's search for and attempt to create an identity than on a testing of character. In the guidebook automobile tours and in its oral history project the FWP tried to help Americans look at and listen to what for many travelers would have been previously unimagined aspects of American life. The emphasis in the guides, however, was not on social documentary trying to remedy problems by so moving readers that other peoples' hardships would become of such concern to them that they felt compelled to address them. Rather the focus was on culture, American ways of life. Cultural differences were celebrated on the assumption that no one group had a superior way of life that could be defined as the American way, that in fact every American's sense of identity and nationality would be enriched if they could see and incorporate as part of themselves the life of their fellow Americans, if they could comprehend the reality of others.

The Federal Writers wanted to use roads as a way for Americans to learn about the pluralistic culture in which they lived. The writers aimed to bring into the road, a symbol of shared public space, aspects of diverse group traditions and thus create a new sense of American identity and national community. Yet, already in the thirties the more widely-shared the public space, the more likely "visible" aspects of differing traditions would not be present. National FWP director Henry Alsberg concluded that by themselves the FWP guidebooks provided only a sketch, not a portrait of American culture. To complete the sketch he proposed the FWP focus on folklore and ethnic groups, capturing in the first person accounts of people evidence about their history and traditions, their consciousness, not readily discernible in the built environment. The Tennessee FWP did not collect urban and industrial folklore as some other state units did. That does not mean it is not there to be discovered. Nor did Tennessee Federal Writers undertake what the FWP called social-ethnic studies. They could have interviewed Greek, Jewish, Italian, Lebanese, and Chinese-Americans living in Tennessee. The guide describes the Pinch in Memphis without mentioning that in the thirties Memphis Jews living in the Pinch had recreated many aspects of the life they had lived in eastern Europe. The importance of black-white divisions should not obscure ethnic diversity in Tennessee and its significance yesterday and today. It is easy to assume that only people who display their traditions in public spaces have traditions that differ from the majority. Consciousness, however, is more complex than tangible things. Studies show that education and travel has heightened, rather than diminished, the regional consciousness of white Southerners.[58]

The Tennessee Federal Writers interviewed former slaves and ordinary Tennesseans—farmers, factory workers, maids, merchants. And some who explore Tennessee through the guide may want to continue with these materials that the FWP officials thought provided the next step in the rediscovery of American culture. The FWP played on the theme that interviewing ordinary people had a democratic import and that the reader needed to both acknowledge the importance of undistinguished individuals and that these individuals were fellow citizens. The FWP tried to create a sense of community between the traveler and the place he visited, between a person being interviewed and the reader.

In the American Guide Series the Federal Writers described numerous distinct but nevertheless American places located in a meaningful landscape in which the tourist could use the automobile as a vehicle for the discovery and exploration of American diversity. No longer, as one critic then commented, "will the traveling motorist have any excuse for regarding the road as merely the shortest distance between two points."[59]

The Federal Writers left us this guide to their Tennessee and ours—this invitation to travel, to explore, to rediscover a part of America. It is an invitation worth accepting.

NOTES

1. Archie Hobson, ed. *Remembering America: A Sampler of the WPA American Guide Series* (New York: Columbia Univ. Press, 1985), xi.

2. Bernard DeVoto, "The Writers' Project," *Harper's Magazine* (Jan. 1942), 222, and "New England Via the WPA," *Saturday Review of Literature,*" 18 (May 14, 1938), 4; Lewis Mumford, "Writers' Project," *New Republic,* 92 (Oct. 20, 1937), 306–307.

3. United States Federal Works Agency, *Final Report on the WPA Program: 1935–1943* (Washington, D.C.: U.S. Government Printing Office, 1947), iii, 63.

4. Edwin Massengill, former member of the North Carolina FWP, telephone interviews, Raleigh, N.C., Feb. 25 and 28, 1972; Claude Dunnagan, former member of the NCFWP to the author, March 8, 1973; Edwin Bjorkman, state director, to Harriet Works Corley, Greensboro, N.C., district supervisor, Aug. 19, 1936, Box 32, Federal Writers' Project files, Works Progress Administration records, Records Group 69, National Archives, Washington, D.C. (hereinafter FWPNA). Biographical statement by Aswell, no date, Univ. of North Carolina Press Papers, Southern Historical Collection, Univ. of North Carolina (hereinafter Press papers) and by Toler, May 2, 1939, Federal Writers' Project, Papers of the Southeast Regional Director, William Terry Couch, Southern Historical Collection, Univ. of North Carolina (hereinafter FWP-Couch Papers).

5. McDaniel to Couch, Jan. 20, 1939, FWP-Couch Papers; copies of the frequent letters that Henry G. Alsberg, national FWP director, sent in the early part of 1936, inquiring about Negro employment on the state projects and prodding state directors to hire black workers, are in the FWP-Couch Papers, and the letters he sent again in 1938 are in Box 201, FWPNA.

6. "Notes on the FWP with special reference to the American Guide," Sept. 17, 1936, Records of the FWP relating to Henry G. Alsberg and George W. Cronyn 1935–1939, Records Group 69, Central Correspondence files of the WPA, National Archives, Washington, D.C. Microfilm prepared by the General Service

Administration, 1968, and available from Washington State Univ. (hereinafter Alsberg-Cronyn files).

7. Wilma Dykeman, *Tennessee: A Bicentennial History* (New York: Norton, 1975), 129.

8. Francis Wright, *Views of Society and Manners in America,* ed. Paul R. Baker (1821; rpt. Cambridge, Mass.: Harvard Univ. Press, 1963).

9. Clipping *Kansas City Star,* Dec. 3, 1936, Box 83, FWPNA.

10. Robert E. Corlew, et al., *Tennessee: A Short History* (Knoxville: Univ. of Tennessee Press, 1981), 500; FWP, *Tennessee: A Guide to the State,* (New York: Viking, 1939), 76, 89; Gilbert C. Fite, *Cotton Fields No More: Southern Agriculture 1865–1980* (Lexington: Univ. of Kentucky Press, 1984), 207, 184–85, 189, 208; Pete Daniel, "The Transformation of the Rural South, 1930 to the Present, *Agricultural History* 55 (July 1981), 231–48. See also Jerrold Hirsch, "From the FSA Files: The Rural Landscape of the Thirties," in Doug Swaim, ed., *Carolina Dwelling, Toward Preservation of Place: In Search of the North Carolina Vernacular Landscape,* vol. 26 (Raleigh: Student Publication of the School of Design, 1978) 241–50.

11. These trends are examined in David Goldfield, *Cotton Fields and Skyscrapers: Southern City and Region, 1607–1980* (Baton Rouge: Louisiana State Univ. Press, 1982), Michael J. McDonald and William Bruce Wheeler, *Knoxville, Tennessee: Change and Continuity in an Appalachian City* (Knoxville: Univ. of Tennessee Press, 1983), Don H. Doyle, *Nashville: In the New South, 1880–1930* (Knoxville: Univ. of Tennessee Press, 1985).

12. The standard works on the genesis, growth, and demise of the Federal Writers' Project are William F. McDonald, *Federal Relief Administration and the Arts, The Origins and Administrative History of the Arts Projects of the Works Progress Administration* (Columbus: Ohio State Univ. Press, 1969); Jerre Mangione, *The Dream and the Deal: The Federal Writers' Project, 1935–1943* (Boston: Little, Brown, 1972); and Monty Penkower, *The Federal Writers' Project: A Study in Government Patronage of the Arts* (Urbana: Univ. of Illinois Press, 1977). Three unpublished dissertations offer additional information. See Kathleen O'Connor McKinzie's "Writers on Relief, 1935–1942" (unpublished Ph.D. diss., Indiana Univ., 1970); Ronald Warren Taber, "The Federal Writers' Project in the Pacific Northwest: A Case Study" (unpublished diss., Univ. of Washington, 1969); and Ronnie W. Clayton, "A History of the Federal Writers' Project in Louisiana" (unpublished Ph.D. diss., Louisiana State Univ., 1974). For a different approach see Jerrold Hirsch, "Portrait of America: The Federal Writers' Project in an Intellectual and Cultural Context" (unpublished Ph.D. diss., Univ. of North Carolina at Chapel Hill, 1984).

13. J. Hector St.John de Crevecoeur, *Letters from an American Farmer* (1782; rpt. New York: Albert & Charles Boni, 1925), 54; Robert Wiebe, *The Segmented Society: An Introduction to the Meaning of America* (New York: Oxford Univ. Press, 1973), 90, 95. Grace Overmeyer, *Government and the Arts* (New York: Norton, 1939), 112.

14. The literature on romantic nationalism, cultural pluralism, and cosmopolitanism is ample. I have relied heavily on the following secondary sources: Charles C.

Alexander, *Here the Country Lies: Nationalism and the Arts in Twentieth Century America* (Bloomington: Indiana Univ. Press, 1980); John Higham, "Ethnic Pluralism in Modern American Thought," and "Another American Dilemma," in *Send These To Me: Jews and Other Immigrants in Urban America* (New York: Atheneum, 1975), 196–246; John Higham, *Strangers in the Land: Patterns of American Nativism* (New York: Atheneum, 1963); David Hollinger, "Ethnic Diversity, Cosmopolitanism and the Emergence of the American Liberal Intelligentsia," *American Quarterly,* 27 (May 1975), 133–51; Gilman M. Ostrander, *American Civilization in the First Machine Age, 1890–1940* (New York: Harper & Row, 1970); Richard Weiss, "Ethnicity and Reform: Minorities and the Ambience of the Depression Years," *Journal of American History,* 66 (Dec. 1979), 566–85; Terry A. Cooney, "Cosmopolitan Values and the Identification of Reaction: *Partisan Review* in the 1930s," *Journal of American History,* 68 (Dec. 1981), 580–98; and Jane DeHart Mathews, "Arts and the People: The New Deal Quest for a Cultural Democracy," *Journal of American History,* 62 (Sept. 1975), 316–39. Many of the interviews done by the FWP have not been published, but a number of volumes provide an introduction to the work they did. See FWP, *These Are Our Lives* (Chapel Hill: Univ. of North Carolina Press, 1939); Tom Terrill and Jerrold Hirsch, *Such As Us: Southern Voices of the Thirties* (Chapel Hill: Univ. of North Carolina Press, 1978); B.A. Botkin, ed., *Lay My Burden Down: A Folk History of Slavery* (Chicago: Univ. of Chicago Press, 1945); George P. Rawick, ed., *The American Slave: A Composite Autobiography,* 19 vols. (Westport, Conn.: Greenwood Press, 1972–76). Ann Banks, *First Person America* (New York: Knopf, 1980).

15. Warren I. Susman, "The Thirties," in Stanley Coben and Lorman Ratner, eds., *The Development of an American Culture* (Englewood Cliffs, N.J.: Prentice-Hall, 1970), 183; Robert Berkhofer, "Clio and the Culture Concept: Some Impressions of a Changing Relationship in American Culture," in Louis M. Schneider and Charles M. Bonjean, eds., *The Idea of Culture in the Social Sciences* (Cambridge, England: Cambridge Univ. Press, 1973), 77–100.

16. "Manual for a Guide to Composite America, Social-Ethnic Studies," July 10, 1938, Box 191, FWPNA; pamphlet "The American Guide and the American Guide Manual: Their Task—To Introduce America to Americans," n.d., Box 74, FWPNA. The term "composite America" was used repeatedly in conjunction with the social ethnic studies and "The Portrait of the Negro as American" was a study that Negro affairs editor, Sterling Brown, directed. See also Joseph S. Roucek, Caroline F. Ware, Morton W. Royse, "Approaches to the Study of Nationality Groups in the United States: Summary of the Discussion," in Caroline F. Ware, ed., *The Cultural Approach to History* (New York: Columbia Univ. Press, 1940), 86–89, and Hirsch, "Portrait of America," 523–61.

17. For a representative statement of this theme see "The American Guide and The American Guide Series: Their Task—To Introduce America to Americans" [1938?], Box 50, FWPNA.

18. For a description of the development of an exclusive, reactionary, racist form of cultural nationalism, see George L. Mosse, *The Nationalization of the Masses:*

Political Symbolism and Mass Movements in Germany from the Napoleonic War Through the Third Reich (New York: H. Fentig, 1975). New Deal officials saw a pluralist version of cultural nationalism as an alternative to totalitarianism. This theme is clearly developed in ch. nine, "Cultural Diversity in American Life," in U.S. National Resources Committee, *The Problems of a Changing Population,* Report of the Committee on Population Problems to the National Resources Committee, May 1938 (Washington, D.C.: United States Government Printing Office, 1938), 224–52. B.A. Botkin, national FWP folklore editor, was a contributor to this study.

19. Henry G. Alsberg, "Federal Writers' Project and Education," *Journal of the National Education Association,* 25 (March 1936), 86.

20. Mabel Ulrich, "Salvaging Culture for the WPA," *Harper's,* 177 (May 1939), 656. Katherine Kellock, "The WPA Writers: Portraitists of the United States," *American Scholar* 9 (Autumn 1940), 474; George Cronyn to all editors state guide, "Subject: Checking State MS.," Jan. 14, 1937, Alsberg-Cronyn files.

21. Alsberg to Edwin Bjorkman, state director, N.C. FWP, Jan. 6, 1936, Box 114, FWPNA; Henry G. Alsberg, "The American Guide," n.d., Alsberg-Cronyn files; "Have You Discovered America," n.d., Box 70, FWPNA; FWP, "The American Guide Manual"; Alsberg to A.F. Cleveland, vice-president in charge of traffic, Association of American Railroads, Oct. 5, 1935, Box 83, Division of Information files, Works Progress Administration records, Records Group 69, National Archives, Washington, D.C. (hereinafter, WPA). Press release, Seattle, Washington WPA, June 26, 1938, Box 83, Division of Information files, WPA, Alsberg, "Have You Discovered America?" n.d., Box 70, FWPNA; Cronyn to Rolls Ogden, ed., *New York Times,* Jan. 28, 1936, Alsberg-Cronyn files; Cronyn to W.T. Couch, southeast regional director, Sept. 28, 1937, FWP-Couch papers.

22. Alsberg to A.F. Cleveland, Oct. 3, 1935, Alsberg-Cronyn files. The idea that the lack of adequate American guides was a national embarrassment was one of the frequent reasons FWP officials gave to justify their existence. See, for example, "For: Writers' Digest," Feb. 15, 1939, Box 83, Division of Information files, WPA; "The First WPA Guide," *Saturday Review of Literature* 15 (Feb. 27, 1937); "Prospectus, The American Guide," n.d., Box 74, FWPNA; "Notes on the Federal Writers' Project with Special Reference to the American Guide," Sept. 17, 1936, Alsberg-Cronyn files.

23. Alsberg, "New Guide to America"; "Have You Discovered America?" n.d.; "Prospectus, The American Guide," n.d., Box 74, FWPNA; "Notes on the Federal Writers' Project with Special Reference to the American Guide," Sept. 17, 1936, Alsberg-Cronyn files.

24. Unsigned, "General Criticism of Material on Hand, New Mexico Points of Interest," June 18, 1936, Box 109; Supplement No. 15 to The American Guide Manual," Sept. 15, 1936, Box 70; Supplement No. 11C to "The American Guide Manual," Sept. 19, 1936, Box 69, FWPNA; McKinzie, "Writers on Relief," 74–84, provides additional details about the manuals.

25. Supplementary Instructions Nos. 11C, 11B, and 11G, to the *American Guide*

Manual, Sept. 19, 1936, July 25, 1936, October 17, 1938, Box 69, and Supplementary Instructions Nos. 15 and 16, the "American Guide Manual," Sept. 15 and Oct. 21, 1936, Box 70, FWPNA. Letters from national FWP officials to state FWP directors offer specific advice about what types of material to place in the introductory essays and what types is in the tours. For example, Alsberg to Paul C. French, state director, Pennsylvania FWP, April 23, 1936, Alsberg-Cronyn files.

26. "Have You Discovered America?" n.d., Box 74, FWPNA; for example, the phrase "Seeing America First" is used as a section heading in "Prospectus, the American Guide," n.d., Box 74, FWPNA. The movement to "See America First," is referred to in unsigned letter to Fiorello LaGuardia, May 16, 1936, Box 11, FWPNA. FWP, "American Guide Manual"; "General Criticism of Material on Hand: New Mexico Points of Interest," Box 109, FWPNA; Supplementary Instructions No. 15 to the "American Guide Manual," Sept. 15, 1936, Box 70, FWPNA. Alsberg to Harrison Parkham, May 8, 1939; unsigned criticism and editorial comment, "Wisconsin Agriculture," Feb. 24, 1938; Alsberg-Cronyn files. Alsberg to Maurice Howe, state director, Utah FWP, May 25, 1936, Box 69 FWPNA.

27. This aspect of the guides is analyzed in Hirsch, "Portrait of America," 119–57.

28. Writers' Program, *The Ohio Guide* (New York: Oxford Univ. Press, 1940), 133; unsigned criticism, "West Virginia: Literature and the Arts," June 25, 1939, Box 189; unsigned criticism of the Oklahoma art essay, June 9, 1937, Box 189, FWPNA; "Story of American Art Told in the American Guide Series," June 3, 1939, Box 83, Division of Information files, WPA; "Suggestions Pertaining to the Guidebook Art Essays", n.d., Box 188, FWPNA; FWP, *California: A Guide to the Golden State* (New York: Hastings House, 1939), 159; FWP, *Delaware, A Guide to the First State* (New York: Viking, 1938), 143–44.

29. Supplementary Instructions No. 3 to the "American Guide Manual," Dec. 16, 1935, Box 69, FWPNA; unsigned, "Vermont Architecture Essay," March 1, 1937, Box 190, FWPNA; Seidenberg, "Ohio, Cleveland Architecture," Dec. 14, 1936, Box 189, FWPNA.

30. Hirsch, "Portrait of America," 149–57.

31. Mary Hornaday, " 'New Light on America' Folklore and Detail about the Past and Present of the United States are to be made available in the American Guide, a volume being prepared as a WPA Project." *Christian Science Monitor,* Nov. 11, 1936; clipping also in Box 460, WPA general file series, Works Progress Administration records, Records Group 69, National Archives, Washington, D.C. WPA.

32. Frederick Gutheim, "America in Guide Books," *Saturday Review of Literature* 24 (June 14, 1941), 5.

33. Critique of Baedeker guide to the United States, n.d., Box 83, Division of Information files, WPA.

34. In thinking about travel books as literature, I have benefited greatly from Paul Fussell, *Abroad: British Literary Traveling Between the Wars* (New York: Oxford Univ. Press, 1980), which is broader than the subtitle indicates and constitutes a

stimulating discussion of the travel genre in general. See especially pp. 37–50, 57, 62–64, 168, 202–15. In addition to Fussell, I have found the following works helpful in thinking about the cultural and social meaning and function of travel: Victor and Edith Turner, *Image and Pilgrimage in Christian Culture: Anthropological Perspectives* (New York: Columbia Univ. Press, 1978), 7–8, 15, 39. Dean McCannell, *The Tourist: A New Theory of the Leisure Class* (New York: Schocken Books, 1976), 46, 125, 150. Valene L. Smith, ed., *Hosts and Guests: The Anthropology of Tourism* (Philadelphia: Univ. of Pennsylvania Press, 1977) and Michael S. Schudson, "On Tourism and Modern Culture," *American Journal of Sociology,* 84 (March 1979), 1240–58, a review essay treating these works.

35. D.W. Meinig, "Symbolic Landscapes: Some Idealizations of Ordinary Landscapes," in Meinig, ed., *The Interpretation of Ordinary Landscapes: Geographical Essays* (New York: Oxford Univ. Press, 1979), 178.

36. Writers' Program, *Texas: A Guide to the Lone Star State* (New York: Hastings House, 1940), 570, 631.

37. For an extreme example of the condescending outsider's tone see the essay on black folkways in FWP, *Mississippi: A Guide to the Magnolia State* (New York: Viking, 1938), 76–86.

38. Supplementary Instructions No. 7 to the "American Guide Manual," Box 69, FWPNA; Walter Pritchard Eaton, "Guides to the Beauties of New England: Writers on Relief Create a Series of American 'Baedekers,' " *New York Herald Tribune Books,* April 24, 1938, pp. 1–2; Supplements to the "American Guide Manual" indicated how national FWP officials constantly thought of their readers as tourists. The following works offer some help in understanding the differences between the local color movement and the regionalism of the 1920s and 1930s: Henry Shapiro , *Appalachia On Our Mind: The Southern Mountains and Mountaineers in the American Consciousness, 1870–1920* (Chapel Hill: Univ. of North Carolina Press, 1978), 6–8; Jay Martin, *Harvests of Change: American Literature, 1865–1914* (Englewood Cliffs, N.J.: Prentice-Hall, 1967), 81–164; Especially important is Michael C. Steiner, "The Regional Impulse in the United States, 1923–1941" (unpublished Ph.D. diss., Univ. of Minnesota, 1978).

39. As quoted in John Foster, *The Life of Charles Dickens* (London: Cecil Palmer, 1928), 370.

40. Alsberg to Lewis Mumford, Oct. 4, 1938, Box 195, FWPNA.

41. Richard Pells, *Radical Visions and American Dreams: Culture and Social Thought in the Depression Years* (New York: Harper and Row, 1973), 316. Penkower, *The Federal Writers' Project* pushes the critical portrait thesis and gives much attention to censorship.

42. Warren I. Susman, "History and the American Intellectual: Uses of a Usable Past," *American Quarterly,* 26 (Summer 1964), 244, 245–48.

43. Stanley Coben, "A Study in Nativism: The American Red Scare of 1919–20," *Political Science Quarterly,* 79 (March 1964), 52–75; John Higham, *Strangers in the Land: Patterns of American Nativism* (New York: Atheneum, 1963).

44. Martin Dies, "Immigration Crisis," *Saturday Evening Post,* 207 (April 20, 1935), 27; Hirsch, "Portrait of America," 214–58.

45. Roosevelt quoted in "American Guide Week Planned for November 10 to 16th," *Publishers' Weekly,* 140 (Oct. 11, 1941), 1463–64.

46. Paul Bergeron, *Paths of the Past: Tennessee 1770–1790* (Knoxville: Univ. of Tennessee Press, 1979), 101–104; Corlew, *Tennessee,* 513.

47. As quoted in Pete Daniel, "The Transformation of the Rural South," 237.

48. As quoted in Michael J. McDonald and John Muldowny, *TVA and the Dispossessed: The Resettlement of the Population in the Norris Dam Area* (Knoxville: Univ. of Tennessee Press, 1982), 263–64.

49. Edwin C. Hargrove and Paul C. Conkin, eds., *TVA: Fifty Years of Grassroots Bureaucracy,* (Urbana: Univ. of Illinois Press, 1983), x.

50. McDonald and Muldowny, *TVA and the Dispossessed,* 217–35, 268–70.

51. Sterling A. Brown, Arthur P. Davis, and Ulysees Lee, eds., *The Negro Caravan: Writings by American Negroes* (New York: Dryden, 1941), 825; see Hirsch, *Portrait of America,* 41–50, 523–61, for an examination of national FWP officials' thinking about the contributions and participation approach to studying American minorities.

52. Goldfield, *Cotton Fields and Skyscrapers,* 194.

53. T.S. Eliot, *After Strange Gods: A Primer of Modern Heresy* (New York: Harcourt, Brace, 1934), 15, 20.

54. For an historical overview of the development of evolutionary and relativistic theories of culture see George Stocking, *Race, Culture, and Evolution: Essays in the History of Anthropology* (New York: Free Press, 1968), 64–90, 195–233.

55. See Alexander Krappe, "American Folklore," in B.A. Botkin, ed., *Folk Say: A Regional Miscellany* (Norman: Univ. of Oklahoma Press, 1930), 291–97. On the impact of evolutionary anthropology on folklore studies see Alan Dundes, "The American Concept of Folklore," *Journal of the Folklore Institute,* 3 (Dec. 1966), 226–49, and his "The Devolutionary Premise in Folklore Theory," *Journal of the Folklore Institute,* 6 (June 1969), 5–19.

56. Botkin, "The Folk in Literature: An Introduction to the New Regionalism," in *Folk-Say: A Regional Miscellany* (Norman: Univ. of Oklahoma Press, 1929), 12. "The Folkness of the Folk," *The English Journal,* 26 (June 1937), 464–65, 469. See also B.A. Botkin, "Manual for Folklore Studies," Aug. 15, 1938, Box 69, and "Social-Ethnic Studies Manual," Sept. 1938, Box 191, FWPNA.

57. My view of Whitman and the problem of creating an American epic has been influenced by James E. Miller, *The American Quest for a Supreme Fiction: Whitman's Legacy in the Personal Epic* (Chicago: Univ. of Chicago Press, 1979), ix, 31–43, and Roy Harvey Pearce, *The Continuity of American Poetry* (Princeton: Princeton Univ. Press, 1961), 59–63, 69–83, 210–20.

58. Most of this material has not been published; however, Banks, *First Person America* provides a good sampling. For an analysis of the social-ethnic materials see

Hirsch, "Portrait of America," especially pp. 523–609. On the regional consciousness of white Southerners see John Sheldon Reed, *Southerners: The Social Psychology of Sectionalism* (Chapel Hill: Univ. of North Carolina Press).

59. "Tooling Down This Side of America," *New York Times Book Review,* March 20, 1938.

For Further Reading About Tennessee

Bergeron, Paul. *Paths of the Past: Tennessee, 1770–1970.* Knoxville: Univ. of Tennessee Press, 1979.

Connelly, Thomas L. *Civil War Tennessee: Battles and Leaders.* Knoxville: Univ. of Tennessee Press, 1979.

Corlew, Robert E., et al. *Tennessee: A Short History.* Knoxville: Univ. of Tennessee Press, 1981.

Dykeman, Wilma. *Tennessee: A Bicentennial History.* New York: Norton, 1975.

Egerton, John. *Visions of Utopia: Nashoba, Rugby, Ruskin and the "New Communities" in Tennessee's Past.* Knoxville: Univ. of Tennessee Press, 1977.

Lamon, Lester C. *Blacks in Tennessee: 1791–1970.* Knoxville: Univ. of Tennessee Press, 1981.

______. *Black Tennesseans, 1900–1930.* Knoxville: Univ. of Tennessee Press, 1977.

Luther, Edward T. *Our Restless Earth: The Geologic Regions of Tennessee.* Knoxville: Univ. of Tennessee Press, 1977.

McDonald, Michael J., and John Muldowny. *TVA and the Dispossessed: The Resettlement of Population in the Norris Dam Area.* Knoxville: Univ. of Tennessee Press, 1982.

Norton, Herman. *Religion in Tennessee: 1777–1945.* Knoxville: Univ. of Tennessee Press, 1981.

Satz, Ronald N. *Tennessee's Indian Peoples: From White Contact to Removal, 1540–1840.* Knoxville: Univ. of Tennessee Press, 1979.

Terrill, Tom E. and Jerrold Hirsch, eds. *Such As Us: Southern Voices of the Thirties.* Chapel Hill: Univ. of North Carolina Press, 1978.

Williams, Frank B., Jr. *Tennessee's Presidents.* Knoxville: Univ. of Tennessee Press, 1981.

Wolfe, Charles K. *Tennessee Strings: The Story of Country Music in Tennessee.* Knoxville: Univ. of Tennessee Press, 1977.

Young, Thomas Daniel. *Tennessee Writers.* Knoxville: Univ. of Tennessee Press, 1981.

Federal Works Agency

WORK PROJECTS ADMINISTRATION

F. C. HARRINGTON, *Commissioner*

FLORENCE KERR, *Assistant Commissioner*

HENRY G. ALSBERG, *Director of the Federal Writers' Project*

Preface

Nearly four centuries ago, in 1541, the area now known as Tennessee was described by the Gentleman of Elvas, chronicler of De Soto's expedition. Vastly more complex and comprehensive than this early narrative is the present account, compiled by the Federal Writers' Project of the Work Projects Administration. *Tennessee: A Guide to the State* attempts to define the State in its important aspects—social, economic, historical, cultural—and to picture the life of its people against their natural background. The writers have aimed not only to supply visitors from outside the State with information that may increase their interest, but also to give Tennesseans a ready source through which their understanding of their native territory may be deepened and enriched.

The task has not been easy. Many phases of Tennessee life and history had not previously been studied, and for the purposes of this volume much original research was necessary. Accuracy demanded that, wherever practicable, existing documents be checked against their sources.

Compilation of such a work would have been next to impossible without the generous help given to the Project by various public and private agencies and by many individuals. Space is lacking in which to mention all to whom appreciation and gratitude are due.

The Project is especially indebted to Jennings Perry, editor of the Nashville *Tennessean,* for reading and criticizing the entire manuscript and for his advice during its preparation; to Dr. Charles S. Johnson, of Fisk University, for his help in preparing the article on "Negroes in Tennessee"; and to the following persons for reading and criticizing parts of the book in its final form: Sam F. Brewster, State Commissioner of Conservation; Dr. Willis Baxter Boyd, Director of State Information; Walter F. Pond, State Geologist; James Bailey and John Caldwell, of the State Department of Conservation; E. S. Draper, Director of the Department of Regional Planning Studies of the Tennessee Valley Authority.

Among others who have furnished information and criticized parts of the manuscript dealing with matters in their particular fields are: *History*—Dr. Robert White, Mrs. John Trotwood Moore, Mrs. Reau Folk, the late Judge John R. DeWitt, Meriwether Lewis, P. H. Hicks, Mrs. Clyde Braley; *Geology, Archeology and Natural Resources*—L. C. Glenn, R. W.

Johnson, Kendall E. Born, Dr. George I. Whitlatch, T. M. N. Lewis, H. D. Ruhm; *Flora and Fauna*—Dr. Harry S. Vaughn, Dr. H. M. Jennison, Howell Buntin, Damon Headden, James O. Hazard; *Education and Government*—Dr. R. R. Vance, Dr. Thomas Elsa Jones, W. C. Davidson, J. E. Anderson; *Folklore*—Dr. George Pullen Jackson, Dr. C. S. Pendleton; *Architecture*—Henry C. Hibbs, Wilbur Creighton; *General Information*—Donald Davidson, Mary Rothrock, Mrs. Brainard Chaney, Dr. A. F. Kuhlman. Other acknowledgments are made in the bibliography.

For their aid and cooperation we are indebted to the newspapers, libraries, chambers of commerce and other civic organizations of the State; the State Planning Commission; the Nashville Automobile Club and the Tennessee Valley Authority.

This volume was begun under the directorship of Colonel A. P. Foster and continued almost to its completion under Charles J. Elder, former State Director.

WILLIAM R. MCDANIEL, *State Director*
JAMES R. ASWELL
WILLIAM H. BUNCE } *Editors*

Contents

	PAGE
PREFACE	lxiii
LIST OF ILLUSTRATIONS	lxvii
LIST OF MAPS	lxxi
GENERAL INFORMATION	lxxiii
CALENDAR OF EVENTS	lxxvii

I. Tennessee: The Background

CROSS SECTION OF A THREEFOLD STATE	3
NATURAL SETTING AND CONSERVATION	7
THE FIRST AMERICANS	27
HISTORY AND GOVERNMENT	43
INDUSTRY AND COMMERCE	65
AGRICULTURE	74
THE WORKING MAN	81
TRANSPORTATION	91
TENNESSEE VALLEY AUTHORITY	98
NEGROES IN TENNESSEE	104
RELIGION	111
EDUCATION	120
SPORTS AND RECREATION	128
FOLKLORE: THE LIVING PAST	134
WRITERS OF TENNESSEE	145
ARCHITECTURE	155
THE ARTS	167

II. City and Town

NASHVILLE	179
MEMPHIS	206
KNOXVILLE	232
CHATTANOOGA	251
JACKSON	270
COLUMBIA	274
KINGSPORT	279

III. *Tours*

		PAGE
TOUR 1.	(Roanoke, Va.)–Bristol–Knoxville–Cleveland. [US 11E, US 11]	289
	Section a. Bristol to Knoxville	
	Section b. Knoxville to Cleveland	
TOUR 1A.	(Roanoke, Va.)–Bristol–Kingsport–Knoxville. [US 11W]	308
TOUR 1B.	Bristol–Mountain City–Elizabethton–Johnson City. [US 421, STATE 67, US 19E]	315
TOUR 2.	(Appalachia, Va.)–Kingsport–Johnson City–(Asheville, N. C.). [US 23, US 23–19W]	320
TOUR 3.	(Middlesboro, Ky.)–Cumberland Gap–Morristown–Junction with US 70. [US 25E]	326
TOUR 4.	Junction with State 33–Tallassee–Chilhowee–(Topton, N. C.). [US 129]	330
TOUR 5.	(Williamsburg, Ky.)–Jellico–Knoxville–Sevierville–(Asheville, N. C.). [US 25W, STATE 35, STATE 71]	332
	Section a. Kentucky Line to Knoxville	
	Section b. Knoxville to North Carolina Line	
TOUR 5A.	Junction with US 25W–Norris Dam–Knoxville–Maryville–(Chatsville, Ga.). [STATE 33]	343
	Section a. Junction with US 25W to Knoxville	
	Section b. Knoxville to Georgia Line	
TOUR 5B.	Junction with State 71–Kinzel Springs–Maryville. [STATE 73]	356
TOUR 6.	(Somerset, Ky.)–Oneida–Dayton–Chattanooga–(La Fayette, Ga.). [US 27]	359
	Section a. Kentucky Line to junction with US 70	
	Section b. Junction with US 70 to Georgia Line	
TOUR 7.	(Glasgow, Ky.)–Nashville–Columbia–Pulaski–(Athens, Ala.). [US 31E, US 31]	366
	Section a. Kentucky Line to Nashville	
	Section b. Nashville to Alabama Line	
TOUR 7A.	Nashville–Lewisburg–Pulaski. [STATE 11]	383
TOUR 7B.	Columbia–Lawrenceburg–(Florence, Ala.). [STATE 6]	386
TOUR 8.	(Hopkinsville, Ky.)–Springfield–Nashville–Monteagle. [US 41E, US 41]	391
	Section a. Kentucky Line to Nashville	
	Section b. Nashville to Monteagle	
TOUR 8A.	Murfreesboro–Shelbyville–Fayetteville–(Huntsville, Ala.). [US 241]	404

PAGE

TOUR 9. (Russellville, Ky.)–Clarksville–Martin–Union City. [STATE 13, 76, 54, 22] 407

TOUR 10. (Mayfield, Ky.)–Martin–Jackson–(Corinth, Miss.). [US 45E, 45] 412

TOUR 11. (Fulton, Ky.)–Union City–Dyersburg–Memphis–(Sena Cobia, Miss.). [US 51] 417

TOUR 11A. Dyersburg–Tiptonville–Reelfoot Lake–(Hickman, Ky.). [STATE 78] 423

TOUR 12. (Asheville, N. C.)–Knoxville–Crossville–Nashville–Memphis (Little Rock, Ark.). [US 70] 430
- Section a. North Carolina Line to Knoxville
- Section b. Knoxville to Nashville
- Section c. Nashville to Memphis

TOUR 12A. Crossville–McMinnville–Murfreesboro. [US 70A] 464

TOUR 12B. Junction with US 70–Centerville–Lexington–Junction with US 70. [STATE 100, STATE 20] 471

TOUR 13. (Murphy, N. C.)–Cleveland–Chattanooga–Pulaski–Junction with US 70. [US 64] 474
- Section a. North Carolina Line to Chattanooga
- Section b. Chattanooga to Pulaski
- Section c. Pulaski to Selmer
- Section d. Selmer to junction with US 70

TOUR 14. (Hopkinsville, Ky.)–Clarksville–Pleasant View–Nashville. [US 41W, STATE 112] 493

TOUR 15. (Albany, Ky.)–Jamestown–Crossville–Chattanooga. [STATE 28, 27] 496

TOUR 16. (Albany, Ky.)–Livingston–Cookeville–Monteagle. [STATE 42, US 70–Alt., STATE 56] 506

GREAT SMOKY MOUNTAINS NATIONAL PARK 513

IV. Appendices

CHRONOLOGY 521

SELECTED BIBLIOGRAPHY 529

INDEX 537

Illustrations

IRIS, THE STATE FLOWER Page 2

Photograph from Tennessee Department of Conservation

CANE CREEK FALLS, FALLS CREEK STATE PARK 9

Photograph from Tennessee Department of Conservation

RACCOON 16

Photograph from Tennessee Department of Conservation

AN EXAMPLE OF SEVERE SOIL EROSION 23

Photograph from Tennessee Department of Conservation

AIR VIEW OF TERRACED LANDS, A SOIL CONSERVATION PROJECT 25

Photograph from Tennessee Department of Conservation

SEQUOYAH AND HIS ALPHABET 41

Photograph by C. B. King

ANDREW JACKSON 51

Photograph by L. C. Handy Studios

CHICKAMAUGA CREEK, BATTLE OF CHICKAMAUGA, SEPTEMBER, 1863 57

Photograph by U. S. Army Signal Corps

THE CAPITOL, NASHVILLE 63

Photograph by E. C. McGlynnan

MARBLE QUARRY, NEAR KNOXVILLE 69

Photograph by W. Lincoln Highton

THE MEMPHIS WHARF 72

Photograph by Poland

RUST COTTON PICKER IN ACTION 77

Photograph from Rust Cotton Picker Co.

COTTON PICKERS 83

Photograph from Farm Security Administration

DECK HAND ON RIVER BOAT 89

Photograph from Farm Security Administration

OLD RIVER PACKET AT THE NASHVILLE WHARF 95

Photograph from Nashville Chamber of Commerce

POWER—THE CASCADE OF THE CLINCH RIVER 99

Photograph from Tennessee Valley Authority

KITCHEN IN A NORRIS HOME 101

Photograph from Tennessee Valley Authority

FIRST GROUP OF FISK JUBILEE SINGERS (1871) 107

Photograph from Fisk University

MEHARRY MEDICAL COLLEGE (NEGRO), NASHVILLE 109
Photograph from Meharry Medical College

ST. MARY'S CHURCH, MEMPHIS 117
Photograph by W. Lincoln Highton

VANDERBILT UNIVERSITY, NASHVILLE 123
Photograph by C. P. Clark, Inc.

SCHOOL CONSTRUCTED BY WPA 127
Photograph from Works Progress Administration

DUCK HUNTING IN REELFOOT LAKE 131
Photograph from Tennessee Department of Conservation

FISHING IN A GREAT SMOKIES STREAM 133
Photograph by Thompson's, Inc.

WOMAN CARDING 137
Photograph from Farm Security Administration

MONDAY 142
Photograph from Tennessee Valley Authority

FORT NASHBOROUGH, NASHVILLE 157
Photograph by W. Lincoln Highton

THE STERRICK BUILDING, MEMPHIS .163
Photograph by W. Lincoln Highton

DIXIE HOMES, A FEDERAL HOUSING PROJECT FOR NEGROES, MEMPHIS 165
Photograph from U. S. Housing Authority

ABUNDANCE, MURAL IN POST OFFICE, CLARKSVILLE 171
Photograph from Treasury Department Art Projects

SIGNATURES OF THE CUMBERLAND COMPACT 183
Photograph from Tennessee Historical Society

SCARRITT COLLEGE, NASHVILLE 199
Photograph by Henry C. Hibbs, Architect

AIR VIEW—DOWNTOWN MEMPHIS 208
Photograph from Tennessee Department of Conservation

SLUM DWELLERS, MEMPHIS 213
Photograph from U. S. Housing Authority

SHELBY COUNTY COURTHOUSE, MEMPHIS 218
Photograph by Tuttle

ROBERTSON TOPP HOME, MEMPHIS 223
Photograph by W. Lincoln Highton

IDLEWILD CHURCH, MEMPHIS 226
Photograph by W. Lincoln Highton

GATEWAY, BLOUNT MANSION, KNOXVILLE 243
Photograph by W. Lincoln Highton

CHURCH STREET M. E. CHURCH, KNOXVILLE 245
Photograph by C. P. Clark, Inc.

THE "GENERAL," CHATTANOOGA 258
Photograph by "Chattanooga News"

OCHS MEMORIAL TEMPLE, CHATTANOOGA 263
Photograph by W. Lincoln Highton

MULE DAY PARADE, COLUMBIA 275
Photograph by Gilbert Orr

THE SAMUEL POLK HOME, COLUMBIA 277
Photograph from Tennessee Department of Conservation

MAKING CELLULOSE ACETATE 281
Photograph from Tennessee Eastman Corp.

THE NETHERLANDS INN, KINGSPORT 285
Photograph by W. Lincoln Highton

THE OLD TAVERN, JONESBORO 293
Photograph by W. Lincoln Highton

ANDREW JOHNSON TAILOR SHOP, GREENVILLE 299
Photograph by W. Lincoln Highton

HAWKINS COUNTY COURTHOUSE, ROGERSVILLE 313
Photograph by W. Lincoln Highton

COUNTRY SAWMILL 322
Photograph from Tennessee Department of Conservation

MOUNTAIN FARMER 325
Photograph from Tennessee Valley Authority

A HANDICRAFT SHOP 333
Photograph by W. Lincoln Highton

IN A GRIST MILL 337
Photograph from Farm Security Administration

NEWFOUND GAP 343
Photograph from Tennessee Department of Conservation

NORRIS FREEWAY 347
Photograph from Tennessee Valley Authority

DEFIANCE 357
Photograph from Tennessee Department of Conservation

RAYON THREAD, OLD HICKORY MILLS 373
Photograph from E. I. du Pont de Nemours & Co.

HAYNES HAVEN, NEAR COLUMBIA 380
Photograph by E. C. McGlynnan

OX TEAM IN THE MOUNTAINS 387
Photograph from Tennessee Department of Conservation

CEMETERY, STONE'S RIVER NATIONAL MILITARY PARK, NEAR MURFREESBORO 400
Photograph by W. Lincoln Highton

TENNESSEE COLLEGE, MURFREESBORO 403
Photograph from Tennessee College

SHARECROPPER'S FAMILY 408
Photograph from Tennessee Valley Authority

WEIGHING COTTON 418
Photograph from Tennessee Valley Authority

GOING TO THE GIN 421
Photograph from Tennessee Valley Authority

SAND BAGS STRENGTHEN A MISSISSIPPI LEVEE 425
Photograph from Meharry Medical College

BARN 433
Photograph by W. Lincoln Highton

ROADSIDE FUR MARKET 440
Photograph by W. Lincoln Highton

CROSSVILLE 443
Photograph from Resettlement Administration

THE HERMITAGE, HOME OF ANDREW JACKSON, NEAR NASHVILLE 450
Photograph from Tennessee Department of Conservation

OPOSSUM 460
Photograph from Tennessee Department of Conservation

RESTING 465
Photograph by Wood

RURAL SHOPPING CENTER, WOODBURY 470
Photograph by W. Lincoln Highton

TENNESSEE'S LARGEST PECAN TREE—NATCHEZ TRACE FOREST 475
Photograph from Tennessee Department of Conservation

TENNESSEE CAVERNS, NEAR CHATTANOOGA 481
Photograph from Tennessee Caverns

SHARECROPPER'S CABIN 487
Photograph from Tennessee Valley Authority

ONE-ROOM COUNTRY SCHOOL 497
Photograph from Farm Security Administration

MAKING SORGUM MOLASSES 501
Photograph from Tennessee Valley Authority

FALL CREEK FALLS 504
Photograph from Tennessee Valley Authority

INTERIOR OF CUMBERLAND HOMESTEAD 511
Photograph from Farm Security Administration

A SMOKY MOUNTAIN VIEW 515
Photograph by Thompson's, Inc.

OLD WATER MILL IN THE GREAT SMOKIES 517
Photograph from National Park Service

Maps

DOWNTOWN NASHVILLE	*Pages* 186 *and* 187
DOWNTOWN MEMPHIS.	216
DOWNTOWN KNOXVILLE	240 *and* 241
DOWNTOWN CHATTANOOGA	260
REELFOOT LAKE	427

General Information

Railroads: Interstate roads are as follows: Alabama Great Southern R.R. (AGS), Clinchfield R.R. (Clinchfield), Central of Georgia Ry. (C. of Ga.), Chicago, Rock Island and Pacific Ry. (Rock Island), Illinois Central R.R. (IC), Gulf, Mobile & Northern R.R. (GM&N), Louisville & Nashville R.R. (L&N), Mobile & Ohio R.R. (M&O), Nashville, Chattanooga & St. Louis Ry. (NC&ST.L), Southern Ry. (S.Ry.), Tennessee Central Ry. (TC), Missouri Pacific R.R. (MP), St. Louis-San Francisco Ry. (Frisco), St. Louis-Southwestern Ry. (Cottonbelt). *(See TRANSPORTATION MAP.)*

Highways: Total mileage: 69,713; all kinds of paved roads: 2,294; treated gravel: 1,782. State has a highway patrol. Gasoline tax 7¢.

Bus Lines: Interstate bus lines: Airline Motor Coaches, Arkansas Motor Coaches, Atlantic Greyhound Lines, Bowling Green-Hopkinsville Bus Co., Capitol Motor Lines, Carolina Coach Co., Consolidated Coach Lines, Crescent Stages, Crown Coach Co., Dixie Greyhound Lines, Eastern Michigan Motorbusses, Eastern Tennessee & Western North Carolina Motor Transportation Co., Fuqua Bus Lines, Greyhound Lines, Rufkin-Beaumont Bus Line, McKee Bus Lines, Missouri-Arkansas Coach Lines, Missouri Pacific Trailways, Mooney Port Arthur Bus Line, National Trailways System, Ohio Bus Line Co., Queen City Coach Co., Red Ball Bus Co., Short Way Lines, Southeastern Greyhound Lines, Southern Limited, Tennessee Coach Co., Tri-State Transit Co., Washington Motor Coach System.

Local Bus Routes: Cason-Miller Bus Co., Central Bus Lines, Cherokee Motor Coach Co., Consolidated Bus Lines, Gibbs Bus Line, Lewisburg Bus Lines, Ray Bus Lines, Smoky Mountains Stages, Washington County Bus Line.

Air Lines: American Airlines (Boston to Los Angeles) stop at Nashville and Memphis; American Airlines (Nashville to Washington) stop at Knoxville and Bristol. Eastern Air Lines (Chicago to Miami) stop at Nashville and Chattanooga. Chicago and Southern Air Lines (Chicago to New Orleans) stop at Memphis. *(See TRANSPORTATION MAP.)*

Waterways: No regular scheduled passenger transportation service in the

State. There are, however, occasional excursions on the Cumberland, the Tennessee, and the Mississippi.

Motor Vehicle Laws (digest): No maximum speed. No licenses required for visitors for 30 days; minimum age for drivers, 16 years. Hand signals must be used. Personal injury or property damage should be reported to highway patrol immediately, and drivers must stop and render all possible assistance.

Prohibited: Spotlights, parking on highways, passing streetcars on L. (in cities or towns); drivers must come to full stop while streetcars are loading or unloading passengers, unless at safety zones. Cars and semi-trailers must not be more than 35 ft. in length. *(Local traffic regulations under general information in large cities.)*

Accommodations: First-class hotel accommodations in cities. Tourist camps are plentiful near urban centers, scarcer in rural sections. Urban sections of East Tennessee well supplied with tourist accommodations, both camps and resort hotels. Some places open all year; others for tourist season only.

Climate and Equipment: State as a whole has cool spring and very warm summer; cold weather from November until March. Winter temperature for brief periods drops to zero. Tourists passing through Tennessee en route to far South should have a heavy coat. Because of favorable spring and fall temperature throughout southern highland region, vacation season is much longer than in most other recreation regions of United States.

Drinking Water: Although water from open springs and wells has been declared impure by State health department, it is used by local people without ill effects.

RECREATION AND CONSERVATION AREAS

(Projects now [1939] in the process of development are marked with an asterisk.)

National Parks: Chickamauga and Chattanooga National Military Park, near Chattanooga *(see Chattanooga);* Fort Donelson National Military Park, near Dover *(see Tour 9)*; Shiloh National Military Park, near Stantonville *(see Tour 10);* Stones River National Military Park, near Murfreesboro *(see Tour 8);* Great Smoky Mountains National Park, near Knoxville *(see Tour 5).*

State Parks: Chickasaw State Park, near Henderson *(see Tour 10);* Cove Lake State Park, near Caryville *(see Tour 5);* Grundy Forest State Park, near Tracy City *(see Tour 16)*; Cedars of Lebanon State Park, near Lebanon *(see Tour 12)*; Natchez Trace State Park, near Lexington *(see Tour 12B)*; Pickett State Park & Forest, near Jamestown *(see Tour 15)*; Standing Stone State Park, near Livingston *(see Tour 16)*.

State Forests: *Bledsoe State Forest, near Pikeville; *Lewis State Forest, near Hohenwald; *Marion-Franklin State Forest, near Sewanee; *Morgan State Forest, near Wartburg; *Stewart State Forest, near Dover.

State Game Preserves: Buffalo Springs Game Farm, near Rutledge *(see Tour 1A)*; *Headdon Lakes Game Preserve, near Tracy City; Reelfoot Lake Game Preserve, near Tiptonville *(see Tour 11A)*.

Recreational Demonstration Areas: Fall Creek Falls Recreational Demonstration Area, near Pikeville *(see Tour 15)*; Montgomery Bell Recreational Demonstration Area, near Dickson *(see Tour 12)*; Shelby Forest Recreational Demonstration Area, near Memphis *(see Tour 11)*.

Farm Security Administration Area: Cumberland Homesteads Park, near Crossville *(see Tour 15)*.

TVA Parks: Big Ridge Park, near Knoxville *(see Sports and Recreation)*; Norris Park, near Norris *(see Tour 5A)*; Pickwick Dam Reservation, near Pickwick *(see Tour 10)*.

Fish and Game Laws (digest): Trout (Brook, Brown, Rainbow)—open season May 1 to July 4, September 1 to October 15, 7 inches. Creel limit 10 per day. Black Bass (Largemouth, Smallmouth and Spotted, or Kentucky Bass)—June 1 to February 28, 11 inches. Creel limit 8 per day. Walleyed Pike (Pike perch—Jack Salmon)—June 1 to February 28, 15 inches. Creel limit 5 per day. Muskellunge (Silver Jack)—June 1 to February 28, 20 inches. Creel limit 5 per day. Yellow Bass and White Bass—all year, 10 inches. Creel limit 20 per day. Crappie—all year, 8 inches. Creel limit 20 per day. Rock Bass and Warmouth Bass (Black Perch and Goggle Eye)—all year, any size. Creel limit 20 per day. Sunfish and Bluegills (Bream, Sun perch, etc.)—all year, any size. Creel limit 25 per day. Catfish, Buffalo and Drum—all year, 15 inches. No limit. Sturgeon and Spoonbill—all year, 30 inches. No limit. Bullheads, Gar, Grinnel, Suckers, Mullet, Red Horse, Black Horse, Carp, Goldfish, Shad, Herring, Eels, no closed season, no size limit, no creel limit. Mosquito Fish (Gambusia) no open season.

Exceptions: No closed season on Reelfoot Lake or on private lakes. Resident Fishing licenses, $1.00, Hunting and Fishing, $2.00, non-resident fishing, seven day trip, $1.00, annual, $3.00. Women not exempt from license. Children under 16 exempt. *(Get local regulations.)*

Open Season for Hunting: Quail and grouse, November 25 to January 25, both dates inclusive. Bag limit on quail 12 per day, on grouse 4 per day. Wild turkey, November 1 to January 1, inclusive. Bag limit 3 a season. Waterfowl, coots, gallinules, Wilson snipe or jacksnipe, November 1 to January 31. Bag limit 15 per day. (Subject to Federal Regulation.) Doves, black-breasted and golden plover, greater and lesser yellowlegs, September 1 to December 15. Bag limit 15 per day. (Subject to Federal Regulation.) Male deer, December 1 to December 15, inclusive. Bag limit 1 per season. Raccoons, muskrats, minks, skunks, opossums, otters, weasels and gray foxes, November 1 to February 1, inclusive. No bag limit. Squirrels, June to January, inclusive. Bag limit 10 per day. Rabbits, November 25 to January 25, inclusive. No bag limit.

Liquor Regulations: Package sales legal on county option. Beers and light wines legal.

Prohibited: Digging in archeological sites, picking wild flowers, chopping trees in State and National Park areas; also prohibited on private property without permission from the owner.

Poisonous Plants, Reptiles, and Insects: Poison ivy found throughout Cumberland and Appalachian Mts.; some species will kill cattle. Poisonous species of mushrooms found in damp low sections of West Tennessee and along streams in other sections of the State. Mosquitoes in all sections where there is standing water. Black widow spiders few, but found in all sections. Rattlesnakes in all rocky and wooded sections. Copperheads mostly in the lowland woods; few on mountains. Cottonmouth moccasins in large rivers, but scarce.

Calendar of Events

("nfd" means no fixed date)

Jan.	1	State-wide	National Emancipation Day (Negro)
	10	Knoxville	University of Tennessee Relay Races
Feb.	1st week	Grand Junction	National Field Trials for Bird Dogs
	15	Jackson	Amateur Field Trial Association Meet
	4th week	Knoxville	Southern Basketball Tournament
	nfd	Nashville	Golden Gloves Tournament
Mar.	4th Sun.	Nashville	Sermon on Prodigal Son
	nfd	Franklin	Jack, Jennet, and Stallion Show
	nfd	Memphis	Tri-State Basketball Tournament
	nfd	Nashville	State Teachers Association Meets
Apr.	1st Fri.	State-wide	Arbor Day
	1st Mon.	Columbia	Mule Day Festival
	2nd week	Knoxville	Southern Fox Hunters Association Meet
	4th week	Nashville	Iris Festival
	30	Springfield	Tulip Show
	30	Colliersville	Cheese Carnival
	nfd	Dyersburg	West Tennessee Cotton Carnival
	nfd	Old Hickory	Middle Tennessee Field Trials
May	1	Bristol	Dogwood Festival
	3	Liberty	Song Festival
	1st Sun.	Post Oak	Meeting of Old Harp Singers
	nfd	Ashwood	Pilgrimage to Bishop Otey's Shrine
	nfd	Memphis	Cotton Carnival
	nfd	Humboldt	Strawberry Festival
June	12-13	Nashville	State Shoot Meet
	21	Chattanooga	Pigeon Racing Association Meet
	24-26	Murfreesboro	Middle Tennessee Educational Association Meets
	nfd	Nashville	Institute of International Relations Meets

July	4	Knoxville	Tennessee Valley Boat Club Races
	4	Lawrenceburg	Picnic and All-Day Singing
	10	Knoxville	Junior Aviators Tournament
	20	Knoxville	National Association of Negro Musicians Meets
Aug.	8	Knoxville	Hole-In-One Tournament
	8	State wide	State Emancipation Day (Negro)
	2nd week	Greenbrier	Smoky Mountain Hiking Club Annual Meet
	21	Knoxville	4-H Club Meet—University of Tennessee
	nfd	Memphis	Doc Huttum's River Marathon
Sept.	2nd week	Murfreesboro	Rutherford County Fair
	2nd week	Maryville	Blount County Fair
	2nd week	Fayetteville	Lincoln County Fair
	2nd week	Jackson	Madison County Fair
	3rd week	Nashville	Tennessee State Fair
	4th week	Sevierville	Sevier County Fair
	4th week	Pulaski	Agricultural Fair
	4th week	Dresden	Sweet Potato Festival
	nfd	Memphis	Mid South Fair
	nfd	Chattanooga	Tri-State Fair
Oct.	20	Martin	Weakley County Singing Convention
	3rd week	Tellico Plains	Wild Boar Hunt
Nov.	2nd week (alt. yrs.)	Nashville Knoxville	Vanderbilt vs. University of Tennessee Football Game

PART I

Tennessee: The Background

IRIS, THE STATE FLOWER

Cross Section of a Threefold State

TENNESSEE is an agricultural State, and the culture of its people has grown out of their struggle with the earth. This is true despite the rapid growth of industry, for even the urban areas are dominated by the traditions of farm life. With few exceptions, the cities largely retain the flavor of country towns.

East, Middle, and West Tennessee, the three geographical divisions, in many ways are like separate States. Although the people are alike in heritage and in general attitude, there are striking sectional differences fostered by the lay of the land. West Tennesseans may differ as much from East Tennesseans in manners and customs as the people of the Appalachian Mountain regions differ from those of the Mississippi Delta.

Between the North Carolina line and the Cumberland Plateau is East Tennessee, an upland region whose high mountains, thickly wooded foothills, broken knob country, and narrow valleys have made it, until recent years, the most shut-in section of the State. Here are the hazy ramparts of the Great Smokies, the gaunt ridges of the Unakas and the Clinch Mountains; and in the Tennessee Valley is Norris Dam, one of the chief units of the Tennessee Valley Authority's vast project. This region is the home of the mountain folk, "our contemporary forefathers," descendants of the pioneers of British, Huguenot, and Pennsylvania German stock, who built their log cabins deep among the ridges. Often the butt of absurd and distorted jokes and stories, these rugged people, isolated in their mountains, are content to live precisely as did the first white settlers. Some of them resented the TVA resettlement program and the bringing in of outlanders with newfangled ideas—even though it promised to give unheard-of advantages to their children and to save land made almost worthless by erosion.

Throughout East Tennessee the cabins of old frontier days, with their little porthole-like windows and dog-trots (open runways), still stand, bearing the scars of Indian tomahawks and bullets. Tucked away in the hills, too, are ancient water mills with slow, moss-covered wheels, to which mountain boys still come on muleback with a turn of corn to be ground into meal. Even in their simple pleasures these mountain folk cling to the past. Quilting and husking parties, fiddling, singing, and dancing are among the popular pastimes.

In politics, as in most things, the East Tennessean shows his independence, for here in an otherwise normally Democratic State is a strong Republican district that regularly chooses Republican representatives in both State and Federal elections. To the East Tennessean, West Tennessee is almost as far away and unknown as Missouri. He looks upon this western section as a swamp and resents the weight of the powerful Shelby County political machine in State-wide elections. What West Tennessee is for, he's "agin." The TVA is a recent exception.

Knoxville, seat of the State University, is the western gateway to the Great Smoky Mountains National Park and the Cherokee National Forest, former hunting ground of the Cherokee. Surrounding Chattanooga are famous battlefields: Lookout Mountain, Missionary Ridge, Walden's Ridge, Orchard Knob, and Chickamauga. These two industrial cities have attracted much northern capital, and their populations are a blend of mountain blood and "furriner" or Yankee.

Middle Tennessee, hemmed in by the looping Tennessee River, is a gently rolling bluegrass country, fertile, well watered, and famous for its fine livestock—blooded horses and mules—and its dark-fired tobacco. The heart of the State, it is rich in tradition and history, and its inhabitants hold to the customs of the Old South. Hardly a day passes that some mention of the War between the States and of a pioneer incident is not made by a city or county paper. The great Indian mounds of the Harpeth and Cumberland Rivers are links with a more distant past.

Most of the towns are old, and in them and along the highways of the countrysides are ante-bellum homes, some in decay. Descendants of the State's founders proudly cling to their traditions. Nashville, capital of the State, was in 1780 the scene of the drafting and signing of the Cumberland Compact, whereby 256 pioneers set up an independent government. Near by are the Hermitage, home of Andrew Jackson, and the town of Smyrna, birthplace of Sam Davis, youthful hero of the War between the States. Sixty miles south of Nashville is Pulaski, where the original Ku Klux Klan was formed in 1865.

It is for its cultural pre-eminence that Middle Tennessee is perhaps best known. With few exceptions, such as the University of Tennessee at Knoxville and Southwestern at Memphis, the State's leading educational institutions are in this division; here are Vanderbilt University, George Peabody College for Teachers, the University of the South, Ward-Belmont School, and the three Negro institutions—Fisk University, Meharry Medical College, and Tennessee Agricultural and Industrial State Teachers College.

Between the Tennessee River and the Mississippi is West Tennessee, which was the land of the Chickasaw and the "last frontier" of the State. With its rugged hills, rich valleys, and deep black bottoms, this section leads agriculturally. Most of the farms are now small, and berries and vegetables have become important rivals of cotton and corn. At intervals the bottoms are at the mercy of flood waters. In this section a good deal of the free-and-easy spirit of the frontier remains, and white and Negro accept good luck and bad philosophically. Because cotton has always dominated its economy, West Tennessee has the largest Negro population. In two counties (Haywood and Fayette), Negroes outnumber the whites.

There is a newness about most of the towns. With the exception of Bolivar, Brownsville, Somerville, La Grange, Troy, Moscow, and a few others, they have virtually been rebuilt within the last twenty-five years. Memphis, on the Mississippi near the Arkansas boundary line, is the metropolis of the division. It has the atmosphere of the cosmopolitan West, and its annual Cotton Carnival draws visitors from everywhere. In the center of the region is Jackson, made famous in song and story as the home of Casey Jones.

The long history of Tennessee has left its landmarks here. On the steep bluffs of the Mississippi, in the walled city of Cisco on the south fork of the Forked Deer River, and along the Tennessee River near Pittsburg Landing are the remains of the earthworks raised by the Mound Builders. In the northwestern corner is Reelfoot Lake, formed by the New Madrid earthquake of 1811–12; in the southeastern section, Shiloh battlefield recalls the tragic war years, and the TVA'S Pickwick Landing Dam represents present-day development.

Throughout Tennessee, particularly in the great rural counties—some of them older than the State itself—traditional allegiance counts heavily. County traditions, too, are so strong that the individual, however far he migrates, continues to feel loyal to his native county and usually identifies himself with his section. Ask a Tennessean where he lives, and he does not say, "I'm from Dyersburg," but rather, "I'm from Dyer County in West Tennessee."

Back of this tradition is a strong sense of family, kin, and clan. Blood relationship may often mean more than wealth or ability. Family connections, even the wider and vaguer ties, may influence county and local politics and business affairs. When Jim Tuttle announces for county office, all his kinfolk start electioneering for him. "These Tuttles are thick as blackbirds in a wheat field." Let Cousin Jim get into trouble and the Tuttle army rallies to his aid.

The Tennessean as a voter is, for the most part, independent in local politics; it is hard to dictate to him his selection of a candidate for public office. But in regular elections the rural sections are seldom able to overcome the strength of the well-organized urban districts. In the past few years machine politics has tended to penetrate each county, and frequently the rural folk "line up" with their city cousins when they feel that they will be benefited by the policies of the group.

Tennesseans' lives are unhurried. Though they may complain about weather, poor crops, bad business and politics, beneath all is a certain feeling of security. The farmer will leave his plowing, the attorney his lawsuit, the business man his accounts, for a moment's or an hour's conversation with stranger or friend. With his good-tempered easiness of manners, the Tennessean has a democratic feeling of equality. His mind, unlike his bed, does not have to be made up each morning, for his judgment and dignity proceed from himself. Whether of farm, mountain, or city, he is like the Tennessee farmer who, after hearing Martin Van Buren speak, stepped up, shook the President's hand, and invited him "to come out and r'ar around with the boys."

Natural Setting and Conservation

A NOTED Tennessee orator used to declare: "Our great State is the *multum in parvo* of all the lands lying between the ramparts of the Alleghenies and the majestic currents of the mighty Mississippi. Within its borders flourishes every shape of beast and bug, every variety of tree and flower found from the blue waters of the Gulf to the somber snow-laden forests of Canada." Couched in less sweeping language, this would not be the exaggeration it seems. A relief map shows Tennessee as a succession of mountain slopes, the worn-down remnant of the towering Appalachian chain of remote geologic time. From the crests of the Great Smokies the land drops westward in a series of ever lower ridge and plateau systems to the Mississippi bottoms.

Roughly a parallelogram in shape, with an east-west length of 432 miles and a width of 106 miles, Tennessee is bounded on the north by Kentucky and Virginia, on the east by North Carolina, on the south by Georgia, Alabama, and Mississippi, and on the west by the Mississippi River, which separates it from Arkansas and Missouri. Of the total area of 42,022 square miles, 335 are water surface.

The State divides naturally into three general regions: upland East Tennessee, Middle Tennessee with its foothills and basins, and low flat West Tennessee. Often called "three separate States within common boundaries," these "Grand Divisions" coincide with three rather distinct cultural and political units, and differ sharply in climate and natural life. In upper East Tennessee the climate, vegetation, and animal life approximate those of New England; in the plateau and basin regions of Middle Tennessee they parallel those of Ohio; West Tennessee, except for scattered hilly sections, is of the Deep South.

A more exact break-down on the basis of physiographic features divides the State into six regions. The first includes the Unaka and Smoky Mountains extending along the North Carolina border. The Smokies, reaching at some points an elevation of 6,600 feet above sea level and covering an area here of approximately 2,000 square miles, are broken by many coves and valleys along their length and breadth. The second region, flanking the Smokies, is the Great Valley of East Tennessee, thirty to sixty miles wide. The valley floor is composed of a succession of minor ridges and valleys, beginning on the northeast as a continuation of the Shenandoah Valley and slanting southwest into Georgia and Alabama. Viewed from the Smokies on the east or the Cumberland Mountains on the west, this bottom melts into a common plain, although its ridges rise 300 to 800 feet above the valley floor. A region of fat soils and prosperous farms, the valley covers more than 9,000 square miles, drained by the Tennessee River and its tributaries. Rising a thousand feet above the Great Valley, and forming an abrupt escarpment on its eastern edge, is the third region —the Cumberland Plateau. Many early settlers were turned back by this seemingly impassable barrier. The western edge is notched and scalloped by coves and valleys which are separated by finger-like spurs pointing toward the northwest. The southern half of this area of more than 5,000 square miles is deeply cut by the Sequatchie Valley. These three regions lie in East Tennessee.

Middle Tennessee includes the fourth and fifth regions. The fourth is the Highland Rim, which merges into the western edge of the Cumberland Plateau and includes the elevations bordering the western part of the Tennessee River. With an area of 9,300 square miles, this section is largely a plain, furrowed by ravines and traversed by streams. Within the Highland Rim is the Central Basin, the fifth region. It is elliptical in shape and covers 6,450 square miles. With an average altitude 400 feet lower than the highlands, it is one of the best agricultural regions in the State.

The plateau of West Tennessee, the sixth division, extends from the Tennessee River to the line of bluffs overlooking the bottomlands of the Mississippi. The valley of the Tennessee River has a broken and irregular surface of about 1,200 square miles, averaging twelve miles in width. The sloping terrain drops gradually toward the Mississippi River. The Bottoms comprise 950 square miles of low, flat terrain studded with lakes. The largest of these, Reelfoot Lake, in the northwest corner of the State, occupies a depression, sixty-five square miles in area, formed by the earthquake of 1811–12. In sections of the plain lying below the high water of the Mississippi, back-waters and underground seepage have formed many swamps and marshes. At Fulton, Randolph, and Memphis the river undercuts the foot of the upland to form protruding bluffs.

There are four principal iron areas in the State: the eastern belt extending along the slopes of the Great Smokies; the "dyestone" or red iron

CANE CREEK FALLS, FALLS CREEK STATE PARK

district which forms a belt skirting the eastern bases of the Cumberland Plateau and Walden's Ridge; the Cumberland Plateau; and the western belt, a wide strip of west Middle Tennessee from Kentucky to Alabama.

At present the leading minerals are: coal, phosphate, clay, zinc, copper, sand and gravel, marble, and sandstone. Of these, coal is the most important, with a normal yearly output of 4,000,000 tons. One of the largest coal areas in the United States is the Cumberland Plateau belt, comprising 4,400 square miles. The Copper Basin in East Tennessee produces more copper and sulphuric acid than any other region east of the Mississippi

River. Marble and Crab Orchard stone (quartzite) are quarried in large quantities. In the production of phosphate rock Tennessee is second only to Florida. Clay suitable for brick making is found throughout the State. Gold and silver, although found in Tennessee, do not rank high in the State's mineral resources.

Three great drainage basins are formed by the Tennessee, Cumberland, and Mississippi Rivers. The Tennessee is formed near Knoxville by the confluence of the Holston and French Broad Rivers and is joined by the Clinch River and countless smaller streams. Flowing southwest into Alabama, it loops north across the State again, absorbing the waters of Middle Tennessee's Elk and Duck Rivers. With its tributary web of streams, the Tennessee drains more than half of the State's total area. Northern Middle Tennessee is drained by the Cumberland River, which rises in Kentucky and empties into the Ohio above the mouth of the Tennessee. West Tennessee drains through a maze of sluggish streams, swamps, and lakes directly into the Mississippi.

There is an annual rainfall of 40 to 50 inches throughout Tennessee, and an average of 155 clear days, 100 partly clouded, and 110 wholly clouded. Few severe droughts occur, or rainy spells protracted enough to damage crops. In the east, the mountains turn the eastward flow of the upper air currents and redistribute their moisture. The long valleys between the highlands serve as flues for the main air currents, which in summer blow north or northeasterly and in winter reverse their directions. Although this topography tends to check the velocity of windstorms, Tennessee was subjected to a series of tornadoes between 1914 and 1933, two of which were violently destructive.

Lying on the border of the great continental air currents, the State—except in Upper East Tennessee—never gets the full force of blizzard weather, or the extremely low temperature produced by the downrush of cold air fields from Canada. However, from the middle of December to the end of March, there are spasmodic periods, rarely more than a week in duration, when the temperature drops to 15 or 20 degrees above zero. During the winter months rain, sleet, snow, freeze, and thaw may occur in succession within 24 hours, and may be preceded or followed by spring-mild spells. The autumn rainy season rarely, if ever, causes flood, but the heavy rains of March and April swell the water courses and inundate the lowlands, causing considerable flood damage.

Some sections of Middle and West Tennessee are visited by periods of moist heat during the summer. But for the most part the surge of warm air from the Gulf and the southwestern plains is modified by the time it reaches the State. In East Tennessee, and to a lesser extent in hilly regions to the west, summer is a succession of pleasantly warm days and invigorating cool nights.

The Record in the Rocks

Rock strata in the State represent all geologic eras and almost every period within these eras. The high mountains along the northeastern border of Tennessee are composed of the oldest rock in the State. These formations, with their largest area in southeastern Carter County, date back to the pre-Cambrian period. The only volcanic heritage from ancient time is in the Norris Basin, where there are two small areas of eruptive rock, and a three-foot bed of volcanic ash in Middle Tennessee. Along the eastern and southeastern border is a belt of conglomerates, quartzites, and slates ten to twenty miles wide, extending from the point where the French Broad River enters the State to the Georgia line. These rocks are of unknown age, probably belonging to an early period in the Paleozoic era; their formation probably antedates the period of known vertebrate existence. Resistant to erosion, they constitute Tennessee's highest and broadest mountain mass. East of Maryville this formation, giving the Great Smokies their height and rugged outlines, begins to push upward over masses of dolomite (probably Upper Cambrian), which is exposed in several Townsend region coves. Cocke County has a peculiar granite, named unakite for the Unaka Mountains. It lacks mica content and contains an unusual mineral, epidote, that gives it a greenish tinge.

The rocks in the Great Valley of East Tennessee consist of sandstones, shales, limestones, and dolomites, all of which developed as marine sediment. These rocks represent the first three periods of the Paleozoic era—Cambrian, Ordovician, and Silurian. Together these periods form what has been called the "Age of Invertebrates," when the only life was shell-forming sea animals and buglike crustaceans. There are also rocks in the northeastern edge, near the Virginia border, that seem to constitute a slight development of the fourth period, the Devonian, known as the "Age of Fishes," and the Mississippian period. Along the west side of the valley runs a layer of fossil iron ore which belongs to the Silurian period, the third stage in the Paleozoic era and the period of the first air-breathing animals. In the center of the valley are long outcroppings of marble from the immediately preceding period, the Ordovician; and at various geological levels there are great quantities of chert, formed of sediment under sea water. Throughout the valley are rocks, mainly limestones and shales, similarly placed but of different periods, as shown by the fossils in the various layers. The strata originally were laid down almost horizontally, but during subsequent mountain-building revolutions have faulted into folds, sometimes 300 miles long, running from southwest to northeast. Ridges in the valley with long even tops usually are of sandstone or chert; those that consist of a series of rounded knobs are shale. The ridges are frequently capped by shale. Between the ridges are limestone or dolomite formations.

Along the western edge of the Great Valley is a narrow belt of Devonian black shale, called Chattanooga shale, which is invaluable as a key rock. Resting against this Chattanooga shale, and exposed frequently along the eastern and everywhere along the western margin of the Cumberland Plateau, are rocks that date from the Mississippian epoch, a time when tree ferns, huge mosses, and primitive flowering plants were dominant. The lower formation, known as Fort Payne, consists generally of silica and chert; the middle and upper parts are largely sandstone, shales, and coal. Five-sixths of the Cumberland Plateau is composed of conglomerates, sandstones, and shales of the Pennsylvanian epoch, the next above the Mississippian. It was during this epoch that amphibious reptiles and primitive backboned land animals came into existence. The rocks of almost the entire area lie in relatively level strata and contain bituminous coal.

The Highland Rim is mostly limestone, similar in age and formation to the rocks of the Cumberland Plateau's western margin. All the formations lie flat, except those of Well's Creek Basin in Stewart County, where rocks dating back to the Cambrian and Ordovician periods are exposed.

The floor of the Central Basin, also, is formed mostly of flat-lying limestones and shales of the Ordovician periods, to which the Great Valley marble belongs. In the upper levels these rocks contain commercial phosphates. On the northern and western sides of the basin, as also in the western valley of the Tennessee River, there are also limestones of the later Silurian and Devonian periods.

Overlappping the western edge of the Highland Rim, basal rocks of the Cretaceous period outcrop in a belt, twelve to thirty-five miles wide, along the edge of the Western Tennessee plain from Mississippi to Kentucky. This belt dips west at a low angle beneath the succeeding Tertiary rocks, which were formed in the Cenozoic (Recent Life) era prior to the glacial epoch. The Tertiary rocks are initiated by a belt of leaden gray clay, a few miles wide and one hundred to two hundred feet in thickness, running north from Middleton to Huntingdon and Paris and on into Kentucky. The formation is cut across by sandstone dikes that give evidence of earthquakes in one of the epochs of the Tertiary period.

Over the leaden clays, to a depth of a thousand feet or more, lie soft light-colored sands, with layers of white pottery clays and occasional beds of lignite, in which the texture of fossilized wood can often be discerned. These sands are covered by a widespread layer of yellow gravel, twenty feet or less in thickness, topped by a layer of sandy or loamy soil that thickens westward. Along the bluffs that border the Mississippi flood plain, this soil grades into typical loess—a wind-laid deposit from glacial times—becoming as much as forty to eighty feet thick. Still more recent alluvial deposits form flood plains and terraces along the streamways of the State.

Because of the lack in formational representation from several periods of the Mesozoic era, there is written in Tennessee rocks no record of the thousands of years during which early marine life disappeared, and the dinosaurs and flying and swimming reptiles reigned supreme. Nor is there evidence in the State of the first appearance of birds. The second period of the Paleozoic era, the Ordovician (said to go back 62,000,000 years), is well represented in the Great Valley of East Tennessee and the Central Basin. In fossil remains and in mineral composition the Ordovician rocks of these two areas are dissimilar, although a few formations and species are common to both. The lower rocks of this period in the Great Valley are rich in molluscoid snails and slugs, of which many species have been collected. In the Central Basin these rocks have long constituted a classic collecting ground. Nearly the entire invertebrate kingdom is represented in the area in the vicinity of Nashville. The corals and bivalve shellfish are especially notable. Here the middle rocks are almost ideally exposed and are actually crowded with fossils. Numerous highway and railroad cuts, quarries, and hillside slopes afford excellent exposures.

The Silurian, or third, period in the Paleozoic era is represented especially in parts of the western valley of the Tennessee River. This age was dominated by shell-forming sea animals, but saw also the rise of fishes and of reef-building corals. Scientific investigation of the area uncovered the fossil territory in Hardin, Decatur, and Perry Counties, and the sponges found here are well known to paleontologists. Waldron shale in Middle Tennessee has yielded fossilized aquatic marine animals, corals, seashells, and mollusks. A small part of the Devonian period is recorded near Camden, in Benton County, in one of the best exposed sections in North America. Almost perfect specimens have been collected in the chert of this region. Bivalve shellfish were the most numerous, and the Birdsong shale is prolific in mollusk forms. The Carboniferous period, the last in the Paleozoic era, has left some interesting marine animal forms—starfish and sea urchin types—in the region about Nashville. Fossilized Carboniferous plants include ferns, club-moss, and reed-like growths.

Of the Mesozoic era, Upper Cretaceous fossils are unusually numerous in the western part of the State, particularly in Hardin, McNairy, Chester, and Henderson Counties. The sands of Hardin County have yielded a few excellent plant impressions and partly or completely silicified wood. Chalk knobs in eastern McNairy and Chester Counties are frequently covered with specimens of large mollusk-like snails. Particularly in the McNairy County sand formations, perfectly preserved animal fossils of this period are found to an extent so far unequaled in any other single North American region. At one site on Coon Creek more than 350 species were collected from a single horizon. The fauna of the McNairy sand formations is essentially molluscan, but there are vertebrate remains. Notable among them are the mosasaurs, large marine lizards with long snake-like bodies, lizard-like heads, and paddle-shaped limbs.

The Cenozoic (Recent Life) era is represented in Tennessee principally by the Eocene, the first epoch of the Tertiary period, and by the Pleistocene, or glacial, epoch of the Quaternary period. The remains of the Eocene—the epoch during which the higher orders of plants began to develop, and birds and mammals to displace the giant reptiles—are mainly centered in West Tennessee. They are found in the Porters Creek clay near Middleton, the Holly Springs sand at Puryear, and the Granada sand in the Somerville vicinity. Collectors report excellently preserved fossils of plants and some mammals in this area, as well as in the Reelfoot Lake region and in Shelby County.

The Pleistocene also is represented in the western part of the State. This epoch, popularly known as the Ice Age, brought about great changes in animal life. Many mammals became extinct; man began to dominate the earth. The ice sheet stopped many miles north of Tennessee, but huge hairy mammoths, long-tusked mastodons, and giant sloths, driven southward by the advancing glaciers, ranged the State, and may have remained until the coming of prehistoric man. At least bones and teeth of these animals, found in caves and alluvial deposits, may be taken as evidence of their existence in this area during the glacial epoch—the opening scene in the Age of Man.

Animal Life

When Boone and Scaggs hunted in Tennessee, great herds of bison grazed in the river bottoms; elk and Virginia deer ranged through the forests and canebrakes; black bears were plentiful everywhere; and wolves, panthers, and lynxes followed the trails of the hoofed animals. Beaver colonies built their dams and mud houses in some of the smaller streams and there were vast flocks of birds and game fowl. So rich in game was the region that parties of Iroquois from the Great Lakes and Choctaw from the Gulf Coast, as well as Cherokee from the Great Smokies and Chickasaw from the Mississippi bottoms, came here for months of summer hunting. Tennessee was the Land of Peaceful Hunting, a neutral ground where ancient tribal hatreds were temporarily forgotten. The Indians were not wasteful hunters; they killed only for food and clothing—and even then they ceremoniously asked pardon of Uncle Bear or Brother Bison. The white settlers had little of the Indians' fellow feeling for wild things. They slaughtered them as prodigally as they slashed and burned the forests and squandered the wealth of the soil.

Today, of all the hoofed animals, only the Virginia or white-tailed deer remains. Ranging wild in the East Tennessee mountains and protected by law, they are now on the increase. Black bears also live in the high Smokies and the southern or bay lynx is fairly numerous in heavily wooded sections of the State, where it manages to hold its own in spite of intensive hunting.

The red fox and the gray are still common in all parts of the State. Next to the fox, the skunk and opossum are probably the best known of the fur bearers and are found even in the woodlots close to towns. Other fur bearers are raccoons, minks, and muskrats; cottontail rabbits, in almost any brier patch or brush pile; and gray and red squirrels, in the oak and hickory woods. All the smaller mammals—such as field and wood mice, gopher rats, weasels, woodchucks, and chipmunks—are numerous. The otter, once a valuable fur animal in the State, is now rare.

A newcomer to the forests of East Tennessee is the Russian wild boar, locally called the "Rooshian" wild hog. These large and savage hogs are believed to have escaped from a North Carolina estate during a forest fire in 1910. Since that time they have spread through the mountains to the headwaters of the Tellico and Citico Rivers.

Some of the birds once plentiful in the State have completely disappeared. The passenger pigeon, the Carolina parakeet (sometimes called

RACCOON

the Cumberland parrot), the ivory-billed woodpecker, and the prairie chicken, which the pioneers shot by the wagonload, are now extinct. Notwithstanding this wholesale slaughter, bird life is still plentiful, and perhaps more varied in Tennessee than in any other inland State. This is due in part to the diversified character of the land and the many different kinds of climate, but the chief reason is that thousands of birds cross Tennessee on their migratory flights between the North and the South. Ornithologists have recorded 316 species in the State; of these, 163 are summer residents, about 100 are found only in winter, and the rest live here the year round.

The American national bird, the bald eagle, lives in the wild regions of the Cumberland Plateau and the marshes of the Reelfoot Lake area. The golden eagle, which the Cherokee called the "king of birds," is rare, but a few still find sanctuary in the Great Smokies. The northern raven, vanished from most of the eastern States, also inhabits the ridgecrest of the Smokies.

The great blue heron, slate-gray rather than blue in color and more than four feet in height, is fairly common along the water courses, where it builds untidy-looking nests of sticks in the treetops. Living in large colonies, herons return year after year to the same nests. In a huge heronry at Reelfoot Lake thousands of nests are visible in the tops of the high cypress trees. Reelfoot Lake is also visited during the year by nearly all species of North American wading or swimming wild fowl. Numerous along all the State's water courses is the green heron, known variously as "shikepoke" and "fly-up-the-creek."

The largest game bird of Tennessee is the wild turkey, still to be found in the eastern mountains. Protected by game laws and reared in State hatcheries, this bird is now assured a permanent place among the game birds of the State. Grouse and quail are also raised and distributed in many areas. The ruffed grouse, often called "pheasant," is fairly plentiful in the scrub oak forests of the Cumberland Plateau, and in most East Tennessee counties. Recently the ring-necked pheasant has been introduced in several areas. The bobwhite, swiftest of the quail family and the most numerous game bird, is widely distributed throughout the State, as is the dove.

The official State bird is the mocking bird, found in all parts of the State, and often called "the singin'est bird in the world." The robin, another famous songster, is even more numerous. The northern variety winters in the South, returning to its nesting places in early spring; a subspecies lives in Tennessee throughout the year. Other birds which remain in Tennessee the year round are the bluebird, killdeer, meadow-lark, cardinal, towhee, screech owl, red-tailed and sparrow hawk, Carolina chickadee, whip-poor-will, flicker, various kinds of woodpeckers (locally known as peckerwoods), and the Carolina wren, whose ringing voice is most often heard at dawn and twilight.

In season, most American migratory birds east of the Rockies visit the State. Of the geese, the Canada type is the most numerous, but snow and blue geese also come through. Ducks of twenty-three varieties are abundant in autumn. Among the winter visitors from the North are the horned lark, and the junco, or "snowbird," one of the most numerous of this group, which nests in the high mountains along the eastern border. Spring migration brings from farther south more than half the total number of birds that nest and raise their young in Tennessee. A number of local breeding birds travel to South America to spend the winter. One of the most punctual migrating birds is the purple martin, which leaves for the South about August 25, and returns between the first and tenth of March.

The Tennessee Ornithological Society, founded in 1915, publishes in Nashville a quarterly journal called *The Migrant.* Its members take a bird census each Christmas at Nashville, Memphis, Reelfoot Lake, Knoxville, Johnson City, and other points in the State. In 1933, the society sponsored the publication of Albert F. Gainer's *A Distributional List of the Birds of Tennessee,* the only comprehensive study of birds in the State.

Because of the many different types of water areas in Tennessee, there are many places suitable for the propagation of all common American inland fishes. In the Cumberland and Duck Rivers are found catfish, buffalo fish, drum, and bass. While most of the species of game fish are native to Tennessee waters, the rainbow trout was brought from the mountain streams of the western United States and the brown trout from Germany and England. The rainbow and brook trout thrive in the deep clear pools of the mountain streams. Polychrome garters and dice are found in these waters during the spring and summer months, their bright colors disappearing after the spawning season, which lasts from late March to early June.

Waters throughout the State are well stocked with the large-mouth black bass which, with the small-mouth bass and pike, frequent the Tennessee River and its tributaries, the Holston, and the French Broad. The blue, or channel, catfish, weighing as much as thirty pounds and found in all waters, is most prolific in the streams and lakes of West Tennessee. The "yellow cats" grow to enormous size. Some weighing as much as one hundred pounds have been caught in the Mississippi and Tennessee Rivers and their tributaries. Other fish are the jack salmon, red-horse, spoonbill cat, crappie, rock-bass or goggle-eyed perch, bream, German carp, and several species of sunfish and catfish. There are several hatcheries where bass, trout, and other desirable fishes are propagated for restocking purposes. This work is carried on by the State, in cooperation with the Federal government and the Tennessee Valley Authority.

The common reptiles of the State are lizards, turtles, frogs, and thirty kinds of snakes. Only the rattlesnake, the copperhead, and the cottonmouth moccasin are venomous. The common rattler, called diamondback, is found throughout the State, especially in the wooded areas on rocky outcrops near timber or on the "balds" of the lower altitudes. The copperhead generally inhabits bush regions. The pilot black snake, one of the swiftest of serpents, often attains a length of from six to seven feet. King snakes, including the red and scarlet king and the brown king, are prevalent in all sections, and perform valuable service by destroying venomous snakes, rats, mice, and moles.

Forests and Plant Life

Great forests once covered most of Tennessee, but today less than one-tenth of the primeval stand remains. Scattered over the State, however, are patches of virgin timber, mostly hardwoods; these huge oaks, tall elms, and stately beeches testify to the great size of the original stand. Second-growth forests are coming up on the cut-over lands. Sycamore, basswood, cherry, walnut, hickory, locust, and maple grow in practically all sections of the State except the high Appalachians. Widely distributed are the hackberry, a small-leaved hardwood, and the persimmon. The conifers appear only in certain areas. The consumption of walnut for gunstocks during the World War and the present demand by cabinet makers have almost exhausted the supply of this tree in Tennessee.

The largest stands of virgin timber are in East Tennessee. Here are hemlock, pine, spruce, southern balsam (Frazier fir), and many hardwoods such as oak, maple, silverbell, and cherry. The tulip tree, or yellow poplar, Tennessee's State tree, reaches its largest growth in this region, often attaining a height of 200 feet.

Middle Tennessee has two principal forest growths—the cedar glades of the Highland Rim, where the soil is shallow, and the scrub oak barrens of the Cumberland Plateau. Growing in low places and along the banks of streams are sweet gum, poplar, willow, and sycamore.

In the swampy bottomlands of West Tennessee the plant life is similar to that of the Deep South. Here remain some stands of the magnificent first-growth timber that originally made Memphis a leading hardwood market of the Mississippi Valley. The largest species of tree in this area is the cypress, which lives to a great age and reaches a height of one hundred and fifty feet. It grows in water-covered places, "breathing" by means of hard, hollow, tumor-like growths called "knees" which are sent up from the roots. The river birch, the pecan tree, the water elm, the water maple, the swamp locust, and the tupelo, or cotton gum, are found in the western lowlands. The chinquapin, a rare tree, with fruit closely resembling the chestnut, also grows here. This region is the natural habitat of the catalpa or "catawba," a fast-growing tree with purple, yellow, and white flowers and large heart-shaped leaves.

Towards the end of the nineteenth century timber which had hitherto been considered commercially worthless—gum, cypress, chestnut, elm, and persimmon—came into demand. Tennessee, with more than one hundred and fifty varieties of trees, has supplied the lumber market with these types of wood for many years.

Fire and wasteful lumbering have taken their toll of the timber regions. Protective grasses have been uprooted from the slopes by overgrazing and by the plow. Erosion has resulted from these careless methods, and today (1939) fourteen million acres in the State need reclamation. Much of this land is now unproductive, but most is suitable for reforestation. Planting of hickory, persimmon, walnut, honey locust, and mulberry is encouraged, since these trees produce commercially valuable timber and also provide food for hogs and chickens during most of the year. State nurseries are producing millions of seedlings, principally black locusts, for use in erosion control. These will develop into a new kind of forest, widely distributed.

Forests are being established by the State forestry division, working in cooperation with the U. S. Forest Service, the Tennessee Valley Authority, and other Federal agencies. These forests provide demonstration areas for fire control, wildlife replenishment, water and soil conservation, and reforestation. Unwisely cleared and depleted agricultural lands are also being reforested by farmers, with technical and financial aid from State and Federal agencies.

The redbud and the dogwood, small flowering trees, add splashes of pink and white to the green hillsides in the spring, the blooms lasting for several weeks. Throughout the woodlands are wild grape vines, climbing to great heights among the tree trunks. The summer grape grows on dry or rocky ground, the winter variety on rich moist lands, especially along river banks. Other vines are the pink wildbean, the passionflower, and the trailing arbutus. Woodbine and poison ivy are widely distributed.

Tennessee's wild flowers range from the violet, growing on a tiny stem, to the large blossoms of the magnolia, a popular lawn tree in many parts of the State. From summer to late fall the fields bloom with dandelions, daisies, black-eyed Susans, goldenrod, wild asters, gentians, and Jerusalem artichokes. Flowering early in the moist woods, where they are protected by leaf mold, are the saxifrage, hepatica, anemone, dutchman's breeches, wild bleeding-heart, bloodroot, firepink, and blue phlox (sweet William). Later appear the jack-in-the-pulpit (Indian turnip), bluebell, shooting star, wood sorrel, and wild geranium.

More than three hundred of Tennessee's 1,500 plants are used for medicinal purposes; about one hundred have commercial value. Goldenseal, hepatica, digitalis, and ginseng are among the best known; they are found in many parts of the State, particularly in the mountain regions.

Johnson grass, a quick-spreading, hardy grass much detested by farmers, and the common varieties of weeds grow in all sections.

Perhaps the best known of the mountain flora is the rhododendron, ranging in color from white to deep purple. At Roan High Bluff (6,287 altitude), is a rhododendron garden, an outstanding display of the shrub in its natural setting. There are fifteen known species of trillium (wake robin) in the Smokies. The earliest to bloom, and the most vivid, is the variety with a dark crimson V at the base of a white petal. The yellow trillium, indigenous to the Appalachians, is common in the shaded foot-hill forests. Flame azalea, varying from red to orange and from gold to light yellow, the white and pink azalea, and the wild honeysuckle touch the mountain slopes with spots of color. Here, also, grows the sand myrtle, native of the sandy pine barrens of New Jersey, and found nowhere else in Tennessee. Mountain laurel covers many miles of mountainside and borders the streams. Peculiar to the highlands is the "burning bush," called by the mountain folk "hearts-a-bustin'-with-love," because of its brilliant berries in autumn. The evergreen holly with its scarlet berries grows in profusion.

Lush grass and weeds cover the mountain glades and even flourish on the high slopes, giving to the rounded tops of some of the mountains the name "grassy balds." Ferns are numerous and grow very large.

The soil of Middle Tennessee is ideal for the cultivation of the State flower, the iris, and the Nashville Iris Association was formed in 1931 to foster its planting and cultivation. Along the boulevards and streets, and in parks and gardens, the blue, white, and purple blossoms appear by the millions annually, justifying Nashville's designation as the "Iris City."

The yellow jasmine, celebrated in the literature of the South, thrives in the southern parts of Middle Tennessee and as far east as the Great Appalachian Valley. Over much of the Central Basin grows bluegrass, which makes the Middle Tennessee region one of the finest grazing lands in the country. Muscadines, as well as the other varieties of wild grapes, grow in the central and western portions of the State.

Interspersed with the oaks of the Plateau region are numerous shrubs. Itea, a member of the willow family, large-flowering hydrangea, Carolina allspice, narrow-leaf crabapple, hazelnut, buttonbush, chokeberry, arrowwood, and southern buckhorn grow where the gravelly soil supports a poor growth of larger trees. On the rock outcrops of the cedar woods are crustose lichens, simplest form of plant life.

Native here, also, are the pink stonecrop and pitcher's sandwort, and the taller plants, such as the daisy fleabane, wild senna, and coralberry. Among the vines are the trumpet honeysuckle and the Virginia creeper. Wild flowers common to much of Middle Tennessee are the spring-beauty, dragonroot, firepink, Indian-tobacco, lamb's lettuce, ground cherry, Venus' looking-glass, hop clover, wooly-leaf dutchman's pipe, shepherd's purse, horse-nettle, mouse-eared chickweed, dwarf evening primrose, violet wood sorrel, Illinois mimosa, common yarrow, and the flameflower, which blossoms only on clear days.

In the moist woodlands of West Tennessee are lilies and orchids, of which one species, the pink ladyslipper or moccasin flower, is said to be fast disappearing because of ruthless picking. There are water lilies in the lagoons; and Indian rye, formerly harvested by the aborigines, furnishes food for the migrating flocks of ducks and geese. The common grasses of the region are rushes, cattails, and swale grasses.

Soil Conservation

The story of Tennessee cannot be understood without reference to the types of soil that have determined the development of the State's three natural divisions. East Tennessee's early political dominance was due solely to first settlement. Although there were many fairly rich farmland pockets in the uplands, much of the soil was so thin that the people were able to force from it only the barest subsistence. The stream of immigration turned toward Middle and West Tennessee, where soils were deep and rich. Here a prosperous agricultural economy came into being. Inevitably Tennessee's cultural and political center also shifted westward.

In the Great Smoky Mountains there are still numbers of good small farms where the mellow sandy soil is similar to that of the Gulf Coast, while in the East Tennessee Valley the soil, formed of disintegrated limestone-marble and shale with an admixture of flint-like chert, yields well to careful farming methods. Thousands of tiny "patch-farms" are scattered through the uplands and, in spite of wasteful lumbering operations, the poorest ridge soils still support fine stands of timber. Two-thirds of the Cumberland Plateau is covered with forest, mostly second-growth scrub. The soil is thin, porous, and unproductive. Possibly the poorest land in the State is found on the inner part of the Highland Rim. Here a skim of earth overlies porous siliceous limestone through which the vitality of the soil "leaches out." The tenacious cedar grows well in these barrens and there is fair pasturage for cattle, but the land can never be made valuable for farming.

AN EXAMPLE OF SEVERE SOIL EROSION

About 40 per cent of the Central Basin, which has been called "The Garden of Tennessee," is used as bluegrass pasturage. The soil has been formed of rich, soluble limestone, and is remarkably productive. The valley of the Tennessee River is given over to medium-sized farms on moderately fertile soil.

The West Tennessee slope differs from the other divisions in that it lacks stone outcrops or free rock. Although the hill section is subject to gully and ravine erosion, there are many large and productive farms. The soil is light, siliceous, and fertile. The flat alluvial bottom lands of the Mississippi, composed of sand, silt, and clay, possess great fertility. The soil is light, porous, and many feet deep. In most of the area large plantations produce enormous yearly crops of cotton and corn with no apparent sign of exhaustion. Much swampy forest land has not yet been cleared.

As early as 1854, the State agricultural bureau warned that excessive "mining" or one-crop cultivation of the soil would finally lead to economic disaster. Farmers following this practice grew one crop year after year without letting the land lie fallow or rotating crops to build up the soil. In 1857 Charles Dod, Jr., predicted that erosion would doom Tennessee agriculture. Two years later Commodore Matthew Fontaine Maury urged erosion control. However, the period was one of prodigal shortsighted waste and little was done to check the menace. Today 85 per cent of all land in the State has been damaged to some extent by erosion. In 1935 the State planning commission made a survey which revealed that three million acres had been practically ruined for cultivation by deep gullies, and that 75 to 100 per cent of the surface soil had been taken from eleven million acres by sheet erosion. In sheet erosion a thin cover of topsoil washes away during heavy rains. The severity of sheet erosion, which occurs on all lands not protected by a crop of heavy-rooted vegetation, depends on the degree of slope to the terrain and the type of soil. Shoe-string erosion is also responsible for much damage. Gullies, started by little rain rills, are gouged out to such a depth that it becomes almost impossible to fill them. Slip or landslide erosion, Tennessee's third principal type, is frequent where shale soils predominate. Water accumulates between soil and bedrock until the undermined soil slides downhill, or collapses into sink-holes.

Contour cultivation, hillside terracing, and planned crop rotation (with careful selection of crops that hold the soil) constitute the best method of fighting sheet erosion. Winter cover crops like clover and grasses have been found beneficial. Gullies, which rarely occur in forest lands or in fields growing alfalfa or Japanese clover (lespedeza), are best fought by building wooden, metal, wire, brush, or stone check dams at proper intervals. Black locust trees are frequently planted to hold the soil. Japanese clover, serving as a legume to enrich the soil, is an effective cover crop. Nothing can be done to remedy landslide erosion, once it has occurred; but landslides can be prevented by proper ditch drainage of susceptible areas.

Soil conservation and erosion control in Tennessee now embrace nearly 100,000 farms with a land area of nine and one-half million acres, or about half of the farm acreage in the State. The university's extension service and the three Federal agencies—the Agricultural Adjustment Administration, the Tennessee Valley Authority, and the Soil Conservation Service—are collaborating in what is considered the most comprehensive conservation program ever attempted in the United States.

A principal land program of the TVA is that of erosion control, carried on in cooperation with farmers. Civilian Conservation Corps boys, supervised by the watershed protective section (the forest division of the

AIR VIEW OF TERRACED LANDS, A SOIL CONSERVATION PROJECT

TVA), do much of the control work on private property; owners must furnish teams and materials, and sign an agreement to maintain the project for five years. So actively have Tennessee Valley farmers cooperated that by 1936 more than one hundred thousand check dams had been built and eighteen million seedlings planted. Reforestation is employed only in the most badly eroded sections. Elsewhere the first two steps of control suffice—the building of check dams and diversion ditches, and the planting of cover crops.

Where cotton and other crops requiring cultivation between the rows are grown, terracing is advocated in addition to readjustment of the crop cover. Terracing associations, usually underwritten by responsible local agencies, purchase large motor-driven grading machines which are operated on a communal basis.

Much of the soil in the eroded areas is too far gone to support even grass crops without plant food. The manure of horses, mules, cattle, and sheep is scrupulously conserved, but this source of home fertilizer has been greatly reduced in recent years with the increased use of motorized farm machinery. Cotton seed hulls, a valuable home product, are rarely used because the farmers prefer to sell them and buy commercial fertilizer. The best home method of fertilizing the soil consists of growing legumes and other plants to be turned under as green manure in a carefully planned rotation of crops. Perhaps one-tenth of the farmers in the State allow a field to rest every third or fourth year, as part of their rotation system. But very few, during this rest period, plant a cover crop which is to be turned under. The common practice is to let the selected field lie fallow, producing the common weeds and grasses indigenous to the region.

To meet the need for cheap phosphate in the valley, Nitrate Plant No. 2, at the Muscle Shoals project of the TVA, produces a new triple superphosphate and a still newer metaphosphate from the raw phosphate rock found in Middle Tennessee. Farmers throughout the valley have organized soil conservation clubs and are demonstrating the value of this fertilizer in growing the most effective control crops—grasses for pasturage or hay, legumes in mat planting, and small grain. In demonstration areas farmers receive fertilizer free through the State agricultural extension service and farm organizations.

Erosion control not only saves reservoirs and checks flood damage, but helps the farmer escape the one-crop system which has impoverished him and exhausted his land. Reforestation provides nut and fruit crops and a continually renewed supply of timber. A cover crop of grass or legume in eroded fields provides pasture for livestock. The change from a one-crop method of farming means less silt in the river, more money in the farmer's pocket, and better food for folk who have too often existed on corn pone, sorghum, and sowbelly the year around.

The First Americans

EARLY in prehistoric times wandering tribes of aborigines—the remote ancestors of the historic Indians—entered the territory that is now Tennessee. Successive waves of migration followed, and many diverse groups came into contact with one another. Some were cave dwellers who subsisted by hunting and fishing, and some were agricultural tribes who made excellent pottery and lived in large fortified towns.

Probably the cave dwellers were the first comers. They settled along the water courses where fish and game were plentiful and where caves and overhanging cliffs afforded natural dwellings. With their crude weapons they may have hunted the last of the mastodons. The sites of their homes are marked by fire-cracked stones, flint chips, and arrowheads, by ash beds and refuse pits, fragments of pottery and implements of stone and bone. Caves showing signs of occupancy are especially numerous at the headwaters of the Cumberland River and its tributaries; others are found in the Tennessee and Duck River valleys.

In the cliffs along Obed and Wolf Rivers there are rock shelters similar to the Pueblo communal ruins in the Southwest. That the caves housed hunters rather than farmers is evident from the quantities of animal bones found on the sites. In some instances burned human bones are present.

The prehistoric Indians also used caves for burial purposes. Indicative of a higher type of Stone Age culture are the partially mummified human remains, interred in a sitting position in baskets of cane, that have been found in widely separated areas. The bodies were wrapped in bark matting, tanned deer-skin, and cloaks or mats of woven feathers. The workmanship of these articles shows considerable mechanical skill.

In pre-Columbian America, maize or corn was a basic food, and the fertile valleys of Tennessee, then as now, produced good crops. The tribes that cultivated maize left behind them remarkable earthworks which show their advanced skill and industry. These people are generally referred to as the Mound Builders. Unquestionably they were Indians, possibly the ancestors of the Muskhogean linguistic stock—the group that includes the Creek, Chocktaw, and Chickasaw. In the mounds, the levels of occupation overlap: the prehistoric merges into the historic. In the lower strata are found only pre-Columbian artifacts; in the upper strata articles of European manufacture are present.

The Tennessee phases of the Mound Builder culture include stone fortifications and palisaded villages, earthworks that served as foundations for ceremonial buildings, cemeteries, and reservoirs. Dome-shaped burial mounds are numerous, and in scattered places about the State are a few earthworks that appear to be effigy mounds, fashioned to represent birds or animals.

The most prominent of the earthen remains are the pyramidal mounds, often elaborately terraced, with level tops. Notable examples are the huge Pinson Mounds in Madison County, the largest of which is some seventy feet high, and the Great Mound Group in Cheatham County. Pyramidal mounds, always associated with important sites, all show indications of having once supported ceremonial buildings of some kind, probably temples or town houses. The resemblance of these terraced ceremonial house mounds to the pyramids of ancient Mexico is striking. This and other evidence suggest a cultural link between the Mound Builders of Tennessee and the civilized Mayan people of Central America and Mexico.

Excavations have revealed post molds where the logs that formed the walls of the ceremonial buildings once stood, and also wattle-work and hard-packed smooth floors. Altars or fire basins, composed of clay and sand, are usually found in these structures. Both square and round types of altars have been uncovered, the different shapes apparently representing two different cultures. When the mounds were high, an inclined ramp led up to the buildings. These ramps were constructed of clay into which were set cedar logs to provide a foothold.

One peculiarity of the prehistoric Tennessee burials is the striking development of stone graves, usually made from flat pieces of limestone or from slaty sandstone. The builders evidently believed in an after life, for shell spoons and artistic pottery vessels, many of which represent bird, animal, and human figures, are found with the bodies. The vessels apparently contained food and drink so that the deceased might not go hungry on the long journey to the Spirit Land. Other implements or ornaments buried with the bodies include copper breastplates, soapstone and clay tobacco pipes, strings of fresh water pearls, sea shells, bone awls, round gaming stones, and pottery disks. The presence of sea shell and copper indicates well-established trade routes.

Although the stone grave form of burial is widespread over the State, it is most frequent in the valleys of the Tennessee and the Cumberland

Rivers. The typical Cumberland graves are rectangular coffins, in which the body is extended full length on its back. In the Tennessee Valley, stone-slab graves have been discovered in which the skeletons lie in a doubled-up position. Remains of another group or tribe, who buried their dead in hexagonal or almost circular stone-slab graves, with the bodies closely flexed, have been found. The skeletal remains are of both long-headed and round-headed types of people. It is believed that the builders of the numerous mounds also built the stone graves, which occur both in mounds and in cemeteries.

Collections of prehistoric Indian relics from mounds and graves are on exhibit at Vanderbilt University and at the Memorial Building Museum at Nashville. The Museum of Natural History and Industrial Arts in Memphis also has an exhibition of Mound Builder relics.

The depicting of human and animal figures in terra cotta and stone is one of the chief phases of prehistoric culture in Tennessee. Specimens found in the area show the high level to which the art of pottery making was carried, and the perfection with which the difficult art of chipping flint was practiced. There are huge ceremonial swords, scepters, maces, and monolithic axes with handle and blade made from a single piece of polished stone. The art of painting as practiced by these ancient Indians is shown in their pottery decorations and in picture writing upon the smooth faces of rock walls overhanging the rivers.

Engravings upon copper and sea shell ornaments are traced with remarkable skill. Ornaments worn suspended from the neck, known as gorgets, are beautifully engraved with intricate designs depicting human, animal, and mythical figures, many of them quite conventionalized. A common motif is the rattlesnake, which is sometimes both winged and plumed as in Mexico. Gorgets cut from conch shells were usually circular in shape and concave from the curve of the shell. In size they range from a few inches to nearly a foot in diameter. Large marine shells were also utilized for bowls and cups.

Both shell and grit tempered pottery have been found in large quantities. Pottery types include corded, paddle-stamped, stippled, smooth, polychrome, and painted ware. Vessels with smooth rims are found; other types are curved-rim and loop-handled ware. Many bowls and water bottles are modeled to represent human and animal figures. Effigy ware is frequently found with burials.

On the Little Tennessee River many of the graves contain the remains of historic Indians, but there are some burials which appear to represent an older and different culture, perhaps that of the Uchees (Yuchis). In

East Tennessee many of the skeletons are found in flexed positions in pits that were lined with bark and covered with lids of bark supported by wooden cleats. The dead, in many cases, were buried under the floors of the dwellings.

Artifacts, pottery, and skeletal remains from East Tennessee are housed at the University of Tennessee at Knoxville. Many of these relics were found during recent excavations conducted jointly by the Works Progress Administration, the Tennessee Valley Authority, and the University of Tennessee.

The Mound Builders, if not the ancestors of Indians living within the State in historic times, certainly exerted cultural influence upon all the later groups that entered the area. Historic tribes in Tennessee were reported by early explorers to have used mounds as foundations for town houses. A number of eighteenth-century village sites contain Mound Builder remains in their lower levels. Either the later tribes were builders of mounds themselves, or they moved in and occupied the sites of the earlier peoples.

Historic Indians

The first Indians encountered by Europeans in Tennessee belonged to two great linguistic groups—the Muskhogean and the Iroquoian. The Koasati, a tribe identified with the Creeks, were in the southeastern region through which Hernando De Soto's Spaniards pushed on their futile search for treasure in 1541. The Cherokee, a detached Iroquoian tribe, lived on the upper reaches of the Tennessee River, claiming all the central and eastern portions of the present State as their hunting ground. Some authorities contend that De Soto passed through the southernmost towns of the Cherokee during his march to the Mississippi.

The Muskhogean still occupied the Tennessee Valley in the seventeenth century, but they later migrated south and joined the main Creek Nation. Early French maps gave the name of "Cusatee" or "Kasquinombo" to the Tennessee River and located the Cusatee or Kasquinompa Indians near the present site of Chattanooga and the Cherokee on the headwaters of the river.

West Tennessee was the domain of the Chickasaw—another Muskhogean tribe—whose main villages were in northern Mississippi. It was doubtless to this tribe that De Soto's aide referred when he stated that "they presented the Governor (De Soto) 150 conies (rabbits), with the clothing of the country, such as shawls and skins." The Chisca, also mentioned in the De Soto narratives, were a small Algonkian tribe living on the Cumberland Plateau.

A century and a half after De Soto's explorations the English, entering Tennessee from the east, and the French, coming down the Mississippi, found the Chickasaw and Cherokee occupying substantially the same sites where the first explorers had found them. The Shawnee, late comers, lived along the lower Cumberland Valley, in an area claimed not only by the Chickasaw and the Cherokee, but also by the powerful Iroquois Confederacy of New York.

Land trails and waterways formed the Indians' system of communication and transportation. The dugout canoe, hollowed and shaped from a single tree by means of fire and stone adzes, was the craft used by all the tribes of Tennessee. Bark canoes were rare, although a few were occasionally obtained through trade with the northern tribes. Besides numerous footpaths of their own making, the Indians incorporated into their system the wide, hard-packed trails trodden by the wood bison, leading to every corner of the wilderness. Beginning in the Creek country of Alabama and Georgia, the Great Indian Warpath entered Tennessee near Chattanooga and followed the Great Valley of East Tennessee northward. Over this well-worn trail, on missions of peace and war, came the Creek, Cherokee, and Chickasaw from the south and the Iroquois and Algonkians from the north. Another famous Indian trail was the Natchez Trace, running from near the vicinity of present Nashville to the towns in Mississippi.

The Chickasaw and the Cherokee were typical southeastern village tribes. They raised large crops of vegetables and tobacco in small gardens and in village farms that were owned in common. Indian corn or maize was the leading crop, and the Green Corn Dance or "Busk" was a yearly festival. In April and May strawberries were gathered in the open prairies along the stream banks, and in summer great quantities of blackberries on the hillsides. When autumn came stores of hickory nuts, walnuts, and pecans were laid by for winter use, one family often having more than a hundred bushels of hickory nuts. Huckleberries, wild plums, persimmons, wild grapes, and muscadines were gathered and preserved; many wild plants and roots were also utilized for food. The forest supplied the Indians with meat of many varieties—turkey, deer, bear, buffalo, and small game. The streams abounded in fish and mussels.

Before the arrival of the whites, the Indians had no domestic animals except the dog. By the middle of the eighteenth century, however, the Cherokee and Chickasaw had obtained horses, swine, and chickens from the English settlers and were raising livestock in considerable numbers.

The most common type of Indian house was circular or rectangular; it was built of thick posts set upright in the ground with smaller posts between, all bound together with split cane or switches and plastered with clay. Strips of bark and thatched grass were used to cover the roof; hard-packed ground or clay formed the floor. A raised hearth in the center contained the cooking fire, and above it, in the roof, was the smoke hole. "Hot houses" for winter were made of heavy timbers, plastered with clay. Every village had its town house, in which the priests performed sacred ceremonies and the chiefs held their councils. Here the braves gathered to drink a tea of herbs called the "black drink" before taking the war trail. The town house was big enough to hold several hundred persons, and the whole village often met there for entertainments and dances. Early explorers, describing the Cherokee council houses, spoke of them as resembling sugar loaves—circular in shape with rounded tops.

From stone, wood, shell, and bone the Indians skillfully contrived the necessary household utensils and the implements used in war, hunting, and fishing. Beautifully ornamented pottery, wooden bowls, and spoons and saucers made from shell have been found on various sites. The fisherman was provided with basketry traps, weirs, nets, spears, bone hooks, and harpoon-like arrows; the hunter, with long flat bows, arrows of both wood and cane—some with fire-hardened tips and others with points of stone, bone, or antler—and blow-guns of cane or of grooved pieces of wood bound together. Stone axes and knives and scimitar-shaped hardwood clubs were the weapons of the warrior.

After the advent of white traders in the latter half of the seventeenth century, many of these implements and utensils were replaced in whole or in part with European trade goods. As early as 1673 many of the Indians had guns, axes, hoes, knives, metal arrow points, glass beads, and double glass bottles in which they kept their powder.

Widespread among the tribes was the game of "ball play," from which lacrosse is derived. Another game enjoyed in some form by all the southern Indians was "chungke," played with round stones (called "chunky" stones) and smooth sticks.

In summer the Indian men wore only deerskin breechcloths and moccasins, but in cold weather they added shirts made of skin, robes of fur, and fringed leather leggings that reached from thigh to ankle. More decorative garments were the feather robes and the mantles woven from various fibers and from the hair of buffalo and opossum. The women wore short deerskin skirts and covered their shoulders with fur shawls in winter.

Various dyes were used, but black and vermilion were the favorite colors for clothing and blankets.

John Wesley recorded an interview with a young Chickasaw chief in which the Indian told him that his people believed in four beloved things above: the clouds, the sun, the clear sky, and He that lives in the clear sky. The Great Spirit, the creator of all things, was called by the Chickasaw "The Beloved One Who Dwelleth in the Blue Sky," and by the Cherokee "The Great Man Above." Each warrior had his own guardian spirit or totem. The sun, the thunder, and the four winds were powerful gods of the upper air, and certain animals were thought to possess magical powers. Medicine men or priests combined sorcery with healing practices. Tobacco was used in religious ceremonies, and the spirit of the corn was honored by special religious rites. To a great extent the Indians were fatalists, accepting death as a matter of course and submitting to events without complaint; sometimes, it is recorded, they sang at the approach of death by torture.

The Chickasaw were the foremost warriors of the South. Compared to neighboring nations they were small in numbers, but so warlike and so well organized that no tribe or combination of tribes was able to withstand their attacks. With the Chickasaw, as with most American Indian tribes, descent was in the female line. Within the nation were subdivisions or phratries, which in turn were composed of clans or gentes. No marriage took place between individuals of the same clan. The tribe was governed by chiefs or headmen, whose personal endowments entitled them to leadership.

Quite distinct from the Chickasaw racially and yet similar in many ways were the Cherokee, one of the largest of the southern tribes. Their legends tell of migration southward from the region of Lake Erie, but they had dug themselves deeply into their historic sites when first encountered by white men. In colonial times the Cherokee territory was divided into three parts or settlements: Towns in the northwestern corner of South Carolina and the neighboring portions of Georgia; the Middle Towns in the southwestern North Carolina; and the Upper Towns (known as the Overhill Towns because they were across the mountains from the Carolina Colonies) along the Little Tennessee and Tellico Rivers. This area contained important villages, among them the capital of the Cherokee Nation, Chota (Echota), some thirty miles south of the present Knoxville. Chota was a "white" or peace town where bloodshed was forbidden.

Cherokee government was democratic, with a leading man acting as head chief or "emperor" of the whole nation. Honorary titles could be earned by warriors who were brave in battle and wise in council. Men too old to fight and women who were very wise were given the name of "Beloved." Among the Cherokee the women had their own council, composed of the leading women of each clan, with the Beloved Woman of the Nation at its head.

Ensign Henry Timberlake, a young British officer who went among the Cherokee on a good will mission in 1761, described the Cherokee as "of middle stature, of an olive color, tho' generally painted, and their skins stained with gunpowder, pricked into very pretty figures. The hair of their head is shaved, tho' many of the old people have it plucked out by the roots, except a patch on the hinder part of the head, about twice the bigness of a crownpiece, which is ornamented with beads, feathers, wampum, stained deer's hair, and such like baubles."

Entirely different from the Cherokee and Chickasaw were the Shawnee of the Cumberland Valley. A wandering tribe of the far-flung Algonkian stock, these people seem to have migrated into the Cumberland Valley just prior to the beginning of the eighteenth century. In customs and language they were typically Algonkian, although they had evidently acquired some of the cultural traits of their southern neighbors.

The presence of the Shawnee in the Cumberland Valley was resented by both the Cherokee and the Chickasaw, who desired to keep the region as their hunting preserve. Repeated raids by these tribes and by the Iroquois finally drove the Shawnee from their villages on the Cumberland in about 1714. They moved northward and settled in the Ohio Valley, from which location they frequently sent war parties against the southern tribes and against the white settlers in Tennessee.

At the beginning of the eighteenth century English traders were well established in Tennessee territory. They lived in the Indian towns, taking part in the life of the village, many of them marrying Indian women. James Adair, best known of these adventurous Englishmen, entered the Indian trade about 1735. To him is due the credit for much of our knowledge of the culture of the Tennessee Indians. An educated thoughtful man and a keen observer, Adair spent forty years among the southern tribes, and recorded his observations in his book, *History of the American Indians.*

In the colonial period the rates of exchange in the fur trade were agreed upon by a board of commissioners and influential chiefs. The Indian country was divided into hunting districts, one district being allotted to a trader. The rates varied from time to time but, for the most part, were well regulated until independent traders flocked into the Indian country.

Beaver fur and deer skins were the principal articles received from the Indians.

A trader's pack train seldom consisted of fewer than fifteen or twenty horses, and pack trains of more than a hundred horses were not uncommon on the "Great Trading Path" from Charleston to the Cherokee country. Established in the Indian town, the trader lived in backwoods luxury, a person of importance in the village. When he won the confidence and admiration of the tribesmen, he was usually chosen by some warrior as "particular friend." The pact, symbolized by a complete exchange of clothing and even names, was lasting, and many a white man owed his life to his particular friend.

The English outnumbered the French in the Cherokee country, but a few French traders came to the Overhill Towns and attempted to gain a foothold there. In 1730, a bold stroke of diplomacy on the part of Sir Alexander Cuming (Cumin) won for the English the friendship of the Cherokee. Going into the Cherokee country on his own initiative, Cuming completely overawed the tribesmen and talked them into signing a treaty. He designated Chief Moytoy of Great Tellico as Emperor of the Cherokee, but reserved allegiance through himself to the British King. The Indians were greatly impressed and agreed to become subjects of King George II. Cuming then took to England a group of Indians, including the young Overhill warrior who later became the famous Attakullakulla (Little Carpenter). The King received the chiefs with great ceremony, presented them with gifts and assured them of his love and protection. In return the Indians pledged the King their loyalty and support.

The Chickasaw were the only tribe on the lower Mississippi friendly to the English and hostile to the French. When the French destroyed the Natchez, the Chickasaw received the remnant of that tribe into their nation. Free passage of the Mississippi was an important step in the French plan to keep the English settlements hemmed in along the Atlantic seaboard, and because Chickasaw warriors captured French supply boats on the Mississippi, destruction of the tribe became a fixed policy of the French.

In the spring of 1736, Sieur de Bienville moved northward from New Orleans with his troops and warriors of the Choctaw Nation, hereditary enemies of the Chickasaw. Major d'Artaguette, with another army of white soldiers and Indian braves, came down from the Illinois district, of which he was then governor. The two armies were to meet in the Chickasaw country and exterminate the tribe. English traders rushed to the Chickasaw villages from Charleston to aid their allies. D'Artaguette landed at Prudhomme Bluff and followed the Chickasaw War Trail southward to the nearest village, where he was decisively defeated by the Chickasaw and the British traders. Six days later Bienville was forced to retreat.

In 1740 the French built Fort Assumption on the Lower Chickasaw Bluff (site of Memphis) as a base of operations against the Chickasaw. A temporary peace was patched up, but the Indians continued to ambush French convoys on the Mississippi. In 1752 Marquis de Vaudreuil led an expedition of 700 soldiers and a large force of Choctaw into the Chickasaw country, but was forced to retreat. The Chickasaw remained the masters of West Tennessee.

Christian Priber, a German Utopian reformer and an agent for the French, appeared among the Overhill Cherokee in 1736. He crowned Moytoy of Great Tellico, then head chief of the Cherokee Nation, "Emperor" of his Utopia, which he called "Paradice." Ludovick Grant, a well-known trader and liaison officer among the Cherokee for Governor Glen of South Carolina, attempted to arrest Priber but the Cherokee would not allow it. Officers sent from South Carolina also failed, and barely escaped with their lives. Priber was finally taken (1743) by Creek traders on his way to the French Fort at Mobile. He was turned over to the English colonial authorities, who sent him to prison in Georgia, where he spent his remaining days. His Utopian plans collapsed, but his influence continued for a long time in Great Tellico.

Regulations to curb whisky trading, which by this time had become an abuse, were drafted by the English in 1751. They provided "that no trader shall carry rum into the nation, unless it be a few bottles for his own use, but that a quantity be lodged in the fort sufficient to supply each district with two keggs in the year, and that it be given to them gratis at two different times; to wit, one Kegg at the Green Corn Dance and one Kegg when they return from their Winter Hunt."

Actual hostilities between the French and the English began in 1754. After long-drawn bickering between South Carolina and Virginia, the latter colony, in answer to Cherokee requests, built a fort near Chota in 1756. The colonial governments still could not reach an agreement and the fort was never named or garrisoned. The following year South Carolina completed and garrisoned Fort Loudoun, five miles west of Chota on the south bank of the Little Tennessee River. At the time Fort Loudoun was completed (1757) the Cherokee, who had been wavering toward an alliance with the French, turned to the English.

In the spring of 1759 reports of negotiations between the Cherokee of Great Tellico and the French came from the Overhill country. To the

Overhill town of Settico came Great Mortar, a Creek chief friendly to the French, who made an alliance with Chief Moytoy. War parties left Settico and fell upon the North Carolina settlements in the Yadkin and Catawba Valleys.

Old Hop, the emperor or principal chief, and Attakullakulla tried to prevent a war with the English, but the French and their Creek allies kept up their intrigues with the Overhills. These "bad talks" continued until Governor Lyttelton of South Carolina, fearing war with the whole Cherokee Nation, authorized the stoppage of their ammunition supplies. Oconostota, the Great Warrior of Chota, and thirty-one chiefs, returning from Charleston where they had gone for "peace talks," were made prisoners and taken under military guard to Fort Prince George. Attakullakulla went to Charleston and finally secured the release of Oconostota and two chiefs.

In January 1760 the Overhills, led by Oconostota, made an unsuccessful attack on Fort Prince George, where their tribesmen were imprisoned. Runners, painted red, carried war messages throughout the nation. In March, Old Hop, the friendly leader, died and Standing Turkey was elected head chief. The whole Cherokee Nation now took the warpath. Attakullakulla, alone of all the headmen, remained loyal to the English. The warring tribesmen attacked Fort Loudoun, cut off communications, and after months of siege forced the starved garrison to surrender. On the trail back to the settlements the soldiers were ambushed by the Cherokee; some twenty of the garrison, including the commandant, Captain Paul Demore, were killed on the spot and the rest were made prisoners. Following the Indian custom of "special friendship" for a white brother, Attakullakulla rescued his friend Captain John Stuart, second in command of the garrison, and helped him to escape to Virginia. British troops and colonial militia finally conquered the Cherokee, and by a treaty made November 9, 1761, the Indians surrendered Fort Loudoun.

It was in this year that Timberlake and Sergeant Thomas Sumter visited the Cherokee. Their host on the journey was Ostenaco, or "Judd's Friend," a war chief of the Overhill Cherokee. When the expedition returned to Virginia, Governor Fauquier sent Ostenaco with two of his warriors and an interpreter to England with Timberlake and Sumter. In London the young Virginians and their Cherokee friends were entertained at fashionable resorts, visited by the nobility, and received at court by King George III. Sir Joshua Reynolds painted Ostenaco's portrait, and the three Indians posed for him in a group. After a two-month stay in England, the Cherokee were brought back to America by Sumter. Timberlake remained in England and two years later published his memoirs, which present an accurate picture of Indian life in that period. The visit of Ostenaco, like that of Attakullakulla in 1730, greatly strengthened British influence among the Cherokee.

The British King's proclamation of 1763 guaranteed the Cherokee their territory west of the Appalachians, but the land-hungry settlers paid little heed to their government's treaty boundaries and steadily encroached on Indian land. By the treaty of Fort Stanwix in New York on November 6, 1762, the Iroquois conveyed to the English their claim to the hunting grounds bounded by the Ohio and the Tennessee Rivers. By the Treaty of Hard Labour, made in the same year between the English and Cherokee, the southernmost limit of the boundary line between the Virginia and the Cherokee lands was declared to be a point thirty-six miles east of the Long Island of the Holston River in East Tennessee. In 1770, by the Treaty of Lockabar, a thirty-mile strip of Cherokee land was purchased by Virginia. When a survey made in 1771 showed definitely that the white settlements were not in Virginia but on Cherokee land, the settlers, rather than move, leased all the land along the Watauga for about $5,000 in merchandise. Similar leases were made of lands along the Nolichucky and in Carter's Valley.

In 1774 Lord Dunmore's War broke out in Virginia, and the Cherokee, roused by war embassies of northern Indians, grew restless. As a nation they did not take the warpath, but there were frequent brushes between young braves and bands of settlers. The Transylvania Land Company of North Carolina purchased from the Cherokee in 1775 their claim to the lands lying between the Kentucky River and the Cumberland for $50,000 in merchandise. But the Cherokee, as a tribe, were by no means unanimous in their acceptance of this agreement, and many of them bitterly resented the transaction. The American Revolution, which began one month after the land purchase, gave the disgruntled faction a chance to regain the lands taken from them and to prevent any further settlements south of the boundary line. Led by Dragging Canoe, they "lifted the war axe."

After two years of fighting the Cherokee met the commissioners of Virginia and North Carolina on the Long Island of the Holston—their sacred treaty ground—and made peace with the white invaders. In a formal treaty made at the Long Island in July 1777, the Cherokee ceded a large area to North Carolina and Virginia and agreed to remain neutral during the Colonies' war with England.

Dragging Canoe's followers, refusing to accept as final the loss of lands in East Tennessee, moved westward to Chickamauga Creek and there established villages. These hostile Cherokee, who became known as the

Chickamauga, were joined by Shawnee warriors from the Ohio, by Creeks from Alabama and Georgia, and by white outlaws. Their war parties struck at the outlying settlements continually, ranging far and wide over the frontier. Colonel Evan Shelby led an expedition against them in 1779, burned their towns, and captured horses and supplies. Later the Indians left Chickamauga Creek and established the Five Lower Towns, west of Lookout Mountain, with Nickajack Cave as their stronghold.

After peace was made between England and America, all Indian attacks ceased for a time. Boundaries were established by the Hopewell treaties with the Cherokee in 1785 and the Chickasaw in 1786, and Indian titles to land in Tennessee were recognized by the United States.

In 1791, William Blount, Territorial Governor, called the Cherokee to a conference at White's Fort, the present Knoxville. The new boundary line between the Cherokee lands and those of the whites in Tennessee was agreed upon. In addition to surrendering land, the Indians granted to the whites the use of the Tennessee River and the road through their lands on the Cumberland Plateau. In return the United States Government gave a certain amount of goods and agreed to pay an annuity of $1,500.

In 1792 a group of Cherokee leaders met representatives of the United States at Chota in a peace council; but while the council was in session militiamen attacked the Indians, killed several, and wounded Hanging Maw, the head chief, and his wife. Peace negotiations were broken off; the Cherokee as a nation joined the Chickamauga and the Creek in war against the whites.

The Chickamauga continued to raid the frontier until Major James Ore led the Nickajack Expedition into their country in 1794 and completely broke their power. They came back into the Cherokee Nation and ceased to exist as a separate tribe. The defeat of the northern tribes by American troops, and the surrender of Spanish territorial claims, placed the Indians under the sole jurisdiction of the United States.

During the first quarter of the nineteenth century the Cherokee were as civilized as the border whites. They had large farms and orchards, owned Negro slaves, and raised cattle, sheep, and horses. They used progressive farming methods in growing cotton, tobacco, corn, wheat, oats, potatoes, and indigo. Most of the cotton their women made into cloth for their own use; the surplus was shipped to New Orleans. They sold the garrisons in the Indian country fresh milk, butter, eggs, and apples. Their territory had good horse paths and wagon roads.

In 1804 the Reverend Gideon Blackburn opened a Presbyterian school for the Cherokee near the village of Sale Creek. In 1817 a school known as the Brainerd Mission, near the present site of Chattanooga, was established by the Reverend Cyrus Kingsbury, a Congregational missionary.

From 1805 to 1819 various treaties were made with the Cherokee and the Chickasaw. In 1818 the Chickasaw ceded all the West Tennessee territory to the United States except a tract four miles square on Sandy River and a few individually owned tracts. In return, the United States agreed to pay $20,000 annually for fifteen consecutive years. In 1823 the reserved lands were also transferred to the United States and the Chickasaw left the territory. It was the proud boast of their tribe that they had never lifted up the war axe against people of the English-speaking race.

In 1825 more than 13,000 Cherokee still occupied their ancestral lands. Some 6,000, however, lived west of the Mississippi River in Texas and Arkansas, having migrated from Tennessee because of dissatisfaction over the treaties made with the whites. Oolooteka, from Hiwassee Island—leading chief of this western band—had adopted young Sam Houston as his foster son, calling him the Raven. After resigning the governorship of Tennessee, Houston became a leader of the western Cherokee and was given full citizenship in the Nation. Going to Washington as the ambassador of the Cherokee, he preferred charges against dishonest Government agents, succeeded in having them removed, and then returned to take an honored seat in the National Council of the Cherokee.

To George Gist or Guess, better known as Sequoyah, belongs the credit for making the Cherokee into a literate people. Sequoyah, a half-breed Cherokee, was a skillful silversmith as well as a hunter and trader. In 1818 he began to devise an alphabet for his people. Using letters and figures from an old speller, without relation to their meaning in English, and inventing other symbols, he built up a syllabary of 85 characters capable of expressing all the sounds in the Cherokee language. In 1821 the tribal leaders adopted Sequoyah's alphabet and within a few months both the eastern and western bands of the tribe were learning to read. In 1828 the *Cherokee Phoenix,* a newspaper in Cherokee and English, was published. In commemoration of Sequoyah's invention, the giant Sequoyah (Sequoia) trees of California were named in his honor.

In 1827 the Cherokee adopted a written constitution modeled after that of the United States. It was the intention of this civilized tribe to continue to be a self-governing nation within the territorial limits of Tennessee and the three adjacent States, where they still owned some 10 million acres of land. But the whites wanted this land, and they began to take it, sometimes by force. Treaties were ignored and the Indians were subjected to many persecutions. Georgia declared Cherokee laws to be void within her

SEQUOYAH AND HIS ALPHABET

territory and all Indians therein subject to her authority. In 1832 the United States Supreme Court denied Georgia's right to do this, but the court's authority was defied. Andrew Jackson, then President, took no action to compel obedience to the supreme judicial authority of the United States and to the treaties that the Government had made with the Cherokee.

Congress authorized the President to offer western lands in exchange for the Cherokee territory east of the Mississippi. Led by John Ross, their principal chief, the tribe as a whole refused to accept the proposed removal. Repeatedly delegations went to Washington to plead their cause, but the President refused to aid them, and Congress turned a deaf ear to their petitions. Despairing of successful opposition to the United States, a faction of the tribe under the leadership of John Ridge decided to accept the removal. A preliminary treaty was made in March 1835, but the Cherokee Council, influenced by Ross, rejected it. On December 29, 1835, however, a minority of the tribe signed the Treaty of New Echota, and the United States Senate quickly ratified it.

By this treaty of removal all Cherokee land east of the Mississippi was ceded to the United States for $5,000,000. In addition the Government was to give the Cherokee 15,000,000 acres of land in the Indian territory. In March 1836 a supplementary treaty was made whereby the United States agreed to pay the Indians an additional $1,000,000, and the Cherokee were to leave Tennessee within two years.

The John Ross party vigorously protested, contending that the treaty did not represent the will of the majority, but the Government was determined that they should accept it. Troops were sent into the Cherokee country to make them vacate. Forts were built and the Indians were herded into them until final preparations were completed for their forced removal.

In the summer of 1838 a number of Indians were sent by boat to their new home; others went by wagon train. But many deaths, from disease and the heat, delayed the removal until autumn. In October the Indians were assembled at Rattlesnake Springs, near the present site of Charleston. After a tribal council—the last one held in Tennessee—they were divided into thirteen detachments, each in charge of two Cherokee officers, and the great removal began. The suffering endured by the evicted Cherokee on their long forced march gave to their route the name of the Trail of Tears.

Not all the Cherokee submitted, however. Homesick for their native hills, more than 1,000 escaped from the forts and fled into the remote mountain regions. Their descendants now occupy the reservation in North Carolina.

History and Government

IN THE summer of 1540 the Indian villages in the valley of the Tennessee River were ransacked by a strong mounted company of Spaniards from Florida. Before entering Tennessee, they had followed Hernando De Soto through what is now Georgia and the Carolinas, believing that somewhere in the vast reaches of the wilderness there would be treasure cities to plunder. From the Tennessee valley the Spaniards moved westward for almost a year. Many of them—including grim, iron-willed De Soto—had looted with Cortez in Mexico or Pizarro in Peru and, as a matter of course, they massacred the Indians and burned their villages when they failed to find gold. They followed bison trails and Indian trade-paths, wandering south at times into Alabama and Mississippi. In April 1541 the remnants of the party planted the flag of Spain on the bluffs of the Mississippi River and made camp near the present site of Memphis. After raiding Chickasaw villages nearby for food and mussel pearls, they crossed the river to continue searching for the will-o'-the-wisp gold they were never to find.

More than a century passed before there is record of another white man entering the territory. In 1673 a woods ranger named James Needham was commissioned by Abraham Wood, Virginia trader, to scout the possibility of trade with the Overhill Cherokee whose towns lay along the Little Tennessee and Tellico Rivers. Accompanied by Gabriel Arthur, an indentured servant, and several Indians from the Cherokee Lower Towns, Needham twice crossed the mountains into Tennessee. On the second trip he was killed by the Indians.

In the year that Needham and Arthur were in the valley of the Tennessee, Joliet and Marquette with five companions beached their canoes under the Lower Bluffs and were hospitably received in the Chickasaw villages north of the present Memphis. Other white men, French and English, may have found their way into Tennessee, but the next recorded visit was that of La Salle in 1682, when Fort Prudhomme was thrown up near the mouth of the Hatchie River on the First Chickasaw Bluff. A crude arrangement of earthworks and palisades occupied for only a short time, the fort soon fell into ruin.

A deserter from La Salle's expedition, Martin Chartier, who wandered into Middle Tennessee and joined a band of Shawnee in the lower Cumberland Valley, left the valley with the tribe in 1692. Soon afterward a second Frenchman, Charles Charleville, set up a trading post in an old Shawnee stockade at French Lick, half a mile from the bluff upon which the little frontier town of Nashville was to be built nearly a century later.

During the period of conflicting claims that followed, Spain included Tennessee with the Province of Florida on the strength of De Soto's journey. The French based their claim to the entire Mississippi Valley on La Salle's explorations and the activities of traders from Louisiana and Canada. The English claim was derived from the Virginia and Carolina grants, which had indefinite limits westward.

After Needham's trips among the Cherokee, the English lost no time in spreading their influence west to the Mississippi. Although French traders continued to visit Tennessee, their importance waned rapidly as more English traders came over the mountains and settled among the Cherokee, usually marrying into the tribe. This persistent penetration by the English robbed the Spanish and French claims of real force.

When Virginia was partitioned in 1663, Tennessee became a western part of Carolina; thirty years later a further division left Tennessee within the jurisdiction of North Carolina. Ideas about the region remained vague well into the middle of the eighteenth century. The Upper Tennessee Valley, which Virginians thought was within their boundaries, was not explored until 1748, when Dr. Thomas Walker, sent out by the Loyal Land Company of Virginia, penetrated the territory to the present Kingsport. Two years later Walker with a party of Long Hunters (probably already familiar with the region) came down the upper Holston Valley, followed well-beaten bison trails westward, and crossed the Clinch River. From this point Walker and his wilderness scouts pushed north into Kentucky through the great mountain pass which he later named Cumberland Gap in honor of the Duke of Cumberland.

When the French and Indian War broke out, the Overhill Cherokee petitioned the colonial governments of Virginia and South Carolina to build and strongly garrison a fort in their country. Virginia acted first. Major Andrew Lewis led a party into the Overhill country and built a fort near Chota, the Cherokee capital. The South Carolinians, refusing to cooperate with the Virginians, set about building a fort of their own. The work was pushed to completion in 1757 by British regulars and militia from South Carolina, under the command of Captain Paul Demore. Named Fort Loudoun in honor of the Earl of Loudoun, commander of the British forces in America at the time, this was the first Anglo-American fort garrisoned west of the Alleghenies. The Virginia fort at Chota was never occupied.

No sooner had the garrison taken possession than traders, artisans, blacksmiths, and small farmers began settling in the region protected by the fort. Many of them brought their wives, and "undoubtedly the first child born in the West to parents of the Anglo-Saxon race saw the light of day in the little community." Fort Loudoun remained the westernmost English outpost for three years. Abandoned at the outbreak of the Cherokee War, it was reoccupied by the North Carolinians after the British victory of 1761. Trade with the Cherokee was resumed and white men could again travel unmolested through the Overhill region.

Even during the height of the war a few wilderness scouts had been hunting in Tennessee and Kentucky. The most noted of these was Daniel Boone, whom the Indians both feared and admired. When Richard Henderson of North Carolina, one of the first great American land speculators, became interested in East Tennessee and Kentucky lands, he sent Boone in 1760 to find desirable sites for settlement. A year later another land-hunter, Elisha Walden, explored the Clinch and Powell Valleys.

Increasing numbers of Long Hunters, seeking lands for Henderson and other speculators, came into Tennessee. In 1765 and again in 1770 Henry Scaggs passed through the Cumberland Gap and explored the bluffs where Nashville now stands. In the next four years parties led by James Smith, Kasper Mansker, and Isaac Bledsoe extensively explored this region. One of the parties found Timothe DeMonbreun, an Illinois Frenchman, operating a trading post in a cave on the Cumberland River. When early Nashville grew up almost at his front door, DeMonbreun became one of its leading citizens.

Meanwhile actual settlement of Tennessee began in 1769, when William Bean built his cabin on Boone's Creek near the Watauga River and several families from North Carolina joined him. Bean's settlement and those in Carter's River Valley (1771) and on the Nolichucky River (1772) were known as the Watauga Settlements.

Isolated in a mountain wilderness and almost entirely ignored by North Carolina, the people of the Watauga Settlements soon felt the lack of organized government. In 1772 they formed the Watauga Association and elected five magistrates to make and administer law. The records of the Association are lost and little is known about it. It is certain, however, that the Watauga constitution was the first to be written and adopted by independent white Americans.

The Wataugans had no legal title to the lands they occupied. Until March 17, 1775, the region was part of the Cherokee country, but on that date Richard Henderson's newly created Transylvania Land Company purchased an immense tract of nearly 20,000,000 acres from the Indians. Immediately the Transylvania Company resold the Watauga territory to its settlers. Title was taken by Charles Robertson as trustee for the community.

At the outset of the Revolutionary War the Wataugans organized themselves into a military district which they named for George Washington. They requested annexation to North Carolina and in 1777 the petition was granted. Washington District was incorporated as Washington County, including the whole of the present State, and in 1779 Jonesboro was platted as the county seat.

In the same year Colonel Evan Shelby marched from Watauga against the Chickamauga, a hostile branch of the Cherokee, and defeated them near the present Chattanooga. In 1780 news came across the mountains that Major Patrick Ferguson and a British force of about twelve hundred men, most of them loyalists, were raiding westward. The Over-Mountain men of Watauga rallied at Sycamore Shoals under John Sevier and, as they trailed eastward, were reinforced by Shelby's Indian fighters and a force of Virginians led by Colonel William Campbell.

On October 7 they attacked the British entrenchments on King's Mountain. The frontiersmen used the Indian tactics they knew so well, creeping from tree to tree, sniping at the British. Ferguson and about six hundred of his men were killed while the Americans lost only twenty-eight men. This, the only battle in which the Tennessee settlers took part, marked the turn of the tide in the South.

While war was going on in the East, the migration of settlers into Middle Tennessee began. Henderson's Transylvania Company had been denied title to its purchases within Virginia's territory, so Henderson and his associates made plans to exploit other lands believed to lie within North Carolina's western boundaries. The Cumberland River region was picked for the first settlement. Here Nashborough was founded in 1780.

The tiny settlements of Watauga and the Cumberland were in an extremely precarious position. They were not even upon the frontiers of North Carolina, but hundreds of miles in the wilderness beyond the frontiers and open to Indian attack from the east, north, and south. In 1784 they petitioned the Assembly of North Carolina for the "salutary benefits of government." But North Carolina immediately ceded the entire Over-Mountain territory to the Federal Government, "for the frontiersmen were always on the verge of war with the Indians and in case of trouble they would require protection." Congress was given two years in which to accept or reject the grant.

News of North Carolina's action aroused great indignation in the settlements. Delegates from Washington, Sullivan, and Greene Counties met at Jonesboro and discussed a working plan for an independent western state to be called Franklin. In the same year (1784) a constitution, patterned after that of North Carolina, was adopted.

Concurrently the North Carolina Assembly had repealed its act of cession, but the Franklanders, as they called themselves, refused to undo their work. A general assembly met at Greeneville in March 1785, and chose officers to act under Governor John Sevier.

For four years there were continual clashes between Franklin officials and those sent over the mountains by North Carolina. When Sevier's term as governor expired, no new election was held, and the State of Franklin collapsed.

Left unprotected again, the territorials organized "The Government South of the Holston and French Broad Rivers." The constitution and laws of North Carolina were adopted, the Franklin officers were continued in power, and various delegations were chosen. This government functioned until 1790, when Congress accepted the second offer of cession and brought into being "The Territory of the United States South of the River Ohio," commonly known as the Southwest Territory. The Territorial government, administered largely by Presidential appointees, with William Blount as Governor, operated for nearly six years. Knoxville was selected as the seat of the government in 1792, a year after the town had been platted.

On July 2, 1791, Blount made the Treaty of the Holston with the Cherokee, who placed themselves under the protection of the United States and agreed to the extension of boundaries for white settlements. In the same year the Knoxville *Gazette* was temporarily set up at Rogersville and soon afterward moved to Knoxville. Four years later a wagon road was completed across the Cumberland Plateau between Knoxville and Nashville.

Tennessee had now exceeded by more than a fourth the population necessary for the formation of a state, and the constitutional convention, which met in Knoxville on January 11, 1796, petitioned Congress for admission to the Union. Here was drawn up the constitution which

Thomas Jefferson called "the least imperfect and most republican" to be adopted by any of the States.

Congress delayed action and the impatient Tennesseans organized their State government before the authority had officially been granted. John Sevier, frontier dandy, soldier, land-speculator, and the most powerful political figure in the region, became the first governor. The legislature, meeting at Knoxville on March 29, 1796, elected as United States Senators William Cocke, an East Tennessee follower of Sevier, and stiff, tory William Blount of Middle Tennessee. To fill the one seat in the House of Representatives another of Sevier's men was elected, a swaggering high-tempered lawyer from Middle Tennessee—young Andrew Jackson.

Three months later, June 1, 1796, Congress admitted Tennessee to the Union, but refused to seat Cocke and Blount because they had been elected prior to the State's admission. The two Senators were reelected at a special session of the legislature, and the three Tennesseans took their seats in Congress on December 5, 1796.

In the following year Blount became involved in one of the gravest scandals of the time. A European war between the new Republic of France and Great Britain was imminent. Blount's sympathies were with Britain. He took part in a scheme to recruit in Tennessee partisan fighters for Britain and planned to send them on raids into Louisiana and Florida. A letter from him on the subject fell into the hands of an enemy and was published in the newspapers. On July 8, 1797, Blount was charged with treason and expelled from the Senate. The date for an impeachment trial was set, but the matter was dropped on a technicality because of Blount's great popularity in the West.

Settlement of Tennessee proceeded rapidly. Home-seekers poured in from the Carolinas, Virginia, Pennsylvania, and even New England. They came with Revolutionary War land-grants, either earned in service or purchased from veterans or speculators. (Often these grants were forgeries.) Many of them came simply as squatters. The old Wilderness Road and Avery's Trace were congested with "movers" during the summer months—great topheavy Conestoga wagons drawn by oxen, broad-tired farm wagons piled high with household goods, and crude sledges with runners of hickory or oak; befrilled gentlemen astride blooded horses, rawboned farmers on hairy plow-nags, peddlers and merchants with their trains of donkeys, immigrants too poor to afford horse or ox plodding through the dust clouds with their meager belongings and children on their backs—all moving west toward the promise of land in Tennessee. Other thousands came by keelboats, poled up the Cumberland and Tennessee from the Ohio.

The newcomers were often misled and swindled by shrewd first settlers who dominated the State, but they kept coming. By the end of the century the wilderness had retreated before them to the Mississippi bottomlands. From the eastern mountains to the western counties of Middle Tennessee towns had sprung up, each with its public square and log courthouse, its church that served as a schoolhouse on weekdays, its gristmill, distillery, smithy, and general store. Roads webbed the forestland, connecting outlying farms and villages with the towns, where, presently, the courthouses and churches were of brick or stone and the log dwellings sheathed with clapboards.

In 1800 the Great Revival swept the State like a wind-driven grass fire and thousands of converts came singing and shouting to the mourners' bench. Although the movement reached its climax and waned within a year, it never died completely, and has remained a force to be reckoned with. The brawling ferment of frontier days began to pass. But the men whose characters the frontier had molded were, in turn, to leave the mark of the frontier upon American policies and life. To them was due half a century of aggressive national expansion. Largely through them there was an abrupt shift in political tone from the benign and essentially English rule-from-above ideal of Washington's time to the easy folksy manner of the backwoods and to a booming devotion to the common people.

Chief among the new politicians was Andrew Jackson, in whom the virtues and vices of the frontiersman were strong. So completely did this spare, sandy-maned figure with hot blue eyes and hair-trigger passions overshadow the State that for more than three decades the history of Tennessee—except for minor side-glances—was, in effect, the biography of Andrew Jackson.

As the protegee of William Blount and Governor Sevier, Jackson succeeded Cocke in the Senate in 1798. Within a year, however, he resigned, when Sevier offered him the appointment as judge of the Tennessee Superior Court of Law and Equity. From Blount and Sevier and their manipulations of State affairs Jackson received a full education in political realism, which he was not long in applying. In 1800, through the support of Archibald Roane, who had succeeded Sevier as Governor, Jackson defeated Sevier in an election for the post of Major General of the Tennessee Militia. The resulting feud between Sevier and Jackson was the bitter theme of State politics for several years.

An outstanding feature of this was a legislative investigation of Sevier for complicity in a large-scale land fraud, launched in 1803 by Governor Roane as the trump card in his campaign for reelection against Sevier. Despite Jackson's powerful backing, Roane failed in the inquiry and lost the election. The legislature, though condemning Sevier's part in the frauds, took no action against him.

By the time the War of 1812 broke out, Andrew Jackson's political stature in Tennessee dwarfed that of all rivals. His noted hatred for the British further increased his popularity, and volunteers flocked to the colors to serve under him. When it was rumored that a British force was sailing up the Mississippi to Natchez, Jackson led his militiamen by forced marches to the threatened point. The invasion failed to materialize and the volunteers returned home. During the long hard marches of this campaign the raw militiamen received invaluable training, and Jackson won a passionate devotion from them which was to serve him in politics as well as in war.

In the same year the Creeks, incited by British agents, took the war path and massacred the garrison at Fort Mims, near Mobile. Governor Willie Blount, half-brother of William Blount, called out 3,500 volunteers. Jackson, still suffering from wounds received in a fight with Jesse and Thomas Benton, again mustered the volunteers and struck south into the Indian country. After a quick campaign, the Tennessee militia broke the power of the Creek Confederacy at the Battle of Tohopeka.

Late in 1814, when the war with England was near its close, a strong British fleet blockaded the Gulf Coast. Once more Jackson led the Tennessee volunteers southward, this time to threatened New Orleans. The townsfolk and militia barely had time to build breastworks of cotton bales across the seaward approach to the city before British troops began landing from their transports, anchored at the mouth of the river. In the close formations they had used against the French in Spain, the British attempted to carry the breastworks by assault. The Tennessee riflemen, crouching and firing behind their cotton bales, shattered each wave of attackers before it could come within volleying distance. As in the Battle of King's Mountain, the British losses were heavy, while only a handful of Americans fell.

Jackson emerged from the battle a national hero. He was appointed major-general of the United States Army in the South, and in 1818 conducted a minor war against the Seminoles in Florida. The war resulted in the formal cession of Florida to the United States.

In 1818 the Federal Government purchased from the Chickasaw all their lands east of the Mississippi and Jackson acted with Governor Shelby

ANDREW JACKSON

This portrait of the President was drawn from life, September 23, 1829, by James Barton Longacre. The reproduction is from an old wet plate photograph of the original by Mathew B. Brady, owned by the L. C. Handy Studios, Washington.

of Kentucky as a Government agent during the negotiations. Before the country was opened to settlement, he acquired with John Overton and James Winchester a tract of land at the mouth of the Hatchie River. Here the town of Memphis was laid out and lots sold. Subsequently there was some scandal about land-titles, and Jackson—who already had presidential ambitions—sold out to Overton and Winchester.

As early as 1822 Nashville newspapers had been proposing Jackson for the presidency and he was a candidate in 1824, when Adams was elected. During the next four years State politics became inseparable from Jackson's presidential campaign. Running against Adams in 1828, he was elected by an overwhelming majority. Only five per cent of the Tennessee vote went to Adams.

Although Jackson was a landed proprietor, he made himself the spokesman for the average citizen and the foe of the vested interests of the day. During his eight years in the White House, reaction to his policies was unrelenting. The story of his smashing of the Bank of the United States, his championing of Peggy O'Neal, his feud with John C. Calhoun, his lampooned Kitchen Cabinet, and all the storm and clash that surrounded him in Washington are not State but National history. Throughout his presidency, he found time to direct politics in Tennessee, even to minor town and county elections.

In 1829 there was a serious break in the ranks of Jackson's party within the State. William Carroll, who had served with Jackson during the Creek and Louisiana campaigns and had thrice been Governor of Tennessee, entered the race against Governor Sam Houston, also an old comrade of Jackson, who was running for reelection. Both were very popular and both declared themselves in accord with Jackson and his policies. Lacking genuine campaign issues, Carroll and Houston were forced to fall back on invective. However, Jackson let it be known—without a direct statement—that he favored Houston's candidacy, and the result of the election seemed a foregone conclusion.

Suddenly, in March 1829, Houston resigned his post as Governor. Dropping his campaign, he went to Arkansas to join the Cherokee, with whom he had spent much of his youth before they were removed from East Tennessee. His flight was due to trouble with his wife; the details have remained obscure.

Carroll was elected without opposition. He wrote to Martin Van Buren, "I got clear of opposition in a most unaccountable manner. Poor Houston . . . He rose like a rocket and fell like a—stick!" Houston lived with the

Cherokee until 1833, when he went to Texas. He became one of the leaders in the Texans' revolt against Mexico and was elected first President of the Republic of Texas.

During the decades that followed Jackson's inauguration, Tennessee became politically and economically the most important State in the Mid-South. Manufacturing and commerce flourished as the State became more thickly settled. The first steamboat made its way up the Cumberland to Nashville in 1819, and a year later the second Bank of the State of Tennessee was established. In 1834 the State constitution was revised by a convention meeting in Nashville. One of the most important changes provided that property be taxed according to the value placed upon it by assessors. Free Negroes were disfranchised, relieved of the poll tax, and exempted from military service. The new constitution was approved by popular vote in March 1835.

By 1830 the Cherokee Indians of East Tennessee had become industrious farmers and slave-owners. The easily mastered Cherokee alphabet, invented by Sequoyah (George Gist), had made them a literate people with their own newspapers and books. Under threat of military action by the Federal Government, they signed away their territories in Georgia and Tennessee in 1835, and within three years had been moved west of the Mississippi. The Cherokee domain became public land and was thrown open to homesteading and purchase.

During this period public attention was focused upon improvement of transportation facilities. An internal improvement act was passed in 1830, setting aside $150,000 for State-wide development of roads and rivers. Cotton, wheat, and the steamboat brought wealth and power to the people of Middle and West Tennessee, and in 1843 the State capital was permanently established at Nashville. However, restless thousands of Tennesseans—many of them younger sons and late-comers—moved into the Ohio country, Alabama, Mississippi, Arkansas, and especially into Texas. The independence of Texas was won largely by transplanted Tennesseans and Kentuckians, and Tennessee furnished a majority of the volunteers who fought in the Mexican War. Andrew Jackson continued to dominate national politics until his death in 1845. His candidate, Martin Van Buren, succeeded him in the White House and one of his followers, James K. Polk, was elected President in 1845.

As early as 1831 the legislature had granted six railroad charters and during a period of twenty years there were numerous abortive attempts to establish railways. But not until 1851, when the Nashville and Chattanooga line began operating, was there effective rail service in Tennessee. Other lines followed and by 1850, when the population had passed the million mark, there were 1,622 miles of rail in use.

Meanwhile the life of the people had lost much of its broad pioneer roughness. In every township the sale of public lands provided funds for free schools and in 1832 twenty-five per cent of the school-age population was enrolled. Although the law specifically demanded that there should be no distinction "between rich and poor" the free schools were, in fact, regarded as "poor schools." Those who could possibly afford it sent their sons and daughters to the many private schools which sprang up throughout the State.

A State library was established in 1853, and Return J. Meigs was appointed State librarian in 1856. Though a superintendent of public instruction had been appointed in 1836, it was not until 1854 that property was taxed for support of the schools. Andrew Johnson, Governor at the time and a strong believer in mass education, forced a reluctant legislature to pass the law. As the century passed the halfway mark, there were more than fifty newspapers and periodicals in the State. Tennessee's progress in agriculture was recognized in 1851 at the Great Exhibition in London and four years later the first Biennial State Fair was held at Nashville.

The dispute over slavery grew bitter during the 1850's. When North Carolina ceded the Over-Mountain territory to the United States, there had been a specific provision "that no regulations made or to be made by Congress shall tend to emancipate slaves." There had, however, always been a fairly strong anti-slavery element in Tennessee, and when the first constitution was adopted in 1796 nearly 2,000 Tennesseans petitioned the convention to abolish slavery after 1864.

As early as 1797 the Knoxville *Gazette* was urging that an abolition society be organized. The Manumission Society of Tennessee was formed in 1815 at Lost Creek, Jefferson County, by the Reverend Charles Osborn, who later established, in Ohio, the *Philanthropist*—a journal partly devoted to anti-slavery propaganda. An early member of the Manumission Society was Elihu Embree. Though a slaveholder, Embree founded the Manumission *Intelligencer,* a weekly which was succeeded by his monthly *Emancipator.* These were the first periodicals in the United States exclusively devoted to abolition. After Embree's death in 1820, Benjamin Lundy took up the work and began publishing the *Genius of Universal Emancipation* in Ohio. In 1822 Lundy transferred his paper to Greeneville, Tennessee, and continued his activities there until 1824, when he moved to

Baltimore to collaborate with William Lloyd Garrison. Out of these efforts grew many anti-slavery societies. Most of the early pioneer preachers were strong abolitionists, and "as late as 1827, East Tennessee alone contained nearly one-fifth of all anti-slavery societies in the United States and nearly one-sixth of the total membership." Despite this, Tennessee churches joined the pro-slavery ranks when the Methodists, Baptists, and Presbyterians split on the slavery issue.

At the outset of the War between the States there were 7,300 freedmen as compared with 275,719 slaves. The ratio of slaves to white population was then one to twelve in East Tennessee, one to three in Middle Tennessee, and three to five in West Tennessee. By 1856 only one person in East Tennessee owned more than one hundred slaves, but in West Tennessee eighty-six owners had this number or more. People in the central and western parts of the State were divided over the slavery question up to the very threshold of the war. East Tennessee, abolitionist in sympathy, was strongly pro-Union even after Tennessee seceded.

The Wilmot Proviso, introduced in the United States House of Representatives during the Mexican War period, asked that slavery be prohibited in any territory acquired as a result of the hostilities. Never passed by Congress, it became the basis of a major political battle, and the center of dispute at the Southern Convention which met on June 3, 1850, in Nashville. The aim of this group, meeting in nine-day session, was to determine "the best means of securing the constitutional rights of the South, and the preservation of the Union as it is, a blessing to ourselves and our descendants."

Henry Clay had proposed that California be admitted as a free State and that the remainder of the Mexican cession be slave territory. John Bell, a Tennessean, also proposed a plan for compromise. Congress ignored the resolutions of the Southern Convention and passed the Clay Compromise. On November 11, 1850, seventy delegates representing ten States met again in Nashville. Here only the Tennessee delegation fought for acceptance of the Compromise, resolving that it was unjust to the South but would be accepted by the southern people as proof of their "attachment and devotion to the Union." Their resolution was rejected.

Ante bellum politics in Tennessee was a strange hodgepodge. Andrew Johnson, a Democrat, was a strong Unionist and William G. Brownlow, the whip-tongued Whig, was as violently pro-slavery and anti-abolitionist as he was pro-Union. The State's political alignment was well demonstrated in the presidential election of 1860. The northern wing of the Democratic party had nominated Stephen A. Douglas and the southern wing, John C. Breckinridge. John Bell was the candidate of the conciliatory and hastily formed Constitutional Union Party. Abraham Lincoln was the nominee of the Republican Party, then seeking to prevent the extension of slavery. When Tennessee's votes were counted the result was: Bell, 69,274; Breckinridge, 64,709; Douglas, 11,350; Lincoln, 0.

The conviction was widely held in the South that Lincoln's election would menace the rights of the southern slave-owners. Following his inaugural address, the three cotton States still in the Union withdrew and joined the Confederate States of America. In Tennessee, where both Union and abolitionist sentiment was fairly strong, there was much hesitation about taking the final step. Governor Isham G. Harris called a special session of the General Assembly, which voted to submit the matter to a referendum at a special election on February 9. Brownlow and the other anti-secessionists staged a brief but vigorous campaign, and the result of the election was strongly pro-Union.

However, a wave of pro-slavery sentiment followed the tours of impassioned orators such as General Felix Zollicoffer. A few weeks later, after the actual outbreak of hostilities at Fort Sumter, Governor Harris called another extra session of the General Assembly to meet April 25 in Nashville. Stating that Lincoln had "wantonly inaugurated an internecine war" upon the people of the South, he urged immediate action. The assembly adopted a formal declaration of independence, and directed the Governor to form a military league with the Southern Confederacy. After waiting to ratify the Governor's action, the assembly called a popular referendum on June 8 to decide on affiliation with the Confederacy. By more than a two-thirds majority the people approved secession. Owing to the energetic efforts of Brownlow, Andrew Johnson, and the other unbending pro-Union men, East Tennessee showed a decided majority (18,000) in favor of the Union.

On June 24 Governor Harris issued a proclamation dissolving all connection with the Federal Union. Military headquarters for the three State divisions were established at Union City, Nashville, and Knoxville. President Davis appointed Leonidas Polk to command in Tennessee and, in September, Albert Sidney Johnston, placed in command of the Western Department, arranged a line of defense to keep Federal troops out of Tennessee.

General Grant broke the Confederate line on February 16, 1862. He captured Fort Donelson on the Cumberland River and declared martial law. On March 3 President Lincoln appointed Andrew Johnson as Military Governor of the State, with the rank of Brigadier-General.

CHICKAMAUGA CREEK—BATTLE OF CHICKAMAUGA, SEPTEMBER, 1863

Important among the engagements, estimated at from 300 to 700, fought in Tennessee, were the battles of Shiloh, April 6-7, 1862; Murfreesboro (Stone's River), December 31, 1862–January 2, 1863; Chickamauga, September 19-20, 1863; Chattanooga, Lookout Mountain, and Missionary Ridge, November 23-25, 1863; Franklin, November 30, 1864; and Nashville, December 15-16, 1864. Some of the bloodiest battles of the war were fought on Tennessee soil, some with most far-reaching results. The death of the Confederate general, Johnston, on the opening day at Shiloh, "was a tremendous catastrophe" and is believed to have "prevented the utter rout or capture of Grant's army on the night of the 6th"; but with the dawn of the 7th the chance was gone, and at noon the Confederates were in full retreat. The struggle at Murfreesboro was terrific, costing each side about one-third of its strength, but left the Union forces in comparatively quiet possession for many months. Chickamauga, where "the pale river of death ran blood," saw a Confederate victory, with great possibilities, turned into a bloody checkmate by the stand made by the Union general, George H. Thomas, later known as the "Rock of Chickamauga." The Chattanooga campaign secured to the Union the entire Mississippi Valley. A year later, at Franklin, the Confederates assaulted "with the valor of desperation," losing several generals and 6,000 men, but failed in their objective, and a fortnight later the Battle of Nashville, a Union victory, resulted in the retreat of the Confederates from Tennessee and contributed to the ultimate defeat of the Southern cause.

Tennessee, occupied by Union forces, was not included in the Emancipation Proclamation of 1863. Slaves in the State were set free February 25, 1865, by an amendment to the State Constitution. Three days after the emancipation amendment was passed by the legislature, Andrew Johnson resigned as Military Governor to become Vice President of the United States. The inauguration of William G. ("Parson") Brownlow as Governor on April 6, 1865, began the period of reconstruction with the radical party dominant.

On March 3, 1865, Congress established the Freedmen's Bureau which had largely grown out of General Grant's appointment of John Eaton, in 1862, as supervisor of Negro affairs in Tennessee. Eaton, later State and United States Commissioner of Education, was made Assistant Commissioner of the Bureau. Within seven months 75 schools were established in Tennessee with 14,768 pupils and 264 teachers. The most noted of the Negro schools founded in the Reconstruction period is Fisk University, opened on January 9, 1866, through joint effort of the American Missionary Association, the Western Freedmen's Aid Commission, and the Freedmen's Bureau. Normal schools for teachers were provided, along with the free grade schools.

In 1867 the legislature enacted a law providing separate schools for Negroes at State expense. However, the Bureau was soon disrupted by an influx of crusading ministers, teachers, and politicians working at cross-purposes. Agitators inflamed the Negroes to arrogance and acts of violence, which caused the whites to organize extra-legal terroristic groups for the suppression of their former slaves. Chief among these was the Ku Klux Klan, organized in 1868 by Confederate soldiers at Pulaski, in Giles County *(see Tour 7)*. The Klansmen surrounded their "Invisible Empire" with crude ceremonies designed to awe the superstitious Negroes. Torchlight parades, sinister warnings, floggings, and lynchings quickly cowed the former slaves and drove out of the State the carpetbaggers and scalawags who had exploited them. Declaring that its purpose had been accomplished, General Nathan Bedford Forrest, the Grand Cyclops, disbanded the Ku Klux Klan in March 1869.

President Andrew Johnson issued a proclamation on June 13, 1865, declaring the insurrection of Tennessee at an end, since the State had announced itself in harmony with the Presidential policy and the Thirteenth Amendment. But an element in Congress refused to support the President, in the hope of strengthening the Republican Party in the South and in the belief that the Negro needed protection from the southern whites. It was not until March 23, 1866, after considerable debate, that the State was finally readmitted to the Union.

Conditions improved gradually throughout the State, especially after Brownlow, who had been elected United States Senator for the term beginning March 4, 1869, resigned the governorship. Governor DeWitt C. Senter, who took oath on February 25, 1869, pardoned many Confederate soldiers still in prison, brought the military occupation of Middle and West Tennessee to an end, and called a convention (1870) for the amendment of the Constitution.

Among the difficulties faced by the State in the decade following 1870 was a series of plagues and epidemics. The worst of these, yellow fever, came in 1878, taking thousands of lives, principally in Memphis. With more than 5,000 fatalities, 25,000 persons in crazed flight, and 5,000 more sheltered in concentration camps, Memphis was in such sorry straits that the city charter was revoked until 1891. Colonel J. M. Keating, who stayed at his post as editor of the *Appeal* throughout the epidemic, directed relief work for what he described as "the horror of the century, the most soul-harrowing episode in the history of the English-speaking people in America."

The State debt, totaling $35,000,000 after the Brownlow administration, was cut approximately in half by 1872.

In 1886 two brothers Robert L. (Bob) Taylor, Democrat, and Alfred A. (Alf) Taylor, Republican, campaigned across the State in a hotly debated but good-humored race for the governorship, called the "War of the Roses." Bob won the election and served two successive terms and a third term six years later, but Alf had to wait until 1921 before he became Governor.

The years between Governor Bob Taylor's second and third terms were especially eventful. The Coal Creek Strike, Tennessee's first major labor disturbance, occurred in 1891–92. Use of convict labor by the mine operators precipitated a series of strikes affecting mines throughout the State and causing numerous casualties. The convict-lease system was abolished and other grievances of the miners adjusted *(see THE WORKING MAN).* On May 12, 1892, the three-mile cantilever bridge over the Mississippi at Memphis, a project recommended since 1857, was opened with elaborate ceremony. With even greater fanfare the Chickamauga and Chattanooga National Military Park was dedicated September 18-20, 1895. It commemorated the valor of both armies in the War between the States.

During Governor Bob's third term, Tennessee celebrated its hundred years of statehood with an exposition in Nashville held from May to December 1897. A year later the State sent four regiments to the War with Spain. One of these, the First Tennessee, saw service against Aguinaldo in the Philippine Islands.

Conflict over liquor had been growing since the Reconstruction period. The act of 1877, prohibiting the sale of liquor near institutions of learning, was broadened ten years later, but State-wide prohibition, by amendment to the constitution, was defeated. Gradually, following the act of 1899 which granted local option to towns of less than 2,000, the law was extended to cover communities up to 5,000, and in 1907 all cities and towns in the State were included. By 1908 only Memphis, Nashville, Chattanooga, and Lafollette remained legally wet.

State-wide prohibition became the issue in the Democratic primary of 1908 with Governor Patterson, who opposed the movement and favored local option, receiving the nomination over Edward W. Carmack. While Patterson was winning reelection at the polls, Carmack continued his battle for prohibition in the Nashville *Tennessean,* of which he had become editor. His bitter editorials brought about a dispute with Colonel Duncan Cooper, a friend of the Governor. In an encounter with Cooper and his son Robin, Carmack was killed. Cooper was tried for murder and convicted, but was immediately pardoned by Governor Patterson, and the case against Robin was nolle prossed. Patterson's standing was so weakened by his pardon of Cooper that a State-wide prohibition law was enacted in January 1909 over his veto.

Tennessee became a dry State July 1, 1909, but the fight left a shattered Democratic Party. In 1910 Ben W. Hooper became the first Republican Governor since 1880, and for four years led a vigorous battle to secure enforcement of the prohibition law, despite connivance of State and municipal officials with the liquor interests. During Hooper's second term,

Republican and independent members of the legislature mustered the quorum necessary for legislation and defeated repeal.

When the United States entered the World War Tennessee lived up to its name, the "Volunteer State," won in the Mexican War. Almost 100,000 men enlisted. Represented in 43 divisions, Tennesseans were most numerous in the 27th and the 30th (Old Hickory). The Old Hickory Division, which included the 59th and 60th Infantry Brigades, participated in breaking the Hindenburg line, and was given ten citations by the English and American High Command. Sergeant Alvin C. York of Pall Mall, Fentress County, was called by General Pershing the outstanding hero of the A. E. F.

In 1919 Tennessee passed a law protecting factory workers from industrial hazards and in the following year earned her latest nickname, "the Liberator," when the State's vote for women's suffrage became the decisive one in adding the Nineteenth Amendment to the Federal Constitution.

Governor Austin Peay, who served in 1923–27, abolished about fifty bureaus and departments, putting all activities of the State under eight major departments which, with few alterations, have functioned ever since. He was also responsible for the State's greatest period of highway construction and was instrumental in establishing the Great Smoky Mountains National Park.

In 1926, when the Tennessee Republican Committee met, charges of political patronge brought State politics to national notice. The political stew boiled over again during the administration of Henry Horton, who succeeded Austin Peay as Governor in 1927. Horton was reelected for two more terms. During his last term a bank scandal, involving a number of prominent Tennesseans, rocked the State from end to end. With State funds to the amount of $6,000,000 in closed banks, the impeachment of Governor Horton was suggested; but after months of public hearings, the investigating committee voted against impeachment.

A bitter political struggle in 1932 resulted in the defeat of Lewis S. Pope by Hill McAlister. During the same year coal miners went on strike at Wilder, and the National Guard was called out to stop killings and property damage.

McAlister reduced the State's annual expenditures, and appointed a commission to make an exhaustive study of educational conditions. Federal and State relief measures and the building program of the Tennessee Valley Authority reduced unemployment during the years following 1933.

The TVA, established in 1933, is one of the most important chapters in the history of Tennessee. An area small enough to be placed under unified control, yet transcending State boundaries, the Tennessee Valley has become the proving ground for one of the most comprehensive social experiments in America. Knoxville as headquarters, with Norris Dam twenty miles north, is at present the center of the TVA's activities *(see Tennessee Valley Authority)*. A unified, long-range program is rapidly transforming the great valley of the Tennessee River—which flood waters and wasteful farming were turning into a desert—into a land of plenty where industry, agriculture, and human values may take their place in a balanced economy.

In 1936 the convict-lease law was repealed, and the Workman's Compensation Law was passed at a special session of the legislature. Early in the following year Mississippi floods caused large property damage in West Tennessee. Labor troubles continued, with the largest strike at the aluminum plant at Alcoa.

State politics again came into national prominence in 1937. Governor Gordon Browning, who succeeded McAlister, called a special session of the legislature and forced through his Unit Bill for proportional suffrage among counties. He met with bitter opposition within the Democratic Party, and the Unit Bill was made a political issue during the Democratic primaries in 1938. In that year the Tennessee Supreme Court invalidated the Unit Bill. Browning was defeated for reelection by Prentice Cooper in one of the bitterest elections ever held in the State.

Government

The original Constitution of Tennessee, 1796, gave suffrage to every free man, allowed free Negroes the right to vote, permitted freedom of speech and of the press, and guaranteed the right of trial by jury. Future legislators were forbidden to permit any "tendency to lessen the rights and privileges" of the people, or to require a religious test as qualification for public office. This last provision was retained in both the later constitutions.

The revision of 1834 promoted education and, like the earlier constitution, recognized slavery. The new version was regarded as adequate until 1870. A new constitution, drawn up in that year, granted the Governor the power of veto, provided for a supreme court, chancery, and circuit courts, and "such inferior tribunals as the legislature may deem advisable." Intended to serve for only a few years, the constitution has been in force ever since. Except for the clauses recognizing the abolition of slavery, for-

THE CAPITOL, NASHVILLE

bidding future laws for "the right of property in man," setting up a judiciary, forbidding State participation in public investments, and giving suffrage to Negroes, the present constitution is substantially the same as the one it superseded.

Laws in Tennessee are made by the General Assembly, consisting of a Senate and a House of Representatives which convene every two years. There are thirty-three Senators and ninety-nine Representatives, all elected for two-year terms. To become a law a bill must be read on three different days and passed each time in the house where it is sponsored, with the same procedure repeated in the other house; it must then go to the Governor for final approval.

The appellate court, reorganized in 1925, operates in each of the three divisions of the State and has final authority in civil cases. Lesser judicial agencies designed to meet the needs of a growing population, rural and urban, have been established from time to time.

Recommendations of the Tennessee Planning Commission resulted in the Reorganization Bill (1936) which centralized executive control in the office of the Governor. This administrative rearrangement provided more efficient means for carrying out programs of social security, conservation, public works, health, education, and financial management. The newest of nine departments directly under the Governor is the department of conservation. The nine commissioners administer 81 divisions and boards. There are also 27 special commissions, principally involving the professions, appointed by the Governor. For the ten-year period ending June 30, 1936, there was a total disbursement of nearly $500,000,000, with 47.56 per cent of the tax dollar going to highways and highway bridges, 18.58 per cent to education, 7.48 per cent to penal and charitable institutions, and 26.38 per cent to all other activities.

There are 34 counties in the eastern, 40 in the middle, and 21 in the western division of the State. In these 95 counties all the functions of State and city government are duplicated in administrative detail.

Industry and Commerce

FOR more than a century before pioneer homeseekers began coming over the mountains into Tennessee, English and French fur traders had been carrying on a brisk and profitable commerce with the Indians. The English traded chiefly with the Cherokee in the East and the Chickasaw along the Mississippi bluffs, and the French with the Shawnee in Middle Tennessee. By 1755 the fur trade between Tennessee and the English colonies alone amounted to a million dollars annually.

Fur seekers who followed Indian tradepaths through Tennessee played a role more important than that indicated by these figures. Their accounts of the rich wilderness beyond the mountains turned men's minds westward and gave first impetus to the great wave of immigration that began in 1768. Trading posts, such as Charleville's on the site of Nashville, John Overton's post at Chickasaw Bluffs, and John Ross' at Chattanooga, were almost invariably followed by settlements.

Though food in the pioneer period could be had from the soil and the game-teeming forests, and salt from numerous salt springs and "licks," the problem of obtaining cloth garments and tools was more difficult. To meet it, itinerant merchants with caravans of pack horses established trade routes throughout the territory. Because of an almost total absence of money, trade between merchant and pioneer farmer, and between farmer and farmer, was largely carried on by barter. On the whole the trader and peddler drove hard bargains, exchanging pot metal rifles, likely to explode at the first charge, poorly soldered utensils, and adulterated powder for the frontier farmer's prime peltries. As fur-bearing animals grew scarce, by-products of the pioneer home—bacon, corn, lye-soap, sorghum-sugar and molasses, and strong whisky—became the medium of exchange, along with Spanish silver, which trickled in as river trade with Louisiana began to assume importance.

By 1790 better trade routes and lessened danger from the Indians were making necessities, and even some luxuries, cheaper and more abundant. Stores, such as Peter Norrison's in Knoxville and Lardner Clark's in Nashville, were well stocked with goods, ranging from bright gewgaws for the Indian trade to high-grade carpenter's tools, English and Pennsylvania rifles, fine French powder, pure pig-lead for bullet molding, gold jewelry and watches, imported shawls, and Philadelphia kid gloves. However, each pioneer community had so nearly become a self-sufficient unit that improved communication with the East did not bring a parallel commercial expansion.

Milling provided the State with its first established industry. A grist mill was set up on Buffalo Creek in 1775, and some meal and flour was shipped to New Orleans and the Atlantic Coast. Other mills followed shortly: on Little Limestone Creek in East Tennessee; on White's Creek, Mill Creek, and on a barge in the Cumberland River near Nashville; one in Palmyra, run in conjunction with a distillery; a fulling mill on Yellow Creek; and a powder mill in Sumner County. These, like other "first" industries in the area, converted existing crops or natural resources into processed necessities.

When wheat became one of the largest cash crops in the 1830's, flour milling became the most important industry. It retained this supremacy until 1845, when competition from the prairie regions of the Middle West forced wheat to be abandoned as a major crop in Tennessee. Later it was discovered that Tennessee's hard wheat made a damp-resisting flour which would remain sweet during shipment but had a great capacity for water absorption in baking. This quality made it especially suitable for tropical countries and the industry revived on the export trade.

The textile industry, also dependent upon agriculture for its raw materials, dates back to 1791, when John Hague, of Manchester, advertised in the Knoxville *Gazette* that the machines in his spinning mill on the Cumberland were "in order for carding, spinning and weaving." A venture into silk-worm culture, begun by Dr. Frederick A. Ross, of Kingsport, in 1850, died in an experimental stage. It remained for wool and cotton to put textile manufacturing on its feet.

One of the earliest cotton mills was established in Lebanon. In 1846 it was operating 2,000 spindles, 21 carding machines, and 40 power looms, turning out 1,000 yards of cloth a day. But as competition from better cotton lands in the lower South drove most of the farmers of the State to other crops, the industry declined until the War between the States virtually destroyed it. During Reconstruction, however, it was seen to have new possibilities. In 1880 a woolen mill in Tullahoma was turning out $1,000,000 worth of cloth a year. Other plants were established in Knoxville, Nashville, and Jackson. By 1900 textile manufacturing had climbed back to fifth place among the State's industries.

During the next twenty-five years the textile industry grew steadily. In 1925 the establishment of a rayon plant in Old Hickory, near Nashville, gave it tremendous impetus. The Old Hickory plant, which later added the manufacturing of cellophane, is now one of the largest in the country, with an annual output of 25,000,000 pounds of rayon and 25,000,000 pounds of cellophane. Among other synthetic-yarn plants which have been established, the second largest is at Elizabethton.

The land, which produced the agricultural wealth of Tennessee during its early years, has likewise been the foundation of much of its industrial wealth. Some of Tennessee's earliest industries were founded on iron. In East Tennessee small forges and bloomeries, supplied by crude mining operations, were turning out bar iron, nails, and tools as early as 1785. But the iron resources of the State were not extensively exploited until coal was discovered. Tennessee iron was soon being shipped to Louisville, Cincinnati, and Pittsburgh, where it was in demand for the manufacture of steam engine boilers. Further expansion came when railroad transportation was made available in 1854. By 1860 a total of 75 bloomeries and forges, 71 furnaces, and four rolling mills were in operation. The iron industry in Tennessee boomed briefly in filling demands for war materials needed by the Confederacy, but Union occupation of the State brought it sudden disruption. After Reconstruction, the industry was revived and grew steadily until 1929, when iron and steel production totaled $3,100,000. Since then the industry has drifted toward stagnation. The small and scattered units in Tennessee could not compete with the newer and more efficient plants of the Birmingham area, and by 1935 the production figures had dropped to $28,438.

Coal fields of East Tennessee, first worked in 1814 near the site of Rockwood, yield a high-grade bituminous type valuable for coking purposes. Because mining costs are low and the supply plentiful, this coal has been an important factor in the State's industrial development. Tennessee coal fields show no parallel to the sharp decline in the iron mining areas. There is at present an annual production of more than 3,500,000 short tons, much of it for domestic use.

Tennessee quarries twenty varieties of marble; the monotone is best known because of its massive structure, soft color, and complete crystallization, which permits a high polish. In the early quarries drilling was done entirely by hand. The blocks, roughly dressed at the quarry, were hauled by sledge to the nearest boat landing. In 1857 the first quarry south of the Potomac River to use derricks and channeling machines was opened near Rogersville. The second largest marble quarry in the United States and one of the world's largest plants for producing finished marble are in Knoxville.

Profitable amounts of other minerals have been extracted and processed in Tennessee. Barites reached a peak value of $345,000 in 1925. Chert and flint from Tennessee were substituted for the usual Belgian supply when the World War curtailed that source. Lignite, limestone, manganese, petroleum and natural gas, pigments, tripoli, fuller's earth, mineral waters, and even gold have been produced at a profit. Bauxite has been mined experimentally and there are extensive reserves near Chattanooga.

The last mentioned industry makes use of the Tennessee River hydroelectric development. The raw materials are imported from surrounding states where reserves have already been mined and equipment is set up. To date, cryolite—the "flux" necessary for the electrolytic refining of aluminum —must be brought from Greenland, where the only exploited deposits exist.

Since the recent development of phosphate rock deposits, discovered in Tennessee in 1893, the State ranks second to Florida in production of this valuable fertilizer material. The present annual output is valued at $2,500,000. Availability of cheap Tennessee Valley Authority electric power has fostered the building of several large chemical plants in the Middle Tennessee phosphate regions. Other leading mining industries include copper, sulphuric acid, and zinc.

Upon the forests of the State is based an extensive lumber industry. One of the largest plants for finishing hardwood floors is in Memphis; another is in Johnson City. Many cedar products, including pencils and buckets, are manufactured in increasing quantities in Middle Tennessee. From a small beginning in 1792, the distillation of wood by-products has grown into an industry with a $60,000,000 yearly output. The principal products are tannic acid, paper pulp, photographic films, celluloid, varnish, and dyes.

Starting with the Knoxville *Gazette,* which began operation in Rogersville in 1791, printing and publishing have been important industries in the State. The southern churches established their publication headquarters in this centrally situated area. More than 300 publications are now printed in Tennessee; Nashville and Kingsport are the centers of the industry.

In 1860, the end of the ante bellum period, the first ten industries ranked roughly in this order: flour and meal, iron, lumber, leather, steam railroad and agricultural machinery, cotton and wool textiles, printing,

MARBLE QUARRY, NEAR KNOXVILLE

coal, copper, and spirits. At that time about one-third of the wealth of the State was represented by slaves and slave-operated farms.

The War between the States brought industry to a standstill. However, despite currency depreciation and destruction of property, there was a 72 per cent increase in output from 1860 to 1870, most marked in grain milling, publishing, lumber products, and woolen goods; much of this production had hitherto been outside the State. Production figures for grain milling doubled betwen 1870 and 1879, with conversion of forest products next in importance. Industry in general showed a steady increase.

By the turn of the century, the size of factories had greatly increased, while many of the small industries had gone under. Though flour and milling still ranked first, textiles had made large gains. Tobacco and cottonseed products ranked seventh and eighth respectively, and coal, copper, and spirits had lost their places among the first ten industries.

The future industrial pattern of the State was visible in outline. Centers for lumber manufacturing, iron works, tobacco factories, market and distribution points, were already located. Urban manufacturing was increasing much faster than rural, with the greatest increase noted in knit goods. New industries, such as cottonseed and soy bean processing and fertilizer manufacturing, were making strong beginnings.

The development up to the World War paralleled that of the country at large. Industries grew out of such newer food preparations as sweetening sirups, lard compounds, and vegetable oils. During the World War a powder plant at Jacksonville (now Old Hickory), near Nashville, boomed for a short time, then died. Later it was reestablished as a rayon and cellophane plant, and its present payroll amounts to $10,000,000 annually.

The U. S. Census for 1920 listed a total of 7,245 establishments. They had a combined payroll of $65,741,045 for 75,446 persons and paid $225,-951,368 for raw materials to produce $374,038,316 worth of goods. In order of value of products, they ranked: lumber and timber, flour and grist mills, knit goods, cars and general shop work, food preparations, printing and publishing, tobacco products, cottonseed products, foundries and machine shops, cotton goods, furniture, confectionery, patent medicines, cloth bags, coffee and spices, meat products, men's clothing, leather, chemicals, marble, ice, fertilizers, carriage and wagon parts and construction, mineral and soda waters.

The development of banking supported the growth of commercial endeavor and stimulated the earliest industrial efforts. Establishment in 1807 of the Bank of Nashville, first in the State, supplied local enterprise with credit. From 1811, with the foundation of the Bank of the State of Tennessee in Knoxville, to 1819, the State went through a period of inflation and wildcat banking which resulted in the suspension of specie payments by all but the State Bank of Knoxville. Banking became a political issue involving private interests, the "Old" and "New" State Banks, the United States Bank (which had been outlawed in the State in 1817), as well as public lands and school funds. However, a general price rise in 1826 allowed all but the original Bank of Nashville to resume specie payments.

The failure of the Nashville institution caused the repeal of the 1817 law and allowed the establishment of the U. S. Bank there in 1827. With the closing of the "New" State Bank in 1829, a system was evolved strong enough to carry through the 1838 panic and survive the railroad and school fund scandals of the times. Credit was nearly swept away during the War between the States, and in 1865 only three or four Tennessee banks were solvent. A nationally reorganized system of money and banking played an important part in Reconstruction.

In 1826 the State's first insurance company was formed in Nashville. The insurance companies, like the banks, were linked with school funds and followed a course parallel to that of the banks. Continued confusion in these fields resulted in regulatory control passing into the hands of a combined State Department of Insurance and Banking in 1923. In 1931 Tennessee led the twelve southern States in new insurance written, averaging $119.25 per capita, and was second in per capita coverage.

Economic Tennessee in general follows its geographic divisions, with commercial activity for the surrounding regions centering in neighboring cities and towns. Nashville and Memphis are predominantly commercial cities; Knoxville and Chattanooga are more industrial. In these four cities, which contain two-thirds of the urban population of Tennessee, are establishments representing nearly every commercial and industrial interest in the State.

In East Tennessee are the railroad towns of Erwin and Harriman. Knoxville draws on farming, textiles, mining, processing of marbles, and the rayon activities of Elizabethton, to the northeast. Kingsport has developed as an industrial community in the past two decades. Mines support much of the activity of Rockwood, Maryville, and Alcoa. Greeneville and Morristown are burley-tobacco centers, while Cleveland and Lenoir City depend on the agricultural activity of the outlying farms, as do the smaller market and mining towns located on the highways. Chattanooga, a manufacturing center, concentrates on heavy metals and textile finishing, and has a trade area which includes northern Georgia and Alabama.

THE MEMPHIS WHARF

Nashville is the financial, wholesale, and distribution focus for Middle Tennessee; the surrounding towns serve their local trade areas in the same way. Springfield and Clarksville, to the northeast, are important tobacco markets. Columbia, to the south, is significant as a mule and livestock market, as well as for the trade from a rich agricultural and phosphate mining area. Dickson and Bruceton, on the railroads and highways, have several manufacturing plants. Lawrenceburg is again becoming active as a phosphate mining town.

Industrial activity of West Tennessee is mainly in Jackson and Memphis, the latter drawing on Mississippi and Arkansas as sources of supply for woodworking, cotton handling, cottonseed processing, and drug manufacturing. Memphis, the railroad hub of the South, is the largest inland cotton-handling port in the country. Jackson is also a railroad center and, like the smaller towns of Paris, Dyersburg, and Humboldt, attracts trade from the surrounding farm areas.

Occasionally some communities have offered new industries preferred tax rates for a period, but in general this has not been the trend. On the whole, there is a wide diversification of activities, as shown by the U. S. Census of Manufactures for 1935. The total value of products was $531,-338,490. The 2,011 establishments employed an average number of 116,-624 wage earners for the year, and paid out $86,714,390 in wages.

More than five hundred banks and insurance affiliates served as a buffer of credit and protection for these activities. With economical transportation available by land and water, and cheap hydroelectric power being developed by the TVA, the State is a likely field for further industrial expansion.

Agriculture

THE Great Seal of the State of Tennessee fittingly symbolizes Agriculture and Commerce, the twined warp upon which Tennessee's past and present have been woven. Even in prehistoric times the region supported an agricultural people, the Mound Builders, whose culture, like that of the Mayas of Central America, was based upon maize. Archeologists have unearthed their granaries and the baskets of corn which they buried as offerings with the dead.

Later the Cherokee and Chickasaw occupied the old village sites of the Mound Builders, and tilled the same cornfields in much the same simple manner.

The white hunters and trappers who came into the region in the early eighteenth century usually "hit a lick of farming" during the summer months. Along their routes they cleared small patches of ground in the crude Indian fashion and planted them with seed which they had likely bartered from the Indians. Months later they returned to harvest what crops chance had given them. Thus they provided themselves with corn and vegetables to go with their venison and bear meat.

In 1769 farmers from backwoods Virginia and Carolina began crossing the mountains to settle the fertile lands described by the hunters and trappers. Their farms were at first small and almost entirely self-sufficient. Plows, axes, hoes—often crude makeshifts—were their only iron tools. Practically every necessity was either grown on the place or made from materials from the surrounding hills and forests. This self-sufficiency remained a characteristic of small farmers in the State for generations and still persists to a degree remarkable in an age when the country has largely become one vast interlocked economic system.

From the first, corn was the chief crop because it was easily cultivated and because its prolific growth was favorable to hog raising. Thus Tennessee's first agricultural exports were bacon, lard, and corn whisky, all of which could be marketed readily in New Orleans, Baltimore, and Philadelphia. Wheat and tobacco were soon added to the list of money crops and were exported in small quantities. Crops produced for home consumption included cotton, hemp, flax, indigo, timothy hay, and vegetables.

In East Tennessee, a high tumbled plateau area broken by innumerable narrow valleys and steep ridges, the size of the farms was limited. Middle Tennessee, however, was a region where hills were low and valleys wide, and the pioneer farm patches could grow as fast as the forest was cleared. Here large farm holdings became the rule. Because of this development—dictated by topography—Middle Tennessee was particularly suited for the wheat boom which came just after the turn of the century.

When it was discovered that Tennessee wheat matured early enough to be shipped to eastern markets ahead of the northern crop, farmers turned to wholesale wheat growing. The fever spread even to the small farmers of East Tennessee. But over-production brought collapse of the market, and Tennessee never regained its early lead as a wheat-growing region.

Farmers in East Tennessee—except for those in the fertile valley of the Tennessee River—returned to the pioneer type of small subsistence farms. In Middle Tennessee the farmers retained the system of specialized farming and its large profits. Many began raising tobacco and fruit as cash crops. Others turned to stock raising and dairying on the bluegrass pasture lands of the Central Basin where the mild climate minimized feeding costs. Arabian horses were imported as early as 1825, and Middle Tennessee became noted for breeding them. There was a growing demand for the sturdy Tennessee mule.

By 1810 improvements in the cotton gin and spinning machinery had created an enormous demand for cotton, and farmers in the middle part of the State feverishly planted it in their pastures and old wheat fields. Though some cotton was grown in East Tennessee, the quality was generally poor and the boom affected the region little. West Tennessee, with its tremendously fertile bottomlands hitherto left to the Chickasaw and a handful of white trappers and squatters, was ideal for cotton growing. In 1818 the region was purchased from the Chickasaw and settlers flocked in. Land was swiftly cleared, and by 1825 West Tennessee—the lower section in particular—had become one of the cotton growing centers of the Mid-South. Cotton showed a decline in Middle Tennessee during this period. Here the farmers could not compete with the vast crops produced by the slave-gang system of the newly cleared sections within the State and in Alabama and Mississippi.

With the lines of development clearly laid out for each division—small subsistence farms in the east; dairying, livestock raising, tobacco, and truck farming in the central part; and large-scale cotton production in the west—Tennessee entered upon an era of agricultural prosperity that continued until the War between the States. In 1854 the State's first agricultural bureau was formed with Governor Andrew Johnson as president, and in the following year the first biennial fair was opened. Even before that, Tennessee farmers received international recognition at the Great Exhibition in London, where Colonel John Pope was given first place in the cotton exhibit, and Mark Cockrill received the same rating for his sheep. The census of 1860 showed approximately 82,000 farms under cultivation, with nearly seven million acres, valued at 340 million dollars.

Four years of war virtually wiped out the development of three-quarters of a century. The losses sustained by farmers were estimated at $115,-000,000, exclusive of the losses of their slaves, who constituted one-third of the value of farm property in 1860. Not for forty years were farm values restored to the 1860 level.

During the Reconstruction period the farm tenancy system had its beginning in the State. Farmers, forced to borrow, found themselves unable to take up mortgages that fell due. With no other means of livelihood, they became tenants on the farms they had once owned. Most of the freed slaves also became tenants. There was a sharp decline in the size of the average farm, partly because sales of land to raise funds for operating expenses greatly reduced individual holdings. The 1860 average of 251 acres dwindled by 1900 to 91. The 1929 depression caused further shrinkage, bringing the average (according to a 1935 census) to 73 acres. However, until 1930 the value of the land itself increased, reaching a peak valuation of $743,222,363 in that year. By 1935 the valuation had fallen to $556,000,000 and the proportion of tenants had materially increased. Of the 19 million acres in 273,783 farms, about one-third were in crops. Gross income, including livestock, approximated $164,000,000 in 1935. The average cash income of $600 was about the same as the Kentucky figure and higher than in most Southern States. Farmers now (1939) constitute 62.8 per cent of Tennessee's population. Of these, 18.18 per cent are sharecroppers, while 27.4 per cent rent farms outright and furnish their own stock and seed.

Corn always has been the leading crop in value and volume. For more than 50 years the State has had a yearly average of three million acres in corn. In 1935 the crop amounted to more than 60 million bushels. One-third of the corn grown is the high-yield variety known as Neal's Paymaster. It is interesting to note that until 1904, when W. H. Neal of Lebanon developed this variety, most Tennessee farmers had been growing the same type of corn planted centuries before by the mound builders. The major part of the Tennessee crop is consumed in the region of its

RUST COTTON PICKER IN ACTION

production. Sweet sorghum, from which thick brown molasses is made, is grown throughout the State and is one of the most important locally consumed crops.

Cotton, the second most valuable and the main cash crop, can be grown at a cost of as little as three cents a pound on some of the bottomland plantations, and with an occasional profit of from six to twelve cents on the pound. Production volume has varied considerably, with an almost continuous downward trend in the past few years. In 1936 the State produced 431,000 bales, averaging 500 pounds each.

Next in rank is the hay and forage crop, with a production in 1935 of 1,620,453 tons valued at $20,279,751. This includes timothy, planted since pioneer days; alfalfa and all types of clover, abundant in East Tennessee and in the Central Basin; and many other plants, such as millets, orchard grass, vetch, soybeans, cowpeas, Sudan grass, and Austrian peas. Tennessee farmers were pioneers in the introduction of lespedeza (Japanese clover), under the direction of the University of Tennessee College of Agriculture. Lespedeza has developed rapidly and constitutes an important new cash crop.

Tobacco has in recent years become the fourth most valuable crop in the State, second only to cotton in cash returns. Burley tobacco predominates in East Tennessee and the darkfired variety is generally planted in Middle Tennessee. The largest tobacco market in the State, at Greeneville, handles about 12,000,000 pounds a season, or about one-fifth of the entire burley crop of Tennessee, Virginia, and North Carolina. The principal markets for dark tobacco are at Clarksville and Springfield. The combined 1935 crop of burley and darkfired tobaccos was estimated at more than 94 million pounds, valued at nearly $12,000,000.

The discovery that Tennessee hard wheat produced a damp-resisting flour which was highly water-absorbent in baking revived wheat production to some extent. It has never regained its former place and now ranks fifth in importance. In 1936 the 454,000 acres sown in wheat harvested 4,858,000 bushels.

Although Henry and Weakley Counties produce more than two-fifths of Tennessee's sweet potatoes, this crop can be grown in almost any part of the State. It did not become a commercial crop, however, until the curing house made possible shipment without decay. Tennessee's Nancy Hall sweet potato is widely in demand on the national market. The Irish (white) potato, among the first crops planted in Tennessee, was also difficult to market for many years. Since 1922, when the State Department of Agriculture put into effect a system of certifying seeds and standardizing varieties, spring and fall crops have been produced regularly. The average yearly production exceeds 5 million dollars. Middle Tennessee is noted for its peanut crop, which is more than 500,000 bushels annually. In only two other States, Virginia and North Carolina, are more peanuts produced.

The Tennessee peach, maturing immediately after the Georgia crop and before that of the northern States, is grown principally in Anderson, Bradley, Hamilton, Knox, and Roane Counties. Apple trees thrive on the Cumberland Plateau and in parts of the Unaka Range and Smoky Mountains. One orchard near Mt. Le Conte produces 30,000 bushels in a normal season. Strawberries, the chief berry crop, are shipped from many parts of the State. The principal areas devoted to its cultivation are Gibson and Sumner Counties. About 16,000 acres are cultivated annually, yielding approximately 18 million quarts. Tennessee's wide variation in climate makes possible the production of both the cherry, which flourishes in extremely low temperatures, and the fig, which requires sub-tropical warmth.

Truck gardening and the specialized production of vegetables for canning factories constitute an important source of cash income in many localities, especially in Gibson and Cocke Counties. One of America's largest vegetable canneries began business about 1902 in Cocke County. Tomatoes, the principal cannery crop, yield as much as $500 an acre in favorable years.

Tennessee, with about six million acres in pasturage, is well adapted to livestock raising and dairying. Most of this land is well watered and can be grazed all year. The purebred beef cattle industry, introduced in 1917, brought many excellent Angus, Hereford, Shorthorn, Polled, and Durham herds into the State. Five herds have won grand championships at international livestock exhibitions.

The coming of the motor age has dwarfed what was once another leading industry in the Central Basin—the breeding of thoroughbred horses. The number of horses on farms decreased from 333,000 in 1910 to 151,000 in 1936. But the Tennessee mule is still in great demand. In 1936 an estimated 291,000 mules were at work on Tennessee farms.

Sheep have been kept by many farmers since the early days, but only recently has it been discovered that the State's early spring gives Tennessee shippers of young lambs a distinct advantage in northern markets.

The early importance of hog raising has not diminished. From 1850 to 1860 Tennessee raised more hogs than any other State in the nation, with an average annual production of 3,000,000 heads. The industry never reached that dominant position again, although it is still an important factor in the farm program. In 1936 there were in Tennessee nearly one million hogs, valued at $8.40 per head.

Tennessee pioneered in testing milk for butterfat, to check the practice of watering. In 1889 Major W. J. Webster, of Columbia, made the first officially recorded butterfat test in the United States. In cooperation with the Bureau of Dairy Industry of the United States Department of Agriculture, the State Extension Service undertook a systematic regulation of dairy conditions, and national manufacturers of evaporated, condensed, and powdered milk, and of milk products were attracted to Tennessee. Such rapid progress was made that in 1925 the State's dairy products were valued at 40 million dollars. The decline in the price of milk during the depression, however, greatly reduced the value of both herds and products.

Another major source of cash income for the farmer is poultry. The combined value of eggs and poultry in 1935 exceeded $16,000,000. East Tennessee, with its small farms, leads the State; Morristown, in the northeast, and Cookeville, in Middle Tennessee, are among the largest poultry-shipping centers in the country.

Cooperative marketing of farm products is carried on in Tennessee in two divisions. One comprises the large incorporated associations with hundreds and sometimes thousands of member producers, who confine themselves to major products, or to those grown in considerable volume. The other consists of producers from a county or group of counties, who form smaller organizations in their own localities for joint marketing.

In 1877 a group of sheep-growers formed the Goodlettsville Lamb Club, the first lamb pool organized in the United States, and made its first sale in May 1878. One of the first southern cooperative creameries began operation in 1910 at Winchester, in Franklin County. Earlier, more than five unsuccessful attempts had been made to establish cooperative creameries.

Today there are fewer cooperative associations in Tennessee than was the case some years ago. Trucking facilities enable growers to haul their products to market at convenient times rather than wait for the periodic shipments of cooperative associations. In this way, too, they get their money immediately. Marketing by associations usually requires a ten-day period before cash for the products can be received.

Under the direction of the State Department of Agriculture and with the cooperation of the University of Tennessee College of Agriculture, the Tennessee Valley Authority, and county demonstration agents, Tennessee farmers have made great strides. Methods of cultivation have been improved, better seeds and more efficient equipment have been utilized, and grades of products have been standardized. Farms on the whole are fertile, but in some sections, particularly in the Unaka Range and the Cumberland Plateau, the land is poor. Through the efforts of the Farm Security Administration, however, most of this area may be restored as forest land and the farmers who have been trying to work it moved to more fertile sections.

One of the most important current factors in the development of agriculture in the State is the Tennessee Valley Authority. In addition to its hydroelectric and soil conservation programs, it has been instrumental in improving living conditions on the farms in the State by encouraging the widespread use of electricity. Complete electrification of the rural districts, a goal which the present program seems likely to attain in the near future, promises a new era of scientific agriculture not only to the Tennessee Valley but to Tennessee as a whole.

The Working Man

RICH natural resources and almost unlimited possibilities for cheap electric power seem destined within the next few decades to sweep Tennessee into the main stream of industrialism. The transition period has already begun. But thinking in terms of the group—the natural corollary to mass-production—has shown only rudimentary signs of development. The working man is still an individualist, carrying over into his new industrial environment the traits of the small farmer and tenant. His employer tends to think and act in terms of land ownership. In general, the relationship between employed and employer rests on a man-to-man footing, in the old tradition of agrarianism. This one fact, the key to many a paradox, must be borne in mind in any discussion of the Tennessee working man, his past, present, and future.

Until at least 1820 the Tennessean lived in a frontier region. Of his 422,000 neighbor Tennesseans, one-fifth were Negro slaves. The largest city, Nashville, had but 3,000 persons and throughout the State only 7,680 devoted themselves to manufacturing, mostly of locally consumed necessities. From the mountain coves of East Tennessee to the Mississippi bottomlands, the remainder of the working men—roughly 100,000—were engaged in farming.

Great plantations, worked by slave gangs and based on a cotton economy, were slow in obtaining a foothold in Tennessee. Only the bottomlands of West Tennessee were ideally suited to the plantation, but even here the people were too typically yeomen in character to fall naturally into the system. The Tennessean of ante bellum days was inclined to continue the small farming practices of his immigrant fathers. The census of 1850 showed 118,941 farmers, none of whom were classified as planters. In significant contrast are the census figures of South Carolina for the same year: 8,407 planters, as against 32,898 farmers.

In the mountains of East Tennessee, frontier conditions lingered; few slaves were owned and the farmer found it necessary to do all tasks about his farm with only such help as his family could give. And as for most of the necessities, he became accustomed to the philosophy of "make it yourself or do without."

Artisans were of such importance in early Tennessee towns that they are estimated to have constituted at least 10 per cent of the population. But two factors were at work to doom the influential craftsman class. As a rule, the artisan who had come into the State worked at his craft only long enough to buy land. And the hard system of apprenticeship, virtual peonage, was failing rapidly in this new country. Newspapers of the time carried many advertisements offering rewards for the capture of runaway apprentices. But few were returned to their masters; the temper of the people was against it.

In Middle and West Tennessee Negro slaves began to assume increasing importance. As early as 1808 Montgomery Bell, of Nashville, advertised for "ten Negro fellows" to man his iron works on the Harpeth River. Even earlier a few slaves were employed in crude mining operations in East Tennessee. Nashville and many smaller towns kept Negroes for municipal repair and scavenger work. With the coming of the steamboat and railroad, large numbers of company-owned Negroes furnished the unskilled labor. Very soon Negroes began filtering into the artisan class as well. So many white craftsmen had become landowners that by 1802 "when General James Winchester built his stone house, Cragfont . . . near Gallatin . . . he had to import working men from Baltimore to do the interior finishing." Most of the ante bellum homes, churches, and public buildings were the work of slave artisans and laborers. The slaves fell heir to brick making and brick laying, carpentry, blacksmithing, and metal working. Principally, however, they were agricultural workers or domestic servants.

The white farm hand at that time could draw $8.67 per month with board. A day laborer got 58¢ per day; 43¢ if he boarded in. Carpenters commanded $1.38 per day, and female domestics, of whom there were few, $1.00 per week. Behind all these was the threat that the work they did could be equally well done by the slaves, who could be hired from their masters or owned at two-thirds the cost of white labor.

Reconstruction for the South meant a readjustment for the Tennessee working man. Faced with fallow fields and run-down industries, he had to enter upon what was almost a second pioneer period.

Many of the freed Negroes migrated to the cities in search of work, or to the North. They made places for themselves in a few industries—mining, iron- and steelwork, the railroads; and in service and trades—as domestic servants, laundresses, and porters. However, in the main they became "the proletariat of the odd job" or returned to the soil as hands or "croppers" and later as tenants.

COTTON PICKERS

The small white farmer rented land, if his own had been lost, and began life again in the only manner he knew. Money was scarce; capital was in the North. The landowner needed a cash crop to meet his obligations, but the tenant, Negro or white, saw little cash from one year's end to another. His family of from six to ten persons, living in a ramshackle shanty, worked from dawn until dusk. He sank ever deeper in debt to the commissary, which in turn was in debt to the wholesaler. The owner himself could buy in no way but on credit. The result was a vicious circle from which it was difficult for either the tenant or the landowner to escape.

This condition grew in West Tennessee and to a lesser degree in the middle counties. Tenant-operated farms constituted 30 per cent of those within the State by 1890 and had increased to 40 per cent in 1900.

E. E. Miller, editor of the *Southern Agriculturist* for many years, voiced the plight of the tenant farmer in "The Cropper Speaks":

And twice a farm I've tried to buy
But couldn't gather, low nor high,
The cash I had to have in hand
To get possession of the land.

* * *

A slave to toil that has no end
And does not help the lot to mend.

By 1900 the same fundamental forces were at work in East Tennessee. Mills, factories, and mines attracted small farmers from "leached-out" mountain farmsteads. Although the pay was low and conditions deplorable in light of the present day, the worker at least did not face prolonged starvation and attendant pellagra for himself and his family.

The textile mills, often poorly ventilated fire-traps, were crowded with machinery, and little provision was made for the safety of workers. Children worked beside the women and men. Company-owned mill towns were monotonously alike—hideous rows of flimsy boxes, roofed with tar paper and as innocent of comfort as of plumbing. Away from the town, the houses of the poor whites became empty of young folk. They had gone to the mills, sometimes as children on contracts signed by the parents in order to supplement their own earnings. The scale of wages and hours had been improved but there were still many working from 40 to 75 hours a week for wages ranging from $1.63 to $15.00.

In early deeds-registries several "Labor Temples" are entered, but these were purely fraternal amusement halls. With the background of an agricultural, landholder-controlled economy, there was little opportunity for a united labor movement. In the urban areas only, where the Memphis and Nashville Typographical Union locals were formed before the War between the States, did labor organization make headway. The Knights of Labor, which organized locally in 1867 and was never highly effective in the State, merged with other national organizations to form the Federation of Organized Trades and Labor Unions in 1881. In 1886 the objectives of this group were amplified and the name changed to the American Federation of Labor, which, after 1893, became the dominant labor organization. The "big four" Brotherhoods (Locomotive Engineers, Locomotive Firemen, Trainmen, and Conductors) were organized in 1882. Though they co-operate with one another, none of the four is affiliated with the American Federation of Labor or the recently formed Congress of Industrial Organizations.

Through the country at large, labor organization throve in industrial centers that were crowded with European immigrants. In Tennessee there has never been more than three per cent foreign-born population, and strikes grew from spontaneous protests against existing conditions rather than from organized labor. Attempts by outsiders to direct or advise the strikers were often met with indifference, suspicion, and at times hot resentment.

Between 1880 and 1887 there were thirty-two strikes, principally in the textile and metal industries, of which twenty were organized and seventeen succeeded. The causes were various: wage reduction, working with Negroes, and employment of non-union labor.

The first major strike in the State's history took place in the summer of 1891 among the miners of the Tennessee Coal, Iron and Railway Company at Coal Creek and Briceville. A principal complaint was the "yellow dog" contract which the miners were compelled to sign, pledging themselves to remain unorganized. Unable to reach an agreement with the operators, the miners struck.

Then the company brought in convict labor, as it was permitted to do by a legislative act of 1865, empowering the prison authorities for a period of fifteen years to lease convicts to the operators. Although leasing of convicts was condemned by progressives as vicious, the system had gathered strong momentum. In opposing the system purely from the standpoint of the threat to their livelihood, the miners incidentally forced the harsh picture upon public attention.

On July 14, 1891, Coal Creek miners marched on the convict camp at Briceville, overpowered the guards, and put the convicts on a train for Knoxville. Governor Buchanan arrived with the State militia and returned the convicts. On July 20 the miners a second time compelled the convicts to return to Knoxville.

An armed group of miners released more than 300 convicts at Tracy City in August 1892, burned the stockade, and put the convicts on a train for Nashville. In the next few days similar steps were taken at Oliver Springs and Inman. The State militia was mobilized, and during a running battle at Coal Creek there were many casualties. The State was aroused, and the Tennessee Coal, Iron and Railway Company ceased using convict labor. In 1895 leasing was finally abolished, though prison shops and the State-owned Brushy Mountain coal mines continued operation under the account system "by which the State itself undertook production with prison labor and marketed the product to the general public."

The building trades, metal and shop workers, and other crafts were gathered into the American Federation of Labor during the years 1900–1920. The World War boom, with its campaign for cooperation between capital and labor, brought about further unionization. When the United Garment Workers, an A. F. of L. affiliate, called its 1914 convention in Nashville, dissension among the delegates resulted in a split within the ranks, out of which came the Amalgamated Clothing Workers. This organization later affiliated with the Congress of Industrial Organizations.

One of the first conflicts, if not the first, in the Southern textile field broke out March 12, 1929, when 800 employees of the American Glanzstoff Corporation, rayon manufacturers at Elizabethton, walked out in a fumbling strike, poorly organized and not under union leadership. They demanded wage increases and the company ordered the plant closed the following day. On March 19 the adjoining plant, under the same management, was also closed and its 3,000 employees joined the ranks of the strikers, all native Americans. The courts quickly granted injunctions against the strikers and two companies of National Guardsmen were rushed to Elizabethton by Governor Henry Horton. On March 22, after the strikers had joined the A. F. of L., a settlement was reached and the mills reopened. However, on April 15 the workers walked out again, charging discrimination against the union. On May 6 the plants reopened with National Guardsmen present to quell disorders and prevent property damage. When later in the month the company agreed to arbitrate workers' grievances and recognize the right of union affiliation, the strike ended.

On July 8, 1932, some 600 members of the United Mine Workers at Wilder and Davidson came out on strike, when the Fentress Coal and Coke Company refused to renew their contracts. No wage increase was demanded; the strike was for union recognition. The company fought the miners with evictions, injunctions, imported strike breakers, and National Guardsmen. State troops were withdrawn when the company refused the services of the State Commissioner of Labor as arbitrator. The union had agreed to accept the decision of the commissioner or any arbitration board appointed by the Governor.

In 1933–34 the industrial towns of East Tennessee, predominantly textile, were the scenes of numerous strikes and labor disputes. Strikes occurred in Chattanooga, Rockwood, Harriman, and Knoxville. Wages and hours were finally agreed upon, the unions recognized, and the workers went back to the factories. Several of the mills, however, have never been reopened.

In the latter part of December 1936 the Zenith Coal Mine, 18 miles from Jamestown, refused to recognize the United Mine Workers Union and closed. It reopened March 8, 1937, with a few non-striking workmen. The sheriff was wounded by snipers; non-striking miners were fired on in their company quarters. On June 17 the general manager of the mines was killed from ambush and the commissary clerk wounded. State troops were dispatched to the scene and order was finally restored.

The fabricating plant of the Aluminum Company of America at Alcoa ceased operations on May 18, 1937, when 3,000 workers led by the A. F. of L. demanded a wage increase. On July 8 non-striking workers returned under police protection. A pitched battle between strikers and police took place; two men were killed and twenty-one wounded. The National Guard was ordered out and remained on the scene until the strikers returned to work July 12, under an agreement negotiated by the representative of the A. F. of L. Demands of the strikers, however, had not been met.

Little legislation affecting labor directly was contained in the State's constitutions of 1796 and 1834. Only two articles in the bill of rights touched on the subject. One prohibited the imprisonment of debtors except in cases of proven fraud. The other declared monopolies to be "contrary to the genius of a free State." It was on grounds of piety, rather than from a consideration of workers' rights, that work on Sunday was prohibited by an act in 1803.

The first law directly influencing organized labor was enacted in 1875. It limited the conditions under which an employee might enter into a contract. Child labor laws were passed as early as 1893, making it unlawful to employ a child less than twelve years of age in workshops, mines, mills, or factories. In 1901 this law was amended to read "children under fourteen," and to limit work to a weekly maximum of sixty-two hours. An act of 1897 made provision for sanitary conveniences in places of employment for women, and subsequent laws have further amplified these requirements.

Protective mine laws, passed as early as 1881, placed restrictions on slopes, washrooms, lamps, and inspection. The acts of 1897, and later ones, attempted to control company stores and issuance of scrip. The protection afforded mechanics and landlords was extended to shield the laborer from attachment of future wages and to give him a lien on corporations for wages due. Various successive commissioners of labor declared that, as it was impossible to get operators to furnish information on which to base legislation, it was obvious that existing laws could not be enforced.

Before the World War, laws were passed concerning wages, exempting them from garnishment, prohibiting misrepresentation of wages by prospective employers, and requiring payment in legal money at least twice a month on definitely stated paydays. Other special laws prohibited false advertising for purposes of getting labor; plumbers, electricians, and loan companies had to be licensed; employment agencies were regulated. In 1915, in a State report on prison conditions, it was "deemed desirable" for Tennessee "to retire from the whole system of contracting or leasing the labor of convicts."

Children were considered in various bills of 1911. The age limit was raised, work hours reduced to fifty-eight weekly, work certificates required, and the employment of children forbidden in hazardous occupations, including virtually all work in which machinery was used. In 1915 a mothers' pension law represented the beginning of a type of legislation that had received much attention from organized labor and social workers. Further legislation provided for examination of the qualifications of foremen in mines, workshops, and bakeries.

Laws passed in 1919 gave police power to factory inspectors and established food inspection. These were amplified in later enactments. The system of contracting for the output of prison shops was changed so that, in theory, convict labor would not compete directly with free labor. Further child labor regulations went into effect in 1921, the year that the Mothers' Pension Law was amplified. A vocational rehabilitation law made the State eligible for Federal grants for this purpose.

Labor leaders consider that the greatest stride made by Tennessee during the post-war prosperity period was the Workmen's Compensation Law, passed in 1911 and amended in 1923. Amendments to this and other laws made during the twenties strengthened labor's position in the State.

Current legislation has kept pace with Federal leadership in recognition of the plight of workers in the lower income brackets. Disputed decisions of the Labor Relations Board are reviewed in the courts, and compensation cases are heard daily before the bar. The Unemployment Compensation Law, Tennessee's first step toward social security, was enacted in December 1936 at a special session of the legislature. The Tennessee State Employment Service has developed from the national services begun as relief measures in 1933. An industrial hygiene unit of the State Department of Health was organized in 1937 to study occupational diseases and outline

DECK HAND ON RIVER BOAT

a program of prevention and control. The prison industries contract law was repealed in 1937, but a two-year extension was granted to mines and a one-year time limit to other prison contracts still in force. In 1937 the use of coal and coal products mined and processed by convict labor on State property was prohibited, except for State or charitable purposes. Use of prison-made goods was also limited to State institutions.

Federal grants of assistance in construction, through the Civil Works Administration, the Public Works Administration, and the Works Progress Administration, have been utilized by most communities to relieve unemployment. In many PWA contracts awarded under this program there have been provisions concerning hours and rates of pay.

Two-fifths of all Tennesseans worked for a living in 1930, according to reports of the University of Tennessee extension service. Men outnumbered women four to one. There were 273,783 farmers in 1935 (U.S. Census), of whom 239,387 were white and 34,396 Negro. Of the total, 46.2 per cent were tenants. For the three State divisions, tenancy ran as high as 63 per cent in West Tennessee, 42 per cent in Middle Tennessee, 32 per cent in East Tennessee. A report of the division of workshop and factory inspection for 1930 listed 1,988 firms employing 113,885 persons, of whom 71,059 were men (15 of these were boys under sixteen years of age) and 42,826 women.

Unionization in Tennessee has made its chief headway in railroads, trades, mines, mills, and pressrooms. The A. F. of L., which was the dominant influence until the advent of the C. I. O. in 1936, had central labor councils in Memphis, Jackson, Nashville, Chattanooga, Knoxville, and Johnson City. The State Federation of Labor directs the A. F. of L. legislative program and maintains a legislative agent at the State Capitol during the sessions. A few trade schools are sponsored by the unions. At the Pressmen's Home, near Rogersville, there is a hospital as well as a trade school.

When the schism between craft and industrial unionism resulted in the formation of the C. I. O., the numerical strength of the United Mine Workers in East Tennessee assured its recognition as an influence. Since then, organizational activity within the State has paralleled that of the nation. Independent unions are in the minority. Company unions function in a few places. Chattanooga, perhaps the most highly industrialized city in the State, is the best organized in its labor activities. Memphis is predominantly an A. F. of L. city. Both the C. I. O., through the clothing and textile workers, and the A. F. of L., with its older craft unions, claim supremacy in Middle Tennessee. East Tennessee, with miners and mass industry workers, is predominantly C. I. O. territory.

Today the working man, agricultural or industrial, lives in a changing environment. New industries born of TVA and industrial farming are reshaping Tennessee's old agrarian system. The sons and daughters of the small farmers, forced by circumstances to tend machines, are now writing the history of labor in Tennessee.

Transportation

THE first white traders drove their pack trains over bison and Indian trails, using light canoes or rafts to cross deep streams. The Wilderness Road, blazed by Daniel Boone in 1775 to open up the Transylvania settlement in Kentucky, was the first road platted by a white man in the Tennessee territory. It led from the North Carolina line into Tennessee, passing near the site of Kingsport and through the Cumberland Gap into Kentucky. From Kentucky a branch circled southward, reaching the Cumberland River at the site of the present Nashville. The term "trace" was used for trail or road by the Southern pioneer.

In 1785 North Carolina, of which the territory was then a part, ordered a road built from the lower end of Clinch Mountain to Nashville. Blazed by Peter Avery, the route entered the Cumberland Plateau at Emory Gap, near Harriman, and crossed the plateau to the Cumberland River. In 1791 the treaty between the United States and the Cherokee Nation granted that "the citizens and inhabitants of the United States shall have a free and unmolested use of a road from the Washington District to the Mero District."

In 1795 a road from Kingston to Nashville, authorized by the Territorial legislature, was completed. After plans to finance the venture by a lottery had failed, the legislature agreed that the Territory should pay up to $1,000 for the actual construction and establish toll rates for upkeep of the road.

In 1799 a tavern keeper of Knoxville, named Chisholm, advertised a post route between Knoxville and Abingdon, Virginia, with trips made once every three weeks. Newspapers and letters were carried for subscribers for an annual fee of $2.50 each.

In 1801 treaties were made with the Chickasaw and in the same year a similar treaty was negotiated with the Choctaw. As a result of these two treaties the southwest frontier obtained use of the Natchez Trace, the Chickasaw "Path of Peace," which linked long fragments of trails and bypaths into one continuous thoroughfare, connecting Nashville with Natchez on the Mississippi, and ultimately by river with New Orleans.

By the treaty of October 27, 1805, the Cherokee granted the Federal

Government a mail route through their territory. Similar agreements were reached with the Creek and Choctaw. The Indians owned and operated all inns and ferries on the intersecting roads, charging a nominal rate for their services.

By 1804 county courts were permitted to build roads and bridges and to establish ferries. At points where building a free bridge would impose too great a tax on the people, the courts had power to build toll bridges and private companies were chartered to build toll roads. The State's first bids for road cutting were received in 1804 for a road linking Tennessee with the "most convenient port in Georgia." The first macadamized road, built in 1831, stimulated the demand for turnpikes of this type. In 1836 an act was passed whereby the State would subscribe one-third of the stock of any properly organized company incorporated for the building of turnpikes. Although several companies had previously built roads in Middle Tennessee, this act of the legislature had a marked effect on transportation in this section. The old roads radiating from Nashville were turned into a system of turnpikes. East Tennessee did not fare as well, for the topography of that section prevented profitable ventures of the kind. By 1840 the building and administration of turnpikes (principal thoroughfares) had almost entirely slipped into the hands of private organizations, who exploited the toll gate system and made few improvements. There were at one time 900 road companies, some of which existed into the twentieth century.

During hostilities between the North and South the marching and counter-marching of armies with their trains of artillery and supply wagons churned the roads of the State into miry, rutted tracks almost impassable for wheeled vehicles. In 1865, county courts were authorized to levy taxes for the improvement of highways. Men from eighteen to thirty were required to pay a three-dollar road tax; or they might work from three to six days a year on the road, if they were able-bodied. In this fashion State roads were maintained until 1907, when the legislature voted surplus school funds to be used for road upkeep. Since no surplus existed, a State commission of public roads was appointed to study the situation. A program of county bond issues and special taxes, resulting from these investigations, transformed the old turnpikes into an excellent system of public roads. Advocates of a property tax to maintain public roads have abandoned the plan in recent years, and revenues from gasoline and motor vehicle fees are used for the purpose.

By the Cherokee treaty of 1791 the Indians agreed to allow the whites free and unmolested navigation of the Tennessee River. One of the earliest commercial river passages was advertised in a Knoxville paper in 1795 by John McFarlane, who notified "all persons who wish to sail with me to New Orleans in one of my boats to be ready within two months." This marked the beginning of a new day for travel and commerce.

As early as 1801, following the passage of laws for freeing the rivers of obstructions, a company was authorized to make the Nolichucky River available for extensive boat traffic. Toll houses were set up to levy one dollar a ton from each craft that passed, and frequently lotteries were employed to raise funds for channel clearing.

In 1807 the Nashville *Impartial Review,* contrasting land and water transportation, pointed out that a merchant who floated 2,000 tons of produce from Murfreesboro to Nashville (a distance of about 34 miles), at a cost of $9.50, had saved $150.50 by choosing the water route.

Flatboats or keelboats were loaded with goods at Knoxville or Nashville and floated to downriver markets along the Tennessee, Cumberland, and Mississippi. These boats, made of heavy timber and steered with long sweeps, were capable of carrying large cargoes and were often "fitted up comfortably with apartments, and in them ladies, servants, cattle, horses, sheep, dogs, and poultry are floating in the same bottom under the same roof."

When the cargo had been disposed of in New Orleans and other southern markets, the larger boats were sold to timber merchants because it was impossible to work them back up the river; the boatmen returned home overland.

In 1819 the first steamboat on the Cumberland, the *General Jackson,* underwritten by a group of merchants seeking to establish quicker communication with New Orleans, puffed up the river to Nashville, and docked on March 11. Steamboat transportation ushered in a new era, and Nashville became the shipping center of the State. Because the dangerous Muscle Shoals of the Tennessee lay between Knoxville and the Mississippi, much of Knoxville's early commercial importance passed to Nashville. As steamboats increased in size and number, channels became a problem.

In 1830 the legislature voted $150,000 to be divided between roadmaking and channel clearance. East Tennessee improved the channels of the Tennessee River and its major tributaries. The building of a portage railway past Muscle Shoals in Alabama made this waterway to the Mississippi accessible to commerce. The Cumberland remained, however, the main water artery into Middle Tennessee until the Illinois Central Railroad was built. The lower Tennessee River and the Mississippi were immediately accessible to the cotton-growing region, and here the steamboat was an important link in the plantation system. On March 3, 1828, the first steamboat, the *Atlas,* reached Knoxville. By 1831 there was fairly regular steamboat service on the upper Tennessee and Holston Rivers during the periods of high water in autumn and spring. Not until 1890, however, when the Federal Government built two canals at Muscle Shoals, was the upper Tennessee navigable the year round. Wilson Dam, completed in 1925, solved some of the remaining problems, though Colbert Shoals, between Florence and Riverton, Alabama, was troublesome until the Tennessee Valley Authority began its program of river control in 1933.

After 1900, use of the State's waterways declined rapidly. Though long-haul freighting was still, in some cases, cheaper by water, the railroads became the chief carriers. However, waterway traffic is today reviving somewhat because of improved methods of mass freight-hauling by tug and barge fleet.

In 1936 more than two million tons of freight were handled on the Tennessee alone. A flotilla of 218 barges was operating on the Tennessee, Cumberland, and Mississippi Rivers, mostly between Tennessee ports and New Orleans. The TVA is now building dams and developing other projects for a nine-foot low-water channel on the Tennessee through its entire length, and on the Cumberland for a distance of 516 miles.

The wave of railroad building which swept the country in the 1830's met at first with little response in Middle and West Tennessee, served as they were with an adequate system of waterway communication. East Tennesseans, however, were fervent advocates of railroad construction. Hemmed in between the Alleghenies on the east and the Cumberland Mountains on the west—over which it was then impossible to build good highways—the people of East Tennessee were at a tremendous economic disadvantage. The railroad was the only solution. The *Railroad Advocate,* said to have been the first paper in the United States devoted exclusively to railroad promotion, began publication at Rogersville on July 4, 1831.

In 1836 the legislature voted that any railroad company which raised two-thirds of its stock should receive the remaining third from the State. The LaGrange and Memphis, the only company eligible for aid under these terms and the first line in the State, sent its first train on an exhibition run at Memphis in 1842. The road extended only ten miles out of the city and the company soon failed. This and the collapse of various promotion schemes in East Tennessee, where construction work had begun as early as 1837, led to a short-lived reaction against railroads. But as a result of the Southern and Western Convention held in Memphis in 1845 to

OLD RIVER PACKET AT THE NASHVILLE WHARF

foster railroad construction, the State issued bonds to grant loans for railroad building.

Rail communication was completed between Knoxville and Dalton, Georgia, by way of the Nashville and Chattanooga Railroad in 1856. This road is now known as the Nashville, Chattanooga and St. Louis. The east coast and the Mississippi were linked together by the Memphis and Charleston Railroad, completed in 1857. Ten years later the Louisville and Nashville Railroad connected the State directly with the North.

Like the highways, railroads were heavily damaged during the War between the States. Legislative efforts to restore adequate train service by loans to the railroads were largely frustrated through loss of these funds by speculation. With three-fourths of the State debt represented in railroad bonds, large sums were voted to encourage railroad development, but only a small amount of the money was actually used for this purpose. When large foreign loans were floated to meet the interest on the public debt, a number of railroads combined to refuse interest payments to their stockholders in order to force due coupons into the market at lower rates. These were bought and later used to discharge their obligations.

In East and Middle Tennessee, railroad branch lines reach into mining, forest, and farming regions; and most of the State's enormous soft-coal production comes over lines from the coal fields of the Cumberland Mountains. Main lines of the Nashville, Chattanooga and St. Louis Railway connect Chattanooga, Nashville, Memphis, and Paducah, Kentucky, each on a different large river, separated by hundreds of miles. Connections between these cities have been established only by surmounting many and varied natural obstacles—badly drained swampland in West Tennessee and high plateaus and rivers in other sections.

Through passenger trains connect the principal cities of Tennessee with St. Louis, Chicago, Cincinnati, Washington, Pittsburgh, Philadelphia, and New York, as well as Miami, New Orleans, and all principal points in the South and Southwest. Transcontinental service is operated from Memphis westward.

Despite the excellent railroad system many communities are more than twenty-five miles from a railroad, and eight counties are entirely without rail service. For this reason the development of motor transport service was encouraged, and today this form of transportation reaches virtually every point in the State. Motor coaches are operated by 50 companies, and trucks by more than 300. During 1935, 507 coaches covered a total of 13 million miles, and 987 trucks carried freight for approximately 10 million miles.

As early as 1877 Tennessee had—for one day at least—an air mail service. On July 17 of that year mail bearing the specially engraved "Balloon Stamp—Five Cents" was dropped from the balloon *Buffalo* two miles from Nashville, picked up, and carried back to the city post office, to be delivered through the regular channels. Forty-five years later, in June 1922, the first official Government air mail in the South was dispatched from Nashville to Chicago in a wartime "Jenny."

The first scheduled airline operations in Tennessee were inaugurated December 1, 1925, between Atlanta and Evansville, by way of Chattanooga and Louisville. The second line started April 27, 1930, with terminals at New Orleans and St. Louis. The next year Fort Worth was connected with Cleveland by way of Nashville and Memphis, and in 1934 the Nashville-Washington section opened to complete the Southern Transcontinental line.

Tennessee had twenty-three airports and landing fields in 1932. At this time the Civil Works Administration undertook seventeen airport projects, later continued by the Works Progress Administration. Five have been completed, at Cookeville, Jackson, Jellico, Lebanon, and Milan.

The WPA program is responsible for five additional major airports. These are at Memphis, Chattanooga, Nashville, Knoxville, and McKellar Field, a point equidistant from Bristol, Kingsport, and Johnson City.

Tennessee is situated where the main commercial lines cross the region south of the Ohio and east of the Mississippi. The transcontinental air route between New York and Los Angeles traverses the entire length of the State; the through passenger planes make their first stop at Nashville. There are two main north-and-south Continental lines, the Chicago-Miami route by way of Nashville and the Chicago-New Orleans route via Memphis.

Tennessee Valley Authority

THE Tennessee Valley, drained by the Tennessee River and its tributaries, is an area of approximately 41,000 square miles, including parts of seven States—Tennessee, Kentucky, Virginia, North Carolina, Georgia, Alabama, and Mississippi. The major portion of the valley lies in Tennessee *(see Tour 5A)*. The Tennessee Valley Authority was created by Congress in 1933 to develop the Tennessee River system in the interest of navigation, flood control, and national defense, and to generate and sell surplus electricity to avert waste of water power. Properties in the vicinity of Muscle Shoals, Alabama, were transferred to the Authority. TVA's integrated water control program requires not alone the proper use of water resources, but, of necessity, the conservation and preservation of the land resources of the region.

The TVA is an independent Government corporation managed by a board of directors. Its activities are directed from headquarters at Muscle Shoals, Alabama, though administrative offices have been set up elsewhere as needed. A contact office, with a small staff, is maintained in Washington, D. C.

The Muscle Shoals project in Alabama, with the Wilson Dam and power house, and the two nitrate plants, was begun as a war measure under the National Defense Act of 1916. Actual construction, however, did not start until late in 1918, and the war was over before the project could be carried out. The problem of what to do with this wartime investment remained unsolved until the project was incorporated into the general program of the TVA.

A significant element in the creation of the TVA was the establishment of a regional authority transcending State lines. In taking this action Congress showed an awareness of the growing trend toward regional and national planning and an understanding of the fact that many of the problems of the Tennessee Valley could not be solved by the States acting alone.

POWER—THE CASCADE OF THE CLINCH RIVER

For more than a century the Federal Government has promoted navigation in its inland waterways. Flood control is intimately related to navigation improvement. Effective measures require Federal rather than State or local action, and call for the expenditure of large sums for construction work. The development of electricity through water power, as Theodore Roosevelt pointed out more than forty years ago, provides a potential source of income with which the costs of both navigation and flood control may be met.

In carrying out the purposes for which it was created, the TVA has undertaken three general, interrelated programs: control and proper use of water resources, conservation and preservation of land resources, and a more widespread use of electrical power. Its work has been carried on with the cooperation of many Federal and State agencies, particularly the agricultural extension services of the land grant colleges and universities.

Specifically, the control of water resources called for the construction of a system of dams. These are designed to maintain a nine-foot navigation channel from Paducah, Kentucky, to Knoxville, Tennessee—a distance of about 650 miles—and to reduce destructive floods. Four dams are already completed: Wilson Dam (finished before the creation of the TVA) and Wheeler Dam (1936), in Alabama; Pickwick Landing Dam (1938) on the Tennessee, and Norris Dam (1936) on the Clinch River in Tennessee. Hale's Bar Dam, also in Tennessee, which was bought from private interests in August 1939, is being tied in with the general control system. Five dams are now under construction: Guntersville, in Alabama; Chickamauga, in Tennessee; Hiwassee, in North Carolina; Gilbertsville, in Kentucky; and Watts Bar, in Tennessee. Projects proposed by the TVA, but not yet begun, are Coulter Shoals, in Tennessee; and Fontana, North Carolina.

Electric power, generated at the completed dams, was being sold at wholesale (as of September 1, 1939) to nearly 100 municipalities, and cooperative associations, serving more than 325,000 consumers. The Authority was distributing power directly to retail consumers in four areas on a temporary basis, pending transfer of the systems to local agencies. In addition, four large industrial companies were using TVA power under individual contracts. As provided in the Tennessee Valley Authority Act, power is sold to consumers at low rates. Experience of municipalities and corporations distributing TVA power has shown that this results in increased consumption and affords a fair and useful comparison of how much the public should pay for electric service. Special attention has been given to promoting the use of electricity in rural areas. Almost 7,000 miles of rural line were in operation on June 30, 1939, most of them owned and operated by cooperative associations and municipalities. More than 85 per cent of the total represented the construction of new lines carrying power to areas previously without service. The usual procedure, the Authority reports, has been for the Rural Electrification Administration to lend the capital, and for TVA or some other agency to build the line, under contract with the local body which operates it.

Cooperation with other Federal agencies has been more strikingly developed in carrying out the third general division of the TVA program—conservation and preservation of land resources. This has meant, by implication, measures for promoting the welfare of the population of the valley, estimated at 2,500,000, with an additional 4,000,000 persons inside the sphere of its influence. The U. S. Department of Agriculture, including the Agricultural Adjustment Administration and the Forest Service, the Civilian Conservation Corps, and State agricultural experiment stations and extension services are among the agencies that are working with the TVA, through local organizations of farmers, to carry out a

KITCHEN IN A HOME AT NORRIS

well-rounded program of rehabilitation for both the land itself and for its people.

Improved types of phosphate fertilizer, produced at Muscle Shoals, are tested and demonstrated by farmers in soil-conserving and fertility-building practices. The neighbors, who select the test-demonstrators, adapt results to their own farms. Legume cover crops and terracing are used. Land devastated by gully erosion is reforested.

The effects of this land-use program on the lives of the people are obvious. The region is predominantly agricultural and, as the productiveness of the farms decreases, the plight of their owners becomes ever more desperate. The availability of improved phosphates for large-scale tests and demonstrations and of low cost electricity is enabling farmers to work out procedures aimed at a sustained agriculture, to reduce drudgery in the home and on the farm, and to enjoy modern conveniences that electricity makes possible.

Educational and recreational programs have been established in cooperation with local educational agencies for TVA employees and their families in the towns that lie within the Authority's jurisdiction. Perhaps less important, but nonetheless significant, are the opportunities for employment on the construction projects and the standards set by the TVA in handling its large labor force. Workers are employed on the basis of special tests developed in cooperation with the United States Civil Service Commission. They are entitled to organize according to their own preferences, and labor and management work together on employee problems. Since construction work is necessarily temporary, the TVA's job training program not only contributes to work efficiency but allows employees to prepare themselves for other work when the TVA job is finished. During the fiscal year ending June 30, 1938, approximately 8,000 job training meetings were held with an attendance of 63,071, and 4,034 adult education meetings drew an attendance of 79,129.

All possible assistance is given to families forced to move from the reservoir areas. Records indicate that, in general, they have improved their lot. In moving these people, due regard was paid to their natural feelings, for in many cases they left homes occupied by their families for more than a century. The story is told of one family who resisted removal because it would entail extinguishing the hearth fire that had been burning continuously for three generations. The TVA cut the Gordian knot by keeping the fire going while it moved the family to its new home.

In its program for flood and navigation control, for land reclamation, and for cheap electric light and power the TVA is substituting order and design for haphazard, unplanned, and unintegrated development. Through its social and educational activities it is bringing to this region a consciousness of its own rich natural and human resources. But the results of this program may be even more far reaching. "If we are successful here," said President Roosevelt in his Message to Congress on Muscle Shoals, "we can march on, step by step, in a like development of other great natural territorial units within our borders." For this, as well as its more tangible objectives, the TVA is of national importance.

Negroes in Tennessee

LITTLE is known concerning the coming of the first Negroes to Tennessee, but there is reason to believe that they were in the territory much earlier than is commonly supposed. It is probable that Negroes were with De Soto when he camped near the present site of Memphis in 1541, since they were known to have been with him when he left Spain the previous year. A century later the French are reported to have sent "an army of 1,200 white men and double that number of red and black men who took up their quarters in Fort Assumption, on the bluff of Memphis." The next Negro to set foot on Tennessee soil seems to have been with Colonel James Smith and a group of Long Hunters who explored the Cumberland country in 1766. Known to history merely as "Jim," this "mulatto lad" inspired a stanza in Colonel Smith's diary. Another "negro fellow" accompanied James Robertson in 1779 when he came down from the Holston Settlement to the site of what is now Nashville.

The new settlers brought Negroes with them and by 1790, when the first census was taken, there were 3,417 slaves in the Territory. Six years later, when Tennessee became a State, there were 10,613 Negroes in a population of 77,282. As a result of the invention of the cotton gin and the rapid growth of the cotton industry, slavery was widely expanded between 1790 and 1835. By 1840 Tennessee had 183,057 slaves whose per capita value was about $550 as compared to less than $100 in 1790.

According to Caleb Patterson, "slavery nowhere in the United States reflected physiographic features more distinctly than in Tennessee." East Tennessee, with its small farms and its independent struggling yeomen, had few slaves; Middle Tennessee, with larger estates and commercial interests, had a larger number; West Tennessee, the richest cotton region of the State, had the highest concentration of Negroes.

The lot of the Tennessee slave was perhaps less unfortunate than that of many of his brethren. Tennessee's slave code guaranteed the Negro shelter, food, clothing, and medical attention. It protected him when he ceased to be useful, gave him the right to contract for his freedom, and in 1835 granted him the right of trial by jury—a privilege accorded to slaves in only four other States. The preponderance of small farms was also advantageous to the slave. Here the absentee landlord system was never prevalent. The small farmer, in close contact with his slaves, was considerate of their welfare. As a result of more direct association with the whites, greater diversification of tasks, and more responsibility in their performance, slaves in Tennessee (like those in the mountain area generally) were often more developed mentally than those in typical plantation States.

Slavery in Tennessee, however, was not without its darker side. Traders imported considerable numbers of Negroes from other sections to be resold into the Southwest. Nashville, the capital, did a thriving business and Memphis was the slave-trading center of the Mid-South. The trader's exhortation to "buy more Negroes to raise more cotton to buy more Negroes to raise more cotton" was taken as sound advice. Although between 1826 and 1855 there were laws against it, the domestic slave trade continued.

From the first, however, there were those who opposed slave trading. Before 1830 Tennessee was a center of abolition activity. The attitude of the people toward the Negro was reflected in legislation and judicial decisions, in organized societies, in the churches, and in abolition literature unusual for the time and section. By 1827 Tennessee contained more antislavery societies than did any other State except North Carolina. Here also was published in 1819 the first forthright abolition periodical in the United States. Among the enthusiastic workers for freedom, Benjamin Lundy, founder of the *Genius of Universal Emancipation* and later associated with William Lloyd Garrison, was prominent. Many churches and some educational institutions engaged actively in the crusade for emancipation. Various societies worked to improve conditions for slaves and free Negroes, to eradicate the domestic slave trade, to effect gradual abolition and colonization; and the more uncompromising groups wished to abolish slavery immediately.

Although abolitionist activity continued intermittently after 1834, increasing demand for slave labor in the western part of the State, and in the cotton-producing valleys of East Tennessee, was accompanied by a growth of pro-slavery sentiment in the State as a whole. By 1855 Statewide sentiment was pro-slavery.

The number of free Negroes in Tennessee had increased from 361 in 1801 to 4,555 in 1831. In that year "defensive legislation" was enacted providing that no slave should be emancipated unless he should leave the State immediately. Negro suffrage was abolished in 1834. Aside from the fact that the free Negro was permitted to attend private schools in Memphis and Nashville, to receive religious instruction, to sue and be sued, to make contracts and inherit property, and to enjoy legal marriage, no rights of citizenship remained to him after 1834. A sort of inmate on parole, he was both socially and economically proscribed.

In spite of the numerous restrictive measures against them, a great number of free Negroes prospered. One of these was a Negro who lived in Nashville in the early 1800's and supplied many whites and Negroes with vegetables from his garden. Upon the occasion of the wedding of his daughter he invited all the prominent white people in town—and "they all went," including General Andrew Jackson and Dr. McNairy, who "danced the reel with the bride." Among those who showed unusual progressive traits were "Black Bob," noted tavern-keeper; "Free Joe," who in 1824 established a colony where his people "enjoyed freedom within a stone's throw of one of the largest slave marts in the world"; and Joe Clouston, who had considerable money, property, and "more than a hundred slaves."

In the vote of 1861 on secession from the Union practically all the eastern counties were opposed, while most of the western and middle counties were in favor of secession. The relationship of cotton to this vote was as marked as was the relationship of the vote to the high Negro population proportion in the different parts of the State. Tennessee was the last State to secede and the first to return. Excluded from Lincoln's plan for emancipation in 1861, it was the only State to free the slaves by popular vote.

After emancipation many Negroes in Tennessee, as elsewhere in the South, migrated to the cities near by and to the urban areas of the North in search of work. Some of them made places for themselves in industries—in mining, iron and steelwork, and the railroads. Others found work in service and trades, as domestics, laundresses, and porters. The bulk of the race, however, was confined to odd jobs or returned to the soil as "croppers" and later as tenants. Some of the Negroes bought farms and homes; others, with accumulated savings, opened businesses. There were apparently few dependents among the freedmen in the State as a whole.

The Negro population has consistently followed the economic fortunes of the three divisions of the State. Since 1880 the State has shown a gradual decline in the proportion of Negroes in the total population, but this decline has been unevenly distributed. There are no Negroes in Union County (East Tennessee) while 73 per cent of the population in Fayette County (West Tennessee) is Negro. In 1930, Negroes numbered 9 per cent of the population in East Tennessee, 34.8 per cent of that in West Tennessee, and 18.3 per cent of the population in the entire State.

FIRST GROUP OF FISK JUBILEE SINGERS (1871)

The story of the Negro in Tennessee cannot be told from census statistics alone. Negroes in the State have accumulated church property valued at about eight million dollars. They own farms worth $10,249,910, and their 33,655 owned homes have an estimated value exceeding $43,000,000. They manage through small retail enterprises to do a volume of business of about $9,000,000 annually. This excludes three large religious publishing houses, an insurance company, and several banks and plants for manufacturing lighting fixtures. The Baptists, the African Methodist Episcopal Church, and the Colored Methodist Episcopal Church have developed publishing businesses—the first two in Nashville, the third in Jackson.

As laborer and as artisan, the Negro has been a significant factor in the development of agriculture and in the building of cities. Many of the fine old mansions, which stand today after more than eighty years, were built by hired slave artisans, and some of the modern structures that are the pride of business were built by the free descendants of these artisans. Negroes excel even today as stone and brick masons.

One of the most prominent of Tennessee's Negro citizens is J. C. Napier, who in 1939 passed his ninety-fourth birthday. His father was a free Negro in Dickson County, and son of the founder of the Napier Iron

Works. Napier, an attorney and banker, has served as a member of the Nashville School Board, and was appointed Register of the United States Treasury under President Taft. In Memphis, Napier is honored by a school, a park, and a court which bear his name.

Between 1865 and 1905, Negroes were affiliated with almost every department of the government in Memphis. Outstanding in politics is R. R. (Bob) Church, of Memphis, whose position has been strategic because of the numerical influence of the Negro voters in West Tennessee. His sister, Mary Church Terrell, became a prominent national leader in the organization of Negro women's civic clubs throughout the country.

Perhaps the most dramatic character in law and politics was Samuel A. McElwee. While still a student at Fisk University he campaigned for a seat in the legislature and won election in January 1883. He was famed for his eloquence, won many friends and success as a criminal lawyer, a field in which few Negroes had found opportunity.

Many of the founders of Negro businesses, as well as the founders of families of importance in the State, started as barbers, caterers, draymen, and hucksters. Their children received the benefits of formal education and in many instances went into the professions. An outstanding example is Lewis Winter, who was born a slave but became a chief produce dealer in the South and amassed a large fortune.

Tennessee has an unusual number of important educational institutions for Negroes. The missionary associations of the several major Christian denominations sent teachers to the Negroes immediately after the War between the States. Baptist, Methodist, and Congregational missionary societies opened schools in 1866. The American Baptist Home Mission Society established Roger Williams University, the American Missionary Association established Fisk University, and Walden University was founded as Central Tennessee College by the Freedmen's Aid Society of the Methodist Episcopal Church. All these schools were located in Nashville. The first missionary work of an educational character undertaken by the Freedmen's Mission of the United Presbyterian Church was McKee School in Nashville, which later developed into Knoxville College (1875). In 1876 Meharry Medical College was founded as part of Walden University. At present there are six Negro major institutions of higher learning; and one normal and junior college.

The earliest professional men received their training in the institutions of the North and then became active in the Negro educational institutions of the State. One of these was the late Dr. F. A. Stewart, a graduate of the Harvard Medical School, who had a distinguished career in medicine.

MEHARRY MEDICAL COLLEGE (NEGRO), NASHVILLE

An outstanding Negro physician in Tennessee and one of the most prominent in the South was Dr. Robert Felton Boyd, who was graduated from Meharry in both medicine and dentistry in the early eighties. The Mercy Hospital (now the Hubbard Hospital of Meharry Medical College), owned by Dr. Boyd, was the first in Nashville established for the care of Negroes. He served for many years as professor of gynecology at Meharry Medical College, and was active in political and civic affairs.

Other Tennessee Negroes who have distinguished themselves include Dr. William Sevier, an early Meharry graduate, who later became dean of Negro pharmacists throughout the country; Dr. W. A. Hadley, another of the early graduates of Meharry, who combined the practice of medicine with public school teaching, and for whom one of Nashville's Negro schools is named; and Dr. Mordecai W. Johnson, president of Howard University.

The shifting economic patterns and fortunes of the State have kept the Negro population in active ferment, struggling for survival and status. The Negroes in this, as in other States, must carry a double task: they must overcome a late start in civic and economic participation and the traditional handicaps of low income, inadequate educational facilities, and some lingering doubt as to their capabilities; at the same time they must make their own constructive impress upon the total life of the State. The extent to which this has been done in the past indicates not only the vitality of the Negro population itself, but also the dominance in the State as a whole of the disposition toward encouraging such development.

Religion

ALMOST half of Tennessee's 2,616,556 population are active churchgoers today, with the Baptists, Methodists, Presbyterians, and Churches of Christ comprising, in the order named, nearly 90 per cent of the combined church membership. Unquestionably the State is one of the chief strongholds not only of Protestantism but of Fundamentalism in the United States. These parallel forces have taken major roles in shaping the history of Tennessee and the character of its people.

Among the North Carolinians of the Watauga and Holston settlements in the 1770's were many Scotch-Irish Presbyterians. They welcomed preachers of that faith, such as the Reverend Charles Cummings, who held a meeting in Watauga as early as 1777. In the following year Tidence Lane, a Baptist, and Jeremiah Lambert, a Methodist, visited the East Tennessee settlements.

More successful than either Presbyterians or Baptists in early Tennessee were the Methodists. The Wesleyan doctrine, that all men were equal and each the master of his own destiny, was identical with the democratic philosophy of the frontiersman. Moreover, the circuit system introduced into Tennessee by Bishop Francis Asbury in 1778, when he organized the first Methodist conference west of the Alleghenies at Half Acres, had among the Protestant groups no equal for effective evangelization of a backwoods people. The circuit rider, equipped with Bible, hymn book, and wiry pony, rode the wilderness traces to isolated settlements and farmsteads, sharing the want or plenty of the people, speaking their language, and respected by them as a man among men.

The Methodists also had lay or local preachers who worked on the land six days in the week and served without pay.

At first, however, none of the churches was strong enough to influence greatly the lives of the settlers, for most of them had long been out of touch with civilization and knew or cared little for formal creed. Lorenzo Dow, the somber Methodist Savonarola, voiced the opinion held among churchmen generally when he said that Tennessee was "a Sink of Iniquity, a Black Pit of Irreligion." The unrelenting grind of daily life in a wilderness dictated for the pioneer settler some violent emotional outlet, and he found it in hard drinking and gargantuan carousing. He was extremely unlikely to adopt any religion which did not provide a compensatory release for his emotions. This accounted for both the form and the success of the Great Revival, a wave of mass religious hysteria which swept the western frontier in the early nineteenth century.

The Great Revival had its beginning in services known as camp meetings. In the new settlements buildings large enough to house even small audiences could seldom be found, so many preachers began holding their meetings in the open fields and in brush arbors or straw pens in the woods. From miles around the people came, bringing their food and drink, their children, slaves, and dogs, as much for the pleasure of getting together, gossiping, and love-making with their far-scattered neighbors as to hear the preaching.

These meetings were growing in popularity throughout Tennessee and Kentucky during the last decade of the eighteenth century. Only a spark, a sense of unity and direction, was needed to touch off the flame of revivalism.

In the summer of 1800 country folk of the Red River section of southern Kentucky flocked by the hundreds along the route of James McGready, a Presbyterian minister with a reputation for being a powerful exhorter. His fiery sermons made such an unprecedented number of conversions that other preachers rode in from central Kentucky and Tennessee to hear and assist him. Afterward, they returned home with high enthusiasm for McGready's methods.

One of them, a Methodist named William McGee, persuaded Baptists and Presbyterians to join him in a five-day meeting at Drake's Creek, in Middle Tennessee. The venture was wildly successful. Bishops McKendree, Whatcoat, and Asbury, touring Tennessee after the second western annual conference of the Methodist Episcopal Church, stopped and preached with McGee. Vastly impressed, they and other preachers who had visited Drake's Creek organized similar meetings. From these, in turn, new evangelists scattered. The movement spread like an epidemic, and before the year was out the entire region had been affected. Camp meetings sprang up everywhere. Farmers left their plowing, merchants their shops, drovers their herds, and blacksmiths their forges, to attend.

The backwoods evangelists were, in their way, as adept with fire-and-brimstone as had been the great preachers of Puritan days, and the congregations responded with muscular spasms known as the "jerks." They leaped and crawled and rolled on the ground, pounded each other, wept, moaned, and screamed in gibberish as they wrestled with the Devil.

"Presently," wrote Peter Cartwright, one of the foremost evangelists, "the gloom would lift, a smile of heavenly peace would break forth, and conversion always followed."

Meetings went on for days, often for weeks. At the height of the revival, preaching continued through the night in the ruddy flickering glare of bonfire and torch. When one preacher was exhausted, another took his place and in the larger gatherings as many as seven or eight might be exhorting at the same time. Between sermons there was singing. "Not since the Crusades," wrote an English traveler, "has the Christian world witnessed the like of these massed hundreds singing their hymns under the open sky with such deep and crashing fervor that the earth underfoot and the very hills rock and tremble."

A stern uncompromising austerity accompanied the revival. It became the rule of the day for men and women to sit on opposite sides of the gathering place because "there was no marriage in Heaven." Dancing, parties, and instrumental music were largely abandoned by the people. Methodist Bishop McTyeire, preaching in a Bristol church where a melodion was used, declared, "When you brought that ungodly box of whistles in here, you brought the devil with it!"

In the beginning there was nearly complete tolerance among the denominations. Methodists, Baptists, and Presbyterians joined in the meetings and their ministers took turns preaching. However, only the Methodist Church had officially espoused the movement. Many Baptist leaders had looked upon it with suspicion, and the central Presbyterian organization had condemned the new revivalism sharply, but no group on the frontier could long have stood aloof and retained its membership against the headlong sweep of the Great Revival. It was join or die, and join most Baptist and Presbyterian preachers did—though as individuals rather than as church representatives.

After a climactic series of meetings at Cane Ridge, in 1802, the revival in Tennessee lost its first irresistible momentum. Dissension between the denominations appeared. The Methodists sang:

> I'll tell you who the Lord loves best—
> It is the shouting Methodist!

The Baptists replied:

> Baptist, Baptist, Baptist—
> Baptist till I die.
> I'll go along with the Baptists
> And find myself On High!

Strong backwashes from the Great Revival were felt repeatedly for more than forty years, but as a unified movement it was virtually dead in Tennessee by 1810. Preachers were soon devoting much time to tirades against competing churches. Peter Cartwright called one of these a "trash trap." Another preacher characterized his rivals as "hirelings, caterpillars, letter-learned Pharisees, Hypocrites, varlets, Seed of the Serpent, foolish Builders whom the Devil drives into the ministry, dead dogs that cannot bark, blind men, dead men, men possessed of the Devil, Rebels and enemies of God!"

Disputes also arose within the three pioneer denominations. The earliest occurred among the Presbyterians. Without official sanction the Cumberland Presbytery, of Middle Tennessee, had been very active in the revival and had tripled its membership in the first year. There were not enough men with the required education to meet the sudden demand for preachers. In 1802 the Cumberland Presbytery began licensing as pastors men of little or no education, a practice severely criticized by Presbyterians in the East. Another source of discord was the Wesleyan flavor which had crept into the doctrine preached by Tennessee Presbyterians because of their close association with the Methodist revivalists. On these and other points the Cumberland Presbytery was voted out of the main body in 1809. Attempts at reconciliation failed and a year later representatives of the Middle Tennessee congregations met in Dickson County and formed the Cumberland Presbyterian Church. By 1850 there were more Cumberland Presbyterians in the State than members of the parent church, and branches had been established in other southern and mid-western States.

Conflict also developed among the Baptists. From the first dispute came the Baptist Church of Christ (1808), which held to a modified Calvinism and practiced foot washing. This group also spread beyond the boundaries of Tennessee. In 1825 there was a second division when seven hundred members withdrew to form the Bethel Association. Later this group affiliated with the Church of Christ, which had been founded in Kentucky when the followers of Barton Stone and Alexander Campbell joined forces. The Church of Christ made such wide gains in Tennessee that by the middle of the century it was fourth in numerical strength.

Several denominations, strong in other parts of the country, were not substantially represented in early Tennessee. A Lutheran church was organized in Sullivan County in the last decade of the eighteenth century. During the revival period several congregations of Germans from Pennsylvania and North Carolina were formed. They remained within the jurisdiction of the Synod of North Carolina until the Synod of Tennessee was established in 1820.

Roman Catholic priests are known to have traveled into Tennessee on church missions as early as 1810. Eleven years later Bishop David and Father Abell held formal masses for Catholics settled in Nashville; and here, in 1830, a Roman Catholic parish was formed and a church erected. The Diocese of Nashville—which included the entire State—was organized in 1837 and the Right Reverend Dr. Pius Miles consecrated as its first Bishop. Bishop Miles, an indefatigable missionary, was largely responsible for the formation of many parishes throughout Tennessee.

Not until 1827 was there a Protestant Episcopal church in Tennessee. This church was established by the Reverend James H. Otey at Franklin. Several factors account for the late coming of the Episcopalians to Tennessee. As has been noted, many of the first settlers were Scotch-Irish of the Covenanter strain, with a heritage of enmity toward the established Church of England. In Revolutionary times the Over-Mountain people identified the Episcopal Church with the Royalist cause. Nor did the church authorities take advantage of the Great Revival; erudite and conservative, they frowned on the spectacular emotionalism of the movement. In Tennessee the Protestant Episcopal Church gained most of its communicants in towns and cities and among well-to-do land owners. The Reverend Otey, who became first Bishop of the Diocese of Tennessee in 1834, lived to see the development of twenty-six parishes with approximately 1,500 communicants. He was one of the founders of the University of the South at Sewanee, which has had marked influence on the religious thought and general culture of the entire South.

Negroes attended most of the pioneer churches, where galleries or sections in the rear were provided for them, and they participated actively in the camp meetings. It was during the revival period that many of the great Negro spirituals were first sung. Early circuit riders and evangelists frankly condemned the institution of slavery. Especially outspoken were the Presbyterians. Their dominance in East Tennessee accounted for that section as a center of abolition sentiment, as much as did economic considerations. Generally speaking, the Methodists and Baptists adopted a more compromising attitude; they attempted to humanize rather than abolish the system. From 1800 on, the three main denominations directed increasing effort to missionary work among the Negroes. By 1839 nine missions, devoted exclusively to this work, were receiving $2,700 annually from the State in addition to church contributions. At that time, one-fourth of the Baptists in Tennessee were Negroes, and there were many slave preachers of great ability.

John C. Calhoun, debating in the Senate with Daniel Webster in 1850, declared that the churches were the strongest ties holding the Union together. But six years before that, one of the most important of these ties had weakened. During the 1844 General Conference of the Methodist Episcopal Church, in New York, feeling had run high between Northern and Southern delegates, and an abolitionist majority had passed strong resolutions condemning slavery. In the following year, the Southern body withdrew and formed the Methodist Episcopal Church, South (Southern Methodist Church), with headquarters and an independent publishing house at Nashville.

In 1845, for reason practically identical, the Southern Baptists broke away and set up the Southern Baptist Convention. Both the Church of Christ and the Baptist Church of Christ were to remain undivided because most of their communicants were within the Confederate States.

Although in 1861 the Presbyterians, meeting in Philadelphia, adopted spirited resolutions to remain loyal to the Union, the Presbytery of Memphis withdrew later in the year and urged concurring Presbyteries to meet for the purpose of organizing a Southern association. This became the Presbytrian Church in the U. S., as distinguished from the Presbyterian Church in the U. S. A., and was popularly known as the Southern Presbyterian Church. The various groups of Presbyterians in Tennessee were, on the whole, Southern sympathizers.

In general the Episcopalians followed their State into the Southern ranks. Bishop Leonidas Polk laid aside the cloth to become a general in the Confederate Army. Other Episcopal clergymen, among them Bishop Otey, opposed secession. Nevertheless, no official severance took place.

There were many examples of chaplains in the Army of Tennessee, conspicuous for their services to the wounded and dying, friend and foe alike. But between the branches of the disrupted churches partisanship was bitter. The Holston Conference of the Methodist Church, South, in northeastern Tennessee, expelled five of its members for disloyalty to the Confederacy. These five linked their fortunes with the northern Methodists and joined in voting their erstwhile brethren guilty "of a crime sufficient to exclude them from the kingdom of grace and glory."

As the Federal forces took possession of territory in Tennessee, southern preachers—regarded as the best recruiting officers for the South—were arrested indiscriminately, particularly in Nashville, and northern ministers "carpet-bagged" their way into the vacant churches. The Methodist Publishing House in Nashville, a flourishing business, was seized by the Federal authorities and converted into a government printing office.

At the close of the war, the rift between Northern and Southern

ST. MARY'S CHURCH, MEMPHIS

branches of the Methodists and Baptists had grown too serious to be healed. No reunion of the Northern and Southern Presbyterian churches was sought.

Beginning in 1866, Negro Baptists began setting up their own congregations. In the same year the Southern Methodists sanctioned the organization of the Colored Methodist Episcopal Church, which was shortly followed by two other Negro Methodist groups—the African Methodist Episcopal Church, and the African Methodist Episcopal Zion Church. The Cumberland Presbyterian Church, Colored, was established in Murfreesboro in 1869. First in number of Negro communicants were the Baptist churches, with the three Methodist groups in second place, and the Cumberland Presbyterians third.

Though a Hebrew congregation had been organized in Memphis in 1852 and another in Nashville in 1853, not until after the war were there more than 500 Jews in the State. During the period of Reconstruction the number of Jews tripled and synagogues were built in Chattanooga and Nashville.

Between 1870 and 1890 wide rifts over the use of instrumental music in worship appeared among the congregations of the Church of Christ, each of which was an independent, self-governing unit. The non-instrumentalists retained the name Church of Christ while those in favor of instrumental music organized as the Christian Church.

At the end of the century the early evangelistic zeal of the chief Protestant denominations had notably lessened. The rapid increase in church membership which had followed the Great Revival and continued through Reconstruction times was checked, and emphasis was on church organization, Sunday School work, foreign missions, and educational programs. Revivalism, however, was still fairly vigorous in rural sections and even invaded urban areas when powerful evangelists such as Sam Jones toured the State. In the main, lesser groups fell heir to the revival movement and kept it very much alive—especially in the uplands where frontier conditions persisted. Sects and subsects appeared, held their camp meetings, declined, split, and died or merged with new groups.

Sentiment for union of the two principal branches of the Presbyterians grew strong in 1903. After several conferences, the parent church modified its doctrines in a manner agreeable to the Cumberland branch, and in 1907 a nominal affiliation was effected.

The latest effort toward church unification was made in 1937–38 by the Northern and Southern branches of the Methodist Episcopal Church. In November 1938, leaders of the two groups met in Nashville and drew up final plans for the union. The measures of the conference were approved by a majority of the delegates.

Proportional numerical strength among the four principal denominations in the State has remained relatively the same as in 1890, though there has been an increase in total church membership of more than half a million. The latest U. S. census *(Religious Bodies: 1926)* shows 56 denominations and branches in Tennessee, with 8,556 churches and an overall membership of 1,018,033.

On the whole, the churches have shown a growing interest in promoting better understanding between Negroes and whites, and in programs for the benefit of the underprivileged. A trend toward cooperation among the Protestant bodies has been fostered by the State-wide interdenominational Sunday School Association. Union meetings and joint work in civic movements have become more frequent each year.

Education

THE first settlers in Tennessee had little time or use for book-learning, but they did have a wide and thorough education in the lore of rifle, plow, and broadax—learning which cleared and peopled a wilderness.

Such schooling as there was lay in the hands of a few clergymen, usually Presbyterians who had joined their Scotch-Irish congregations from North Carolina and Virginia. In summer, when children could be spared from farm work, the local preacher kept school in the community church-courthouse, a rough one-room log cabin with a packed clay floor and slab benches. Here for a few weeks the children struggled with ciphering, writing, and learning to read from a great leather-covered Bible.

A departure from this sketchy between-planting-and-harvest schooling was made by the Reverend Samuel Doak in 1780, when he began conducting graded classes in a log outbuilding on his farm near Jonesboro. The first regular school west of the Alleghenies, it was chartered three years later by North Carolina as Martin Academy, in honor of Governor Alexander Martin. In 1785 the charter was confirmed by the legislature of the short-lived State of Franklin. About the same time the North Carolina Assembly chartered, as Davidson Academy, the meeting house near Nashville where the Reverend Thomas Craighead had gathered a class of boys.

The Constitutional Convention of 1796 made no provisions for public education, and for a decade the small academies that a dozen or so ministers had set up, after the example of Doak and Craighead, were the only schools in Tennessee. In these "literary institutions" matters of conduct and morals were stressed as much as familiarity with the English classics, Latin, Greek, and oratory: the prized hallmarks of a gentleman's education. They ranged in quality from little backwoods establishments with almost illiterate teachers—who accepted payment in food, wood, or help about the place—to expensive town schools conducted by the most pontifical and flowery of scholars. The best of these prepared the sons of the land-holding gentry for Harvard and Yale, and for politics; the worst gave doubtful prestige and rather muddled minds to the sons of solvent small farmers. So strongly did the system of private academies entrench itself that by 1889 more than 500 had received charters from the State, and nearly a third of these were actually operating.

In 1806 the United States Congress had directed that 600 acres of good land in each Tennessee township should be reserved and sold for the support of public schools. This requirement was largely ignored. Of the 6,500,000 acres which should have been set aside, only 23,000—and these so poor that they sold for as little as one cent an acre—were actually converted into school funds. Money realized from land sales was insufficient to establish a single school. A tentative effort toward the establishment of common schools was made in 1815, when the State legislature passed an act "to provide for the education of orphans of those persons who have died in the service of their country." In 1823 a few thousand dollars were appropriated for pauper schools, and five years later half the proceeds from the sale of public lands between the Hiwassee and Little Tennessee Rivers was allotted to a common school fund. The scant income from the Hiwassee lands supported only a handful of extremely ill-equipped schools. They were taught by political appointees, minor bandwagon followers who often were barely able to sign their names.

Every year or so between 1823 and 1854 the General Assembly passed some ineffective act "to establish a system of common schools in Tennessee." By 1840 the State was spending for public education a little less than 50 cents a year for each white child; a fourth of the adult white population was illiterate. Inevitably, the Negroes were overwhelmingly illiterate, though here and there a bright slave child was allowed to study with his master's children or was taught by some liberal clergyman.

Private academies, meanwhile, had multiplied and flourished. Three of the older ones assumed the dignity of colleges even before the State had been admitted to the Union. Greeneville College, which had been the Reverend Hezekiah Balch's school, was chartered in 1794. In the same year Blount College was established at Knoxville, to succeed the Reverend Carrick's seminary. One of the earliest nonsectarian and coeducational schools in the United States, Blount College was named for the Territorial Governor, whose daughter Barbara was among the women enrolled. The school became in succession: East Tennessee College, East Tennessee University, and the University of Tennessee. In 1795 Samuel Doak's Martin Academy was chartered as Washington College.

Maryville College was begun in 1802 as the log-cabin school of the Reverend Isaac Anderson. Several appeals for a charter were refused by the legislature, for Anderson was active in politics and had made powerful enemies. The charter was not granted until 1842. Davidson Academy, chartered as Cumberland College in 1806, later became the University of Nashville, and eventually fathered the present George Peabody College for Teachers, the leading school of its kind in the South.

Before the close of the first quarter of the nineteenth century, several academies for girls had been established in the State. The more fashionable and prosperous of these were in Nashville—Price's College for Young Ladies, the Misses Martha and Fanny O'Bryan's school, Ward's Seminary, the Belmont School for Girls, and the Nashville Female Academy. Here came the daughters of wealthy Tennesseans to be taught manners and morals, and to read such books "as are considered proper for the sensibilities of the female intellect." In summing up his system of education, Dr. Collin Elliot, the Methodist minister who conducted the Nashville Female Academy, wrote: "We educate the girl according to God's Word and the demand of every fiber of her mind to be a wife, to be a mother. Then in after life, circumstances determining, she may do anything a female body, mind, and soul may do."

Public schools begged for funds in vain until the administration of Governor Andrew Johnson. The "Little Tailor of East Tennessee," who had learned to read after he was grown, was a passionate advocate of public education. In his message to the legislature of 1853, Johnson said: "At the present period, and for a long time past, our common schools have been doing little or no good, but on the contrary have been rather in the way than otherwise. There is one way that the children of the State can be educated . . . and that is to levy and collect a tax from the people of the whole State." Against stiff opposition, Johnson's bill for the support of schools by direct taxation was passed on February 28, 1854. Subsequent legislation standardized the method of examining teachers and authorized the employment of women teachers on an equal footing with men. For the first time Tennessee had public schools that functioned.

During the decade before the War between the States Nashville and Memphis set up free public school systems, with graded grammar courses and four years of high school. Operating funds were secured from municipal poll taxes and levies on real and personal property.

In 1857 the Protestant Episcopal Church established the University of the South at Sewanee, a village on the Cumberland Plateau, and proposed to introduce the English tradition of education. Soon after the war began, the uncompleted university buildings were burned by Federal raiders.

The war brought the machinery of formal education to an abrupt halt in Tennessee. Academies and colleges, drained of able-bodied young men,

VANDERBILT UNIVERSITY, NASHVILLE

shut down. State and municipal public school systems were disrupted. After the Confederates were driven out of Tennessee, school and college buildings were commandeered as Federal barracks and hospitals, or were used to house the Negroes who flocked in the wake of the liberating armies.

In the years of Reconstruction public attention was centered on repairing material damage and little thought could be spared for the problems of education.

While the Republicans controlled the State, the post of superintendent of public instruction was created, county superintendents were appointed, school taxes were levied, and special schools for Negroes were put into operation. As soon as the Democrats returned to power, in 1869, these measures were repealed. In 1873, however, the legislature passed bills which substantially incorporated the earlier measures.

Concurrently, academies and colleges were evolving into their present forms. Between 1865 and 1900 some of the State's leading private schools began operating—Montgomery-Bell Academy, St. Cecilia Academy, and Ward-Belmont School, at Nashville; Webb Preparatory School, at Bell Buckle; Morgan School, at Petersburg; and several military schools for boys.

The Fisk School for Negroes, founded at Nashville by the American Missionary Society in 1866, developed into a normal school and was chartered in 1867 as Fisk University. It has become one of the country's foremost institutions of higher education for Negroes. Associated with Fisk and using the same library facilities is Meharry Medical College, the world's largest Negro institution of its kind, founded in 1865 by the Methodist Episcopal Church. Fisk University and Meharry Medical College have been leading factors in advancing Negro education in the South, and in uniting the efforts of the two races in developing an educational program for the Negro.

As was the case with other colleges in Tennessee, Vanderbilt University, at Nashville, was founded as a church school. Chartered in 1872 as the Central University of the Methodist Episcopal Church, South, it was endowed by Cornelius Vanderbilt in 1873 and reopened as Vanderbilt University. The Methodist Church relinquished control in 1914.

In 1875, with money voted by the legislature and an endowment from the George Peabody Trust Fund, Peabody Normal School was established as a department of the University of Nashville. Shortly afterward the normal school absorbed the university and became George Peabody College for Teachers. One of the three ranking teachers' colleges in the United

States, the school is noted today for its advanced methods and its extensive experiments with new techniques of child training. Its graduate teachers hold key positions throughout the South.

When the University of the South was reorganized in 1876, law and medical departments were included; later these branches were discontinued. In addition to the academic and theological schools of the present university, there is a preparatory school, the Sewanee Military Academy.

The legislature designated East Tennessee College, at Knoxville, as the University of Tennessee in 1879. By the terms of the act, it became "a part of and the head of the public school system of the State."

After publication of the 1870 census figures on illiteracy, interest in public education increased in Tennessee. In 1893 the legislature provided for tax-supported secondary schools, and in 1899 county courts were empowered to set up county high schools. With the expansion of the school system, the power of the county courts over local schools increased. The magistrates approve county school budgets, audit school expenditures, and require quarterly reports from the county boards of education.

In 1909, with one-fourth of the State's revenue allotted to education, four teacher-training institutions were established—three for whites and one for Negroes; funds for the consolidation of schools, vocational education, and libraries were increased. Four years later one-third of the State's income was set aside for educational purposes, and school attendance was made compulsory. Meanwhile the number of local school-board members throughout the State had been reduced from 10,000 to 600.

Consolidation of schools began in 1924 in counties where declining population has made it increasingly difficult to maintain efficient schools. By 1933, 324 consolidations had been made; but since then cuts in appropriations have retarded this trend. At the close of the school year of 1934 there were still approximately 3,000 one-room schoolhouses in the State, comprising almost one-half the total number of elementary schools. At this time there were 617 high schools, 545 of which were for white students. Two hundred and ten high schools which do not give a full four-year course offer further possibilities for consolidation.

Tennessee's anti-evolution law and the Dayton trial that was its aftermath are best understood if viewed as indications of a social problem caused by the swift imposition of a system of public education, compulsory and uniform, upon a people long accustomed to private and denominational education—or to no education at all. When the Tennessee fundamentalist found himself compelled by law to send his children to a tax-supported State school, where doctrines were taught that seemed to him a denial of Scripture, he rebelled. This rebellion, characteristically blunt and straightforward, led to the adoption of prohibitive legislation. On March 21, 1925, the General Assembly passed a bill sponsored by John Washington Butler, a farmer, making illegal the teaching in tax-supported institutions of any theory concerning the creation of man which disagreed with Holy Scripture. While discussions of the bill in the legislature were extremely facetious, and the sponsors of the Scopes test case did not themselves take the matter too seriously, the popular tension which followed indicated much support for the law.

Dayton became the scene of a drama that centered national interest on Tennessee. The episode was exploited by newspapers and by partisans as a conflict between religion and science, or between a progressive ideal of education and sheer backwardness. Rather, it was a struggle between those who conceived of democratic education as purely and wholly a State function and those who were doubtful of the State's capacity to assume complete control of such a function. Though efforts to repeal it have failed, the anti-evolution law is to some extent a dead letter today.

Illiteracy remains one of the State's major problems. In 1930 the percentage of rural illiteracy was 8.8—twice as high as that in the urban areas. At this time there were 18,536 persons between the ages of 10 and 20, and about 127,000 persons 21 years old and over, who were illiterate. Of the total number, 87,406 were native whites and 57,251 were Negroes. The marked decrease in the illiteracy rate for the total population between 1920 and 1930—from 10.3 to 7.2—as well as the consistent increase in school attendance during the same decade, indicates definite educational progress. In 1930, 71.7 per cent of native white persons 7 to 20 years old, or 466,220, and 64.6 per cent of the Negroes within this age group, or 91,268, were attending school.

Among institutions doing special work in vocational training are Lincoln Memorial University at Harrogate, the Pi Beta Phi Settlement School at Gatlinburg, and the Cumberland Homestead Project at Crossville. The Alvin C. York Agricultural Institute is supported by the Fentress County Board of Education in cooperation with the State board. The College of Agriculture of the University of Tennessee combines practical and theoretical training in farming. Although emphasis is placed on training boys and girls for farm life, most of the graduates are drawn into more lucrative positions as teachers and demonstration agents.

Seven institutions of higher learning are administered as part of the public school system in Tennessee: the State university at Knoxville, with medical and dental schools at Memphis and a junior college at Martin; the

SCHOOL CONSTRUCTED BY WPA

three units of the State Teachers College at Johnson City, Murfreesboro, and Memphis; the Tennessee Polytechnic Institute at Cookeville; the Austin Peay Normal School at Clarksville; the Tennessee School for the Blind, at Nashville; the Tennessee School for the Deaf, at Knoxville; and the Agricultural and Industrial State Teachers College for Negroes at Nashville.

The last-named institution, opened in 1909 as a normal school, is the largest land-grant college for Negroes in the United States and the second largest Negro educational institution in the world. There are three other four-year colleges and two junior colleges for Negroes in the State.

Under the rehabilitation program of the WPA, adult classes have been organized throughout the State. Primarily organized to give employment to unemployed teachers, these classes taught 7,448 adults to read and write during the 1937–38 school term. There are 17,750 white and 7,853 Negroes enrolled in the adult classes; the white teachers number 311 and the Negro 133. Health, citizenship, and homemaking are taught in addition to reading and writing.

Sports and Recreation

TENNESSEANS have been sportsmen since the days when the pioneers delighted in long hunts and horse racing, wrestling and shooting matches. Though the frontier is long since gone, the State's vast stretches of forest, mountain, and marshland still attract those who love the outdoors. The Great Smokies and the Cumberlands offer magnificent panoramas from skyline hiking trails; the wooded hills and rolling blue grass meadows are ideal for camping, horseback riding, and motoring; and Reelfoot Lake is famous for fishing and duck hunting. Under a vigorous program of conservation the Virginia or white-tail deer, once nearly extinct, is fairly numerous and may be hunted in several counties. Black bear, protected by closed seasons, are found in the wilder parts of the Great Smokies and the Unakas.

For Tennessee's newest big game animal—the Russian wild boar, locally called "Rooshian" wild hog—the ancient sport of boar hunting has been revived. The annual boar hunts, held in the fall in the Cherokee National Forest, are conducted by the State game and fish division in cooperation with the U. S. Forest Service. Because the animals are not yet numerous enough to permit indiscriminate hunting, only 108 participants are drawn by lot from the appplicants. Three methods of hunting are used, each having its special difficulties and fascination. In shooting from a "stand," the hunter takes a position on a vantage point, while guides with two or more dogs drive the boar within shooting distance. Stalking or still hunting is difficult because the crackling of dry leaves underfoot usually warns the keen-eared boars of the hunter's approach. When jumped by the dogs, the "Rooshians" strike through brush-grown ravines and over laurel-covered mountain slopes. The chase, sometimes lasting for miles, calls for unlimited stamina from both dogs and men, and ends with the hog at bay, slashing at the hounds with razor tusks that will rip an unwary dog to ribbons.

Smaller game animals are abundant in the State. For those who like to shoot cottontail rabbits the near woodlands and back pastures afford good hunting ground. The first chill of autumn brings squirrel hunters into the oak woods, and trapping of small fur bearers—mink, muskrat, and weasel—is widespread during the open season. To 'coon hunters nothing quite equals the night chase under a harvest moon, when two eyes glowing like embers high up in a basswood crotch mean that the game is treed. The deep-toned bay of redbone hounds in full cry is music to the fox hunters who gather around campfires on frosty evenings and argue heatedly about "whose dog's ahead." 'Coon dog trials are held in Chester County each year.

The mounted hunt clubs "ride to the hounds" in the old English fashion from November to April, and act as occasional hosts to the National Fox Hunters' Association. The One-Gallus Fox Hunters' Association, composed of farmers and casual fox hunters who maintain no kennels, meets at various places in Middle Tennessee.

Wild turkeys are plentiful, and are hunted in open season. These fine game birds and bobwhite quail are raised at the State Buffalo Springs Game Farm, near Rutledge, and released on protected land.

In the eastern uplands the ruffed grouse, skyrocketing from cover with a startling thunder of wings, is game worthy of any hunter's gun. Ring-necked pheasants are becoming a popular game bird, taking the place of grouse in the lowlands. Game technicians are experimenting with the propagation of chukar and Hungarian partridges. For the average man, who does not go far afield, bobwhites and doves form the bulk of the daily bag, and hundreds of hunters take to the open with bird dogs and shotguns every season. Annual field trials for bird dogs, sponsored by the National Field Trials Association, are held at Grand Junction, in Hardeman County. On the Hobart Ames Plantation—24,000 acres of rolling land, well stocked with quail—sportsmen from all parts of the country enter their champion pointers and setters to compete for national honors.

Reelfoot Lake is on America's greatest flyway of migratory waterfowl, and practically every variety of wading and swimming bird rests there during north and south flights above the Mississippi Valley. Geese, ducks, coots, and snipe in thousands roost at the lake and in the adjacent marshes, and may be taken in season. Sportsmen are assured their bag limit of teal, redheads, and mallards. Swans, wood ducks, and eider ducks, because of their dwindling numbers, are under the strict protection of the U. S. Biological Survey, which has control of all migratory birds and game refuges. Since taking over the region in the early part of the present century, the State has spent $450,000 to preserve and improve this sportsman's paradise, now known as the Reelfoot Lake Game Preserve. The game and fish division maintains a large clubhouse and cabins for fishermen and hunters.

When the Reelfoot earthquake shook the bottom of the Mississippi in

1811, fish of practically every variety known in the Central States were swept into the lake with the backward-rushing river. Today the great pool with its acres of sunken snags swarms with large mouth bass, bream, crappie, carp, bluegill, and buffalo fish. The underwater trees make ideal lurking places for tremendous "spoonbill cats" and huge "loggerhead" turtles. Fly fishing, plug casting, and still fishing enthusiasts meet at Reelfoot and use their favorite methods. Other lake sports are gigging for bull frogs, and shooting water snakes among the dead tree trunks, where motionless water turkeys sit above on the bare branches and the only sound is the swirl of the water as the guide paddles the canoe.

About three million fish are reared yearly at the State hatcheries at Springfield and Morristown and placed in streams and lakes throughout the State. The U. S. Bureau of Fisheries also operates two hatcheries in Tennessee at Erwin and Flintville.

In the clear, swift mountain streams, brook and rainbow trout are plentiful and the rapids and pools are ideal for fly casting. Anglers try for small mouth bass, jack salmon, drum, and catfish in the more sluggish waters of the Cumberland and the Tennessee. Small streams and brooks are well stocked with perch and "pumpkinseed" sunfish, usually the first fish to dangle from the homemade rod of the young American angler.

To develop recreational opportunities and conserve or restore natural resources, State parks and forests have been established under the jurisdiction of the Tennessee department of conservation. Most of them have comfortable cabins, swimming and other facilities. In these areas, totaling more than 100,000 acres, and in the State's game preserves animal and plant life are protected and developed.

Pickett State Park and Forest was the first to put into effect the present program linking conservation and recreation. The area consists of 11,500 acres of wild land on the rugged Cumberland Plateau, where 100-foot rock walls tower above brawling streams, and giant magnolias shade the banks of a 15-acre lake. Natchez Trace Forest State Park, on the western plateau, is being developed both as a resort and a fish and game refuge. Half of its 42,000 acres are gullied badlands, now being reclaimed; the remainder are thickly grown with sedge, sumac, and mixed second-growth hardwood. Three lakes have been constructed with beaches, boathouses, and overnight cabins. Among other State areas now being developed are Morgan, Marion-Franklin, Bledsoe, and Chickasaw forests, Chickasaw Forest State Park, and the Lebanon Cedar Forest State Park, containing one of the largest groves of cedar in the Central Basin.

In the Mississippi bottomlands the National Park Service administers

DUCK HUNTING ON REELFOOT LAKE

the Shelby Forest Recreational Demonstration Area, twelve thousand acres of jungle-like swamps, forests of beech, cottonwood, cypress, and willow. Another Federal owned recreational demonstration project is Falls Creek Falls, fifteen thousand acres of the wildest land in the Cumberlands. Foot trails and a road give access to the falls, a 256-foot curtain of water tumbling over a mighty sandstone cliff.

Foot trails, bridle paths, and campsites are being established in Federal and State areas, and this program is opening up vast roadless sections of the State for nature study, hiking, horseback riding, and camping. Organized hiking clubs and other outdoor groups sponsor trips into the wild parts of the State. In Eastern Tennessee some of the clubs are affiliated with the Appalachian Trail Conference, which maintains the Maine-to-Georgia skyline trail along the crest of the Appalachians.

In Norris Park, a development of the Tennessee Valley Authority overlooking Norris Lake, bridle paths and foot trails have been laid out in the valleys, and stables, picnic areas, and an outdoor theater have been established on the lakeshore. Other TVA developments are Big Ridge Park, a rugged region of limestone ridges, on an impounded arm of Norris Lake; and Pickwick Dam Reservation, an area of rolling wooded hills bordering Pickwick Reservoir.

For those interested in history, the National military parks—Chickamauga and Chattanooga, Shiloh, Fort Donelson, Stones River, and the Meriwether Lewis National Monument—are popular. Caverns with magnificent rock formations have been developed under private management and are open to the public at nominal rates. The most notable of these are Craighead Caverns, Jewel, Ruskin, Dunbar, Nickajack, and Lookout Mountain Caves.

With the development of lakes and river courses, interest in boating is increasing. Outboards are in use on the principal rivers, and regattas and races are held regularly. Swimming facilities are available for residents and tourists at the State's lake and river beaches, which are among the finest to be found in the South.

A unique sport, drawing enthusiastic crowds of participants and spectators, is the "turkey shoots" of the mountain people, stemming from the rifle contest of pioneer times. Scorning modern breech loaders, the contestants use long-barreled cap and ball "hog" rifles, patterned after the famous guns of the frontiersmen. Indeed, in the high Smokies riflemen still use flint-lock Dechard rifles that saw duty in the Revolutionary battle of King's Mountain. The prize may be a turkey, a hog, or a side of beef. These "old time shootin' matches," most popular in the mountain regions, are also held in other parts of the State.

The four professional baseball teams—Nashville, Memphis, Knoxville, and Chattanooga—are members of the Southern Association. Softball teams are sponsored by business organizations, factories, unions, and churches all over the State. Leagues have been formed in all localities, and many municipal parks provide free facilities for night games. Collegiate and high school football is popular; the annual games played by Vanderbilt, Tennessee, and Sewanee university teams draw enthusiastic crowds.

The horse and riding shows which are features of State and county fairs are well attended by city and country folk alike. The Plantation Walking Horse, bred originally for planters and overseers to ride while directing work in the fields, is an especial favorite. With its three easy gaits—the walk, the running walk, and the canter—it is an ideal mount for use and pleasure. In Marshall and Bedford counties, where the Walking Horse is bred in great numbers, an extensive network of bridle paths spreads through the rolling hill country. Each spring, usually in April, cavalcades

FISHING IN A GREAT SMOKIES STREAM

of men, women, and children take to these paths for trips that range from weekend jaunts to rides lasting two weeks or more. The recently inaugurated Ride-a-thon—a two-day horseback trip over the country trails—has proven popular. Plans are in the making for a State-wide system of bridle paths. In most of the cities and larger towns there are riding clubs and stables where horses may be rented.

Most of the county fairs feature horse races, automobile racing, shows, and midway amusements in addition to a variety of exhibits. Large crowds are drawn every year to the iris festival at Nashville, the dogwood festival at Knoxville, the strawberry festival at Bells and Humboldt, in Crockett County, and the rhododendron festival at Gatlinburg. Two outstanding yearly events are the Memphis Cotton Carnival with its Mardi-Gras revelry and Mule Day at Columbia, an all-day celebration in honor of the "orneriest and workingest work-critter living."

Folklore: The Living Past

THE Tennessee that the tourist knows, with its standard highways and hotdog stands, its industrial areas, cities, and hustling chambers of commerce—all smoothly integrated in surface America—is much like the tourist's Maine or Ohio. But there is an older Tennessee, resistant to the leveling force of an age of radio, motion pictures, mass printing, and rapid transit, and taking its folkish pattern from habits, beliefs, and art forms rooted in the remote past of the British Isles. To an outsider these folkways may seem merely odd survivals of the quaint or decadent. They are more than that: they are the earthy Tennessee of Davy Crockett and Andy Jackson, grown old but still hale and hearty.

Though the folkways of Tennessee are part of the general regional culture of the South, they belong to the upland and border area rather than to the Deep South and the Seaboard. Folkways persist most vigorously in isolated mountain and hill regions and in rural sections, but their influence is still felt in the cities and among people of all classes, whites and Negroes. Some of the traditions and beliefs are State-wide; others are peculiar to mountain, Negro, or rural communities.

The speech of Tennesseans is rich in racy and vigorous folk idiom, derived from times when the English language had not yet been starched and formalized with definitions and rules of grammar. In the speech of the unlettered, especially in the mountains and hill country, there is often the metrical surge and flow of the Old Testament and of the Reformation hymns that the people sing. "My mind went a-rambling like wild geese in the West." "I went down to Chattanooga, where the smoke runs up to the sky." "I am not fitten for to knock at her door."

Backcountry folk are prone to use parts of speech in strange ways—nouns as verbs, verbs as nouns, adjectives and adverbs as nouns or verbs. "I've got them weary dismals today," moans the hillman. "Granny Tatum's standing on the drop-edge of Yonder and we'll soon be laying her down in her silent grave." Of a jealous lover they say: "Oh, he's heartburning the worst kind over that little gal." A quicksand stream is a "miring branch"; a gossip is a "bone-carrier"; a tirade is a "clapper-clawing." If a man is reserved, he is "offish" or "uncomeatable." An extravagant lie is a "ripper," a "snorter," a "screamer." A person who changes his mind often is called a "fly-up-the-creek" or a "whip-around."

Often there is a broad vein of humor in the folk expressions of the people. "I'm so hungry I could eat a bull—and it bellering!" "He's as lazy as the hound that leaned against the fence to bark." "She's as ugly as a mud fence dabbed over with toad frogs."

Thousands of Tennesseans still judge character by physical traits catalogued by generations of observations. "You watch," they say, "and see if politicians don't most usually always have big noses. You take a man with stubby fingers. He masters his way through the world and he's bull-stubborn. Take a man that grays early. Most likely he's a fine fellow and will lend you money. A blue-gummed Negro is a killer and his bite is as poisonous as a copperhead's. A dimple in a girl's chin is a mighty bad sign, means the devil within. But a dimpled man is a good steady sort of fellow and can be trusted. Don't know why it is, but rich men most usually are hairy. Any man who talks to himself has money in the bank, but he won't lend you any."

The old weather signs have vital meaning in the lives of rural people and farmers watch them closely. "You can always tell there will be a storm," they say, "when cats and rats play after sundown. A sure sign of rain is when a rooster crows at night. Frost will come as sure as judgment just six weeks after you hear the first July fly. It never fails when birds flock on the ground that a wind storm is brewing up, and when fires commence spitting there'll be a soon fall of snow."

"When it comes to farming," they will tell you, "I'd sink down to beggar-trash in no time if I didn't know the things I learnt from my daddy and he learnt from his daddy about farming. Suppose you plant potatoes near onions. Well, the onions will put their eyes out. I've never seen a garden that throve good unless it was planted in the full of the moon. You've got to be careful and don't thank a man for gift seeds or they will perish in the ground. If it thunders while the fruit trees are in bud, the orchard won't yield to amount to anything. If a hen is set in the light of the moon the eggs will hatch roosters that you can't noways keep out of the house. Don't ever set a hen during a run of wind or the chickens will cackle, crow, and sing till you're half crazy. If you'll mark the bottom of the churn with a cross or drop a dime into it, the butter will come quicker. If you want to keep your horses and cows from catching distemper, tie a strong billygoat in the stalls with them. Always plant peppers when you're good and mad at your wife and give your gourd seeds a hard cussing or they won't come up."

The old wives say: "It ain't no sort of ailments except the pneumonia and bad fever sickness that you can't treat at home just as good as any doctor a-living. Nothing on this earth better for a cut than some turpentine to burn out the poison and a binding of fat bacon to heal the soreness or maybe draw out rust and splinters. You could pay five dollars a bottle for cough medicine and it wouldn't do no better than a dose of coal oil and sugar. Want to get shet of warts? Well, let a black calf lick them three times on three days and fare-ye-well warts. You drink water boiled with a silver dollar and your hives will leave you."

"Now, when it's babies," they say, "it's just rightdown foolish to try to go by a book. Say a young woman goes by the book. She pays no mind to what her old mother tells her. She maybe goes to town and sees a scary movie show. Then what? The baby's born with a birth-scald on his face. When a child is born, you dasn't sweep under the bed nor take the ashes out of the fireplace for a good month if you want the mother to live. If you want the child to rise in the world, make sure you take it upstairs before you take it downstairs. Let your baby look into a mirror before it's a month old and it'll have trouble teething. Say you want to know what sort of man your boy-child's going to be. Well, when he's exactly one year old take and set him in the middle of the floor. Put things like a Bible, a hammer, a piece of money, and a snake's tongue around him. Watch which one he picks up first. Is it the Bible? He'll be a preacher. The hammer? A carpenter. Money? A banker. Snake's tongue? A lawyer."

"These fresh younglings they send here to teach school now vow it ain't a thing to luck signs," they say, shaking their heads. "But don't you believe it! I've seen many a thing that the books don't tell. Now, it's a mighty mean thing to hear an owl screech at midnight. A man's got to tie a knot in a towel or stick a shovel in the fire, or he'll foul his times and seasons. If you bite your finger nails on Sunday, you are bound to be sick unless you wear something blue for a week. If you count flowers on a grave, you will die unless you swallow as many minnows as there were flowers. If, unbeknownst, you burn cherry wood, or lightning-struck wood in your stove, you better be quick to burn thornwood, or the Lord help you! It's terrible bad luck to sit in a chair backward or lay a broom on the bed, or tear up a Bible, or turn a chunk around in the fireplace."

Love and marriage customs are rich in folk beliefs. "On the first day of May," they will tell you, "a girl can hold a mirror over a well and see her future husband. But she won't catch a husband at all if she ever sits on a table. Let a boy find a girl's knife or nail file and she will be his wife. If a girl and boy bump heads, they will become lovers before six months are

WOMAN CARDING

out. Sleep with a beef bone under your pillow for nine nights and you will marry the person you dream of on the ninth night. You can set your shoes crosswise under your bed and dream of your sweetheart. September marriages will be happy. Marry during a rain and you will turn sour on your husband or wife."

Sitting up with the dead has its own peculiar customs. "They's three main things you've got to be mighty careful about," they say. "First off, it's the blackest sort of luck for any member of the family to sit up with the departed. They's death in it. Be sure that every mirror is taken down or turned to the wall. If any of the folks sitting up was to see the coffin in the mirror, it's death to them. And cats! Lord, don't let a cat come near the remainders! Cats is the devil's own and they'll sure steal the soul of the departed if they can get up into the coffin."

The lives of most rural folk revolve about the churches, which are not merely places of worship but also social clubs, news exchanges, and marriage marts. Country church "sociables," picnics, and "Summer Association" meetings are in essence folk festivals.

After "laying-by" time in the summer the rural folk take things easy. There are visiting in the community, all-day fishing trips, which end with fish fries on the river bank, ice-cream and strawberry suppers, squirrel stews, and barbecues *(see Tour 10)*. As late summer approaches, preparation is begun for the Big Meeting. Women cook for weeks in anticipation of "visiting company." Singing school masters from far-gone places like Arkansas, Missouri, and Texas have taught their schools at a dollar a head, and now folk know enough about reading shaped notes to make the music good during the meeting. The Sunday community singings and the monthly all-county sings at the county courthouse have "shook the crimps out of voices." The Big Meeting is the crowning point of the summer—two weeks of fiery sermons, sweet music, prayer, shouting, conversion, baptism, dinner on the ground, visiting and courting.

Every county seat has its "Liars' Bench"—the worn steps of the courthouse or the curbing on its shady side—where on Saturdays and first Mondays *(see Columbia)* farmers in town to market their produce gather with townsmen to swap tall tales, and talk politics, women, and religion. In each county is one man outstanding as a wit. Trade days find him on the court square surrounded by howling men and boys. In national and local news he is well informed, and his humorous comments "make folks clear" on otherwise perplexing questions. People will say, "Don't miss first Monday, because Tom Siler will be on hand. That man's a rich card, a Joe Darter for a fact! Ain't nothing he don't know and ain't nobody he can't mock down to the point of nothing." Politicians, lovers, church folk, and the like fear the quips of such a man, but they admire him and are always on hand to hear his latest.

In general, there is no sharp line of cleavage between the substance of Negro and white folk beliefs. The Negro has absorbed and modified many white folk beliefs, as he borrowed speech and religion. However, his temperament and vivid imagination have given this old European lore a new richness of imagery and a naïve freshness authentically his own. The humorous philosophy which often underlies his life brightens for him circumstances that would be unrelieved bleakness for the whites. The Negro's powerful folk instincts have softened the hard angularity of his adopted religion. His Lord is made in man's own image: an all-wise, benevolent, and thoroughly human deity. Some of the traits of the Calvinist God are transferred to the devil—and even the devil is sometimes an "old rip," malicious but amusing, rather than a foul fiend. The weight of evil power rests with witches and the vague rabble of dark forces which prowl the night. These things are true, of course, only of the uneducated Negro. The high school or college graduate follows the urban *mores*.

Negro religious services are highly emotional, and in many Negro churches of the rural sections dancing is one of the most important elements in the worship. These dances and the songs accompanying them are called "reels." Although they are tabooed in the city congregations, it is in general considered proper to dance, provided the feet are not crossed, as "hit ain't railly dancin', lessen de feets is crossed." The Baptist churches in many places follow the old custom of baptism. Dressed in white robes, the minister, his assistants, and those to be baptized march into the water. A man called a "feeler" goes ahead of the minister with a pole, feeling the way for the others, so that there may be no "pit falls." After a suitable place is reached, the applicants for baptism march to the minister and are immersed. As a rule they come from the water shouting, while the onlookers on the banks of the creek chant a dirge-like melody.

Belief in "cunjur" lore, an offshoot of voodoo, is fairly widespread among Tennessee Negroes. Its influence is strongest in West Tennessee where both white and Negro folkways have much in common with those of the Deep South. Cunjur spells, which may consist of anything from a muttered rigmarole of African words to scattering graveyard ("goober") dust, are relied on to accomplish a variety of things for believers. Cunjur doctors will sell you "hands" or "tobies" enabling you to detect witches and ward off their spells. Through cunjur you can cause rain, find lost property, wither the tongue of your gossiping neighbor, win your sweetheart's love, and drive your enemy insane or to the grave. It can force your debtors to pay you and your creditors to forget you, make your wife fecund or barren, cause the fish to bite, and the mosquitoes to forage elsewhere. The power of cunjur is as limitless as its user's desires.

"Cunjur doctors" are often marked by physical peculiarities that add to their professional reputations. One such man who lived near Memphis had kinky hair on the sides of his head, but straight hair on top, a lucky mole on his right arm, and three birthmarks on his left arm declared to represent the Father, Son, and Holy Ghost. He was chicken-breasted, indicating that he would never have tuberculosis, and had been born with a caul over his face.

Cunjur doctors do a thriving business in the Negro districts of Memphis and Nashville. They traffic chiefly in good luck charms, love powders, cure-alls, and spells to insure winnings in the numbers game. Though there are many skillful Negro physicians in the towns, wrinkled red-eyed old men and women ply their trade of herb-doctoring and cunjuring in tenement districts just as they do in the most isolated swamplands.

Rural Negroes are little concerned with luck charms for gambling. Their endless struggle is with witches, "ha'nts," and the like. Though ha'nts are feared, some of them are merely prankish or bothersome. But all witches are deadly dangerous and feared utterly. Among the whites, belief in witches has largely disappeared. The Negro has a double heritage of witch lore—Celtic and Teutonic from England, and a jumble of beliefs from many African peoples. A witch can take any form. The most common is the traditional toothless old hag. But the cur-dog slouching across the road, the whickering owl that perches in your yard, a cat, a snake, a fish, or even a stone may be a witch in disguise. When a witch fastens on you, you are doomed to a terrible death unless you can find a spell to rid yourself of her. The witch comes to you in the night and rides you. In the morning you find your hair plaited into stirrups and your face scratched, and you feel as if you have had a savage beating. Good charms against witches are salt sprinkled about the house, especially in the fireplace, black pepper carried on the person, sulphur matches thrust into the hair, or the left hind foot of a graveyard rabbit in the pocket. Unless the witch is particularly powerful, a Bible under your pillow will keep her at bay. She must count every word before she can begin riding you, a task she can never finish before dawn. The best way to prevent harm from witches is never to offend anyone suspected of witchcraft.

The uneducated Negro clings religiously to many old death customs. If a person dies hard, his ghost will return to haunt the family. Nothing must be overlooked to make the dying of your kin as "easy" as possible. The bed must never be placed "cross-way of de world," but always with the head toward west so that the spirit can flow out with the mystical east-west currents of the earth. If this does not help, the pillows are removed, because a bed containing the feathers of a fowl protects the life spark. When anyone is suffering greatly, it is better to shift him to a strange mattress to hasten the end: it is dangerous even for a well person to sleep on a strange mattress.

The custom of holding several funerals for one person is not uncommon; and after the main funeral and the burying have taken place, a funeral service may be conducted by each lodge or association to which the deceased had belonged. Many a Negro will pay dues to a lodge all his life so that he and his relatives may be "laid away" in style. A preacher often has his funeral preached in each church which has been under his pastorate. Because rural Negroes cannot always get together on short notice, a body will sometimes be buried on the day after death, and the funeral services held several months later. Occasionally, when a person dies penniless, preachings will be held for several days over the body until enough money has been collected to satisfy the undertaker. To keep the spirit from coming back again, the cup and saucer used in the last illness are placed on the grave. The medicine bottles are sometimes turned upside down with loosened corks on the grave so that the contents can soak into the ground.

In every locality are men and women, Negroes and whites, who are oral libraries for neighborhood history and gossip. They can quote exhaustively from all important sermons and political speeches for years back, and have at their tongues' tip a great variety of jokes and anecdotes. They will tell you long circumstantial tales of the War of the Roses, when Fiddling Bob Taylor and Uncle Alf Taylor, brothers and political enemies, campaigned against each other for the governorship. They will tell you of the roaring sermons of Evangelist Sam Jones and of how he fought the saloon keepers and gamblers with Scripture and fist. They will tell of famous railroad wrecks, the teething troubles of children dead these many years, and they will grow eloquent on Bryan's last stand at Dayton. And from the mountains of East Tennessee to the Mississippi lowgrounds they will tell you the eerie tales of Old Kate, the Bell Witch of Robertson County, who tormented John Bell to his grave and cowed Andrew Jackson. There are stories of ghosts and badmen, of lovers, family feuds, and political killings —all true folk tales, edited and garnished by thousands of tellings. Tennessee's finest contributions to folk tale are undoubtedly the legends that

MONDAY

grew up around the exploits of Davy Crockett as bear and 'coon hunter, marksman, politician and wit, lover, mighty drinker, and spinner of tremendous yarns.

The white folk music of Tennessee, like the rest of its white folk culture, belongs to the large upland region of the southeast. It is best understood by observing it in its various functional forms. It may function, for example, as the joy of the individual or the small casual group, the religious gathering, the "singing," the dance, and the play-party—a gathering where singing games are played.

The ballad ("love song" or "ballet") is still perhaps the strongest type of traditional song in Tennessee. These may be very ancient, like "Little Hugh," "Lord Lovel," and scores of others; or they may be more recent compositions in the ancestral ballad manner, like "Springfield Mountain," "Jesse James," "The Death of Floyd Collins," "Mr. Bryan's Last Fight," and "Casey Jones." The production of these ballads seems endless. Every new happening of enough importance to arouse widespread note and ruffle the feelings of the country folk is almost sure to bring a ballad in its wake.

Typical of the recent compositions are the "badman" songs, one of the best of which—"Stagolee," or "Stack O'Lee"—comes from Memphis. Stagolee is pictured thus:

> Stagolee was a bully man, an' everybody knowed
> When dey seed Stagolee comin' to give Stagolee de road.
>
> (Refrain)
>
> Oh, dat man, bad man, he gives his wife his han'—
> "Goodbye, darlin', I'm going to kill a man."

The song gives a detailed account of the murder and of the capture of Stagolee, followed by the court scene, which does not reveal Stagolee's fate. The song ends with,

> Stagolee cried to de jury, "Please don't take my life,
> I've got three little chillun an' one little lovin' wife."
> O, dat man, bad man, Stagolee done come.

Another typical Negro folk song, relating the sinking of the Titanic, was composed by an old western Tennessee Negro:

> It was sad when dat great ship went down—ship went down,
> It was sad when dat great ship went down—ship went down;
> Women, wives, and little children los' their lives—los' their lives,
> It was sad when dat great ship went down.

The ordinary Negro prayer is really a spontaneous song, since it is often intoned as a sort of chant. In moments of earnestness, stilted phrases are laid aside and prayers for particular individuals are moaned, with direct mention of particular besetting sins. Sorrow is expressed in the same fashion. There is a large group of regular Negro church songs known as "moans" because they are pitched in the sing-song fashion of prayer or grief. Tragedies and catastrophes are made themselves for chants, much like a deacon's prayer or "the "moan" of the convert who has just "come through" and vividly describes his trip to hell and heaven.

The dance song has practically given way to the dance fiddle tune without words. The "old fiddler" of Tennessee is far from extinction, and he still fiddles such strains as "Natchez under the Hill," and the "Arkansas Traveler," "Turkey in the Straw," "Turkey Bone Buzzer," and "Pop Goes the Weasel"—tunes of hoary age. More recently the old fiddler has associated himself with guitar and banjo players to form "hillbilly bands" which have done their part in entertaining radio listeners. Related to the dance, and less subject to the disapproval of churchly folk, is the play-party. Though now less prevalent than in earlier times, when social diversions were fewer, it is still played to the singing of "Hog Drovers," "The Miller's Lot," "Slop the Hogs," and "Possum Pie," and like swinging games.

Many songs are composed and sung on the basis of "calls" and " 'sponses," as:

> Leader (call): Oh, where you runnin' sinnah
> Audience ('sponse): No hidin' place down here!

"Note singing" and "book singing" are rapidly replacing the "jump-up" songs among the Negroes. Individual Negro composers pass out printed copies of their songs, usually called ballads, which are learned and sung by rural congregations until it is almost impossible to separate the old from the new. Even here the creative impulse is not ended—the ballads usually come without music and a tune has to be improvised, the lines often being modified to fit the melody. This improvisation, called "chooning it," is done with surprising quickness and ease.

The religious folk impulse finds expression in the spirituals, both white and Negro *(see MUSIC)*. Particularly as developed by the Negro, these folk songs are now a unique and significant part of American music.

Writers of Tennessee

THE literature of the early settlers is found in the written forms with which they transacted the business of their everyday lives. These trail-clearers, fort-builders, and Indian-fighters gave historians of a later day the framework of their collective biography in the various documents they published.

The first writers, in the professional sense of the word, were concerned with religious and political controversy, history, and law. J. G. M. Ramsey, a physician and scholar, wrote the one-volume *Annals of Tennessee* (1853), a valuable and detailed source of information on pioneer life and government. Through his newspaper and broadside writings he was instrumental in the building of the first steamboat in Knoxville and in securing the first railroads for East Tennessee. John Haywood, of Nashville, justice of the State supreme court, was the author of the widely known *Civil and Political History of the State of Tennessee* (1823). His *Natural and Aboriginal History of Tennessee* (1823), a book now all but forgotten, is sought by collectors.

Charles Todd, a Presbyterian minister and newspaper editor, is believed to have been the State's first novelist. His *Woodville, or, The Anchoret Returned* (1832) is wholly a product of Tennessee. At a date when book-publishing was considered the exclusive province of the northeastern States, this 278-page novel was published from the printing shop of F. W. Heiskell in Knoxville, on thin linen stock that came from an East Tennessee paper mill. The book's pages differ in size, but the type is uniform and clear. *Woodville* contains little local color. The author states in his preface that, since the novel's characters and scene have "true-life" origin, he judges it honorable not to be explicit. Therefore, the village S—— "is situated in a lovely valley and immediately on the shore of a beautiful river." The emotions of his characters Todd describes in the ponderous and moralistic style of the early nineteenth century.

In pioneer days, when an editor could term a fellow citizen a "low-born loon" with no fear of legal aftermath, newspapers in Tennessee were usually one-man affairs. A printer by profession, the publisher aired his own opinions and gathered his paper's news. The pioneer newspaperman set up his business in centers of State or Territorial government. The birth of the newspaper was often due to some cause vital to the community's growth (such as agitation for railroads). When the cause was won or lost, the newspaper ceased to exist. Or, if rumor reached the publisher's ears that some settlement was having a livelier contemporary history than the community in which he was then working, he moved his newspaper there.

George Roulstone, a New Englander, published the State's first newspaper, the Knoxville *Gazette,* at Rogersville, November 5, 1791. As soon as the Indian troubles subsided—these having prevented the paper's first issue from being published in Knoxville—Roulstone moved his newspaper to that center of State government and there continued its publication.

Mark Twain's "Journalism in Tennessee," with its uproarious account of fist fights, duels, and horse whippings among editors, was small exaggeration. Well toward the close of the last century Tennessee editors were an outspoken and violent breed. Characteristic of the vituperative type of editor was W. G. (Parson) Brownlow who contributed forcefully to early journalism. From 1843 when Brownlow's *Whig,* published in Jonesboro, won its fight against Andrew Jackson and the Democratic supremacy, his papers continued to be storm centers of political and religious turmoil. The *Whig* was removed to Knoxville in 1849; and in 1861, because its editor openly supported the Unionist cause, the paper was suppressed by the Confederates. Brownlow resumed publication of the paper in 1863 when Union forces took possession of Knoxville; its publication was continued in that city until 1869. Brownlow was successively editor of the *Daily Chronicle,* the *Independent Journal,* and the Knoxville *Whig and Rebel Ventilator*—a title later changed to *Weekly Whig and Chronicle.* "Cry Aloud and Spare Not," the belligerent motto of the paper, adequately characterized its editorial policy.

The first verse published in Tennessee appeared in the early newspapers; poems by the editor and literary subscribers were used as fillers or given column space on the last page of these four-page folios. In Colonel James Smith's *Account of Remarkable Occurrences,* published at Lexington, Kentucky, 1799, is what is believed to be the first poem composed in Tennessee territory. Smith, with four others, explored the Cumberland down to the Ohio in June 1776. At the mouth of the Tennessee three of the adventurers turned homeward, but Smith and a Negro boy continued their journey into Tennessee country. Smith received a severe cane stab in his foot and, while he waited for his injury to mend, he composed the poem that appears in his reminiscences.

David Crockett, Tennessee bear hunter, politician extraordinary and hero of the Alamo, was one of the first humorists of the South and a trail blazer for the American school of humorous writing. A thorough Tennessean, Crockett knew the State from Hangover Mountain to Reelfoot Lake. Although there is much controversy over the authorship of *A Narrative of the Life of David Crockett, of the State of Tennessee . . . Written by Himself* (1834), the vital brawny qualities of the Colonel are unquestionably present in this hair-raising classic of the Southern frontier.

After his defeat in the race for Congress against Andrew Jackson's candidate, Crockett announced to the opposition, "You can go to hell, I'm going to Texas." There he wrote *Col. Crockett's Exploits and Adventures in Texas* (1836). In this book, in his autobiography, and in *An Account of Col. Crockett's Tour to the North and down East* (1835), Crockett describes how he drank, hunted, speculated, begot children, farmed badly, and, when settlers built cabins near him, moved farther into the wilds.

Little of permanent value was achieved in the fields of fiction, poetry, biography, or journalism until after the War between the States, but George Washington Harris and Opie Read further developed the humor of the mountains and the canebrakes. Harris, the first Tennessean to write realistically of the Appalachian mountain folk, introduced the lank uncouth East Tennessee mountaineer, Sut Lovingood, a chronic drunkard and "a nat'ral born durn'd fool," whose main purpose in life was to raise "perticklar hell." Readers of the *Sut Lovingood Yarns* (1867) were delighted with a kind of humor that depended on rowdy and ludicrous situations. The tortuous dialect, which all but requires a key, foreshadows the writing of Nye, Nasby, and others of the bucolic and red-flannel era of American life. Harris also wrote political articles.

Opie Read, of Nashville, the author of *Len Gansett* (1888), *A Kentucky Colonel* (1890), *The Jucklins* (1896), and numerous other novels, reports the customs and manners of earlier Tennessee in an easy conversational style. His pathos and humor, depending upon stock situations and obvious play on words, are in the vein of newspaper feature writing. Several of Read's novels were published in the *Arkansas Traveler,* of which he was the founder and editor (1883–91). After removing from Little Rock to Chicago, he wrote his autobiography, *I Remember* (1930).

The principal novelists of the late nineteenth century used the State as a background for romantic fiction, and of these John Trotwood Moore and Charles Egbert Craddock (Mary N. Murfree) are the best remembered. Moore, who came from Alabama in 1885, described Middle Tennessee in the years before and immediately after the War between the States. In

The Bishop of Cottontown (1906) he attacked the system of child labor in Southern cotton mills. Miss Murfree chose the region of the Great Smokies for her pictures of a backwoods people and their never-ending struggles for existence. *Drifting down Lost Creek,* and *The Prophet of the Great Smoky Mountains* (1885) are representative works.

Maria Thompson Daviess wrote of the Nashville region—Harpeth Valley, Providence Road, and Paradise Ridge. Her characters are kind-hearted, gentle country-folk who live in an aura of optimism. Some of the novels are propaganda for movements dear to the author; *The Tinder Box* (1917) deals with woman suffrage and *Over Paradise Ridge* (1915) with the back-to-the-farm movement. Henry Sydnor Harrison, of Sewanee, wrote several sympathetic novels about middle-class people. *Queed* (1911) and *V.V.'s Eyes* (1913) were best sellers.

The "lost cause" was a favorite subject of Tennessee poets of the period after the War between the States. Virginia Frazer Boyle, of Memphis, romanticizes the antebellum and wartime South in *Love Songs and Bugle Calls* (1906). Against the same background Abram J. (Father) Ryan, one of the prominent poets of the Confederacy, wrote mystic and devotional verse. Father Ryan saw action in the Tennessee campaigns, and in "The Conquered Banner" and "Sword of Robert E. Lee" he proclaims his unreconstructed sentiments.

Walter Malone, of Memphis, wrote serious verse and nature poems, profuse in imagery. "Opportunity"—a standby of expression teachers—found in his *Songs of East and West* (1906) and a lengthy narrative in verse, *Hernando De Soto* (1914), are his best known. Will Allen Dromgoole, of Nashville, wrote of the cabin dwellers of East and Middle Tennessee. For years she conducted a weekly page known as "Song and Story" in the Nashville *Banner.* In prose and poetry she used the dialects of the Negro, the mountaineer, and the "po' white trash." *The Heart of Old Hickory and Other Stories of Tennessee* (1895) and the *Doll's Funeral* juvenile verse, are representative of her work.

Many editors and historians made valuable contributions to the understanding of Tennessee. Albert Virgil Goodpasture, whose histories are source books for early State history, was co-author, with William Robertson Garret, of the *History of Tennessee, Its People and Its Institutions* (1900).

Will T. Hale, of Clarksville, editor of the Memphis *Commercial Appeal,* Nashville *American,* and Knoxville *Sentinel,* described the rural sections, and in dialect verse and prose interpreted the homely philosophy of Tennessee villages and farms. Among his best known works are *Showers and Sunshine* (1896), poems; *The Backward Trail* (1899), stories of the Indians and the Tennessee pioneers; and *Great Southerners* (1900), biographical sketches.

Robert Love (Bob) Taylor, editor of the *Taylor Trotwood Magazine,* was a humorist of the old school. *Gov. Bob Taylor's Tales* (1896) contains "The Fiddle and the Bow" and some of his most quoted lines. Almost every Tennessean knows at least one Bob Taylor yarn. C. P. J. Mooney, editor of the Memphis *Commercial Appeal,* wrote in defense of the interests of the farmers of Tennessee and the mid-South.

The *Sewanee Review,* founded at the University of the South in 1892, claims to be the oldest quarterly in the United States in continuous publication. Among its famous editors have been William Peterfield Trent and John Bell Henneman. Under William S. Knickerbocker, its present editor, the *Sewanee Review* has published much competent literary criticism during the past decade.

Many of the younger Tennessee writers show a lively and skeptical interest in State history, past and present, and a large part of their efforts has been directed toward reinterpreting the South of the War between the States. In biographies of statesmen and military leaders, panoramic novels, and volumes of poetry, they patiently vivisect the period and its people. Commonly they are protagonists of the South, but with no rose-colored conception of the aristocratic tradition of the Old South. The modern writer breaks with the past, and his sentence structure is as unconventional as his viewpoint. He gives his attention to the everyday life of the common people, too frequently disregarded or depicted romantically in earlier Southern literature. In direct and vigorous prose that often has a stark beauty, these writers tell the story of sharecropper, politician, mountaineer, and frontiersman. If the scene of the book is contemporary, the bitter details may have their origin in the author's own life.

Of first rank among genre writers is T. S. Stribling, of Clifton, realist of the Tennessee and North Alabama hills. His novels, written in a straightforward, forceful style, deal with the moral codes, social practices, and economic conditions of Southern life. Stribling's first novel, *Birthright* (1922), his *Teeftallow* (1926) and *Bright Metal* (1928) are all set in Middle and West Tennessee. Two adventure novels, *Fombombo* (1923) and *Red Sand* (1924), and the short story collections, *Strange Moon* (1929) and *Clues of the Caribees* (1929), have a Venezuelan background. Stribling's most important work is the trilogy, *The Forge* (1931), *The Store* (Pulitzer Prize novel, 1933), and the *Unfinished Cathedral* (1934). The trilogy presents the rise of unscrupulous Miltiades Vaiden from middle-class Baptist farmer to storekeeper, cotton speculator, banker, and High-Church Methodist, and the retribution that overtook him when a poor-white enemy dynamited him in the unfinished cathedral that was to have been his monument.

Harry Harrison Kroll, of Murfreesboro, has written of the East Tennessee Mountains in *Three Brothers and Seven Daddies* (1932) and of the West Tennessee cotton country in *The Cabin in the Cotton* (1931). His vivid, often crude technique achieves a striking realism. His latest novel, *I Was a Sharecropper* (1937), is autobiographical. In 1938 one of Kroll's short stories appeared in the O'Brien collection of best stories. *Fish on the Steeple* (1935) by Ed Bell, of Smithville, is a well-written story of everyday life in a small mountain town in East Tennessee. Bell's style is starkly realistic.

Two West Tennesseans who have written with understanding of their section are Ridley Wills, of Brownsville, and Jennings Perry, of Jackson. Wills' two novels, *Hoax* (1922), the life of a young man from the age of eighteen to twenty-seven, and *Harvey Landrum* (1924), a psychological study of chinless Harvey Landrum, who tries to conceal a sense of inferiority behind a false front of bravery, are written in a frank but restrained prose style. Perry's *Windy Hill* (1926) is a love story with Jackson for its background.

Caroline Gordon (Mrs. Allen Tate), of Clarksville, writes of the Middle Tennessee planters before and after the War between the States. *Penhally* (1931) and *Aleck Maury, Sportsman* (1934) are her earliest novels. *None Shall Look Back* (1937) is a careful study and evaluation of the war in the eastern section of the State. Her latest novel is *The Garden of Adonis* (1937), in which she deals with the tenant-farmer situation. Miss Gordon has received a Guggenheim fellowship, and her short stories have appeared in the O. Henry and O'Brien collections.

Evelyn Scott, of Clarksville, has made outstanding contributions in the fields of fiction, poetry, and autobiography. Although Evelyn Scott is concerned more with the portrayal and analysis of emotions than with political, military, or social events, the war background of her Civil War novel, *The Wave* (1929), is lucidly and authentically presented. Her prose works include her autobiographical *Escapade* (1923); the novels *The Narrow House* (1921), *The Golden Door* (1925), *Migrations* (1927), *Blue Rum* (1930); a collection of short stories, *Ideals* (1927); and two books for children, *In the Endless Sands* (1925), written in collaboration with Cyril Kay Scott, and *Witch Perkins* (1929). Two volumes of her poetry have been published: *Precipitations* (1920) and *The Winter Alone*

(1930). In *Background in Tennessee* (1937), Evelyn Scott gives a frank account of the social life and customs in her native State.

Maristan Chapman, of Chattanooga, writes of the Cumberland Mountain folk. Among her outstanding novels are *Happy Mountain* (1928), *Homeplace* (1929), *Glen Hazard* (1933), and *Eagle Cliff* (1934), written in collaboration with her husband, John Stanton Higham. (Chapman is Mrs. Higham's maiden name, and Maristan is a combination of Mr. Higham's middle name and his wife's given name.) All of these books are distinguished by simplicity of style and intuitive understanding of the mountain people. The characterizations and descriptions have a quiet charm, a lightness and freshness of approach.

John Porter Fort, of Chattanooga, has written with power and sincerity of the under-privileged groups. His *Stone Daugherty* (1929) and *God in the Straw Pen* (1931) show a deep understanding of pioneer life, and especially of the early revival movement. His first novel, *Light in the Window* (1928), deals with the development of an idealistic young Southerner.

Roark Bradford, of Memphis and West Tennessee, presents the Southern Negro with more realism and appreciative understanding than did many earlier writers. *Ol' King David an' the Philistine Boys* (1930) and the John Henry stories (1931) are the result of years of study and association with the workers of plantation, river, and city. In 1927 Bradford's short story, "Child of God," won the O. Henry Award; *Green Pastures,* Marc Connelly's stage adaptation of Bradford's *Ol' Man Adam and His Chillun* (1928) was awarded the Pulitzer Prize in 1930. His latest book, *The Three Headed Angel* (1936), has the Tennessee hills for its background.

Negroes who have been concerned with problems of their race are George Lee (*Beale Street;* 1934); Thomas Talley (*Negro Folk Rhymes;* 1922), George McClellan (*The Pathway of Dreams;* 1916), and Thomas O. Fuller (*A Pictorial History of the American Negro;* 1935).

Poetry of the period revolves around the Fugitive group, which was organized at Vanderbilt University in 1922, under the leadership of John Crowe Ransom, Donald Davidson, Ridley Wills, Merrill Moore, and Allen Tate. These poets have announced that "to the last degree in their poems they are self-convicted experimentalists." Through the *Fugitive,* a magazine of poetry published for three years at Nashville, the group has left its mark on present-day thought in the South. The work of Ransom, a student of John Donne, was first appreciated in England. The author of three books of poetry, *Poems about God* (1919), *Chills and Fever*

(1922), and *Two Gentlemen in Bonds* (1927); the religious work, *God Without Thunder* (1930); and numerous critical articles, he has received many poetry awards and a Guggenheim fellowship. Davidson is thoroughly Southern in his critical essays and in his two volumes of lyric and narrative poetry, *The Tall Men* (1927) and *Lee in the Mountains and Other Poems* (1938). Merrill Moore, of Nashville, adapts the sonnet form to modern thought in his *The Noise that Time Makes* (1929) and *Six Sides to a Man* (1935).

An outgrowth of the Fugitives is the Agrarian group. In the anthology *I'll Take My Stand* (1930), "all articles tend to suggest a Southern way of life against what may be called the American or prevailing way; and all as much as agree that the best terms in which to represent the distinction are contained in the phrase, Agrarian versus Industrial." In *Who Owns America? A New Declaration of Independence* (1936), jointly edited by Herbert Agar and Allen Tate, twenty-one essayists suggest what they believe to be the best means of bringing about adjustments necessary to save the democratic way of life. The Tennessee Agrarians include Ransom, Tate, Davidson, Frank Owsley, and Lyle Lanier.

One of the ranking critics in the South is Dr. Edwin Mims, head of the English department of Vanderbilt University and contributor to the *Dictionary of American Biography,* the *Encyclopedia Britannica,* and other scholarly publications. Dr. Mims has made a special study of the poetry of Sidney Lanier. *The Advancing South* (1926) and *Adventurous America* (1929) are excellent presentations of his critical opinion.

Dr. Walter Clyde Curry, a member of the Vanderbilt English department, is an authority on Chaucer and Shakespeare. His *Chaucer and the Medieval Sciences* (1926) is a close study of Medieval medicines and the part they played in the *Canterbury Tales. Philosophical Patterns in Shakespeare* (1937) is the most recent work in his series of literary interpretations.

Samuel Cole Williams, of Johnson City, has made significant contributions to Southern historical writing in his *Early Travels in Tennessee* (1926–28), *The Lost State of Franklin* (1930), *Beginnings of West Tennessee* (1933), *General John T. Wilder* (1935), and *Dawn of Tennessee Valley and Tennessee History* (1937). His accounts of pioneer life and government are carefully documented and accurate and show a broad outlook, free from provincialism. Judge Williams' lifetime connection with the State bar furnished first-hand material for his *History of Codification in Tennessee* (1932). He has edited *Timberlake's Memoirs* (1927),

Adair's History of the American Indian (1930), and an eight-volume *Annotated Code of Tennessee* (1934–35).

Philip Hamer, of Knoxville, is the author of the four-volume *Tennessee, a History* (1933), which is recognized as a standard work. Colonel Austin P. Foster, of Nashville, a man well-versed in Tennessee history, wrote (with John Trotwood Moore) *Tennessee, the Volunteer State* (1923), a book that is both readable and useful. Dr. Robert White, of Nashville, is a student of contemporary life. His *Tennessee, Its Growth and Progress* (1936) has been adopted by the State textbook commission for school use. *The Sequel of Appomattox* (1921), by Walter L. Fleming, of Nashville, is a study of Reconstruction days. Frank Owsley, of Nashville, has described in *King Cotton Diplomacy* (1931) the Confederacy's long and unsuccessful effort to gain the friendship and support of Europe. Robert Selph Henry, a native of Clifton, has given an authentic interpretation of the war period in *The Story of the Confederacy* (1931) and *The Story of Reconstruction* (1938).

George Fort Milton, Jr., editor of the Chattanooga *News,* is the author of *The Age of Hate* (1930), a biography of Andrew Johnson, and *The Eve of Conflict* (1934), a study of Stephen A. Douglas and the "needless war." Andrew Nelson Lytle, of Murfreesboro, author of the biography, *Bedford Forrest and His Critter Company* (1931), has also written a fine historical novel of the War between the States, *The Long Night* (1936), in which the Battle of Shiloh is vividly described. Among Tennesseans who have written biographies of Andrew Jackson are James Parton (*A Life of Andrew Jackson;* 1859–60), and Samuel G. Heiskell (*Andrew Jackson and Early Tennessee History;* 1918). Richard Halliburton, of Memphis, with *The Royal Road to Romance* (1925), *The Flying Carpet* (1932), and other books of travel, has appeared regularly on the best-seller lists. T. H. Alexander, of Franklin, writer for the Nashville *Tennessean,* is one of the leading contemporary columnists in the State.

Of late years Tennessee newspapers have become almost indistinguishable from other standard papers published in the United States. The Nashville *Tennessean,* the Nashville *Banner,* the Knoxville *Journal,* the Chattanooga *Times,* or the Memphis *Press-Scimitar* might well be printed in Seattle, Miami, or Bangor, so far as style and makeup are concerned. Only on the editorial pages are found traces of the vigorous individualism which was the hallmark of Tennessee journalism in the early days. As late as 1908, Edward Ward Carmack, editor of the Nashville *Tennessean,* was assassinated in the heart of the downtown district of the capital city because of his strong anti-liquor editorials.

Among present-day Tennessee papers of pre-Civil war vintage are the Memphis *Commercial Appeal* (1840), the Nashville *Tennessean* (1812), the Franklin *Review Appeal* (1813). Influential among county papers are: the Clarksville *Leaf-Chronicle* (1808), the Athens *Post-Athenian* (1838), the Columbia *Herald* (1850), the Gallatin *Examiner-Tennessean,* the Pulaski *Citizen* (1854), and the Cleveland *Banner* (1854). The drift of population to the cities has caused a sharp decrease in the number of county papers. At the same time, due to consolidation and the economic depression, the total number of the State's news publications has declined rapidly. From 302 in 1913 there remained only 181 in 1937; of these, 148 are weekly and 33 are daily papers.

The South's native contribution to music has received interesting treatment by Tennessee writers. *Folk Songs of the American Negro* (1915), the work of John Wesley Work, Sr. (completed by his son, John Work, Jr., of Nashville), is the first serious study by a Negro of the musical expression of his race. In the same field JamesWeldon Johnson's *The Book of American Negro Spirituals* (1929) is widely known. Dr. Johnson, who was a resident of Nashville, was a poet and scholar, as well as a writer and collector of songs. His talents are represented by *The Autobiography of an Ex-Colored Man* (1912), a novel; *God's Trombones* (1927), seven Negro sermons in verse; and *Along This Way* (1933), an autobiography. George Pullen Jackson, of Nashville, made a detailed study of mountain folk music in *White Spirituals in the Southern Uplands* (1933). W. C. Handy, of Memphis, composer of the "St. Louis Blues," is the author of *Blues, an Anthology* (1926), a study of jazz.

The folk background of this literature of music and the general interest in genre writing may indicate the trend of Tennessee literature of the future.

Architecture

THE pioneer settler came to Tennessee from Virginia and North Carolina, with ax, adz, wedge, frow, and drawknife as carefully included in his traveling kit as were his gunpowder, metal, and mold. His first buildings were by no means places of comfort and refinement, but they were stanchly built.

These early one-room log cabins were cell-like structures about twelve by sixteen feet in size. The logs varied from one to two feet in diameter, but were dressed down to a thickness of about six inches, giving the walls a flat surface both inside and out. Their corners interlocked and they were sawed off flush to make a sharp angle. Spaces between the logs were chinked with chips and mud. The cabin floor was hard-packed dirt. The first fireplaces were of dressed logs; the fireback was of earth, pounded until it became nearly solid. Chimneys were of wattled saplings daubed with mud. The simple pitch roof was covered with hand-split shingles that were held in place by weight poles. In rare instances the cabin was two stories high, with a second floor overhang, following the medieval method of timber construction. The larger settlements had fortresses where everyone could gather in case of attack. These were usually stockade-enclosed groups of log houses. Fort Nashborough, originally built in 1780 by James Robertson and his party, has been reconstructed on its original site in Nashville under the supervision of Joseph W. Hart. It is an accurate reproduction of the pioneer log fort.

A gradual refinement of the one-room log cabin took place. Puncheon floors of split logs replaced dirt packing, rock fireplaces supplanted those of sapling and mud construction; and, as Indian attacks slackened, windows replaced loopholes. Still at a disadvantage for want of tools and devices, the pioneer found it difficult to enlarge his home. Since heavy logs were hard to frame, it was simpler to build another cabin than to make an addition. Thus came the "dog-trot" or "breezeway" houses: two separate identical cabins, six to twelve feet apart, with a roofed over passage between. The pioneer had chanced upon a happy expedient. The open passage or dog-trot, though somewhat breezy and cold during the winter, was comfortable and convenient during the summer months. The dog-trot house is the traditional building type of the isolated hill folk. It is also often used in more or less crude form by sharecroppers and tenant farmers, as well as by small farm owners throughout the State, chiefly because, in addition to other advantages, it is inexpensive and easy to build. Architects have classified the dog-trot house as Tennessee's principal indigenous architectural type and have found ways in which to modernize it, using the fundamental plan as the basis for their improved designs.

All log cabins did not evolve into dog-trot cabins. There were many in which there was no improvement, while in others the settlers added rooms by interlocking or by a double wall. Such forms, however, were exceptions rather than the rule. After sawmills were established many cabins were clapboarded, and some became the nuclei of larger and more pretentious dwellings.

Planed boards were first used in 1792, when William Blount built one of the first frame houses west of the Allegheny Mountains. This house, referred to as the Mansion, is described in *Ramsey's Annals* as "finished with some taste, and the grounds better improved than any in town."

Seth Smith, who came to the Watauga section from Pennsylvania in 1791, designed and constructed the first stone house in the State. He was a stone-mason, but in the execution of his work he was perforce also the architect and contractor. He built four stone houses in or near Limestone, Tennessee, which answered the dual purpose of settlement-fort and residence. The Gillespie house, built in 1792, is the only one of these structures still in a good state of preservation. In renovating this house there have been introduced some departures from the original design. Originally, the house was a plain two-story structure with simple pitch roof and little if any detail. The walls, which have not been altered, are of limestone, thirty inches thick at the foundation, twenty-four inches thick at first floor level, and eighteen inches thick at second floor level. Interior walls are of wood stud construction; the flooring is of random width and length pine, laid on hand-hewn joists. The roof, its lines since altered by the addition of dormers, was originally of hand-split shingles laid on round posts or trunks of small trees.

Rock Castle, near Hendersonville, might well have been the first stone house in the State had not its construction been delayed for seven years by an Indian massacre, in which the original artisans were killed. This seven-room stone structure, designed and constructed by Gen. Daniel Smith, a surveyor, was one of the first houses in the State to show architectural planning, being influenced by the Georgian Colonial homes of the Eastern Seaboard, from which General Smith had orginally come.

FORT NASHBOROUGH, NASHVILLE

The early years of the nineteenth century were marked by the gradual use of hand-made brick. Buildings throughout the new State began to take advantage of the unusually abundant natural resources, principally limestone, quartz, and the plentiful brick and enamel clays. Styles followed in somewhat crude fashion the late Georgian Colonial mode of the Eastern Seaboard. They were plain structures and, though lacking in many of the classical embellishments of their prototypes in Virginia, the Carolinas, and certain regions of the Middle Atlantic, they were large and substantial. On his flatboat journeys to New Orleans, the Tennessean saw a type of construction that appealed to him. He liked the long verandas of the Spanish builders and decided to incorporate them in his own home. Cragfont, near Gallatin, built by Gen. James Winchester in 1802, is one of the first examples of this type. The house was built in the form of a "T" with the stem forming the back wing. The main section was Georgian Colonial in treatment, but the wing included first and second floor Spanish galleries extending the full length on each side.

By 1825, construction in Tennessee showed signs of improved planning. Wealthy planters, aided by details and plans appearing in early architectural books, began to build pretentious homes. They superintended their own operations and employed slave labor almost exclusively. Among the early carpenters and contractors to enter the State were Samuel Cleage and his son-in-law Thomas Crutchfield. They came from Virginia, bringing their families and many skilled slaves. All along their route they secured contracts and erected houses, their slaves making brick and hewing lumber. A similar firm was formed by Joseph Rieff and William C. Hume, who settled in Nashville. The most noted example of their work was the rebuilding of the Hermitage in 1835. This lovely estate, built for Andrew Jackson, retains all the flavor of the antebellum architecture and is typical of the Tennessee planter's home.

The thirty-five years from the beginning of steamboat transportation to the War between the States marked a period of great prosperity in the South. The land was fertile, cotton and tobacco were in great demand, rivers were becoming crowded with traffic, and the large plantation owners engaged in elaborate home-making projects which gave the State its famous antebellum architecture.

The Tennessee plantation home, like those of other southern States, was dressed up in borrowed finery. It followed no single style; instead, such details were incorporated as best suited the planter's taste. The result was a fusion of styles, representing in most instances a combination of Williamsburg, Natchez, and New Orleans Garden District influences. The house was usually large with a classic façade designed in the manner of Jefferson's Classical Revival, as well as in the more strictly classic manner of the Greek Revival of the 30's and 50's. Oversized rooms, high ceilings, winding stairs, large rear galleries, and temple-like porticoes, beautifully colonnaded, were the dominant features. Gardens were landscaped, and the slave quarters, set apart like a small seigniorial village, sometimes housed more than a hundred Negroes. Ante bellum architecture featured both square shafts and round columns, but fluted shafts with Ionic capitals predominated. There were first and second floor porches as well as the single veranda, large Spanish galleries as well as delicate Italian balconies.

In 1825 Thomas Baker built Foxland Hall, five miles south of Gallatin, possibly the best-preserved building of its period in this section. The sturdy two-story brick structure is designed in the Greek Revival style with massive columns across the entire façade reaching up to the roof. Fairview, one mile closer to Gallatin, was erected seven years later by Isaac Franklin and was known in its day as "the finest country home in Tennessee." The original section of the house was Georgian Colonial, but a few years later an addition was made that was definitely Spanish. This fusion of design is easily explained, for besides his 5,000-acre plantation in Tennessee, Franklin owned several large plantations in the Felicien Parish of Louisiana, where Spanish architecture was widely used.

Some of the best examples of the ante bellum Greek Revival architecture are in Maury County, just south of Columbia. Among these are the three Pillow homes, built by the sons of Gideon Pillow. Clifton Place, Pillow-Bethel Place, Pillow-Haliday Place, all still in use, follow the same architectural plan, large brick structures featuring a central entrance façade in the general classic mode. The three Polk homes, built by the sons of William Polk, are also in the Greek Revival style but vary in plan. Each son, it seems, tried to outdo the other in building his home. Rattle and Snap, the last of the Polk mansions, was completed in 1845. This is an unusual structure, with ten magnificent Corinthian columns extending the full height of the spacious two-story front. The interior is columned, and features two spiral stairways and also two dining rooms that, on special occasions, were opened into one great banquet hall.

Public buildings as well as homes underwent a change at this time. Many new buildings were erected to replace those already outmoded. Churches and schools, heretofore housed in cabins, were given more ambitious settings. Business houses were built in rows of three- or four-story buildings with little or no variation except perhaps in the treatment of window or doorway detail. A number of these buildings still exist in the business sections of the cities, changed only by remodeling of the lower story.

Maj. A. Heiman was one of the first skilled architects to make Tennessee his permanent home. He designed the huge suspension bridge that spanned the Cumberland River at Nashville until 1862, when it was destroyed by the retreating Confederate forces. His works, for the most part, were in the castellated Gothic Revival style, and he designed a number of homes as well as public and semi-public buildings in this style. This style was contemporary with the Greek Revival and played a significant part in the romantic movement of the early nineteenth century. The best example of his work, still in existence, is the Castle Building, now a part of Austin Peay Normal School at Clarksville. He was employed to design the State capitol, but the plans of William Strickland, one of America's greatest early architects, were accepted instead.

Strickland, an outstanding exponent of the Greek Revival in America, acquired his architectural training under the renowned Benjamin Latrobe. In 1836 Strickland had been one of the organizers and the first president of the American Institution of Architects, the organization which anticipated the later founding (1857) of the American Institute of Architects. His classic designs in Philadelphia, which included the Merchants Exchange (1845), the United States Naval Asylum (1827), the United States Mint (1829), and restorations at Independence Hall (1828), had brought him fame. He was acknowledged as America's first native born and educated architect of note. The State capitol at Nashville, an original adaptation of Greek forms to a public building, is regarded as one of Strickland's best works.

The capitol conforms in every respect to Strickland's original design, as may be seen from a comparison with his report to the State legislature on May 20, 1845. The dimensions, according to the architect, were to be, including the porticoes, 232 feet by 124 feet, with a surrounding flagged terrace or platform 18 feet in width. "The architecture of the building consists of a Doric basement, four Ionic porticoes, two of eight and two of six columns four feet in diameter, surmounted by a Corinthian tower in the center of the roof, the whole height of which is to be 170 feet from the summit of the site. The porticoes are after the order of the Erechtheum, and the tower from the Choragic monument of Lysicrates in Athens. . . ."

When Strickland died, April 7, 1854, his body was buried in a vault in the north wall, where he had prepared his own resting place. The capitol, completed by his son, Francis, has been in constant use since 1853, when it was first occupied by the legislature.

During the nine years of Strickland's life in Tennessee his services were in great demand. He was a master of Greek design, and expressed himself in many structures in that mode. He demonstrated his versatility in designing a few luxurious houses in the manner of Italian villas, while the First Presbyterian Church in Nashville is reminiscent of Egyptian architecture. His influence on Tennessee architecture has been such that public buildings consonant with the capitol are favored throughout the State; similarly, his domestic designs have had a wide influence.

The firm of Wills and Dudley, of New York, designed Holy Trinity Church (1852) and the Church of the Advent (1857–1866), both in Nashville. These edifices are still acknowledged as the purest examples of the Gothic Revival style in the State. Holy Trinity is suggestive of the English village parish church. It is a small, blue limestone building with exposed roof trusses of polished cedar. The Church of the Advent, now the property of the Christian Science Church, is designed in the Pointed Gothic style. It is larger than Holy Trinity, and is constructed of native limestone, with a high pitched roof, the first roof entirely of slate put up in Tennessee.

West Tennessee was the last section of the State to be settled. Memphis was not laid out until 1819, and for thirty years the future western metropolis could boast no buildings of architectural significance. But during the decade before secession there was a considerable building boom. A number of architects had by this time settled in Memphis, and the directory of 1859 listed James B. Cook, Calvin Fay, Fletcher and Winter, P. H. Hammerscold, and Morgan and Baldwin, as trained architects. These men were responsible for a marked improvement in domestic and ecclesiastical architecture, and developed a superior type of commercial building. In Memphis the most noted buildings of the ante bellum period are the Greek House, the Hunt-Phelan Place, the Pettite Home, the Robertson-Top Home, the Gayoso Hotel (since altered), Chelsea Church, Calvary Episcopal Church, St. Mary's Catholic Church, and Irving and Adams Blocks.

The War between the States blotted out prosperity in the South. Many of the homes and buildings throughout the State were left in ruins, landscaped gardens were mutilated, public buildings, churches, and schools were converted into buildings of war—arsenals, hospitals, and the like. Of the beautiful homes that remained, few could be maintained in their former splendor. Large plantations were divided, and rented or sold as it became impossible to maintain them. The small farm, the tenant farm, and the sharecropper farm came to Tennessee. There were few if any noteworthy buildings on these smaller farms; the majority were either log cabins or one-room rip-sawed board-and-batten shacks.

Recovery was a long time getting under way and for this reason architectural excesses of the Queen Anne and Victorian styles, flourishing in the rest of the country in the eighties, did not make much headway in the South. Toward the end of the nineteenth century, when building was revived in Tennessee, designers had returned to Georgian Colonial and Classical Revival models for inspiration. The Chicago Exposition (1893) contributed to a countrywide return to the classic mode; the Centennial Exposition (1897), at Nashville, brought it to Tennessee. It was at the latter fair that the Municipal Art Gallery, a full-sized model of the Parthenon in Athens, was built. Intended to be only a temporary structure, this building was constructed of wood and plaster, but stood out in such singular beauty that it was left standing at the close of the exposition. In 1922, it was rebuilt in the exact Athenian dimensions and now bears the name of its prototype, the Parthenon. Architects for the reproduction were Hart, Freeland, and Roberts; sculptors were Geo. J. Zolnay, Belle Kinney, and Leopold Scholz.

The designs of public and semi-public buildings are based upon America's two dominant schools of architecture: the neo-Classic, led by McKim, Mead, and White; and the neo-Gothic, led by Cram, Goodhue, and Ferguson. Government buildings in the State are usually of modified Greek design, though somewhat bare for lack of sculpture. In each county seat is a "square," of one or two square blocks, in the center of which stands a courthouse with porticoes or fluted colonnades at two or sometimes all four sides. A number of college buildings are modifications of Jeffersonian Classicism, influenced by the University of Virginia, their design accentuated by colonnades and pedimented porticoes. But in the other group are the recent churches and colleges that tend to follow the Gothic style, with cloisters of sturdy piers and groined cross vaulting, deeply recessed windows and doors, buttressed walls, and pinnacled towers. Some of these, further accentuated by walls of varicolored sandstone, are the Church Street M. E. Church at Knoxville, Scarritt College at Nashville, Southwestern Presbyterian University and the Idlewilde Presbyterian Church at Memphis, and the University of the South, at Sewanee. Scarritt and Southwestern are two works of Henry C. Hibbs of Nashville, who in 1929 was awarded the gold medals of the American Institute of Architects for excellence in ecclesiastical and educational architecture, respectively.

THE STERRICK BUILDING, MEMPHIS

There are few skyscrapers in Tennessee. The Sterrick Building, in Memphis, completed in 1930, with 29 stories above street level and a height of 364 feet, is the tallest in the State. Designed by Wyatt C. Hendrick, the structure is Gothic in detail and conforms to the modern set-back type. In the city shopping centers, plain fireproof buildings with brightly colored fronts are generally favored. The tendency is to remodel the exteriors of the old business houses, and very few completely new buildings are erected in the congested trading areas.

The inclination in Tennessee, as elsewhere, is for the exclusive sections of cities to edge toward the suburbs. Many of the modern homes in the suburban areas are of the traditional antebellum mode, similar to the old plantation homes but smaller in scale. In the rural sections, suburban city architecture is imitated wherever possible, but on smaller farms rough frame houses continue to be in vogue. Many old log cabins are still in use in the isolated areas, some with raised roofs and added lofts. Dog-trot houses have been developed with main central chambers in place of the former runway. Throughout most of the State, utility is becoming almost as decisive a factor as it was in pioneer days, and there is a marked return to the small one-family house that more than matches the development of the apartment dwellings in the larger cities.

At the present time (1939), Tennessee is experiencing a more rapid development in construction than at any other time previous to the War between the States. This new era of building has been brought about by the combined Federally assisted projects and the Tennessee Valley Authority. The principal housing project of Tennessee is the Cumberland Homestead, 3.5 miles southeast of Crossville. This is one of the subsistence homesteads established in 1933 by the National Recovery Act, whereby a stranded population was reestablished on farming lands and unemployed workers removed from congested areas. The site is a 10,000-acre plot on the eastern edge of the Cumberland Plateau, more than half of which is suitable for farming and almost one-fourth destined to remain in permanent forest. The homesteader secures complete ownership of his property by paying a small rental for about twenty years. He chooses his home from several standard designs. Each house is built of local stone, with shingle roof and wood trim. Many of the building materials are obtained on the land.

Slum clearance and housing projects in the larger cities have also made great headway. Compact project houses, by prominent architects, have modern conveniences. They are row houses, comprising four to six units and so arranged that each unit has individual yard space and private front and

DIXIE HOMES, A FEDERAL HOUSING PROJECT FOR NEGROES, MEMPHIS

rear entrances. The units comprise from two to five rooms, the larger ones having a second story. The architects have shown a preference for a modified Georgian Colonial style in the design of these projects; a two-story central portion of four units is flanked on each end by a one-story wing. The interiors are so arranged as to utilize to the best advantage each foot of floor space. Electric refrigeration and stoves are provided. Heat (furnished from a central heating plant), water, and electricity are included in the rent.

The future architecture of the Tennessee Valley is indicated by the city of Norris, where a new standard for rural existence is being set. This town was born of the practical necessity of housing about 1,500 men engaged in the construction of the dam. Preliminary plans determined the street network possible in the hilly terrain, and three focal points were established: a community center, a construction camp, and a shop center. Around these points the streets with 350 houses were laid out. Arrangement, comfort, and modern equipment were the principal concerns of the architects. American precedent and local customs were taken into account, but the stress was on economy and residential convenience. For variety in appearance the exteriors were finished in brick, concrete, stone, shingle, and board-and-batten. Of the various designs employed, the favorite was a modern adaptation of the dog-trot dwelling. Here kitchen and dining quarters are on one side, sleeping quarters on the opposite side, with the center—an open passage in the log cabin days—arranged as the living room. The loft or low second story is used for spare bedrooms or storage. Electrical equipment has been provided to an extent unusual for moderately priced homes, including in many cases electrical heating.

The dams and power plants of the Tennessee Valley Authority deserve mention in any consideration of Tennessee architecture. These towering masses of concrete and steel are impressive and modern in form, harmonious in lighting and color scheme. Technicians of the Authority have succeeded in combining economy with significant design by well-studied organization and proportioning of spaces and masses, and by renouncing all surface detail and embellishment.

The Tennessee builder has been slow to recognize architectural fads, but encourages the development of proven styles. This accounts for recent architectural achievements of decided quality, seen in the State's suburban residential houses and in ecclesiastical and educational buildings.

The Arts

AS IN all pioneer territories, early settlers in Tennessee were concerned primarily with things other than art; and even when some measure of civilization had been achieved, portraiture was the only type of painting in demand. The pioneer folk of Tennessee produced, however, an exceedingly rich assortment of handicrafts and domestic patterns. Spinning, hand-weaving, furniture-, broom-, and basket-making, and coverlet-making—an intimate and especially prized art of the mountain folk—constituted Tennessee's earliest and most native participation in American art.

Painting and Sculpture

Not until past the first decade of the nineteenth century is there record of a professional artist in Tennessee. William Edward West came from Philadelphia, where he had studied under Sully, and spent several years in various parts of the State, finally making his home in Nashville. He excelled in "fancy cabinet portraits"; and in 1822, under the patronage of a local admirer, West went to Europe, where he painted many portraits, including likenesses of Lord Byron and Percy Bysshe Shelley, and exhibited at the Royal Academy. He was a close friend of Washington Irving and illustrated *The Pride of the Village* and *Annette Delabre.* In 1843, West returned to Nashville, where he remained until his death in 1857.

The "man of a thousand portraits," Washington Cooper, moved from Washington County to Nashville in 1830. By 1838 he was at the height of his popularity and was kept continually busy with commissions. During his most active years he averaged thirty-five portraits a year, painting governors, bishops, master Masons, and members of leading Nashville families. He died in 1889 at the age of 87. His younger brother, William Brown Cooper, also painted portraits, and the similarity of their signatures caused considerable confusion between the works of the two artists.

About 1850 James Cameron, who painted landscapes as well as portraits, came to Chattanooga from Scotland. He built his home on a bluff which has been called "Cameron Hill" in his honor. His *A View of the Bluff and Valley,* painted in 1859, hangs in the Chattanooga Public Library.

Here, as in all his paintings, Cameron's close attention to realistic detail is evident.

In 1869, a young man named Melchior Thoni came from Switzerland and soon established himself in Nashville as a woodcarver and cabinet-maker. Among his many sculptural enterprises, Thoni designed and carved the first wooden animals to stand upon a "Flying Jenny" (merry-go-round).

John W. Dodge, a noted nineteenth century miniaturist, moved from New York to Cumberland County, where he engaged in apple culture on a large scale until his death in 1893. Portraits by Dodge include studies of Andrew Jackson, Henry Clay, Daniel Webster, and Thomas Marshall.

Several Tennessee artists gained wide recognition in the nineties. The most famous of these was George De Forest Brush, who was born in Shelbyville in 1885. Brush studied at the National Academy of Design in New York and with Gérôme at the Ecole des Beaux Arts in Paris. His paintings of Indian life as well as the later group portraits of his wife and children have been highly praised. Among his Indian works *Silence Broken, Mourning Her Brave,* and *The Sculptor and the King* illustrate his dignified composition and his sincere and elevated imagination. *In the Garden* (Metropolitan Museum, New York), *Mother and Children* (Pennsylvania Academy), and *Family Group* (Art Institute, Chicago) represent his domestic phase.

Other Tennessee artists who emerged in the nineties were Charles Frederick Naegele, a Knoxville portrait painter who studied with Collier, Sartain, and Chase; and Willie Bettie Newman, of Murfreesboro, who worked under Laurens, Bachet, Bouguereau, and Constant. Miss Newman lived in Normandy and Brittany for some time and painted peasant life there; in 1900 she received honorable mention at the Salon. Frank Wilbert Stokes of Nashville, who studied under Thomas Eakins at the Pennsylvania Academy, Ecole des Beaux Arts, and at Colarossi's and Julian's Academies, was the artist member of the Peary North Greenland Expedition in 1892 and 1893–94. Later he was a member of both the Swedish Antarctic and the Amundsen-Ellsworth Expeditions. Two well-known expedition paintings by Stokes are *Return of Commander Byrd and Floyd Bennett from the North Pole* and *Departure of the "Norge" for the North Pole.* In 1907, he did the mural decorations for the American Museum of Natural History in New York City. Sara Ward Cooley, Nashville artist, studied in Paris and received several exhibition prizes in Europe and America. A later artist is Matilda Lotz, of Franklin, who was educated in San Francisco and Paris. She has exhibited in America, England, Vienna, and Budapest. Rhea Wells and McCullough Partee are widely known as illustrators.

The historic Gayoso Hotel in Memphis houses a series of interesting murals by Newton Alonzo Wells (1852–1923) portraying episodes in the life of Hernando de Soto and events associated with the exploration of the Mississippi River. In the lobby of the Hermitage Hotel in Nashville is an excellent collection of murals, including a narrative in twelve paintings devoted to the Confederate Soldier in the War between the States, by Gilbert Gaul (William Gilbert), a noted genre painter (1855–1919). Among the country's noteworthy murals are those on the walls of the library at Fisk University, painted in the 1930's by Aaron K. Douglass, well-known Negro artist. Conceived in terms by symbolic rather than realistic presentation, the murals, whose theme is the history of the Negro, are in marked contrast with other murals in the State. Fisk University also exhibits the Baldridge Collection, a gift of Samuel Insull, which constitutes one of the most complete records of Negro life and types to be found in America. Cyrus Le Roy Baldridge spent fourteen months in Africa making these drawings, which fall into sixty-eight descriptive groups of nearly three hundred studies.

During the past few decades, efforts have been made to stimulate local interest and activity in art. The Brooks Memorial Art Gallery in Overton Park, Memphis, established in 1916, has been visited by more than 45,000 persons in a single year, and conducts a comprehensive program of exhibitions and education. In 1936 the Brooks Memorial Art League, with the assistance of the Works Progress Administration, succeeded in setting up a systematized art library, the first in the State. Another important institution in Memphis is the James Lee Memorial Academy of Arts. This school, founded in 1925, is already prominent in the South as a free center of instruction in the arts. It has a large student enrollment, and the City of Memphis and the Memphis Art Association contribute to its support. The Art Gallery of the famous reproduction of the Parthenon in Nashville contains the Cowan Collection of Paintings, which includes work by Benjamin West, William Chase, Winslow Homer, Albert Ryder, and George Inness. The pediment sculptures of the building are the work of Belle Kinney Scholz and Leopold F. Scholz, and the metopes are by George Julian Zolnay.

In December 1933 the Federal Government set up an art project in Tennessee, and within one month forty painters, sculptors, and print makers received commissions for murals, portraits, regional industrial scenes, and depictions of historic streets and buildings. After two months of activity, however, the project was brought to a close. In some cases local interests secured the paintings or sculptures for use in public buildings. The board of park commissioners in Memphis appropriated funds for the completion of a series of mural sketches on the walls of the Museum of Natural History. Active centers of the Federal Art Project, set up in 1935, include today the Anderson County Federal Art Center at Norris, the University of Chattanooga WPA Federal Art Gallery, and the LeMoyne Federal Art Center at LeMoyne College (Negro) in Memphis. These centers have gained the support and cooperation of local institutions and individuals, and their exhibits, lectures, and classes in arts and crafts have awakened wide popular response. These governmental enterprises have helped to revive interest in local art and have touched new sources of artistic energy.

Handicrafts continued to survive in the mountain regions of Tennessee long after machine production had destroyed them in other sections of the United States. The preservation of indigenous crafts and their further development have been the concern of the Southern Handicraft Guild, with which several Tennessee handicraft centers are affiliated. The Federal Art Project centers have also devoted much effort to instruction in and encouragement of native crafts.

An exciting event in the art world was the recent "discovery" of William Edmunson, a Negro carver of tombstones in Nashville. The sculpture of this genuine folk artist has been exhibited in the Museum of Modern Art in New York City and has been much commented upon in the press. Edmunson's Biblical figures, with their sculptural solidity and genial fancy, have struck an original note in modern American art.

Typical of contemporary trends in Tennessee art were the State selections for the National Exhibition of American Art at Rockefeller Center, May 1936. These consisted of two sculptures by Harold Cash of Chattanooga and a group of paintings, the majority of which were by Nashville artists. Cash, born in Chattanooga in 1895, has worked in Paris under modernist influence.

Thomas Puryear Mims, Nashville sculptor, has shown heads, figures, and decorative work in various exhibits in New York and elsewhere. Outstanding in his work are character interpretations of the Tennessee Negro, farmer, and backwoods types. Hugh Poe, of Knoxville, is recognized mainly for his pastels, though his oil portraits hang in many Tennessee homes and a group of his murals decorate the walls of Culver Military Academy, Indiana. The oils and lithographs of Alene Gray Wharton, of Nashville, are notable for their stylized characterization of mountain villages and common folk.

F. Louis Mora

ABUNDANCE, MURAL IN POST OFFICE, CLARKSVILLE

Outstanding among Tennessee cartoonists are Carey Orr and Joe Parrish, now of the Chicago *Tribune,* Tom Little and John Cross, of the Nashville *Tennessean,* and Jack Knox, of the Memphis *Commercial-Appeal.*

The following artists are listed in *Who's Who in American Art* for Tennessee in 1937: Mayna Treanor Avent, Frank M. Baisden, Charles Cagle, Sarah Ward Conley, Edith E. Flisher, J. H. Goodrich, Howard Henry, Ella Sophonisba Hergesheimer, Irene Charlesworth Johnson, J. B. Jordan, Lalla Walker Lewis, Bessie Dawson McGavock, Karl Oberteuffer, Ernest A. Pickup, Bertha Potter, Mrs. Fay S. Rule, C. M. Said, L. Pearl Saunders, Elisabeth Searcy, Jascha Shaffran, Myrtis Smith, Rosalie Sandheimer, Clarence A. Stagg, Ann Williams.

Music

A fiddler, old Ned Jacobs, was the first settler in Lebanon, and two other fiddlers, equally famed in pioneer stories, were among the first comers at Bledsoe Station and Nashville. Ballads, fiddle tunes, and spirituals—both white and Negro—were an integral part of early Tennessee life and have continued to hold a place of importance. From them have developed the State's two most significant contributions to American music, the spiritual and the blues.

The mountain people of East Tennessee sing songs of every type, survivals of old English and Scottish ballads, native folk songs, and tunes of recent origin. Cecil J. Sharp, the English folksong collector, writes of the wealth and variety of mountain folksong in his *English Folk Songs of the Southern Appalachians,* and says: "I found myself for the first time in my life in a community in which singing was a common and almost as universal a practice as speaking."

A great body of spiritual songs came into existence during the first decades of the nineteenth century as part of the Wesleyan trend in rural religious life. Some of the tunes were adaptations of chants used in medieval times and others were borrowed from popular ballads. The "white spirituals," as these religious songs are called, gathered strength through the old-time singing schools and the shape-note song books, such as the *Sacred Harp* (1844) and *Harp of Columbia* (1849). White spirituals are still heard in "big singings" in the Tennessee Valley and in the hill country from the Virginia to the Alabama line. Farther to the west they are sung in the Primitive Baptist churches.

The Negroes gave themselves enthusiastically to this manner of singing, and lent to the songs so much of their peculiar racial talent, that many white spirituals have been widely accepted as of Negro origin. The best of the spirituals, such as "Swing Low, Sweet Chariot" and "Go Down, Moses," are true Negro creations, both words and tune. Even in cases where spirituals can be traced to earlier white songs, the Negro has invariably bettered the tunes and often transformed a doggerel text into excellent poetry. Some melodies that are thought to have been first sung in Tennessee are "Has Anbody Here Seen My Lord?" "I'm All Wore Out A-Toiling fo' de Lawd," "I'm Troubled in Mind," "My Brudder's Died and Gone to Hebben," and "When the Lord Called Moses."

The non-religious songs of the Negro mirror his attitude on everyday life. Among the better known of these are "Sweet Tennessee," "I'm on My Last Go-Round," "Here Come Dat Inshawnce Man Collectin'," "Make Me a Pallet on de Floor," and "Joe Turner." Whether the Negro is working on the levee, in the cotton fields, at the washtub, or "just workin'," bodily rhythm accompanies his singing. Improvised tunes lighten the burden of labor. "Dis Ol' Hammer," "Don't Grieve about a Dime," "Working My Blame Head Off," and "Push-uh-Push" are work songs current in Middle Tennessee.

The whites also have their work songs, brought into mill town life from their mountain homes. Old traditional melodies are often used with new words, telling of unions, strikes, and current events. Government activity in the Tennessee Valley has called forth many new verses for the old-time tunes. One of these, set to an old English tune, runs like this:

My name is William Edwards
I live down Cove Creek way
I'm working on the project
They call the TVA

The government begun it
When I was just a child,
But now they are in earnest
And Tennessee's gone wild.

* * * * *

Oh, see them boys a-comin'
Their government they trust
Just hear their hammers ringin'
They'll build that dam or bust.

Music lovers are uncovering and preserving some of the traditional folk songs that had been nearly lost. This work has been stimulated by the folklore and historical societies throughout the State and by the Old Harp Singers, formed in 1932 by Dr. George Pullen Jackson of Vanderbilt University. The tours and radio broadcasts of this organization have done much to arouse public interest in folk music.

The Fisk Jubilee Singers have probably done more than any other group to preserve the Negro spirituals and stimulate interest in this form of American music. The chorus was first organized in 1867 by George L. White, treasurer of Fisk University. He recognized the strange, compelling beauty of the songs sung by the students, almost all of whom were former slaves, and believed that the world, too, would recognize and acclaim them. Encouraged by the success of local concerts, he planned extended tours in the hope of winning friends and funds for the young school. The group, then called the Colored Christian Singers, visited practically all the large cities in the North, the British Isles, and the principal countries of Europe in the 1870's. They were entertained by nobility and royalty, and everywhere their songs aroused first curiosity, then deep interest and admiration.

The work of collecting, harmonizing, and interpreting the spirituals, originally done by northern white men, was gradually taken over by the Fisk students, alumni, and faculty. Authentic dialect was introduced; new songs were discovered and added to the repertoire, among them the present favorites, "Little David, Play on Your Harp," "Witness," "All God's Chillun Got Wings." John W. Work, a member of the university faculty, and his brother Frederick collected spirituals in rural communities, which they published in *New Jubilee Songs* (1905). *Folk Songs of the American Negro* (1915), by the same authors, and Thomas W. Talley's *Negro Folk Rhymes* (1922) also gave this folk music permanent form.

The secular or "sinful" Negro folk songs, known as blues, in which the singer mulls over his troubles, gave rise to another form of music, likewise unique but entirely different in mood. In 1909, William C. Handy, a Negro musician of Memphis, wrote the "Memphis Blues," taking his cue from these songs. The piece, originally called "Mr. Crump" and written as a campaign song for Ed. Crump, who was running for mayor, was immensely popular and Memphians continued to whistle the tune long after the election. Handy followed his first success with the "St. Louis Blues" and the "Beale Street Blues," and inaugurated an era of blues songwriting throughout the country. These commercial blues, with their syncopated rhythm and definite melodic idioms, have exerted a strong and distinct influence on jazz and swing music, and indeed on most contemporary American composition.

Tennessee's vigorous interest in folk music is complemented in urban communities by an active musical life, which found expression in concerts and musical instruction even during the early years of the nineteenth century. Fisk Female Academy, in Overton County, established a music department in 1816; a decade later the Nashville Female Academy and the Knoxville Female Academy followed suit; and in 1836 the Nashville Academy of Music was founded. In the 1850's Jenny Lind appeared under the sponsorship of P. T. Barnum, and Adelina Patti toured the State with the famous Norwegian violinist Ole Bull.

Symphonic music was first brought to Tennessee by Theodore Thomas in the 1870's. Thomas also directed the Memphis Festival Concerts of 1884, sponsored by the Memphis Conservatory of Music and the Mozart Society, and still remembered as one of the musical high lights of this period.

Through the last decades of the nineteenth century and approximately up to the time of the depression, the principal cities of the State were visited by touring opera companies. Memphis for a time had two opera seasons, played by the San Carlos Company of New York and the Chicago Opera Company.

Women's club organizations have played an active part in developing musical appreciation in Tennessee. In 1916 musical activities were merged to form the Tennessee Federation of Music Clubs, which by 1937 included 137 groups.

Among Tennessee's early composers were Henri Christian Webber, a German, who settled in Nashville in the 1850's, and wrote "Blow, Bugle, Blow," "The Storm," and "Centennial March"; Julius C. Meininger, author of "Golden Rays" and "Silver Rays"; and Mrs. E. L. Ashford, whose *Organ Instructions* is said to be the first book of its kind to be translated into Chinese and used in China as a textbook.

Present-day Tennessee composers include Arthur Nevin, Burnet C. Tuthill, and Patrick O'Sullivan of Memphis; C. Roland Flick and Alvin S. Wiggers of Nashville; and Roy Lamont Smith of Chattanooga. Harry

Philbin, the blind composer, and Lyle Tomerlin, both of Memphis, have written popular song hits. Many Tennessee singers have gained national reputations, among them Grace Moore, James Melton and Bessie Smith.

The Theater

Hampered at times by the enmity of religious leaders and, to a lesser degree, by economic difficulties and epidemics of cholera, the theater's development was slow but insistent. The first recorded performance in Nashville was given on December 4, 1807, thirteen years after the last Indian raids in that locality. The program, following the generous custom of the time, was a double bill made up of a drama, *The Child of the Nation, or Virtue Rewarded,* and a farce, *The Purse, or the Benevolent Tar.*

Early in 1816 Samuel Drake, who had come from Albany, New York, to establish theaters in the "western frontier" of Kentucky, included Nashville in his circuit. The following year the old Salt House was converted into the Market Street Theater, and here Drake's company inaugurated a regular theatrical season, opening on July 10 with the comedy *The Soldier's Daughter*. Noah M. Ludlow, in charge of the company, began the next season with *Speed the Plough* and *The Day after the Wedding.* His wife, Mrs. Mary Squires, of Franklin, was probably Tennessee's first professional actress. In 1818 the Thespian Society of Nashville, of which Sam Houston was secretary and Andrew Jackson and Felix Grundy were honorary members, asked Ludlow to direct their activities. In the same year the State's first visiting star, William Jones, of the Park Theater in New York City, played in Nashville and became the idol of the town. James H. Caldwell, a well-known manager, who was competing with Ludlow for popular support, built the city's second theater in 1826.

Sol Smith's Thespians toured the State in 1829, making stops of a week to twelve nights in the leading settlements. Their performances were usually well patronized, despite ministerial warnings that "a brimstone roasting awaits theater-goers." But Smith tells of three consecutive nights in Greeneville, when he played in competition with a Methodist camp meeting, and had a paid attendance of six, five, and seven persons, respectively. Of one of his earlier tours Smith wrote: "The Methodists had raised their banner before us and got possession of all the money and all the hearts of the young folks."

During the nine years from 1830 to 1839 there were 700 performances of 296 plays in Nashville alone. Church opposition, however, had grown so strong by 1839 that the Mill Creek circuit of the Methodist Church resolved "that the practice of attending such places is contrary to the letter and spirit of our discipline and is highly criminal." Tennessee newspapers of this period were full of "the theater controversy."

The forces for and against the theater seem to have been evenly matched. Traveling companies toured the State, and the vacant log cabins and crude platforms which served the early players began to give way to theaters with well-equipped stages. Signor Mondelli, of the New Orleans Theater, is said to have been in Nashville during the 1830's, giving plays with scenic effects which included "real waterfalls, moving boats, storms, and forest settings."

Drama flourished during the War between the States. Stars, such as John Wilkes Booth, Maggie Mitchell, John E. Owens, and Helen Western, played regularly in the Nashville theaters, and provided welcome entertainment in these difficult years. The early Reconstruction period saw the decline of the legitimate theater and the rise in popularity of minstrels and variety shows, which constituted more than half of all theatrical productions by 1875.

Many new theaters were built in the later Reconstruction years, including Staub's Theatre in Knoxville, the Vendome in Nashville, the Lyric Theatre in Memphis, and the Bijou in Chattanooga. These presented the best available legitimate productions. In Tennessee, as elsewhere, road shows became more infrequent after the turn of the century. Most of the old-time theaters were gradually taken over by the movies, though here and there a few still housed occasional stock offerings or road shows. Today the few companies that tour the country make stops in Tennessee and are given enthusiastic support.

But the place left vacant by the decline of the glamorous legitimate theater of a former generation has been filled by the little theater movement. This has been successfully promoted in all the large cities. The leading college towns have drama guilds, usually under academic auspices. The Tennessee Playmakers is the only non-professional group with more than local affiliations. Directed by Frederick Kleibacker, of Nashville, it embraces twenty-four school, college, and Y.W.C.A. units in Middle Tennessee. The Nashville Community Playhouse, Inc., is the strongest single dramatic organization in the State, combining the city's twenty little theater groups; it offers a regular program of the best Broadway plays. The Memphis Little Theater, directed by Eugart Yerian, with auditorium and laboratories in the Memphis Art Museum, has won national attention by the professional quality of its performances.

PART II
City and Town

Nashville

Railroad Stations: Union Station, 10th Ave. and Broad St., for Nashville, Chattanooga & St. Louis Ry. and Louisville & Nashville R.R.; 1st Ave. S. near east end of Broad St. for Tennessee Central Ry.
Bus Stations: Union Station, 517 Commerce St., for Southeastern Greyhound, Dixie Greyhound, Lewisburg Bus Line, Inc., Consolidated Bus Lines, Tennessee Transportation Co., Tennessee Coach Co., and Ladd Motor Coach; 143 6th Ave. N. for Waller Bus Line.
Airport: Municipal Airport, 7.5 m. S.W. on US 41, for American and Eastern Air Lines. Taxi fare 75¢. Ticket office for American Air Lines, Hermitage Hotel; for Eastern Air Lines, Andrew Jackson Hotel.
Streetcars and Busses: Streetcar fare 5¢, bus fare 7¢. Busses for East Nashville stop on Deaderick St. and 4th Ave.; all others stop on Church St.
Taxis: 25¢ for first mile, 10¢ for each additional half mile, one to four passengers.

Accommodations: Eleven hotels, four for Negroes; tourist homes, tourist and trailer camps.

Information Service: AAA, Hermitage Hotel, 6th Ave. & Union St.; Bus Station, 517 Commerce St.; Union Depot, 10th Ave. and Broad St.

Radio Stations: WSM (650 kc.); WLAC (1470 kc.); WSIX (1210 kc.).
Theaters and Motion Picture Houses: Ryman Auditorium, 115 5th Ave. N., local productions and occasional road shows; Community Play House, Hillsboro and Carlton Ave., one play monthly during winter and spring; four first-run motion picture houses; ten neighborhood houses; three for Negroes.
Football: Vanderbilt "Commodores" of Southeastern Conference, Dudley Field, entrance 223 26th Ave. S. and on Natchez Trace.
Baseball: Nashville "Volunteers" of Southern Association, Sulphur Dell, 916 5th Ave. N.
Wrestling and Boxing: Hippodrome, 2613 West End Ave.
Tennis: Shelby Park, 20th St. and Shelby Ave., 10 courts; Centennial Park, 26th and West End Aves., 7 courts; East Park, 7th and Russell Sts., 2 courts; Richland Park, 46th and Charlotte Aves., 4 courts; Reservoir Park, 8th & Argyle Aves., 3 courts; Hadley Park, 1032 31st Ave. N., 2 courts; McFerrin Park, 601 Meridian St., 2 courts; Vanderbilt University, Garland Ave., 7 courts.
Swimming: Shelby Park; Centennial Park; Cumberland Park, Wedgewood and Rains Aves.; for children only, East Park; Richland Park; Morgan Park, 6th Ave. N. and Hume St.; South Park, Lindsley Ave. and University St.
Boating: Shelby Park, boats 25¢ an hour.
Golf: Municipal Golf Courses, Shelby Park, 18-hole course, $1.50, 9-hole course free; Centennial Park, 9 holes, free; Percy Warner Park, Belle Meade Blvd., 9 holes, 35¢; Richland Golf Course, Elmington Ave., 18 holes, $1.05 weekdays, $1.55 Sat., Sun., and holidays; Belle Meade Country Club, Belle Meade Park, 18 holes, $2; Oriental Country Club, Caldwell Lane 9 holes, $1.

Annual Events: Golden Gloves Tournament, Feb.; Iris Festival, Apr.; State Fair, Sept.; Horse Show, Sept.

NASHVILLE (498 alt., 153,866 pop.), the capital and second city of Tennessee and the seat of Davidson County, extends raggedly on both banks of the Cumberland River near the center of a great bowl-like valley formed by a chain of knobby ridges. Though an industrial city, Nashville generally retains the easy-going quality of the old South. The capstone of the city is the State capitol, on a high hill overlooking Victory Park. Surrounding the park are Government and office buildings, hotels and restaurants. On the other three sides of the capitol are ornate brick mansions, reminders of the days of belles in crinoline, dashing young bucks on blooded horses, carriages with liveried coachmen, and bowing Negroes. Many of these gaunt structures have been replaced by State buildings, those that remain have fallen to the status of cheap rooming houses.

Downtown Nashville is a crowded area of stores, restaurants, and theaters. Office buildings, bright with glass and chromium-steel, tower over brick structures that antedate the War between the States, and traffic moves slowly along narrow streets. The oldest business houses are on the public square, near the river.

Nashville has many industries but few exclusively industrial sections. The wholesale district, stockyards, a bridge company, and other large corporations are near the river. Ranging east and west from it are shoe factories, lumberyards, stone and cement works, a feed mill, and a snuff factory. On the west side of the city are nurseries, foundries, ice and chemical plants, railroad shops, cotton and flour mills, brickyards, and numerous small industries.

On residential streets Southern Colonial mansions in old-fashioned gardens stand beside Victorian and modern English-type homes on landscaped lawns. Along many of the older streets are rows of large brick houses with high windows, shuttered from within. Towers and cupolas with elaborate iron and woodwork reflect the taste of a former day.

The outlying parks and shaded campuses, and the suburban residential sections of Belle Meade, Green Hills, and Harpeth Hills give way to wide stretches of fertile farm lands, usually overhung by blue haze.

Hundreds of varieties of trees grow in Nashville. Gardening is a favorite pursuit, and enthusiasm for iris growing has led to the development of numerous private and public gardens that are visited by iris lovers from all over the country. The American and English Iris Societies have awarded 20 honorable mentions, four awards of merit, and two Dykes Medals to Nashville iris growers.

Nashville's schools annually attract more than 4,500 non-resident students. A free night school, various business colleges, and trade schools offer training in special lines. Lectures and concerts are presented almost every day in some college or auditorium.

About three-fourths of the population is of English stock, with an intermingling of German, Scottish, or Ulster Irish blood. The foreign-born group is small, but native-born descendants of immigrants have taken an active part in the growth of the city.

Nearly one-fourth of the population is Negro. Fisk University, State Agricultural and Industrial College, and Meharry Medical College have made the city an educational center for Southern Negroes. The principal Negro business streets are Cedar, Fourth Avenue North (Black Bottom), and Jo Johnston. Their homes, ranging from lowly shacks to well-built modern houses, are in Salem Town, Mount Nebo, Trimble Bottom, Rock Town, Bush Bottom, and Black Bottom.

According to archeologists, mound builders erected their earthworks in the Nashville region long before the voyages of Columbus or even Leif Ericson. Traces of their cemeteries and villages are still found in the vicinity.

The first Indians encountered by white explorers in the vicinity of Nashville were the Shawnee, a small wandering band of Algonquian stock, whose palisaded villages occupied the bluffs along the river. Intermittent raids by war parties from Kentucky and Alabama forced the Shawnee to move into the Ohio Valley early in the eighteenth century.

In 1767 five Long Hunters (so called because they spent months at a time on hunting expeditions) from East Tennessee, entered the valley, then returned home with glowing tales of its fertility and abundance of game *(see HISTORY AND GOVERNMENT)*. In 1770 Kasper Mansker organized and led another party of Long Hunters through the Cumberland country to find the best spots for settlements.

Richard Henderson, one of the greatest land speculators of the period, acting through his agent, Daniel Boone, made the Transylvania Purchase in 1775. North Carolina and Virginia opposed the sale and Henderson lost the Purchase. However, a tract of 200,000 acres, part of which lay in the Cumberland Valley, was granted to Henderson as compensation.

In the spring of 1779 Henderson sent James Robertson, whom Andrew Jackson called "The Father of Tennessee," into the valley to investigate the reports of the Long Hunters, and to blaze the way for another land promotion scheme. Robertson found the country all that the hunters had declared—rich soil, heavily timbered, and well drained by the Cumberland River and smaller streams. Selecting a site at "French Lick," or "Big Lick," now Sulphur Dell baseball park, Robertson and his party built a few cabins and planted a field of corn in Sulphur Bottom near the Lick. Leaving three men to guard the crops, Robertson and the others returned to Watauga and purchased the site from the Transylvania promoters, title being taken by Robertson as trustee for the community.

In the fall of 1779 the return trip to the new settlement began. One party, led by Robertson came overland, driving a herd of horses, cattle, and sheep. They reached the Bluff on Christmas Day, 1779, crossed the ice-covered Cumberland and made preparations for their families.

The other party bringing the women, children, and household goods, came by flatboat down the Tennessee to the Ohio, and up the Cumberland to the settlement. The flotilla of 30-odd flatboats, headed by the *Adventure* under the command of Col. John Donelson, reached its destination on April 24, 1780, after an extremely hazardous journey.

The new settlement consisted of seven stations or forts along the Cumberland River with a total population of 300. The French Lick station, called Fort Nashborough for Gen. Francis Nash, a Revolutionary veteran, was the center community. The Cumberland Compact, providing for a government by a council of representative "Notables" or "General Arbitrators," was drawn up and signed by 256 of the settlers. Two men chosen from each station formed a Committee of Guardians of which Robertson was the head.

In 1784 the Legislature of North Carolina set aside a 250-acre site on the west side of the Cumberland River, which included Fort Nashborough and the other stations. It was named Nashville because of prejudice against the English-sounding "Nashborough." Settlers came in great numbers along the Wilderness Road to the new town. They were not molested by the main body of the Cherokee, but the Chickamauga, a branch of the Cherokee, who harbored white renegades and strays from hostile tribes, refused to make peace. The Chickamauga raided along the Wilderness Road and sent strong war parties against the Cumberland settlement until an expedition under Maj. James Ore crushed the tribe.

In 1787 Nashville's first newspaper, the *Tennessee Gazette and Mero District Advertizer,* was established by a Kentucky printer named Henkle. Two years later the *Rights of Man,* or the Nashville *Intelligencer,* a weekly newspaper, was published.

By 1790 Nashville was a trade and manufacturing center with mills, foundries and gun smithies, supplying frontier traders and settlers. In 1802 George Poyzer established a plant for the manufacture of cotton spinning machinery and opened a spinning mill. The town was chartered as a city in 1806 with a mayor and six aldermen. The State legislature met here from 1812 to 1817 and from 1827 to 1843; on October 6 of the latter year Nashville became the State capital.

With the coming of the first steamboat in 1818 Nashville entered upon a profitable era of river trade. By 1825 the population had reached 3,460, a stone bridge spanned the Cumberland, and the town had become a shipping center for cotton. It was in this year that Lafayette visited Andrew Jackson at the Hermitage and was entertained in Nashville at an elaborate civic banquet. In 1850 a suspension bridge was built and the Granny White Turnpike incorporated. The Nashville, Chattanooga & St. Louis Railway was completed in 1854, though most of the city's freight was carried by steamboat between Nashville and the river ports of the Ohio and Mississippi until the end of the century.

The Southern Convention, "to decide the best means of securing constitutional rights of the South, and the preservation of the Union as it is," met in Nashville, June 3, 1850. Nine Southern States, represented by 175 delegates, met in the McKendree Church. During the nine day session the Wilmot Proviso and other compromises were discussed. After Congress disregarded the resolution adopted by the Southern Convention and passed the Compromise of 1850, 70 delegates representing seven States again met in Nashville, November 11, 1850. Only the Tennessee delegates fought for the Compromise *(see HISTORY AND GOVERNMENT).*

With the secession of South Carolina, Georgia, and Alabama, and the election of Jefferson Davis as President of the Confederacy in 1861, Nashville citizens organized home protection squads, suspended courts, and appointed a postmaster for the Confederate Government.

During the War between the States most able-bodied men were enlisted in the Confederate Army, and their families at home endured bitter priva-

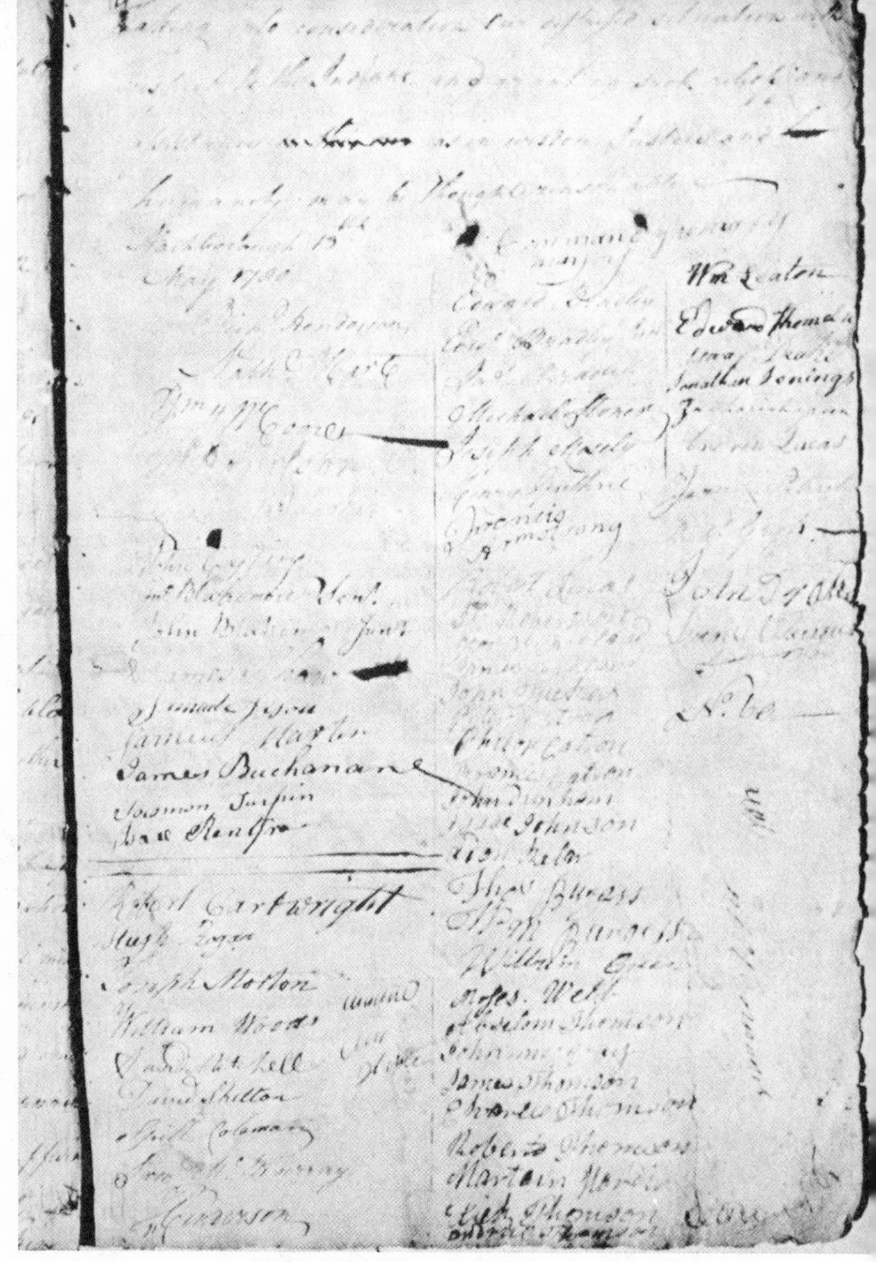

SIGNATURES OF THE CUMBERLAND COMPACT

tions. In the winter of 1862 actual warfare crept southward from the Kentucky line toward Nashville, and on February 16, news that the Federals had captured Fort Donelson, 70 miles down the Cumberland, threw the city into panic. Families prepared to flee south; the legislature convened and speedily adjourned to Memphis, taking the archives and public monies with it *(see MEMPHIS)*. On February 17, Gen. Albert Sidney Johnston's army began retreating through Nashville. All day the narrow streets echoed with the sound of marching feet, the clatter of hoofs, and the rattle of gun carriages over the cobblestones. During the night of February 18 General Floyd, who had been left in the city to cover the retreat, destroyed the bridges over the Cumberland in spite of frantic protests from the townspeople. Five days later the Confederate rear guard withdrew when Federal skirmishers, in advance of the army under Gen. Don Carlos Buell, appeared on the east bank of the river. Next day Mayor Cheatham and a committee of councilmen surrendered Nashville.

In March, 1862, Andrew Johnson, then United States Senator, was appointed Military Governor of the State of Tennessee. When the mayor and city council refused to take the oath of allegiance to the Union, Johnson replaced them with Loyalists. The city was placed under martial law, and newspapers and other properties were confiscated.

General Buell moved south to the Tennessee River, leaving the city in the custody of Gen. Theodore Rousseau, who was succeeded by Gen. James S. Negley. In the following autumn Nashville was headquarters for Gen. William Starke Rosecrans and later for Gen. George H. Thomas and Gen. Ulysses S. Grant.

When Gen. Thomas Hood succeeded Gen. Joseph E. Johnston as commander of the Confederate Army facing General Sherman in Georgia in 1864, he was ordered to strike northward into Tennessee, to capture Nashville and cut off Sherman from his source of supplies, but he moved so slowly that General Thomas had time to make heavy troop concentrations at Nashville.

Hood encountered a Union force under Gen. John Schofield at Franklin, and forced him to retreat to Nashville. On December 2, 1864, Hood began throwing up earthworks on the hills south of the city. For days rain and snow kept the ground so boggy that the armies merely skirmished. On December 15, there was a freeze and Thomas attacked, smashing Hood's left wing and forcing him back to the Overton Hills, between the Franklin and Hillsboro Pikes. On the 16th Thomas again attacked. Late in the afternoon the Confederate line collapsed and a general retreat began. Hood's army, crumbled in morale and depleted by wholesale desertion, was virtually destroyed as an effective fighting unit.

Nashville, as State capital, was the seat of the Unionist State Government. A. E. Alden, a carpetbagger, was elected mayor, and his friends filled the city council. The "Alden Ring" instituted a thorough system of public plunder, boosted the tax rate, and issued and sold checks, warrants, and duebills in the name of the city. When the citizens appealed to the courts, Chancellor James O. Shackelford refused to hear them, for he, too, was one of the "ring."

In May, 1868, A. S. Colyar, publisher of the *Union and American*, managed to examine the city's books and publish what he found. The people of Nashville pushed through another suit; the Aldenites packed their carpetbags and caught the first train north. Nashville was freed, but every note and bill made by the "Alden Ring" had to be redeemed at face value.

During the struggle for economic recovery, Nashville suffered two cholera epidemics. The first, in 1866, stopped business and the town was practically deserted. Though attempts were made to conceal the second epidemic in 1873, thousands left the city. The *American* in an editorial advised: "Use sulphur in your socks, one-half teaspoonful in each sock every morning. This will charge your system with sulphurated hydrogen which is a bar to cholera." The epidemic took about 1,000 lives. The mortality rate reached a peak of 72 deaths on Friday, June 20, since known locally as "Black Friday."

When it was discovered that more deaths occurred among those drinking well and spring water than among the people who drank city water, the board of aldermen provided for public hydrants.

Not until 1875–76, when a great business boom began, did Nashville begin to regain lost ground. By the later part of 1876 railway traffic had greatly increased, and the Cumberland River again became an important waterway. Packet and freight lines operated from the wharf at the foot of Broad Street, and blocks of warehouses were built.

On May 1, 1897, President McKinley officially opened the Centennial Exposition, celebrating Tennessee's 100th anniversary as a State, by pressing a button in the Nation's Capital, which fired a gun in the exposition grounds in Centennial Park, Nashville. Nashville floated an exposition bond issue of $100,000, to run for 20 years, the Federal Government appropriated $130,000, and $500,000 was raised by public subscription. The exposition buildings were grouped around a plaster reproduction of the Greek Parthenon. During the six months that it remained open, the exposition was visited by more than 6,000,000 people, including President McKinley.

Between 1900 and 1910 the city's population increased from 80,865 to 110,361; and from 1920 to 1930, from 118,342 to 153,866. These boom periods followed improvements in transportation, the establishment of numerous new industries, and the growth of Nashville as an educational city. Economic expansion has been steady but less rapid than before the turn of the century. New and diversified industries have been established, and some of the older plants have been consolidated.

Although East Nashville suffered a disastrous fire in 1916 and a tornado in 1933, it quickly recovered, and new buildings now cover the devastated area.

POINTS OF INTEREST

1. VICTORY PARK, 6th Ave. N. between Cedar and Union Sts., extending to 7th Ave. N., is divided into two sections, each surrounded by a paneled cement wall, ornamented at intervals by tall pillars and flower re-

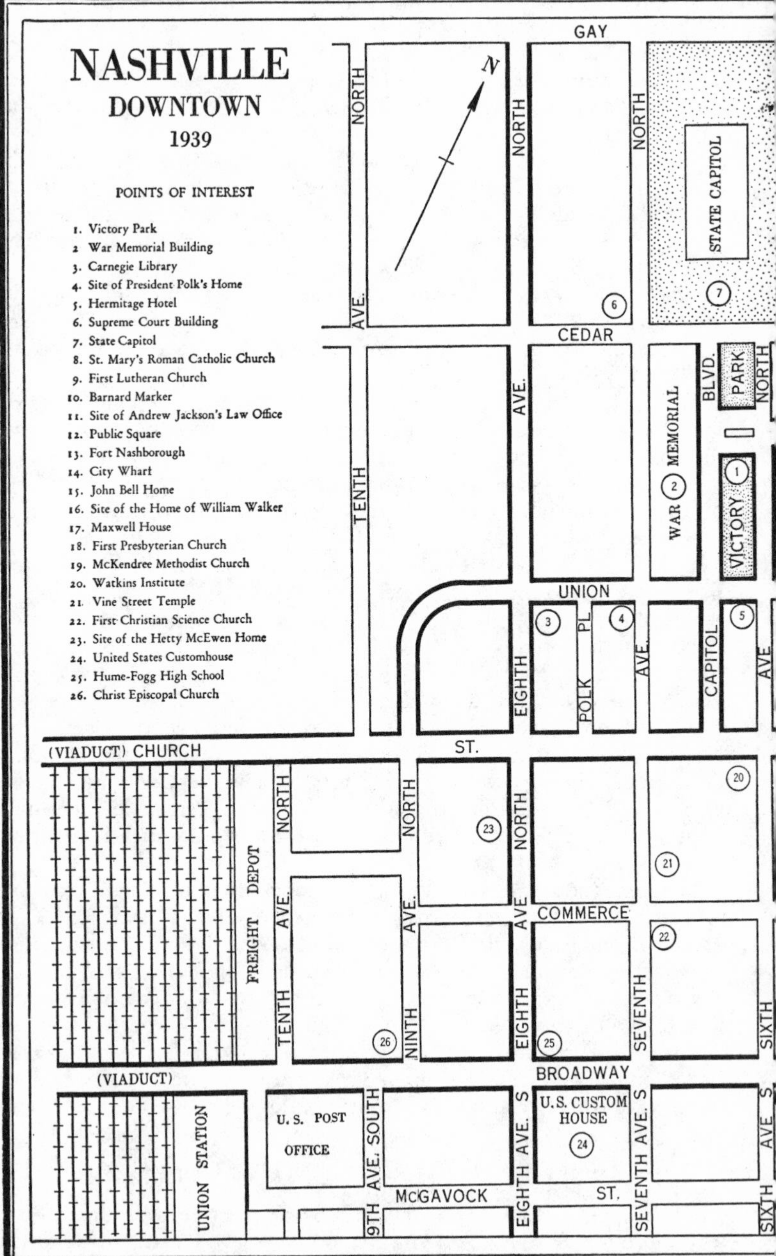
NASHVILLE
DOWNTOWN
1939
POINTS OF INTEREST
1. Victory Park
2 War Memorial Building
3. Carnegie Library
4. Site of President Polk's Home
5. Hermitage Hotel
6. Supreme Court Building
7. State Capitol
8. St. Mary's Roman Catholic Church
9. First Lutheran Church
10. Barnard Marker
11. Site of Andrew Jackson's Law Office
12. Public Square
13. Fort Nashborough
14. City Wharf
15. John Bell Home
16. Site of the Home of William Walker
17. Maxwell House
18. First Presbyterian Church
19. McKendree Methodist Church
20. Watkins Institute
21 Vine Street Temple
22. First Christian Science Church
23. Site of the Hetty McEwen Home
24. United States Customhouse
25. Hume-Fogg High School
26. Christ Episcopal Church
N
GAY
CEDAR
UNION
(VIADUCT) CHURCH
ST.
COMMERCE
BROADWAY
(VIADUCT)
MCGAVOCK
ST.
NORTH AVE.
NORTH
NORTH
TENTH
STATE CAPITOL
WAR MEMORIAL
VICTORY
PARK
BLVD.
NORTH
POLK PL
AVE.
CAPITOL
AVE
EIGHTH
FREIGHT DEPOT
TENTH AVE.
NORTH
NINTH AVE.
NORTH
EIGHTH AVE
SEVENTH
SIXTH
UNION STATION
U. S. POST OFFICE
9TH AVE. SOUTH
EIGHTH AVE. S
U.S. CUSTOM HOUSE
SEVENTH AVE. S
SIXTH AVE S

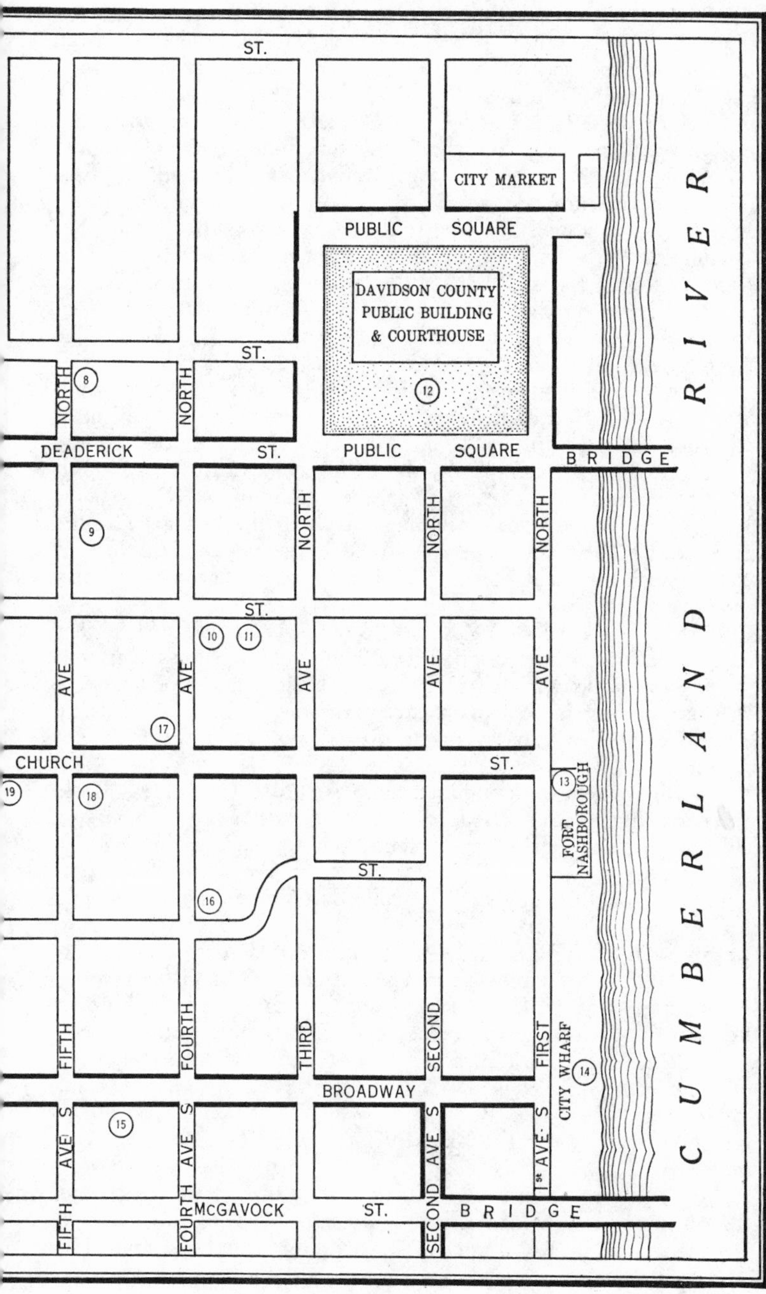
ST.
CITY MARKET
PUBLIC SQUARE
DAVIDSON COUNTY
PUBLIC BUILDING
& COURTHOUSE
ST.
NORTH
NORTH
DEADERICK ST.
PUBLIC SQUARE
BRIDGE
RIVER
NORTH
NORTH
NORTH
ST.
AVE
AVE
AVE
AVE
AVE
CHURCH
ST.
FORT
NASHBOROUGH
ST.
CUMBERLAND
FIFTH
FOURTH
THIRD
SECOND
FIRST
CITY WHARF
BROADWAY
FIFTH AVE S
FOURTH AVE S
SECOND AVE S
1st AVE S
McGAVOCK ST.
BRIDGE
8
9
10
11
12
13
14
15
16
17
18
19

ceptacles. Stone seats are placed along graveled walks bordered by closely-clipped hedges. In the south section is a large fountain. The American Flag flies over one section, the State Flag over the other.

2. The WAR MEMORIAL BUILDING *(open 8:30-4:30 weekdays),* Capitol Blvd. between Union and Cedar Sts., extending to 7th Ave. N., completed in 1925, is a three story neo-Classic limestone structure, designed by McKim, Mead & White, with Edward Daugherty of Nashville as associate. The main entrance, a spacious central court, joins the north and south sections. Wide stone stairs lead to the Doric east portico, with large fluted columns and a pedimented entablature. In the center of the court is a BRONZE STATUE of a young man, by Belle Kinney and Leopold Scholz, which symbolizes the strength and valor of war. Large bronze tablets, at the western side, bear names of 3,400 Tennessee World War dead. The MEMORIAL AUDITORIUM, on the south side, seats, 2,200.

The WORLD WAR MUSEUM *(open),* in the basement of the south wing, contains a large collection of helmets, machine guns, rifles, and uniforms captured from the Germans by Tennessee troops, weapons used by the Allies, and battlefield photographs by the U. S. Signal Corps.

The STATE HISTORICAL MUSEUM *(open),* adjoining the World War Museum, contains Tennesseana, including a copy of the first issue of the Knoxville *Gazette* (first newspaper published in Tennessee), trophies of the Mexican War, historical portraits, and battle flags. The museum also houses the State Archives.

3. The CARNEGIE LIBRARY *(open 9-9 weekdays; 2-6 Sun.),* SE. corner 8th Ave. N. and Union St., designed by Albert Randolph Ross, was constructed 1903–04. Following the conventional classical design of Carnegie libraries, this building is very plain except for the division of walls by pilasters, and a circular stairway of the Regency mode at the main entrance.

On the north wall of the children's room is a MURAL by Mrs. Marie Barton Taylor of scenes from the legend of King Arthur.

The library contains more than 160,000 volumes, and Nashville daily papers dating back to 1818. A business branch in the chamber of commerce building, contains an extensive collection of books on economic theory and business problems.

4. The SITE OF PRESIDENT POLK'S HOME, SW. corner Union St. and 7th Ave. N., is occupied by the Polk Apartments. Felix Grundy, twice a United States Senator, built the original mansion and after his death in 1840 the property was sold to President Polk, who remodeled it.

5. The HERMITAGE HOTEL, SW. corner 6th Ave. N. and Union St., has in the lobby 20 paintings of Confederate scenes, by Gilbert Gaul (1855–1919).

6. The SUPREME COURT BUILDING *(open 8:30-4:30 weekdays),* NW. corner 7th Ave. N. and Cedar St., is in the neo-Classic style with modified Greek detail. Its outer walls are of white marble with base and terrace of polished granite. The façade is accentuated by deeply recessed panels between large square pilasters. The building is by Marr and Holman of Nashville.

7. The STATE CAPITOL, Cedar St. between 6th and 7th Aves. N., and extending to Gay St., is on Capitol Hill, the highest point in the city.

In 1811 a neighbor bought a cow from Judge George W. Campbell and was unable to pay for it. "But I'll tell you what," the neighbor said, "I've got a pretty fair rifle gun and I own old Cedar Knob up yonder. Write my debt off your books and you can have them." Campbell agreed. Thirty-three years later the city bought Cedar Knob from Judge Campbell for $30,000 and presented it to the State as the site for the Capitol. The building was finished in 1855, the terrace completed in 1859. The crest of the hill was removed to a foundation of solid rock; blocks of fossilized limestone for the building, from 4½ to 7 feet thick, were quarried by prisoners and slaves. The cost of the building exceeded $1,500,000.

In 1862, the building placed under a heavy guard and surrounded by a stockade, was renamed Fort Johnson, headquarters of Federal activities. Union soldiers badly damaged the grounds.

The building, designed by William Strickland, who lived in Nashville from 1844 to 1854 *(see ARCHITECTURE)*, follows the plan of an Ionic temple. The pedimented Ionic porticos on each façade are modeled after those of the Erectheum at Athens, each having eight fluted columns, with hand-carved capitals of solid stone. The east and west porticos have six Ionic columns, surmounted by parapets. Strickland was buried in a recess in the north portico wall. The long gable of the roof is broken by a central tower, the upper portion designed in the manner of the Choragic Monument of Lysicrates in Athens.

The main entrance is through the south portico. Surmounting the check-blocks of the stairs at each front are ornamental lamp posts. Three figures —two maidens, representing morning and noon, and a youth holding a torch, representing night—are grouped around the posts.

The first floor occupied by the executive offices has a hall the length of the building and a transverse hall. A marble staircase leads to the Hall of Representatives, the Senate Chamber, and the State Library. The main floor of the Hall of Representatives, 64 by 97 feet, is flanked by committee rooms, above which are the public galleries. Extending from the gallery parapets to the ceiling are fluted columns, with decorative capitals, carved from solid blocks of stone. The Senate Chamber ceiling is adorned with radiating panels. A gallery on three sides is supported by Ionic columns with solid shafts of variegated marble. Portraits of noted Tennesseans are hung on the walls of the library, which has a fine collection of Tennesseana.

Walks wind through the capitol grounds and a driveway curves around the hill. Old cannon, used in fortifying the capitol during the War between the States, are spaced along the upper terrace.

Inside the southwest entrance is Julian Zolnay's bronze MONUMENT TO SAM DAVIS, the boy hero of the Confederacy *(see Tour 8)*. Among contributions for the monument, received from every State in the Union, was a generous gift from Gen. G. M. Dodge, before whom Sam Davis was court-martialed.

Directly below the south entrance portico stands the bronze STATUE OF

EDWARD WARD CARMACK, by Nancy Cox McCormack. Carmack was a United States Senator from 1901 to 1907. In 1908, as editor of the Nashville *Tennessean,* he vigorously attacked the administration of Governor Malcolm R. Patterson. Championing prohibition, Carmack exposed a number of the "wet" administration's shady deals. The politicians warned him to "lay off." Carmack's scorching editorials and exposes continued. One of his main targets was the influential Duncan Cooper, of Nashville. On the evening of Nov. 9, 1908, as Carmack was walking along Seventh Avenue between Church and Union Streets, Cooper and his son shot Carmack and left him dead on the sidewalk. Duncan Cooper was convicted of murder, and the Tennessee Supreme Court confirmed the sentence. At the gates of the penitentiary the warden presented Cooper with a full pardon from Governor Patterson.

Before the east entrance portico is the bronze equestrian STATUE OF ANDREW JACKSON by Clark Mills, 1880.

The TOMB OF JAMES KNOX POLK AND MRS. POLK, near the northeast corner of the capitol, designed by William Strickland, was built on the grounds of the Polk home and removed here when the house was torn down in 1893.

8. ST. MARY'S ROMAN CATHOLIC CHURCH *(open 6-6 daily)* 330 5th Ave. N., is a gray brick structure of Greek Revival style, designed by William Strickland in 1844 and completed in 1847. The façade, faced with limestone blocks, has a half portico supported by two fluted Ionic columns. Surmounting the structure is an octagonal tower topped with a circular cupola. The cupola, like that of the Capitol, is designed in the manner of the Choragic monument of Lysicrates. The paneled walls of the interior are acoustically treated. The ceiling, of square panels and classical mouldings, is decorated with murals of the life of Christ. In a niche is the high altar of Botticino marble. The statues of the Virgin Mary and St. Joseph, and the holy water fonts are also of marble. Oil paintings of the sufferings of Christ hang between the stained-glass windows.

The history of St. Mary's goes back to the 1820's when the Holy Rosary—the first Catholic Church in Tennessee—was erected in Nashville. When the congregation moved to St. Mary's, the Holy Rosary Church was converted into a hospital.

The tomb of Bishop Pius Miles, who was largely responsible for building St. Mary's, is beneath the high altar. Father Abram Ryan, the "Poet Priest of the South," was an assistant pastor from 1864 to 1865.

9. The FIRST LUTHERAN CHURCH *(open 8-12 daily),* 312 5th Ave. N., of brick with stone trim, designed in the castellated Gothic Revival mode by Maj. A. Heiman, was completed in 1838. The art-glass memorial windows, dedicated to early members, were imported from Germany before the World War. Built for a Baptist congregation, the building was purchased by the Lutheran Church in 1884.

10. The BARNARD MARKER, SE. corner of Union St. and 4th Ave. N., identifies the site of the studio of E. E. Barnard (1857–1923). Barnard, the first to photograph the Milky Way, discovered 16 comets and the fifth satellite of Jupiter.

11. The SITE OF ANDREW JACKSON'S LAW OFFICE, 333 Union St., from 1789 to 1896, is occupied by a drugstore.

12. The PUBLIC SQUARE, Deaderick St. between 1st and 3rd Aves. N., extending to Cedar St., was set aside by the assembly of North Carolina in 1784. The first building was a one-story log jail, with whipping post and pillory, and in 1789 local Methodists erected a stone church, also used as a courthouse and public meeting place.

The DAVIDSON COUNTY PUBLIC BUILDING AND COURTHOUSE *(open 8-4 weekdays),* in the center of the square, replaced the courthouse built in 1857–58. The eight-story, air-conditioned building is constructed of reinforced concrete on a steel framework, with walls of buff limestone. The base and peristyle are of granite and the corridors are wainscoted with marble. Designed in the Greek Revival style with Doric detail, by Woolwine and Herons, the building was completed in 1937. The south entrance, which has a *salle de pas perdue* (Fr., hall of lost footsteps), opens on a terrace with two fountains.

In the main lobby are four MURALS by Dean Cornwell. The murals—*Statesmanship, Commerce, Industry,* and *Agriculture*—are painted on a background of red, silver and gold. Faintly sketched on the first two is a map of Nashville, on the other two a map of Davidson County. At the bottom of each mural are medallions of local historical events.

City and county administrative offices are on the first, second, and third floors; the Chancery Court rooms, the Bar Assembly Hall, the Quarterly Court room, offices of the Clerk and Master, and the committee rooms on the fourth; the Circuit Court rooms, office of the Circuit Court Clerk, jury and witness rooms on the fifth.

The Criminal Court is on the sixth and seventh floors. The top floor houses the sheriff's office and the jail.

The CITY MARKET *(open 7-6 Mon.-Fri., 7 a.m.-9 p.m. Sat.),* fronting the square on the north side, was designed by Henry C. Hibbs of Nashville in the Classical Revival style, and completed in 1937. Window frames and sashes are of steel, the roof is of copper, and the interior has a five-foot wainscoting of glazed tile and a terrazzo floor. The market contains stalls, restaurants, and rest rooms.

On the streets adjoining the market house farmers line up their wagons, loaded with fresh country produce, everything from wild fox grapes, persimmons, and sorghum molasses, to "pyor" honey, split-bottom chairs, cut flowers, and fresh cider.

13. FORT NASHBOROUGH *(open 9-4 daily),* 1st Ave. N. and Church St. built in 1930, is a model of the fort built by James Robertson and his party on this site in 1780. Joseph J. Hart, of Nashville, was the architect.

Inside a stockade of black locust logs are the log blockhouses chinked with mud. The houses have hand-split shingles, puncheon floors, and handmade furniture of the period.

The fort was the scene of an ambuscade by the Chickamauga on April 2, 1781. The previous night, the war party had crept to the edge of the woods that fringed the fort. Soon after sunrise three painted bucks jumped from cover, fired toward the fort, and ran back into the woods. Col. James

Robertson set out with 20 mounted men to drive them off and his party was allowed to pass through the first line of the ambush. As they approached a hillside, near what is now the corner of Third Avenue and Demonbruen Street, the Indians attacked. The white men took shelter behind their horses, and returned the fire. Mrs. Robertson, realizing the men had been trapped, ordered the gates opened and the settlers' pack of bear-dogs loosed. The great mastiffs, trained to hate Indians, attacked the war party. The Indians ran in all directions, allowing Robertson and his men to dash to safety. The following day the Indians attempted to storm the fort, but were driven off by a swivel cannon, loaded with scrap iron, bits of chain, and stones.

14. The CITY WHARF, Broadway and 1st Ave., was a transportation center during the 1800's when most of the city's freight was carried by boat. In the early 1900's, with a network of railroads across the State, water transportation practically ceased, but in the thirties barge and tugboat lines renewed activity on the waterfront.

On warm Sunday afternoons, a motley crowd predominantly country folk, gathers on the north corner of Lower Broad across from the wharf, for the "free-for-all preachings," a custom of 20 years standing. Anyone, Negro or white, man or woman, fundamentalist or atheist, is free to have his say. The audience, for the most part, is made up of people restlessly awaiting their turns to preach. They clutch battered Bibles, which they leaf through and quote from at an instant's notice. Almost without exception they have tried and discarded the standard sects.

One of the men who preaches here regularly says: "The only place you can get the truth is on the street as God told his people to go into the highways and the hedges. There's not any truth in the churches these days because God is not there." Each preacher hopes to found his sect and gather a following at the Sunday preachings. Often ten or twenty preachers stand on the curb, on packing cases, and in truck beds, all preaching at the same time. Gradually the crowd extends up Broad as far as Second Avenue and spills down across First Avenue to the wharf. Preachers mount boxcars and the loading-apron of the warehouse. They stand on the hoods of cars and perch on the first story window ledges of the produce houses. Some lure listeners by mouthing French harps or strumming banjoes and guitars. Others whoop until a group collects. There is a constant crossfire of heckling between preacher and listeners. Furious men rush up to the preacher and shake fists, Bibles, and canes under his nose. Some ignore the preaching and draw aside to roar Scriptural quotations into each other's faces. The preaching continues until about 9 o'clock at night, when the people, satiated and subdued, begin to leave. By 10 o'clock the corner is deserted.

15. The JOHN BELL HOME, 413 Broadway, built in 1857, has been remodeled for business houses. John Bell, born near Nashville on February 15, 1797, was a member of the House of Representatives (1827–41), appointed Secretary of War by President Harrison (1841), and was a member of the United States Senate (1847–59). Bell opposed secession and kept Tennessee in the Union until Fort Sumter was fired on; then reluc-

tantly he threw in his lot with the South. In 1860 Bell was nominated for President on the Constitutional Union Party ticket, but was defeated by Lincoln. He won the votes of Tennessee, Kentucky, and Virginia.

16. The SITE OF THE HOME OF WILLIAM WALKER, NE. corner 4th Ave. N. and Commerce St., is indicated by a marker. William Walker, the "Grey-Eyed Man of Destiny," soldier of fortune, was born May 8, 1824, in the plain brick house that stood here. Walker, a doctor and newspaper editor, joined the gold rush of 1849. After leading an unsuccessful filibustering expedition into Sonora, Mexico, he recruited a second band, landed in Nicaragua, and seized the government. As President of Nicaragua, he was unofficially recognized by the U. S. Government. In 1860 Walker invaded Honduras and was captured by British marines. Turned over to the Honduran authorities, he was executed by a firing squad at Truxillo. The Government of Honduras refused requests to return his body to Nashville.

17. The MAXWELL HOUSE, NW. corner 4th Ave. N. and Church St., a four-story brick hotel, was designed by Francis W. Strickland and built by Col. John Overton. The building, started in 1859 and completed ten years later, was named Maxwell House for the colonel's wife, Mary Maxwell Overton.

According to tradition, one day when Colonel Overton was riding along Church Street, he noticed a crowd in a roadside field, gathered around a red-faced auctioneer in a beaver hat who was standing on a stump "making a mighty gobbling miration." To the colonel, who had just left the taproom of the Nashville Inn, the auctioneer's gestures seemed to indicate a cow tethered near the stump. Mellowly noting that the cow was a heavy milker, Overton called out a bid of $15 and rode on. The next day he was notified that his bid was high; he had bought, not a cow, but the lot upon which he later built the Maxwell House.

The hotel was so out of proportion to the town that it was called "Overton's Folly." Service quarters on each floor were in the center of the building, and all rooms were on the outer side. The façade on 4th Avenue was adorned by a colonnaded portico two stories high with a balcony used as a reviewing stand. For years every parade in the city passed by this entrance.

During the War between the States the unfinished building was used by Confederate and Federal troops as barracks and prison. In the spring of 1867, at a Ku Klux Klan convention held in the hotel, plans for the Klan's operation were laid under the very noses of the carpetbag administration. A constitution was written and Gen. Nathan Bedford Forrest was made Grand Wizard, the chief officer.

A nationally known brand of coffee, originally manufactured in Nashville, was named for this hostelry.

18. The FIRST PRESBYTERIAN CHURCH *(open 8-5 daily)*, SE. corner Church St. and 5th N., is a gray brick structure designed in a modified Egyptian style, by William Strickland. Between the towers, each 104 feet high, is a half portico with two Egyptian columns supporting a delicate

pediment. The auditorium is decorated in the manner of an Egyptian temple.

In the first church, built on the site in 1816, Andrew Jackson was presented a sword by the State of Tennessee for his services at the Battle of New Orleans. This Church, which burned in 1832, was replaced by a second building, in which James K. Polk was inaugurated Governor of Tennessee. In 1838 this building was likewise destroyed by fire, and the present one constructed. During the War between the States the Federal army used the church as a hospital.

19. The McKENDREE METHODIST CHURCH *(open 8-5),* Church St. between 5th and 6th Aves. N., constructed of brick and stone, is Italian Renaissance in design, with low square towers and dome. The memorial windows, copied from religious paintings, depict the life of Christ. The Methodist congregation originally worshiped in Nashville's first church, erected on the Public Square in 1789. In 1807 the building was torn down, and for five years services were held in the county jail. In 1812 a church was built on the northeast corner of Broad Street and 8th Avenue, where the congregation worshiped until the present building was completed in 1912.

20. WATKINS INSTITUTE *(open 9-9 daily)* 605 Church St., built in 1885 in the Victorian Gothic style, was endowed by Samuel Watkins, Nashville philanthropist, to furnish free instruction. Mr. Watkins left in trust to the State of Tennessee a lot and $100,000 in cash with which to erect a suitable building. The free night school was opened in 1888. In 1902 Mrs. Ann E. Weber gave in trust to the State two valuable storehouses on Fifth Avenue to augment the work. A day school was started in 1924. Special elementary work, art courses, and commercial and trade courses are offered, as well as full high school work. Evening lectures are given in sociology, modern literature, and other advanced courses.

The NASHVILLE ART MUSEUM *(open 10-5 weekdays, 2-5 Sun.),* on the second floor, has historical paintings by Paul De La Roche; miniatures by John Dodge; landscapes by Charles Warren Eaton; paintings by Lillian Genth, a pupil of Whistler; and a collection of rare Dresden and Spode china. There are also murals by Charles Cagle, former art teacher at Watkins Institute.

21. The VINE STREET TEMPLE, Hebrew Reform *(open 9-5 daily),* 136 7th Ave. N., is a brick structure of Byzantine style, designed by W. Dodson in 1876. The stone-trimmed walls are topped with a massive, bulblike dome surmounted by smaller domes of similar style. The Byzantine detail is also carried out in the interior.

22. The FIRST CHRISTIAN SCIENCE CHURCH *(open 10-5 daily),* 120 7th Ave. N., built 1856–1881, is of pointed Gothic style, designed by Wills and Dudley. Its buttressed ivy-covered walls are of random rubble stone. During the War between the States construction was suspended, and service was held in the basement until 1866. The building was erected by the Episcopal Church of the Advent, and purchased by the present congregation in the early 1900's.

23. The SITE OF THE HETTY McEWEN HOME, 117 8th Ave., N.,

is occupied by business houses. Hetty McEwen, a beloved eccentric and outspoken individualist of the 1860's, whose grandfather fought at King's Mountain, staunchly opposed secession. When Tennessee left the Union, Mrs. McEwen had a flagpole erected in her front yard and raised the Stars and Stripes. Throughout the war she was allowed to fly the Union flag, for while she was flaunting it, she was busy night and day cooking food, knitting socks, and furnishing lodging for Confederate soldiers.

24. The UNITED STATES CUSTOMHOUSE, Broadway and 7th Ave. S., is of pointed Gothic style. The basement is of granite and the superstructure is faced with cream colored limestone. The three-story building is surmounted by a Gothic tower, which extends 190 feet above the sidewalk. The entrance façade is ornamented with devices symbolizing the progress of the United States. It was designed by William A. Potter, government architect. Begun in 1875, the building was completed in 1881. The interior is arranged for the Federal courts, customs offices, and other government offices.

25. HUME-FOGG HIGH SCHOOL, NE. corner Broadway and 8th Ave. N., is on the site of the first meeting place in Nashville of the Tennessee legislature. From 1812 to 1815 a Methodist church on this site was used by the State legislature in lieu of a State capitol.

26. CHRIST EPISCOPAL CHURCH *(open 8-5 daily)*, 900 Broadway is a Victorian Gothic sandstone building with cut-stone trim, designed by H. Kimball, and built 1887–1892. Gargoyles resembling those of old English cathedrals ornament the exterior. Two small pieces of stone are in the southeast vestibule, one from the old York Minster, the other from the ruins of Pompeii. Heavy polished oak doors open into the nave of the church, and the pews are of carved oak.

27. The ROMAN CATHOLIC CATHEDRAL OF THE INCARNATION *(open 6 a.m.-midnight daily)*, 2011 West End Ave., a group of three buildings, is designed in the manner of ecclesiastical architecture in Rome. The cathedral proper recalls the Church of San Martino; the tower resembles the campanile of the Church of San Damase; and the detail of the rectory and the cathedral school, which flank each side of the cathedral, is similar to that of the Farnese Palace. The buildings are of buff-colored brick with red tile roofs and are connected at the rear by cloisters. The interior woodwork is of solid oak, the hardware of specially designed brass; the holy water fonts are miniature copies of those by Michelangelo in St. Peter's, Rome; and the high altar is copied after that of San Martino in Lucca, Italy. Designed by Aristide Leonard of Rome, Italy, construction was supervised by Bishop Thomas Byrne.

28. CENTENNIAL PARK, West End Ave. betwen 25th and 28th Aves. N., is a 134-acre landscaped tract, formerly called West Side Park. The name was changed in 1897, when the exposition marking the hundredth anniversary of the State's entrance into the Union, was held there. Buildings were not completed in time for the exposition to be held in 1896 as originally planned. The park has a swimming pool, tennis and croquet courts, a golf course, and horseshoe lanes.

The KIWANIS MEMORIAL, facing West End Ave. near the 25th Ave.

entrance, is a sculpture group in bronze by Julian Zolnay of Palermo, Italy. On the marble pedestal two tablets are inscribed with the names of Davidson County's World War dead. The Roumanian Government obtained permission to reproduce this memorial.

The following points of interest are on the driveway circling the park and are listed in sequence starting from the right hand entrance.

The PROW OF THE OLD BATTLESHIP TENNESSEE (L) is a reproduction of the figurehead on the U. S. S. *Tennessee,* of Spanish-American War days, loaned by the Secretary of the Navy, at the request of Capt. Albert Gleaves, 1910.

The *JAMES ROBERTSON MONUMENT* (L) is a roughly-hewn shaft of solid stone on a plain-hewn stone pedestal. Bronze plaques give brief biographies of James and Charlotte Reeves Robertson.

On tree-bordered WATAUGA LAKE (L) live 23 species of water fowl.

In the GREENHOUSE *(private)* are three rare trees: The bread-fruit, a tropical food tree; the ornamental banana; and the dwarf banana, planted in the park during the Tennessee Centennial Exposition in 1897. The greenhouse furnishes plants for all city parks.

In the JAPANESE GARDEN (L) are a grotto, a statue of Buddha, several Japanese pagodas, 45 varieties of plants, and a small lake, covered in season with water lilies.

The PARTHENON *(open 10-6 weekdays; 2-7 Sun.)* (L), is a steel-and-concrete reproduction, by Hart, Freeland, and Roberts, of the Athenian Parthenon. The present building, 228 feet long, 101 feet wide, and 65 feet high, was opened in 1931 replacing the plaster structure erected in 1897 for the centennial anniversary. The Doric columns of the peristyle are more than six feet in diameter, and the double bronze doors weigh 15 tons. Ninety-two metopes in high relief, reproduced by George J. Zolnay, decorate the Doric frieze and 54 classic statues, executed by Belle Kinney and Leopold Scholz, adorn the tympana of the pediments.

In the west room are casts of the original pediment sculptures of the Parthenon in the British Museum. The reproductions for the Ionic frieze of the Nashville Parthenon were made by Belle Kinney and her husband, Leopold Scholz, of Nashville.

The Gowan Collection of sixty-three oil paintings by American artists is in the basement. The paintings were chosen to represent a cross section of American art from the Colonial period to the present.

The JOHN W. THOMAS MEMORIAL (L) is a 10-foot pedestal of solid white marble, designed by Enid Yandell and erected by employees of the Nashville, Chattanooga and St. Louis Railway in 1907. A bronze plaque gives a brief biography of Thomas (1830–1906), president of the Tennessee Centennial Exposition.

29. The NATCHEZ TRACE MARKER, West End Ave. facing Centennial Park, is at the junction of the old Wilderness Road from Knoxville and the Natchez Trace Road to Natchez, Mississippi *(see TRANSPORTATION)*. Originally the Natchez Trace was used by the Chickasaw, Choctaw, and other Southern tribes as a path to the rich hunting grounds of Tennessee

and Kentucky. In 1801 treaties with Chickasaw and Cherokee Indians provided for the opening of a wagon road from Nashville to Natchez. The road was completed in 1807. The Natchez Trace is being restored as a national highway (1939).

30. VANDERBILT UNIVERSITY, entrance West End Ave. at 23rd Ave. S., is one of the South's foremost educational institutions. On the 76-acre campus, which is landscaped with more than 50 varieties of trees, weathered brick buildings of Victorian Gothic architecture stand side by side with modern stone-and-brick structures designed in the Collegiate or Oxford Gothic mode. Winding paths along the grass beneath the ancient trees are in contrast to the concrete walkways with their trim curbs.

The college was chartered in 1872 as Central University by the Methodist Episcopal Church South and continued under Church control until 1914. In 1873 Bishop Holland M. McTyeire secured from Cornelius Vanderbilt of New York an endowment for the University of $500,000. Mr. Vanderbilt subsequently increased his endowment to one million dollars, and the name was changed to Vanderbilt University.

The university opened with four general departments, Academic, Biblical, Law, and Medical, but because there were not enough students available with the necessary scholastic requirements, a department was added for preparatory classes. This department was discontinued in 1887. The University consists of six schools: Arts and Science, Law, Engineering, Religion, Medicine, and Nursing.

When the medical department of the University of Nashville was acquired by Vanderbilt in 1874, new buildings were erected, equipment was purchased, and entrance requirements raised. In 1913 Andrew Carnegie gave $200,000 for the erection and equipment of a laboratory, and a year later he made an endowment of $800,000. In 1919 the General Education Board (an organization that handles Rockefeller philanthropies for educational purposes) appropriated $4,000,000 for a complete reorganization of the School of Medicine. Operating funds were provided by a joint endowment of $3,000,000 from the General Education Board and the Carnegie Corporation. The Rockefeller Foundation also appropriated $100,000 to be used over a period of five years for the School of Nursing. The Abraham Flexner lectureship, to bring outstanding American and European scientists to lecture at the school, was established in 1927 through a gift of $50,000 from Bernard Flexner of New York. Other large contributions were endowments of $3,500,000 for the School of Medicine, and $4,000,000 for the Vanderbilt University Hospital, made by the General Education Board in 1929.

The MEDICAL COLLEGE AND HOSPITAL, of modified Gothic design, is the work of Coolidge and Shattuck of Boston. It is planned in a series of connected squares enclosing courts. The building contains wards with 350 beds, an extensive out-patient department, surgeries, laboratories, lecture rooms, medical library, museum, and administrative offices.

KIRKLAND HALL, the Administration Building, named for Chancellor Emeritus James H. Kirkland, contains the School of Law, the Academic Library and the THRUSTON COLLECTION OF ANTIQUITIES AND MINERALS *(open by permission)*, presented by Gen. G. P. Thruston, Tennessee archeologist. The collection includes ancient pottery, idols, clay pipes, shell spoons, vases, articles made of copper, and a collection of rare gems (booklet available). With the exception of the minerals, most of the collection was taken from prehistoric graves in and around Nashville.

The STATUE OF COMMODORE VANDERBILT, by G. Moretti, cast in bronze and of heroic proportions, stands in front of the main entrance of Kirkland Hall.

GARLAND HALL, named for Landon C. Garland, first Chancellor of Vanderbilt University, contains a MUSEUM *(open on application)* of rocks, fossils, maps, and charts, including complete sets of topographic and geologic maps issued by the United States Geological Survey. The geology and physics libraries are also housed in the building.

Among other buildings are Alumni Memorial Hall, the recreation building; Wesley Hall, the School of Religion; Furman Hall, the chemistry department; Mechanical Engineering Hall; Science Hall; the Observatory; Buttrick Hall, biology department; Mark Kirkland Hall, the School of Nursing; and Calhoun Hall.

DUDLEY STADIUM, a short distance west of the campus, seats 22,000. Home football games of the "Commodores" are played here. It was named for William L. Dudley, professor of chemistry and early head of athletics at the University.

31. GEORGE PEABODY COLLEGE FOR TEACHERS, 21st Ave. S. and Edgehill Ave., has twelve principal buildings on a 50-acre campus. Built to conform to the campus plan, designed in 1911 by Ludlow and Peabody, the buildings, facing a landscaped quadrangle, are of Classical Revival design with temple-like façades. Crowning the hill is the Social Religious Building, with its graceful columns and huge dome, designed by Ludlow and Peabody and constructed in 1914. Connected with this building by circular colonnades are the East and West Dormitories (1921–23), designed by Henry C. Hibbs. On the west side are: the Graduate Dormitory (1929), designed by Raymond Hood; the Fine Arts Building (1927); and the Administration Building (1925), by McKim, Mead and White; and the Library (1918), by Henry C. Hibbs. On the east side are the United Daughters Memorial (1933), designed by Granberry Jackson; the Psychology Building (1914); the Industrial Arts Building (1914); and the Home Economics Building (1914), by Ludlow and Peabody. On the north facing the group is the Demonstration School (1925), designed by McKim, Mead and White.

Under the name of the University of Nashville, the college was founded in 1875, as a State Normal School and in 1889 the name was changed to Peabody Normal College because of financial aid from the estate of George Peabody of Massachusetts. It was incorporated under its present title in 1909; and was moved in 1914 to the site it now occupies. The college was the first institution in the South established for the sole purpose of teacher-training. Junior College, Senior College, and graduate courses leading to M. A. and Ph. D. degrees are offered. The college, which is co-educational, has an average enrollment of 1,000.

SCARRITT COLLEGE, NASHVILLE

The COHEN MEMORIAL MUSEUM *(open 9-4 weekdays),* on the right of the campus, the gift of Mrs. George Etta Cohen of Nashville, contains many canvases, costly porcelains, rare laces, old silver, tapestries, china, and antique furniture. The college art department has classrooms in the basement. The marble in the stairway and halls was imported from Carrara, Italy.

32. SCARRITT COLLEGE, 1008 19th Ave. S., consisting of four units connected by cloisters, is on a nine-acre campus. Designed by Henry C. Hibbs of Nashville, and completed in 1928, the building of varicolored quartz stone forms the three sides of a quadrangle and opens on a court. Single bricks and red and green stone slabs set in the walls at intervals accentuate the natural color of the quartz. The dominant feature of the building is the well-proportioned tower with its pinnacled corners and cut-stone trim. In 1929 Hibbs received the gold medal of the American Institute of Architects in recognition of this ecclesiastical design.

In 1887 Belle H. Bennett, President of the Women's Missionary Council of the Methodist Episcopal Church, South, conceived the idea of a training school for missionaries. In May 1890 the Woman's Board of Foreign Missions of the church authorized the establishment of the institution.

Dr. Nathan Scarritt gave a tract at Kansas City, Missouri, where the college was dedicated in 1892, as the Scarritt Bible and Training School, with an enrollment of three. In 1923 the Scarritt School was moved to Nashville, its scope broadened to include all church workers, and the name changed to Scarritt College for Christian Workers. Senior college courses leading to a bachelor's degree and graduate courses have been organized in three fields: community and family service, social work, and religious education.

33. WARD-BELMONT COLLEGE, 16th Ave. S. and Belcourt, for young women, has as its main building, Belmont, the former home of Col. J. A. S. Acklen, built in 1850, and at that time considered one of the finest private homes in the South. The building is designed in the manner of an Italian Renaissance villa, with wrought-iron balconies and window guards imported from Italy. Other buildings have been added, facing the garden in the rear and forming a quadrangle with one open side. The circular flower beds, many of the walks, and the outdoor tea houses of iron grill work have been retained in their original setting. The statues on the grounds once stood in the old Acklen garden. The water tower, used during the War between the States as a signal tower, houses the carillon bells, a gift in 1929 from the alumnae of Ward's Seminary, Belmont College, and Ward-Belmont.

Ward Seminary was established in 1865 by the Reverend William E. Ward. It was first housed in the Kirkman Building, near the State Capitol, then on the present 8th Avenue. In 1890 Belmont College was established in the Acklen home by Miss Ida E. Hood and Miss Susan L. Heron, and when they retired in 1913 the two schools were united.

34. FORT NEGLEY *(open at all hours),* Chestnut St. and Ridley Blvd., erected by Federal Gen. James S. Negley of Pennsylvania in 1862, was re-

stored in 1937 by WPA. The original plans made by Brig.-Gen. James St. Clair were used. Many of the walls and much of the foundation of the abandoned fort were found intact when the restoration was made. The large stone and iron building, with its complex polygonal plan, stands on the summit of the hill. Two bomb-proof basements are roofed with iron. The guns of Fort Negley opened the Battle of Nashville in 1864.

During the Reconstruction Period the abandoned fort was used as a meeting place by the Ku Klux Klan. The musty crypts and debris-littered galleries were well suited to midnight gatherings, and sentries on the parapets could warn against the approach of troops. All efforts of the Union Army of Occupation to stamp out the Klan failed. By 1870 the last of the carpetbaggers and "scalawags" had left town, and Grand Wizard Nathan Bedfort Forrest ordered the Klan dissolved. As a gesture of defiance, the final "Konclave" of the Nashville chapter was announced in the newspapers and by handbill. Gov. DeWitt Clinton Senter issued orders to the Union troops garrisoned in Nashville to break up the demonstration, and the city police, augmented by special deputies, were also called out. Warnings to the Klan were posted, and the police and troops had orders to shoot to kill if the proposed march through the city was attempted.

Ignoring this, a picked troop of Klansmen gathered at Fort Negley and, in full regalia, circled west of Nashville to the Charlotte Pike and came into the city by Cedar Street. Thousands turned out to watch the parade whose route would pass directly by Capitol Hill. Troops in battle formation were drawn up on the capitol grounds, where a heavy iron chain had been stretched across the Cedar Street entrance. Ranks of policemen were stationed on both sides of the street and when the robed column cantered up the hill, the order was passed along to policemen to draw their weapons. The order was not carried out, for at that moment each of them felt the muzzle of a pistol poked into the small of his back. Behind every policeman stood an armed Klansman in civilian clothes. The Klansmen reached the chain and halted. One of them dismounted and broke the chain with a sledge hammer. The Union officers on Capitol Hill, sensing from the inaction of the police that something was wrong, withheld fire. The Klansmen cantered past the capitol and swung west through the heart of town. Then they rode on out to Fort Negley where, after the last ceremonies, they burned their robes and ritual books and rode home. (This well-known Nashville story is treated by Mrs. S. E. F. Rose in her book, the *Ku Klux Klan.*)

35. CITY CEMETERY, Oak St. and 4th Ave. S., when opened in 1822, was surrounded by a peaceful woodland, but now factories crowd close to its walls.

In the cemetery is the simple boxlike tomb of James Robertson, founder of Nashville; and the tombs of Charlotte Reeves, his wife, and Felix Robertson, their son (the first white boy born in Nashville). Here also is buried William E. West, friend of Washington Irving and portraitist of European celebrities *(see PAINTING AND SCULPTURE)*. William Carroll, former Governor of Tennessee, and William Driver, who gave the name "Old Glory" to the National flag, are also buried here.

Over the graves of John Kane, stone cutter at the capitol, and Sarah Ann Gray, wife of William Walker, are monuments designed by William Strickland.

36. HOLY TRINITY CHURCH (Negro), 6th Ave. S. and Ewing St., is constructed of native blue limestone with a trussed roof of varnished cedar. Designed by Wills and Dudley (1852), the building resembles an old English parish church. The altar is of cedar adorned with a crown of thorns. Founded by Charles Tomes as the first mission of Christ's Church in Nashville, Holy Trinity was given to its Negro members in 1908. Singers from Fisk University frequently furnish music for the services.

37. The SITE OF THE WILLIAM DRIVER HOME, 511 5th Ave. S., is occupied by a dwelling. In 1831 Captain Driver, master of the brig *Charles Daggett,* was presented with an American flag by his mother and some neighbor girls in Salem, Massachusetts. As the flag was unfurled from the masthead, the young seaman exclaimed, "I'll call her 'Old Glory.' " Driver came to Nashville in 1837, bringing the original "Old Glory" with him. On special occasions it was hoisted in front of his home. During the War between the States, Driver was strongly Union in sentiment. His house was searched repeatedly in an effort to find the flag, which had been sewed into a quilt. When the Federals took the city in 1862, the captain brought the flag from its hiding place and hoisted it.

38. SUNNYSIDE *(private),* Kirkwood Lane and 12th Ave. S., was built by Mrs. Jesse Benton in 1840 and is one of the finest examples of antebellum architecture in Middle Tennessee. Plans for the home were drawn by Thomas H. Benton, brother of Jesse. The two-story structure was designed in the Jeffersonian Classic style; the central portion constructed of clapboards over the original logs, and the portico with large square columns. White brick wings were added in the 1920's by the present owner, Col. Granville Sevier, foster grandson of Mrs. Benton.

The house was in the line of fire during the Battle of Nashville. After the battle the marks of 42 Minie balls were found in the front portico and door.

39. WESTWOOD *(private),* 2712 Westwood Drive, derived its name from two family names, West and Wood. The house is built of large wooden blocks, cut from timber on the estate, and painted white to resemble stone. Four galleries, supported by slender fluted Corinthian columns with delicate acanthus leaves, surround the house. There is a balcony over the entrance and wrought-iron railings enclose the lower half of the balcony and the galleries. The overseer's house and the stone spring house are still standing. Westwood was the home of Robert Woods, whose wife was the daughter of Edward West, an experimenter with early steamboat engines. His son William West, the artist, lived here for many years.

40. DAVID LIPSCOMB COLLEGE, 4 *m.* (Granny White Pike bus), is a co-educational institution supported by a private foundation in the interest of the Church of Christ. Specializing in Christian education, it is one of the oldest institutions of its kind and is one of the few schools in the country that include Bible study every day. The natural beauty of the shaded 40-acre campus has been enhanced by effective landscaping. The

red brick buildings, trimmed with white limestone, have classic façades of modified Greek Revival mode. The oldest structure on the campus is the president's house, the former residence of David Lipscomb. This building and the Burton Gymnasium, the latter designed by C. K. Colley and constructed in 1923, were the only two structures spared in a fire of 1929. In 1930, Harding Hall, which was designed by R. E. Turberville and constructed about 1900, was remodeled by George Waller. Elam Hall and Sewell Hall were also designed by Waller and constructed in 1930.

Founded in 1891 as the Nashville Bible School, the first session was held in a rented building on Fillmore Street. In 1903, David Lipscomb, co-founder with J. A. Harding, gave his farm as a permanent location and in 1918 the name of the institution was changed to David Lipscomb College. Elementary, high school, and junior college courses are given. In 1936–37 the enrollment was 500.

41. SHELBY PARK of 361 acres, at the E. end of Shelby Ave., contains several log houses, and the municipal Iris Garden, with more than 500 varieties of iris. It is equipped with baseball and soft ball diamonds, tennis courts, a swimming pool, a golf course, children's playgrounds and numerous picnic areas.

42. CHEATHAM PLACE, 1564 9th Ave. N., is a PWA housing and slum clearance project. On the 21-acre site are 352 apartments in two-, three-, and four-room units. Designed by the Nashville Allied Architects, the buildings are plain and symmetrically arranged in landscaped courts. Kitchens are designed to provide efficiency in working space and are supplied with modern appliances. A community building provides social rooms, clinic rooms, and office.

43. ANDREW JACKSON PLACE, 1457 Jackson St., is the site of the PWA Negro housing project, designed by the Nashville Allied Architects. The houses are simple in design, carefully planned, and well built. There are individual yards and garden plots. The homes cover only about 20 percent of the entire site, the remainder of the land being used for yards, gardens, and play space.

44. FISK UNIVERSITY (Negro), Jefferson St. and 17th Ave. N., has a campus of 40 acres, with 20 buildings.

The American Missionary Association of New York City and the Western Freedmen's Aid Commission of Cincinnati assisted by Gen. Clinton B. Fisk, then in charge of the Freedmen's Bureau in Tennessee, founded Fisk University. The institution was opened in 1866 as Fisk School, with John Ogden as its first principal. In 1867 the school was chartered as a university.

For 70 years Fisk devoted its efforts to building a college of liberal arts and sciences, but now (1939) more attention is given to training leaders among the American Negroes. Bachelor of arts, bachelor of music, and master of arts degrees are granted.

JUBILEE HALL, is a brick L-shaped structure, six stories in height, and Victorian Gothic in style, the oldest and largest building and the center of University life. It was built in 1876 with part of the money made by the first group of Jubilee Singers. The group was organized in 1867 by George L. White, treasurer of Fisk, and was known as the Colored Christian Singers. In 1871 the chorus of seven women and four men students made an extensive tour of the larger northern cities, Europe, and the British Isles. Their singing of Negro spirituals was so enthusiastically received that the proceeds of the tour amounted to more than $150,000, sufficient to purchase the university campus and build Jubilee Hall. Under the name of the Fisk Jubilee Singers, successive choral groups have continued at intervals to tour the Old and New Worlds, and to give radio concerts.

The UNIVERSITY LIBRARY *(open 8-5:30 weekdays)*, designed by Henry C. Hibbs, is of modified Gothic design, constructed of reinforced steel and concrete faced with red brick and cut-stone trim. Murals by Aaron Douglas, prominent Negro artist, portray the progress of the Negro in America. Reading room space provides for 300, and a tower stack accommodates the 175,000 volumes.

45. MEHARRY MEDICAL COLLEGE (Negro), 1005 18th Ave. N., adjoining Fisk University, is on a campus covering six blocks. Meharry took its name from the descendants of Alexander and Jane Meharry, who with the aid of Dr. R. S. Rust, original founder of the school, contributed liberally to its support. The four buildings of red brick with cut-stone trim, are Collegiate Gothic in style, designed by Gordon and Keelber (1930–31). The main building houses the hospital, school of medicine, school of pharmacy, school of dentistry, dental hygiene department, and a school for nurses. Organized in 1876 as the Medical Department of Central Tennessee College, the name was changed in 1900 to Meharry Medical College of Walden University, and in 1915 it became an independent college. Doctor of medicine and doctor of dental surgery degrees are given. Three years' work is offered in pharmacy and in nursing.

46. TENNESSEE AGRICULTURAL AND INDUSTRIAL STATE TEACHERS COLLEGE (Negro), 3300 Centennial Blvd., on 80 acres overlooking the Cumberland River, has a group of buildings, in simple Greek Revival style, with low gabled roofs and Doric porticoes. The college opened as a State normal school in 1912, but became an accredited teachers college in 1922 with a four-year training course. In 1937 the State legislature authorized the school to grant the degree of master of arts. The A. & I. Concert Singers specialize in classical music and spirituals and sponsor a musical drama each spring.

47. In CHEROKEE PARK, 62nd St. and Louisiana Ave., is the TREATY OAK, under which, in June 1783, the white settlers of Middle Tennessee headed by James Robertson, met delegations from principal southern tribes in a peace council lasting three days. The tree, its six-foot trunk protected by an iron fence, is estimated to be at least 350 years old.

Around Treaty Oak were the camp grounds where Tennessee's soldiers were mustered for every war from Jackson's Creek campaign in 1813 to the Spanish American War in 1898.

POINTS OF INTEREST IN ENVIRONS

Glen Echo, *6.3 m.;* Rock Castle, *19 m. (see Tour 7, sec. a);* Melrose, *3.9 m.;* Peace Monument, *3.8 m.;* Travelers Rest, *7.4 m. (see Tour 7, sec. b);* Site of Home of John Haywood, *7.9 m. (see Tour 7A);* West View, *3 m. (see Tour 8, sec. a);* Camping Grounds of Irish Nomads, *3.5 m.;* Municipal Airport, *7.7 m. (see Tour 8, sec. b);* Buchanan Station, *5.4 m.;* DeMonbreun Cave, *5.9 m.;* Two Rivers Farm, *7 m.;* Clover Bottom, *10.1 m.;* Tulip Grove, *12.8 m.;* Hermitage, *13 m. (see Tour 12, sec. b);* Belle Meade Estate, *6 m. (see Tour 12, sec. c);* Percy Warner Park, *8.7 m. (see Tour 12B).*

Memphis

Railroad Stations: Grand Central, 535 S. Main St. and Calhoun Ave., for Illinois Central R.R., Chicago, Rock Island and Pacific Ry., and St. Louis-San Francisco Ry.; Union Station, Calhoun St. between S. 2nd and S. 3rd Sts., for Southern Ry., Louisville & Nashville R.R., St. Louis Southwestern Ry., Nashville, Chattanooga & St. Louis Ry., and Missouri Pacific R.R.
Bus Stations: Greyhound, 161 Monroe Ave., for Dixie Greyhound, Southwestern Greyhound, and Oliver Bus Lines; Missouri Pacific Terminal, 269 S. Main St., for Missouri Pacific Transportation Lines, and for Missouri-Arkansas Lines; 122 S. 3rd St., for Arkansas Coach Lines; 156 Monroe St., for Tri-State Transit Co.
Airport: Memphis Municipal Airport, 10 m. SW., Airways Blvd., for American Airlines, Inc., Chicago and Southern Airlines, and Southern Air Service, Inc. Taxi fare 75¢ from downtown. City ticket office, Peabody Hotel, Union Ave. at 2nd St.
Streecars: Local busses, street cars and coaches, Main St. Uniform fare of 7¢, with transfers to all lines.
Taxis: 25¢ for first 1.5 miles, 10¢ for each additional half mile. Flat rate of $2 per hr.
Boats: Excursion boats for short trips during summer, at wharf, foot of Beale Ave., and Riverside Drive. A boat makes three trips daily between President's Island and the foot of Wisconsin Ave. (fare varies).
Traffic Regulations: Speed limit 25 m. p. h. Observe National Traffic Code. All cars using Memphis streets for more than 30 days must bear guest tags. All-day parking allowed between Riverside Drive and river.

Accommodations: Thirty hotels, two for Negroes; tourist camps.

Information Service: Dixie Motor Club, Hotel Peabody, Union Ave. at S. 2nd St.

Radio Stations: WHBQ (1370 kc.); WMC (780 kc.); WMPS (1430 kc.); WREC (600 kc.).
Theaters and Motion Picture Houses: Ellis Auditorium, Main St. and Exchange Ave., road shows and opera. Memphis Little Theater, Museum of Natural History and Industrial Arts, Tilton Road facing Central Ave. Four first-run, 33 second-run motion picture houses, three for Negroes.
Baseball: Russwood Park, Madison Ave., Southern Association (Class A).
Wrestling: Each Monday at Ellis Auditorium, Main St. and Exchange Ave.
Swimming: Municipal Pool, Fairgrounds at E. Parkway, S. of Central Ave.; Memphis Country Club Pool, Southern and Goodwyn Aves.; E. End, 2016 Madison Ave. (Fairgrounds Car No. 2); Malone Pool (free), N. Main St. and Saffarans Ave.; Washington Pool (for Negroes), N. 2nd St. and Marble Ave.; Clearpool, 10 m. S. on US 78; Maywood Pool, 17.5 m. on US 78; Harbin's Pool, 10 m. S. on US 51.
Golf: Overton Park, N. Parkway, Poplar Ave., E. Parkway, 9 holes, free; Riverside, S. end of Riverside Blvd. and W. end S. Parkway, 9 holes, free; Alicia Gold Club, 2629 Poplar Ave., 9 holes, 25¢; McLean-Vallentine Golf Club, N. McLean Ave., one block W. of Vallentine, 9 holes, 25¢; Galloway, 18 holes, 50¢.
Tennis: Beauregard Park, Jefferson Ave., at Waldron (30¢ per hour on three courts, no charge on nine), night tennis (40¢ per hour); Galloway Park, Walnut Grove Rd. just N. of Poplar (30¢ per hour); Mid-South Fairgrounds, E. Parkway (free); Alicia Tennis Courts, E. Parkway just S. of Poplar Ave. (40¢ per hour).
Free Circus: South entrance Overton Park, between N. Parkway and Poplar Ave. (daily summer, 10:30 a.m. and 2:30 p.m.; Sundays the year round at 2:30 p.m.).

Annual Events: Cotton Carnival, May, and Mid-South Fair, September; Horse shows, Mid-South Fairgrounds, spring and fall; Southern Amateur Tennis Tournament, during Cotton Carnival in May.

MEMPHIS (320 alt., 253,143 pop.), largest city in the State, is a metropolis for Tennessee, Mississippi, and Arkansas. On the Fourth, or Lower Chickasaw Bluff, east bank of the Mississippi River, Memphis flattens out from its 40-foot elevation to the black cotton lands and the rolling forested country of the Wolf River on the north and east and Nonconnah Creek on the south. Its position on the banks of a great river that like the Nile, flooded the delta lands each spring made the name Memphis an appropriate choice.

Now an industrial center, the city still has much of the glamour of early river days. The names of buildings and streets recall the Chickasaw Indians, De Soto, and the roaring days when ranks of steamboats nosed into the landing and sent pungent woodsmoke rolling over the city. Along the cobblestoned river front of Wolf Harbor are wharves and warehouses. Cable transportation systems swing out over the water, and with the massed railroad tracks form river and rail connections for lumber, steel, and cotton products. Shanty-boats are moored to the sloping willow-tangled banks of Mud Island, which rises in the center of the harbor. Below the island the steel spans of the Harahan and Frisco Bridges reach to the Arkansas shore.

Overlooking the Wolf and Mississippi are Jefferson Davis and Confederate Parks, Cossitt Library, and the Federal building. From the weathered cotton-office buildings of Front Street the business district climbs eastward toward lofty new office buildings. The central section of downtown Memphis, with Main Street as a base and with the tall Sterrick and Exchange buildings looming above, has the appearance of any thriving metropolis, except that the crowds move with less push and hurry, and groups are more apt to gather on the broad sidewalks to talk. The tower of the Columbian Mutual Tower Building rises above Court Square, where shoppers pause to feed the squirrels and pigeons. The flavor of the older city grows stronger along upper North Main and lower South Main and adjacent streets. Here the fruit stands, antique and curio shops, and musty second-hand bookstores and pawnshops display their wares on counters along the sidewalks. The first floors of many buildings are deserted. Doors hanging ajar on warped hinges show sagging littered stairs to second-story living quarters.

The principal avenues lead northeast from the river past Crosstown, the mid-city business area, to join the Parkway, a double-laned, oak and maple-shaded drive which, with Riverside Drive, encircles the city and passes the spacious wooded parks.

Business and office structures, apartments and their minor satellites, the soft drink stand, "hamburger joint," and filling station, have obliterated much of the former grandeur of the queer, castle-like homes of the Victorian era. The few that remain are bedraggled rooming houses whose former occupants have retreated to the newer residential sections along the Parkway, in Chickasaw Gardens, Red Acres, and Hein Park.

AIR VIEW—DOWNTOWN MEMPHIS

For the first hundred years of its history Memphis was nothing more than a river boom town on the borderline of the West. Settlers were too busy amassing fortunes to take the time for building stately homes. For this reason there are few old mansions in the city. Only in the last two decades have restricted residential areas been laid out. These areas have grown rapidly and are like neat little villages in the suburbs. Gravel drives wind past homes of Georgian Colonial, English Tudor, and Spanish mission style.

Near the river and in North and South Memphis are the large blocks of factory buildings, lumber yards, and cotton compresses. The homes in these districts, rows of duplicated houses, are similar to those found in any industrial center.

The Cotton Carnival, a 1931 revival of the Mardi Gras celebrations of 1872–1901, presents the story of the city in pageantry. Sponsored by a non-profit civic organization, the carnival each May dramatizes the story of cotton and serves to center national attention on Memphis and its leading product.

King Cotton and his Queen of Beauty, selected in secret committee, reign for four days over a court chosen by leading clubs and by 40 cities throughout the Tri-State area. The colorful and impressive entry of their majesties on the royal barge laden with hundreds of bales of cotton opens the revelry—pageants, street parades, carnival balls, street dancing, beauty reviews, races, shows, tournaments, and many private parties.

The Cotton Carnival celebration assumed a more serious nature in 1935 with the presentation of the National Cotton Show at the Mid-South Fairgrounds, in which leading cotton manufacturers of the country participate. The displays tell the story of cotton in all its phases, from planting through production to the many finished products.

The Negro plays his part in "The Negro Sings," the Beale Street section of the fiesta. The Negro floats are made in the manual training departments of their schools. Their three-day revel, parades, and "sings," beginning the second day, are a vivid part of the ceremonies. Included in the Negro division of the carnival are the coronation parade and dance on Wednesday, lawn tea and oratorical contest on Thursday, and the children's parade, track meet, jubilee parade, and ball on Friday.

Through their physical labor the Negroes have helped build Memphis on the bluff, and they love the town. The Negroes' old "lonesome songs" inspired the "blues" of W. C. Handy. In the Bluff City they have found a place to grow, as attested by their homes, schools, churches, and business houses. Memphis is the center of an agricultural section in which Negro labor predominates, and more than one-third of the city's population is Negro. Although the death rate for Negroes exceeds the birth rate, the Negro population continues to increase because of a strong influx from the surrounding country. There is also a large transient Negro population.

The Chickasaw lived on the Fourth or Lower Chickasaw Bluff long before 1541, when they were visited by De Soto and his gold-seeking expedition. The Spaniards first stopped at Quizquiz, identified by most historians as the lower Chickasaw Bluff. Then De Soto moved to a nearby town, Chisca, where he first saw the Mississippi River, May 21, and called it the River of the Holy Ghost.

The bluff was not again visited by white men until 1673 when Joliet and Marquette stopped to trade with the Indians. La Salle followed in 1682 and built Fort Prudhomme on the First Chickasaw Bluff, above the mouth of the Hatchie River. Then France, Spain, and England began a long struggle for control of the bluffs, which commanded the Mississippi River. Neither intrigue nor force succeeded in winning the Chickasaw as French allies. In 1763, the French ceded to the English the eastern part of the Mississippi Valley, including the site of Memphis.

During the next two decades Spanish influence grew strong among the Chickasaw. The Spaniards of Louisiana planned to use the tribe as a buffer against the growing Cumberland Settlement in Middle Tennessee. There was, however, a strong party among the Chickasaw, led by the half-breeds John Turner and James Colbert, which used the Lower Chickasaw Bluff as a base for raiding Spanish river commerce. Turner visited the Cumberland Settlement and persuaded Gen. James Robertson that the encroaching power of Spain should be stopped. Robertson led a force to the bluff in 1782, and established a depot where the Chickasaw could be given supplies to offset Spanish bribes. In 1794 John Overton, temporary agent for Indian affairs, established a trading post at the bluff.

As late as 1795 Gayoso, Spanish Governor of Louisiana, led troops to the bluff to prevent the Cumberland settlers from building forts. A detachment of United States Regulars forced their withdrawal.

When Capt. Isaac Guion, leading a force of Regulars to Natchez in 1797, stopped to distribute goods to the Chickasaw, he secured land on the bluff for the erection of Fort Adams, a United States Army post named for President John Adams. The bluff remained in Chickasaw control until 1818, when the western territory was ceded to the United States.

In 1783–1786 North Carolina granted John Rice and John Ramsey 5,000 acres of land on the site of Memphis. Though North Carolina had no legal claim to the land, this fact was ignored because the Revolution had drained the State treasury. Rice was killed by the Indians, and John Overton bought his grant for $500. Overton conveyed half of his interest to Andrew Jackson, who made over part of his interest to James Winchester.

Immediately after the Indian treaty (1818), Jackson, Overton, and Winchester made plans for laying out a town. Having selected the site because of the high bluff over the Mississippi and the excellent landing at the mouth of Wolf River, they marked out 362 lots. General Jackson, severely criticized for his interest in this technically shady land operation, sold his claims to John C. McLemore in 1823.

Memphis was settled rapidly, chiefly by North-of-Ireland Scots, Scotch Highlanders, and Germans from East and Middle Tennessee, who had come originally from North Carolina, Virginia and South Carolina. The North-of-Ireland Scots were adventurers, politicians, and land speculators, while the Highlanders and Germans were thrifty farmers, mechanics, and home builders.

The town was incorporated December 9, 1826, by an act of the State legislature. Under the leadership of John Overton $100 was subscribed in 1827 to establish a newspaper, the Memphis *Advocate and Western District Intelligencer*. The *Western Times and Memphis Commercial Advertiser* began publication in 1831 and the Memphis *Gazette* in 1834.

Among the first industries were gunsmithing and blacksmithing. Stores, repair shops, and sawmills were operating by 1830; cotton warehouses and mills followed.

Large cotton plantations were laid out and hundreds of slaves brought up river from the market at New Orleans. Barges and flatboats, the first carriers of river commerce, were manned by hard-bitten "bullies," who fought pirates on the river and brawled among themselves in every waterfront tavern. In 1812 the *New Orleans,* first steamboat on the Mississippi, made a trip from Pittsburgh to New Orleans. The first steamboat line from Memphis to New Orleans began operation in 1834. Because of its central position on the Mississippi, Memphis was designated as a port of customs in 1850. Though fires, explosions, river piracy, collisions, and wrecks made shipping and travel by steamboat hazardous, packet lines prospered, and Memphis became one of the busiest ports in America.

Stagecoach service from Nashville to Memphis and on to Little Rock was established in 1829. In 1843 a telegraph line to New Orleans was opened. The LaGrange & Memphis Railroad, begun in 1839, made an exhibition run of six miles in 1842. The line was never completed, and the sheriff sold the engine, coaches, and rails. The Memphis & Charleston Railroad, connecting the town with the Atlantic Coast, was completed in 1857.

Between 1850 and 1860 Memphis grew from a town of 6,427 to a city of 33,000.

With the outbreak of the War between the States in 1861, Memphis became a Confederate military center under Gen. Leonidas Polk. Commerce, trade, and manufacture were suspended. Early in 1862 Memphis was made the temporary State capital because Nashville lay unprotected before advancing Union troops.

On June 6, 1862, the city was seized by Union forces under Commodore C. H. Davis after the brief but decisive Battle of Memphis. Seven of the defending Confederate fleet of eight boats were sunk by the Union fleet of six armored gunboats, four rams, and 20 other boats. The battle, watched by the population from the bluffs, now Chickasaw and Confederate Parks, lasted only 90 minutes. Commodore Davis entered the city and raised the Stars and Stripes over the courthouse. The city remained in Union control until after the war, though there was a brief, spectacular Confederate raid led by Gen. Nathan Bedford Forrest in August 1864.

While they imposed martial law, the Federal commanders issued a number of military orders. Merchants had to obtain Federal permits to do business; families of men in the Confederate Army were driven out or imprisoned. In July 1865, military authority over municipal affairs was ended by order of Gen. John E. Smith.

At the close of the war Memphis was without money, credit, or crops. The suddenly altered labor situation, wild price fluctuations, and the generally unsettled condition of the country made normal readjustment impossible. Then came the yellow fever epidemics of 1867, 1873, and 1878. The heaviest blow fell in the last epidemic. More than 25,000 fled within the first two weeks, and 5,000 more sought refuge in camps near-by.

Memphis became a pest-hole. As deaths mounted, the streets were deserted except for the "dead wagons." Bodies lay rotting in the streets where they had fallen. The criminal element of the city ran wild. Looting and killing, terrific drunken brawls, gun battles, and rape were common. Not more than 20,000 people remained in the city; 14,000 were Negroes, of whom 946 died. The higher fatality was among the 6,000 whites, of whom 4,206 died. Surrounding towns speedily quarantined Memphis. At Columbus, Kentucky, armed citizens turned back a train on the Mobile & Ohio Railroad.

The spread of the disease was due to ignorance of its cause. At the time the general medical belief was that it was caused by a "parasite of vegetable nature" so tender that frost would destroy it. They properly diagnosed standing water, sluggish sewage, garbage, dumps, and hot weather as breeders, but failed to recognize the mosquito as the carrier.

Relief was undertaken by the Howard Association (generally called the Howards), the contemporary Red Cross which had originated about 1857 among clerks in a New Orleans store. The work was financed by gifts totaling $417,000 in money and more than $500,000 in provisions. Roman Catholic sisters and priests also took courageous part in the relief work, prominent among them being Father J. A. Kelly.

During the worst of the epidemic Anna Cook ("Madame Annie"), who kept the noted Mansion House brothel on Gayoso Street, turned out her girls and took yellow fever patients into her elegantly furnished rooms. An expert in the treatment of disease, she personally superintended the nursing of patients. She contracted the disease and died in September 1878.

The "heavy black frost and ice one-sixteenth inch thick" of October 20, 1878, ended the epidemic. Yellow fever had killed thousands, but it had awakened the people to the urgent need for sanitation. A complete sewage system was installed, and artesian wells were sunk to eliminate use of river water. Other rigid measures were adopted to prevent return of yellow fever.

The aftermath of the epidemic in Memphis was worse than the dismal days of Reconstruction. Surrendering its charter to the State, the city was made the Taxing District of Shelby County. The leaders of the movement gave two reasons: they wanted breathing time to recover before paying the city debt; they felt that municipal government in this country was a failure. The legislature provided a government composed of a legislative council of eight members: the board of fire and police commissioners, and the board of public works—elected by popular vote.

Then trade boomed and by 1890 Memphis had grown in population to 64,589. In 1893 the State restored the charter.

The first railroad bridge across the Mississippi River south of St. Louis was built at Memphis in 1892, followed by Harahan Bridge in 1909. The bridges brought increased trade with the Southwest, and Memphis became the greatest inland cotton market and hardwood lumber center in the world.

Wealthy planters retired from their delta lands and settled in Memphis to become cotton factors and lumber dealers. The expanding river town drew tradesmen, professional men, and laborers. From small towns and plantations Negroes poured into the Bluff City. Many opened businesses and became independent; the majority of them worked as laborers in cotton, lumber, and construction. Many foreigners settled in Memphis, among them Italians, who at present are among the civic leaders.

The Mississippi flood of January-February 1937 imposed upon Memphis the huge task of providing for an estimated 50,000 to 60,000 refugees. Bewildered sharecroppers, fisherfolk, and river-town people from Mississippi, Arkansas, and Tennessee—most of them suffering from hunger and exposure—poured into Memphis by train, truck, rescue boat, and "footback." Through the efforts of every available civic and social agency, a rescue program met practically every human need from the moment of registration to the departure of the last refugee group.

SLUM DWELLERS, MEMPHIS

At the Mid-South Fairgrounds, the largest refugee camp, barracks were erected, and the adjacent Fairview High School was converted into a major base hospital. The sick were cared for in the wards of John Gaston, Baptist, Methodist, St. Joseph's, U. S. Veterans, and Marine Hospitals. Eight hundred and six patients were listed as refugee emergency cases; 2,089 were immunized against typhoid fever and smallpox. In addition to the fairgrounds camp, 14 school buildings were converted to refugee service. Negro refugees were provided for in the north hall of Ellis Auditorium.

The "rivergees" sang:

> Down at the Fairgrounds on my knees,
> Prayin' to the Lord to give me ease—
> Lord, Lord, I got them high-water blues!

Edward Hull Crump (Boss Ed), a notable figure in Tennessee politics, took a leading part during the flood. He donned a pair of high-topped boots and went out to the levee to encourage the workers. Negroes of the chain gang sang loudly when they saw him:

> Oh, the river's up and cotton's down,
> Mister Ed Crump, he runs this town.

"Do you think the levee will break?" A visitor asked one of the foremen. "Hell, naw!" was the reply. "Why are you so damn sure?" "Mister Crump say it won't."

To some of the Negroes and poor whites, the experience was a holiday. Many of them had never been more than a few miles from home. Social workers found hundreds who did not know their last names or the State and county from which they had come. Used to an unvarying diet of "sow bosom," sorghum, and corn mush, they devoured fruits and good beef with the wonder of children drinking their first pink circus lemonade. People warped and stupefied by pellagra responded quickly to balanced diet and left the refugee camp cured.

The increasing demand for cotton, cotton products, lumber, and lumber products have continued to bring different lines of transportation to Memphis. Today the city has ten railroads, four steamship lines, two U. S. Customs bonded warehouses, eleven general warehouses, and five freight forwarders. All of its four large banks maintain foreign trade departments.

The U. S. Engineers Flood Control project is directed from Memphis. The extensive engineering work is considered a Memphis unit despite the fact that the offices, warehouses, and materials are on the Arkansas bank of the river. The commanding officer maintains headquarters and residence in Memphis and most of the engineers and workmen live in Memphis and commute to their work across the river.

The Port of Memphis annually exports to all parts of the world, but mainly to Europe, Central and South America, merchandise valued at more than $250,000,000. Foreign commerce is approximately 10 per cent of the gross transaction of the district. The valuation of imports is only slightly less.

Thousands of tons of freight annually pass through the city for redistribution. Principal items of export are raw cotton, cottonseed products, and lumber and wood manufactures. Memphis is the largest non-manufacturing steel distribution center in the South. The city leads in the production of cottonseed products. An immense grain storage elevator, with river and rail connections, handles grain from the central, western, and northwestern States. A large quantity of oil is relayed from the fields of the Southwest by river tankers for redistribution.

Natural gas is piped from the Monroe, Louisiana, fields. The City of Memphis, which purchased the utilities company in 1938, has contracted with TVA for the purchase of power from Pickwick Dam or Muscle Shoals.

The commission form of government was adopted in 1909. Among Memphis' municipally owned public services are the water works, airport, park, and recreational facilities valued at $12,000,000, and viaducts spanning all dangerous railway crossings. Memphis was one of the first cities to create and completely equip a motor inspection bureau. Its system, providing for compulsory quarterly inspection of all motor vehicles, was established in 1934 and has been followed by ten other cities. In 1927 Memphis took first rank in safety among cities of America under 500,000 population.

POINTS OF INTEREST

1. GOODWYN INSTITUTE *(open 8-10 weekdays)*, SW. corner Madison Ave. and S. 3rd St., is a seven-story structure of steel, stone, brick, and terra cotta. The spacious lobby has tiled floors, lofty columns, and wide marble steps with elaborately decorated marble newels. The institute, which houses an auditorium, library, and office, was founded in 1907 as a memorial to William A. Goodwyn, philanthropist, who lived in Memphis most of his life. At his death, in 1889, he left $473,940 for its establishment and maintenance. A series of free lectures by authorities in various fields and concerts by leading artists are given annually. The lecture season extends from October through March.

2. The STERRICK BUILDING, NE. corner Madison Ave. and N. 3rd St., is a 29-story building, Gothic in detail and designed in modern setback style. Erected in 1929–30 by Ross Sterling, former Governor of Texas, the building was designed by the engineer-architect, Wyatt C. Hedrick. Sterrick is a combination of the names Sterling and Hedrick.

3. The SITE OF THE JEFFERSON DAVIS HOME, 129 Court Ave., is marked by a bronze tablet. Jefferson Davis, President of the Confederacy, lived here from 1867 to 1875.

4. The SITE OF THE IRVING BLOCK, N. 2nd St. at Court Ave., is occupied by modern business houses. The original buildings were constructed in 1860 when iron fronts (the façades faced with cast-iron) were not common in Memphis. This section of town was notably tough, and iron slats were used to cover the windows. On September 12, 1861, the block became a Confederate hospital, and at the occupation of Memphis by the Federals, in 1862, was converted into a prison where citizens and Confederate prisoners of war were incarcerated. Among them were ladies of fine families. A report on the prison by Judge Advocate General J. Holt to President Lincoln reads: "According to a report of inspection made to Colonel Hardie By Lieut. Col. John F. Marsh, 24th Regiment Veterans Reserve Corps, under date of April 28, 1864, the prison which is used for the detention of citizens, prisoners of war on their way north, and the United States soldiers awaiting trial, and which is located in a large block of stores, is represented as the filthiest place the inspector ever saw occupied by human beings. The whole management and government of the prison could not be worse. Discipline and order are unknown. Food sufficient but badly served." Lincoln abolished the prison the following year.

5. COURT SQUARE, N. Main St. between Jefferson and Court Aves., extending to N. 2nd St., is the most noted of the original four squares laid out in 1819 for public use by the proprietors of Memphis. Bronze Tablets commemorate Walter Malone's poem, "Opportunity," and the Confederate prison history of Memphis.

A FOUNTAIN, a copy of Canova's celebrated statue of Hebe in the art gallery at Leningrad, is in the center of the square. Designed by J. B. Cook, the fountain was presented to the city by a group of citizens in 1876.

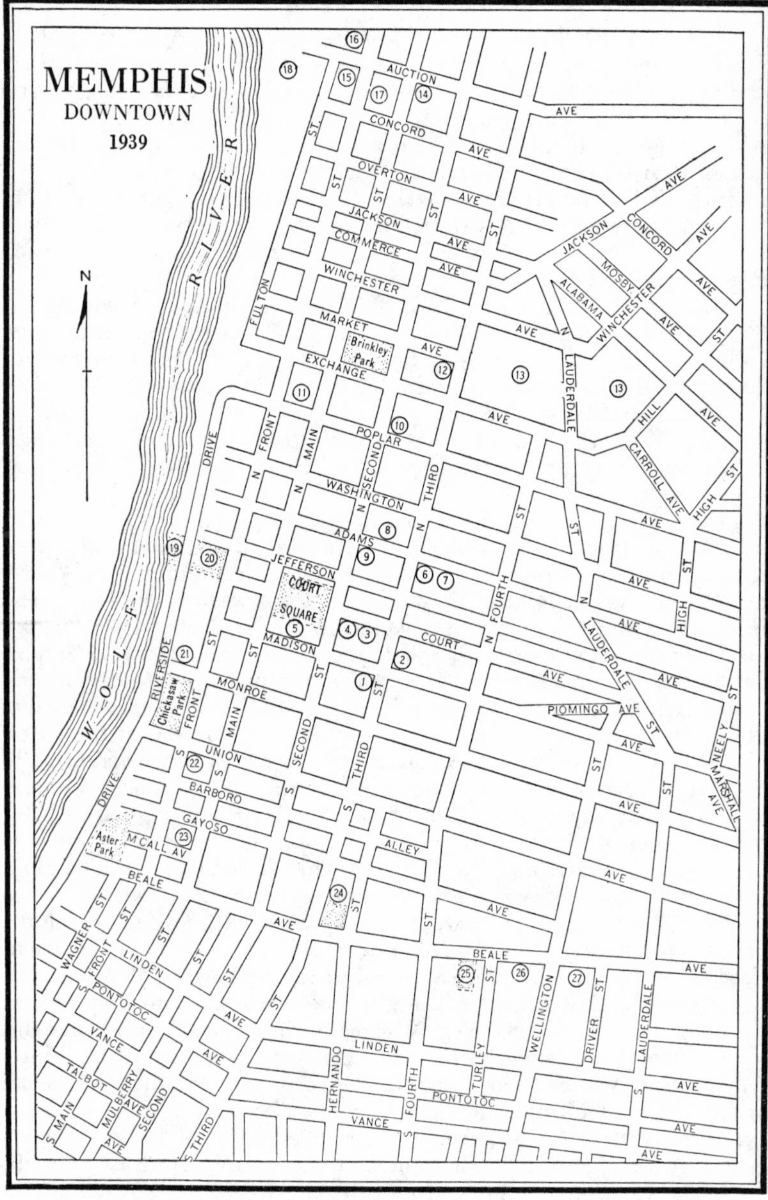
MEMPHIS
DOWNTOWN
1939
N
WOLF RIVER
AUCTION
CONCORD
OVERTON
JACKSON
COMMERCE
WINCHESTER
MARKET
EXCHANGE
Brinkley Park
POPLAR
WASHINGTON
ADAMS
JEFFERSON
COURT SQUARE
COURT
MADISON
MONROE
UNION
BARBORO
GAYOSO
M CALL AV
Aster Park
Chickasaw Park
RIVERSIDE DRIVE
BEALE
ALLEY
LINDEN
PONTOTOC
VANCE
TALBOT
MULBERRY
WAGNER
FRONT
MAIN
SECOND
THIRD
FOURTH
HERNANDO
TURLEY
WELLINGTON
DRIVER
LAUDERDALE
FULTON
ALABAMA
MOSBY
HILL
CARROLL AVE
HIGH ST
NEELY
MARSHALL AVE
PIOMINGO AVE

6. ST. PETER'S ROMAN CATHOLIC CHURCH, SE. corner Adams Ave. and N. 3rd St., erected in 1843, is Victorian Gothic in style with rose windows of Bavarian glass. In 1852 stone buttresses and arches were added to the original brick structure. In 1935 two coffins were discovered beneath the altar. One, of wrought iron, contained the body of Father J. H. Clarkston, who died in 1849; the other, the body of Father J. A. Kelly, a hero of the yellow fever epidemics.

7. The MAGEVNEY HOME *(private)*, Adams Ave. between N. 3rd and N. 4th Sts., is a gable-roofed, clapboarded cottage, built more than a century ago. The first Holy Mass in Memphis, the first Catholic marriage, and first Catholic baptism took place in this house.

8. The SHELBY COUNTY COURTHOUSE *(open 7-6 daily)*, Adams Ave. between N. 2nd and N. 3rd Sts., designed in the neo-Classic style by James Gamble Rogers of New York and completed in 1909, is a blue Bedford limestone structure. The Ionic columns of the long south portico rest on pedestals equal in height to the heavy balustrade. The long lines of the cornice are interrupted at intervals by lions' heads. The apex of each pediment supports a colossal head of Minerva. On the cornice of the north front are six figures (double life-size), representing *Integrity, Courage, Mercy, Temperance, Prudence,* and *Learning*. Life-size groups carved in high relief on the webs of the pediments represent *Canon Law, Roman Law, Statutory Law, Civil Law,* and *Criminal Law*. Flanking the entrance are massive pedestals with seated figures of heroic size, cut from single blocks of Tennessee white marble, representing *Wisdom, Justice, Liberty, Authority, Peace,* and *Prosperity*. All the sculptures were designed by J. Massey Rhind.

Seven kinds of marble, from Vermont, Pennsylvania, Alabama, and Tennessee, have been used on the interior. The gray floor of the corridor

---

KEY TO MEMPHIS DOWNTOWN MAP

1. Goodwyn Institute
2. The Sterrick Building
3. The Site of the Jefferson Davis Home
4. The Site of the Irving Block
5. Court Square
6. St. Peter's Roman Catholic Church
7. The Magevney Home
8. The Shelby County Courthouse
9. The Calvary Episcopal Church
10. The First Methodist Church
11. The Ellis Municipal Auditorium
12. St. Mary's Catholic Church
13. Lauderdale Courts
14. Auction Square
15. The Union Compress Plant
16. The Site of the Old Forts
17. The Site of Old Bell Tavern
18. The Jones and Laughlin Steel Plant
19. Jefferson Davis Park
20. Confederate Park
21. Cossitt Library
22. The Cotton Exchange Building
23. The Gayoso Hotel
24. Handy Park
25. The Beale Street Baptist Church
26. The Hunt-Phelan Home
27. The Old Robertson Topp Home

SHELBY COUNTY COURTHOUSE, MEMPHIS

and the base and high wainscoting are of veined Tennessee marble. Slender marble pilasters rise in pairs to support the paneled ceiling. In the south corridor is a marble bust of Andrew Jackson, done from life by John Frazee in 1835.

9. The CALVARY EPISCOPAL CHURCH, SE. corner Adams Ave. and N. 2nd St., with its square tower has been a landmark in the business district since 1844. The chancel was added to the original Gothic structure about 1881. Jefferson Davis worshiped here after the War between the States.

10. The FIRST METHODIST CHURCH, NE. corner N. 2nd St. and Poplar Ave., built in 1886, is a gray stone building in the Victorian Gothic style. The pulpit and Bible were given by old "Uncle Ben" Abernathy, a former slave, who served as church sexton for years. The church stands on the site of Wesley Chapel, the first religious structure in Memphis.

11. The ELLIS MUNICIPAL AUDITORIUM *(open for special attractions),* N. Main St. at Poplar Ave., with a seating capacity of 12,500, was designed in the Italian Renaissance style by Charles Oscar Phiel of Memphis. The main floor, planned with ample circulation around the auditorium, receives all ramps and stairs except those from the galleries. The

auditorium is used chiefly for conventions, and occasionally for operatic and theatrical performances.

12. ST. MARY'S CATHOLIC CHURCH, SW. corner Market Ave. and N. 3rd St., is a Gothic structure of stuccoed brick, designed by Frank Foster of Memphis. Built in 1864–70, it was the second Roman Catholic Church in Memphis.

13. LAUDERDALE COURTS, N. 3rd St. between Exchange and Winchester Aves., extending to Alabama Ave., is a slum clearance project for white tenants. The red-brick buildings are of modified Georgian Colonial design. There are 400 apartment units and each of the two main buildings houses 66 families.

PINCH, the section north of Market Avenue, was once the bitter enemy of South Memphis, or Sodom, a rivalry, that retarded the city's growth. In the 1830's, the North Memphis people, who lived on Catfish Bay, a small lake north of Jackson Street, were termed "Pinch Guts," because they were scrawny and underfed and "pinched their guts" with their belts for lack of food. North Memphis became known as "Pinch." In retaliation the Pinchites called South Memphis "Sodom" because of its alleged wickedness. The use of these words caused fierce street brawls. People of the Bluff kept away from "Smoky Row," the main thoroughfare of Pinch, where the gamblers, prostitutes, and flatboatmen hung out at Paddy Meagher's Bell Tavern, Sam Stodgen's Place, and the Pefraza Hotel. John A. Murrell came to town and found a wife on Smoky Row *(see Tour 12).* David Crockett, on a political tour, gave a moonlight whisky party on the river bank, one of the wildest drunken brawls ever thrown on the bluff. Fanny Wright, a tall rawboned English woman, stalked about the streets, raising her fog-horn voice to damn marriage, the Bible, and anyone opposed to freeing the slaves *(see Tour 12, Sec. c).*

14. AUCTION SQUARE, SE. corner Auction Ave. and N. Main St., is one of the four original squares laid out in 1819. Slaves were auctioned from an old stone block, no longer here. A stone slab with a bronze marker records that in 1797 Capt. Isaac Guion took possession of the site in the name of the United States.

15. The UNION COMPRESS PLANT *(open 8-4 Mon.-Fri., 8-12 Sat.),* N. Front St. at Auction Ave., one of the largest cotton compresses in Memphis, operates its own switch engine and has 10 miles of standard railroad track, with storage facilities for 500 cars. The high density attachment, a mechanical device for compressing bales of cotton for export shipment, is one of its many features. The plant occupies a part of the old Navy Yard.

16. The SITE OF THE OLD FORTS, NW. corner Auction Ave. and N. Front St., now occupied by the MEMPHIS DOG POUND *(open 8-6 daily),* is the center of the most disputed area in the early settlement of Memphis territory. On this site, in 1739, Jean Baptiste le Moyne de Vienville assembled his followers and built Fort Assumption, and in 1795 Don Manuel Gayoso de Lemos, a Spaniard, built Fort San Fernando de las Barrancas, named for the Prince of the Asturias. He sent Benjamin Foy, a Hollander and experienced Indian trader, to guard the fort and to keep

in contact with the Chickasaw. In 1797 the U. S. Government, ruling that Gayoso's fort constituted an invasion, sent Isaac Guion to the bluff. He found the fort removed to the other side of the river, and built Fort Adams on the site; it was later named Fort Pike. In 1801 a better location two miles down the bluff was found and there Capt. Zebulon M. Pike built Fort Pickering, named for the Secretary of State under Washington.

17. The SITE OF OLD BELL TAVERN, N. Front St. between Auction and Concord Aves., is a vacant lot. The tavern was run by Paddy Meagher, a well-known gambler and friend of Andrew Jackson, when Memphis was young and boisterous. Said to have been erected in 1819, this was the only place where visitors could be accommodated at the time.

18. The JONES AND LAUGHLIN STEEL PLANT *(open 8-4 Mon.-Fri., 8-12 Sat.),* along Wolf River betwen Auction and Concord Aves., has an electrically operated telpherage system, a form of automatic cable transportation for loading and unloading barges. This system extends 800 feet from the pipe yards out over the river. The system and the word "telpherage" were introduced by Flemming Jenkins. This also is the SITE OF THE OLD NAVY YARD, constructed by the Government in 1846. In 1854 it reverted to the city. Though the Government spent $1,000,000 on the Navy Yard, it built no vessels and fitted only one, the *Allegheny.* Part of the original stone yard wall still stands.

19. JEFFERSON DAVIS PARK, Riverside Dr. at Jefferson Ave. commemorates the President of the Confederacy, who lived at Memphis for a number of years after the war. The park occupies the SITE OF DE SOTO'S SHIP YARD, where, as tradition relates, the Spanish explorer built barges to transport his expedition across the Mississippi River in 1541. A marker gives the history.

20. CONFEDERATE PARK, N. Front St. and W. Court Ave., memorializes the Battle of Memphis in the War between the States. From the west edge of the park there is a view of the river, Riverside Drive, Jefferson Davis Park, the Memphis Yacht Club, boathouses, Mud Island, and the Harahan Bridge.

The broad river recalls the boom days of river traffic. Then the *Robert E. Lee,* the *Stacker Lee,* the *Kate Adams,* and other broad beamed side-wheelers and lean, sleek stern-wheelers made wild, reckless races to carry the region's commerce on the river, and many times "busted their bilers" in an effort to get there first. Gaudy showboats were heralded by the shrill music of the calliope. Excursion boats with gay parties made leisurely trips to New Orleans. Flashily-dressed gamblers and befrilled and be-ribboned belles awaited the arrival of a new packet. Shiny black Negroes, chanting their folk melodies, carried bales of cotton across swaying "tote-planks" to the decks for a down-the-river ride, while the river front was aswarm with monster cotton drays drawn by heavy mules or horses, four and six to a team. Three drays, low-swung on powerful wheels and axles, were capable of handling a mighty burden of bales. Levee and plantation workers from the lowlands of Mississippi and Arkansas crowded the waterfront at night to drink throat-burning rum and sometimes fight with fine-pointed dirks, pistols, and glinting razors, or wandered to the uptown saloons to spend their wages before returning to workday drudgery.

21. COSSITT LIBRARY *(open 9-9 weekdays; 2-6 Sun.),* S. Front St. at foot of Monroe Ave., the only free, tax-supported library in Memphis serving both city and county, was founded in 1888 as a memorial to Frederick H. Cossitt by his daughters. The original building, constructed of Lake Superior red sandstone, was designed by M. L. B. Wheeler of Atlanta, in the Romanesque style, and completed in 1893. In 1924 three more stories of concrete block were added. Parapets and walls form an effective background, and a red gronolith pavement leads up to the portals of the building.

The library contains 238,443 volumes that include a special collection of 1,500 volumes on Memphis and Tennessee; a music collection of 1,200 volumes containing scores, librettos, operas, and anthems; the oldest and most complete record of Memphis newspapers from 1836 to 1939; and the Bayard Cairns Library on architecture. The city also supports six community branches, one Negro branch, and a library for the blind, in Braille.

22. The COTTON EXCHANGE BUILDING *(open 8-4 Mon.-Fri., 8-12 Sat.),* SE. corner Union Ave. and S. Front St., founded in 1873, is the official organization of the Memphis cotton trade, and the economic heart of the city. The Memphis Merchants Clearing Association established the first known cottonseed "pit" in January 1929. From here quotations on cottonseed and cottonseed meal are flashed throughout the world. "Cotton Row," that section of Front Street running south from the Memphis Cotton Exchange Building at 67 Union Avenue, is honeycombed with offices of cotton factors, and is the central market place of the cotton-producing area. The Mississippi Delta, together with the adjacent uplands, ships as much as two and a quarter million bales of cotton annually.

23. The GAYOSO HOTEL, 139 S. Main St., opened in 1844, was named for Don Manuel Gayoso de Lemos, Spanish explorer and last governor of the Spanish territory in Louisiana. For 50 years the main entrance was on Front Street, overlooking the Mississippi River but was changed when Main Street became the principal thoroughfare. During the War between the States the hotel served as headquarters for Confederate and Federal armies. At the time of Gen. Nathan Bedford Forrest's strategic raid upon the Federal forces, in August 1864, his brother, Capt. William H. Forrest, rode his horse into the hotel, which was being used as headquarters by the Federal Gen. Stephen A. Hurlbut. A BRONZE PLAQUE describing the incident, and MURALS by Newton Alonzo Wells (1852–1923), depicting the life of De Soto, are in the hotel lobby. Among the cherished relics are two gold candelabra and a magnificent clock that once belonged to Sarah Bernhardt.

24. HANDY PARK, Beale Ave. and S. 3rd St., a small grassy square, is the scene of the Negro Cotton Fiesta during the Memphis Cotton Carnival.

BEALE STREET (official name Beale Avenue), noted in song and story as the center of Negro life in Memphis, begins at the De Soto Fish Dock on the Mississippi River and runs for one mile to East Street.

On Beale Street in 1909, W. C. Handy, Negro composer and originator of the "blues," wrote and first played "The Memphis Blues." In the Beale Street Blues he tells what Beale means to the Negro:

The Seven Wonders of the world I have seen
And many are the places I have been;
Take my advice, folks, and see Beale Street first.
You will see pretty browns dressed in beautiful gowns.
You will see tailor-mades and hand-me-downs;
You will meet honest men and pick-pockets skilled,
You will find that business never closes until
Somebody gets killed.

You will see hog-nose restaurants and chitterling cafes
And jugs that tell of by-gone days.
You will see golden balls enough to pave the New Jerusalem.
I would rather be there than any place I know.
It is going to take a sergeant just for to make me go—
I am going down to the river maybe by and by,
'Cause the river is wet and Beale's done gone dry.

Beale Street has produced more than its quota of notable Negroes. Through the efforts of men like Robert Church, Sr., early financier, Robert Church, Jr., lawyer and politician, and George Lee, writer, Beale Street developed from a poverty-stricken area into one of wealth and standing. Negroes have built up businesses of their own and have advanced the education of their race. They have organized insurance companies, banking establishments, and schools; Negro lawyers, doctors, and real estate men have gained the respect of their professions.

The blocks between Main and Third Streets are crowded with pawnshops, clothing stores, fruit stands, restaurants, doctors' offices, and photographic studios. Traders and merchants display goods on the sidewalks in front of stores. Smooth-tongued barkers entreat passersby to stop and inspect bargains.

On East Beale Street "conjure" doctors and medicine men still ply their trades. They offer luck bags to wear around the neck, containing strange mixtures to cure diseases and drive away trouble. Love powders, packets of "goober" or graveyard dust, and black and white cat bones are among the charms offered for sale.

Of the famous old establishments still in operation under their original names are Peewee's Place, formerly owned and operated by Vigelio Maffi Peewee, Italian gambler, and now a favorite gathering place for musicians; the Panama Club; and Hammitt Ashford's Place.

On Saturday Beale Street is thronged with country Negroes from Arkansas, northern Mississippi, and western Tennessee, who arrive early and bargain for clothing, groceries, fish, and pork chops. Saturday night belongs to the cooks, maids, houseboys, and factory hands.

The "underworld" block, from Hernando Street to Fourth Street, is packed with social clubs, movie theaters, beauty parlors, and lunch rooms. Though quiet and peaceful in daytime, at night "we stomps the daylights into the flo'." Street walkers and guitar players stroll up and down the avenue. Pickpockets and gamblers weave in and out of the crowd. The air

ROBERTSON TOPP HOME, MEMPHIS

is thick with the smell of fried fish, black mud from the levees and plantations, and whisky trucked in from the moonshine stills of swamps and hills. From the pianos in crowded honkeytonks comes the slow, "hesitation" beat of the blues, or the furious stomp of swing music.

Beale Avenue was once an exclusive residential section, occupied by wealthy, influential families, who built magnificent homes and entertained lavishly. Ladies and gentlemen of the old South passed along the street in carriages driven by liveried servants. After the ravages of the War between the States and the yellow fever epidemics, the wealthiest families moved farther out into the eastern part of the city, and Negroes began to take possession of the street and the surrounding territory.

25. The BEALE STREET BAPTIST CHURCH, Beale Ave. between S. 4th and Turley Sts., is Victorian Gothic in style, of brick and gray stone, with two rectangular towers, on one of which is a statue of John the Baptist. Built 1865–69 by Negro labor, it was the first Negro Missionary Baptist Church in America. Ulysses S. Grant delivered an address from its pulpit while on a visit to Memphis after the War between the States.

CHURCH PARK AUDITORIUM, a two-story stuccoed structure on the church grounds, was built by the City of Memphis in 1929 as a Negro community center and named for Robert Church, Sr., the early Negro financier.

26. The HUNT-PHELAN HOME *(private),* 533 Beale Ave., is an impressive red-brick Greek Revival house with a monumental Ionic portico. Erected in 1835, it sits back on a lawn planted with trees that break the view from the street. Leonidas Polk, Confederate general, occupied this home in 1861 during the organization of the "Provisional Army of Tennessee." It was seized by Federal troops during their occupancy of Memphis, used by General Grant as headquarters in 1862, and converted into a Federal hospital in 1863. Jefferson Davis, Andrew Johnson, and other notables of that period were entertained by the owners before and after its occupancy by Union forces.

27. The OLD ROBERTSON TOPP HOME *(private),* 567 Beale Ave., built 1837–38, is a massive two-story structure adorned with a pedimented Corinthian portico. It was designed by P. H. Hammarskold of Memphis. One door is of carved, hand-hewn beveled oak.

28. FORREST PARK, NE. corner Union Ave. and S. Manassas St., contains an EQUESTRIAN STATUE OF GEN. NATHAN BEDFORD FORREST, the Confederate cavalry leader. It was designed by Charles Henry Niehaus and cast in bronze in Paris. General Forrest and his wife are buried in front of the monument.

29. The UNIVERSITY OF TENNESSEE HEALTH DIVISION, 874 Union Ave., includes the Colleges of Medicine and Dentistry and the Schools of Pharmacy and Nursing, concentrated around the John Gaston Memorial Hospital. The division was established in Memphis in 1911 when health units in Nashville, Memphis, and Knoxville were consolidated. The Anatomy, the Pharmacy, and the Library Buildings are Collegiate Gothic in style, built of reinforced concrete and faced with dark variegated brick and limestone trim. The architects were Jones and Furbinger of Memphis.

30. The IDLEWILD PRESBYTERIAN CHURCH, NW. corner Union Ave. and Evergreen St., constructed of a combination of rubblestone from Arkansas, and stone from Vermont, Massachusetts, and Tennessee, is English Gothic in style. Its two towers rise with arches and buttresses above the western transept to a height of 150 feet. The main entrance is of cut stone with sculptured panels of characters and symbols of sacred history. The interior, with massive stone piers lining the auditorium, recalls the Lincoln Cathedral in England; the roof is formed by handhewn oak arches and trusses. Stone tracery of delicate design further ornaments the richly colored stained glass windows. Joining the church and Sunday School building is a seven-arched cloister, where an outdoor auditorium and stone pulpit are used for summer services. Pfiel and Awsumb were the architects.

31. OVERTON PARK, N. Parkway, between N. McLean Blvd. and E. Parkway, extending to Poplar Ave., is a memorial to John Overton, one of the city's founders. The 355-acre park contains 100 acres of virgin forest interlaced with drives and bridle paths, and large landscaped open spaces for recreation, camping, picnicking, and open-air drama.

The ZOOLOGICAL AND BOTANICAL GARDENS AND FREE CIRCUS *(open 9-6 daily; circus performances 10:30 and 2:30 weekdays during summer; 2:30 Sun. year round)*, are at the south entrance. The zoo occupies 47 acres. An hour-long, 18-act circus for children, maintained by the Memphis Park Commission, is put on by zoo attendants, former circus trainers. The circus is complete, with educated ponies, trained dogs and monkeys, clowns, stunts, miniature merry-go-round, Ferris wheel, pony track and other circus features. A grandstand seats 1,000.

The DOUGHBOY MONUMENT, near Brooks Memorial Art Gallery, erected in 1926, is a massive bronze of an American soldier of the World War advancing with fixed bayonet, sculptured by Mrs. Nancy Coosman Hahn of Memphis. A bronze marker bears the names of Memphis and Shelby County soldiers killed in the conflict.

The BROOKS MEMORIAL ART GALLERY *(open 9-5:30 weekdays, 2-5:30 Sun.)*, near the Poplar Ave. entrance, is a white marble structure designed in the Italian Renaissance style by James Gamble Rogers of New York, 1915. Paintings by Del Garbo Raffaellino, Thomas Sully, and Cecilia Beaux are in the permanent collection. The building was a gift to the city from Mrs. Samuel Brooks, of Memphis, in memory of her husband. The gallery has monthly circulating exhibits of oils, water colors, miniatures, and ceramics.

32. SOUTHWESTERN, THE COLLEGE OF THE MISSISSIPPI VALLEY, N. Parkway at University Blvd., is a small Presbyterian college, owned by the Synods of Alabama, Louisiana, Mississippi, and Tennessee. On the campus of 100 acres are seven buildings of Collegiate Gothic design. These buildings, arranged in a quadrangle, are built of variegated sandstone. The roofs are of thick, green-colored Vermont slate. The deeply set steel casement windows, made in England, contain small delicately tinted glass panes. Doorways are deeply recessed and molded. The paneled interior woodwork is of oak. Incorporated in 1875 as Southwestern Pres-

IDLEWILD CHURCH, MEMPHIS

byterian University, at Clarksville, Tenn., the school was moved to Memphis in 1925, and renamed Southwestern.

In 1929 the competitive medal of the Southern Chapters of the American Institute of Architects was awarded to Henry C. Hibbs, of Nashville, architect-in-chief, for his work in designing the buildings at Southwestern.

Among the college's early professors of theology was the Reverend Joseph R. Wilson, father of Woodrow Wilson, whose portrait hangs in the administration hall. Tutorial courses similar to those of the Oxford plan were made a part of the curriculum in 1931. The college is co-educational, with an average enrollment of 400.

33. The MUSEUM OF NATURAL HISTORY AND INDUSTRIAL ARTS *(open 9-4:30 weekdays, 2:30-5:30 Sun.)*, 275 Tilton Rd., the "Pink Palace," is built of Georgian pink marble with gray marble trim. It is a 21-room house of modified Georgian style, designed by Hubert McGee of Memphis. On its 25-acre grounds are an artificial lake and extensive rose gardens. The exhibits include 2,000 stuffed birds; a collection of eggs; the Harvey E. Miller exhibit of North American mammals, which has 14 specimens either extinct or so rare that killing is prohibited even for scientific purposes; the Paul Rainey exhibit of big game from Africa; the Charles Scott collection of 60 heads of bear, elk, and moose; 400 firearms from the earliest wheellock to the most modern gun; a Mound Builders collection; marine collections; Indian and Mexican relics; Confederate and other relics; American and foreign dolls; and early American glass.

Built as a residence by Clarence Saunders, founder of the Piggly-Wiggly Stores, in 1923–24, the house was purchased by the city for public use in 1925. The Little Theater is housed in the former swimming pool.

34. WEST TENNESSEE STATE TEACHERS COLLEGE, NE. corner Southern Ave. and Patterson St., has 13 buildings on a campus of 82 acres. The Administration Building, Library, Gymnasium, and Science Buildings are of modified Georgian Colonial design. The college is co-educational and offers work leading to a B.S. degree. The average enrollment is 600 students.

35. LE MOYNE COLLEGE, 807 Walker Ave., one of the oldest Negro colleges in the South, was established in 1871 by the American Missionary Association, under whose jurisdiction it remains. The buildings and a small endowment came from a $20,000 gift of Dr. Julius Le Moyne, philanthropist of Washington, Pennsylvania. The college is co-educational and confers the A.B. and B.S. degrees. The average enrollment is 385.

36. ELMWOOD CEMETERY, NE. corner Walker Ave. and Neptune St., is the oldest cemetery in Memphis still in use, and was the official burial ground for the Confederate dead. At Elmwood are the graves of Mrs. Dorothea S. Winston, Patrick Henry's oldest child by his second marriage; John S. McLemore, who bought Andrew Jackson's part in the John Rice grant on which Memphis now stands; and Walter Malone, the poet.

37. RIVERSIDE PARK, Riverside Blvd. and S. Parkway, is a natural wooded park of 427 acres, bordering the Mississippi River for a mile and a half along high grassy bluffs, with picnic grounds, golf links, an artificial lake, and pavilions. Below the bluffs the broad river flows between the Ten-

nessee shore and President's Island and curves away into dense forests to the South. Drives twist through woodlands of giant trees and deep ravines.

38. PRESIDENT'S ISLAND, reached by boat from the foot of Wisconsin Ave., named for President Jackson and first called Jackson's Island, is the largest island in the 2,500-mile course of the Mississippi River. Twelve miles long, it covers approximately 32,000 acres of shifting sands, cottonwoods, and fertile farming land. The surface of the small fishing lakes is covered with ducks during the season. Great numbers of rabbits and squirrels are in the woods and brush. The island is divided into small farms, owned and operated by Memphis people, chiefly Negroes. The largest farm is near the center of the island and contains 970 acres. Cotton, corn, vegetables, and pecans are grown, and chickens, turkeys, hogs, and mules are raised. Church services are held at irregular intervals in a one-room schoolhouse, built on stilts for protection during the high water.

During the early history of Memphis, Jackson bought a small farm on the island, with Paddy Meagher, one-time proprietor of Bell Tavern, in charge. When Meagher moved back to Memphis, Jackson disposed of the farm. After the Holly Springs, Mississippi, disaster in 1863, a camp was set up on President's Island for all Negro refugees in the western section of Tennessee. In April 1865, 1,568 refugees were on the island, all incapacitated for hard labor, and the majority unfit for any duty. Before the flood, in the spring of 1865, which caused considerable suffering and loss the Freedmen's Bureau furnished labor and wages for all who were able to work at wood cutting, coal burning, and in sawmills. The more feeble raised vegetables, cotton, and corn. Schools were built. A tent was raised for orphan children, and a Negro woman was put in charge; sick and destitute orphans were rounded up, bathed, and clothed. In the fall of 1865, the tent was replaced by a house, with six acres of land for a garden and playground. The older girls were taught to sew, wash, and cook, and the boys to cultivate the garden. The Freedmen's Bureau ended its main work in 1869, and the Negroes were gradually absorbed into various occupations.

The island was for a while headquarters for moonshiners. Years ago the river changed its course and ran through what is now the middle of the island. It washed out a graveyard at the southern tip and undermined a saloon at the foot of Wisconsin Avenue in Memphis. Coffins and barrels of liquor floated downstream together.

Gen. Nathan Bedford Forrest farmed a large tract of land on the island in 1875–76, and while there contracted a fatal illness from drinking impure water.

39. DE SOTO PARK, W. end of Colorado Ave., formerly known as Jackson Mound, is the place where Hernando De Soto and his followers are thought to have discovered the Mississippi River, May 21, 1541. Under the Chisca Mound, which apparently supported the chieftain's lodge, is a cave used as a powder magazine during the War between the States. A bronze tablet records the history of the site.

40. HARAHAN BRIDGE, spanning the Mississippi at the western end of Virginia Ave., built first in 1909 and rebuilt in 1915–16, was the first vehicle and railroad bridge across the Mississippi River south of Cairo, Ill.

It is a fireproof steel cantilever truss bridge more than a mile long, double-tracked for railroad traffic, and carries more than 3,500 cars daily. The engineer was Ralph Modjeska.

RIVERSIDE DRIVE, intersection of Virginia Ave. and Delaware St., affords a good view of the river with its barges and boats, river-and-rail terminals, coal tipples, telpherage systems, and the Harahan and Frisco Bridges.

41. CITY ISLAND, formerly Mud Island, reached by wharf boats at foot of Madison, Union, or Monroe Sts., is a peninsula-like body of willow-covered land, extending down the Memphis harbor to a point opposite the foot of Beale Avenue. The island was built up by an eddy that deposited mud and gravel against the stern of the *Aphrodite,* a gunboat used in the Spanish-American War. The gunboat, with a full crew on its way from New Orleans to St. Louis, had to anchor at Memphis for six or eight months in 1910 because of low water. When high water came, and the boat departed, a small sandbar had formed off the foot of Court Avenue. Each rise added to the island; in 1913, when the Mississippi reached a high stage, the island was built up about 25 feet.

Subject to overflow, it would have ruined shipping at this point had not the United States flood control engineers diverted the Wolf River southward from the regular point of confluence with the Mississippi River, causing it to flow by the Memphis harbor between the island and the river front. The improvements of the Wolf River channel have greatly enlarged the harbor space. Yearly dredging is necessary to keep the harbor open. Mud Island has been farmed at intervals, and unsuccessful efforts have been made to establish squatter's rights. Annual overflows have kept all but squatters off the island. The dense willow thickets harbored many moonshine stills prior to repeal. A few straggling shanty-boats remain around Mud Island, their occupants the gypsies of the water. Clannish and friendly to river people, but contemptuous and suspicious of land people, they are vagabonds who live meagerly by selling fish in season. During flood times, as Old Man River laps far out into the bayou country to form a great inland sea, the island vanishes. In 1919 the Supreme Court placed title to the land in the City of Memphis.

42. The AMERICAN SNUFF PLANT *(open by permission),* NW. corner N. Front St. and Keel Ave., is the largest strong snuff factory in the country.

Users of snuff habitually judge the strength of the product by the number of "knobs" (glass bubbles), on the bottom of the brown jars. Four "knobs" mean very strong; three, fairly strong; two, medium; none, weak. How this belief became prevalent is not known. The "knobs" have nothing to do with the "power" of the snuff, since it is bottled in only one grade.

43. The CHELSEA AVENUE PRESBYTERIAN CHURCH, Chelsea Ave. and N. 6th St., a brick and stone structure, was erected in 1860. When the Federals occupied Memphis, Gen. U. S. Grant took possession of the church and made a second floor hospital for Union soldiers and the lower floor a storage place and a stable for army mules and horses. The

first pastor, Edward Porter, served as chaplain in the Confederate Army. The original second floor pews are still in use.

44. The CHALFANT DOCK STEEL PLANT *(open 8-4 Mon.-Fri., 8-12 Sat.),* Thomas St. and Plum Ave. (river terminal at foot of Auction Ave. on N. Front St.), occupies 20 acres. The telpherage system is used for loading and unloading steel products. The plant occupies the site of the noted North Memphis Driving Park, where race-horse history was made by the record-breaking Dan Patch in 1903, when, driven by Ed (Pop) Geers, he paced his most sensational mile of the year against his own record of 1:59, finishing the mile in 1:55, with the last 1/8 in 13-3/4 seconds, a 1:50 clip.

45. DIXIE HOMES, NW. corner Poplar Ave. and Decatur St., is a slum clearance PWA project for Negroes, and contains 28 one-story and 48 two-story houses. The area accommodates 633 families.

46. ST. MARY'S EPISCOPAL CATHEDRAL (GAILOR MEMORIAL), 714 Poplar Ave., founded as a missionary chapel in 1857, is of white stone, Gothic in design, erected in 1926. The stained glass windows of the nave were designed and executed by Len Howard. The altar, reredos, altar rail, and chancel rail, are of Barcelona marble carved in Italy. The altar is a memorial to four Sisters of St. Mary who died in line of duty during the yellow fever epidemics. The reredos was erected to the memory of Sister Hughetta (Snowden), also a leading figure of that distressing period. A silver communion service, presented by Jefferson Davis to the Episcopal Church of Arlington, Tennessee, is one of the cathedral's most treasured possessions. Set into the wall of the western transept is a stone from the balustrade surrounding the pool of Bethesda in Jerusalem. Another stone, part of a column from the Abbey of Glastonbury in England, is set into the wall of the eastern transept.

An arched cloister joins the cathedral to the DIOCESAN HOUSE, headquarters of the Episcopal Church in Tennessee. In this stone structure are the offices of the Bishop and other church executives and a valuable library of religious books. Oil portraits of bishops include an original by William Cooper, English painter (1858–1934).

47. ST. AGNES COLLEGE, 697 Vance Ave., was established in 1851 by six Sisters of St. Dominic. The present building, a four-story brick structure of Victorian Gothic architecture, was erected in 1901. Tents pitched on the campus in 1862 served as General Sherman's headquarters. It is the only woman's college in Memphis and the only Catholic College in Tennessee.

48. The FEDERAL COMPRESS AND WAREHOUSE PLANT *(open by permission),* S. end of S. Lauderdale St., is one of the largest cotton compressing plants in the world. Representatives from all principal nations have been sent here to study arrangements and operation.

A flat bale of cotton as it comes from the country gin is 27 inches wide, 54 inches long, and 48 to 50 inches high, weighing about 500 pounds. If sold to an American spinner, the bale is compressed to a density of 22 to 24 pounds per cubic foot, a standard bale. If the cotton is to be exported, the bale is compressed to 32 to 35 pounds per cubic feet, in order to obtain lower ocean freight rates; it is then called high density cotton.

49. RUST COTTON PICKER PLANT *(visitors by appointment)*, 2369 Florida St., a single story brick building, manufactures mechanical cotton picking machines.

The motorized picking machine, which may prove to be the greatest development in the raw cotton industry since Whitney's invention of the gin, is the culmination of plans conceived by John D. and Mack D. Rust of Memphis. The brothers are said to have obtained their idea when they noticed their mother wetting her fingertips while picking up raw cotton.

The Rust machine consists primarily of an endless belt carrying several hundred smooth wire spindles automatically moistened. The spindles pass in a rotary motion over the bolls, the moisture causing the cotton to adhere; the cotton is then stripped from the spindles and delivered by suction fan to a container. The first model, which has been improved upon annually, was built in 1928. Standardized models are now in use in several southern states and sample machines have been sold to the Russian and Argentine governments.

Because the widespread use of the machine will displace thousands of cotton pickers the Rust Foundation, supported by profits of the concern, has been set up in an effort to rehabilitate the unemployed.

POINTS OF INTEREST IN ENVIRONS

Shelby Forest Park, *20.7 m.* *(see Tour 11).*

Knoxville

Railroad Stations: Broadway and Western Ave. for Louisville and Nashville R.R. Depot St. one block east of Gay St., for Southern Ry., Tennessee Central Ry., and Tennessee and North Carolina Ry.
Bus Station: Terminal, 326 Gay St., for Greyhound, White Star, Tennessee Coach, Smoky Mountain Transit Lines, and the East Tennessee and Western North Carolina Lines.
Airport: McGhee-Tyson Municipal Airport, 13.4 m. S. via State 33, for American Airlines. Taxi fare $1, time about 45 minutes.
Streetcars and Busses: Electric Cars, trackless trolleys, and motor busses. Fare 10¢, five tokens 30¢, unlimited weekly pass $1.25. Free transfers except to parallel lines. U. S. mail boxes on all types of street transportation.
Taxis: Inter-city rate, 15¢ for first half mile or fraction, 10¢ for each additional half mile. Long distance, 20¢ per mile.
Traffic Regulations: Parking meters in business area; local traffic code free at Public Safety Building, 409 N. Broadway.

Accommodations: Fourteen hotels; tourist camps on outskirts.

Street Nomenclature: Streets run north and south with dividing line at Jackson and McCalla Aves. Avenues run east and west with dividing line at Central St.

Information Service: Knoxville Chamber of Commerce, 621 Gay St.; East Tennessee Auto Club, 920 Gay St.; Tourist Bureau, 811 Broadway; TVA Information Office, New Sprankle Bldg., 508 Union St.

Radio Stations: WNOX (1010 kc.); WROL (1310 kc.).
Theaters and Motion Picture Houses: Lyric Theater, 802 Gay St., road shows and opera. Twelve motion picture houses; one for Negroes.
Wrestling: Lyric Theater, Market Hall Auditorium.
Baseball: Southern League games, Smithsonian Stadium, Caswell Park.
College Athletics: University of Tennessee "Volunteers," Southeastern Conference games in season, Shields-Watkins Field, University Campus.
Swimming: Whittle Springs Hotel grounds, Whittle Springs Rd. between Mineral Springs Ave. and Iowa Ave.
Golf: Municipal course, adjoining Whittle Springs Hotel, Whittle Springs Rd. between Iowa Ave. and Underwood Place, 18 holes, 25¢.
Tennis: 28 free municipal courts. Information at Welfare Dept., City Hall, Western Ave. and Broadway.
Riding: Chilhowee Riding Academy, Chilhowee Park, on US 11 about 3 m. east of business area; Silver Stables, Whittle Springs Hotel grounds, Whittle Springs Ave. at city limits (off N. Broadway); Sequoyah Riding Academy, Bluff View Rd. in Sequoyah Hills, 3 m. W. on US 11 and 70; Sherrill Riding Academy, 11 m. Kingston Pike (US 70 and 11).

Annual Events: Southeastern Basketball Tournament, last week in February; Appalachian Golf Tournament, last week in June; boat and automobile races, July 4; Tennessee Valley A. & I. Fair, last week in September; Burley Tobacco Market opens for season first week in December.

KNOXVILLE (933 alt., 105,802 pop.), seat of Knox County, is on the broad but rather shallow Tennessee River, which is formed four miles east of the downtown section by the junction of the Holston and French Broad Rivers. The city extends fan-wise from the river banks into the nearby hills, with the Chilhowee and the Great Smoky Mountains in the distant background.

The business district is crowded upon a plateau of 240 acres and is approached by narrow, steep streets. On Gay Street, the principal business thoroughfare, modern office and mercantile buildings rub shoulders with old-fashioned arcades; a skyscraper hotel looks down on one-story business houses of another day; and a modern bus terminal pours thousands of shoppers into the street. A block west of Gay Street is the Market Square where a free market for farmers has been maintained since 1853.

Knoxville's industries are scattered over various parts of the city, with the largest groupings along the river front, and along the tracks of the two major railroad systems. South of the river are marble mills; sand and gravel concerns are along both banks, with barges and small boats forming a considerable river traffic. The wholesale district, including the clothing factories, are along the eastern main line of the Southern Railway, with the smoke-begrimed iron and steel foundries farther out. The lumber yards form a rather well-defined group in northeast Knoxville.

Knoxville is the only city in the United States that has mail collections from streetcars and busses. In 1913 a post office inspector suggested that mail boxes be attached to the cars; permission for the innovation was granted as an experiment, and has never been rescinded. Anyone can stop a streetcar at any time to drop a letter in an outside slot; the boxes are cleared at stated hours throughout the day.

The Sequoyah Hills and Holston Hills subdivisions have many modern homes, but elsewhere in the city are old houses with Victorian architectural features, newer homes built to suit the owner's taste without reference to the one next door, and just plain houses. Most of the residential streets are lined with trees.

The Tennessee Valley Authority, a Federal regional planning project, with navigation, flood control, power distribution, and soil conservation as its principal objectives has had important cultural and economic effects on Knoxville. In 1933, the TVA established offices in Knoxville and more than 1,000 families moved in to become a part of the town. The Authority has made heavy purchases of local materials and national interest in the TVA program has attracted many tourists *(see TENNESSEE VALLEY AUTHORITY)*.

The early settlers, traders from North Carolina and Virginia, were more concerned with developing the settlement as a trade center than with the plantation and slave system. This concern for industrial development, vigorously pursued as part of the town's reconstruction program after the War between the States, has set a definite stamp on the character of the community that distinguishes it from most other Southern cities.

The Negro population of Knoxville is only 16.2 per cent of the total, a ratio that has been practically the same since the city was founded. The average Knoxville Negro today is a descendant of "free persons of color" and has had a century of experience in adjusting himself to freedom.

Negro business men operate two weekly newspapers, real estate and insurance agencies, furniture and grocery stores, restaurants, and other business concerns. Some are professional men. The majority, however, are skilled or common laborers or are in domestic service. The principal residential areas are East Knoxville and Western Heights, with most of the Negro business houses on the eastern section of Vine Avenue. The Negroes have their own churches and schools, and one institution of higher education—Knoxville College.

The first recorded journey by Anglo-Americans through the region of the present Knoxville was made in the early winter of 1761. Ensign Henry Timberlake, Sergt. Thomas Sumter, and John McCormack, an interpreter, came down the Holston and the Tennessee on a goodwill mission to the Overhill Cherokee. Eighteen years later Col. Evan Shelby and a band of frontiersmen, returning from a raid against the Chickamauga, camped for one night within the present city limits. The following year the flatboat flotilla of Col. John Donelson passed down the river on the voyage to the Cumberland settlement.

In the summer of 1783 James White, a former captain in the Continental Army, Robert Love, also a Revolutionary soldier, and F. A. Ramsey, a surveyor, explored the Knoxville region, looking for land on which to enter claim. Two years later the State of Franklin established Sevier and Caswell Counties, including the Knoxville area in the latter county. In 1785 the Dumplin Treaty between the Franklin government and the Cherokee was signed and new hordes of settlers poured into East Tennessee.

In 1786 Captain White built a story-and-a-half log cabin on a hill near the present Farragut Hotel, and became the first permanent settler of Knoxville. Later he added three more cabins and the four were connected by a high palisade of logs, making a frontier outpost that was called White's Fort.

During the next five years settlers, claiming the land North Carolina was giving as a bonus to its Revolutionary soldiers, flocked into the Knoxville region. White's Fort became a repair and restocking point for westbound wagon trains.

William Blount, commissioned Governor of the Territory South of the River Ohio, came to Tennessee in 1790 and established his headquarters at White's settlement. The Treaty of the Holston was made with the Cherokee and, with the Indian land cession, became effective. At Blount's suggestion Captain White laid out streets, and the new town was named Knoxville in honor of Maj. Gen. Henry Knox, Secretary of War.

In 1792 Knox County was laid off from parts of what was then Greene and Hawkins Counties, with Knoxville as the county seat. During the next few years the town grew steadily. Roads were built in the county, more cabins and a courthouse were erected. Knoxville, in the last years of the eighteenth century, was a frontier jumping off place, with grog shops and taverns, smithies and harness shops doing constant business. The town was a rowdy resort of teamsters and flatboatmen, soldiers and westward-bound emigrants.

The Knoxville *Gazette,* a weekly newspaper, established in 1791, was moved from Rogersville, where it had been first published by George Roulstone. In 1792 the *Gazette* had the following to say, in describing the favorable position of Knoxville as a shipping point for regions south and west:

> . . . It is the most eligible spot in the possession of the United States for a REPOSITORY of goods for supplying the Cherokees, Chickasaws, Choctaws and perhaps the Creeks, too. The land carriage to it from either of the above mentioned towns (Philadelphia, Baltimore, Richmond), and from Alexandria, is nearly as cheap as from Philadelphia to Fort Pitt, and the passage down the Holston and Tennessee to the places most proper to trade with those nations, is shorter and safer than from Fort Pitt down the Ohio and up the Tennessee.

The one and only Indian scare came in September 1793 when the troops were all absent. Captain White organized the citizens to meet the Indians but the war party did not attack. They turned instead to Cavet's Station eight miles below Knoxville and there killed thirteen persons.

A ferry to the settlements south of the Tennessee River began operation in 1793, and the First Presbyterian Church was organized that year. A post office with semi-monthly mail service to Washington was established in 1795. The same year a wagon road from Knoxville to Nashville was completed. On June 1, 1796, Tennessee was admitted to the Union with Knoxville as its first capital. The constitution of 1796 provided that the first general assembly of the new State should be held in Knoxville, "and may adjourn to such a place as they think proper, until the situation of this State will permit the fixing of a permanent seat of government, which shall be established as nearly central as convenience will permit." Knoxville continued as the capital until 1812, when the State government was moved to Nashville. The legislature, however, convened in Knoxville again in 1817 and remained there two years, when once more the seat of government was moved, this time to Murfreesboro. In 1843 the State government was permanently established in Nashville.

For the first decade, Knoxville was merely a frontier town on the south fork of the Wilderness Road, where frontiersmen stopped on their way West, to buy fresh supplies. James Weir, who visited Knoxville in 1798, wrote:

> It was County Court day when I came. I saw men jesting, singing, swearing; women yelling from doorways; half naked Negroes playing on their 'banjoes,' while the crowd whooped and danced around them. Whiskey and peach brandy were cheap. The town was confused with a promiscuous throng of every denomination—blanket-clad Indians, leather-shirted woodsmen, gamblers, hard-eyed and vigilant. My soul shrank back to hear the horrid oaths and dreadful indignities. . . . There was what I never did see before, viz., on Sunday, dancing, singing, and playing cards.

Knoxville in these early days was often plagued by outlaws, the most notorious of which were the Harpe Brothers—Micajah (Big Harpe) and Wiley (Little Harpe)—who were said to be quadroons. Driven from their native North Carolina in 1797, they settled on Beaver Creek, about eight miles west of Knoxville, and frequented the town on trade days. People near Beaver Creek began missing hogs and sheep. At the same time Harpe hams and mutton became well known in Knoxville stores. The Harpes were arrested but escaped with their women into Kentucky. They were not merely highwaymen; invariably they killed, and usually tortured their victims. After murdering an enemy's wife and baby in Kentucky, Micajah Harpe was trailed by a posse and in July 1799 (according to Robert M. Coates' *Outlaw Years)* he was wounded by gunshot and while still conscious his head was hacked off with a butcher knife by the husband of the slain woman.

Little Harpe escaped and joined the bandit Samuel Mason. Later he and another member of the gang brought Mason's head, rolled up in a ball of blue clay into Natchez and demanded the reward offered for the outlaw. Before the money was paid, however, Harpe's identity was suspected. A Knoxville man named John Bowman, who had cut the outlaw during a brawl in Knoxville, made the identification absolute and Harpe was hanged in Greenville, Mississippi, on Feb. 8, 1804.

Among Knoxville's first industrial establishments were grist mills, sawmills, tanyards, cotton-spinning factories, wool-carding mills, and a brass foundry, all of which were on the banks of the two swift-flowing creeks east and west of the business area. No effort was made to exploit the near-by coal, iron, and marble deposits, which were known to exist, because wagon transportation to markets was too expensive. Steamboat navigation to New Orleans was inaugurated as early as 1828, but an obstruction in the channel of the Tennessee River at Muscle Shoals made this form of transportation unreliable.

The growth of the town was slow in comparison with the rapid increase of population in the State. Knoxville had a population of only 2,076 in the census of 1850, and the census bureau of 1860 considered it such a small town that its inhabitants were not enumerated separately from Knox County.

The East Tennessee & Georgia Railroad, completed in 1855, gave rail connection to the South via Chattanooga. A branch line of the East Tennessee & Georgia Railroad, completed in 1856, provided connections with Nashville, and in 1858 the East Tennessee & Virginia Railroad was completed to Bristol on the Virginia boundary. This was the last link in a continuous line of railroads from Chattanooga to the East. But the War between the States temporarily stopped further development.

Because the majority of East Tennesseans were loyal to the Union during the War between the States—their farm holdings were small and few of them owned slaves—a Confederate army of occupation, numbering about 10,000, was sent into East Tennessee early in 1861 and established headquarters at Knoxville. About 1,500 Union sympathizers were arrested and, after trials by military courts, most of them were sent to prisons in the Lower South. Thousands of Unionists fled the section for protection to the hills of Federal-held Kentucky.

All Confederate troops were withdrawn from the Knoxville area during August, 1863, to be mobilized at Chattanooga. About the same time, an army of 20,000 Union troops, under the command of Maj. Gen. A. E. Burnside, marched from Kentucky into Tennessee. Upon Burnside's arrival at Knoxville, some townspeople turned out in the streets to greet him, but the majority of citizens watched his entry from behind drawn blinds.

During November, 1863, a Confederate army of 10,000 veterans of Gettysburg, and 5,000 cavalrymen, under command of Gen. James A. Longstreet, struck toward Knoxville from Chattanooga to capture or destroy Burnside's forces. The Union forces stubbornly resisted Longstreet's advance until fortifications around the city could be completed. Several severe rear-guard actions were fought 13 miles west of the city and on November 19 the siege of Knoxville began. The Union troops faced starvation when the Confederates blocked their supply lines. Rations were first cut in half, and at the last reduced to a cracker a day for each man. When the Confederates received information that Gen. W. T. Sherman was on his way with 25,000 men to relieve Burnside, Longstreet attempted the capture of Knoxville by assault. But the attack, made against Fort Sanders at dawn on November 29, was repulsed with heavy loss to the Confederates. A few days later the siege was raised, and the Confederates went into winter quarters near Morristown.

Property damage in Knoxville was enormous. The railroad shops, industrial plants, and the homes north of the railroad tracks were burned by Union troops on a sortie during the siege. All public buildings, and many private homes in the city, were badly damaged by troop quartering and shell-fire.

When peace came, restoration was rapid. Scores of Union soldiers returned to make Knoxville their permanent homes and established some of the leading business houses. Many skilled Welsh and German workmen immigrated to Knoxville and skilled laborers came from northern States. New buildings were erected, new industries were founded, the railroads were rebuilt, trade with other cities was re-established, and a public school system adopted. Knoxville's population, less than 3,000 in 1860, increased to almost 10,000 in 1870.

The next thirty years brought further industrial development. Wood and iron plants, marble quarries, foundry and machine companies, and cotton and woolen factories were established, and by 1900 the population had grown to 36,637.

During the World War period there was further industrial expansion and a marked increase in banking capital. An act passed by the legislature in April, 1917, expanded the city limits from 3.9 to 26.4 square miles. This resulted by 1920 in an increase of 114 per cent over the population of 1910.

Cotton textiles, marble, and hardwood furniture, in the order named, lead in local production and in the number of persons employed. Other industries include the manufacture of porcelain, flour, cement, concrete pipe, steel products, agricultural implements, wood veneer, thermostatic control devices, drop-bottom mine cars, and mucking machines for drilling underground tunnels.

Most of the laborers in Knoxville's industries are native whites from farm and mountain areas; very few of the semi-skilled workmen are organized.

Knoxville has three tobacco warehouses. The season for tobacco auctions begins about the second week in December and lasts for about three months, depending on weather conditions. Tobacco sales in 1937–38 totalled $1,610,000.

Knoxville's electric light system is municipally owned. In 1938 the city purchased the local system from the Tennessee Public Service Co., and contracted with the TVA for the supply of power. In a transaction completed at the same time, the TVA acquired the company's facilities in the outlying districts.

POINTS OF INTEREST

1. The SITE OF BLOUNT COLLEGE, SE. corner S. Gay St. and W. Clinch Ave., is marked by a bronze plaque on the Gay St. side of the Burwell Building. Blount College, named for Governor William Blount, and incorporated by the Territorial Assembly in 1794, was the third institution of higher learning west of the Allegheny Mountains and was co-educational from its beginning. Dr. Samuel Carrick was its only president and Barbara Blount, a daughter of the Governor, was among its early graduates. In 1807 it was chartered as the East Tennessee College, which later became the University of Tennessee.

2. The FIRST PRESBYTERIAN CHURCH, 620 State St., of neo-classic design and constructed of yellow brick with limestone trim, completed in 1901, houses the oldest church organization in Knoxville, and is the third building erected on the site. The church was organized about 1793 and Capt. James White, founder of the city and one of the church's first presiding elders, donated the site. The original building, finished in 1816, was replaced in 1852 by a second structure. In September, 1863, on the first Sunday after Burnside's army occupied Knoxville, the pastor, the Reverend W. A. Harrison, was arrested by Union officers as he left his pulpit and charged with sedition, treasonable utterances, and inciting the citizenry of Knoxville to rebellion against the United States. Later he was released and escorted south. From September 1863 until May 1, 1866, the church was used by the Union Army as barracks, hospital, quarters for refugees, and as a school house for Negro children. In the graveyard, a marble slab marks the GRAVE OF WILLIAM BLOUNT, the first Governor of the Territory South of the River Ohio while a bronze tablet on the original footstone marks the GRAVE OF JAMES WHITE. The GRAVE OF DR. SAMUEL CARRICK, first pastor of the church and president of Blount College, is also here. Many inscriptions read: "Consort of" or "relict of" instead of the usual modern inscription "wife of" or "widow of."

3. The HUNTER-KENNEDY HOUSE *(private)*, 216 E. Church Ave., erected in 1820, by James Kennedy of Pennsylvania, is a two-story, brick post-Colonial house with a handsome cherry staircase leading to large bedrooms on the second floor. The house was once the center of a complete self-sustaining economic community. Mr. Kennedy kept his Negro slaves busily employed producing nearly all the commodities required by the

community. The remains of a gristmill, for which power was generated by the water of First Creek, stand near the house. An enormous smokehouse yet intact is evidence of the generous food supply of an ante-bellum slave plantation. During the occupation of Knoxville by Burnside's army, Union officers were quartered in the house, but members of the family were allowed to remain.

4. The JACKSON HOUSE *(open by permission),* 1000 State St., built in 1800 of red clay bricks made in pioneer kilns, is well preserved. It has thick, ivy-clad walls, a small front porch with an iron grill balcony, and ornate exterior details. The interior walls are finished with the original plastering of sand, lime, and hair. An old copper press stands in the brick-floored basement, once a kitchen and dining room. A secret stairway is built in a little closet in an upper-story room. The old "witch door" with its double cross paneling is a reminder of the tradition that such a cross prevented the entrance of mischievous witches.

The house was owned by Dr. George Jackson for 50 years, and is now the property of descendants of Casper Aebli, who came to the United States from Switzerland in 1865 and later purchased it.

5. The BLOUNT MANSION *(open 9-12, 1-4 Mon.-Fri.),* SW. corner State St. and W. Hill Ave., the first frame house west of the Alleghenies, was built in 1792 by Governor William Blount. Of simple Georgian Colonial design, the house has a two-story central portion between one-story wings. The grooved clapboards are painted white and the windows have green shutters. An old-fashioned garden, enclosed by a picket fence, surrounds the house and a wide brick walk leads from the gate to the main entrance.

The large rooms have hand-made mantelpieces, chair-rails, and wide-paneled doors. The East Room, built in 1799, has walls of light buff plaster with white doors and trim; an old Adam mirror hangs above the high mantelpiece, grooved in diamond-shaped design.

In this room are portraits of William Blount, Willie Blount, his half-brother, Henry Knox, and John Sevier, and steel engravings of Louis Philippe as a young boy and as King of France. The room also contains a large secretary-desk which belonged to the family of Thomas Jefferson, and a large illuminated English Bible and Prayer-Book combined, dated 1751.

KEY TO KNOXVILLE DOWNTOWN MAP

1. Site of Blount College
2. First Presbyterian Church
3. Hunter-Kennedy House
4. Jackson House
5. Blount Mansion
6. Chisholm's Tavern
7. Knox County Courthouse
8. Lyric Theater
9. Cumberland Hotel
10. Lawson McGhee Library
11. Summitt Hill
12. Market House
13. Park House
14. Dickinson-Atkin House
15. Church Street M. E. Church
16. Henley Bridge

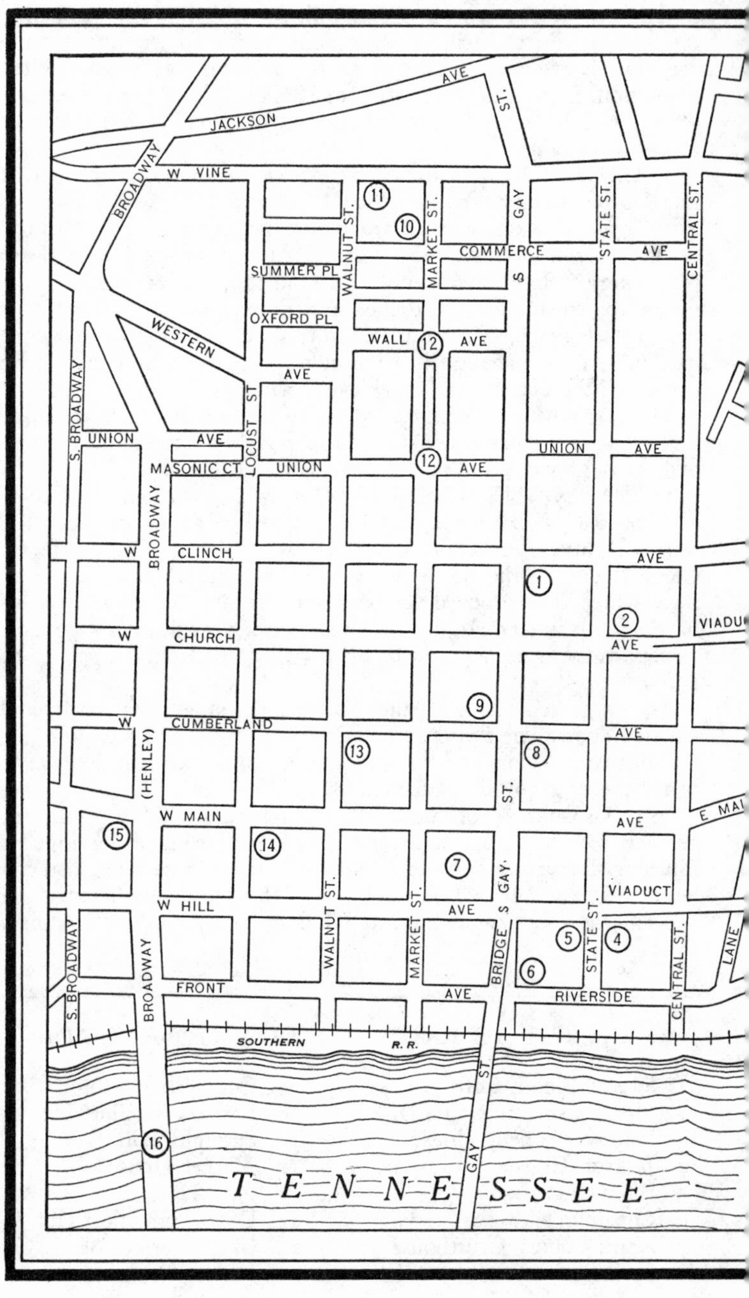
JACKSON
AVE
ST.
BROADWAY
W VINE
WALNUT ST.
MARKET ST.
GAY
STATE ST.
CENTRAL ST.
COMMERCE
AVE
SUMMER PL
OXFORD PL
WESTERN
WALL
AVE
S. BROADWAY
UNION
AVE
LOCUST ST
MASONIC CT
UNION
AVE
UNION
AVE
W
CLINCH
AVE
BROADWAY
W
CHURCH
AVE
VIADU
W
CUMBERLAND
AVE
(HENLEY)
ST.
W MAIN
AVE
E MAI
S GAY
VIADUCT
W HILL
AVE
LANE
BRIDGE
FRONT
AVE
RIVERSIDE
SOUTHERN
R. R.
GAY ST
T E N N E S S E E

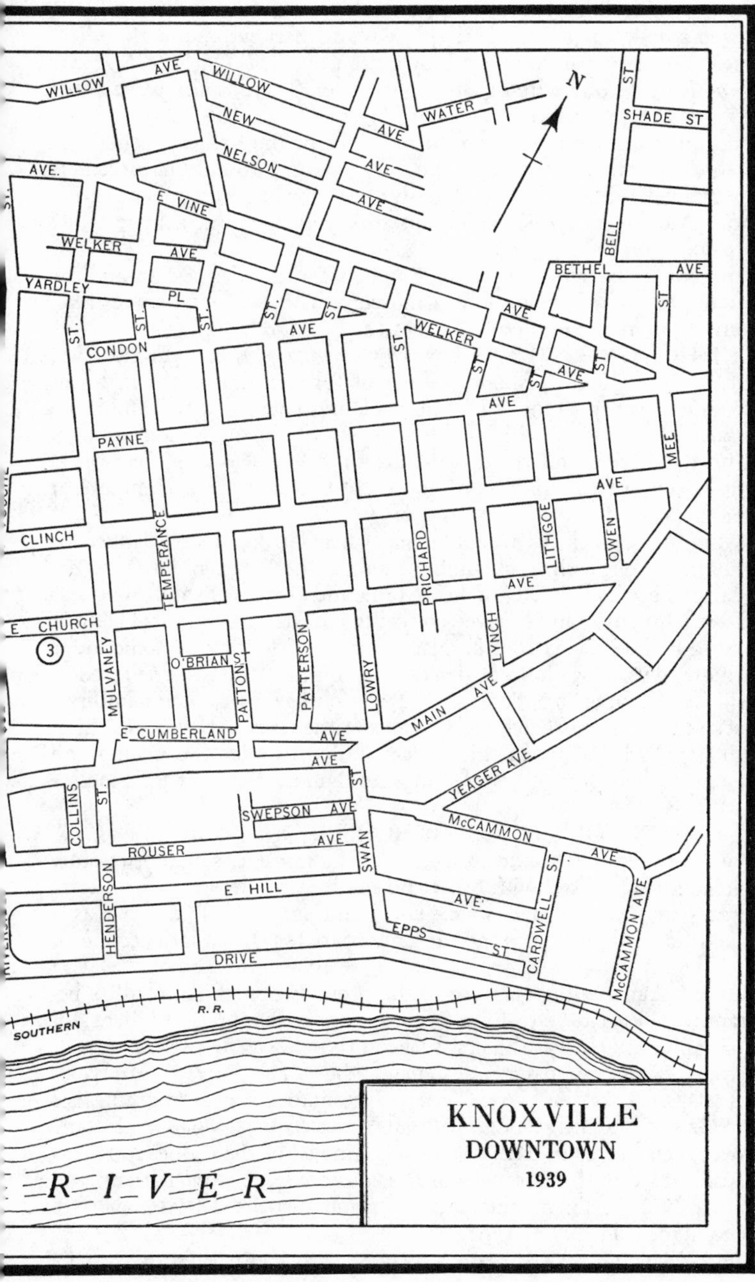
WILLOW AVE
WILLOW
NEW AVE
WATER
NELSON AVE
AVE
SHADE ST
AVE.
E VINE
WELKER AVE
YARDLEY
PL
BELL ST
BETHEL AVE
CONDON ST
AVE
WELKER
AVE
PAYNE
MEE
AVE
CLINCH
TEMPERANCE
PRICHARD
LITHGOE
OWEN
AVE
E CHURCH
3
MULVANEY
O'BRIAN ST
PATTON
PATTERSON
LOWRY
LYNCH
MAIN AVE
E CUMBERLAND AVE
AVE
ST
YEAGER AVE
COLLINS ST
SWEPSON AVE
McCAMMON AVE
ROUSER AVE
SWAN
HENDERSON
E HILL AVE
EPPS ST
CARDWELL ST
McCAMMON AVE
DRIVE
SOUTHERN R. R.
R I V E R
KNOXVILLE
DOWNTOWN
1939

In the adjoining bedroom are a tester-bed with a pine cradle beside it; John Sevier's desk, upon which Dr. J. G. M. Ramsey wrote the *Annals of Tennessee;* and two paintings by Lloyd Branson, *The Old Block House* and *Bonny Kate,* second wife of Governor Sevier. There is also a chair that once belonged to John Adair.

The dining room, or pine room, to the right of the hallway, contains a trestle table set with pewter, and a hunter's board with antique decanters and white china fruit dishes. On a Welsh dresser or hooded cupboard from the Smoky Mountains are an enormous turkey platter and a huge white porcelain soup tureen.

A trap door leads from the passageway between the East Room and the bed chamber to a lower room, now a museum. The exhibits include treasures from old pioneer families of Tennessee.

6. CHISHOLM'S TAVERN *(open by permission),* 217 Front Ave., was built by Capt. John Chisholm, soldier of fortune, during the first year of Knoxville's history (1792). It is built of logs covered with hand-hewn weatherboards and fitted with wooden pegs and square-headed wrought nails. The foundation and cellar walls are of field stone three feet thick. At the gable end of the three-story house are two huge pent chimneys of baked brick.

From the main porch, two double, six-paneled front doors, flanked by fluted pilasters and with a five-light transom above, open into the entrance hall. The woodwork is of heart pine and there are solid pine, six-paneled "witch doors" and twelve-foot ceilings. The "great room", left of the entrance hall, has a six-foot fireplace opening. The first Masonic lodge of Knoxville, with Gov. John Sevier as Worshipful Master, is believed to have held its early meetings here. Local tradition has it that Louis Philippe was attacked by a vicious batch of bed bugs at the tavern. He greased himself with hog lard, but when this remedy failed to allay the itching and stinging, he rushed outdoors screaming, and jumped into the Tennessee River

7. The KNOX COUNTY COURTHOUSE *(open 7-6 weekdays),* W. Main Ave. between S. Gay and Market Sts., is a massive, square, two-story steel frame structure faced with brick and marble and decorated with terra cotta friezes in the Victorian style. The building, erected in 1885 as a county courthouse, also houses the supreme court for the eastern section of the State.

A MARBLE ARCH at the entrance to the grounds honors Knoxville's beloved family physician, Dr. John Mason Boyd, who practiced here for more than 50 years. He was the first surgeon to successfully perform a panhysterectomy. A stone marker designates the SITE OF THE MILITARY BLOCKHOUSE, erected in 1793. The two monuments near the entrance mark the GRAVE OF JOHN SEVIER AND HIS SECOND WIFE. The tombstones placed over their graves in Alabama before removal of their ashes to Knoxville are imbedded in the east walls of the courthouse. A stone marker, 100 feet south of the Sevier monument, commemorates the TREATY OF THE HOLSTON, signed on July 2, 1791.

8. The LYRIC THEATRE, 802 S. Gay St., was constructed in 1871 by

GATEWAY, BLOUNT MANSION, KNOXVILLE

Peter Staub, consul from Switzerland to the United States, who was later naturalized and appointed consul from the United States to Switzerland. It was formally opened as Staub's Theater in 1872 with the presentation of *William Tell,* by local talent.

9. CUMBERLAND HOTEL, 723 S. Gay St., erected in 1854 as Schubert's House, occupies the SITE OF JOHN STONE'S LOG TAVERN. Since 1792 this site has been occupied by a series of taverns and hotels, and was the gathering place of the elite for many years. Remodeling abolished the "elegant barroom, spacious ballroom, and commodious lobby with a large open fireplace," but the large rooms with huge ceilings remain as they were built.

10. The LAWSON McGHEE LIBRARY *(open 9-9 weekdays, 2-6 Sun.),* 217 Market St., is the second building occupied by the library since it was established in 1885. Of modified Georgian Colonial design, the present building is of white brick and terra-cotta construction. It was designed by Grant B. Miller and presented to the city in 1917. Chas. M. McGhee, founder of the library, named it for his daughter, May Lawson McGhee. In the basement is the C. M. MCCLUNG HISTORICAL COLLECTION, about 6,000 volumes of history and genealogy of the Southern States —one of the finest collections of early books, maps, and documents in the South.

11. SUMMIT HILL, W. Vine Ave. between Market and Walnut Sts., was occupied by a battery of Confederate artillery, manned by troops and citizen volunteers for the defense of Knoxville against a Union cavalry raid on June 21, 1863. This hill was an excellent position for defense during the days of open warfare. The Union artillery was superior in range to the Confederate and fired successfully upon Summit Hill from a knoll more than half a mile away.

12. The MARKET HOUSE, Market St. between Wall and Union Aves., is on a tract of land donated to the city in 1853 by William G. Swan and Joseph A. Mabry to be maintained as a free market for farmers. The building, Romanesque in design, was constructed in 1897 of red brick trimmed with white Knoxville Marble. The stalls in the Market House are leased to the merchants, and in the central aisle 104 tables are allotted free to farm women for the display of their produce. In this section and on the free curb market outside, where farmers sell their wares from wagons, trucks, and cars, no produce that has been "jobbed" is permitted for sale. An auditorium on the second floor seats about 1,000.

MARKET SQUARE and its environs form a town within a town. Here, only one block from Gay Street, the talk is of the weather, of the price of corn, of stockbreeding, and other matters important to the farmers. At noontime, the women who run boarding houses on the second floors of the buildings around the square descend to the street and clang their old-time hand bells. Meals in these houses are 15 cents for "all you eat." The two ten-cent movie houses on the square exhibit western films.

13. The PARK HOUSE *(open 9-5 daily),* 422 W. Cumberland Ave., of brownish-red brick in post-Colonial style, is typical of the large dwellings erected by wealthy builders in pioneer days. L-shaped in plan, it con-

CHURCH STREET M. E. CHURCH, KNOXVILLE

sists of two stories above a raised basement, with a narrow arcaded and latticed porch in the angle of the ell. John Sevier, first Governor of Tennessee, began the house in 1798, but financial reverses compelled him to abandon it after the foundation and part of the first story were completed. James Park, later mayor of Knoxville, bought and completed the house. It is now used as an infirmary.

14. The DICKINSON-ATKINS HOUSE *(open by permission),* 518 W. Main Ave., begun by Perez Dickinson in 1830, was purchased and completed in 1901 by C. Brown Atkins, Knoxville manufacturer. This two-story white house of post-Colonial architecture with stuccoed walls stands far back from the street at the end of a spacious garden and lawn. Leon Beaver of Knoxville was the architect.

15. The CHURCH STREET M. E. CHURCH, SW. corner W. Main Ave. and Broadway, completed in 1932, is of neo-Gothic design. The exterior walls are faced with quartz stone of various hues; the stone trim is of Indiana limestone carved in the traditional Gothic manner. The roof is covered with a variegated gray-green slate. The pews of oak, between aisles paved with sandstone, are of a classical pattern of the Middle Ages. Barber and McMurray of Knoxville were the architects.

16. HENLEY BRIDGE spans the Tennessee River at the south end of

Broadway. It is 1,800 feet long and 300 feet above the low-water mark. The bridge affords an excellent view of the Knoxville business skyline and the University of Tennessee campus.

17. The UNIVERSITY OF TENNESSEE, W. Cumberland Ave. between Hunter and 15th Sts., occupies a 40-acre campus with a quadrangle of buildings crowning "The Hill," flanked by a number of other buildings at a lower level. Buildings erected since 1917 conform to the Collegiate Gothic style. These newer buildings, designed by Barber and McMurray, Knoxville, are constructed of variegated brick with limestone trim. On the grounds on the north and south sides of Cumberland Avenue are exceptionally fine old trees. Among the rare imported specimens are copper elms and gingkos.

The University of Tennessee was established in 1794 as Blount College. By an act of the General Assembly in 1807, Blount became East Tennessee College, which in turn was chartered in 1840 as East Tennessee University, assuming its present name in 1879.

For thirty years prior to the War between the States the annual enrollment was about a hundred. The military tradition has been strong from the beginning, and as the result of a petition by the students a military department was established in 1843. During the War between the States, the university was closed because most of the faculty and the student body volunteered in Confederate or Union armies. Both forces used the buildings for barracks and hospital.

East Tennessee University was selected by the General Assembly in 1869 as a beneficiary of the Morrill Land Grant Act, and as a result a College of Agriculture was set up and the military department re-established. The College of Liberal Arts began to offer graduate courses in 1872, and in the following year courses for teachers were added to the curriculum. A summer session, noted as "The Summer School of the South," was opened in 1880. Classes in education and engineering soon developed into separate colleges, and the law school was organized in 1889.

While Blount College had been co-educational, women were denied admission by its successors. Not until 1893 did the university again admit women. With this development domestic science courses made their appearance and there is now an excellent School of Home Economics.

Experiments in extension courses were inaugurated in 1897 and instruction for nonresidents now constitutes a widespread function of the university. The School of Commerce was established soon after the World War, and separate pre-medical and pre-dental courses were offered shortly thereafter. The Colleges of Medicine and Dentistry and the Schools of Pharmacy and Nursing are in Memphis *(see MEMPHIS)*, and the Junior College of Agriculture, Home Economics, and Industrial Arts at Martin *(see Tour 10)*. The annual enrollment is about 6,000.

The university is outstanding in agricultural experiment, maintaining experimental stations at Nashville, Jackson, Columbia, Clarksville, and Knoxville. Through these stations the university has given aid in modern farming methods to the rural folk of the State, with experiment and discovery often of Nation-wide benefit. It has also cooperated with the TVA in the rehabilitation program in the Valley of East Tennessee.

The UNIVERSITY LIBRARY *(open 8-10 weekdays; 6-8 Sat.),* 1401 W. Cumberland Ave., built in 1931, is Collegiate Gothic in style, constructed of concrete faced with variegated brick and limestone, with cast-iron trim. The most notable architectural features are the tall tower at the southwest corner, the broad stone staircase encircling a massive pier with a groined ceiling above, and the large reference room on the east side of the second story. This room, 35 by 135 feet, has a ceiling 28 feet above the floor and large windows on three sides. Huge concrete beams, resting on stone columns, support the roof. The ceiling above the staircase and the beams of the reference room and delivery hall are decorated with murals, the work of Hugh Tyler of Knoxville. Barber and McMurray, of Knoxville, were the architects, and Grant C. Miller the consulting architect.

A huge oil painting of a scene in the Great Smoky Mountains, regarded as one of the best examples of the work of Charles Christopher Krutch, hangs in the main hall of the second floor. The painting was a gift from Miss Lou Krutch, a sister of the artist, and friends. The library contains approximately 133,000 volumes and an extensive collection of bound magazine files. The AUDIGIER ART COLLECTION *(open 2-5 Sun.)* occupies two especially designed tower rooms in the library building. Consisting of oil paintings, sculpture, oriental rugs, early Italian furniture, and antiques, the collection was presented to the University by L. B. Audigier as a memorial to his wife.

The BIOLOGY BUILDING *(open 8-6 weekdays),* on the first lower level of "The Hill," contains a collection of 36,000 specimens gathered in the Smokies by university botanists. There are 20,000 varieties of ferns and flowering plants, 5,000 mosses and their relatives, 400 lichens, and 10,600 fungi, replacing the original collection, which was destroyed in the Morrill Hall fire of 1934.

SHIELDS-WATKINS FIELD, at the south level of the campus, was named in honor of W. S. Shields, of Knoxville, for many years a trustee of the University, and Mrs. Shields, whose maiden name was Alice Watkins. Mr. and Mrs. Shields donated the fund that bought the property. The seating capacity of the stadium is 35,000. Under the east side, bedrooms for about 200 male students are being constructed. The field is the scene of football games of "The Volunteers" and of the weekly dress parade and review of the university's R. O. T. C. regiment.

18. TYSON MEMORIAL HOUSE *(open 9-5 daily),* 839 16th St., a commodious structure of Georgian Colonial design, now a recreational and religious center for University students, was once the home of L. D. Tyson, wealthy manufacturer of Knoxville, and in his later years, United States Senator from Tennessee. In the World War, General Tyson commanded the 59th Brigade, 30th Division, A.E.F. After his death the home was donated to the Tennessee Diocese of the Episcopal Church by his daughter Mrs. Kenneth Gilpin. The house contains living rooms, a chapel, and a library. Episcopal services are held in the chapel, but students of all sects are welcome to the home.

19. MELROSE *(open 9-9 daily),* 1702 Melrose Place, of Classical Revival design with Tuscon detail and long French windows in the lower story, was built by Negro slave labor during the early 1850's. The brick walls, two and a half feet thick, are covered with stucco and the eaves project three feet from the walls on all sides of the house. The outstanding feature of the interior is an unsupported spiral stairway.

Melrose was built in 1858 by John J. Craig of Florence, Alabama, who named it Lucknow, but did not himself live in it. The house stood between the contending lines in the sixties and many soldiers of both sides died within its walls.

In 1865 it was bought by O. P. Temple and was then named Melrose in memory of his mother-in-law's old home near Melrose Abbey, Scotland. Later, the home was turned into apartments.

20. UNIVERSITY OF TENNESSEE EXPERIMENTAL FARM *(open 9-5 weekdays),* 2600 Kingston Pike, occupies 1,200 acres on both sides of the Tennessee River. The one principal building, H. A. MORGAN HALL, of Collegiate Gothic design, is of red brick with limestone trim. Northeast of this building is an unusually large lysimeter laboratory consisting of 350 units housed in the two hillside houses and an underground tunnel. Soil-leaching tests are conducted by trained laborers under the direction of a staff of scientists.

21. LONGUEVAL *(open by permission),* 2602 Kingston Pike, built in 1823, is a two-story post-Colonial structure of hand-made brick. At the front entrance the drive winds among huge oaks and other native trees. The flower and vegetable gardens slope in terraces down to the river. In the gardens are crepe myrtle, fragrantissima, sweet alyssum, heliotrope, lemon balm, rosemary, rue, sage, tansy, thyme, nepeta, bee balm, rose geranium, lemon verbena, sweet lavender, and Confederate jasmine.

The rooms of the house are spacious, the ceilings high. The walls are paneled, and a stairway branching two ways from a narrow balcony leads to the bedrooms on the second floor.

Originally known as Crescent Bend from its position on the river, Longueval, meaning "long view," as it was finally called, was the plantation home of Drury P. Armstrong, merchant, banker, and planter. During the winter Armstrong housed bees in his cellar to keep them warm. Armstrong's lands extended across the present Kingston Pike and for some miles on both sides of the Tennessee River, then known as the Holston. A slight depression indicating the wagon road to a privately owned ferry is still discernible south of Kingston Pike.

22. BLEAK HOUSE *(private),* 2800 Kingston Pike, named for the novel by Charles Dickens, is a two-story brick structure painted gray and adorned with a cupola. Gen. James A. Longstreet made his headquarters here during the siege of Knoxville. Union artillery fired upon the house and damaged it slightly, a number of Minie balls being still imbedded in its walls. Opposite the house are serpentine walls of brick, modelled after those designed by Thomas Jefferson at the University of Virginia.

23. The SANFORD ARBORETUM *(open 9-5 weekdays),* 2890 King-

ston Pike, rear of the A. F. Sanford home, is a non-commercial collection of more than 2,200 varieties of dwarf trees and shrubs. All specimens bear embossed metal tags, which give the common and scientific name of the plant, its native country, and the date of transplanting.

24. KNOXVILLE COLLEGE, 1400 College St. one of the oldest institutions for Negro instruction in the South, had its inception in the Freedmen's Missions. After a survey of points in Tennessee and South Carolina the college was established on its present site in 1875 by the United Presbyterian Church of America. The church took over a school for Negroes run by R. T. Creswell and hired an extra teacher for the more than 100 pupils already enrolled.

From the original class of impoverished Negro children and adults, housed in a one-room abandoned grocery store, there has evolved a college of 28 buildings on a beautiful campus of 20 acres, a part of the 90-acre tract owned by the college. There is an average attendance of more than 300 men and women students, representing 21 States. The faculty is bi-racial.

The red-brick buildings, three and four stories high, are trimmed in wood and stone, and the campus, with elms and maples, occupies the site of the encampment of the Confederates under General Longstreet during the siege of Knoxville. The ADMINISTRATION BUILDING is in the center of an informal amphitheater of similar buildings. A few buildings were erected of bricks made in the college's own brick kiln by former students.

The CARNEGIE LIBRARY *(open 8-5 and 7-9 weekdays; 10-12, 2-4, and 7-9 Sat.),* and MACMILLAN MEMORIAL CHAPEL, the latter erected in 1913 by the Second United Presbyterian Church of Allegheny, Pa. and named in honor of the Reverend W. E. MacMillan, are of neo-classic design.

Knoxville College confers bachelor degrees in academic subjects and in music.

25. BROOKSIDE MILLS *(open 9-4 weekdays; guides),* 300 block Baxter Ave., is one of the largest cotton textile mills in the South. It consists of four principal units, employs approximately 5,000 persons during prosperous years and, when operating at maximum capacity, consumes about 100,000 bales of cotton annually. The plant manufactures a large variety of textiles, including challis, lawns, piques, organdies, voiles, poplins, moires, calicoes, corduroy, and broadcloth.

26. NATIONAL and OLD GRAY CEMETERIES, Broadway between Tyson and Cooper Sts., extending to Bernard Ave., adjoin each other. National Cemetery, founded by the Government in 1863 for interment of Union soldiers killed in East Tennessee, also contains the graves of Spanish-American and World War veterans. In Old Gray Cemetery are the graves of Gov. W. G. (Parson) Brownlow, editor of the *Whig,* Unionist leader, and Radical Republican; Horace Maynard; L. D. Tyson, United States Senator and Brigadier-General in the World War, and William Gibbs McAdoo, father of former United States Senator W. G. McAdoo, of California.

POINTS OF INTEREST IN ENVIRONS

Indian Cave, *26.8 m. (see Tour 1A)*; Smoky Mountains National Park, *38 m. (see Tour 5)*; Norris Dam, *26 m.*; Fort Loudoun, *35.1 m. (see Tour 5A)*; Cavet Station, *10.4 m.*; Middlebrook, the Hazen-Webb Home, *10.8 m.*; Charles McClung House (States View), *16.4 m.*; Campbell Station, *15.5 m.*; Admiral Farragut's birthplace, *22.7 m. (see Tour 12)*.

Chattanooga

Railroad Stations: Union Station, W. 9th and Broad Sts., for Nashville, Chattanooga & St. Louis Ry. and Tennessee, Alabama & Georgia Ry. Terminal Station, Market and 14th Sts., for Southern Ry. and Central of Georgia Ry.
Bus Station: Union Bus Terminal, Market, Broad, and 10th Sts., for Greyhound, Capitol, Tennessee Coach, Motor Transportation, Smoky Mountain Stage, Cherokee, Chickamauga and Thomas Lines.
Airport: Lovel Field, Municipal Airport, 8 m. NE. on US 64, for Eastern Air Lines. Information office at Read House. Taxi fare 75¢; time 20 minutes.
Streetcar and Bus Service: Cars and busses to all parts of city and suburbs from Market St. Fare 7¢ for cars, 7¢ and 10¢ for busses; 20¢ to Lookout Mountain via St. Elmo bus.
Incline Railway: Lookout Mountain Incline Ry., St. Elmo St. at Tennessee Ave., round trip 40¢.
Taxis: 15¢ first mile, 10¢ each additional half mile; zone rates approximately same as mileage.
Traffic Regulations: Speed limit 25 m. p. h., 30 m. p. h. on boulevards and through streets; no left turns on Market St. at 7th, 8th, 9th Sts. Traffic regulations, published by Chattanooga Safety Council, obtainable at City Hall.

Accommodations: Fourteen hotels; three for Negroes; tourist camps.

Information Service: Chattanooga Automobile Club, Hotel Patten, 11th and Market Sts.; Chamber of Commerce, 819 Broad St.

Radio Stations: WDOD (1280 kc.); WAPO (1420 kc.).
Theaters and Motion Picture Houses: Memorial Auditorium, McCallie Ave. and Lindsay St., all types of theatricals. Two first-run motion picture houses; 10 second-run, two Negro.
Wrestling: Memorial Auditorium.
Baseball: Engel Stadium, east side O'Neal St. between E. 3rd and E. 5th Sts. (Southern Association).
Football: Chamberlain Field, University of Chattanooga.
Polo: Fort Oglethorpe Polo Association.
Swimming: Municipal Pool, Warner Park, McCallie Ave. at viaduct (fee 25¢); McCallie Lake, McCallie School (fee 10¢ and 25¢).
Golf: Municipal Course, at Brainerd E. of Missionary Ridge where US 11 crosses city limits, 18 holes, 40¢.
Tennis: Free courts: Warner Park, McCallie Ave. at viaduct, 12 courts; Riverside Park, N. bank of Tennessee River between Market and Walnut St. Bridges, four courts; Citizens' Park, E. 5th and Lansing Sts., two courts; Lincoln Park (Negro), Central Ave. and Blackford Sts., three courts.

Annual Events: January 1, Emancipation Day (Negro); February 22, Chattanooga *Times* five-mile foot race; April 1 (week), Baylor Relays, Baylor School; April (3rd week of even years), University of Chattanooga Institute of Public Affairs; early May, Music Festival; early Spring, Chattanooga Flower Show; June 21, National Pigeon Racing Association races; mid-September, Chattanooga Tri-State Fair, Fort Oglethorpe Horse Show.

CHATTANOOGA (674 alt., 119,798 pop.) lies near the border of Georgia on the sharp Moccasin Bend of the Tennessee River, in a valley walled by Missionary Ridge to the east, Signal Mountain to the northwest, and Lookout Mountain to the southwest. The ridges are so steep that tunnels were blasted througth them for the main highways into Chattanooga.

Steep crosstown streets rise from Market and Broad, the two main north and south thoroughfares. In the shopping center tall buildings with the straight simple lines of modern architecture crowd heavily ornamented structures of the late 1890's. Tied up at the foot of Market Street are houseboats, motor launches, and outboards. Occasionally an old stern wheeler churns along the Tennessee past the waterfront. Just south of the business district the city is divided by the railroad tracks connecting the Union Station with the Terminal Station. The area south of the tracks is mainly industrial—iron and steel works in South Chattanooga, woodworking plants in East Lake, and textile mills in Rossville, Georgia.

Residential sections reach far up the gaunt ridges, where the nights are cool even in summer. The more elaborate homes are on Lookout Mountain, Missionary Ridge, and Signal Mountain. North of the river and closer to the business district are residential North Chattanooga and Dallas Heights. On some of the downtown streets old dwellings are wedged between apartment houses and office buildings.

Negroes make up nearly one-third of Chattanooga's population. Houses range from well-kept bungalows, duplexes and small tenement houses in Churchville, in some sections of College Hill, and on East 8th Street, to the ramshackle shelters of South Chattanooga and Tannery Flats, where seven or eight families live in a single dwelling.

Many Negroes work in factories, foundries, and in domestic service, while others are engaged in business. A place has been found for Negroes in local political organizations, a procedure simplified under the direction of an inter-racial committee. Typically Negro are the all-day and all-night dances on the southwest side and the rummage sales at Five Points. There are Negro lodges of Masons and Knights of Pythias, a local chapter of Alpha Phi Alpha fraternity, Y.M.C.A. and Y.W.C.A., and churches of many denominations.

Long before the Cherokee built villages along Chickamauga Creek, Indians were planting corn and building towns in the vicinity of Chattanooga. Aboriginal remains, including earthen mounds, midden deposits, and cemeteries, have been found along Moccasin Bend, on Williams Island, and along Riverside Drive. Recent archeological investigations indicate that these first inhabitants were of Muskhogean stock. When the Muskhogeans first entered the region is not known, but it is certain that they occupied the valley for many years, and that they were still in the valley in 1540, when De Soto arrived.

Even in prehistoric times, Chattanooga was an important junction of many lines of communication. Over Lookout Mountain passed the Great War Path, following the valley of East Tennessee into the Deep South. The Shawnee Trail began at Williams Island and struck north into the Cumberland Valley. The Suck Creek Trail roughly followed the present Suck Creek Road.

French traders established a post in the area and maintained trade with the Indians for half a century. Competing with them were English traders, whose outpost, Fort Loudoun, was on the Little Tennessee River. When the Cherokee and Creek besieged Fort Loudoun in 1761, the French at New Orleans sent a supply boat up the Tennessee to aid the Indians. The boat could not navigate the "Suck" of the Tennessee, however, and the goods were sold to the Indians near present Chattanooga. When the tide of Anglo-Saxon immigration began to pour over the mountains, the French traders left the valley.

With the outbreak of the American Revolution the Cherokee turned unsuccessfully against the settlers. Dragging Canoe, a young war chief, led the recalcitrants from upper East Tennessee to the vicinity of Chattanooga. Joined by other hostile Indians and by white outlaws, they became known as the Chickamauga. From this region their war parties struck at outlying settlements until they were feared all along the frontier. The Nickajack Expedition, led by Maj. James Ore in 1794, finally broke their power. They ceased to exist as a separate tribe and rejoined the Cherokee Nation.

In 1803 John Brown, a half-breed Cherokee, established a ferry at the south end of Wiliams Island, which he operated until the removal of the Cherokee in 1838 *(see Tour 13 sec. b)*. The ferry was on a stage route across Lookout Mountain, the only passageway between the South and the eastern markets.

After the treaties of 1805–1815 Chattanooga became a Cherokee trading center, called Ross' Landing, for the Scotch-Cherokee family who operated it after 1815. In 1817 Brainerd Mission was established by the Rev. Cyrus Kingsbury, a Congregationalist missionary, and functioned until the Indian removal of 1838.

The first permanent white settlement at Ross' Landing was made about 1835. The following year the Cherokee removal began, and Ross' Landing was made a military post and a point of embarkation for the Indians. In 1837 the post office was created, and mail service to Washington—ten days distant—was established.

Ross' Landing became the salt-trading center of eastern Tennessee, northern Georgia, and northern Alabama. In time of freshets the salt, imported from King's Salt Works in southwest Virginia, was shipped down the north fork of the Holston River and thence down the Tennessee. In 1838 1,500 barrels of salt sold at $8.50 per barrel. Through that fundamental commodity, Chattanooga began as a trading and shipping point.

In the fall of 1838 the town was laid out and Ross' Landing became Chattanooga. The name is generally believed to derive from the Creek word *Chat-to-to-noog-gee* (rock rising to a point), which seems to describe Lookout Mountain. In 1839 the little community received a charter, and town lots were auctioned. Those near the river sold for as much as $1,680 and seldom for less than $850, while those toward the south brought almost nothing.

The community was not long without a newspaper, for in 1838 F. A. Parham began printing the Hamilton *Gazette,* later the Chattanooga *Ga-*

zette. It is believed that the Hamilton *Observer* antedated the *Gazette*, but no copies are extant. Apparently the first issues of the *Gazette* were set up and printed on the flatboat that brought the press from Knoxville.

By 1841 trade included such commodities as bacon, flour, iron, whisky, and muslins. In 1849 the Western & Atlantic Railroad connected the city with the South Atlantic seaboard. Two years later, when Chattanooga was granted a city charter, 45,000 bales of cotton were coming annually from northern Alabama for shipment to Charleston and Savannah. Chattanooga and Memphis became temporary rivals as cotton markets, a competition that ended in Memphis' favor with the completion of the Memphis & Charleston Railroad through northern Alabama and Mississippi.

Because it was the only town of importance between Kingston and Muscle Shoals, a distance of more than 300 miles, Chattanooga had a river trade out of proportion to its population. Upon completion of the Nashville & Chattanooga Railway in 1854, with its through connection with the Atlantic seacoast via Atlanta, river traffic dwindled. In 1855 railways connected Chattanooga and Knoxville. Two years later the Memphis & Charleston joined Chattanooga with the Mississippi country.

On the eve of the War between the States Chattanooga, while important as a railroad center, was still a very small town, with a total population of 5,545.

As early as 1862 one of the key objectives of Union strategy was to occupy East Tennessee and Chattanooga, to drive a wedge between the Eastern and Western Armies of the Confederacy. Soon after Tennessee seceded, Confederate troops were massed to protect Chattanooga from Union invasion. The first Union move on Chattanooga shortly after the Battle of Shiloh in 1862, was made by Gen. Don Carlos Buell, who advanced toward Chattanooga along the Memphis & Charleston Railroad. He was to keep the railroad in constant repair behind him so that the line to Memphis, his base of supplies, would remain open. But Confederate cavalry troops so constantly raided and destroyed the railroad in Buell's rear that when his advance guard was within artillery range of Chattanooga he had to abandon the campaign. The Confederate invasion of Kentucky temporarily turned Union attention from Chattanooga.

In the summer of 1863 the Union forces renewed their campaign against Chattanooga in an effort to cut the Confederates off from their base of supplies. The Confederates were driven back to the Tennessee River. Here the Union Army was faced by the problem of crossing the river under fire.

Maj. Gen. William Starke Rosecrans sent a small Union detachment to the hills east of Walden's Ridge, north of Chattanooga. The troops marched back and forth in the hills, beat on barrels to imitate the rumble of wagons, and floated wood down river to suggest that bridges were under construction. This led the Confederates to concentrate their strength north of Chattanooga.

Meanwhile, the main Union force moved south of Chattanooga, and crossed the river at Bridgeport and Caperton's Ferry just across the Alabama line. Two units moved up Lookout Mountain, while Rosecrans planned to move south of Chattanooga, cut the Confederates' line of communications and supplies and force them to evacuate the city. But the Confederate commander, Gen. Braxton Bragg, learned of this movement. To protect his line he left the town on September 7 and 8 and took up a position near LaFayette, Georgia. Here he received reinforcements from Virginia and Mississippi. Rosecrans, believing the Confederates in full retreat southward, sent his divided army over different routes to cut them off.

The Confederates were waiting for this move and struck north again. Bragg planned to destroy the divided Union forces and retake Chattanooga.

As the Confederates crossed Chickamauga Creek on September 18, Union cavalry detachments were hurled in their path. Strong Union infantry reinforcements arrived, and next morning fighting began on a large scale. Back and forth in the dense woods above Chickamauga Creek the battle raged, with Confederates gradually pushing the Union troops up toward the Lafayette Road, and on September 20 the Confederates broke through the Union line, forcing many Federals from the field. The remaining Union troops under General Thomas concentrated on Snodgrass Hill and held off the Confederates until nightfall. Then Thomas retreated toward Chattanooga. Of the 66,000 Confederate troops engaged, about 18,000 were killed, wounded, or missing. On the Union side, 16,000 casualties out of 58,000 troops were reported.

After the battle the Confederates surrounded the Union troops in Chattanooga in an effort to starve them into surrendering. News of the disaster of Chickamauga caused the high command at Washington to send all available resources to Chattanooga. Two Union army corps under Gen. Joe Hooker marched from Virginia. On October 23 Grant rushed from Louisville to take command, and captured the Confederate outpost at Orchard Knob. The next day Hooker pushed back the small Confederate force stationed on Lookout Mountain.

On the afternoon of November 24, Hooker's corps advanced through the clouds up the side of Lookout Mountain and attacked Walthall's brigade of Confederates, numbering 1,469. The "Battle above the Clouds" was fought in a thick mist until 2 a.m. November 25, when the Federals withdrew and crossed Chattanooga Creek Valley to Missionary Ridge.

In late November, Bragg spread his troops along a seven-mile line on Missionary Ridge. Sherman arrived with Union reinforcements. The Battle of Missionary Ridge, November 25, began with an unsuccessful Union attack at the north end of the Ridge. Late in the afternoon General Thomas took the Confederate rifle pits at the base of the ridge just east of Orchard Knob, then, without orders, stormed the crest and broke through the Confederate line. A simultaneous Union attack through Rossville Gap forced many of the Confederates off the ridge. Those on the north only left their positions later in the evening. The broken army of

Tennessee retreated through the night into Georgia with Cleburne fighting a rearguard action in the gaps near Ringgold. Bragg fell back to Dalton, 40 miles south of Chattanooga, and established winter quarters.

From September 1863, to March 1866, Chattanooga was a Union military camp and the base for Sherman's Atlanta campaign. After the Union withdrawal, the great accumulation of goods in private hands, bought at peak prices for sale to the troops, had to be sold at sheriff's auction.

At the close of the war Chattanooga's normal population of 1,500 was outnumbered more than two to one by refugees, camp followers and settlers, criminals, and fugitives. Civil authority was weak and corrupt, but in 1867 citizens organized vigilante committees and expelled or subdued the undesirables.

A scourge of smallpox in the wake of the war lasted until the flood of 1867 that washed away homes, industries, and the military bridge, and kept Chattanooga isolated for days. Other epidemics—cholera in 1873, yellow fever in 1878, and smallpox again in 1883—claimed many lives, but only temporarily impeded the city's growth.

In 1878 Adolph S. Ochs moved to Chattanooga from Knoxville, purchased the Chattanooga *Times,* and made it one of the State's most influential journals. Although later identified with the New York *Times,* he retained active control of the Chattanooga paper until his death in 1935.

Abundance of raw material, transportation by water and by rail, and cheap labor was the basis of a successful campaign during reconstruction to attract manufacturing enterprises. The newspapers, supplemented by the legislature, made tempting offers to Northern investors. The first plow factory in the South, founded by Newell Sanders with $3,000 of borrowed capital and purchased in 1919 by International Harvester for $1,000,000, was the outstanding local enterprise. The iron industry boomed in the early seventies, but later disappeared because of outside pig iron competition. In 1887–88 there was a sudden real estate boom, followed by a crash; but with its natural assets and fresh Northern capital, business gradually gained stability.

Chattanooga suffered heavily from the panic of 1893, but took on new life during the Spanish-American War, when the battlefield of Chickamauga was converted into a quartermaster's depot and concentration camp. After the war, expansion was rapid and steady. From 1900 to 1910 the population increased from 31,000 to 44,000; and about the time of the shift (1911) from the old aldermanic system to a commission form of government, there began a ten-year period of increasing migration to the city from the farms and mountains of Tennessee, Alabama, and Georgia.

The 1920 population of 57,895 more than doubled in the next decade. Smoke and congestion caused many to move from the older residential sections of Cameron Hill, Alton Park, and Ridgedale to the suburbs of North Chattanooga, Missionary Ridge, Brainerd, and Shepherd Hills.

Electric power and railroad facilities have figured prominently in the growth of Chattanooga as a manufacturing center. A railroad hub from the beginning, the city is entered by nine trunk lines. The flood of cash during the World War, when thousands of troops were concentrated and trained at Chickamauga Park and Fort Oglethorpe, was also a vital factor in furthering industry.

Chattanooga leads the South in the manufacture of foundry, oil well, and other iron and steel equipment, and in hosiery, furniture, and patent medicines. In 1930 there were 388 manufacturers employing 36,000 workers, producing 1,500 different articles.

Since 1935, the yearly payroll of the TVA in Chattanooga, conservatively estimated at $1,500,000, plus the millions spent by that organization to develop the Chattanooga area, has materially stimulated the economic growth of the city.

POINTS OF INTEREST

1. UNION STATION, W. 9th St., between Broad and Chestnut Sts., is owned by the State of Georgia, but is leased to the Nashville Chattanooga & St. Louis Railway. The stone and brick walls and wooden-arched trusses in the rear shed are part of the original building, designed by Eugene Le Hardy of the Nashville & Chattanooga Railroad and erected by slave labor in 1858.

Under the shed, between the waiting room and the platform at the Union Station, is the *General,* the old woodburning locomotive whose spectacular run on April 12, 1862, was part of a scheme to cut Confederate communications between Chattanooga and Atlanta.

At Big Shanty, near Marietta, Georgia, the Andrews raiders, disguised as civilians and led by Capt. James J. Andrews, a Federal spy, seized the *General* and rushed northward. Conductor W. A. Fuller and another employee gave chase on foot until they found a handcar. At Etowah River, Fuller found a yard engine, the *Yonah.* Andrews lost much time clearing the one-track line of southbound extras, and at Kingston he was almost overtaken by the *Yonah.* The *Yonah* was abandoned because of tangled traffic. Another engine was found and abandoned for the same reason. Near Adairsville, Fuller found the *Texas* and continued pursuit. Seeing that Fuller was gaining, Andrews dropped a burning boxcar on the wooden bridge at the Tennessee Line and rushed into the woods. Within a week all the raiders were captured. Some escaped and others were exchanged for Confederate prisoners. Andrews and seven companions were executed at Atlanta. The *Texas* is in the basement of the Cyclorama Building in Atlanta *(see GEORGIA GUIDE).*

2. READ HOUSE HOTEL, W. 9th St. between Broad and Chestnut Sts., of modified Georgian architecture, was designed by Holabird and Root and constructed in 1926 at a cost of $2,500,000. The building is 12 stories high. The walls of the lobby are paneled with quarter-sawed American black walnut. Read House occupies a site used for hotel purposes since 1847 when the Crutchfield House was established. In 1861 the Crutchfield House was the scene of a quarrel between Jefferson Davis, later President of the Confederate States, and William Crutchfield, a prominent Unionist and later a member of Congress. The two men were separated by friends.

THE *GENERAL*, CHATTANOOGA

During the War between the States the Crutchfield House was used as a military hospital, and bronze tablets donated by the Federal Government and commemorating its services, are in the 9th Street entrance of the present building. In 1867 the Crutchfield House was destroyed by fire. A three-story brick structure was built on the same site and opened Jan. 1, 1872 as the Read House. Under the management of Dr. and Mrs. John T. Read the hotel was well known for its hospitality and splendid cuisine. The "Tin Banquet," given at the Read House in 1888, celebrated the success of the local production of metals.

3. The KENNEDY-RATHBURN-NOTTINGHAM HOUSE *(private)*, 603 Pine St., was built about 1840 by W. F. Ragsdale. It is a large house of Greek Revival design with a two-story central portico sheltering a small second floor gallery. The entrance has a beautifully designed fanlight and sidelights. During the War between the States this house served in turn as headquarters for Col. D. B. Hill, Col. J. B. McPherson, and Col. J. M. Palmer.

4. BOYNTON PARK, at the top of Cameron Hill, end of Park Drive, rises abruptly at the edge of downtown Chattanooga. This hill was utilized during the War between the States by the signal corps of both armies. Cameron Hill, residential section, was named for James Cameron, an itinerant portrait painter, who took up permanent residence there about 1852.

From an OBSERVATION TOWER the Tennessee River is visible for miles in either direction as it curves around Lookout Mountain forming Moccasin Bend, and flows into the Grand Canyon of the Tennessee between Signal and Raccoon Mountains. Missionary Ridge rises to the east, and directly across the river is Stringer's Ridge from which the city was shelled by Union artillery before the evacuation.

5. GRANT'S HEADQUARTERS *(private)*, 110 E. 1st St., is an unpretentious frame structure, built by Thomas J. Lattner in 1839 on one of the highest sites of downtown Chattanooga, overlooking a cliff on the bank of the Tennessee River. Mrs. Lattner and her family went to Georgia during the war-time exodus in the summer of 1863. Grant arrived in Chattanooga October 23, 1863, and took possession of the empty house. It was returned by the United States to the owner, Thomas J. Lattner.

6. FOUNTAIN SQUARE, Lookout St., Georgia Ave. and E. 6th St., a small triangular park, contains the cast-iron FIREMEN'S FOUNTAIN. Erected in 1886 in honor of two department heroes who lost their lives in a Market Street fire, the fountain is capped with a statue of a fully rigged fireman. The CANNON at the apex of the park, captured at Santiago July 16, 1898, commanded the bay and harbor when the *Merrimac* was sunk.

7. The UNITED STATES POST OFFICE AND COURTHOUSE, Georgia Ave., between E. 9th and E. 10th Sts., was designed by Reuben Harrison Hunt of Chattanooga and constructed in 1933–34. This massive structure, with corner pylons and deep aluminum grilled windows, is a striking example of modern architecture. In 1937 the plans were selected

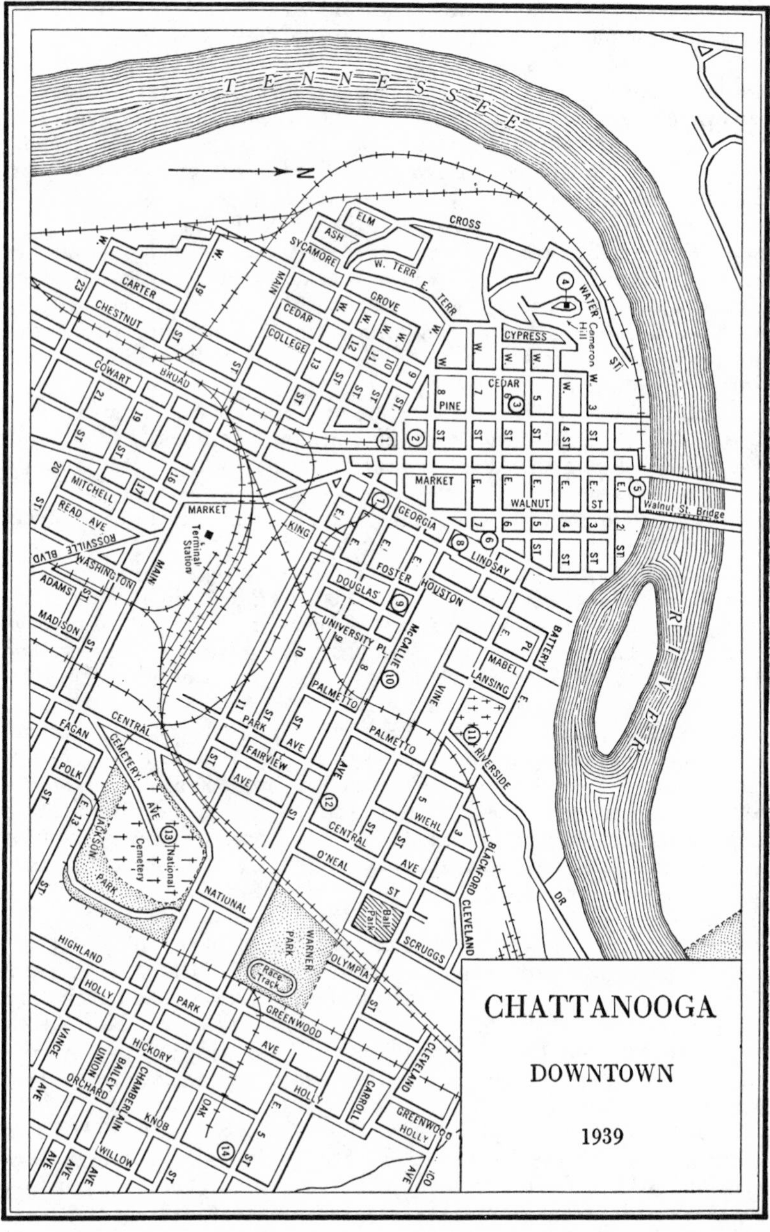
CHATTANOOGA
DOWNTOWN
1939
TENNESSEE
RIVER
N
Walnut St. Bridge
Terminal Station
Cameron Hill
National Cemetery
Warner Park
Race Track
Ball Park

by the American Institute of Architects as one of the 100 distinguished and representative buildings in the United States erected since 1918; plans and photographs were exhibited throughout America and Europe. The first floor houses the Post Office, the upper floors the Federal courts and offices, and a part of the TVA staff.

8. SOLDIERS AND SAILORS MEMORIAL AUDITORIUM *(open during performances),* NW. corner McCallie Ave. and Lindsay St., a seven-story building of modified Italian Renaissance design, covers an entire city block. The hip-roofed front section of the building has a two-story rusticated base pierced with five graceful decked portals. Above these entrances are monumental windows, a long balcony with wrought iron railing, and a series of projecting flag poles.

The building houses a main auditorium, seating 5,500 persons, with a fully equipped stage and an organ; a smaller hall; assembly room; and a large exhibition space in the basement.

9. THE FIRST PRESBYTERIAN CHURCH, SW. corner McCallie Ave. and Douglas St., designed by McKim, Mead and White, in the Italian Renaissance style, was constructed in 1910. The six large art-glass windows in the nave were designed by E. H. Blashfield. Adjoining the church is the Sunday school building of the same design.

The Presbyterian Church of Chattanooga, organized in 1840, held its first meeting in an old log school; a few years later a frame church was erected at Third and Walnut Streets. A larger structure, built in 1851, served as a hospital during the War between the States. After the war, services were resumed there, and continued until the present building was completed.

10. The UNIVERSITY OF CHATTANOOGA, McCallie Ave. between Douglas and Baldwin Sts., covers 15 acres and extends back two squares to Vine St. The site commands a view of the city and surrounding countryside. It is a co-educational institution with an enrollment of about 500 students. The main college halls, forming the quadrangle, were designed by H. B. Downing in the Tudor Gothic style. Established in 1886 under the auspices of the M. E. Church, the institution was called U. S. Grant University. In 1907 this connection was severed and the name was changed.

KEY TO CHATTANOOGA DOWNTOWN MAP

1. Union Station
2. Read House Hotel
3. The Kennedy-Rathburn-Nottingham House
4. Boynton Park
5. Grant's Headquarters
6. Fountain Square
7. The United States Post Office and Courthouse
8. Soldiers and Sailors Memorial Auditorium
9. The First Presbyterian Church
10. The University of Chattanooga
11. The Confederate Cemetery
12. The Julius and Bertha Ochs Memorial Temple
13. The National Cemetery
14. Orchard Knob

The university holds biennial institutes of public affairs, modeled after those of Williams College and the University of Virginia. The 1936 institute, held in conjunction with the university's sesquicentennial celebration, drew representatives of societies, foundations, and other colleges throughout the world.

11. The CONFEDERATE CEMETERY, extending from E. 3rd to E. 5th St. between Lansing and Palmetto Sts., is flanked by the Citizens and Jewish Cemeteries. It is maintained by the Gen. A. P. Stewart Chapter, U. D. C., and the city. Only the graves of veterans buried in recent years are mounded or marked. Tablets commemorating soldiers from various States are erected along the walks.

12. The JULIUS AND BERTHA OCHS MEMORIAL TEMPLE *(open 9-12, 2-4 daily)*, NE. corner McCallie and Fairview Aves., a white marble and brick structure of Classical Revival architecture, was built in 1928 by Adolph S. Ochs in honor of his parents. The architect was Henry B. Hertz of New York, with C. B. Bearden and William Crutchfield of Chattanooga, as associates. Marble staircases lead from the street up to the entrance loggia. The memorial tablets were designed in Paris by Edmondo Quattrachi.

13. The NATIONAL CEMETERY, spreading over 20 blocks with its main entrance at the S. end of National Ave., is the burial place of nearly 15,000 veterans of every war and foreign expedition in the history of the Republic. On the hillsides are magnificent trees planted near the close of the War between the States. Approximately one-third of the graves are those of the unknown dead from Chickamauga and Missionary Ridge. The Andrews Raiders are buried beneath a reproduction of their captured locomotive, the *General*.

14. ORCHARD KNOB *(open 8-5 daily)*, Orchard Knob Ave. between Ivy and E. 5th Sts., a unit of the Military Park, was purchased by the Federal Government in 1894. From this point General Grant and General Thomas directed the Union forces during the Battles of Lookout Mountain and Missionary Ridge (Nov. 24-25, 1863). Rising abruptly from the valley, Orchard Knob is about one mile west of Missionary Ridge, and from it the movements of the Union forces in any direction were visible. The earthworks, behind which Federal cannon were placed after the hill was seized from the Confederates, are well preserved. The guns are mounted as nearly as possible in the position of Grant's signal guns. An account of the military movements is given on historical markers.

LOOKOUT MOUNTAIN TOUR

Chattanooga—Lookout Mt. Bridge—Memory Place—Caverns Castle—Mountain Top—Point Park—Sunset Rock—Fairyland—Rock City—Chattanooga, 12.6 *m.* US 41, 64, and 11 (Broad St.), E. Brow Rd., W. Brow Rd., W. Sunset Rd., Bragg Ave., Fleetwood Dr., Fairyland Rd., and Ochs Hwy., Broad St.

Lookout Mountain rises abruptly at the southwestern city limits. From its peak, Point Lookout, 1,400 feet above the Tennessee River, early

OCHS MEMORIAL TEMPLE, CHATTANOOGA

settlers were warned against Indians. The mountain was a favorite Cherokee hunting ground.

After the Battle of Chickamauga, Lookout Mountain was occupied by Confederate troops besieging the Union Army in Chattanooga; the "Battle above the Clouds" was fought here November 24, 1863, as a preliminary to the storming of Missionary Ridge.

After the National Military Park was created, the War Department acquired two small reservations on Lookout Mountain: Point Park at the summit; and Cravens' Reservation on the northern slope. In the 1920's Adolph S. Ochs conceived and largely financed the Chattanooga-Lookout Mountain Park, 3,000 acres on the eastern and western slopes, incorporated into the Chickamauga and Chattanooga National Military Park in 1935. Two main highways, Lookout Mountain Boulevard and Ochs Highway, pass directly through the park.

Arrangements were completed in 1938 for the erection on Lookout Mountain of the Adolph S. Ochs Observatory and Museum, which will house exhibits depicting the history, geography, and geology of the territory. The National Park Service has agreed to provide the site and the labor, and to maintain the building. The remainder of the cost will come from a family bequest and from local contributions.

Lookout Mountain Township (pop. 1,031), extending along the crest from Point Park S. to the Georgia Line, is a residential section.

CHATTANOOGA, 11th and Market Sts., 0 *m.* Proceed W. one block on 11th St. S. on Broad St. (US 41).

At 2.6 *m.* is junction with St. Elmo St. Left on St. Elmo St. 0.4 *m.* to Tennessee Ave. LOOKOUT MOUNTAIN INCLINE RAILWAY *(round trip 40¢),* operates between the street level and the summit of the mountain. Two electric cable cars run simultaneously, one ascending, one descending, at about 8 m.p.h. The present 4,750-foot incline, the third erected, was completed in 1897. Designed by Jo Conn Guild, Sr., and Lynn White, it was constructed by John T. Crass.

LOOKOUT MOUNTAIN BRIDGE, 3.2 *m.,* built 1934–35, has its outer face 200 feet above the river bank, while the inner side of the bridge is for the most part flush against the palisades. It forms an artificial ledge 1,060 feet long, with the supporting columns joining the sharp inclination of the mountainside from 12 to 60 feet below. Even from this comparatively low elevation there is a widening view of the river to the north, west, and east. Paralleling the highway, the Tennessee River runs in a northwesterly direction forming the heel and toe of Moccasin Bend To the west is RACCOON MOUNTAIN, to the north SIGNAL MOUNTAIN, and to the east Chattanooga with MISSIONARY RIDGE in the far background.

At 3.3 *m.,* is the junction with Lookout Mountain Boulevard; L. from US 41 up the mountain.

MEMORY PLACE (R), 3.7 *m.,* formerly an abandoned rock quarry, was transformed into a garden during the building of the park.

At 3.9 *m.* is a junction with Jo Conn Guild Trail.

This trail leads (L) along the eastern slope and slowly descends to the foot of the mountain. Another trail, part of the Great Indian Warpath, leads (R) around the toe and western shoulder of the mountain to SKIUKA SPRINGS, 5.7 *m.*

CAVERNS CASTLE (R), 4 *m.,* is the entrance and administration building of LOOKOUT MOUNTAIN CAVES *(adm. $1.50, with guide).* Electric elevators operate from Caverns Castle to two levels. Twin Caves, at the 420-foot level, show evidence of long Indian occupancy. Among the many names scratched on the walls is "Andrew Jackson, 1833." During the War between the States the caves sheltered soldiers and civilians. The natural entrance on the bank of the river was sealed by the Southern Railway tunnel through the mountain. In 1928, when an elevator shaft was being sunk through solid limestone, the cave at the 260-foot level was discovered. The route to Ruby Falls, electrically lighted, reveals gigantic stalactites.

In the HALL OF DREAMS the startling formations have an appearance of unreality. RUBY FALLS drop 145 feet in the great chamber at the end of the route, and the entire waterfall is visible. The lower cave is 160 feet below the falls cave.

At 4.9 *m.* is the junction with Cravens Road, dirt.

Right on this road around the end of the mountain to CRAVEN'S RESERVATION, 0.5 *m.,* site of the major part of the "Battle above the Clouds." Monuments and markers in the Cravens' House yard give a clear account of the fighting there.

At 5.4 *m.* is a picnic area.

At 5.9 *m.* is the junction with the Richard Hardy Trail.

Right on this trail is an excellent hiking and bridal path, which runs along the eastern shoulders around the end of the mountain.

At 6 *m.,* the top of the mountain, turn (R) N. on E. Brow Rd.

At 7 *m.* (R) is the upper terminal of LOOKOUT MOUNTAIN INCLINE RAILWAY.

POINT PARK, 7.3 *m.* *(open sunrise to sunset; no automobiles; U. S. guide service, free),* entrance at N. end of E. Brow Rd., is the extreme northern end of the crest and terminates at Lookout Point. The park has an area of 17.5 acres.

In the immediate foreground is MOCCASIN BEND, formed by the Tennessee River as it makes a seven-mile bend, beginning at Cameron Hill, and finally disappearing between Signal and Raccoon Mountains. The peninsula, also known as Moccasin Bend, made by the curve of the river, forms a perfectly shaped foot of huge proportions. The bunion, actually a small hill, is on the top of the extreme right. The ankle, three miles to the north, is slightly more than a mile wide, while the sole, at the base of the mountain, appears to be several miles wide. Hundreds of skeletons in sitting positions have been excavated on the peninsula. This mode of burial, customary with the Creek, indicates that they preceded the Cherokee. Pottery, stone axes, chunky stones, and flint knives are among the relics found here.

To the right of Moccasin Bend Chattanooga is spread like a patchwork quilt. Beyond are the rolling hills of East Tennessee, gradually rising into the Great Smoky Mountains, more than 100 miles away but plainly visible on a clear day. To the west is Raccoon Mountain and to the north Signal Mountain and Walden's Ridge.

UMBRELLA ROCK, on Point Lookout, about 12 feet high, consists of several large stones topped with a great flat slab, forming the umbrella. Indians may have erected it as a shrine, though most geologists agree that the formation is natural.

Several hiking trails begin at the foot of the iron steps descending the palisades. One leads to Cravens' Reservation, and the Bluff Trail (R) runs beneath the eastern palisades.

The cannon at Point Park are in the positions they occupied during the battle. An account of military operations is given on numerous markers. Halfway down the mountain, Robert Cravens, an iron manufacturer, built his home in 1854.

The largest monument is the NEW YORK PEACE MONUMENT, a tall shaft of Massachusetts pink marble. Designed by R. Hinton Perry it rises 95 feet from a simple dignified rotunda and measures 50 feet in diameter at the base. Two bronze figures, one of a Confederate soldier, the other of a Union soldier, with an American flag between them, surmount the shaft. It was erected in 1907.

Left from Park Entrance on W. Brow Rd.

Rock steps at 7.8 *m.* lead down the mountain 200 yards (R) to Sunset Rock, the best point for viewing Lookout Valley and the western mountains.

At 10.1 *m.* R. on Fleetwood Drive.

FAIRYLAND, 10.6 *m.*, a suburban residential section, was named for the weird shapes of the surrounding massive boulders. Roads and trails in Fairyland follow the natural contour of the land and have such names as Gnome Trail, Red Riding Hood Lane, Elfin, Pied Piper, Peter Pan, Mother Goose, Robin Hood, and Tinker Bell. Most of the 400 residents live in houses of native stone and logs, Old English in style.

The FAIRYLAND CLUBHOUSE (L), 11.5 *m.* *(members and guests only)*, on the brow of the hill, affords an excellent view of Chattanooga Valley and the mountains. The Tom Thumb Golf Course, built here and patented in 1927 by Garnette Carter, started the craze that soon swept the country. The Fairyland Golf Course *(private)*, SW. of Fairyland, was designed and built by Seth Raynor

ROCK CITY (R), 11.9 *m.* *(adm. $1 with guide)*, is a natural city of rocks and caves covering 10 acres of lichen-covered sandstone. Three suspension bridges extend from one high bluff to another. A trail leads 3,200 feet through narrow crevices, many more than 100 feet deep, and passes Pulpit Rock, the Lion's Den, Shelter Rock, and crosses a suspension bridge to Lover's Leap. Over the bridge the trail passes Tortoise Shell Rock, through Fat Man's Squeeze, to the 1,000-ton balanced rock and Hall of Mountain King. Rock City is noted for its horticultural display.

At 12.1 *m.* turn R. on Ochs Highway down the mountain. From this road are many excellent views of the valley below.

The OCHS MARKER, 13 *m.* (L), a memorial to Adolph S. Ochs, is at the junction of Ochs Hwy. and Fairyland Rd., which ends here.

The LOOKOUT, 13.3 *m.* (R), is a parking area, with a picnic ground and the mountain behind.

At 15.2 *m.* (L) is a two-story red brick building occupied by the Bee Dee Stock Medicine Company. The duel in the novel *St. Elmo* was fought at the Spring under this building.

South Broad Street, 15.8 *m.,* returns to CHATTANOOGA, 18.5 *m.* (11th & Market Sts.).

CHICKAMAUGA PARK

Chattanooga—Rossville (Ga. State Line)—John Ross House—Fort Oglethorpe—Chickamauga and Chattanooga National Military Park (Administration Building)—Missionary Ridge—Chattanooga, 19.8 *m.* US 27, South Crest Rd., Shallowford Rd., McCallie Ave.

The Chickamauga and Chattanooga National Military Park, an area of 8,456 acres in Tennessee and Georgia, includes the battlefield of Chickamauga, Orchard Knob, Lookout Mountain, and Missionary Ridge.

CHATTANOOGA, 11th & Market Sts., 0 *m.*

At 0.5 *m.* turn L. on Main St.

At 0.7 *m.* turn R. off Main St. on Rossville Blvd. (US 27) to Rossville, Ga., an industrial suburb of Chattanooga. At 4.5 m. the State line crosses the main street in the business area.

The JOHN ROSS HOUSE, (R) 4.7 *m. (private),* home of the noted Cherokee chief, is built of hewn logs, held together by wooden pegs, chinked with mud, and covered with clapboards. The two-story full-length front porch is enclosed by a rustic railing. A stone marker to Ross is in the yard. John MacDonald, a Scottish trader, built the house about 1770. The house was an important Civil War headquarters.

The IOWA MONUMENT, 5 *m.* (L), a marble shaft 50 feet high, has five statues of soldiers, one at the top and four around the base.

FORT OGLETHORPE, 7.4 *m. (speed limit 20 m., open 8-8),* named for the founder of Georgia, became an Army post in 1904. A principal World War training post, it is now the permanent station of the 6th U. S. Cavalry and several smaller units, and the summer camp of National Guard, R. O. T. C., and C. M. T. C. units.

At 8.1 *m.* (R) is a police information booth.

CHICKAMAUGA AND CHATTANOOGA NATIONAL MILITARY PARK, 8.6 *m. (Administration Building. Free U. S. guide service),* largest unit of the park system and site of the Battle of Chickamauga, was created in 1890. Organizations have erected hundreds of monuments, and the Park Commission, with two exceptions, has duplicated the roads of 1863. Three camps carry on reforestation and check soil erosion. Officers from the Army War College in Washington come here annually to study Civil War military tactics.

The KELLY HOUSE *(not open)* is a reconstruction of the one that stood on the Kelly Farm, scene of the severest fighting of September 20, until the battle shifted to Snodgrass Hill. The GEORGIA MONUMENT is on Poe Field near the northern edge of the gap in the Union line through which Longstreet rushed Stewart's division. Seventy-nine feet high, the monument is the largest in Chickamauga Park. The statues around the base represent the three branches of service. A flag bearer surmounts the shaft. Across the road (R) a marker designates the SITE OF THE POE HOUSE, another scene of bitter fighting.

The BROTHERTON HOUSE *(not open),* SW. corner US 27 and Brotherton Rd., a reconstruction, marks the site of the fatal break in the Union lines.

VINIARD FIELD was the scene of the severest fighting of September 19, 1863, when the Confederate left advanced against the Union right. The marked SITE OF THE VINIARD HOUSE is frequently mentioned in battle orders.

WILDER TOWER (Glenn-Kelly Rd.), on Wilder Hill, is the SITE OF WIDOW GLENN'S CABIN, General Rosecrans' headquarters, burned September 20, 1863.

The MONUMENT OF THE FIRST WISCONSIN CAVALRY, across the road, a riderless horse, invariably attracts attention.

The reconstructed BLACKSMITH SHOP was the scene of severe fighting and is mentioned in official reports.

Horseshoe-shaped SNODGRASS HILL, scene of the Battle of the Horseshoe, has a tower affording the widest view of the battlefield. From this point General Thomas directed his attack after Rosecrans retreated.

Retrace on US 27 from Park Office to Crest Road, 11.4 *m.,* which traverses MISSIONARY RIDGE to its termination at Chickamauga Dam *(see Tour 13).* From Rossville Gap northward, Missionary Ridge is lined with beautiful homes. Less than 100 yards wide, the Ridge forms the eastern rim of Chattanooga Valley, 500 feet below.

The Battle of Missionary Ridge, November 24, 1863, lost Chattanooga and East Tennessee to the Union. Both Grant and Sherman were deceived by the maps. Sherman supposedly attacked Missionary Ridge, but he actually took a detached hill. Forces on strongly fortified Tunnel Hill, the key to Missionary Ridge, defied his efforts. To relieve the pressure on Sherman, Grant ordered Thomas' advance against the center. Thomas' troops then made their charge without orders, not waiting to re-form after taking the first line trenches.

BRAGG RESERVATION, 15.1 *m.* (L), is a small circular plot, the site of General Bragg's headquarters. Here in October 1863 Jefferson Davis addressed the Confederate troops. The steel observation tower offers a broad view. The ILLINOIS MONUMENT, a circular marble shaft, has four charging soldiers at the base, and an angel of mercy at the top.

At 16.2 *m.* Shallowford Rd. branches L. from Crest Rd. and runs down Missionary Ridge to McCallie Ave., 16.6 *m.*

MCCALLIE SCHOOL (L), a private military school for boys, established in 1905, is one of the three ranking preparatory schools in the South. Twelve buildings are on the extensive, wooded campus, and three off the campus.

Follow McCallie Ave. (R) to CHATTANOOGA, 11th & Market Sts., 19.8 *m.*

POINTS OF INTEREST IN ENVIRONS

Brainerd Mission Site, *6.8 m.;* Frankstone Inn, *9.5 m.;* Chickamauga Dam, *18.7 m.;* John Brown's Tavern, *8.1 m.;* Tennessee Cave and Obar House, *7.9 m.;* Hale's Bar Dam and Power House, *19.8 m.* *(see Tour 13).*

Jackson

Railroad Stations: Union Station, N. Royal St., for Illinois Central R.R. and Mobile & Ohio R.R.; S. Royal St. for Nashville, Chattanooga & St. Louis Ry.; Poplar Ave. for Gulf, Mobile & Northern R.R.
Bus Station: Terminal Station, E. Chester St., for Greyhound, Gibbs, and local lines.
Streetcars: Fare 5¢.
Taxis: Anywhere in city 10¢.

Accommodations: Four hotels, numerous tourist camps.

Information Service: Chamber of Commerce, City Hall.

Radio Station: WTJS (1310 kc.).
Motion Picture Houses: Two.
Swimming: West End Beach, Neely St., 1.3 m. W. of Public Square on State 20, adm. 20¢. East View pool (Negro), SE. Jackson, adm. 20¢ adults, 10¢ children.
Football: Union University "Bulldogs," Southern Inter-collegiate Athletic Association, Union Field, College St.; Lambuth College "Eagles," Mississippi Valley Conference, Lambuth Field, Lambuth Blvd.
Baseball: Jackson "Generals," Kitty League (professional), Lakeview Park, 2 m. S. on US 45.
Municipal Skeet Traps: (open every Thursday, spring and summer) Jackson Heights Tavern, 3 m. N. on US 45.

Annual Events: Mississippi Valley Conference Basketball Tournament, the Armory, Mar. National Fox Hunters' Association, May, Crawford Springs, 2 m. S. on State 20. Tennessee Amateur Field Trials for bird dogs, spring. Horse Show, sponsored by Meadowbrook Bridle Club, spring; other horse shows at intervals. West Tennessee District Fair, Sept. 12-17.

JACKSON (450 alt., 22,172 pop.), seat of Madison County, a West Tennessee railroad center in the valley of the Forked Deer River, is a city of broad streets and tree-lined avenues. The downtown buildings are grouped around an oak-shaded courthouse square from which the residential streets radiate. The white marble of the new courthouse and the Federal building stands out against the gray and red brick of the earlier structures.

Highland Avenue leads north into a section of Georgian Colonial and modified English Tudor residences. Well-built conservative homes are in the college areas. Two-story Victorian frame houses, weathered to an unsightly brown, stand in parts of the city, especially near the railroads.

Negro shanties center near the railroad tracks, for many Negroes work on the trains, in the shops, or on section gangs. In the better Negro districts, such as those around Lane College, are neat cottages and occasional brick bungalows of more recent construction.

Jackson is entered by five railroads, two of which maintain division shops. The *Rebel,* first streamlined train in the South, runs from Jackson to New Orleans over the Gulf, Mobile & Northern Railroad. Thousands of railroad men live here, and three colleges bring in hundreds of students. The town serves a rich agricultural section, a middle-ground between Northern and Southern farming belts, where crops common to both are raised.

White settlement of Jackson was begun by North Carolinians in 1819, and within three years it had become the county seat. The name of Jackson was chosen because many of Gen. Andrew Jackson's soldiers and numerous relatives of his wife lived in the vicinity.

The town was laid out with streets 90 feet wide and the first courthouse was built of logs. When lots were sold in 1822 the county court allowed $20 to Joseph Lynn for whisky to enliven the bidding. In 1823 Jackson was incorporated as a town and in 1825 the legislature established a land registry office here for the Western District.

In 1833 Jackson had a population of 900. By 1840 the town was a cotton depot for the surrounding region, and in 1845 it was chartered as a city. With the coming of the Illinois Central Railroad in 1858 and the Mobile & Ohio in 1861, the town grew rapidly as a market for lumber, farm products, and furs.

Madison County furnished a company, "The Madison Greys," for the Seminole War of 1836. Jackson was headquarters of Confederate General Beauregard in 1862. The town was used as a supply depot by Union forces under General Grant, between June, 1862, and March, 1863, when it was captured by Gen. Nathan Bedford Forrest on a cavalry raid along the Mobile & Ohio Railroad. The town was occupied by a Confederate garrison until July, 1863, when it was attacked by Union Gen. John P. Hatch with 1,500 men. A shortage of ammunition caused Confederate Col. Jeff Forest to surrender.

Files of Jackson's early newspapers are in the State Library, Nashville. The *Pioneer,* published at Jackson in 1822 or 1823, no copies of which are known to exist, was probably the first newspaper in West Tennessee. The Jackson *Gazette,* first issued in 1824, with Elijah Biglow as editor, became the *Truth Teller* in 1830. In this same year the *Western Tennessee Republican* and the *Southern Statesman* were started. The *Western District Telegrapher* and the *Watchman of the West* were begun in 1838 and 1839 respectively. The *Forked Deer Blade* was founded by J. G. Cisco in 1883. Current publications include the Jackson *Sun,* a daily, and two Negro magazines–the *Christian Index,* a weekly, and the *Western Index,* a bi-monthly. The Colored Methodist Publishing House in Jackson is owned and controlled by the African Methodist Church.

Judge Ben B. Lindsey, eminent juvenile court judge, was born in Jackson in 1869. Bishop Isaac Lane, aged 106 years (in 1938), is a retired Negro Bishop and one of the founders of the African Methodist Church and Lane College. J. G. Cisco of Jackson, was a member of the Confederate Secret Service, newspaper correspondent with Custer's Expedition, and a collector of Tennessee historical lore.

Jackson manufactures steel for bridges, gasoline engines, mattresses, medicines, cotton-seed oil, varnish, paper boxes, and cigars.

POINTS OF INTEREST

The CARNEGIE LIBRARY *(open 9-5 weekdays)*, College and Church Sts., is a two-story brick building with limestone trim. In the children's room is a MUSEUM, equipped by the Smithsonian Institution with geological specimens, fish, birds, and Indian pottery.

The SITE OF THE DUKE HOME is at 518 E. Main St. The two-story brick Georgian Colonial house that stood here till it burned in 1938, was Gen. U. S. Grant's headquarters in 1862.

UNION UNIVERSITY, College St. between Irby St. and Hayes Ave., is a four-year, co-educational Baptist college established in 1875 by consolidation of Southwestern Baptist College at Murfreesboro and West Tennessee College at Jackson. It is on the site of West Tennessee College whose charter was granted in 1846 by an Act of Congress and the Tennessee Legislature, and signed by President James K. Polk. The average enrollment is 400.

The MORGAN-HITCHCOCK PLANT *(open 8-4 Mon.-Fri., 8-12 Sat.)*, Beasley St. between Liberty and Lancaster Sts., is the largest skewer factory in the country. The company also manufactures clothespins, flower and candy sticks, tongue depressors, and other small wooden articles.

The ASHBY VENEER AND LUMBER PLANT *(open 8-4 Mon.-Fri., 8-12 Sat.)*, S. end of Market St., is one of the largest veneer plants in the United States. More than 3,000,000 feet of lumber are used annually in the plant, which also manufactures crates and baskets.

RIVERSIDE CEMETERY *(open sunrise to sunset daily)*, Bolivar St. and Bates Ave., is Jackson's oldest cemetery. Some of the monuments, dated 1817, bear inscription,—"Born in Ireland," "Born in England," or "Born in Virginia." More than 100 slaves are buried in their masters' lots.

LANCASTER PARK, S. Royal St. between O'Connor St. and the city limits, a 40-acre tract, contains two small lakes stocked with goldfish and other ornamental fish. A 550-foot artesian well has water of high iron content, used for medicinal purposes. On the WEST TENNESSEE FAIRGROUNDS the West Tennessee District Fair is held annually. Purse races for trotters and pacers are featured, and there are automobile races, pageants, and the usual carnival shows. The WATERWORKS PLANT *(open 8-5)*, with five wells and a pumping station, produces six million gallons daily.

CENTENNIAL PARK, E. Chester St. near city limits, is a community recreational center with a well-equipped playground.

LAMBUTH COLLEGE, Lambuth Blvd. between King and Maple Sts., is a four-year co-educational college controlled by the Methodist Conference of West Tennessee. Founded in 1924, Lambuth has an average enrollment of 225. The two three-story buildings are situated on an oak-covered campus.

LANE COLLEGE (Negro), Middleton St. between Berry St. and Lane Ave., is an accredited four-year co-educational liberal arts college. It was established in 1880 by the Colored Methodist Episcopal Church of

America, under the leadership of Bishop Isaac Lane. Most of the ten buildings are brick.

CATHOLIC CEMETERY *(open sunrise to sunset daily),* NE. corner Royal and Hardee Sts., is the BURIAL PLACE OF JOHN LUTHER JONES, nicknamed "Casey" for his home town—Cayce, Kentucky. He entered the service of the Illinois Central R.R. at Water Valley, Mississippi, as locomotive fireman in 1888 and was promoted to engineer in 1890. He was famous among railroad men because of his peculiar skill with a locomotive whistle:

> And the switchmen they knew by the engine's moans
> That the man at the throttle was Old Casey Jones.

Substituting for a sick friend, on the *Cannon Ball Express,* Casey was killed in a wreck near Vaughn, Mississippi, on the night of April 30, 1900. The original words of the popular ballad "Casey Jones" were "made up" by an admirer of Casey, Wallace Saunders, a Negro engine wiper in a roundhouse at Canton, Mississippi. Dozens of versions are sung throughout the South.

EDGEWOOD *(private),* S. Royal St., a square two-story frame house of Greek Revival design, was built about 1840 by John R. Campbell. The façade is accentuated by a massive two-story portico with six fluted Doric columns reaching to the pedimented roof. It contains twelve rooms with decorated ceilings. A circular drive through huge old trees leads to the home, which stands on the village site of the prehistoric Mound Builders.

POINTS OF INTEREST IN ENVIRONS

State Forest Nursery, *6.2 m.;* Cisco Indian Village, *14 m.* *(see Tour 10);* John A. Murrell Home, *13.7 m.* *(see Tour 12).*

Columbia

Railroad Stations: High St. joint station, for Nashville, Chattanooga & St. Louis Ry. and Louisville & Nashville R.R.
Bus Station: Bethel Hotel, Garden and 7th Sts., for Southeastern Greyhound Bus Lines and Lewisburg Lines.
Taxis: Fare 25¢ per person; reduced rates for groups.

Accommodations: Three hotels; tourist camps in environs.

Information Service: Bethel Hotel, Garden and 7th Sts., Chamber of Commerce, SW. corner Garden and 7th Sts.

Motion Picture Houses: One.
Swimming: Indoor pool at Columbia Military Academy; outdoor pool for children at Knob Hill (free); Duck River, below dam.

Annual Events: Mule Day, first Monday in April.

COLUMBIA (650 alt., 7,882 pop.), seat of Maury County, is built on the low limestone bluffs of the Duck River in a region of fertile farmland, bluegrass meadows, and rolling wooded hills. Centering in a typically Southern public square and the old grey stone courthouse with its domed clock tower, the town has wide-spaced streets in its business and residential areas.

The center of Maury County's dairy and livestock trade, Columbia boils with activity on the "First Monday" market days each month, and to a lesser extent on Saturdays. The square and adjacent streets are clogged with the trucks and wagons of farmers who pour into town with their families and market produce.

The high point of the year in Columbia is "Mule Day," the first Monday in April, when the largest street mule market in the world is held. The town is thrown open to traders and visitors from all over the United States, and more than 10,000 attend, their cars, wagons, and livestock blocking the streets and roads. Court Square is lined ten deep, and every upstairs store window is filled with people watching the grand opening parade, probably the only one in America with no motorized vehicles. Horses, ponies, and mules draw decorated floats, old-fashioned race carts, speed wagons, and high-wheel sulkies. There are fine mules and horses, and pretty girls riding jackasses. Every newspaper in the State has a reporter wandering through the crowd to gather material for a new story about mules and men.

In the "jockey yard," adjoining the mule mart, whites and Negroes sell crisp brown fish, fried chicken, barbecue, and sandwiches. Medicine-show barkers wave bottles of cure-all tonic at the farmers and city folk who press in close to their platforms. Politicians mix with the crowd, booming

MULE DAY PARADE, COLUMBIA

expansively, shaking hands, slapping shoulders, and kissing babies. Spavined horses are swapped for hollow-horned cows. Moulting roosters of mixed blood are exchanged for white rabbits. Fresh-caught catfish are traded for pocket knives or for dollar watches that won't run.

The mule men are different—ponderously sure of themselves and of the dignity of their profession. They stride deliberately, and poke walking canes ("measuring rods") in the mules' flanks to make them show their points. Shrewd buyers, they move through the crowd appraising here a promising colt, there a sleek, powerful mule, drawling in heavy, authoritative voices. Representatives from foreign governments are often the heaviest buyers. There is the stamping of iron-shod hoofs on the asphalt pavement, an occasional chorus of wild braying, and the voices of auctioneers drumming up purchasers. Events of the day are photographed for the newsreels and broadcast by two national radio chains. Will Rogers wrote of this day: "It ain't anything to see a man come in and trade in a tractor and a three-year-old Buick and $100 down on a span of hard-tails."

Columbia was first settled in 1807, and in that year was made the seat of Maury County. One of the earliest newspapers in the State, *The Western Chronicle,* was founded here by James Walker in 1811. During the same year there was a destructive flood of the Duck River and several Indian scares. In December began a series of earthquakes, continuing at intervals of a few days, until March, 1812 *(see Tour 11A)*. The bewildered settlers thought the place accursed and for a time considered abandoning it.

The town was incorporated in 1817. In January 1861 Maury County voted to remain with the Union, but after Lincoln's call for troops and the beginning of fighting had forced the issue, Columbia abruptly became Confederate in sympathy. During General Hood's Nashville campaign, November-December, 1864, the town was occupied alternately by Union and Confederate troops, but no major engagement took place here.

Columbia has three newspapers. The Columbia *Observer* dates back to 1834, the Columbia *Herald* to 1862, and the *Maury Democrat* to 1882.

Columbia is the trading center of an area where the major crops are wheat, corn, oats, and tobacco. Industrial plants include a large hosiery mill, garment factories, grain mills, building supply houses, a brick manufacturing plant, a marble works, a canning factory, meat packing plants, and a chair factory.

POINTS OF INTEREST

The SAMUEL POLK HOME *(open 9-5 daily; adm. 25¢)*, 301 W. 7th St., was the home of Samuel K. Polk, father of James Knox Polk, eleventh President of the United States. The two-story white brick house with spacious rooms, French windows, and balconies, was built in 1816 by Sam Polk. Offices occupied the building for a while but in 1928 it was purchased by the Polk Memorial Association and restored.

The house contains a collection of Polk relics, which include paintings, engravings, gilt-frame mirrors, glassware, silverware, china, furniture, and the gown supposed to have been worn by Mrs. Polk at the inaugural ball, though the same is said of another in the Smithsonian Institution at Washington. An ivory fan, the gift of her husband, carried by Mrs. Polk at the inauguration, bears miniatures of the eleven presidents from Washington to Polk.

The adjacent house *(private)*, an almost exact duplicate of the Polk home, was built by Sam Polk for his daughter.

The JAMES K. POLK HOME *(private)*, 318 W. 7th St., a two-story frame residence, square in plan, with a gable roof, was built by James K. Polk in the 1820's. Here he entertained Andrew Jackson and Martin Van Buren during the campaign of 1844, in which he was elected President.

The MAYES-HUTTON PLACE *(private)*, W. 6th St. and Mayes Place, was built in 1854 by Samuel Mayes, who, believing the slave question might result in a war, sold all of his slaves and invested his money in a home. This large brick house retains all the flavor of the Southern ante-bellum mansion. A fusion of Greek Revival and Mediterranean architecture, the house is accentuated by a central two-story portico with four large Corinthian columns. This portico shelters a small second-floor gallery, with wrought-iron railings that are almost lace-like. The front doorway forms a trefoil arch with attractive sidelights and fanlight. The large high-ceiled rooms are tastefully decorated, and there is a lovely curved stairway.

THE SAMUEL POLK HOME, COLUMBIA

In GREENWOOD CEMETERY, N. Garden St. near 1st St., beneath tall, somber cedars in a tanglewood of honeysuckle vines, are the graves of the parents of James K. Polk and other early settlers.

The KNOB, end of W. 6th St., a familiar topographical feature of Columbia, has the town reservoir on its summit. This rocky elevation, 200 feet above the city, appears in old histories under the name of Mount Parnassus.

EDWARD F. ("POP") GEERS MEMORIAL PARK is on the lower southern slope of the knob, fronting on W. 7th St. The slope is terraced, and a stone shaft stands to the memory of the noted turfman.

"Pop" Geers maintained a stable near Columbia from 1880 to 1890 where he trained some of the outstanding horses of the day. His greatest record (1:55) was made with Dan Patch, the fastest pacer the world has ever known. In those days Maury County was the heart of a great pacing horse region.

POINTS OF INTEREST IN ENVIRONS

Beechlawn, *3.4 m.;* Haynes Haven, *9.3 m.;* Cheairs House, *9.9 m.* *(see Tour 7).* Mercer Hall, *1 m.;* Columbia Military Academy, *1.3 m.;* Middle Tennessee Experiment Station, *2.2 m.;* Blythewood, *2.4 m.;* Clifton Place, *5.5 m.;* Pillow-Bethel Place, *7 m.;* Pillow-Haliday Place, *7.2 m.;* Hamilton Place, *7.6 m.;* Rattle and Snap, *8.7 m.;* *(see Tour 7B).*

Kingsport

Railroad Station: Clinchfield Railroad Station, Broad and Main Sts., for Clinchfield R.R.
Bus Station: Main St., for Tennessee Coach Co., Eastern Tennessee and Western North Carolina Motor Transportation Company, Tri-State Coach Corporation, and Washington County Bus Lines.
Airport: McKellar Field (Tri-City Airport), south on US 23, 12 m. to junction with Airport Rd., left on this road, 4 m., for American Airlines. Taxi fare from city $2.

Accommodations: Three hotels; overnight homes for tourists on all highways into the city.

Information Service: Rotary and Kiwanis Clubs, the Kingsport Inn on the Circle; Kingsport Improvement Bldg., Shelby and Market.

Motion Picture Houses: Four.
Golf: Kingsport Country Club, 1 m. E. on Bristol Highway, 18 holes, greens fee 25¢.
Tennis: Kingsport Country Club, 1 m. E. on Bristol Highway.
Swimming: Swimming pool at junction US 11W. and 23, 1.7 m. SE. of Circle. Fee 25¢.

KINGSPORT (1,720 alt., 11,914 pop.) is a mountain-circled industrial city on the shores of the Holston River in the heart of the Southern Appalachians. To the east stretches the wall of the Blue Ridge, to the west are the gaunt ridges of the Cumberlands, to the north the rugged Clinch Mountains, while to the south and nearer to the valley loom Chimney Top and the Bays Mountain range, tumbling away southeastward into the ranks of the Great Smokies. These ranges are little changed in some respects since the first pioneers followed the buffalo trails over their timbered heights and built their cabins in the Holston Valley. Farmed first by the Indians and later by white pioneers, the valley of the winding Holston with its fertile bottom lands has long been an agricultural area. Kingsport, a modern city in its industrial development, still bears the marks of its rugged pioneer ancestry.

Although Kingsport had been settled since 1761, the modern city has grown from a small village in 1907, with a population of less than a thousand, to a modern city with a balanced group of industrial units that offer a diversity of employment. Planned as an industrial center, the city received its charter on March 2, 1917. Dr. John Nolan, internationally known engineer and city planner, superintended the designing of the public buildings, homes, and parks. He was assisted by Earl S. Draper who is now (1938) director of the TVA Department of Regional Planning. The aim was usefulness, beauty, and variety in each structure and in the city as a whole. Before a street was paved definite areas were set aside for residential sections, industrial divisions, and business centers. Open areas were left for recreational development as the city grew. Street parkways and parks at intersections were designed; trees were planted throughout the business section.

The principal streets radiate from a circle drive and small park in the geographical center of the city. The U. S. Post Office, of Georgian Colonial design, and six churches are built around this circle.

Local citizens are mostly of English and Scottish stock. The mountain folk who work in the local plants have adapted themselves to an industrial life but in many cases have retained their roots in the land. Some live on the home farm and work in the city. Others cultivate gardens around their urban homes. There has never been any labor strife in Kingsport, a point of pride with local citizens. Having the advantages of a present-day city, Kingsport and its surroundings retain some of the charm of early America. Tucked away in the hills hereabout are old water mills and cabins with wide fireplaces, stone chimneys, and rafters hung with drying herbs. There are only 595 Negroes in Kingsport, most of whom find employment in domestic service.

Dr. Thomas Walker, leader of the first organized exploring expedition into Upper East Tennessee, while following Reedy Creek down to North Fork of the Holston in the early spring of 1750, found a well-marked Indian path that crossed the Holston River at Long Island and extended through what is now the southern part of Kingsport. This was the trail used by Daniel Boone and his party in 1769 when marking out the route of the Wilderness Road.

The first Anglo-American structure on the site of Kingsport was Fort Robinson, built in 1761 near the fording place of the Holston at Long Island. Later, Fort Patrick Henry, erected at the same site in the spring of 1775, was the outpost of white civilization beyond the mountains.

Kingsport was known variously as Island Flats, Fort Robinson, Fort Patrick Henry, the Boat Yard, and Christiansville. The last name was for Gilbert Christian who bought land and intended to build a town. The Boat Yard seems to have been the generally accepted name until 1774 when it was called King's Port because it was used as a port, or boat landing, for the shipping of iron, bacon, salt, and other commodities to towns down the Holston and Tennessee Rivers. Some people credit the origin of the name to William King of Abingdon, Virginia, owner of a salt works, who hauled his product to the Boat Yard for shipment. In 1774 Col. James King established a mill at the mouth of Reedy Creek and later built an iron works and a nail factory. Early settlers met with bitter resistance from the Cherokee, when they began to occupy the valley, but finally defeated the Indians in the Battle of Island Flats in 1776. The battle took place in the cane brakes which covered what now is the heart of the business district of Kingsport. On July 20 of the following year, the treaty of the Long Island of the Holston was made between the whites and the Cherokee.

Situated on a main north and south post road, Kinsport was a busy place in the early nineteenth century. In 1806 the town's industries con-

MAKING CELLULOSE ACETATE

sisted of four powdermills, a charcoal iron furnace and iron works, oil mills for turning out pure linseed oil, tanneries, gristmills, and sawmills.

A minor battle took place at Kingsport, December 13, 1864, during the War between the States. After a day's fighting the Federals captured the entire Confederate force.

The town's development was at a standstill for more than two decades following the war. Manufacturing revived a little in 1885 when David and William Roller and C. N. Jordan established a brick and glazed tile plant. Up to the twentieth century, railroads had ignored Kingsport and followed the valleys to the northeast and southwest. But in 1909 the Holston valley was connected with Cincinnati and the Carolina coast by the Carolina, Clinchfield and Ohio Railroad. Thus Kingsport obtained an outlet to the Great Lakes and the Atlantic.

Civic-minded citizens organized an improvement association to establish a planned industrial city on the flatlands adjoining old Kingsport. The association assembled a select group of industries, chosen for diversification of business, elimination of undesirable and dangerous industries, and to fit the available supply of labor.

Under this scheme a cement plant was erected, followed in succession by a brick oven, extract plant, and a tannery. To take care of the needs of the growing community a power plant was constructed, and by 1917 a hosiery and pulp mill were in operation. Less than a decade later Kingsport had a methanol distillery, a book manufacturing and book cloth establishment, a cotton spinning and weaving mill, and a belting plant. Industries added later included glass and hosiery knitting plants. In 1932 the methanol plant expanded operations to include the manufacture of cellulose acetate for camera films, acetate yarns, and other products. With these major industries have come many smaller businesses.

The University of Tennessee has a co-operative agreement with Kingsport industries whereby students, largely from the engineering and chemistry departments, are given practical training. These students divide their time between the plants at Kingsport and the university and thus gain practical experience in industry while earning a part of their expenses.

Kingsport was the first city in Tennessee to adopt the city manager type of government, and the city charter was approved by the Bureau of Municipal Research of the Rockefeller Institute in 1917.

POINTS OF INTEREST

The BOONE TRAIL or WILDERNESS ROAD SITE, at the Circle, between Sullivan and Watauga Sts., has a bronze plate set in a cobblestone monument shaped like an arrowhead, to mark the route taken by Daniel Boone when he was exploring the Holston Valley in 1769.

KINGSPORT PRESS *(open 8:30-4:30 weekdays),* Roller and Reedy Sts., one of the largest plants in the world manufacturing books exclusively, was established in 1922 to publish a low-priced series of the classics, but in 1925 was remodeled for the production of books of all types. A vocational school with a trained supervisor in charge was operated in connection with the plant for several years.

The plant averages 2,000,000 books a month, and uses more than 30 tons of paper daily in the manufacture of Bibles, fiction, reference and school books, catalogs, and encyclopedias.

Club and recreation rooms, a cafeteria, and a credit union are operated for employees.

The MEAD CORPORATION *(open by appointment)*, W. Main St., manufactures paper for magazines and books, and produces 100 tons of paper daily. The wood used by the Mead Corporation is shipped from seven Southern States, and the Kingsport Press uses a part of the output.

The PENNSYLVANIA-DIXIE CEMENT PLANT *(open on application at office)*, Main St., was established in 1909–1911. The site was chosen because the area possessed an abundant supply of limestone and other materials used in the manufacture of cement. Six kilns produce about 6,000 barrels of cement per day.

The KINGSPORT FOUNDRY AND MANUFACTURING PLANT *(open on application at office)*, Sullivan and Main Sts., organized in 1927, is one of the leading foundries of this region. Gray iron, brass, and semi-steel casting for general job work are produced by the foundry, which also has pattern and machine shops.

The GENERAL SHALE PRODUCTS PLANT *(open 7-4 weekdays)*, Main St., started operations in 1910. Its 31 kilns produce 135,000 bricks per day, with an average annual shipment of 3,800 carloads. Building tile is also manufactured. Shale is dug from a hill behind the plant.

The TENNESSEE EASTMAN CORPORATION *(not open to public)*, 2 miles south of the Circle on State 81, is second in size of the 13 Eastman plants. It consists of 82 buildings covering 372 acres on the Holston River and employs approximately 4,000 people. The plant produces large quantities of cellulose acetate for camera films, acetate yarns and plasters. Among its by-products are "charket," a concentrated fuel made from charcoal, and wood oils used as non-poisonous denaturants and insecticides.

The BORDEN MILLS *(not open to public)*, across from the Tennessee Eastman Corporation, is a subsidiary of the American Printing Co. The mills manufacture over 900,000 yards of cloth weekly. The complete, modern village for the employees, Oakdale, covers 75 acres.

The NETHERLAND INN *(private)*, 2144 Lee Highway, is a three-story structure of stone and frame, with massive chimneys at both ends. A two-story octagonal veranda on the front relieves the severity of the massive gabled structure. The Netherland Inn, known locally as the Old Tavern, was built in 1811 by Richard Netherland, a big slave-holder and land-owner. It was the center for the gay social life of upper East Tennessee in the early nineteenth century and a regular stopping place for Andrew Jackson on his trips from the Hermitage to Washington. Presidents Andrew Johnson and James K. Polk frequently rested there. A bronze tablet on the outer wall gives the date of construction as 1812, but the best authorities place the date as 1811.

On the hill behind the tavern stood the log house in which the brothers,

Gen. Edmund P. Gaines and George S. Gaines, were reared. Edmund Gaines, born in Virginia in 1777, served in the Tennessee militia against the Indians when he was eighteen, and joined the U. S. Army two years later. In 1801 he surveyed "Gaines' Trace," a military road generally following the Natchez Trace between Nashville and Natchez. In 1804, as commander of Fort Stoddart in Alabama, he arrested Aaron Burr. When Burr was tried in Richmond, Virginia, Edmund Gaines was one of the prosecution's witnesses. On leave from the army for several years, he practiced law in Mississippi. He was commissioned a colonel at the outbreak of the War of 1812 and placed in command of Fort Erie which he successfully defended during a long hard siege by a large force of British and Indians. For this he was given a citation by Congress and was breveted major general. He later participated in the Creek and Seminole Wars and in Black Hawk's War. Though he was removed from his command of the Western Department at the beginning of the Mexican War for overstepping his authority, he was vindicated and until his death in 1849 commanded the Eastern Department.

George S. Gaines, Alabama pioneer, was born in North Carolina in 1784. During his young manhood, he traded with the Creek Nation in Alabama and was appointed Indian agent at St. Stephens Post on the Tombigbee River. Trusted and well-liked by the Creek and Choctaw, he prevented their joining Tecumseh and, in 1812, persuaded the Choctaw to aid the United States against the Creek. He was also instrumental in carrying through the Choctaw Purchase. In after years, as a merchant of Mobile, he became wealthy, helped promote the Mobile & Ohio Railroad, and served in the State legislature.

The LONG ISLAND OF THE HOLSTON, where the Treaty of the Long Island of the Holston was signed, divides the river for four miles southwest of Kingsport. Here, in July 1777, the warring Cherokee, after two years of fighting met the commissioners of Virginia and North Carolina, and made peace with the white invaders. William Christian, William Preston, and Evan Shelby represented Virginia. North Carolina sent as its agents, Waightstill Avery, William Sharp, Robert Lanier, and Joseph Winston. From the Overhill towns came the headmen of the Cherokee —grim-faced Oconastota (the Great Warrior of Chota), Old Tassel of Toquah, the Raven of Chota, and peaceful old Attakullakulla (Little Carpenter), the steadfast friend of the whites for more than half a century.

The council fire was kindled and around it gathered Indian chiefs, long hunters in buckskin, settlers, and back country militiamen whose rough overbearing manners sorely tried the Indians' patience. The "good talks" were about to begin when an unknown white man killed an Indian brave named the Big Bullet. Immediately "Peace Island" became an armed camp. The angry commissioners offered $600 reward for the capture of the murderer but he was never found. After the Indians had been calmed by presents "with which to cover the grave of the slain warrior," the conference continued.

The Cherokee ceded to Virginia all of their claims north of a line from a point about three miles west of Cumberland Gap to the Holston River

THE NETHERLANDS INN, KINGSPORT

at the junction with Cloud's Creek. To North Carolina the Indians ceded land north and east of Cloud's Creek to Chimney Top, to the Nolichucky, ten miles below the mouth of Limestone Creek and thence southeastward into the territory of the Cherokee Middle Towns. No white man was supposed to cross these boundaries "on any pretense whatsoever." The Indians refused to give up the Long Island to any person except Col. Nathaniel Gist, with whom they recognized joint ownership. The treaty contained the following memorandum: "That Colonel Gist might sit down upon Long Island when he pleased as it belonged to him to hold good talks on." Col. Nathaniel Gist, son of Christopher Gist, Washington's guide to Fort Duquesne, is said to have been the father of the half-breed, George Guess or Gist (Sequoyah), inventor of the Cherokee alphabet.

It was while serving as a surgeon with the troops at the Long Island in 1776, that one Dr. Patrick Vance discovered a method of treating scalped persons. In one of the Draper Manuscripts (Wisconsin Historical Society collection), Dr. Vance states:

> I have found that a flat-pointed, straight awl is the best instrument to bore with, as the skull is thick and somewhat difficult to penetrate. When the awl is nearly through, the instrument should be borne more lightly upon. The time to quit boring is when a reddish fluid appears on the point of the awl. I bore at first about one inch apart and as the flesh appears to rise in these holes, I bore a number more between the first and second, etc. The scalped head cures slowly. It skins remarkably slow, generally taking two years.

The SITE OF KING'S MILL is at the mouth of Reedy Creek on the south fork of the Holston River. The gristmill, built by Col. James King in 1774, was one of the first water-powered mills in Tennessee and was an improvement over the hand-operated mill and the "hominy pounder" or "slow john," a crude but useful affair that operated by a process of hammering the corn with a wooden beam. Most of the early mills were log buildings, but King's Mill was a fort-like structure built of heavy stone. The water was taken from the creek several hundred feet above and brought down in a trough made from hollow logs split in halves. It fell over a paddle-wheel built on a shaft, on the other end of which was a rude wheel studded with pegs. These pegs served as cogs and meshed with other pegs which were fastened to one of the stones. The corn was ground as one stone revolved upon the other.

King also erected a substantial stone tavern, near the mill and the site became known as King's Mill Station.

POINTS OF INTEREST IN ENVIRONS

Site of Fort Robinson, *2.8 m.;* Rotherwood, *3 m.;* the Old Elm, *3.1 m.* *(see Tour 1A).*

PART III

Tours

Tour 1

(Roanoke, Va.)—Bristol—Johnson City—Knoxville—Athens—Cleveland; US 11E, US 11, the Lee Highway.
Virginia Line to Cleveland, 217.8 m.

The Southern Ry. parallels the route; American Air Lines flies over route between Bristol and Knoxville.
Paved roadbed.
Hotels in towns and tourist cabins and campgrounds at short intervals.

Section a. BRISTOL *to* KNOXVILLE; *131.8 m.*

The northern section of US 11 follows the valley of upper East Tennessee, the route over which passed the westward-moving wagon trains of the pioneers. They came down the valley from southwestern Virginia and over the mountain passes from North Carolina—hardy Scotch-Irish farmers, tired of the clay hills and eager to find richer land. Having already pioneered in the eastern uplands, they were inured to hardship and unafraid of the wilderness. Few of them were slaveholders and as a whole their political interests and sympathies were opposed to those of the plantation owners of the tidewater settlements.

They built blockhouses at strategic points, and grouped their cabins around them. They built well, and their material was so sound and their craftsmanship so skilled that many buildings of the period are still standing. But even before their cabins were roofed their plows had been turning the rich soil of the valleys. Wherever their cabins went up they established schools and organized civil government.

These settlements were made in defiance of the British Proclamation of 1763 which guaranteed the Cherokee their holdings west of the mountains. The Cherokee, angered by continued occupation of their lands by the whites, grew restless, and irresponsible young warriors began to attack groups of settlers. In 1776, a band led by Dragging Canoe, took the war trail against the white invaders. The war continued until 1777 when the members of the Cherokee Nation, with the exception of Dragging Canoe and his followers, signed the Treaty of the Holston *(see FIRST AMERICANS)*.

US 11 crosses the Virginia Line 157.4 *m.* southwest of Roanoke, Va.

BRISTOL, 0 *m.* (1,689 alt., 12,005 pop.), is two municipalities—Bristol, Tenn., and Bristol, Va.—with a total population of 20,845. The State Line divides State Street, the main thoroughfare.

With its busy shopping district, its smoky railroad yards and factories, Bristol is a hustling trading town and railroad junction. Its manufacturing plants produce pulp and paper, leather goods, mine cars, veneer, furniture, and structural steel. Sometimes the soft coal smoke from the factory stacks shuts out the view of the mountains that surround the city, but in the residential areas the view is clear.

Each Bristol has its own first-class post office. Both sides of State Street are usually astir with activity. Country people mingle with city folks, crossing from one State to the other to make their purchases. Business is about equally divided between the two cities.

Bristol is also a shipping point for much of the farm produce of upper East Tennessee. Trucks rumble through the city, and yard engines at the railroad junction are kept busy switching cars of cattle, sheep and poultry from the rails of the Southern to the northbound fast freights of the Norfolk and Western. Many cafes stay open all night and are well patronized by railroad employees and truckmen.

The 1,946 acres that comprise the city site were sold to Col. James Patton for 9 pounds, 7 shillings, and 6 pence. In 1771 Col. Isaac Shelby built a fort here to protect the thousands of immigrants. The place was called Sapling Grove. Recruits gathered for Shelby's campaign of 1779 against the Chickamauga Indians in lower East Tennessee. These troops marched to the Long Island of Holston, and thence to the mouth of Big Creek in the present Hawkins County, where boats were built for the voyage to the Chickamauga towns along the creek of the same name near Chattanooga.

After the Revolutionary War, Col. James King bought Sapling Grove and changed the name to King's Meadows. King, a Londoner and a civil engineer, started an iron works about 1784 and brought John Smith, an expert foundryman, from England to operate it. The plant produced the first nails for the frontiersmen. The quality of the ore used here, its high cost, and the difficulties of hauling it to the furnaces by wagon over poor roads finally reduced the output of the 29 furnaces. Eventually they were abandoned.

In 1852 Joseph R. Anderson learned that a railroad was planned to connect Knoxville and King's Meadows, bought 100 acres of land from the King estate, and laid out the tract. Because he thought his town would be an industrial center, he named it Bristol for the great manufacturing city of the same name in England. A Tennessee charter was granted in 1856 and in the same year a Virginia charter incorporated Goodson across the line, which was named in memory of Thomas Goodson, who had been a business associate of James King.

KING COLLEGE, on King College Road, is a Presbyterian co-educational college, founded in 1867. The campus, comprising 60 acres, is studded with towering beech trees and landscaped with an abundance of dogwood, evergreens, and shrubbery. Seven brick buildings, erected in 1917, form a quadrangle; they are of modified Georgian Colonial design, the work of C. B. Kearfott, of Bristol. This college was named for James King. It confers the degree of bachelor of arts.

To the east of the town is the upper section of the Cherokee National Forest *(see NATURAL SETTING AND CONSERVATION)* of 744,427 acres, a steep and rolling hill country.

Southwest of Bristol US 11E passes through a series of high knobs, that, when seen from the south, resemble the knuckles of the hand.

A marker (L) at 16.8 *m.* calls attention to Rocky Mount.

Left here 0.4 *m.* on a dirt road to ROCKY MOUNT *(private)*, one of the oldest houses in Tennessee, built by William Cobb in 1770. The place was so named because of the outcroppings of varicolored limestone on the site. The two-and-a-half story house, which stands on a hill high above the forks of the Holston and the Watauga, was constructed of hewn white oak logs and roofed with pegged white oak shingles, still in place. At the left end of the main house is a large, outside hipped chimney of home-pressed brick and in the one-story ell is another. The huge rafters are fastened with pegs 8 inches long. The house contains nine rooms and in its early days it was the most impressive structure in the area. The paneled front door is surmounted with a five-light transom; the interior is paneled with pine and the staircase has a walnut handrail.

The garden, one of the first planted in Tennessee, is to the right of the house; it was carefully landscaped in the early days and still contains rock lilies, Provence roses, white and blue violets, lilacs, japonicas, and star of Bethlehem.

Two years after he built this house, William Cobb signed the Articles of the Watauga *(see HISTORY AND GOVERNMENT)* and thereafter his name crops up frequently in the public records of this frontier. When in October 1790 William Blount, appointed Governor of the Territory South of the River Ohio, reached the Watauga settlement, Cobb invited him to spend the winter with him; thus the new Territory was organized from this place.

At 18.8 *m.* the route crosses the Holston River.

At 18.9 *m.* (at the west end of the bridge) is a gravel road.

Right on this road 1.4 *m.* is a junction (R) with another gravel road which leads 0.3 *m.* to the William Bean Cabin Site *(see Tour 2)*.

At 21.8 *m.* is the junction with US 23 *(see Tour 2)*, which unites with US 11 for 3 miles. At the junction is a PIONEER MEMORIAL, surmounted with figures of a pioneer family. Descriptions of historic points of interest in this section are on the shaft.

JOHNSON CITY, 24.5 *m.* (1,717 alt., 25,080 pop.) *(see Tour 2)*, is at the junction with State 67 *(see Tour 1B)* and with US 23 *(see Tour 2)*.

JONESBORO, 32 *m.* (1,695 alt., 1,981 pop.), seat of Washington County and the oldest town in Tennessee, was formally established on Nov. 4, 1779. It was named for Willie Jones (1740–1801), a North Carolina politician who was a friend of the settlers beyond the mountains. Many of the houses, churches and stores have changed little since pioneer days. Local people take great pride in their picturesque town and discourage the remodeling of the stores on the main street.

Washington County, which included all the settlements in what is now Tennessee, was a political subdivision of North Carolina and the first in the United States named for George Washington. The constitutional convention and the first legislative sessions of the State of Franklin *(see HISTORY)* were held in Jonesboro until 1785, when the seat of government of the Lost State was moved to Greeneville. In May, 1779, James Carter began to build the courthouse, a somewhat makeshift log structure with a shingle roof.

From the beginning this was a planned community. No ramshackle cabins were permitted; the owner of each lot had to build "one brick, stone, or well-framed house, 20 feet long and 16 feet wide, at least 10 feet in the pitch, with a brick or stone chimney." Failure to comply with this provision brought forfeiture of the land title.

The middle 1780's were years of confusion here. Many people refused to acknowledge the State of Franklin, preferring to remain loyal to North Carolina; two sets of officials attempted to establish their authority.

The first Court of Magistrates of the State of Franklin dispensed high, middle, and low juctice—and in criminal cases some of its decisions were harsh. A horse thief was branded with an H on one cheek, a T on the other, and nailed to the pillory by his ears for one hour after which, they were cut off. In 1788, at the whipping post in the public square, a woman received 10 lashes for petty larceny. The penalty imposed upon a man guilty of this offense was 30 lashes.

Andrew Jackson, then 21 years old, rode into Jonesboro in May, 1788, and hung out his shingle; he practiced law here about two years and boarded at the home of Kit Taylor, two miles west of town. When, in 1815, a rumor reached Jonesboro that Andrew Jackson had killed the whole English army at New Orleans, and had set sail to take possession of England itself, the townspeople were thrown into a frenzy of pride. One old grandpap threw his hat in the air and yelled, "Whoopee! Hurrah for Andy Jackson! Hell-and-thunder, I knowed he could whip anybody the day I seed him ride that hoss-race at Greasy Cove!" "Andy Jackson, hell-and-thunder" are the words still used in this section to express high feelings.

Jonesboro was the home of William and Matthew Atkinson, who designed (1801–2) the Great Seal of the State of Tennessee *(see HISTORY AND GOVERNMENT).*

In 1840 a spot on Main Street, 100 feet east of the courthouse, was the scene of an encounter between William Gannaway (Parson) Brownlow and Landon Carter Haynes. Brownlow, in his paper, the *Whig,* had printed some bitter things about Haynes, who thereupon had denounced the editor publicly. They fought it out at this spot. When friends separated them Brownlow had a bullet in his thigh, and Haynes' head had been badly battered by the parson's unfired pistol. Haynes was later a member of the Confederate Congress, and Brownlow was Governor of Tennessee (1865–67).

The COURTHOUSE in the center of the town, at Main and Cherokee Sts., was designed by Baumann and Baumann. This two-story brick structure, erected in 1912 is surmounted by a central clock tower in two stages, the first of which is columned. A balustraded parapet surrounds the roof, and there are pedimented porticoes on three fronts.

On the northeast corner of the courthouse lawn is a BOONE TRAIL MARKER in the shape of an arrowhead.

CHESTER INN, or Jonesboro Inn, on the corner of Main and Cherokee Sts., has been a hotel since 1798. A first floor room was for a time the office of Brownlow's *Whig.* Presidents Jackson, Polk, and Johnson, and other notables, including Charles Dickens, have stopped here.

A vacant lot at 203 W. Main St. is the SITE OF THE RUSSELL BEAN

THE OLD TAVERN, JONESBORO

HOUSE. Bean, son of the first permanent white settler in East Tennessee (1770) lived here for about five years. He was a gunsmith whose products were in great demand, and a man of furious temper with little respect for the law. Returning home after a long business trip to New Orleans he found his wife nursing an infant, born during his two-year absence. In a rage he bit the child's ears off. "To mark it so I can tell it from my own," he explained.

The FIRST PRESBYTERIAN CHURCH, 206 W. Main St., was dedicated Aug. 15, 1850. Resting upon a high basement with a panelled entrance, the structure is in the Greek Revival style. Above the simple pediment rises a Victorian steeple with pinnacles on the four corners of the first stage. The first church established in Jonesboro was the Hebron Presbyterian, organized about 1790 by the Rev. Samuel Doak and the Rev. Hezekiah Balch. Martin Academy built in 1816, was used as a church for some years. In 1831 a new house of worship was erected in great haste, that it might be ready for the meeting of the synod of Tennessee, beginning on the 12th of October of that year. This structure was replaced in 1847 by the present one.

After the close of the war the united synod had gone out of existence. Partisan feelings were still high. In March 1868, the Southern members of the congregation withdrew and organized a separate society. Legal proceedings for control of the church property were begun but a compromise was effected, whereby the members of the Northern Church relinquished their claim. They erected a handsome brick structure known as the Second Presbyterian Church.

The METHODIST EPISCOPAL CHURCH, SOUTH, at 215 W. Main St., completed in 1845, is a one-story brick Greek Revival structure with an Ionic portico, having four columns and an unusual arched window in the pediment. A steeple with three stages surrounds the structure. Early in the 19th century the Methodists organized a society in Jonesboro. Their first church was a small brick building, with a brick floor. The seats were rough slabs supported by round pine. This building was torn down after the present church was completed in 1845. At the close of the War between the States the Methodist congregation was also torn by partisan sympathies and for several years the members of the Methodist Episcopal Church North had possession of the property. Through process of law, however, they were in time compelled to transfer the property to the Methodist Episcopal Church South.

At 33.4 *m.* is the junction with State 81.

Left on State 81 is EMBREEVILLE, 7.6 *m.;* R. a short distance from Embreeville to the EMBREE IRON CO. PLANT, built in 1831 and in almost continuous operation since that date. For many years iron was smelted here with charcoal. In 1913 zinc was discovered here, later limited deposits of lead, and in 1934 low grade manganese. The company now mines and cleans lead and zinc. The manganese, like all other deposits in the United States, cannot be refined at a profit. In the beginning the iron works made a variety of articles—nails, wagon fittings, implements, building hardware, and the like. Elijah Embree, who operated the plant after the death of his brother Elihu in 1820, was in need of funds in 1825 and applied to the legislature for a loan of $25,000. In order to encourage the manufacture of iron, the legislature granted the subsidy. This is the only case in which the State has loaned money to a private individual. It took Embree 20 years to repay the money.

At 34 *m.* is the junction with a graveled lane leading between a house and a barn.

Right on this lane 0.3 *m.* to the CHRISTOPHER TAYLOR HOUSE (L). This gaunt structure is a two-story log house sheathed with clapboards; it has an outside chimney of field stone. Andrew Jackson boarded here during the time he practiced law in Jonesboro. Here he kept and trained the horse he rode in his celebrated race against Col. Robert Love at Greasy Cove *(see Tour 2)*.

At 38.1 *m.* is TELFORD.

Right from Telford 2 *m.* to LEESBURG, where the DE VAULT TAVERN was built by members of the De Vault family in 1820. It is a large square two-story brick building with mansard roof and shuttered windows. It has a small two-story pedimented porch with slender white columns. The old bar has been preserved.

At 39 *m.* is the junction (R) with a graveled road.

Right on this road 0.1 *m.* to the LIMESTONE HOUSE (R), built in 1791 by Thomas Embree; it is one of four stone houses in this area designed and constructed by the mason, Seth Smith. The original lines of the steep-roofed two-and-a-half story structure have been somewhat obscured by the addition of a porch across the front and a one-story frame wing. Inside are twin fireplaces.

In 1797 Thomas Embree, who was a Quaker, wrote a letter to the Knoxville *Gazette* urging the organization of a society to promote "a gradual abolition of slavery of any kind." Though the people of East Tennessee were free farmers and as such were hostile to slave labor there is little evidence of a strong abolition movement here until 1814. The temper of the community in 1820 is evidenced in a speech made by Thomas Roan before the Tennessee Manumission Society:

"Slavery is unfriendly to a genuine course of agriculture, turning in most cases the fair and fertile face of nature into barren sterility. It is the bane of manufacturing enterprise and internal improvements; injurious to mechanical prosperity; oppressive and degrading to the poor and laboring classes of the white population that live in its vicinity; the death of religion; and finally it is a volcano in disguise, and dangerous to the safety and happiness of any government on earth when it is tolerated."

Elihu, son of Thomas Embree, established one of the first periodicals in the United States exclusively devoted to the freeing of slaves. His paper, the *Manumission Intelligencer,* a weekly that first appeared in 1819, was succeeded in the following year by his monthly *Emancipator*. The latter, with 2,000 circulation—large for those days—was published until Embree's death in December 1820. Benjamin Lundy took it over in 1822 and moved the publication office from Jonesboro to Greeneville.

WASHINGTON COLLEGE (L), 40.9 *m.,* was chartered in 1795 as successor to Martin Academy, chartered in 1788. Samuel Doak, frontier preacher, founded both schools. He brought the first books into the State, and these on his only horse; he walked. Doak, a Pennsylvania Presbyterian, was a graduate of Princeton University; a contemporary historian described him as "a rigid opposer of innovation in religious tenets, very old school in all his notions and actions; uncompromising in his love of the truth and his hostility to error or heresy; . . . in . . . character, fearless, firm, nearly dogmatical and intolerant. . . ." There was some antagonism to the curricula of some of the early schools in the State, particularly to that of Washington College; in 1823 one contributor submitted a poem to the Knoxville *Intelligencer* which he concluded with the following stanza:

When boys have learn'd that they are made
To heave the earth with plough and spade;
And girls, that they must toil for man,
Make clothes, wash pots, and frying pan;
They're then prepar'd for learning.

But Doak, always firm in his conviction of right, when he was praying with the small band of mountaineers that left Sycamore Shoals to battle on King's Mountain, said: "Oh God, have regard for the souls of the English, for they will be with Thee tonight."

The building is now used as a county high school.

At the southern end of LIMESTONE (1,389 alt., 300 pop.), 44.3 *m.*, on Mill Brook are (R) a series of rapids and a waterfall. There are picnicking spots nearby.

The OLD STONE HOUSE (L), at the center of the town where the highway goes under the bridge, was the home of George Gillispie, an early settler in the Watauga country. The house, inside and out, has been little changed since it was built in 1792. The foundation is 30 inches thick, the first floor walls 24 inches, and the second story walls 18 inches. The cornices are deeply carved with a walls-of-Troy design; about five feet from the floor are small partly-filled apertures, probably former musket loop holes used in those days when houses were not only homes but fortresses as well.

George Gillispie was one of the signers of the petition to the Assembly of North Carolina asking for a separation from the State. This caused the formation of Franklin County. The house served as a marking point in describing the dividing line between Washington and Greene Counties and in outlining the boundary lines of Brown's settlement.

During the Indian depredations of 1777, the Chicakamauga led by Abraham of Chilhowee, planned a surprise attack on Gillispie's Station. The garrison at the station, having been informed of the plans, escaped quickly to Watauga, leaving their cabins and stock to the plunder of the Indians. The present house was built on land fiercely contended for by the Indians and was often attacked by them. The house has been owned and occupied by one family for four or five generations.

Left from Limestone on the paved Crockett Highway to the BIRTHPLACE OF DAVID CROCKETT (1786–1836), 1.7 *m.*, on the banks of the Nolichucky River; the site is in a field (L) between Crockett road and the river. This spot, with its clear spring, was formerly a camp site of the Cherokee Indians.

West of this point is a large area whose main product is burley tobacco, known locally as the 14-months crop. The burley farmer begins to prepare the next year's crop before last year's crop has been marketed. In January he cuts logs and underbrush and piles them in rectangular heaps about 9 feet wide and 300 feet long. Early in February he lights these piles, and the hillsides burst into flames. The bonfires are kept burning for several days to make sure that the ground has been heated to a depth of two or three feet. This process of burning kills insects and vegetation that would harm the young tobacco plants.

Then the farmer sows his seeds, and immediately covers the plot with light canvas to protect them from frost and insects until the plants have attained three leaves and are less susceptible to frost. In summer the plants grow to their full height, giving a bright green radiance to the landscape. Harvesting is done in early fall; the stalks are hung on scaffolds in the fields or under sheds.

In the fall, after the leaves have turned brown, they are stripped from the stalks and tied into "hands," which are bundled and hauled on a damp day—to prevent the leaves from crumbling—to one of the warehouses in the basin where it is stored until auction time. The auctions, which are held from December 1 to March 1, are attended by growers as well as buyers, who listen intently to the monotonous whine of the tobacco auctioneer as he passes hurriedly from one loose-leaf stack to another.

TUSCULUM COLLEGE, 54.1 *m.,* originally Tusculum Academy, was founded in 1818 by the Rev. Samuel Doak after he had resigned as president of Washington College; in 1868 it was merged with Greeneville College. The co-educational institution is now under control of the Cumberland Presbytery. All the buildings are of brick and stone except one wooden structure that was built in 1825, to replace a log house. There are about 250 students.

GREENEVILLE, 58.7 *m.* (1,565 alt., 5,544 pop.), seat of Greene County, was named, as was the county, for Nathanael Greene, the Revolutionary general. Surrounded by a rich agricultural region, noted for its burley tobacco, Greeneville is now, and always has been, primarily a farmers' trade center.

On Saturday farm families flock into Greeneville. Cars, trucks, and mule-team wagons are parked everywhere; people fill the streets and trade is brisk in the stores.

On a hill at the corner of Main and College Streets is the courthouse, its marker-dotted lawn a favorite gathering place. To the west along Main Street are fine old houses; toward the east is the business section; southward stretch stockyards, creameries, poultry houses, coalyards, and largest of all, the warehouses in which from two to three million dollars worth of tobacco is sold annually.

Greeneville was the capital of the State of Franklin during the last two years of its existence (1785–1787). Greeneville College, founded by Hezekiah Balch and chartered in 1794 by the Territorial Assembly, was merged in 1868 with Tusculum College. The first paper published here was the abolitionist *Genius of Universal Emancipation,* edited by Benjamin Lundy, which was a successor to the paper published by Embree at Jonesboro. The Greeneville *Sun,* a daily paper and the *Burley Bulletin,* a monthly tobacco journal, are the present publications.

In 1861, when the Tennessee Legislature adopted the Ordinance of Secession, the loyalists of East Tennessee held a convention here, during which they proposed that East Tennessee be made a separate State.

At the age of 17, Andrew Johnson (1808–75) moved here from North Carolina with his mother and stepfather. Within a few weeks young Johnson, who was a tailor, had made most of the cloth in town into suits. He moved on to Rutledge, but he stayed there only about six months. Hearing that the only tailor in Greeneville had left, he came back here and soon afterward, on May 17, 1827, married Miss Eliza McCardle, who taught him to write and cipher. He entered politics, and in 1829 was elected as an alderman on the Democratic ticket. In 1843 he was sent to Congress as a Representative and served until 1853. He was Governor of Tennessee from 1853 to 1857.

On the day of Johnson's inauguration as Governor, retiring Governor Campbell called at his hotel to take him in a carriage to the ceremonies, but Johnson refused to ride, saying that he was "going to walk with the people." Remembering his own struggle for an education, Johnson in his first message to the State Legislature, requested "a tax of 25¢ on the polls, and two and a half cents on the hundred dollars, of all the taxable property of the State . . . for the common schools."

In 1862, when Union forces had taken possession of most of Tennessee, President Lincoln appointed Johnson Military Governor of the State. He took office as Vice President of the United States on March 4, 1865 and succeeded to the Presidency after Lincoln's death in April of the same year.

His career in Washington was a stormy one. Part of his difficulties arose from the fact that he was a Union Democrat, but the post-bellum Presidency would have been stormy for any man. His program, like that of Lincoln's, was based on the theory that the seceded States had never been out of the Union. The radical Republicans, who dominated Congress, opposed him because he supported the institution of slavery and was a Democrat; the South hated him because he was a Unionist. The lower House brought impeachment proceedings against him on the grounds that he had violated the Tenure of Office Act, but more moderate opinion prevailed in the Senate and the impeachment vote fell one short of the constitutional two-thirds required for removal.

The ANDREW JOHNSON TAILOR SHOP *(open 8 a.m.-4:30 p.m.; free)*, on the northwest corner of Depot and College Sts., back of the county courthouse, is a small frame structure now enclosed in a brick building. Over the door hangs the sign, "A. Johnson, Tailor."

The ANDREW JOHNSON HOME *(open on request)*, on W. Main St., was bought by Johnson while it was still under construction; he completed it in 1851. It stands flush with the sloping street and is a two-and-a-half story brick structure with a many-gabled roof and a long one-story porch on the lower side. This was Johnson's home until his death in 1875. It is now owned by Mrs. Andrew Johnson Patterson, widow of the President's grandson. The parlor furnishings of Johnson's day have been preserved.

The SITE OF THE CAPITOL OF THE STATE OF FRANKLIN, a log house, is commemorated by a bronze tablet in the wall at the front entrance to the courthouse. The State of Franklin, formed a year after the end of the Revolutionary War, lasted until 1788.

On the courthouse lawn is the MORGAN MONUMENT. Gen. John H. Morgan was killed here; it is not definitely known whether he was shot by Union soldiers, who had dashed into town to surprise the Confederates' "Terrible Raider," or was assassinated by a civilian. One version of the affair has it that Morgan was shot in the back by a person not in uniform. Near the Morgan monument is a memorial tablet erected to the memory of Union soldiers who were killed while fighting in this area.

The FIRST PRESBYTERIAN CHURCH, on Main St., one block north of the courthouse, was designed in modified Greek Revivial style by Coile and Cardwell, and was constructed in 1912. Resting on a high basement, the balustraded portico is approached by a wide central stair. Four Doric columns support a simple pediment which is surmounted by a steeple in three

ANDREW JOHNSON TAILOR SHOP, GREENEVILLE

stages. This church is a copy of its predecessor, which was built in 1780.

BOXWOOD MANOR *(open on request)*, 209 Brown's Hill, was built by Joseph Ramsey Brown and his wife, in 1855 to replace the cottage in which they began their married life in 1843. George M. Spencer of Ogdensburg, N. Y., was the architect of the square, many-windowed, central-halled, and ornately trimmed brick house. The ceilings are 12 and 14 feet high. The winding stairway has walnut banisters and handrail, and a ramshorn newel post.

The chief charm of the place is its fine boxwood trees, which were brought from Charleston, S. C., about 1850. The vegetable and flower garden are behind the house.

The nucleus of the SEVIER-O'KEEFE HOUSE is probably the oldest structure in town; this first unit, a two-story log house, was the home of Valentine Sevier, brother of John Sevier, the first Governor. The present white clapboarded structure, which grew up around Sevier's house, piece by piece, has the charm inherent in houses with such a history of slow growth. The bole of the wistaria—81 inches in circumference—draped over the south wall offers its testimony of the house's age. The surrounding gardens are particularly delightful.

Left from Greeneville on State 70 to (R) the BURLEY TOBACCO EXPERIMENT STATION *(open weekdays)*, 4 *m.* This experiment station is operated by the University of Tennessee and the U. S. Department of Agriculture. On the farm of 325 acres experiments are conducted in breeding, growing, curing, and fertilizing burley tobacco, and in disease prevention and control, and in crop rotations. Soil-erosion control is also studied.

There is a view at 64.9 *m.* (R) of Clinch Mountain. At Greeneville the highway swings sharply northwest and crosses a ridge.

BULLS GAP, 75.9 *m.* (1,154 alt., 1,500 pop.),—Bullsgap to the U. S. Post Office Department—was named for John Bull, a gunmaker, who turned out many long rifles, the type that made Tennessee frontiersmen famous for marksmanship. Each rifle was marked with the maker's name, the name of the person for whom it was made, and the date of completion.

RUSSELLVILLE, 82.9 *m.* (300 pop.), is on land awarded Col. James Roddey (Roddye) for services in the Battle of King's Mountain, and was named for his second wife, who had been a Miss Russell. Roddye was a delegate to the North Carolina convention of 1788, a member of the first Tennessee constitutional convention, and a signer of the State's first Constitution.

Left from Russellville on a graveled road 0.5 *m.* to HAYSLOPE, Roddye's home. It was a hewn-log cabin with steep shingled roof and outside fieldstone chimney. The house has been remodeled several times. In early times this house sheltered many leading citizens of the Territory and of the new State. The owner's hospitality was not limited by religious bias; any itinerant preacher was sure of a bed, a meal, and a meeting-room when he reached this place. At one time mass was held in the cabin. Roddye, however, was a member of the Bent Creek Baptist Church which, like other frontier churches, took responsibility for the conduct of its members; on one occasion the congregation reproved him for "the transaction of fighting." At the next meeting, two members appointed to "labor with him" recommended that he be "restored to fellowship in the church when he feels satisfied with himself."

The DEADERICK HOUSE (L), 83.9 *m.,* built prior to 1812 by Judge Charles Deaderick, is reached through a long boxwood walk. Every joining of wood in this large two-story brick house was mitered, spliced, and pegged. The only nails are in the weatherboarding of some outbuildings, and these are of the headless hook type, hand-made. The moldings throughout are of delicate proportions; even the corners of the ceiling joists in the slave quarters were finished with beaded molding. The house is now roofed with block tin, 1/8 of an inch thick. In the carriage house is a small carriage, elaborately carved, painted, and decorated.

MORRISTOWN, 89.3 *m.* (1,317 alt., 7,305 pop.), seat of Hamblen County, was named for three brothers, Gideon, David and Absalom Morris who settled here in 1783.

The town is in a fertile valley enclosed by the Clinch Mountains, where dairying and poultry-raising are of importance. The famous "milk-fed broiler" originated in this area. Carloads of fryers are sent out by rail and a fleet of specially constructed motor-trucks rush chickens and turkeys to New York and other eastern markets. This business is carried on by both private business concerns and by a Farmers Co-operative Poultry Association.

Large amounts of burley tobacco are sold in the town's six warehouses; tobacco is the leading cash crop of the county. There are more than 30 industrial plants which can vegetables, process silk, cotton and leather, manufacture staves and barrel heading, woodworking and finishing, and shell walnuts.

The town owns and operates its own water works and electric lighting system, and utility rates are low.

The MORRISTOWN NORMAL AND INDUSTRIAL COLLEGE, east of James St. at E. 6th Ave., was chartered in 1909, and is the only college with both white and Negro teachers maintained in the South by the Methodist Episcopal Church. The institution, an experimental junior college for Negroes, has about 120 students. Its 10 buildings are on a 7-acre campus and a 320-acre farm.

Since about 1917 the *Progressive Teacher,* a widely circulated magazine, has been printed here at the TRIANGLE PRESS PLANT, which also prints the nationally distributed Augsburg spelling books and some art books.

At Morristown is the junction with US 25E *(see Tour 3).*

1. Left from Morristown on Springdale Rd. to a STATE FISH HATCHERY, 8 *m.,* where 400,000 trout, 100,000 bass, 150,000 bream, and quantities of other fish are hatched annually for distribution in mountain streams of East Tennessee. Spring traps feed the rearing pools, which cover 14 of the 25 acres in the property.

2. Left from Morristown on Valley Home Pike to the JARNAGIN CEMETERY, 2 *m.,* which contains the GRAVE OF DEWITT C. SENTER, Governor of Tennessee 1869–1871, and also a marker in memory of Kiffen Rockwell, World War ace, who was killed in action in France while a member of the Lafayette Escadrille.

At 95.6 *m.* is the junction with a dirt road.

Left on this road to ROCK HAVEN DOLOMITE WELL (R), 2.5 *m.,* drilled 135 feet through solid dolomite, that yields water reputed to have remedial properties.

At 97.5 *m.* is the junction with a dirt road.

Right on this road to PANTHER SPRINGS, 0.5 *m.* Near the spring is a rock with a depression in which early settlers ground corn into meal with the aid of a heavy pestle attached to a beam propelled by the current of the stream. The operation of this device, called a "pounding mill," was slow, but it could be carried on without attention.

FAIRVIEW *(private)*, 102.9 *m.*, is a long two-story brick dwelling (L) with one-story wings and a classic facade of three bays formed by the use of a central recessed two-story portico. The portico has a second floor gallery and a pediment ornamented with a regency star; its octagonal columns have capitals carved in a lotus motif. This house was built in 1850 by Stokely Williams, for his bride. The bricks were made in a nearby clay pit and oven, still in existence. Bricks were also made in these pits to patch the walls during the War between the States; the patched places are noticeable. The barns and outbuildings were constructed at the same time as the house.

At Fairview is the JAMES HOBBY FARM, for the breeding and propagation of small animals and fowl, including guinea pigs, white rats, ground hogs, monkeys, giant white Flemish and Polish hares, 12 varieties of pheasants, several varieties of white turkeys, peafowl, tufted bantams, and breeds of exhibition chickens.

JEFFERSON CITY, 103.4 *m.* (1,117 alt., 1,898 pop.), was formerly called Mossy Creek because it was by the creek of that name. This stream, five miles long, flows swiftly and was used as early as 1840 to provide power for an ax-handle factory, a cotton mill, a woolen mill, and an ironworks. An iron smelter was established here in 1810.

CARSON NEWMAN COLLEGE, in the center of town, is a Baptist coeducational institution that resulted from the consolidation in 1889 of Carson College for men, founded in 1851, and Newman College for women, founded in 1882. On the beautifully landscaped campus are nine brick buildings with classic facades. These are dominated by the ADMINISTRATION BUILDING, completed in 1919 at a cost of more than $100,000, a large structure of red brick trimmed with cut stone. The facade has three entrances of classic design; in the center is a large two-story portico with six Ionic columns supporting a massive pediment; flanking the portico are one-story porticos of the same design. This building contains 23 lecture rooms, the administrative offices, literary society halls, and an auditorium that seats more than 800. The school confers bachelor degrees in arts, science, and science in commerce.

The MAPLES, Branner St. near George St., is built on land granted by the Crown in 1772 to Christopher Haynes. Haynes built a four-room log house, which a few years later was sold to George Branner. Around the Haynes cabin Branner built the present large house of Greek Revival design whose gabled roof extends forward to form the pediment of the two-story portico. The simple lines of the mass have been somewhat destroyed by the forward extension of one-story wings.

1. Left from Jefferson City on Dandridge Pike (State 92), six blocks, to COLONIAL HALL (L) on George St., a large grey brick structure on a seven-acre landscaped estate. The house contains 16 rooms of unusually large size.

2. Left from Jefferson City on Piedmont Rd. to the UNIVERSAL EXPLORATION COMPANY MINES AND MILLS, 1 *m.,* which have a production capacity of about 1,000 tons of zinc daily.

The BRAZELTON HOUSE *(private),* 107 *m.* (R), was built in 1832 by the Quaker major-general, William Brazelton. Brazelton himself drew the plans and supervised the construction and decoration of the long, plain two-story structure, which stands on a high foundation. Two stairways rise from the first floor and the interior has delicate hand-wrought moldings.

In the yard is a pecan tree, more than 100 years old, that still produces soft-shelled pecans. It is 80 feet high and 11 feet in circumference.

NEW MARKET, 107.3 *m.* (1,049 alt., 500 pop.), was settled in 1788. In 1862 about 450 young men from the town and from nearby farms left here, unarmed and unorganized, to join the Union Army. They were captured by Confederates and transported to Tuscaloosa, Ala., where they were held until the war ended.

The HODGSON-BURNETT HOUSE *(open on request),* built of logs and later weatherboarded, was at intervals the home of Frances Hodgson from 1865, when her family arrived from England, until 1875, when she was married to Dr. S. M. Burnett and moved to Washington, D. C. Mrs. Burnett came back to New Market each summer, and two of her early books, *That Lass o' Lowrie's* and *Surly Tim's Trouble,* and her most famous work, *Little Lord Fauntleroy,* were in part written during her visits here.

At New Market is the junction with Indian Cave Road *(see Tour 1A).*

The FRIENDS MEETING HOUSE (L) 109.1 *m.,* is on the site of the Lost Creek Meeting House. From 1809 Quakers of Jefferson County advocated the abolition of slavery and in 1815 they organized the Tennessee Society for Promoting the Manumission of Slaves in the old meeting house on this spot. Branches were organized in many other places in East Tennessee.

The SITE OF TUCKER'S TAVERN (R), 109.6 *m.,* is marked by a chimney standing in a field. The inn was built in 1819 on the stage road between Knoxville and Abingdon, Va., which was the first Federal post road established in Tennessee (1794).

Tucker Tavern was typical of the log-cabin inns of the frontier, where the roads were lonely and long, and the accommodations for travelers meager. The backwoods inn was usually a large two-story log cabin, the second story being merely a sleeping loft. Quite often the tavern keeper spent more time distilling whisky and selling it than in attending to the more prosaic needs of his guests. Travelers carried their own bedding, and also such luxuries as tea, coffee, and sugar. The innkeeper furnished bread and butter, milk, salt and fresh meat, beans, mush, rice and other vegetables. There was little privacy. A traveler who went to bed alone might wake up with several bedfellows packed into the straw-filled loft beside him. A story still survives of the irate landlord who ejected a traveler from his inn because the visitor objected to a towel that fifteen others had used without a murmur.

Tavern rates in 1785 were as follows: "Diet, one shilling; liquor, half pint, six pence; pasture and stable, six pence; lodging, four pence; corn, eight pence a gallon; oats six pence a gallon."

At 110.2 *m.* (R) is the scene of the GREAT NEW MARKET WRECK. On September 4, 1904, two crack passenger trains of the Southern Railway collided. Part of a long, popular hill ballad tells the whole story:

> One autumn morning in Tennessee
> An awful wreck was heard;
> East of Knoxville and New Market
> Was where the crash occurred.
>
> The east and west-bound passenger trains
> Were running at highest speed;
> They struck each other in the curve;
> 'Twas a horrible sight indeed.
>
> The engine crew on the west-bound train
> Their orders had misread;
> About one hundred and fifty were hurt,
> And nearly seventy were dead.

STRAWBERRY PLAINS, 115.8 *m.* (1,150 alt., 500 pop.), a trading point of farmers, was so named about 1788 because of the abundance of wild strawberries nearby.

Left from Strawberry Plains on Jones Road to WATER CRESS FARM, 0.4 *m.,* where is a pond of two and one-half acres, divided into 5 one-half-acre pools. Five to 15 barrels of cress are cut daily from May to October 1.

At 117 *m.* is the junction with paved Mascot Road.

Right on this road is MASCOT, 2.9 *m.,* with the mines and reduction plant of the American Zinc Company, established in 1913. Zinc ore is mined with pneumatic drills and dynamite, and hauled to the surface by mule-drawn tramcars. The mines, from 150 to 250 feet underground, are worked at different levels. The ore is crushed and ground and the asphalerite is separated from the gangue by means of jigs and a flotation process. The mineral is shipped to plants in other States for further treatment, most of it to the American Zinc plant in New Jersey.

At 119.6 *m.* is the junction with US 70 *(see Tour 12),* which unites with US 11E between this point and a junction south of Knoxville.

KNOXVILLE, 131.8 *m.* (933 alt., 105,802 pop.) *(see KNOXVILLE).*

Points of Interest: The University of Tennessee, Blount Mansion, Henley Street Bridge, Church Street Methodist Church, Headquarters TVA, and others.

At Knoxville are the junctions with US 70 *(see Tour 12),* US 129 *(see Tour 5),* State 33 *(see Tour 5A),* and US 11W *(see Tour 2).*

Section b. KNOXVILLE *to* CLEVELAND, *85 m.*

Between KNOXVILLE, 0 *m.,* and the Dixie Lee Junction filling station at 19.8 *m.* south of Knoxville, US 11 and US 70 are united *(see Tour 12).*

At this junction US 70 branches R.; L. on US 11, which winds through a region of low knobby hills timbered with second-growth hardwoods, until it reaches the Tennessee River. South of the Tennessee River the route follows the wide Tennessee River valley, where are rolling farm land, woods, and views of distant mountains. About fifty miles south of Knoxville the route traverses the Sweetwater Valley, which is within the bounds of the greater Tennessee Valley. On the right is the long blue wall of the Cumberlands, and on the left the ridges of the Chilhowie Mountains.

In the valley canning crops are grown extensively, also burley tobacco. Dairying and bee culture are also important means of livelihood, and a tall factory smokestack now rises from almost every small town.

LENOIR CITY, 25.6 *m.* (853 alt., 4,470 pop.), on the Tennessee River south of the mouth of the Little Tennessee, was founded in 1840 by William Ballard Lenoir, who operated one of the first cotton mills in the South. Over the Southern Railway and by truck Lenoir City ships out quantities of hay and grain grown in the rich river bottoms. Lenoir City also has more than 15 factories, most of them small, including chair and hosiery mills. The largest plant is the Lenoir Car Works, in which railroad cars are manufactured.

Right from Lenoir City on Eaton's Crossroad to a large GINSENG GARDEN, 1.5 *m.*, which has more than a million plants in a two and one-half acre plot. A brush-covered wire-net arbor above the plants admits air and rain but excludes the direct rays of the sun. The root of the ginseng, which belongs to the sarsaparilla family, is highly prized in China for its medicinal properties. Most of the crop is shipped to the Orient, where it brings high prices. Five to seven years are necessary for the root to mature. The leaves resemble those of poison ivy.

US 11 crosses the Tennessee River at 31 *m.* on LOUDON BRIDGE *(toll 25¢)* a million-dollar structure.

LOUDON, 31.6 *m.* (782 alt., 2,578 pop.), seat of Loudon County is the outgrowth of a settlement, Blair's Ferry, which was on the north bank of the river. It is the trade and shipping center of a farming area, and has the small hosiery and chair factories usually found in the towns of this area. The JOHN BLAIR HOUSE was built in 1839 on land acquired from the Indian Chief Pathkiller.

The TENNESSEE MILITARY INSTITUTE, (R) 40.7 *m.*, was founded in 1874 by the Reverend John Lynn Bachman. It is a college preparatory school. On the 100-acre campus are buildings and drill grounds on the crest of a hill, tennis courts, athletic fields, and a golf course. The land was purchased in 1909 after the school had outgrown its old plant, and all buildings have been erected since that date. Each year since 1927 this institution has been designated by the U. S. War Department as an honor military school. The MAIN BUILDING is a four-story brick structure with battlemented towers and parapets. The GYMNASIUM is a two-story brick structure of Gothic design.

SWEETWATER, 43.7 *m.* (917 alt., 2,271 pop.), like other points in the Sweetwater Valley, was in the former Cherokee domain. It has several small factories that produce cheese, hosiery, and dresses.

Left from Sweetwater on the Christiansburg Rd. to CRAIGHEAD CAVERNS *(adm. $1; guides),* 1 *m.* The caverns follow an underground river through marble-like rock.

The CLEAGE HOME, 54 *m.,* built some time after 1820 by Samuel Cleage, is a two-story brick house with stepped gable ends and a true one-and-a-half story ell. The entrance has a well proportioned fanlight.

Samuel Cleage learned the trade of brick mason in his youth and was later a successful contractor in Botetourt County, Virginia. Believing that the rapidly developing Tennessee would provide a good field for his trade he proceeded along the old Post Road with a caravan made up of his family and possessions as well as some skilled slaves. The journey was a leisurely one, because he stopped to work at various places along the way. He drew his own plans and supervised construction while his Negroes made bricks, hewed timbers, and turned moldings and chairboards. His party increased in size because he accepted slaves as well as notes and gold in payment. Arriving here shortly after the Hiwassee purchase, by which the territory was acquired from the Cherokee, he obtained some 3,000 acres of land and built his home.

Samuel Cleage and his son-in-law, Robert Crutchfield, became partners. They constructed many of the public buildings and important private residences of East Tennessee.

ATHENS, 58 *m.* (974 alt., 5,385 pop.), seat of McMinn County, is surrounded by wooded knobs. The distant peaks of the Unakas are along the southeastern horizon. Athens is a true courthouse town, and the shady square is filled to overflowing with country people on Saturdays. They come on horseback, in mule-drawn wagons, and in cars spattered with red clay. When their trading is done the men lounge around the courthouse square, swapping gossip and political views while their womenfolk attended the movies. Soap-box evangelists, musicians, and dancing Negro boys add to the holiday air.

In 1835, when the tide of proslavery sentiment was running high in the State, a bundle of abolition papers arrived at the post office here. A number of people united to demand their surrender by the postmaster and made a bonfire of them in the street. The editor of the Athens *Journal* loudly advocated a law against distribution of "these filthy and wicked productions" and State feeling was such that the legislature enacted a law "to prevent the publication or circulation in this State of seditious pamphlets and papers," meaning those advocating the abolition of human chattels.

TENNESSEE WESLEYAN COLLEGE, in the center of town, is a coeducational junior college. It has a 20-acre campus shaded by splendid trees. There are eight buildings of various designs. OLD COLLEGE HALL, a square three-story brick structure, is the oldest on the campus. There are several large frame buildings with mansard roofs built during the President Grant era. The ADMINISTRATION BUILDING, an attractive and imposing brick structure of neo-classic design, has an auditorium seating more than 1,000, a gymnasium, and a basketball court, besides administrative offices and lecture halls.

For the first twenty years of its existence (1867–1887) the institution was called East Tennessee Wesleyan College or University; for twenty years (1886–1906) it was Grant University; for nineteen years (1906-1925) it was the Athens School of the University of Chattanooga. In June 1925 the institution was separated from the University of Chattanooga and again called Tennessee Wesleyan College.

Near Ritter Hall, in the sidewalk on the north of the college, are two trees growing very close together—one an oak, the other a hackberry. A local legend accounts for their position. A young British soldier, who had been wounded at the Battle of Kings Mountain, was nursed back to health by Weena, a daughter of Little Carpenter, the famous Cherokee chief. They fell in love and the soldier was adopted into the tribe; but their happiness was short-lived. A jealous suitor murdered the white man, and Weena, grief-stricken, killed herself. When the two lovers were buried here, Little Carpenter placed an acorn in the white man's hand, and a hackberry seed in Weena's.

CALHOUN, 73 *m.* (893 alt., 300 pop.), on the north bank of the Hiwassee River, was settled in 1819 and named for John C. Calhoun, then Secretary of War.

Under their treaty rights the Cherokee retained the islands in the Chestatee, Tennessee, and Hiwassee Rivers. John McGhee wished to acquire one of these islands in the Hiwassee near here. He owned a rifle that was coveted by Jack Walker, a chief of the local Cherokee. One day the Indian remarked, "The Chief had dream. He dreamed that White Chief had given him his fine gun." McGhee did so. Later, McGhee, taking advantage of the Indian tradition that what was asked for under such conditions must be given, approached the Indian and remarked, "White man dream Indian Chief gave him fine island." After a period of reflection the Indian replied, "Big Chief give you island, but Indian no dream against white man no more."

CHARLESTON, 74.6 *m.* (903 alt., 480 pop.), is opposite Calhoun on the south bank of the Hiwassee River. While this area was still Indian territory—the Ocoee District, ceded to the U. S. in 1819 by the Cherokee —the Indian Agency stood here.

In the summer and fall of 1838 several thousand Cherokee were herded together for the Great Removal to land west of the Mississippi River. At Rattlesnake Springs, 2 miles from Charleston the last tribal council of the old Cherokee Nation was held. After this gathering in October, the Indians began the weary march into western exile, escorted by soldiers of the United States Army. Gen. Winfield Scott was in command of the troops who evicted the Cherokee.

Attention is called to the SITE OF THE HOUSE and the GRAVE OF CHIEF JACK WALKER by a bronze tablet set in a stone wall at 81.8 *m.* The tablet says:

"Location of house and grave of Chief Jack Walker, greatest of his tribe and a servant of our country. Married 1824 Emily Meigs, daughter of Return Jonathan Meigs."

Chief Jack Walker lived on what is known as the Cherokee Farm. At an Indian council at Old Fort, he was accused of treason by his tribesmen and was assassinated on his way home from the meeting.

About 40 feet east is the grave; a hackberry tree stands at one end of it, a block of limestone at the other.

At CLEVELAND, 85 *m.* (873 alt., 9,136 pop.) *(see Tour 13),* is the junction with US 64 *(see Tour 13),* with which US 11 unites to Chattanooga.

Tour 1A

(Roanoke, Va.)—Bristol—Kingsport—Rogersville—Knoxville; US 11W. Virginia Line to Knoxville; 121.3 m.

Paved roadbed; narrow and winding with sharp curves.
Accommodations of all types throughout.

US 11W winds southwestward through a region over which the white settlers and the Cherokee fought bloodily for years. It was a part of the Cherokee Overhill Country, with fertile bottom lands and held several Cherokee towns. US 11W branches west from US 11E *(see Tour 1)* at BRISTOL, 0 *m.* *(see Tour 1)* on the Virginia Line 157.4 miles southwest of Roanoke, Va. and descends into farm lands.

BLOUNTVILLE, 9.5 *m.* (1,700 alt., 1,200 pop.), seat of Sullivan County, was named for William Blount, the first Governor (1790) of the Territory South of the River Ohio. The county, named for Gen. John Sullivan (1740–1795), was organized at the home of Moses Looney on February 7, 1780. Isaac Shelby, appointed colonel-commandant of the new county by Governor Caswell of North Carolina, subsequently became the first Governor of the Commonwealth of Kentucky.

According to tradition, Blountville, among craggy, timbered hills, had been the site of a fort and settlement before it became a town in 1795. It is now surrounded by rich farm land that produces grain, vegetables, and a very fine grade of tobacco.

From the first the people here felt the need of education for their children. In 1806 Jefferson Academy was established in a log structure that in 1836 was replaced by one of brick. In 1837 a Female Academy was established in a building opposite the cemetery.

When the PEARSON HOME was constructed about 1810 it was given a second-story overhang by the cautious owner to enable him to shoot and to pour scalding water on Indians should they attempt to attack the place.

At 21.5 *m.* where US 11W crosses Chestnut Ridge, is the junction with a country road.

Right on this road along the crest of the ridge to spots that offer delightful views of Clinch Mountain and other ridges.

At 22.5 *m.* is the junction with State 81, bituminous surfaced.

Left on State 81 is the village of FALLS BRANCH, 12 *m.*, near a 40-foot waterfall for which the creek and village are named. Near the fall and creek are two water mills. The route between Kingsport and Falls Creek affords a clear view of Chimney Tops and Bays Mountain and follows the narrow gorge of the Nolichucky River through Buffalo Mountain.

At 23.4 *m.* is the junction with US 23 *(see Tour 2).*

KINGSPORT, 24.5 *m.* (1,700 alt., 11,914 pop.) *(see KINGSPORT).*

Points of Interest: The Kingsport Press, Tennessee Eastman Corporation Plant, Borden Mills, and others.

At 27.3 *m.*, by the eastern end of the bridge over the north fork of Holston is a stone monument (L) marking the SITE OF FORT ROBINSON and FORT PATRICK HENRY *(see KINGSPORT).* Right along the north fork 0.3 *m.* on a graveled road to the OLD ROTHERWOOD ELM, plainly visible from the bridge. This old tree has a trunk circumference of 22 feet, and a branch spread of approximately 150 feet. Dr. Thomas Walker mentioned it in the *Journal* kept on his exploration trip through the valley in 1748. A party of French travelers commented with awe on this magnificent elm and Daniel Boone is said to have camped under it on one of his journeys through this region into Kentucky. The spring near its roots supplied water to the estate; the ruins of the cotton mill are nearby.

ROTHERWOOD (L), 27.5 *m.*, is close to the junction of the north and south forks of the Holston River. The house, built in 1850 by Frederick A. Ross for his daughter Rowena, is a massive two-story brick structure with a balustraded hip roof, and is surrounded by a wide balustraded stone terrace; the entrance is protected by a tall two-story portico with balustraded flat roof forming a gallery at the third floor level. This house was constructed a few hundred yards below the site of the first Rotherwood house, built in 1818 and destroyed by fire in 1865. Ross called the grounds that were terraced and landscaped to the river's edge, his "falling gardens." He named his estate for the castle of Cedric the Saxon, and his daughter Rowena for the blond heroine of Scott's *Ivanhoe,* a popular book of the day. Frederick Ross and his large family extended lavish hospitality to some of the most noted men of the day. His carriage was Napoleonic in style, with gray silk upholstery and trappings of pure silver. Ross attempted silkworm culture. He also built a cotton mill on the bank of the North Fork River, but it was a failure and in 1852 he lost his entire estate.

At 51.2 *m.* is the junction with a dirt road.

Left on this road to EBBING AND FLOWING SPRING, 1 *m.* The basin, six or eight feet deep, fills slowly. At intervals of approximately two and a half hours it overflows. At full flow the spring produces about 500 gallons of clear water a minute. When the water reaches its lowest ebb, it suddenly begin to stir slightly; then within eight or ten minutes it is flowing strongly. For a few minutes it holds this heavy flow, and begins to ebb again. On a hill about 300 yards from the Ebbing and Flowing Spring is a burial ground where a monument over the grave of W. A. Lee (1885–1906) bears the familiar inscription:

Remember me, as you pass by
As you are now so once was I
As I am now you soon will be
Prepare for death and follow me.

Beneath the inscription someone has cut a comment into the stone:

To follow you, I am not content
Unless I know which way you went.

At 52.7 *m.* is the junction with State 70.

Right on State 70 to the junction with State 94, 6 *m.;* L. here 3 *m.* to the estate established in 1910 by the International Printing Pressmen's and Assistants' Union; it now represents an investment of more than $1,000,000. It is maintained by appropriation from the regular dues of the union.

The HOME FOR SUPERANNUATED PRINTING PRESSMEN is a large white structure of modified Georgian Colonial design with 240 rooms. Members of the organization, who are 60 and more years old and do not wish to take advantage of the union's pension system, may live here.

Because of printers' susceptibility to tuberculosis, the union also maintains a SANATORIUM here; this large two-story structure has wings projecting forward at an angle and many porches.

The TECHNICAL TRADE SCHOOL supplies instruction without charge to members of the union.

On the ground is a MEMORIAL CHAPEL of Gothic design dedicated to members of the union who were killed in the World War. It is built for the most part of reddish-gray sandstone quarried on the 3,000 acres of land belonging to the union. Among the recreational facilities is a large swimming pool *(open to public in summer).* There is a modern hotel on the grounds, owned by the union.

At 53.6 *m.* is the junction with paved Kepler Station Road.

Left on this road to the little AMIS STONE HOUSE, 3.5 *m.,* erected by Thomas Amis in 1780. The 18-inch walls of field stone formerly had rifleports instead of windows in the upper half-story. In later years Amis' daughter Mary said that she frequently wakened to hear Indians grinding their knives and tomahawks on her father's grindstone. The log kitchen was formerly some distance from the house.

ROGERSVILLE, 54.7 *m.* (1,170 alt., 1,590 pop.), is the seat of Hawkins County. Settlements were made in this area in 1772, three years after the first whites came to live in what is now Tennessee. About 1780 Thomas Amis erected a stone house three miles northeast of this place and in the following year he established a store, a blacksmith shop, a distillery, a gristmill, and a hotel. In 1785, when Joseph Rogers, an Irishman employed by Amis as storekeeper, married Mary Amis, Thomas' daughter, Amis gave the couple the tract of land upon which Rogersville was established in 1786. One of the last acts of the General Assembly of North Carolina that affected what is now Tennessee was the naming of Rogersville as seat of Hawkins County. The county was named for Benjamin Hawkins, U. S. Senator from North Carolina, who, with his colleague, Senator Johnson, executed the deed of cession that conveyed the Territory of Tennessee to the United States on Feb. 25, 1790.

The town is a trade center for an area in which tobacco-growing and livestock-raising are the principal activities. Walnuts are collected nearby in large quantities.

Three of the earliest newspapers in the State began publication here. The Knoxville *Gazette,* which first appeared on November 5, 1791, had been published here weekly by G. Roulstone and R. Fergueson for about a year before the plant was moved to Knoxville. The paper devoted much space to Thomas Paine's *Rights of Man.*

The second issue carried this news story which reveals the state of mind of the whites when meeting the natives whose lands they were expropriating:

"About the 10th inst. a company going through the wilderness to Cumberland was met on the road by a party of Indians. Upon first sight the men, being seven in number, rode off with the utmost precipitation and left the women, four in number, who were so terrified that they were unable to proceed."

A typical *Gazette* advertisement read:

"Mr. James Miller informs his friends and the public that he has just arrived from Philadelphia and Richmond and has brought with him a large and general assortment of goods among which are best rum, wine, brandy, and whisky, a few young, likely Virginia-born Negroes and will pay the highest prices for bear, otter, wild cat, and other kinds of fur."

The *Railroad Advocate,* one of the earliest publications in the United States devoted exclusively to railroad news, first appeared here on June 21, 1831. The *Calvinistic Magazine,* which had a five-year existence, began publication in 1827.

The HAWKINS COUNTY COURTHOUSE is a two-story brick building, with front gable protruding to form a huge pediment supported by four large columns. Surmounting the building is a clock tower that, in turn, is surmounted by an octagonal cupola. The deed for the land here, obtained from the Cherokee, is recorded in the registrar's office. It was signed by Oconastoto, the chief warrior and representative of the Cherokee Nation and Attakullakulla and Savanooka, otherwise Coronah, appointed by the warriors and other head men to represent the nation.

The former MCMINN ACADEMY is on the north side of Main St. at the western end of town; the institution was founded in 1806 and named for Joseph McMinn, who was elected Governor in 1815. The present building, a two-story structure with equally distant classic pilasters, has a circular cupola. After the academy was closed, the building for many years housed the city high school. It is now privately owned.

The ROGERSVILLE INN, constructed about 1782, has been converted into two dwellings at 107 and 108 Rogers St. This inn operated by Thomas Amis, was an important stop on the stage routes. The rooms on the second floor have been little changed since the early days. The former bar room is now a dining room.

At 64.8 *m.* is the junction with a dirt road.

Right on this road to GALBRAITH SPRINGS, 1 *m.* (1,400 alt.). It has been believed locally that the chalybeate water, commonly called "iron water," has medicinal properties. A comfortable hotel and numerous cottages are in a large grove of trees. The resort is a mile from the Holston River, which affords opportunities for excellent bass fishing, as well as for boating and swimming.

At 73.7 *m.* is the junction with an unimproved road.

Right on this road to MOORESBURG SPRINGS, 3 *m.* James Shields and Caleb Witt, who discovered a spring here highly impregnated with iron, deeded it and about two acres of adjacent land "to the sick and afflicted of the State of Tennessee." Any sick Tennessean could build a cabin on the premises and hold the title to it as long as he cared to remain.

At 76.2 *m.* is the junction with a graveled road, and a private lane.

1. Right on this road to TATE SPRINGS, 0.5 *m.* The water of the springs has been bottled and widely distributed. The Indians prized the water as a specific for eye diseases. Because members of several hostile tribes visited the springs it was agreed that sufferers and their friends should come unarmed. The first hotel at the springs was erected by C. O. Tate, for whom the springs were named. Soon after the War between the States, Capt. Thomas Tomlinson purchased the property and built a hotel *(open summers only),* which at one time was a fashionable summer resort.

2. Left here 0.3 *m.* to STONELEIGH *(open).* On a spot marked by a sundial in the back lawn a triple echo can be heard. A tall pine, sketched by Fred Yohn for an illustration in the novel, *The Trail of the Lonesome Pine,* by John Fox, Jr., can be seen from the back lawn. The tree, on the west side of a slight knoll, is surrounded by smaller pines.

BEAN STATION, 77.6 *m.* (1,367 alt., 270 pop.), is at the intersection of the Lee Highway and the Buffalo Trail, now US 25E *(see Tour 3);* these were formerly called the Baltimore International Turnpike and the Louisville-Charleston Highway. The Daniel Boone Trail and the Great Indian Warpath also intersected here.

The crossroads was named in honor of the Bean brothers, William Robert, George, and Jesse, who in 1787 erected a fort to protect settlers from the Indians. The home of the Beans was at one corner of the palisade, which also enclosed a spring. The site of this fort is near the Old Colonial Inn. William and Robert Bean were captains in the militia under John Sevier; George Bean, an artisan, in 1792 advertised in the Knoxville *Gazette* that he had opened a jewelry and gunsmith shop here.

The former WHITESIDE INN, now the Old Colonial, built in 1801 by Thomas Whiteside, was an important hostelry because of its position at the intersection of highways. Drovers moving their stock from Kentucky to the southern markets also stopped here. The first building was frame, but in 1813 Whiteside erected a three-story brick structure. Part of this building has been incorporated in the present hotel.

Plainly visible from the highway, near the hotel, are entrenchments thrown up around an encampment by Confederate troops under General Longstreet during the winters of 1863–64.

CLINCHDALE *(private),* 79.4 *m.,* a comfortable frame house built in 1850, stands in a grove of large cedars. This was the home of John K. Shields, U. S. Senator (1913–1925). His father, James Shields, built the house and practiced law in a small building on the grounds. Behind the house are slave huts, a smokehouse, and a carriage house.

At 81.8 *m.* is the junction with a graveled road.

HAWKINS COUNTY COURTHOUSE, ROGERSVILLE

Right at the end of this road to AVONDALE SPRINGS *(open May 1 to Oct. 1),* 0.7 *m.,* which have water impregnated with various minerals. A small hotel is operated here and there are nine cabins that can be rented.

RUTLEDGE, 86.4 *m.* (1,225 alt., 518 pop.), seat of Grainger County and a trade center, was named in honor of Gen. George Rutledge, the successor of John Sevier as brigadier general of the State militia. The county, named in honor of Mary Grainger, wife of Gov. William Blount, was established in 1796, before Tennessee was admitted to the Union. The permanent county seat was not selected until 1801.

Black-veined marble is quarried near the town.

Left from Rutledge on State 92 to a junction with a dirt road, 3 *m.;* R. here 4.3 *m.* to BUFFALO SPRINGS GAME FARM of 375 acres, in which is a quail hatchery with an incubator and brooder having a capacity of 100,000 birds. Fifty acres of the tract are used for the propagation of wild turkeys, California quail and chicken partridges. Near the eastern corner of the reservation is a large water mill that was built in 1796 and is still in operation.

Along this section of the route the Clinch Mountains (R) and the Great Smoky Mountains (L) are visible. Herds of shorthorn cattle graze on bluegrass pasture land. Large flocks of sheep wander over the hillsides. Poultry farms are numerous. Thousands of acres are planted in peaches and apples.

At 92.4 *m.* is the junction with the paved Jefferson City Road.

Left on this road to a junction with a dirt road 3 *m.;* L. here to BUFFALO SPRINGS GAME FARM, 5 *m.*

RED HOUSE TAVERN, 96.1 *m.* (R), erected in 1796 by Jeremiah Jarnagin, is in good condition today.

At 99 *m.* is the junction with a county road.

Right on this road to LEA SPRINGS, 1 *m.,* an old resort popular because of its iron and sulphur springs. The principal lodge *(open May 15–Sept. 15),* was built about 1830 as a farmhouse. The lake here is well stocked with bass.

At 101.5 *m.* is the junction with a graveled road.

Left on this road to INDIAN CAVE *(adm. $1),* 7 *m.* There are thousands of stalactites and stalagmites here, great masses of dripstone, flowstone, and translucent draperies. Notable among the formations are Vista of Old Pekin, the Pillars of Hercules, the Pass of Thermopylae, and the Grave of the Gnomes. Tradition is that the Cherokee used the cave as a hiding place after defeat at the hands of an Iroquois war party.

The JOHN SEVIER YARDS of the Southern Ry. (L), 111.7 *m.,* built in 1925, have 50 miles of track in a classification yard that can handle 3,500 cars. In normal times 60 trains move in and out of the terminal daily. Modern facilities for the rapid handling of freight are used, including a transfer station for less-than-carload freight moving through Knoxville, a refrigeration station for the storage of perishable goods, and pens in which livestock can be fed, watered, and rested. The yard is built in two units, each with a receiving and a make-up section. Freight trains are carried around Knoxville on a belt line.

At 116.2 *m.* is the junction with US 11-70 *(see Tour 12),* which unites with this route into Knoxville.

Knoxville, 121.3 *m.* (993 alt., 105,802 pop.) *(see KNOXVILLE).*

Points of Interest: University of Tennessee, Blount Mansion, Henley Street Bridge, Church Street Methodist Church, Chisholm Tavern, TVA Headquarters, and others.

Knoxville is at the junction with US 70 *(see Tour 12)*, with US 25W and State 35 *(see Tour 5)*, with State 33 *(see Tour 5A)*, and with US 11E *(see Tour 1)*.

Tour 1B

Bristol—Mountain City—Elizabethton—Johnson City.
US 421, State 67, and US 19E.
Bristol to Johnson City, 76.7 m.

Southern Ry. parallels route between Mountain City and Johnson City.
Graveled roadbed between Bristol and Mountain City; paved between Mountain City and Johnson City.

Southeast of Bristol the route traverses an area lying within the Unaka Division of the Cherokee National Forest and is overshadowed by the Holston and Iron Mountains. About 18 miles from Bristol the highway begins a winding ascent of Holston Mountain, and at several points there are views of hazy hills and green valleys. In season purple rhododendron blooms in profusion on jutting rocks high above the road and in deep gulches far below it. The Appalachian Trail, which extends from Maine to Georgia, crosses the highway along the summit of Holston Mountain.

Between the Holston and Iron Mountains lies Shady Valley—grassy, cool, and quiet. The highway winds from one elevation to another on Iron Mountain. From a gap, on clear days, Grandfather's Mountain and other lofty peaks in North Carolina are visible about 20 miles southeast.

This area was first visited by Daniel Boone, acquisitive frontiersman, whose relentless push into unexplored wilderness has filled pages of Tennessee and Kentucky history. Hotels, roads, creeks, church buildings, and schoolhouses along the route bear the name of this Indian fighter, bear hunter, and trail blazer.

US 421 branches east from US 11 *(see Tour 1)* at BRISTOL, 0 *m.* (1,689 alt., 12,500 pop.) *(see Tour 1)*.

BISHOP'S CAVE (L), 4 *m.*, which extends under approximately 100 acres of land, has a small opening half hidden by hardwood and cedar. Various passages and corridors open into its many chambers, one of which is more than 40 feet in height. Stalactites and stalagmites line a subterranean stream, which flows on the lowest level to its exit in the base of a nearby cliff.

Acres of rhododendrons cover the mountain slopes (R) at 17.1 *m.*

The highway crosses the Appalachian Trail at 19 *m.* Near the highway is a protected spring, 19.3 *m.* (R), near which the U. S. Forest Service maintains a campground.

US 421 crosses the trail of Daniel Boone at 27 *m.*

MOUNTAIN CITY, 34 *m.* (2,418 alt., 1,058 pop.), seat of Johnson County, is a trading center for farmers. Mountain people ride or walk in to this town from their distant cabins to buy supplies with "cash money," or to swap eggs, chickens, butter, and cream for tobacco, sugar, coffee, salmon, bananas, and other "store-boughten" delicacies.

In 1885 the town, first called Taylorsville for an early settler, was given a more picturesque name; it is in a high valley surrounded by mountain peaks. The coldest weather ever registered in Tennessee was recorded here on December 30, 1917, when the thermometer dropped to —30°.

Johnson County, created in 1836, was named for Cave Johnson, Postmaster General during the administration of President Polk. It was the first county in the State to establish a public school under the Tennessee law of 1854, which provided for the support of schools by taxation.

During the summer of 1770 James Robertson, later founder of Nashville, planted a crop on Roan Creek near its junction with the Watauga River. The Roan Creek Baptist Church, the first in the county, was organized in 1794.

Left from Mountain City on a graveled road, known locally as Gasoline Highway No. 2 to a LOG CABIN, 15 *m.,* erected in 1790 by Casper Cable, a Hessian soldier who came here after the Revolutionary War. The GRAVE OF CABLE is in a small plot behind the cabin.

Right from Mountain City on State 67; the route passes through valleys dotted with small villages and attractive homesteads.

At 48.9 *m.* on State 67 is a junction with a graveled road.

Left on this road is BUTLER, 3 *m.* (1,800 alt., 706 pop.), a trading center in a valley formed by a chain of undulating hills and ridges. It was named for Roderick R. Butler, who served several terms in the Tennessee Legislature.

In 1788 Bishop Asbury preached in the vicinity of Butler. He mentions in his journal how "we came on to a dismal place called Roan's Creek."

Right from Butler 12 *m.* on a dirt road to a very rough trail that tumbles down to TWISTING FALLS, known as the Big Falls of the Elk, or Greasy Falls, in the Elk River Gorge. The water of Elk River falls 200 feet in three big leaps. The gorge, which rises 100 feet or more above the stream, is broken by gullies and crevices that prevent close approach to the river. Blackberry bushes, devils walkingstick, smilax, and a few rhododendrons grow close in the brush along the falls.

At 60.5 *m.* is HAMPTON (540 alt., 450 pop.). On an unnamed street in the center of the village is the HARRIS HOME *(open).* This large square two-story brick structure was erected early in the nineteenth century by Elijah Simerly. During the War between the States, it was the home of Nathaniel E. Harris, a Confederate sympathizer. Ostracized by his Unionist neighbors after the war, Harris moved to Georgia where he became prominent in politics; he was the last Confederate veteran elected Governor of Georgia. After war bitterness died down, the Harris family returned here each summer. A great spring in the back yard discharges

7 million gallons of pure freestone water daily and is the source of the municipal water supply of Elizabethton.

Left from Hampton on US 19E, 7.2 *m.*, to a PICNIC GROUND surrounded by laurel, rhododendron, and hemlock.

At 14 *m.* on US 19E is ROAN MOUNTAIN STATION. Right 6.5 *m.* from Roan Mountain on a graveled road to a toll gate at the lower end of a steep, winding road leading 7.3 *m.* to the summit of ROAN MOUNTAIN, which has two peaks, Roan High Bluff (6,227 alt.) and Roan High Knob (6,313 alt.). The north slopes are heavily timbered with second-growth trees, varying from cove hardwood to spruce, according to the elevation. The summit, which is above timber line, offers a view of countless peaks and ridges. On Roan High Bluff is a rhododendron garden. Across the gap from Roan Mountain, SUNSET ROCK (6,133 alt.) rises. The natives cherish the tradition that through the gap between Sunset Rock and Roan the backwoodsmen passed on their way to King's Mountain to defeat Ferguson and his British troops.

One tale about the origin of the name Roan traces it to the Catawba, who were victorious in three bloody battles with invading Indian nations; afterwards, the story is, the flowers that grew on the mountain became crimson. The Catawba, believing these roan-colored flowers were nourished by the blood of the slain, looked upon it as a sign of favor from the Great Spirit.

Right from Hampton on US 19E; at 61.4 *m.* is the western end of DOE RIVER GORGE, which extends 17 miles in a southeasterly direction. The walls rise steeply 1,000 feet above the stream bed, and during rainy seasons many tiny streams cascade down them.

ELIZABETHTON, 66 *m.* (1,575 alt., 12,786 pop.), is the seat of Carter County, which was named for Landon Carter. The town was named for his wife. It is an industrial town in Happy Valley at the confluence of the Watauga and Dee Rivers, an area known as Watauga Old Fields, because there had once been a Cherokee village here. The North American Rayon and the American Bemberg Corporations have plants along the north side of the Glanzstoff Highway about one-half mile west of the courthouse; rayon yarn is manufactured here from Canadian fir pulp, and from cotton linters.

The larger part of the stock of both companies is owned by the German cartel, and the plants operate under their patents. Other industrial products of Elizabeth are twine, lumber, boxes, overalls, and flour.

The SOLDIER'S MONUMENT, on the lawn of the Carter County Courthouse, has an inscription honoring Mary Patton, who made the gunpowder fired by Tennesseans at the Battle of King's Mountain.

A boulder monument on the courthouse lawn marks the spot where the Watauga Association was organized in 1772 *(see HISTORY AND GOVERNMENT)*.

The ALFRED MOORE CARTER HOME, on Elk Avenue, was designed by an architect from New Jersey and constructed in 1819. It is a plain two-story structure from large double-hinge windows, having sixteen panes in the lower sash and twelve in the upper.

The exterior walls are covered with tongued-and-grooved, hand-hewn, hand-planed boards and there is a small two-story porch in front. The interior has carved mantels and trim.

Under a very large sycamore tree at 109 Riverside Drive, a short distance from the courthouse, is a marker that designates the spot where the first court west of the Allegheny Mountains was held in 1772; the sycamore under which it convened was then a young tree. Near the tree at the east end of Hattie St. is a covered bridge built before the War between the States.

Robert L. Taylor (1850–1912) and his brother Alfred A. Taylor (1848–1931), Governors of Tennessee, were born and reared in Elizabethton. The site of the old Taylor homestead is near the rayon plants. Bob Taylor was a lifelong Democrat, Alf an ardent Republican. As young men (1886) they campaigned together as opposing candidates for the Governorship of the State; Bob described their campaign:

"We had dreamed together in the same trundle-bed, and often kicked each other out . . . seen visions of pumpkin pie . . . pulled hair . . . But now the dreams of our manhood clashed . . . With flushed cheeks and throbbing hearts, we eagerly entered the field, his shield bearing the red rose, mine the white . . . The multitude . . . gathered . . . a white rose on every Democratic bosom and a red rose on every Republican breast . . . But when the clouds of war had cleared away . . . I thought of the first speech my mother ever taught me:

Man's a vapor full of woes;
Cuts a caper—down he goes.

Bob was elected and served three terms (1887–91; 1897–99). He was later a United States Senator. His brother was Governor from 1921 to 1923.

As a storyteller and lecturer, Bob Taylor belonged to the school of Mark Twain. His most popular story concerned Bert Lynch, the bully of the mountains, who stayed at an old gristmill and picked fights with anyone who came along. He had whipped Adam Wheezer the week a new minister came to the mountains. As Taylor told the story:

"Brother Billy Patterson preached from the door of the mill on the following Sunday. It was his first sermon in that neck of the woods, and he began his ministrations with a powerful discourse, hurling his anathemas against Satan and sin and every kind of wickedness. He denounced whisky; he branded the bully as a brute and a moral coward, and personated Bert. This was too much for the champion. He resolved to thrash Brother Patterson, and in a few days they met at the mill. Bert squared himself and said:

" 'Parson, you had your turn last Sunday; it's mine to-day. Pull off that broadcloth an' take your medicine! I'm a-gwine to suck the marrow out'n them old bones o' yourn.'

"The pious preacher pleaded for peace, but without avail. At last he said: 'Then if nothing but a fight will satisfy you, will you allow me to kneel down and say my prayer before we fight?'

" 'O, yes; that's all right, parson!' said Bert. 'But cut yer prayer short, for I'm a-gwine to give you a good, sound thrashin'.'

"The preacher knelt and thus began to pray:

" 'O Lord, Thou knowest that when I killed Bill Cummins and John

Brown and Jerry Smith and Levi Bottles, that I did it in self defense. Thou knowest, O Lord, that when I cut the heart out of young Slinger and strewed the ground with the brains of Paddy Miles, that it was forced upon me, and that I did it in great agony of soul. And now, O Lord, I am about to be forced to put in his coffin this poor, miserable wretch, who has attacked me here to-day. O Lord, have mercy upon his soul and take care of his helpless widow and orphans when he is gone.'

"And he arose, whetting his knife on his shoe sole, singing:

" 'Hark, from the tomb a doleful sound;
Mine ears attend the cry.'

"But when he looked around, Bert was gone. There was nothing in sight but a little cloud of dust far up the road, following in the wake of the vanishing champion."

Right 0.7 *m.* from Elizabethton on State 91, a paved road, to the entrance to THE MANSION, the Landon Carter Home *(entrance by permission)*, erected in the latter part of the 18th century. It is a two-story structure of the Georgian Colonial type, with large stone chimneys at each end, and wide hand-hewn clapboards over logs. The hall and some of the other rooms, including the master's bedroom, are beautifully paneled. Many heirlooms are in the house.

John Carter came to Carter's Valley from Virginia before the Revolution, and there opened a store. He traded with both Indians and white settlers; many of the immigrants moving west stopped at his store for supplies. The Tassel, a Cherokee chief, wrote to a Crown officer in North Carolina about Carter: "I received your Talk about Mr. Carter. . . . I will order my young people not to lay out their hunts (trade) with him any more as it greatly hurts our Traders (the French) that has been among us and supply'd us for many years." But Carter continued to trade; after the Indians burned his store, he moved to the Watauga settlement.

Here he quickly became a leader in the movement to form the Watauga Association, and when it had been formed, he was elected to one of the five judgeships, and was also made colonel of the militia. While holding this rank, he defended Fort Caswell with a small group of settlers. Carter, like King Carter in Virginia, prospered exceedingly.

Landon Carter was elected Secretary of State of the short-lived State of Franklin. Later he became involved in a land scandal with John Sevier, then Governor. The two men were never absolved of the accusation, but the illegality of many frontier land titles prevented an outburst of public sentiment. Everyone was speculating in land and grabbing what he could at the time.

At 3.3 *m.* on State 91, at the northern end of the bridge is the junction with a graveled road that runs along the river. Left on this road to another graveled road leading 0.9 *m.* to the DANIEL STOVER HOUSE (R). This two-story frame house, now abandoned, stands in the yard of another two-story frame house. Daniel Stover's wife, Mary Johnson Stover, was a daughter of Andrew Johnson, President of the United States after the death of Lincoln. Johnson visited this house frequently after his retirement, and died here in July, 1875.

The SYCAMORE SHOALS MONUMENT, 69.6 *m.,* is a three-sided shaft of river rocks, erected to mark the place where important events occurred. In 1772 settlers from Virginia and North Carolina built Fort Watauga here as a protection against the Indians; in the same year the Transylvania Treaty with the Cherokee was negotiated at the fort, the Cherokee agreeing to sell to the Transylvania Company the area between the Ohio River and the watershed of the Cumberland. Virginia and North Carolina had no interest in these early settlements, and neither State took any steps immediately to extend its jurisdiction. Realizing the necessity of having some form of government, the settlers met during the spring of 1772, at the site of Elizabethton, and entered into a compact forming the Watauga Association. This compact for self-government was the first made by white men west of the Allegheny Mountains. In 1776 a survey definitely determined that what is now northeast Tennessee lay within the boundaries of North Carolina. Accordingly, the association petitioned the General Assembly of North Carolina to include them within the jurisdiction of that Colony. The petition resulted in the creation of Washington County, which comprised all the area settled by whites in what is now Tennessee.

MILLIGAN COLLEGE (L), 72.5 *m.,* a coeducational and nonsectarian institution, was established in 1881 by Joseph Hopwood, a Kentuckian, on the site of Buffalo Institute, which had been opened before the War between the States. In April 1881, the name was changed to Milligan College to honor Robert Milligan of Kentucky University, a former teacher of Hopwood's.

JOHNSON CITY, 76.7 *m.* (1,717 alt., 25,080 pop.), *(see Tour 2)* is at junctions with US 11E *(see Tour 1)* and US 23 *(see Tour 2).*

Tour 2

(Appalachia, Va.)—Kingsport—Johnson City—Erwin—(Asheville, N. C.); US 23, US 23-19W.

Virginia Line to North Carolina Line, 53.8 m.

Paved throughout. Accommodations at short intervals along the route.

US 23 traverses the region of the Watauga Settlement, established in 1770, and passes the site of the first house erected by a permanent settler in the Tennessee region. It winds through the territory over which Daniel Boone made many scouting trips.

Between Kingsport and Johnson City the foothills of the nearby mountains are rugged and cultivated fields are scattered. South of Johnson City is a fertile valley at the foot of Unaka Mountain. The peaks of the Unaka and the Beauty Spot rim the horizon. Between Erwin and the North Carolina Line the route parallels the Nolichucky Gorge.

The route crosses the Virginia Line, 0 *m.,* 47 miles south of Appalachia.

At 2.7 *m.* is the junction with US 11W *(see Tour 1A).*

KINGSPORT, 3.2 *m.* (1,720 alt., 11,914 pop.) *(see KINGSPORT).*

Points of Interest: Kingsport Press, Pennsylvania-Dixie Cement Plant, Netherlands Inn, and others.

At 4.9 *m.* is the junction (L) with US 11W *(see Tour 1A).*

At 8.2 *m.* the Holston River is crossed; the river affords good bass fishing.

At 9 *m.* is the junction with a graveled road.

Left on this road 0.3 *m.* to the Great Falls Bluffs of the Holston River.

Rising from 450 to 500 feet above the river, the bluffs are covered with willow, alder, mock orange, sycamore and beech, with huge grapevines clinging to the branches. Above the Falls, which are really rapids, is a quiet pool.

At 12 *m.* is the junction with a graveled road. Close to the highway (L) here is a well-preserved pioneer cabin of two rooms separated by an open hallway (dog-trot).

At 14 *m.* is the junction with a graveled road.

Left on this road 1.6 *m.* is (R) a pioneer log cabin with run-way.

At 4.3 *m.* is McKELLAR AIRPORT, serving Bristol, Johnson City, and Kingsport. It was built by the WPA (1936) and is a regular station of the American Airlines. The 200-acre field has two runways, one of 4,000 feet, the other of 3,500.

At 18.7 *m.* is the junction with a graveled road.

1. Right on this road 0.3 *m.* to the junction with Gray Station Road. Right 0.4 *m.* on Gray Station Road to Reedy Creek. A trail leads (L) along the creek 0.4 *m.* to the SITE OF THE BOONE BEAR TREE. The old beech, known as the "Bar Tree," was blown down in 1916; it bore the knife-carved inscription: "D. Boon cilled A Bar On Tree in the yEAR 1760."

2. Left from US 23 on the graveled road, crossing Carroll Creek at 1.4 *m.,* where it empties into Boone Creek. Between the mouth of Carroll Creek and the Watauga, on the right bank of Boone Creek is the FIRST TENNESSEE GRIST MILL (about 1772).

A trail leads 200 yards up Boone Creek to a marker indicating the SITE OF WILLIAM BEAN'S CABIN, on the right bank. A ruined chimney is all that remains of the log cabins built in 1769 by the first settler in the territory.

At 21.1 *m.* is the junction with US 11E-19W *(see Tour 1),* which unites for 3.5 miles with US 23. In the fork of this junction is the MASSENGILL MEMORIAL MONUMENT *(see Tour 1).*

JOHNSON CITY, 24.4 *m.* (1,717 alt., 25,080 pop.), a trade center and shipping point for a lumbering and farming area, partly dependent for employment on railroad division shops, began to grow rapidly after the establishment of the rayon plants in Elizabethton to the east. Large numbers of people who came to work in the Elizabethton plants could not find quarters in the boom city and decided to live here and commute. New stores were opened to accommodate the increased population and various new businesses came into existence—box factories, tanneries, lumber yards and lumber mills. The result is that the center of town, which is cut by the tracks of the three railroads converging here, has a brisk, modern appearance. The homes are on higher ground, many on streets shaded by hardwoods.

The downtown streets are particularly lively on Saturday when everybody for miles around comes in to shop and to see a movie; the moun-

COUNTRY SAWMILL

taineers are easily identified by the dark tan of their lean faces and by the blue jeans they usually wear.

The first settler in the vicinity was David Jobe, who came to the Watauga about 1777, but settlement of the region progressed slowly until 1854, when Henry Johnson, for whom the city was later named, arrived from North Carolina, and opened a store in the settlement then known as Blue Plum. After the East Tennessee and Virginia Railroad, now part of the Southern, built a water tank here in 1858, Johnson saw an opportunity to sell his land at a profit; and at his own expense, he constructed a depot for the railroad. Trains were soon scheduled for a stop at Johnson's Tank, or Johnson's Depot.

During the War between the States the town, then called Haynesville in honor of Landon C. Haynes, Confederate States Senator from Tennessee, saw much military activity but the wartime boom was soon over. After the close of the war Henry Johnson renewed his activities for the development of a city but for some years he was postmaster, depot agent, merchant, hotel keeper, and magistrate. In 1869 a charter of incorporation was granted to Johnson City, and Johnson was elected the first mayor. In 1879 the town charter was revoked, and the community, whose population was then estimated at about 400, became merely a district of Washington County. On March 25, 1885, a new charter was granted and the town took a fresh lease on life.

The SITE OF THE CONFEDERATE TRAINING GROUND was near Lamont and Tennessee Sts. It was also a camp ground of Confederate troops on their way from the deep South to Virginia.

The EAST TENNESSEE STATE TEACHERS' COLLEGE, at the western end of W. Maple St., has a 140-acre campus, 90 acres of which are covered with woods and a farm. The eight buildings of modified Georgian design are constructed of red brick with a limestone trim. The institution, chartered in 1909 and opened in 1911, has since 1927 been a standard four-year college offering the degree of B.S. in education.

The entrance to the U. S. SOLDIER'S HOME *(open 9-5 daily; for guide service apply Administration Bldg.),* is on Lamont St. W. of Harrison Ave. The home is a city within a city, has its own post office, called Mountain Home, its own fire and police departments, waterworks, and telephone system. There are 448 acres of landscaped grounds with many maple and dogwood trees. The 57 buildings, designed by J. H. Freelander of New York, are constructed of brick and stone in the modified Italian Renaissance style.

The institution accommodates 3,500 patients and has an average of 400 hospital cases and 2,000 permanently disabled residents. Handicraft training is given to the residents, who sell their products to visitors. All the paper poppies sold annually by the Veterans of Foreign Wars are made here.

The Soldier's Home was established in 1903 through the efforts of former Congressman Walter Brownlow for the care of aged Union soldiers. After the World War it was used for tubercular ex-service men, and was later converted to its present use.

Johnson City is at the junctions with State 67 *(see Tour 1B)* and with US 11E *(see Tour 1)*.

Right from Johnson City on Knob Creek Road 2 *m.* to a boulder from the Watauga River marking the SITE OF THE NELSON HOUSE where in May 1788, the indefatigable Bishop Asbury preached his first sermon in what is now Tennessee, and organized the first Methodist congregation west of the Alleghanies.

South of Johnson City at 26.8 *m.* on US 23-19W is a junction with a graveled road.

Right on this road to the HAYNES HOUSE, also known as the Tipton House, 0.5 *m.,* built of logs about 1770, and later weatherboarded; it stands today much as it was in 1795. John Tipton, the builder, was a colonel of the Washington County militia and a bitter personal and political foe of John Sevier. He joined with the group that refused to recognize the authority of the State of Franklin. Shortly after Sevier was elected Governor of the State of Franklin, he and Tipton met in Jonesboro, and exchanged blows for some time "with great violence and in a convulsion of rage." They were separated before either could claim a victory. By order of a court sitting under the jurisdiction of North Carolina in the winter of 1788, Sheriff John Pugh of Jonesboro took a number of Governor Sevier's slaves because of non-payment of North Carolina taxes, and sent them from Sevier's Mount Pleasant farm here. Sevier gathered about 150 men and marched to this house where 45 men were guarding the slaves. Sevier gave them 30 minutes to surrender but Tipton and the sheriff refused, and sent for aid. Capt. Peter Parkinson answered the call with a company. Sevier's band opened fire and drove them back. Sevier then laid siege to the house. There was firing on both sides; one of Sevier's men and two on the other, including Sheriff Pugh, were killed. Reinforcements arrived and Sevier's men were driven back to Jonesboro in a blinding snowstorm.

Landon Carter Haynes, who became a Senator in the Congress of the Confederate States of America, bought this property from the grandchildren of Tipton.

At 33.8 *m.* is UNICOI (1,775 alt., 982 pop.).

1. Right from Unicoi to PINNACLE MOUNTAIN, 2.5 *m.* From an observation tower on the summit are views of the Unaka Range and the valleys around Erwin.

2. Left from Unicoi on a delightful loop route, most of which falls within the Cherokee National Forest. This loop leads along Limestone Cove Road to Red Fork Creek. Right here on the Red Fork Creek Road which ascends to the DAVIS SPRINGS PICNIC GROUNDS, 5.1 *m.*

At 8.6 *m.* is the junction with two mountain roads.

Right here along Red Fork Creek on the flank of UNAKA MOUNTAIN, part of the Unaka Range. At 15.8 *m.* is VIEW POINT (5,259 alt.). The mountains were named Unaka (Cherokee, *white*), because of the white haze that clouds the summits. Reindeer moss, painted trillium, Clintonia, wingberries, partridge berries, huckleberries, and blueberries grow profusely on the slopes.

At 18.8 *m.* is the northern end of BEAUTY SPOT, which extends for a mile along the State Line. A 200-yard trail leads to the top of the ridge, the Tennessee-North Carolina Line. Black Mountain is to the south, Roan Mountain to the east, Stone and Buffalo Mountains to the north, and the Bald Mountains to the west. The entire area is carpeted with a thick turf; violets, bluets, wild strawberry, golden ragwort, and mayapples give color in the spring. Hawthorne, dogwood, and other shrubs grow in thick patches. Large maples and beeches of luxurious growth contrast with the gray snags of dead chestnuts. At 22.4 *m.* is a cool mountain spring (L), surrounded by azalea. At 23.8 *m.* is ROCK CREEK CAMP (R), a camping and picnic area.

At 27 *m.* the loop returns to US 23-19W.

At 36 *m.* (R) is a marker calling attention to the SITE OF THE HOUSE OF WIDOW BROWN, which stood half a mile northwest of this spot. On October 10, 1788, John Sevier was arrested by John Tipton in this house. Sevier, then Governor of the State of Franklin, had been charged with treason against the State of North Carolina, and an order for his arrest had remained unserved in the hands of his friend, Judge Campbell at Jonesboro. When Sevier visited Jonesboro to consult military officers concerning a second campaign against the Chickamauga, Colonel Tipton seized the order and made the arrest. With this arrest the independent State came to an end.

A FEDERAL FISH HATCHERY (R), 36.3 *m.*, covers 72 acres and has 30 concrete pools fed by a large spring whose temperature does not vary more than one degree throughout the year. The annual production of the hatchery is 750,000 fry of several varieties.

At 37.9 *m.* is the junction with a graveled road.

ERWIN, 39 *m.* (1,680 alt., 3,623 pop.), seat of Unicoi County, is on the 277-mile Clinchfield R.R., that runs between Elkhorn City, Ky., and Spartanburg, S. C., and cuts directly across four high watersheds. The first name of the town was Vanderbilt, but it was renamed for Dr. J. N. Ervin, a physician of the community who gave one-half the town lots to

MOUNTAIN FARMER

the county so that the town would be made the county seat. Through error the spelling was changed by the U. S. Post Office Department.

The SOUTHERN POTTERIES PLANT *(open to visitors 8-6 weekdays)* manufactures painted and underglazed pottery, producing about 30,000 pieces a day. The clay is imported from six southern states. An affiliated plant manufactures novelties from feldspar.

A CONFEDERATE MONUMENT is at Ohio Ave. and Unaka Way (US 23) south of the courthouse.

The territory surrounding Erwin is rugged, but there are farms in the coves and valleys along the Nolichucky River. Between Erwin and the North Carolina Line, the route is within the boundaries of the Cherokee National Forest.

A marker at 40 *m.* calls attention to the old GREASY COVE RACE TRACK nearby, scene of a race between one of Andrew Jackson's horses and one owned by Col. Robert Love of Jonesboro. When in 1788 Jackson came from the Carolinas to Jonesboro, he brought a fine horse with him and soon challenged Colonel Love to a race. Love's horse had defeated the fastest mounts in Virginia and hundreds of people from Tennessee and Virginia gathered here to see him win again. Jackson's jockey became ill shortly before the race and Jackson decided to ride in his place. When he was defeated, Jackson lost his short temper and quarreled with Love, who in return called Jackson "a long, gangling, sorrel-topped soap stick." Friends intervened and prevented a fight.

At 46 *m.* is the junction with a graveled road.

Left on this road to UNAKA SPRINGS, 0.5 *m.*, a resort that became popular because of its iron and sulphur water. Here is the northern end of NOLICHUCKY GORGE, through which the Nolichucky River runs for about 10 miles. The gorge is about 250 feet wide and barely affords room for the Clinchfield R.R. tracks beside the river.

At 53.8 *m.* US 23-19W crosses the North Carolina Line 58 miles north of Asheville, N. C.

Tour 3

(Middlesboro, Ky.)—Cumberland Gap—Tazewell—Morristown—Junction US 70; US 25E.

Kentucky Line to Junction US 70, 64.9 m.

Southern Ry. roughly parallels route between Cumberland Gap and Tazewell and between Morristown and Newport.

Paved roadbed throughout. Usual small-town accommodations.

US 25E follows the old Wilderness Road between Cumberland Gap and Bean Station. In 1775, after Richard Henderson of North Carolina had organized the Transylvania Land Company, Daniel Boone was commissioned to blaze this trail across the mountains for the benefit of immigrants. This route became the main artery of settlement for much of the Territory South of the Ohio River.

Because of Indian troubles to the north and south, it was the safest route across the mountain, and in time was used by settlers from New England, New York, and Pennsylvania, as well as those from South Carolina and Georgia. From the outbreak of the Revolution to the end of the 18th century, immigrants and the pack trains of traders crowded it. Though relatively free from marauding Indians, the Wilderness Road was slashed by ravines and soft-banked creeks and was often obstructed by landslides and freshets. Many parties had to abandon their wagons at such places as Powell's Valley and continue westward on ox back or on foot. So difficult was the passage that hundreds of families, worn out and discouraged, abandoned their plans for moving farther west and settled in the most desirable cove they could find. From these are descended the mountain clans.

Between Cumberland Gap and Bean Station, US 25E cuts across ridges, striking examples of the abrupt formations of East Tennessee. Many of the hills and ridges have been cut over and are now covered with scrub timber. The fertile, sheltered valleys and coves are inhabited by farmers, some of whom specialize in livestock and poultry raising.

US 25E crosses the Kentucky-Virginia Line 0 *m.,* 3 miles southeast of Middlesboro, Ky., through CUMBERLAND GAP (1,304 alt.), and cuts across a tiny corner of Virginia.

The natural passage through the mountains, long used by the early pioneers as the chief gateway to the west, was called Cumberland Gap by Dr. Thomas Walker when he discovered it in 1750.

A sign at 0.4 *m.* indicates a short path (L) leading to CUDJO'S CAVE *(adm. 50¢ plus tax; special rates to parties of 20 or more; 45 to 75 min. for tour),* which has more than 30 miles of explored passageways and numerous unmapped passages. Water from subterranean streams in the web of caverns is piped to the town of Cumberland Gap. James Townsend Trowbridge used this cave as the locale of his novel *Cudjo's Cave* (1864).

At 0.6 *m.* is the junction with US 58.

Left 1.5 *m.* on US 58 to the junction with the privately maintained Skyline Highway *(50¢ per person in cars; pedestrians free)*; L. 1 *m.* on this road to PINNACLE MOUNTAIN (2,860 alt.), which is divided by the Virginia-Kentucky Line. From its summit, earthworks thrown up around Cumberland Gap during the War between the States are visible, standing out conspicuously. Along the highway are rock formations, called the TURTLE'S BEAK, the ELEPHANT'S HEAD, and the CHIMNEY ROCK, on the crest of the Pinnacle.

At 0.8 *m.* US 25E crosses the Tennessee Line.

CUMBERLAND GAP, 1.1 *m.* (1,304 alt., 369 pop.), named for the nearby pass, is in that corner of East Tennessee first explored by white men.

This place, merely a hamlet at the time, was the scene of much activity during the War between the States because the gap for which it is named was of strategic importance. Since it was the logical route for a Union invasion of East Tennessee, it was fortified by the Confederates under Gen. Felix K. Zollicoffer in May, 1861; but in June of that year Gen. George Morgan and two Union brigades drove the Confederates away. In September a force of Confederates under General Stephenson met Morgan's column in Tennessee and forced them back to the gap. In the meantime, Confederate forces under Gen. E. Kirby-Smith had joined Stephenson and built strong fortifications about four miles from Pinnacle Mountain. There Morgan had mounted a huge cannon, Long Tom, to sweep the Tennessee approach to the gap. Many of his supplies were stored in caves under the Pinnacle, among them Cudjo's Cave. When Morgan learned that the Confederates were maneuvering to turn his flank, he issued orders for a retreat. The Union soldiers gathered everything they could carry and stacked the rest across the gap in an enormous pile to which they set fire. The subsequent explosion and fire checked the Confederate advance with a flame wall that also effectively covered the Union retreat.

In 1863 Union troops under General Burnside met Stephenson in Tennessee and forced him to retreat to the pass, where they surrounded the Confederates and forced them to surrender. Until the end of the war the gap and the town were in Union hands.

It is not known when or by whom the first settlement was made on this site, but it was probably soon after the American Revolution, when thousands of immigrants streamed westward over the Boone trail.

About 300 yards north of the business center is the end of the railroad tunnel, cut through solid rock for a distance of nearly a mile.

The HOLBROOK COLLECTION, at Pinnacle Cafe, contains old postage stamps and also relics of the War between the States, including guns, swords, ammunition, flags, and albums with pictures of Army officers.

HARROGATE, 2.9 *m.* (1,362 alt., 400 pop.), formerly a summer resort, was named for Harrogate, England, by Lord and Lady Pauncefort. After its failure as a resort in 1888, an English promoter, Col. A. A. Arthur, began mining coal here and because of the mines, the railroad from Knoxville to Middlesboro was built in 1889.

Harrogate University, now LINCOLN MEMORIAL UNIVERSITY, was founded in 1897 as a memorial to Abraham Lincoln. Chartered as a university, it functioned as such for a time and then developed into a liberal arts college. The buildings form a quadrangle. There is a shop for trades training and a building for the display of arts and crafts products made by students of the school. The institution has an endowment of about $2,000,000 and 2,000 acres of forest land.

On the campus is a COLLECTION OF ENGLISH PLANTS, brought here by English settlers about 1890. In the DUKE HALL OF CITIZENSHIP *(open weekdays 8-5),* are a number of interesting documents, including a LINCOLN COLLECTION. In the CARNEGIE LIBRARY *(open weekdays 8 a.m. to 10 p.m.; Sundays 2:30-5)* is an INDIAN RELIC MUSEUM and a large collection of historic letters and documents.

At 4.2 *m.* is the junction with State 63.

Right on State 63 to a junction with side lane, 20.6 *m.;* R. here 1 *m.* to the Ellison Farm, from which a trail leads to McLEAN ROCK (2,960 alt.), an overhanging ledge approximately 2,000 feet above the valley. This point offers farspreading views, mountain ridge after mountain ridge to the horizon. At 22.9 *m.* on State 63 is the junction with a narrow road. L. here 0.2 *m.* to the TVA DOAK CREEK REARING POOLS. Picnicking facilities have been provided around the pools. At 32 *m.* on State 63 is the junction with US 25W *(see Tour 5)* at LA FOLLETTE *(see Tour 5).*

There is a view of Powell River (R) several hundred feet below the highway at 5.9 *m.* Farther south US 25E crosses Powell River, south of which is a barren plain with poor, gravelly soil.

TAZEWELL, 13.3 *m.* (1,454 alt., 989 pop.), seat of Claiborne County, is a typical mountain town that has changed little in several decades. It was named for Henry Tazewell, who served in the United States Senate. The town was settled about 1801. People in this county possessed few slaves and when the vote was taken on secession 250 were for it and 1,242 against.

GREYSTONE INN, now a tourist home, is a large stone structure erected in 1810 by William Graham, an Irish immigrant who opened the first store here.

South of Tazewell the country rises in massive ridges; except in the Clinch Valley, the soil is unproductive.

OLD SPRINGDALE CHURCH, 21.1 *m.,* was erected by Baptists soon after they had organized a congregation in 1796.

The highway now crosses Clinch River which, with Powell River, forms Norris Lake *(see Tour 5A).*

The highway ascends the western slope of Clinch Mountain. Rough, stony soil covers the southern slopes and the crest.

MINERAL SPRINGS HOTEL, 34.1 *m.,* is a summer resort.

BEAN STATION, 34.7 *m.* (1,367 alt., 260 pop.) *(see Tour 1A),* is at the junction with US 11W *(see Tour 1A).*

The BAPTIST CEMETERY, 40.5 *m.,* contains a marble slab engraved, "J. Bean killed by Indians, 1779."

US 25E now crosses Holston River; at the southern end of the bridge is the MORRISTOWN MUNICIPAL POWER PLANT *(free picnic grounds, tables, and a spring).* To the south are many fine orchards.

At 44.1 *m.* is a junction with the Bright Ferry Rd. (dirt).

Left on this road to the SITE OF A PAPER MILL, 2 *m.,* built in 1825 on the bank of Holston River for the manufacture of writing, printing, and wrapping paper. It ceased operation in 1861. The mill had two overshot water wheels, 36 feet in diameter. Five hundred horses and mules were used to transport rags for paper making from Baltimore and Cincinnati. Parson Weems' *Life of George Washington,* which first told the cherry-tree story, was printed for Mathew Carey on paper made at this mill, and the book was bound here. There were 120 little houses for workers about the mill.

MORRISTOWN, 46.1 *m.* (1,350 alt., 7,300 pop.) *(see Tour 1)* is at the junction with US 11E *(see Tour 1).*

South of Morristown is the fertile New Market Valley. The long ridge beyond it is cut by deep coves and pockets; occasional gaps allow passage. A commercial company of Kingsport, which owns a large part of this mountain, is conserving the timber by scientific methods.

South of Morristown is one of the few straight stretches on US 25E. The English Mountain is R., the Unaka range ahead. In this valley US 25E crosses the French Broad River. A canning plant at Newport has stimulated the development of truck farming in the fertile valley.

At 64.9 *m.* is the junction with US 70 *(see Tour 12),* 1.5 miles west of Newport.

Tour 4

Junction with State 33—Tallassee—Chilhowee—(Topton, N. C.); US 129.

Junction with State 33 to North Carolina Line, 32.2 m.

Hard-surfaced roadbed except 3 m. near State Line.
Continuous hairpin curves and grades, but route is safe; descend hills in gear.
Limited accommodations.

This route crosses several ranges of the Great Smoky Mountains and skirts the border of the Cherokee National Forest. This mountain region was the domain of the Cherokee, who lived in groups of villages; those in East Tennessee were called the Overhill towns because they were over the mountains from the Carolina settlements. Chota, the capital, Settico, Hiwassee, and Great Tellico were the largest.

The first white men known to have entered the Overhill country were James Needham and Gabriel Arthur, who came into the region from Virginia in 1673 to trade with the Cherokee. Eleazer Wiggan, whom the Indians called The Old Rabbit, had a trading post among the Overhills in 1711. By the second quarter of the eighteenth century nearly every Cherokee village, even those remote from the main trails, was trading with the English. Frenchmen, too, entered the Overhill towns, coming up from Mobile in search of furs, but the bulk of the Cherokee trade went to the Carolina and Virginia traders. Some of the well-to-do whites brought their Negro servants with them into this country. Abram, a Negro who belonged to Samuel Benn, a trader among the Overhills, won his freedom during the Cherokee War by carrying dispatches through hostile Indian country.

In Colonial days travelers crossing the mountains usually followed the Great Indian Trading Path, whose chief feeder came from Charleston, S. C. This deep-trodden route began at Keowee (near the present Pendleton, S. C.), crossed northeastern Georgia to what is now Murphy, N. C., thence passed over the mountain ridges between North Carolina and Tennessee in a northerly direction to what is now Tellico Plains and the Overhill villages.

During the struggle between the French and the English for possession of the region west of the Appalachians, the Cherokee played an important part. The Overhill towns were in strategic positions along the Little Tennessee River. Their warriors could guard the valley against the French or swoop down the mountain passes upon the English back settlements. So the liaison officers of both white nations labored to secure Cherokee allegiance. Council fires burned often in every Cherokee town house; Creek runners, painted red, came up from the French fort in Alabama to urge the Cherokee to take the war trail against the British, while haughty Chickasaw, bitter enemies of the French, arrived to counsel an alliance with the English.

At the request of the Cherokee and to protect their western frontiers, the Royal governments of Virginia and South Carolina each built a fort in the Overhill country. The Virginia fort, built first, in 1756, on the north bank of the Little Tennessee about a mile from Chota, the capital of the Cherokee Nation, was never garrisoned. The following year South Carolina completed Fort Loudoun on the opposite side of the river; it was the first fort in Tennessee occupied by British Colonial troops. Trouble later arose between the English and the Cherokee and in 1760 Fort Loudoun was taken by the tribesmen, and destroyed *(see Tour 5A)*.

In 1761 peace was made and Ensign Henry Timberlake, a young British officer, traveled through the Overhill towns on a goodwill mission at the request of the Cherokee leaders. Afterwards he conducted a delegation of chiefs on a ceremonial visit to England, and the new-made friendship was greatly strengthened.

At 0 *m.* is the junction with State 33 *(see Tour 5A)*, 6 miles south of Maryville.

WILLIAMS SPRINGS, 10.5 *m.*, only a store and a filling station, is across the Little Tennessee River and one mile north of the site of Chota (Echota), capital of the Cherokee Nation before the Revolution. Chota, called the Metropolis, was not only the chief town of the Cherokee, but was also a town of refuge—a white or peace village—so called because blood could not be shed within its boundaries. A person pursued by enemies could find safety there. Cultivated fields now cover the site of the village.

TALLASSEE, 14 *m.* (863 alt., 210 pop.), is a hamlet on the north bank of the Little Tennessee.

CHILHOWEE, 18 *m.* (1,851 alt., 250 pop.), has a post office and a gas station.

The Chilhowee Mountains are about three miles north toward the valley of Little Pigeon River.

At 20.8 *m.* is the western boundary of the Great Smoky Mountains National Park.

At 21.7 *m.* is the junction with a winding graveled road.

Right on this road which runs steeply down hill to CALDERWOOD (1,651 alt., 188 pop.), 0.7 *m.*, on the edge of the river gorge; the town is owned by the Aluminum Company of America. Along the unpaved main street are the homes of the company employees. At the end of this street is a powerhouse and CALDERWOOD DAM, which is 897 feet wide and 205 feet high.

At 23.4 *m.* the route passes along high above the Little Tennessee and offers a view of Calderwood Dam and the nine-mile lake behind it in the steep narrow valley. Many peaks of the Smokies are visible here.

The Aluminum Company of America *(see Tour 5A)* has constructed three large dams in this area *(free guide service at the dam)*. The Tapoco Dam just across the North Carolina Line, six miles from Calderwood, and on the Tuskasegee River, a tributary of the Little Tennessee, is 770 ft. wide and 205 ft. high.

At 32.2 *m.* US 129 crosses the North Carolina Line 40 miles northwest of Topton, N. C.

Tour 5

(Williamsburg, Ky.)—Jellico—La Follette—Clinton—Knoxville—Sevierville—(Asheville, N. C.); US 25W, State 35, State 71.
Kentucky Line to North Carolina Line, 122 m.

Louisville & Nashville R.R. and the Southern Ry. parallel route between Jellico and Knoxville.
Greyhound buses operate between Jellico and Knoxville; Tennessee Coach Co. and the Great Smoky Mountain Transit Co. between Knoxville and Sevierville, Gatlinburg, and points in North Carolina.
Paved roadbed throughout. Hotels in towns.

US 25W passes through an area in which there are rich deposits of coal. The northern part runs through the rugged Cumberland Mountains and the southern part through the Great Smokies. There are many beautiful views of the Tennessee Valley and of the Great Smoky Mountains.

Section a. KENTUCKY STATE LINE *to* KNOXVILLE; *67 m.* US 25W

US 25W crosses the Kentucky Line, 0 *m.,* 16 miles south of Williamsburg, Ky.

JELLICO, 0.3 *m.* (1,025 alt., 1,530 pop.), a border town in the foothills of the Cumberlands, lies at the northern end of a 24-mile ravine that US 25W and the Louisville & Nashville R.R. follow southward. First known as Smithburg, because the name Smith predominated among the settlers, the place was to have been incorporated under the name Jerrico, but through a typographical error in the charter it became Jellico.

Early westbound settlers usually camped here before resuming their journey along the Wilderness Road. Some, tired of traveling and others who felt it unnecessary to go farther to find fertile land, decided to remain here. As early as 1795 there was a small settlement.

In the early days a tavern was usually the first building to appear in such a place. The story is told of how a tavern keeper of the early 1800's, whose house was on the State Line, avoided State officers by running back and forth across the line as the need arose.

In 1880 railroads were built to exploit the coal deposits in the area

A HANDICRAFT SHOP

and the population increased rapidly. Jellico bituminous burns slowly and has a low ash content. Jellico is still a mining town though the nearby deposits have been exhausted. The UNITED STATES MINE RESCUE STATION here conducts a school for miners that teaches first aid in mine rescue work. Teams from the district have annual competitions.

The highway passes the house in which Grace Moore, opera singer and movie actress, once lived. The First Baptist Church, where she sang in the choir, is at the southwest corner of South Main and Church Sts.

Homer A. Rodeheaver, when a youth, worked in his father's mill here. From 1909 to 1931 he was well known as a singer and trombonist in the Billy Sunday revivals.

Right from Jellico on old State 9, Elk Valley Road, to the junction with a graveled road, 1.3 *m.;* R. here 0.2 *m.* to the FALLS BRANCH MINE, 0.2 *m.,* at WOOLRIDGE. It has been in operation since 1882.

South of Jellico US 25W runs through the gorge between heavily timbered hills. From many side gulches swift foaming streams flow over precipices and join the stream that has cut the gorge.

Few dwellings are visible from the highway in this region, though "swing-foot" bridges over the creeks indicate that there are inhabitants. Huge, smutty tipples, in which the mine-run coal is graded, screened, and loaded into cars, are at fairly short intervals; above them are the monitors that dump coal pulled by trams from the pit head.

At 1.8 *m.* is the junction with a narrow, rough dirt road.

Right on this road to LOOK-OFF ROCK (3,500 alt.), 2 *m.* The peak, directly above the highway, can be reached only on foot or on horseback. Seldom visited, this peak offers an excellent view of Jellico, the Norris Dam area, and the Cumberland Mountains in Tennessee and Kentucky.

A SWIMMING BEACH is (L) at 4 *m.*

MORLEY, 8.3 *m.,* surrounds a modern, electrically-operated mine.

Rows of abandoned coke ovens are (R) at 23.6 *m.* In the same cove are Red Row and Green Row, two small mining communities.

At about 24.2 *m.* is the junction with a trail.

Left on this trail up along Big Creek Gap to MORGAN HEIGHTS, 0.5 *m.,* where are the ruins of entrenchments and cannon emplacements made by Confederate troops under Gen. John H. Morgan. There were several skirmishes here during the period when the Confederates were attempting to check advancing Union troops at Cumberland Gap.

LA FOLLETTE, 24.7 *m.* (1,060 alt., 2,637 pop.), is in Powell Valley at the eastern base of the Cumberland Mountains. Part of the town wanders up the mountain side. It was first known as Big Creek Gap, but was renamed for Henry M. La Follette, an Indianan, who was instrumental in having the town incorporated in 1897, when he organized the La Follette Coal, Iron, and Railway Co., and began exploiting coal and iron resources here on a large scale. His company failed but others took over his properties and operated them successfully. After the railroad from Jasper to La Follette had been completed in 1897, La Follette became an important center of coking.

The town grew steadily until 1920 when overproduction, brought on by the World War demand, caused a sharp decline that continued until the TVA established field offices here. The backwaters of the Norris Lake reach to within one mile of the city limits.

Members of the Amalgamated Clothing Workers were locked out of the Washington Shirt Company factory here on May 1, 1937. The dispute between the owners of the factory and the workers continued for six months and was settled by the National Labor Relations Board which ordered reinstatement of the dismissed workers. During the time the plant was closed, the union, co-operating with the Highlander Folk School *(see Tour 16)*, opened a school here for the idle workers. It was successful, and classes are still being held although the students have returned to work.

North and west of La Follette are the Cumberland Mountains. Eastward is the first of the chain of hills that wall Norris Lake.

At 25.7 *m.* is the junction with Demory Road.

Left on this paved road to the junction with another dirt road at 8 *m.* by a brick schoolhouse; L. 2 *m.* on this road to Shanghai Hollow in SHANGHAI BRANCH RECREATION AREA *(boating, fishing)*. The TVA Forestry Division maintains wharves here from which boating trips are made to Norris Dam and Park and Big Ridge Park. A few hundred yards north of the park entrance is a SALTPETER CAVE, in which saltpeter was mined during the War between the States. Some of the equipment, rotted and damp-slimed, remains. In Saltpeter Cave, at the base of the Longmire Ridge, are many kinds of mineral deposits, some still in the process of formation.

JACKSBORO, 29.2 *m.* (1,200 alt., 830 pop.), seat of Campbell County, was named for Capt. James W. Jack, a local hero. Settled by 1795, Campbell County was created through an act of the General Assembly, on September 11, 1806. Iron forges were in operation before the county was incorporated. Among these was a bloomery, or furnace for making malleable iron. Some of the bar-iron was hauled by oxcart to Kentucky and exchanged for Goose Creek salt.

At 32.6 *m.* is the junction with a dirt road.

Right on this road to CARYVILLE, 0.5 *m.*, a shipping point for coal. Between the highway and the town are two lakes formed by the backwaters of Norris Lake.

The bluffs (R) steadily become lower as the route nears Knoxville and the East Tennessee Valley.

VASPER, 34.3 *m.* (1,203 alt., 716 pop.) is a shipping point for coal.

At 38.2 *m.* is the junction (L) with Norris Freeway *(see Tour 5A)*, which crosses Norris Dam.

COAL CREEK, 38.9 *m.* (1,048 alt., 2,000 pop.), was formerly spelled Cole, supposedly for a man of that name. Coal mining is the only important activity in and around the town. There are 16 seams of good bituminous within a radius of 10 miles.

Right from Coal Creek at the First National Bank Building on the Briceville Road, to the junction with a good mine road, 0.5 *m.*; R. on this road 4.5 *m.* to SWAG GAP. From here a two-mile trail leads to the summit of CROSS (or FLAG POLE) MOUNTAIN (3,500 alt.), a long, heavily wooded ridge with outflung spurs. The Great Smoky Mountains, more than 40 miles away, are visible on clear days, with the House and Clinch Mountains, 27 and 29 miles away, prominent in the east.

BRICEVILLE, 3.9 *m.* (1,191 alt., 613 pop.) on the Briceville Rd., is a mining village at the foot of the Cross Mountains.

Left from Coal Creek at the corner drug store, on a winding graveled road, to the junction with a private road, 1.7 *m.;* over a bridge 0.1 *m.* on this road to the SAVAGE ROCK GARDENS *(open),* acres of woodland on the south slope of Coal Creek. The owner has planted and encouraged the growth of native wild flowers and rock plants.

Coal Creek and Briceville were the scene of a coal miners' war in the last decade of the nineteenth century. The miners struck against the leasing of convicts to private industry by the State. In 1899 the penitentiary and its inmates had been leased for a term of six years to the Tennessee Coal, Iron and Railroad Company, and the agreement had provided that the convicts might be worked in the coal mines. Thousands of miners who lost their jobs to convict laborers brought out their squirrel rifles and, reinforced by their mountain kin and by other miners from the Kentucky coal fields, seized the convict stockades at Coal Creek and Briceville. In July, 1891, Governor Buchanan arrived from Knoxville with militia. He made terms with the miners, promising them that their grievances would be adjusted by the legislature, but convicts were sent back into the mines. The miners again seized the stockades and Governor Buchanan once more called out the militia. By a combination of threats and promises he managed to get the miners to evacuate the stockades. The convicts were again put to work. A third time, on August 13, 1892, the miners marched on Briceville and Coal Creek. This time they burned the stockades and freed the convicts. In the following months of intermittent guerrilla fighting a number of miners were killed; in the end, however, they won their point. The convict lease system was abolished.

CLINTON, 48.1 *m.* (850 alt., 3,000 pop.), seat of Anderson County, was first named Burrville in honor of Aaron Burr. By act of the legislature, in 1809, the name was changed to honor Gov. De Witt Clinton of New York.

The area was explored by Virginians in 1761 and settled in 1787. The county was named for Joseph Anderson, one of the three judges of the Territory South of the Ohio River.

Between Clinton and Knoxville the highway crosses a fairly open country in which there are prosperous farms, orchards, and evergreen nurseries. On all sides are hills.

KNOXVILLE, 67 *m.* (833 alt., 105,802 pop.) *(see KNOXVILLE).*

Points of Interest: Headquarters TVA; University of Tennessee and others.

Knoxville is at the junctions with US 11E *(see Tour 1),* US 70 *(see Tour 12),* US 11W *(see Tour 1A),* and State 33 *(see Tour 5A).*

Section b. KNOXVILLE *to* NORTH CAROLINA LINE; *55 m.,* State 35 *and* 71

South of KNOXVILLE, 0 *m.,* a good view of the Knoxville sky line is provided by the Henley Street Bridge. Between Knoxville and Sevierville,

IN A GRIST MILL

State 35 passes through knobby farm land. From many points the Smoky and Unaka Mountains are clearly visible.

At 2.8 *m.* is the junction (R) with State 33 *(see Tour 2)*.

At 5.5 *m.* is a gap in Brown's Mountain, from which, on clear days, there is a view of the Great Smokies. Thunderhead (5,530 alt.) and Gregory's Bald (4,948 alt.) are visible (R) in the distance. The lower range in the foreground is the Chilhowee.

SHOOK'S GAP, 9.7 *m.,* notches a ridge that divides Knox and Sevier Counties. Peace officers of Knox County often place barricades across the gap road to stop liquor runners from transporting moonshine from the mountains into Knoxville. Numerous gun battles have occurred.

At 10 *m.* is the junction with the old Sevierville Pike.

Left on this road to the BATTLE OF BOYD'S CREEK MONUMENT, 8 *m.,* on the site of an important border clash. When Col. John Sevier returned from the Battle of King's Mountain, the Cherokee were on the warpath, so he immediately mustered 100 men and marched swiftly to the Cherokee country. On the third day he surprised a large force of Indians near this place, and gained a decisive victory. After reinforcements had joined Sevier, he forced the Cherokee to sign a treaty of friendship.

The monument stands near the middle of the battlefield, which later became a part of the Chandler plantation. Nearby is the JOHN CHANDLER HOUSE, built in 1825. Chandler came from North Carolina and settled in the valley in 1791.

The nine-room house, built of brick made from clay on the plantation, has never been remodeled though the original windows and doors were destroyed during the War between the States. Still in place are hand-wrought hinges, a built-in cupboard, an old wide stairway, and great open fireplaces. Although the kitchen has been electrically equipped, the kitchen fireplace is still furnished with pot hangers and kettles. The china, pewter, silver dishes, furniture, and quilts of the early days are still in service here.

The road passes through a gap at 11.6 *m.* When open country is reached again, there is a view (R) of the CHILHOWEE RANGE, the most westerly thrust of the Smokies. Several thin veins of gold were once mined in them.

At 12.2 *m.* is the junction with a paved road.

Left on this road to HARRISON-CHILHOWEE INSTITUTE, 0.5 *m.,* founded in 1881, a school accredited by the State; the institute is supported by the Baptists of Tennessee.

MOUNT CHAPMAN (6,430 alt.), a three-pointed peak, is visible at 12.7 *m.* and (L) MOUNT GUYOT (6,621 alt.), the second highest peak in the park.

The edge of the slate knob section, where erosion has worn the hills into dome-shaped formations, is next reached. The knobs, from which timber has been cut, are used for grazing.

MOUNT LE CONTE (6,595 alt.) is visible (R) at 18.9 *m.*

The highway cuts through a rim, 24 *m.,* and the town of Sevierville and the Smokies can be seen.

State 35 crosses the West Fork of the Little Pigeon River, 24.6 *m.* Just below the bridge (L) the West Fork unites with the East Fork.

SEVIERVILLE, 25 *m.* (900 alt., 882 pop.), seat of Sevier County, bears the name of the State's first Governor. Sevier County was established in March, 1785, as part of the short-lived State of Franklin. Because it was south of the French Broad River in territory set aside for the Cherokee by North Carolina, John Sevier headed a commission to make a treaty with the Indians. On May 31, 1785, at Dumpling Creek the Indians ceded the land between the French Broad River and the ridge separating Little River and the Little Tennessee to the white settlers. With the collapse of the independent government, North Carolina, the parent State, refused to extend her jurisdiction south of the boundary fixed with the Indians in the Holston treaty. As a result a fourth Tennessee independent government, the Association South of the Holston and French Broad Rivers, was set up.

The first courts in Sevierville were held in a stable. It is said that this stable was so infested with fleas that itching lawyers had it burned.

In January, 1892, the White Caps, an organization that proclaimed its purpose as law enforcement and adopted the uniforms and tactics of the Ku Klux Klan, was organized here. Their methods were spoken of as "white cappings." Though their avowed purpose was to right miscarriages of justice, the White Caps also carried on private quarrels. After a series of White Cap murders and floggings, the people of the community combined with the public officers in a strenuous fight to break up the organization. Finally in January, 1898, after the conviction of several White Cap leaders on felony charges, the organization was disbanded.

Great Smoky Mountains National Park occupies about one-fifth of the total area of the county along its southern border on the North Carolina Line *(see GREAT SMOKY MOUNTAINS NATIONAL PARK).*

Sevierville is the trading center for a large area in which farming is one of the chief means of livelihood. Lumber is one of the chief commercial industries. There are two large planing mills, a hosiery mill, and a large canning plant here.

The log house on the corner of Main St. and Park Road was built in 1806 and housed NANCY ACADEMY, named for Nancy Rogers, probably the first white child born in the section. The structure is still in good condition.

At the north entrance is the ISAAC THOMAS MONUMENT, honoring a scout in the Battle of King's Mountain, who was the original grantee of the land on which the institution stands.

Right from Sevierville, on Court St., to a large INDIAN MOUND, 0.5 *m.,* on the McMahon farm. *(See FIRST AMERICANS.)*

At Sevierville the route, now State 35-71, turns south, and passes through a valley overshadowed by rugged mountains.

An old-fashioned SWINGING BRIDGE is (R) at 28.1 *m.* The highway bridge crosses the river into the valley of the Little Pigeon where good crops of wheat, tobacco, clover, and vegetables are grown. Owing to the lack of transportation facilities, this region was isolated as late as 1890.

At 29.9 *m.* is the junction with the Wear Valley Road.

Right on this graveled road to the COL. SAMUEL WEAR MONUMENT, 0.5 *m.,* in an open field. Samuel Wear served under John Sevier at the Battle of King's Mountain and was at Yorktown when Cornwallis surrendered.

At 11 *m.* is LINE SPRINGS *(hotel),* a summer resort by mineral springs.

PIGEON FORGE, 31 *m.* (1,142 alt., 212 pop.), an unincorporated town, was named for an old iron foundry on the Little Pigeon River. From the eastern end of the village is an excellent view of the Smokies, Mount Le Conte (R), and Mount Guyot and Mount Chapman (L).

At 34.9 *m.* the route is in the mountains. *(Drive with care; steep grades and sharp curves.)*

At 37 *m.* the highway crosses Norton Creek.

Right along the creek 1 *m.* (no trail) to a GROVE OF LARGE TULIP POPLAR TREES. These trees are six to seven feet in diameter.

GATLINBURG, 38 *m.* (1,550 alt., 550 pop.) *(see also GREAT SMOKY MOUNTAINS NATIONAL PARK),* is a mountain resort at the head of the cove through which the Pigeon River runs. It has three hotels, one of them with 75 rooms, and many other tourist accommodations. The village has taken on new life since the HEADQUARTERS OF THE GREAT SMOKY MOUNTAINS NATIONAL PARK was established here, but it had been attracting visitors since the first decade of the century. Many of the early visitors came to find the products of the handicraft revival, which had been stimulated first by those who rediscovered the charm of primitive products and later by missionary and semiphilanthropic organizations interested in the welfare of the mountain people. Members of these organizations believed that by encouraging and training the craft workers they were reviving a satisfying form of cultural expression, giving to the mountain people a means of decorating their homes and clothing themselves with products far better than they could buy, and providing them with a source of income to supplement the average of $150 a year derived from crops.

Gatlinburg is now only one of many places where such training has been given; the number of trained Appalachian craft workers is now about 15,000. According to a Government survey, however, the results of the movement have been far less satisfactory than those who started it had hoped. Often the people are too poor to keep anything for their own use that will bring in cash. For the most part they lack the sources of raw materials available to their forefathers and must work for the middlemen who can supply them; and these middlemen cannot afford to permit use of the raw stuffs for experiments in designs that may or may not be salable. Moreover, the market for primitive handicraft products is limited; the average customer cannot, or will not, pay much more for goods produced by long hours of handwork than he pays for a machine-made imitation. The average income of the Appalachian handicraft producer is $52 a year. Many of these who formerly spent many days making rugs, quilts, and the like have turned to the production of minor novelties, such as ash trays decorated with poker work, walnut buttons, and other articles that can be turned out quickly.

Gatlinburg shops display patch quilts and hooked rugs in the old designs, fern baskets made of fiber growing in the weaver's cove, and rugs and counterpanes still in the frames of looms.

By the highway (L), just west of the center of town, is a store called the GREAT SMOKY MOUNTAINS MUSEUM, containing a large number of pitchers, toby jugs, and specimens of Tiplet and Ridgway wares.

The MOUNTAINEER MUSEUM *(lectures twice a day; small fee),* along the highway (L) west of the center, contains a large and authentic collection of old domestic and agricultural implements, furniture, guns, beartraps, and other articles long used by mountain people of this region. At one end of the display hall is a very old cabin furnished as it was when it was used as a home.

The BARNES CHEROKEE INDIAN MUSEUM *(open; small fee),* opposite the Mountaineer Museum, has a fine collection of Cherokee Indian artifacts. Among them are about 700 stone axes and tomahawks, more than 300 clay and stone pots and domestic utensils, jewelry and beads of every kind known to the Cherokee Nation, arrowheads, silver breastplates and other ornaments, pipes, bowls, skulls, and complete skeletons.

1. Left on a cove road from the highway at a point east of the center of Gatlinburg. The PI BETA PHI SETTLEMENT SCHOOL, 0.2 *m.,* is sponsored by a sorority that disposes of the handicraft products of its pupils through gift shops and private sales. The school gives expert instruction in craft work. Articles are on sale in a shop on the grounds.

In June an Old Timers' Day is sponsored by the settlement. The program includes "calling" contests for husbands, wives, hogs, cows, and dogs; honors for the oldest man and woman, the handsomest and the ugliest man; ballad, hymn, and Old Harp singing; tale telling, fiddling by individuals and groups; horseshoe pitching, and bow-and-arrow and gun shoots. The picnic dinners at noon represent weeks of preparation and are generously shared with those whose cupboards are bare.

At 0.5 *m.* is HOLSTON ASSEMBLY GROUNDS, at the southern edge of the town, where the Epworth League Institute of the Holston Conference (Methodist) meets annually, during the first two weeks of July. On the 75-acre tract are a baseball diamond and a swimming pool.

The road continues to the large CHEROKEE APPLE ORCHARD (2,581 alt.) unusual at this elevation.

From this orchard are two approaches to the summit of Mount Le Conte *(see also trail from Bear Pen Gap and Alum Cove Creek, this tour).*

a. The old, steep trail leads up 4 *m.* along LeConte Creek; it twists around and over large moss-covered boulders, passing beautiful RAINBOW FALLS, whose waters drop 83 feet from a ledge covered with a dense growth of old buckeye trees. The trail rounds Rocky Spur to the summit of MOUNT LE CONTE (6,593 alt.) where LE CONTE LODGE *($1 a night),* provides 40 rough bunks but no food.

b. The new bridle trail winds 7 *m.* to the summit by easy grades, following Roaring Creek and Fork and passing Rainbow Falls on the way. This trail offers a series of views. The course of Roaring Brook is a long series of cascades, punctuated by at least 7 spectacular falls that are from 30 to 100 feet in height. TWIN FALLS is a cascade in which the water churns in parallel streams for 125 feet over a slanting wall of rock. DOME CASCADE is the uppermost falls.

2. Left from the town to the flats above it, where are the OLD SMOKY RIFLE GROUNDS, 0.5 *m.,* scene of many old-time shooting matches. The riflemen, shooting for the prize of whole beef "set a handicap that wuz mighty hard to jump." They either had to shoot "a crooked bar'l or fire a slut of a gun that'd strip her patchin' or some slow-firer that'd never go off 'tell you'd lay her down." The prizes were sometimes divided: the first might be the hide and tallow, the next the hind quarters, the fore quarters, the remainder, and last the lead from the targets.

3. Left from Gatlinburg on an unimproved road to GREENBRIER COVE, 9 *m.* *(see also GREAT SMOKY MOUNTAINS NATIONAL PARK).*

This cove, one of the largest wilderness areas in the park, is at the foot of Pinnacle Mountain. On the divide above are six peaks with altitudes of approximately 6,000 feet. The SMOKY MOUNTAINS HIKING CLUB CABIN in the Brier, resembling the more comfortable pioneer dwellings, and a few cabins vacated by natives are the only buildings, besides the RANGER STATION, in this section. The Komarek mammal studies *(see NATURAL SETTING AND CONSERVATION)* were conducted here. In this section is the headquarters of a colony of art students from Sophia Newcomb College, New Orleans.

Southeast of Gatlinburg State 71 follows the long valley of the Little Pigeon River.

The road begins a series of ascending curves.

At 39.6 *m.* is a white-and-green marker announcing the Great Smokies Park boundary.

The NATIONAL PARK CHECKING STATION, 40.5 *m.,* is at the junction (R) with State 73 *(see Tour 5B),* part of the favorite scenic loop of Knoxville people. Southeast of this junction State 71 goes over the center of the Smokies on a good graveled road with no blind curves.

There is a view of BULLHEAD (L) at 41.8 *m.,* and of ROCKY SPUR beyond. Both are on spurs of the massive Mt. LeConte.

At 42.2 *m.* are junction with class B Trails (L) to Bullhead and Balsam Point.

The Chimney Tops (R), ragged twin peaks, are visible at 43.3 *m.*

Over the cove are straight stretches of road, then hairpin curves. At intervals are amazing vistas through the shoulders of the mountains, but at other times the road is shut in by towering barriers.

An overhanging rock wall (L), 46.2 *m.,* is about 100 yards from the road; it is called Fort Harry.

At 47.4 *m.* is the site of the old INDIAN GAP HOTEL.

Right from this point on an extremely steep trail that leads to CHIMNEY TOPS (4,740 alt.), 1 *m.,* from which is a view of the valley of the Sugarlands and the peaks on the divide.

At 48.2 *m.* is BEAR PEN GAP.

Left from the gap on a Class A trail to MT. LECONTE 4 *m.* From a small park the trail ascends through dense conifers, whose needles mat the earth thickly. Here are innumerable beds of ferns and wild flowers. Bear pens, heavy "deadfall traps" were at one time a hazard along trails. One mountaineer said, "They might at least stick up a sourwood switch as a warning."

The route runs through a virgin hardwood forest. Here are probably the largest stands of virgin hardwood in the South. Massive Bullhead (L), a spur of Mount LeConte, is visible and an entire mountain slope covered with rhododendrons, is a beautiful sight in the spring.

By Alum Cave Creek, 51.8 *m.,* and Walter Camp Prong of the Little Pigeon River is the junction with the Alum Cave trail, the steepest and shortest trail to LeConte.

Left on this trail which follows Alum Creek and goes up a steep half-mile to ALUM CAVE, 1 *m.* Just below Alum Cave Bluff is (L) Hide-in Rock Ridge.

In Alum Cave, under the immense overhanging Alum Cave Bluff, are deposits of Epsom salts and alum. The cave mouth is a good observation point.

A stand of black birches, a specie usually found in the latitude of Canada is 55.2 *m.* It is possible that these Canadian trees may have grown from seeds brought by migratory birds. Down the gorge is the crest of Chimney Tops (4,740 alt.).

At 55.5 *m.* is NEWFOUND GAP (5,045 alt.), where State 35-71 crosses the State Line 81 *m.* west of Asheville, N. C. The Appalachian Trail crosses the highway here.

Right from Newfound Gap on macadam Skyline Rd., paralleling the Appalachian Trail between Newfound Gap and Clingmans Dome. The old Indian Gap Road, which at 1.4 *m.* appears (L) about 100 yards below the new road, was built by the Cherokee in 1862, to enable Confederate soldiers to haul saltpetre from Alum Cave Bluffs to North Carolina arsenals for the manufacture of gunpowder.

At 1.5 *m.* Skyline Road crosses INDIAN GAP (5,265 alt.), known in former years as Collin's Gap. The Appalachian Trail crosses the highway here. There are excellent views of both sides of the Great Smoky Range.

At 2.7 *m.* the road crosses back into Tennessee and at 3.2 *m.* crosses again into North Carolina.

Clingmans Dome, with a fire tower, can be seen on the sky line (L) at 4.5 *m.*

At 5 *m.* the road again crosses into Tennessee.

BLANKET MOUNTAIN, also with a fire tower, appears (R) at 5.1 *m.* Cove and Rich Mountains are visible (R), and Siler's Bald and Thunderhead Mountain (L).

At 6.9 *m.* is a good view of OCONALUFTEE GORGE (L).

The highest point on the road (6,311 ft.) is at 7.4 *m.*

The road ends at a large parking plaza, 7.7 *m.* A Class B trail to the summit of CLINGMANS DOME (6,642 alt.), about 0.5 *m.* in length, begins R. From the

NEWFOUND GAP

plaza are fine views of the Blue Ridge Range, and the Natahala National Forest and Andrew's Bald in North Carolina.

From the top of Clingmans Dome are visible a number of the highest peaks in the Smokies: Mt. Kephart, Siler's Bald, and Mt. Collins. On some days clouds fill the valleys on both the Tennessee and North Carolina sides, and on the brightest days the blue haze, from which the Smokies derive their name, dims the landscape.

Tour 5A

Junction with US 25W—Norris Dam—Norris—Knoxville—Maryville—Madisonville—(Chatsville, Ga.); Norris Freeway and State 33.
Junction with US 25W to Georgia Line, 122.3 m.

New concrete roadbed throughout.
Limited accommodations.

Section a. JUNCTION WITH US 25W *to* KNOXVILLE; *30.5 m.*

The Norris Freeway traverses the Norris Dam area. This highway is scientifically constructed to eliminate sharp turns, crossroads, and other traffic hazards. The roadside has been landscaped with the co-operation of landowners. Use of the privately owned land for some distance on both sides of the right-of-way is publicly controlled to prevent erection of unsightly roadside stands and billboards. There is a sharp contrast in the landscape along the road. The long, high, unbroken lines of the concrete dam, the bare, angular, steel electric line towers, and the powerhouse of modern design are in a primitive forest. The freeway ascends the hills above Norris Lake in long, sweeping curves until it reaches the summit overlooking the dam.

The Norris Freeway branches southeast from US 25W *(see Tour 5)* at the northern end of Coal Creek.

At 3.9 *m.* it descends to the level of the dam, passing a steel barge (L) that serves as a boat landing. A boat *(fee 50¢)* leaves here at regular intervals for trips on the lake. The freeway crosses the dam.

NORRIS DAM, 5.2 *m. (guard at each end of road over dam will give information),* is of the concrete gravity storage type. Named for United States Senator George W. Norris of Nebraska, it was the first major construction job to be completed by the Tennessee Valley Authority, and began impounding the waters of Clinch River on March 4, 1936. *(See Tennessee Valley Authority.)* Work had begun in 1933. The total cost, including purchase of the reservoir area, was approximately $36,000,000. Norris Dam is 1,860 feet long, 1,570 feet of its length being a solid concrete mass. The remaining 290 feet is an earth-fill dike with a reinforced concrete core wall. The dam is approximately 208 feet thick at the base and 265 feet high from the lowest point in the foundation to the roadway on its top.

Norris Dam has created a reservoir, Norris Lake, which, extending into numerous side coves, has a shore line of approximately 705 miles and is 50 square miles in area; it extends 72 miles up the Clinch River and 65 miles up the Powell. The lake has a storage capacity of 836 billion gallons. Its outline resembles a huge hand, the palm near the junction of the Powell and the Clinch, with fingers spreading out into narrow valleys between tree-covered hills.

The normal level of the lake is 1,020 feet above sea level; a flood could cause the water to rise to 1,052 feet. During dry seasons, when the river below the dam is too low for navigation and power purposes, the lake can be lowered to 955 feet. The level of the lake, or its spillway crest, is controlled by three drum-type gates, each 14 feet high and 100 feet long, through which 205,000 cubic feet of water can be discharged each second. Eight sluiceways, each controlled by vertically sliding gates, can release an additional 37,000 cubic feet a second. The spillway discharges into a concrete hydraulic jump pool that extends 215 feet downstream from the toe of the dam. This concrete pool prevents the downward force of the water from eroding the foundation of the dam.

Surrounding the lake are 117,000 acres of TVA-owned land, purchased primarily to prevent siltation of the reservoir. This land has been developed as a park and stocked with game.

Left from the freeway at the traffic circle to the entrance of NORRIS PARK *(horseback riding, boats, picnicking, fishing, hiking, and swimming available; furnished cabins at moderate rates; see Superintendent of Norris Park at Norris for reservations for tent and trailer camp, 50¢ a night)*. There are 20 miles of bridle paths and trails. A WATER MILL built in 1797 has been carefully restored and is on the bank of Clear Creek, 100 yards east of the freeway.

At the traffic circle the freeway turns R. Near the junction is a HANDICRAFT SHOP that sells rugs, spreads, baskets, pottery, and woodwork made by mountain people.

At 6.3 *m.* is the junction with a paved road.

Right on this road to the TVA FOREST NURSERIES and TVA FISH HATCHERY POOLS, and to the POWERHOUSE, 0.7 *m. (guide service)*, where there is an exhibit showing steps in the construction of the dam, and its operation. From the walkway around the building is an excellent view of the great white face of the dam from below, an impressive sight reminiscent of a frozen Niagara Falls. Next to the building are the geometrical towers of the transmitter through which the two 50,000-kilowatt generators are linked with those of Wilson and Wheeler Dams by a high-tension transmission line 230 miles long.

In simplicity, directness and power of design as well as in the immense scale of the undertaking, Norris Dam may justly be compared with the most impressive works of the Egyptians.

NORRIS, 9.2 *m.* (1,100 alt., 1,600 pop.), on the freeway *(free parking spaces; guides furnished free at the town office between 8 a.m. and 4:30 p.m.)*.

Norris is an unincorporated town owned and controlled by TVA. For matters solely concerning the residential community, the manager has an elected advisory council of nine. The cost of government is defrayed from the rental of houses and business places. The Norris school, in session twelve months a year, uses the standard curriculum of Tennessee. There are extension courses for adults.

Some of the dwellings in the park-like town were built during the dam construction period and were occupied by technical workers. Now many are rented by TVA office workers who commute daily to Knoxville. The individual houses differ greatly in size; there are ten duplexes and six five-family apartment houses. Bricks, stone, cinder blocks, concrete, and wood have been used for the walls, and many houses have various kinds of electrical equipment, even, in some cases, for heating. Experiments have been made with old-fashioned and modern designs, and on the whole, the results have been satisfactory. The chief criticism of architects has been directed against the use of low, slanting roofs that reduce the air space and floor space in some of the second stories.

Two large TVA LABORATORIES are at Norris. One is the hydraulic laboratory, in which models of the Authority's dams are built and extensive engineering tests conducted. The other is the ceramic research laboratory in which experiments are conducted in the use of local kaolin for the manufacture of high-grade porcelain and chinaware.

Near the town on a 1,500-foot RESERVOIR HILL is a rock overlook that affords a sweeping view of the dam and the distant Cumberland and Great Smoky Mountains. On the hill is a picnic area *(ovens, tables, water, sanitary facilities, shelters).*

South of Norris the freeway sweeps through a hilly, forested area. Shrubbery and lespedeza are planted on both sides of the road.

A MOUNTAIN CABIN (L), 12.9 *m.,* constructed of logs chinked and daubed with clay is preserved by the TVA.

At 20.5 *m.* is the junction with State 33.

Left on State 33 to the junction with a paved road 6.4 *m.;* L. here 0.1 *m.* and L. again to BIG RIDGE PARK, 13 *m. (adm. 10¢; swimming, picnicking, boating, fishing; furnished cabins at moderate rates).* This park, covering 3,500 acres, is on the south shore of Norris Lake. Approximately 100 acres have been developed as a recreational area. The country is rugged and picturesque, with many high criss-crossing ridges.

One of the arms of the Norris Lake has been dammed to maintain a constant water level here when the level of the main reservoir is lowered.

On State 33 is MAYNARDVILLE (500 pop.), 14 *m.,* seat of Union County; it was named for Horace Maynard, Member of Congress from 1857 to 1863 and from 1866 to 1875; he was a vigorous and outspoken Unionist. During the early part of the War between the States, sentiment in East Tennessee—where plantations were few—was strong for peace and for remaining in the Union. Maynard interviewed President Lincoln soon after his inauguration and was reassured by the latter's statement that the North did not want to fight. At this time many southerners had been disturbed by Lincoln's inaugural address, so Maynard carried home the message the President had given him.

When in June 1861, Andrew Johnson and other East Tennessee Unionists called a convention to protest against a resolution for secession adopted by the legislature, Maynard was among those present. The delegates adopted a resolution threatening to rise in armed opposition if any attempt was made to coerce East Tennesseans into the Confederacy. Maynard urged the delegates to be more temperate, and rewrote parts of the measure. The resolution became merely a strong protest, without the threats. "We prefer to remain attached to the government of our fathers," the delegates wrote. "The Constitution of the United States has done us no wrong. The Congress of the United States has passed no law to oppress us. The President of the United States has made no threat against the law-abiding people of Tennessee. Under the Government of the United States, we have enjoyed as a nation more of civil and religious freedom than any other people under the whole heaven. We believe there is no cause for rebellion or secession on the part of the people of Tennessee."

In August 1861, Maynard was re-elected to the House of Representatives. He had difficulty in traveling to Washington, but finally arrived safely. Meanwhile, in other parts of the State, resentment grew against the East Tennessee Unionists. Governor Harris wrote to President Davis of the Confederacy: "We can temporize with the rebellious spirit of that people no longer. . . . The arrest and indictment for treason of the ringleaders will give perfect peace and quiet to that division of our State in the course of two months." Soon afterwards, East Tennessee was occupied by a Confederate force of 10,000 men. Maynard, together with Andrew Johnson who had a seat in the Senate, urged President Lincoln to protect the loyalists. Lincoln wrote to General McClellan who, in turn, wrote to General Buell. Buell disagreed and thought it would be unwise strategy to move into East Tennessee. McClellan answered: "For the sake of these East Tennesseans who have taken part with us I would gladly sacrifice mere military advantages; they deserve our

NORRIS FREEWAY

protection and at all hazards they must have it." Weeks passed; finally Lincoln wrote to Buell: ". . . my distress is that our friends in East Tennessee are being hanged and driven to despair, and even now, I fear, are thinking of taking rebel arms for the sake of personal protection. In this we lose the most valuable stake we have in the South. My dispatch, to which yours is an answer, was sent with the knowledge of Senator Johnson and Representative Maynard of East Tennessee, and they will be upon me to know the answer, which I cannot safely show them."

East Tennessee was taken by Union forces; Johnson became Military Governor of the State, and Maynard the Attorney General. Later Maynard was appointed Minister to Turkey, and from 1880 to 1881 was Postmaster General of the United States.

At the southwest end of the town is a MAYNARD MONUMENT.

Right from Norris Freeway on State 33; now the main route.

The marked site of a log blockhouse, ADAIR'S STATION, is (R) at 25.7 *m.* The cabin was built in 1788 by John Adair, an entry taker in Sullivan County who financed the expedition led by Isaac Shelby and John Sevier that defeated the British in the Battle of King's Mountain. Sevier and Shelby obtained the money by promising Adair that it would be repaid by the State. Adair was a member of the Tennessee constitutional convention of 1796.

The SCOTT HOUSE *(open),* 27.8 *m.,* a two-story, ten-room brick structure (R) was built in 1833 by James Scott, a member of Tennessee's first legislature. There are hand-carved fireplace mantels in all of the rooms. The kitchen fireplace is eight feet wide.

The wallpaper of the living room, imported from France, antedates that of the Hermitage by two years; it has seven different patterns, and the colors are still bright, though the room was used as a hospital ward during the War between the States.

Owing to a custom of the second owner, Colonel Ledgerwood, there is a grove with twenty-six kinds of trees. When driving through the country, the colonel would cut a branch from some tree, use it as a buggy whip and on his return stick it in this ground.

KNOXVILLE, 30.5 *m.* (833 alt., 105,802 pop.) *(see KNOXVILLE).*

Points of Interest: TVA Headquarters, University of Tennessee, Blount Mansion, Henley Street Bridge, Church Street Methodist Church, Chisholm Tavern, National Cemetery, Old Gray Cemetery, and others.

Knoxville is at the junction with US 25W *(see Tour 5),* US 11W *(see Tour 1A),* US 11E *(see Tour 1),* and US 70 *(see Tour 12).*

Left from Broadway on Main Ave. to Gay St.; R. on Gay St. to Hill Ave.; and R. from Hill St. on Riverside Dr.

The JAMES WHITE HOME SITE, 1411 Riverside Drive, is identified by a stone marker. White, a Revolutionary soldier and founder of Knoxville, erected his second home here after abandonment of White's Fort. A few feet north of the marker is an elm, about thirty-six inches in diameter, which was standing when Knoxville was founded.

At 2 *m.* is the junction with a paved road.

Right on this road 0.3 *m.* to the CITY WATERWORKS PLANT *(open),* on twenty-five acres of river bottom land. The plant, completed in 1927, has a capacity of 15 million gallons a day.

At 2.6 *m.* is the junction with Dandridge Ave.

Left on Dandridge Ave. 0.2 *m.* to the JOHN WILLIAMS HOME *(open 9-5 week days),* 3700 Dandridge Ave., now the administration building of the STATE SCHOOL FOR THE DEAF (Negro Division). The long two-story brick house has been somewhat changed. It is approached by a boxwood-bordered walk. The house was built by Williams' wife, Melinda, daughter of James White, while her husband was Minister to Guatemala (1825–1828). She made the plans, supervised the burning of the bricks by slaves, and superintended details of construction, without telling her husband what she was doing. His surprise on his return was long a matter of amusement in Knoxville. In room arrangement the house is typical of the early 1800's, a hall runs through the center with large square rooms on each side. To the left of the house is a small brick office.

Williams had recruited and organized the 39th U. S. Infantry from Tennessee volunteers for the Creek War. He was the hero of the Battle of Horseshoe Bend under Gen. Andrew Jackson, who, it is said, exclaimed, "Williams, you have this day made me famous." Williams was United States Senator from 1815 to 1823, when he was defeated by Jackson.

At 4.1 *m.,* R. on Strawberry Plains Pike; at 5.7 *m.* R. on Asbury Rd. and at 6 *m.* L. on Thorngrove Rd.

On Thorngrove Rd. at 7.2 *m.* is the RAMSEY HOUSE *(open by permission),* built in 1797 by Col. F. A. Ramsey, the surveyor who accompanied Capt. James White on his exploring expedition in 1783. The architect was Thomas Hope, of London, who was also an expert cabinetmaker and upholsterer; he had been brought from England in 1752 by Ralph Izard to build his now famous house in Charleston, S. C. In his unprinted autobiography Colonel Ramsey's son, Dr. J. G. M. Ramsey, author of *Annals of Tennessee,* described the house: "It was a large stone structure, with a deep basement and an attic besides two tall stories. Its corners, its arches, the top of the chimneys, and one row of building rock midway between the ground and the top of the square, were built of pure blue limestone, while the walls throughout were built of red granite. Its style was Gothic, long narrow windows, cornices richly carved in wood but painted to resemble stone, massive, elaborately finished and ornamented. At the census of 1800 it was the most costly and most admired building in Tennessee." Even the first stone steps, the threshold of the front door, and some of the window shutters with hand-wrought hinges are still in place. The heavily bracketed cornices are carved with maple leaves. The huge rear chimney has an exterior fireplace. The thick stone walls make the interior cool on the hottest day. The house is now in poor condition.

MARBLEDALE, 8.1 *m.,* R. on Cinder Lane which begins to circle through quarries of the Tennessee Marble Co., and past fields covered with defective marble which is waiting to be crushed into lime. The road returns to Asbury Rd.; R. on Asbury Rd.

The QUARRY AND POWER PLANT OF THE APPALACHIAN MARBLE COMPANY *(open by permission of the superintendent, who acts as guide),* is at 10.1 *m.* Here, in one of the largest marble quarries in East Tennessee, are three types of marble—grey, pink, and rose. The second variety, one of the most beautiful, is a light pink throughout, with flecks of red like tiny drops of blood. It is very decorative and takes a high polish.

This quarry was opened in 1869 by the U. S. Government to provide material for the old Knoxville Post Office and Customhouse at W. Clinch Ave. and Market St.

Every color of marble except pure white is found in Tennessee. The stone most recently exploited is almost jet. This marble absorbs less than half as much water as the best granite. Marble from the Knoxville district has been used in the Morgan Bank and the Grand Central Terminal, New York City, and in the New York State Capitol at Albany.

LEBANON PRESBYTERIAN CHURCH, 10.6 *m.,* is at the forks of the Holston and French Broad Rivers. The small frame structure is on the site of the log church in which the Presbyterian doctrine was first preached in lower East Tennessee. Dr. Samuel Carrick, later founder of the First Presbyterian Church of Knoxville and first president of Blount College, became the minister. He established himself in a house across the Holston River in 1791, and taught as well as preached. Prior to the erection of the log church, his pulpit was an Indian mound at the junction of the two rivers, immediately west of the church. Among the large crowds of pioneers at the all-day services were many Cherokee, who liked the minister.

On the afternoon of September 25, 1793, Dr. Carrick left for Knoxville to aid in its defense against a threatened Indian attack, not even waiting to bury his wife, who had died shortly before. Negro slaves took the body of Mrs. Carrick across the Holston River in a canoe and buried it without religious rites on a little mound at the rear of the church.

In this graveyard are also the graves of Col. F. A. Ramsey and his two wives, Peggy Alexander and Annie Agnew, buried one on each side of him; J. G. M. Ramsey, near his father's tomb; Brig. Gen. John C. Ramsey, C. S. A., his brother, and Reynolds Ramsey, Esq. (1736–1816), who was with Washington at Trenton and Princeton.

Section b. KNOXVILLE *to* GEORGIA LINE; *91.8 m.* State 33

The Chilhowee Mountains (L) parallel the route and obstruct the view of the Smokies.

South of KNOXVILLE, 0 *m.,* at 1.4 *m.* is the junction (R) with State 35 *(see Tour 5).*

At 10.4 *m.* is the junction with Mentor Road.

Right on this road to the REMAINS OF GILLESPIE'S FORT, 0.5 *m.,* which was captured and burned by Indians who killed 30 white men, women, and children here. The place was thereafter called Burnt Station.

At 10.7 *m.* is the junction with a graveled road.

Right on this road to the McGHEE TYSON AIRPORT, 3.7 *m.,* constructed as a WPA project in 1936–37 and sponsored by the cities of Knoxville, Maryville, and Alcoa, though now operated by the municipal government of Knoxville. It was named in honor of Lieut. McGhee Tyson, U. S. Naval flier, who lost his life when his plane went down in the North Sea in 1918.

At 12.9 *m.* is the junction with a paved road.

Right on this road is ALCOA, 1 *m.* (1,040 alt., 5,255 pop.), founded by the Aluminum Company of America in 1913, when it purchased a large tract of land, including all of North Maryville, and began the construction of a first plant.

The little city has wide streets, parks, and school grounds planned on a scale to meet the needs of a future population of 25,000, which was expected when the place was incorporated in 1919. Full development never took place, and many of the buildings are now in bad condition.

The reducing plant here smelts a considerable quantity of the aluminum produced in the United States. Bauxite is shipped in from mines in Arkansas, and cryolite from Greenland. The processing plants were erected here because of the proximity of hydroelectric power sites. Three dams have been constructed, one at Calderwood on the Little Tennessee River *(see Tour 13)*, and the others in North Carolina.

At full capacity the plant produces 130 pounds of aluminum a minute.

In one of the parks is a large swimming pool. There is also a nine-hole golf course with a clubhouse near the eastern city limits.

MARYVILLE, 16.1 *m.* (1,150 alt., 4,968 pop.), named in honor of Mary Grainger Blount, wife of Gov. William Blount, is the seat of Blount County. The early settlers here preempted Cherokee land and therefore had a rather dangerous existence. Blount County, named in honor of Gov. William Blount, first and only Governor of the Territory of the United States South of the River Ohio, was created by the Territorial Assembly, July 11, 1795, from part of Knox County.

In 1807, Sam Houston, later the hero of the Battle of San Jacinto, came from Virginia to a nearby tract with his widowed mother and eight brothers. The family established a store in Maryville. Before many years Sam, wild and impetuous, and, as he said, fonder of "measuring deer tracks to tape," ran away to the Cherokee country.

Maryville's main street runs along the crest of a hill. All the approaches to it are steep side streets. Thus Maryville is more of a "Main Street town" than most of those so described; it is also a blue-Sunday town, no merchandise being sold on the Sabbath.

The BARCLAY MCGHEE HOME *(open)*, 306 Broadway, two blocks west of the post office, is a plain, square, two-story structure with outside chimneys. It was built in 1790. Its high ceilings, paneled doors, carved mantels and wainscoting, and the old porch are characteristic of the more luxurious homes of the period in which it was erected.

The SITE OF FORT CRAIG, around which Maryville grew, is at the corner of Washington Ave. and E. Main St. The stout little structure was built by John Craig about 1785 and became a refuge for settlers along Pistol Creek during Indian attacks. The stockade enclosed about two acres of ground on which was a spring. One attack was repulsed with severe losses to the Indians but none to the defenders.

The HARPER LIBRARY *(open daily, 2 to 6 p.m.)*, at the northeast corner of College St. and Church Ave., is dedicated to the memory of William Harper, who was killed in the World War.

MARYVILLE COLLEGE, on College St. four blocks southeast of the courthouse, was founded in 1819 by the Tennessee Synod of the Presbyterian Church, as the Southern and Western Theological Seminary. When a new charter was taken out in 1842, the name was changed. The 320-acre campus, purchased in 1879, commands a view of the distant Great Smoky Mountains and of the nearby Chilhowees. A farm of 100 acres is operated by the College and another 100 acres has been developed into a recreational park, with a seven-acre botanical garden and an amphitheater.

The college has had only six presidents in 117 years. The endowment fund is about $1,600,000, and its buildings and grounds are valued at about $675,000. The student body is limited to 800. The usual liberal arts courses are offered, but only degrees in the arts and sciences are granted.

The college was one of the centers of anti-slavery sentiment in East Tennessee, partly because the Reverend Isaac Anderson, founder of the institution, often lectured ardently on the subject. In 1838 one of the students wrote that twelve among the student body of thirty were abolitionists. "We have some friends in the country around, among whom we have the privilege of distributing without fear a considerable number of pamphlets," he said. Because English opponents of slavery were contributing to the abolitionist funds, advocates of slavery denounced this activity as "subversive foreign propaganda."

Rules for student conduct at the school are almost as strict as they were when it was founded. Students must attend chapel each morning, and church twice on Sunday. No dancing or smoking is permitted, and women students cannot leave the campus after dark. On Sundays no student is allowed off the campus except to go to church. The low tuition, combined with high educational standards, compensates for the rigidity of the regulations.

In LAMAR LIBRARY on the campus is the flag of the Blount County Women's Home Guards, organized during the War between the States after most of the men in the county had left for military service. A group of young women formed this military company and adopted a flag with thirty-two stars in a blue field. The advance guard of Sherman's troops, on its way to relieve Burnside in the siege of Knoxville, had received word that the Union advance was being opposed and sent out a skirmish line before it was realized that the opposition came from the "Blount County Home Guards, commandeered by Capt. Cynthia Dunn."

At Maryville is the junction with State 73 *(see Tour 5B).*

1. Left from Maryville on the graveled Nale's Creek Road to the junction with another road at 5.1 *m.;* L. here to a junction with a dirt road by an iron gate 5.9 *m.;* R. here 0.4 *m.* to the SAM HOUSTON SCHOOL, in which the young man who was later leader of the Texas Revolution, taught for a time after his stay among the Cherokee. The little log cabin, whose floor boards and ceiling are secured by hand-wrought iron nails, is 20 feet long, 18 feet wide, and about 10 feet high. There is a fireplace and the interior is lighted through an 18-inch opening made by omitting one log.

2. Right from Maryville on the graveled Friendsville Rd. is FRIENDSVILLE, 12 *m.,* settled in 1796 by Quakers from North Carolina and Virginia, but not laid out until 1852. In 1857 the Society of Friends established the Friendsville Academy, which is still in operation. The Friends took a decided stand against slavery, and, though conscientiously opposed to war, many enlisted in the Union Army during the War between the States.

At 14 *m.* is the SITE OF ISH'S FORT, where John Sevier, in 1793, gathered about 300 militiamen to oppose more than 1,000 Indians then moving to attack Knoxville. This thwarted the attack and the war party was driven back into the Indian country.

3. Right from Maryville on a graveled road to the junction with Lewis Ferry Road at MENTOR, 4.5 *m.;* R. here to GILLESPIE'S ARMORED HOUSE, 6.5 *m.,* built of stone in 1802 by the Gillespie brothers, James and Isaac. The stone blocks, averaging two feet in length, are fitted together and form walls no Indian arrows could penetrate.

There are ten bedrooms. The brothers also erected nearby a three-story stone structure for the storage of meats, dairy products, grain and potatoes. These precautions were taken as a protection against a long Indian siege.

4. Left from Maryville on the Montvale Springs Road to MONTVALE SPRINGS, 9 *m.,* the scene of Charles Todd's *Woodville or Anchorer Reclaimed,* the first novel written by a Tennessean. Sidney Lanier wrote *Tiger Lilies* while visiting his grandfather here.

At 22.1 *m.* is the junction with US 129 *(see Tour 4).*

At BRICK MILL, 28.1 *m.,* is the junction with Lanier Road.

Left on this road to LANIER SCHOOL, 3.5 *m.,* at the junction with another dirt road; R. here 1 *m.* to ARMY HEADQUARTERS, 4.5 *m.,* a large brick house used as headquarters by Gen. C. C. Howard during the advance of Union forces from Chattanooga to the relief of General Burnside, besieged in Knoxville by the Confederates.

State 33 crosses the Little Tennessee River 33.3 *m.,* on a toll bridge *(25¢ for car and driver, 5¢ for each passenger).*

At 33.7 *m.* at the southern end of the bridge, is the junction with Fort Loudoun Road.

Left on this dirt road to the junction with another road 0.2 *m.;* R. here and across a bridge over Tellico River to a junction with another road; L. on this road to the SITE OF FORT LOUDOUN, 1.2 *m.* Fort Loudoun was constructed in 1756 by the British as an outpost against the French and as a friendly gesture to the Overhill Cherokee, who were allied with the British. The British wished to retain the aid and sympathy of the Cherokee. The fort became a refuge for Indian women and children when hostile tribes appeared during the absence of the men. The fort was named in honor of the Earl of Loudoun, Lord Chancellor of Scotland in 1641.

Fort Loudoun was designed and constructed by James William Gerald de Brahm, who is said to have been in the service of Emperor Charles VI before coming to America. He was an eccentric person given to intense research in alchemy. His eccentricities, however, appealed to the Cherokee, who held him in high regard. De Brahm in one of his reports wrote: "When the Author arrived with three hundred men at Little Tamothly, on the West Side of the Appalachian Mountains, He went recognizing the Place intended for a Fort; was accompanied by the Captains Raymond Demere, John Stewart, and John Postel; also by the Indian Emperor, (:Old Hope:); the great Conjurer (:Attakulla-Kulla, or Little Carpenter:); and young Beamer, a Mustee, who served as Interpreter; when the Author saw the Place, he observed not only, that a Ridge of Mountains on the NE. side of the River, but also that two Eminences, one to the NW. and another to the SE: commanded the place so that He could not agree to fix upon that Spot seemingly a favorite Place of the Indians, wherefore he had much ado to convince Them of the Impropriety to build a Fort between three commanding Eminences, His Arguments would have required less Force, had the other officers (:who seemingly inclined out of Compliance to the Indians to favor their Choice:) joined the Author, who at last showed the Indians that the Men's very Shoe Buckles were seen from either of these three Mountains, could not serve for A Fort to protect their Old Men, Women and Children, what could not protect its own Garrison. A Rhombus with two Small and two extensive Bastions was the Figure which the Fort would receive from the Bearings of the River and the Mountain, who with a rocky Precipice 41 ft. high from the Waters Superfices terminates upon the Rivers edge; each Poligon extends 300 ft. in Length with a Breast-Work of 21 ft. thick. In the Ditches he directed a Hedge to be planted of young Locust Trees (:a:) which in less than twelve Months time filled the ditch from the Contre Scarpe to the Scarpe, so that there was no Possibility to come to its foot with Intent to cut or burn it down. The Locust Trees are full of Thorns, which are three and four inches long, and out of each Thorn project four other Thorns more, perpendicularly forming a cross, in the manner of a cheval de freis, so that the medling with this Hedge is in every respect impracticable, and renders the Fort impregnable at least against Indians, who always engage naked; each Bostion mounts three Cannons, each Cannon is of 16 ounces Caliber, or bore. These small Cannons were brought with the greatest difficulty, and great expenses over the Apalachian Mountains; the Indian Trader (:one Ellit:) undertook to bring them from Fort Prince George opposite Keewee on the east side of the Apalachian Mountains; Ellit contrived to poise on each Horse a Cannon cross-ways over the Pack Saddle, and lashed them round the Horses Body with Belts (:b:); but as these Horses had to cross a Country full of high Mountains, and these covered with Forests, it would happen, that some times one End of a Cannon did catch a tree, twist upon the Saddle, and drew the Horse down some of which had by these Accidents their Backs broken under the Weight, and lost their lives; the longest journey these horses could make was six miles in a day."

As the work progressed De Brahm and Commander Raymond Demere had a sharp disagreement as to authority, causing De Brahm to leave secretly at Christmas 1756, before the work was completed. A council of war found he had "clandestinely gone away and left the fort unfinished," and Old Hop, the Cherokee Emperor, spoke of him as "the warrior who ran away in the night." The fort was completed under the direction of Captain Demere.

During the construction of the fort the white men occupied huts nearby, and many of them married Indian women. War broke out with the Cherokee, who laid siege to Fort Loudoun in February 1760. The little band inside withstood the attack for five months, though they were forced to eat their horses and dogs.

All attempts to obtain reinforcements having failed, it was agreed to surrender to the Cherokee upon the best terms obtainable. Captain Stuart went to Chota, the home of Oconastota, and negotiated an agreement to capitulate upon the following terms: "That the garrison of Loudoun march out with their arms and drums, each soldier having as much powder and ball as the officer shall think necessary for the march and all the baggage they choose to carry; that the garrison be permitted to march to Virginia or to Fort Prince George, as the commanding officer shall think proper, unmolested; that a number of Indians be appointed to escort them, and aid them in hunting for provisions during the march; that such soldiers as were lame or disabled by sickness from marching be received into the Indian towns and treated kindly, until they recover, and then be allowed to return to Fort Prince George; that the Indians provide as many horses for the garrison as they can for the march which were to be paid for at the end of the journey; that the great guns, powder and ball and spare arms be turned over to the Indians without fraud and delay on the day set for the march of the troops."

In accordance with these terms, the garrison evacuated on August 8, 1760. Accompanied by Oconastota and several other Indians, they marched about 15 miles over the Tellico River Trail toward Fort Prince George, and camped for the night near Cane Creek. At dawn the next morning they were attacked by a large number of Indians, who killed 4 officers, 23 privates and 3 women, and made the rest prisoners. A number of the latter were eventually ransomed and delivered to Fort Prince George, principally through the efforts of a friendly chief.

The old fort is being reconstructed by the WPA.

MADISONVILLE, 44.1 *m.* (875 alt., 926 pop.), seat of Monroe County, was named in honor of James Madison. On record in the COURTHOUSE are many grants and deeds that were made by the Cherokee.

HIWASSEE JUNIOR COLLEGE, established here in 1847, is a self-help institution where most of the students work part-time.

On the north side of the courthouse square is GUILFORD CANNON HOUSE, better known as the Stickley House because Vastine Stickley, a man of local prominence, occupied it for 50 years. It is a large two-story brick structure built in 1846; there is a two-story pedimented veranda in the center of the front and the spiral stairway runs from the first floor to the low attic.

Left from Madisonville, on State 68, is TELLICO PLAINS, 14 *m.* (900 alt., 902 pop.), in the CHEROKEE NATIONAL FOREST *(camping, hunting, and carrying of firearms permitted only in restricted areas; inquire at office of the park Ranger a few yards east of the center of the village).*

According to the diary kept by Louis Philippe, on his travels through Tennessee, he fell from a horse here and was injured. He had himself bled. The results were so satisfactory that the aged chief of the Cherokee, ill at the time, asked that the operation be performed on him. The chief was cured and in grateful recognition of the white man's skill, he invited the Prince to his lodge. A feast was served and the French aristocrat spent the night in the chief's crowded lodge, sleeping between two squaws.

When Louis Philippe became King of France he frequently asked residents of the United States who were presented to him. "Do they still sleep three in a bed in Tennessee?"

The town is on the site of the Cherokee town of Talequah, important in the military, political, and tribal history of the Cherokee Nation. Five important Cherokee treaties were signed here. Indian mounds and relics have been found nearby.

1. Left from Tellico Plains 1.4 *m.* on a graveled road to THE MANSION *(private),* by the Tellico River; it is so called because when built it was the finest home in this part of Tennessee. The house was built around a cabin erected by John Sevier.

About 1824 the cabin was purchased by Elijah Johnson, of New Jersey, whose son had preceded him to the area and had been living with the Indians. The new owner added nine rooms. The ceiling levels of the first floor vary from room to room. A secret underground passageway was constructed between the house and the river. The entrance to this passage was at the top of the house; as a result some of the rooms are oddly shaped.

2. Left from Tellico Plains 11 *m.* on a graveled road to RAFTER; L. from Rafter on White Oak Flats Rd. to the junction with a dirt road, 19 *m.;* R. here into JEFFREY'S HELL, 19.5 *m.,* a game preserve in the Cherokee National Forest. The section is wild, mountainous, and uninhabited, lying between the north and south forks of Citico's Creek and extending eastward almost to the North Carolina Line. There are cliffs, ravines, sharp rocky spurs, and a dense growth of plant life. Although the area has been exploited for commercial purposes, it has retained much of its original wild and freakish character. It received its name when a hunter named Jeffrey ventured too far from camp, and wandered for two days without food. When he finally reached the headwaters of Tellico and was asked where he had been, he replied, "I don't know, but I have been in Hell."

Along the road is much laurel and rhododendron. The rhododendron is from 15 to 20 feet high, and the laurel so dense that it is almost impossible to penetrate the thickets. Several varieties of trillium grow here, also lilies-of-the-valley, wild bleedinghearts, and numerous orchids. The fringe trees grow from 20 to 30 feet high. Scattered along the creeks and in dense beds of rare ferns are the beautiful silver trees.

Wildlife is still abundant in this section of the country. Ruffed grouse, rabbits, wild turkeys and many small game birds and animals are seen. White-tailed deer are being propagated, but are not plentiful. Black bears are frequently shot.

The wild boar of the German Hartz Mountains is found here. They were imported to stock a private preserve but escaped and now run wild. They spread over an 80,000-acre region, now the Tellico Game and Fish Management Area. They have greatly increased in numbers and now furnish exciting sport for hunters; they are vicious fighters, and the females with litters are especially dangerous, sometimes killing or injuring several dogs during the hunt.

The first official Tennessee boar hunt was held in 1936 under the supervision of the State Game and Fish Department and the U. S. Forest Service.

In the fall, a limited number of hunters, whose names are drawn by lot from a list of applicants, gather at Tellico Plains, the headquarters for the hunt. Here mountain guides with packs of trained dogs are available. Three styles common to big-game hunting are used—chasing, stalking, and shooting from a stand. In addition to the regular State hunting license, a special permit issued by the State, costing $5, is required.

ENGLEWOOD, 54 *m.* (850 alt., 1,554 pop.), is a trading center in a fertile farming district.

ETOWAH, 61.8 *m.* (865 alt., 2,516 pop.) a railroad division point, is primarily a trading town for farmers.

Left from Etowah on a dirt road to CHILHOWEE SPRINGS *(hotel and cabins)*, 6 *m.*, on Chilhowee Mountain.

At 68.2 *m.* is the junction with paved State 40, the Kinsey Highway.

Left on State 40 is RELIANCE, 5.9 *m.*; R. here 4 *m.* on a dirt road to SPRINGTOWN, near which Geo. W. Johnson wrote the song "When You and I were Young Maggie."

BENTON, 74.8 *m.* (880 alt., 508 pop.), is the seat of Polk County. An OLD FORT TENNESSEE BLOCKHOUSE has been moved to the center of the town. It was built of hewn pine logs; though its age is not known, the type of construction indicates that it was erected in a very early period of Tennessee history. The upper story contains 32 loop-holes, the lower 28.

Left from Benton 7.5 *m.* on a dirt road to the GRAVE OF NANCY WARD, an Indian woman, who attempted to maintain peace between her people and the aggressive white settlers. She frequently warned the whites of Indian attacks. Nevertheless the Indians held her in high esteem, partly because of her service to members of the tribe. The chiefs conferred upon her the office of "Beloved Woman," gave her the right to be heard in the council, and bestowed on her the power to release condemned prisoners. During the siege of Fort Watauga, Mrs. William Bean, mother of the first white child born in Tennessee, was taken prisoner and condemned to be burnt. She had been carried to the top of a mound when Nancy appeared and released her.

At 80.8 *m.* is the junction with US 64 *(see Tour 13)*.

OLD FORT, 86.8 *m.*, is the former site of the blockhouse that has been moved to Benton.

TENNGA, 91.8 *m.*, a town on the Tennessee-Georgia Line, with a post office in each State, is at the northern end of Bedspread Boulevard, which extends to Dalton and Atlanta, Ga. For miles on both sides of the road are displays of homemade bedspreads, mats, rugs, beach coats, and other articles. Men, women, and children deftly operate needle and hooked-rug frames. Entire families are busy "keeping up the spread lines" for tourists and for mail-order trade from city department stores. The income obtained from this work is relatively low, but many of the families have no other means of earning cash.

Tennga is 16 miles north of Chatsworth, Ga., on Georgia 61.

Tour 5B

Junction with State 71—Kinzel Springs—Walland—Maryville; 40 m. State 73.

Resort accommodations at points both on and near the route.
Surfaced roadbed; winding road, requires slow driving.

State 73 branches southwest from a junction with State 71 *(see Tour 5)*, 2.4 miles south of Gatlinburg; it is part of the Knoxville Scenic Loop, joining State 33 *(see Tour 5A)* at Maryville. Half the route lies within the GREAT SMOKY MOUNTAINS NATIONAL PARK *(see GREAT SMOKY MOUTAINS NATIONAL PARK)*. The road follows the course of Fighting Creek, runs through Fighting Gap until the defile converges with the gap of the Little River at Elkmont, then winds along Little River Gulch. At Townsend it enters Tuckaleechee Cove, and at Walland leaves the foothills through a gap in Chilhowee Mountain to drop down into the Valley of East Tennessee.

Between the junction with State 71 and Walland, State 73 twists through some of the most rugged and picturesque highlands in the East. Between Elkmont and Townsend the road, laid on the bed of a logging railway, follows a clear mountain stream through a gorge whose walls rise sharply. Until a decade ago this gorge was known only to foresters, lumbermen, and mountaineers. A few mountain cabins are visible from the road; each has its truck garden, but sometimes the plot is on such a steep slope that it would seem impossible to plow and cultivate the land. The mountain people cross from the road on swinging bridges to paths that lead into high coves in the gorge.

At 0.3 *m.* south of the junction with US 71 is the junction with a trail.

Right on this trail to HOLY BUTT (2,910 alt.), 2.7 *m.* The trail continues to MOUNT HARRISON (3,000 alt.) 3.3 *m.*, on the northern boundary of the park and overlooking Wear Cove, and affording views of Mount LeConte, the Chimneys and Siler's Bald.

An OBSERVATION POINT (2,089 alt.) is (L) at 2.3 *m.*

At 2.5 *m.*, where State 73 cuts through FIGHTING CREEK GAP (2,300 alt.) is a junction with a trail.

1. Left on this trail to MID'S GAP (2,584 alt.), 1 *m.*, and TURKEY GAP, 2 *m.* At Turkey Gap is a junction with a trail that leads 3 *m.* to SUGARLAND MOUNTAIN.

2. Right from Fighting Creek Gap on this trail to LAUREL CREEK FALLS, 1.4 *m.*, frequently visited because of their accessibility. DEVIL'S CHUTE, 1.8 *m.*, is one of the picturesque spots in the park.

At 2.5 *m.* to CHINQUAPIN RIDGE (3,500 alt.). At 4 *m.* is a junction with a trail that leads (L) 0.3 *m.* to COVE MOUNTAIN (4,091 alt.), which affords a broad view overlooking Wear Cove.

DEFIANCE

At 5 *m.* on the main trail is PHIL'S VIEW (3,700 alt.). At 6 *m.* is MOUNT HARRISON from which return to State 73 can be made by a shorter trail.

At 4.4 *m.* is the junction with a macadam road.

Left on this road is ELKMONT (2,146 alt., 110 pop.), 1 *m.*, a resort *(hotels and cabins)* on a farm once owned by Drury P. Armstrong, Knoxville merchant, whose diary (1844–49) tells of an abundance of game fish, wild fowl, wild animals and large crops here. The railroad of the Little River Lumber Company was the first means of access to the spot. An excursion of the Knoxville Elks caused the place to be called Elks Mountain, but this was later shortened to Elkmont. The Wonderland Club Hotel, built in 1912 and since enlarged, is one of the few resort hotels in the park *(guides available)*.

The Appalachian Club maintains a smaller clubhouse and a number of cabins.

Across the road from the hotel is the entrance to Le Conte, a private camp for boys.

1. Right from Elkmont on Jake's Gap Trail 2 *m.* to the barrier *(cars should be left here)*. The trail follows the old railroad bed. At JAKE'S GAP, 3 *m.*, the trail turns (R) to BLANKET MOUNTAIN (4,609 alt.), 5 *m.*, where panoramas unfold. The fire lookout on the mountain commands a 35-mile view of the western end of the Great Smokies.

The origin of the name of this peak is unknown; some believe it was given because Indians used the mountain as a signal post for sending smoke messages with the aid of blankets; others attribute the name to early surveyors who marked central points for their platting by hanging a blanket on a tree on each summit.

2. Left from Elkmont 4 *m.* on a trail following Little River to Fish Camp Prong, which is followed and crisscrossed by the trail ascending to the Tennessee-North Carolina Divide, 5 *m.* Left (east) is SILER'S BALD on the Divide (5,620 alt.), 6.5 *m.* Other trails are available for descent. The climb up Siler's Bald is not an easy one; it leads nearly 8 *m.* over boulders and through undergrowth. Part of the way this slope is like a well lined with slippery, moss-covered rock. On top of the ridge is a deep, rich loam that frequently reaches the shoetops. Roots of rhododendrons offer perilous foothold, but the flowing branches form a beautiful arch overhead.

On the North Carolina side the view downward shows Forney Ridge and Bear Wallow Knob. A bear wallow, the ideal bathtub of the mountain bear, is formed by soft humus on a moisture-retaining underclay or rock. There is an impressive view down the north front of Siler's Bald into the triangular gulf formed by the Miry Ridge (5,240 alt.) and the Sugarland Mountain. This is sometimes a forbidding vista. Seas of rhododendron cover the impenetrable depths which in winter are sunless and desolate.

At 9.9 *m.* on State 73 is the junction with a graveled road.

Right on this road 1.1 *m.* to a junction with a trail. Left on this trail 0.7 *m.* to ROUND TOP (3,080 alt.). At 1.3 *m.* (R) to WEAR COVE GAP.

At 2 *m.* is LINE SPRINGS HOTEL *(see Tour 5).*

At SINK'S BRIDGE, 11.9 *m.,* on State 73 is a junction with a trail.

Right here following a creek to CURRY HE MOUNTAIN and CURRY SHE MOUNTAIN (3,014 alt.), 1.7 *m.*

Curry He was the mountaineers' version of an unknown Indian word approximating it in sound and, having thus arrived at the name of one mountain, they logically called a neighboring peak Curry She.

At 17.9 *m.* on State 73 is the junction with an unimproved road.

Left on this road that follows the Middle Prong of the Little River to WALKER'S VALLEY, 3 *m.,* where there is a junction with a trail leading 0.7 *m.* (L) to FODDERSTACK MOUNTAIN (2,525 alt.). At 4.5 *m.* on the road is TREMONT (1,925 alt., 50 pop.). COLD WATER KNOB (4,009 alt.) and RUSSELL FIELD (4,876 alt.) are nearby. Radiating from Tremont are the trails to THUNDERHEAD MOUNTAIN (5,530 alt.), GREENBRIER KNOB on the North Carolina Line, JAKE'S GAP (4,474 alt.), and BLANKET MOUNTAIN (4,609 alt.).

State 73 leaves the gorge at TUCKALEECHEE COVE, 19.1 *m.*

TOWNSEND, 21.3 *m.* (1,500 alt., 402 pop.), in Tuckaleechee Cove, was known by the name of the cove until a lumber mill was built here in 1902 by W. B. Townsend. It is a quiet village with many houses facing the river. There is a hotel and a tourist home here.

KINZEL SPRING, 24 *m.* (1,610 alt., 100 pop.), a summer resort established in 1894, lies below four mountains—Matthew, Mark, Luke, and John. Beyond the two hotels cluster cottages, housing a large summer colony.

Left from Kinzel Springs on the improved Cades Cove Rd. At 3.5 *m.* is RICH MOUNTAIN, where is a notable view. The road approaches CADES COVE (1,710 alt.), 10 *m., (two hotels),* from a high rim. The view over the broad flat resembles that over an unrippled lake. This peaceful expanse, two miles wide by six long, spreads between Rich Mountain and the divide. The cove is threaded by Abram Creek, which rushes down through an almost invisible gorge. Over Cades Cove towers Thunderhead. This place is believed to have been named Kate's Cove, for an old Indian squaw.

Miss Mary Noailles Murfree *(see WRITERS OF TENNESSEE),* who was lame, was so eager to see the mountain that she traveled the trails on horseback. Cades Cove is the locale of her books, *The Prophet of the Great Smoky Mountains, Stranger People's Country,* and *The Raid of the Guerrilla,* written under her pen name of Charles Egbert Craddock.

1. Right from Cades Cove on a 3-mile trail that follows Abram's Creek to its union with Laurel Branch, which it then follows to the pool at the foot of ABRAM'S FALLS.

2. Left from Cades Cove on a 7-mile trail that follows Anthony Creek to Bote Mountain and thence (L) to Spence Field on the divide and THUNDERHEAD MOUNTAIN (5,530 alt.).

3. Right from Willie Myer's place at the western end of Cades Cove, on a trail that follows Gregory Ridge to RICH GAP, 4.2 *m.,* and GREGORY'S BALD (4,948 alt.), 4.5 *m.* This area was formerly used for the pasturage of sheep. The descent can be made by several routes.

WALLAND, 29.4 *m.* (250 pop.), with a mineral spring, is in a gap of the Chilhowee Mountains. The settlement grew with the establishment of the England Walton Tannery in 1902. There is a hotel here.

MARYVILLE, 40 *m.* (1,150 alt., 4,968 pop.) *(see Tour 5A)* is at the junction with State 33 *(see Tour 5).*

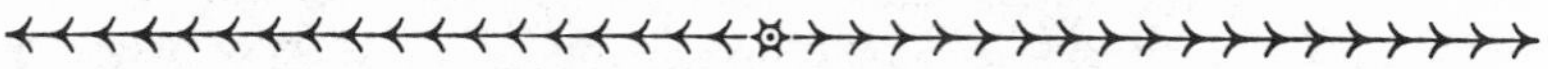

Tour 6

(Somerset, Ky)—Oneida—Harriman—Rockwood—Spring City—Dayton—Chattanooga (La Fayette, Ga.); US 27.
Kentucky Line to the Georgia Line, 139.5 m.

The Southern Ry. parallels US 27 for the entire route.
Paved roadbed.
Usual accommodations.

Section a. KENTUCKY LINE *to* JUNCTION WITH US 70; *69 m.*

US 27 crosses the Kentucky Line, 0 *m.,* 46 miles south of Somerset, Ky., and, for about 60 miles, runs through a beautiful mountain area broken by ragged gulches, through which swift streams and rivers flow. Small timber grows densely along the highway and, during the spring and summer, wild flowers brighten the roadside.

South of Wartburg, US 27 descends circuitously through the valley of the Emory River into that of the Tennessee. Between Harriman and Chattanooga the route passes along the foot of the Cumberland Escarpment (R), which is known locally as Walden's Ridge; it rises 1,000 feet above the valley, forming the western rim of the East Tennessee Valley.

During the heavy immigration to America in the latter part of the nineteenth century, numerous sites in the valley were selected for colonization—some with high idealism and some with hope of gain. Judged by the hopes of their founders, all failed.

ONEIDA, 9.3 *m.* (1,500 alt., 1,382 pop.), the largest town in Scott County, is a shipping point for timber, coal, farm products, and live stock.

Right from Oneida on an unmarked dirt road to INDIAN ROCK HOUSE, 13 *m.*, on the Grassy Fork of Williams Creek. The shelter is created by an overhanging rock ledge. Stones piled up in crude walls and frameworks of poles covered with skins or branches made effective windbreaks. The Indians of Tennessee and Kentucky made this terrritory neutral ground and used it solely for hunting. During the hunting season they lived in this place and others like it. Here they smoked meat, treated skins, and stored their supplies.

At 16.4 *m.* is the junction with graveled State 63.

Left on State 63 is HUNTSVILLE, 2.6 *m.* (1,450 alt., 500 pop.), seat of Scott County. Lumbering is the chief activity.

NEW RIVER, 20 *m.* (1,201 alt., 200 pop.), is a shipping point for coal and lumber.

The principal activity of ROBBINS, 23.5 *m.* (1,370 alt., 500 pop.), is brick making. BARTON CHAPEL was erected in memory of the Reverend William E. Barton, who began his ministry near the site of this church in 1885. The chapel has become a center of social-service work in the community. Barton, who died in 1930, was a lecturer at a theological seminary in Chicago and at Vanderbilt University School of Religion. He was the author of *The Paternity of Abraham Lincoln,* an account of exhaustive research on the question of Lincoln's legitimacy, and of *The Women Lincoln Loved.* His son, Bruce Barton, who was elected to the U. S. House of Representatives in 1937 from the 17th district of New York, is the author of *The Man Nobody Knows.*

At 25 *m.* is the junction with State 52.

Right on this graveled road is RUGBY, 7 *m.* (1,410 alt., 275 pop.), established in 1877 as an experimental colony under the supervision of Thomas Hughes, British author of *Tom Brown's School Days.* The community was intended for Englishmen "recruited from the ranks of mechanics and tradespeople, and for the overplus of intelligent young men for whom there seemed to be no proper occupation at home." As conceived by Hughes, it was to be a place where "a reverent, godly life would grow up and spread over all neighboring regions of the South Highlands." Rugby was selected because of its mild climate and fertile soil. A large acreage was purchased, spreading over parts of Morgan, Scott, and Fentress Counties.

Royalties from the sale of Hughes' books were used in starting the colony. Two months after Hughes' arrival there were 120 colonists. English social customs and sports, such as cricket, Rugby football, and tennis, were introduced. A library of 800 volumes was contributed by American publishers. Later the HUGHES FREE PUBLIC LIBRARY had 7,000 volumes; it is still open. The colony never attained the "slow and steady growth" hoped for by Hughes. His dream that the members living by the "labors of their own hands . . . would be able to meet princes in the gate without embarrassment and self-assertion" never came true. After the project had failed, Hughes wrote to friends in Rugby, "I can't help feeling and believing that good seed was sown . . ."

The Gothic-type RUGBY PARISH P.E. CHURCH, built of wood in the early days of settlement, is still in use. The church organ, manufactured by the London firm of Ralph Allison & Sons, belonged to the Reverend Joseph Blacklock, who left England with his wife and seven sons to settle here. The church has hangings of hand-embroidered silk, a needlepoint kneeling cushion, and a hand-carved alms basin.

The route crosses the ridge at 34 *m.* that is the dividing line between the watersheds of the Cumberland and Tennessee Rivers.

SUNBRIGHT, 36 *m.* (1,216 alt., 500 pop.), is a shipping point for an oil and gas field discovered in 1916; distributing plants are maintained here by two large oil companies.

Lumbering is an important activity here, and both rough and dressed lumber are prepared.

Right from Sunbright on old State 52 to BOONE CAMP *(open 8-4 weekdays; apply at office for pass),* 4.5 *m.,* where there is an oil refinery having a daily productive capacity of 1,200 barrels of gasoline. The gas wells can produce 10 million cubic feet in 24 hours.

Right 5 *m.* from Sunbright on Deer Lodge Pike to DEER LODGE, a small colony of Poles, most of whom are farmers.

At 37 *m.* on US 27 is the junction with a paved road.

Left on this road 0.5 *m.* to the foot of a 2.5-mile trail to PILOT MOUNTAIN (2,700 alt.). Shortly before Christmas 1934, an airmail plane crashed, killing the pilot on the top of this mountain. There is a fine view from a lookout tower.

WARTBURG, 47.5 *m.* (1,373 alt., 350 pop.), named for Wartburg, Germany, is the seat of Morgan County, named for Gen. Daniel Morgan, Revolutionary soldier. Although it is on the Cumberland Plateau, Wartburg lies at the foot of Ward and Byrd Mountains. It was settled in 1845 by Swiss and German colonists, one of whom, Frederic Beneike, established a piano factory here.

Outstanding among these German colonists were Augustin Gattinger and George Dury, brothers-in-law, who arrived in 1849 from Munich. Gattinger became an assistant surgeon in the U. S. Army in 1864, was appointed State Commissioner of Agriculture in 1883, and later published books on botany and mineralogy. His collection of plants, seeds, minerals, and fossils, now at the University of Tennessee, is almost complete for the State. His botanical library of 187 volumes is now at Peabody College. A species of shell Gattinger discovered was named for him.

After Dury settled in Tennessee, he painted portraits of several Americans, including Robert E. Lee and Abraham Lincoln. His portrait of Mrs. James K. Polk hangs in the East room of the White House; several other paintings are in the State Library at Nashville.

Among the first buildings was Immigration House, a large structure in which the colonists lived until land could be cleared and dwellings built. A Lutheran congregation was organized and a church built.

During the gold rush of 1849 a resident of Wartburg, whose name has been forgotten, joined the thousands who went to California. He made a rich strike and returned to Morgan County, bringing with him the fortune in gold nuggets he had found. After a short stay he decided to return to California, and, fearing that someone might rob him, buried the gold somewhere on the bluffs of Big Clear Creek. Returning to California, the miner became ill and sent word of the cache to a relative who failed to find the gold. The miner died in California, and as far as anyone knows his treasure has never been found. Many believe that it is still buried in the vicinity.

1. Right from Wartburg, 1.5 *m.*, on the old Oakdale Road to POTTER'S FALLS, 45 feet high, in Crooked Fork Creek. The water below the falls is fine for bathing.

2. Left from Wartburg on graveled State 62 to the junction with Petros Road, 9 *m.* L. here 2 *m.* to PETROS (1,300 alt., 1,500 pop.), the northern terminus of the Harriman and Northeastern R.R. Petros lies in a deep valley that is in the coal area extending over parts of Morgan, Scott, and Anderson Counties. The name Petros possibly originated by a peculiar blending of the first name of Gov. Peter Turney and the last name of a friend, Ross. In 1893 the State bought 11,000 acres of timber and coal land at Brushy Mountain, near Petros, and established BRUSHY MOUNTAIN PRISON. Convict labor is used to work the mines. Prior to the purchase of this property the State leased the services of convicts to private industry. This practice, however, was later abolished *(see Tour 5A)*.

South of Wartburg the route descends the mountain and passes through the valley of the Emory River into the valley of the Tennessee.

At 59.5 *m.* is the junction with a paved road.

Right on this road is OAKDALE, 1 *m.* (805 alt., 1,123 pop.). Because the town is crowded between Mountain Gap and Big Emory River, the houses are on the sides of steep hills. There is a fine beach by the river.

In the village is a small colony of Melungeons, a dark-skinned people found only in the mountainous region of East Tennessee and western North Carolina.

HARRIMAN, 64.5 *m.* (792 alt., 4,488 pop.), is a neat and prosperous city surrounded by beautiful rolling hills. The town is the trade center of a fertile farming region; its interests center primarily about large hosiery and woolen mills.

In 1845 Col. R. K. Byrd bought large holdings and established a plantation here. He believed that at this place "nature had ordained a town should be," but died five years before it was founded. Nearly fifty years later the East Tennessee Land Company bought 10,000 acres of his land, planning a city that would have a population of 50,000. The only house on the site was the MARGROVE HOME, on Margrove St., which was built of logs in 1810. In 1889 the company platted 343 acres and on Feb. 26, 1890, the first 574 lots were sold at an auction conducted by the president of the land company, Gen. Clinton D. Fisk, who in 1888 had been a candidate for the Presidency on the Prohibition Party ticket. He endeavored to make the city a model of morality and sobriety and the restriction still holds that "every contract, deed, or other conveyance, or lease of real estate by the land company and its successors, should contain and does contain a provision forbidding the use of of the property, or any building thereon, for the purpose of making, storing, or selling intoxicating liquor as such." The Women's Christian Temperance Union had much to do with the early life of the place, which was named for Gen. Walter Harriman, a former Governor of New Hampshire, and incorporated on Feb. 7, 1891.

The first office building of the East Tennessee Land Company on Roane and Walden Sts., became the American Temperance University, from which many prominent people of the section received their degrees. It was later the Mooney School, then Tate School, and is now the CITY HALL.

The CASSELL HOUSE *(private)*, on Cumberland St., holds a fine collection of old furniture, patchwork quilts, hand-made bedspreads, chinaware, and silver. Among the pieces of furniture is a secretary given to Gov. John Sevier as a wedding present. There is an old silver service with an acorn design that was made, like most Colonial silver, of melted money. The Cassells, when they fled from Germany to America to escape religious persecution, brought the silver service with them.

A PUBLIC MUSEUM *(open 2:30-5:30 daily)*, established by Mrs. Daniel Denny, is in the basement of the CARNEGIE LIBRARY, on the corner of Walden and Trenton Streets. It contains articles from China, Japan, and other Oriental countries; old chinaware, stuffed birds and animals, and geological specimens.

Left from Harriman on the Swan Pond Road to the JONES DAIRY FARM 4 *m.*, which has a water mill built by August and Henry Knoblauch, Germans who settled here about 1830. It was originally used for milling corn and wheat but finally fell into disuse. The old wheel has been replaced, and the mill now generates electric power for use at the dairy.

At 69 *m.* is the junction with US 70 *(see Tour 12)*. Between this point and 78.8 *m.* US 27 and US 70 are united *(see Tour 12)*.

Section b. JUNCTION WITH US 70 *to* GEORGIA LINE; *70.5 m.*

South of the junction with US 70 *(see Tour 12)*, 2 miles west of Rockwood, is a BOY SCOUT MEMORIAL, 4.4 *m.*, a beautiful monument erected in honor of a scoutmaster and seven scouts who were drowned in a flood in 1929 while camping at a point near the marker.

SPRING CITY, 13.8 *m.* (766 alt., 1,090 pop.), is in the Tennessee Valley at the foot of Walden's Ridge.

Left from Spring City on State 68 to RHEA SPRINGS, 2 *m.*, whose water was valued by the Indians for its supposed medicinal qualities. They called it the "Home of the Great Spirit," possibly because, as legend says, the water frequently rose with a great swish at midnight—a sign of the power of the healing spirit inhabiting its depths. Just before a sale, slave owners brought their work-worn slaves to Rhea Springs to rejuvenate them and increase their value. The hotel here is a modern log structure.

The HAMPTON GROUP of Indian mounds is on the bank of the river. They include about twenty earthen mounds, a part of the chain of prehistoric earthworks that extended through the Tennessee Valley. A number of them have been excavated, and numerous Indian artifacts have been removed.

DAYTON, 30 *m.* (706 alt., 2,006 pop.), seat of Rhea County, was founded in 1820 by W. H. Smith, a New England schoolmaster. The industrial plants include hosiery mills, an underwear factory, canneries, and a bottle works. Coal mines are operated in the nearby mountains.

At the RHEA COUNTY COURTHOUSE the "evolution trial" of John T. Scopes was held in the summer of 1925. This case, known as the "Monkey Trial," grew out of the alleged violation of a Tennessee statute, passed March 21 of that year, making it "unlawful for any teacher in . . . the State . . . to teach any theory that denies the story of the divine creation of man as taught in the Bible . . ." At a meeting in a local drugstore early in 1925, Dr. George Rappelyea persuaded Scopes, the science teacher in the high school, to stand trial in a test of the new law. Scopes admitted teaching evolution in his general science class. The American Civil Liberties Union offered to finance the trial and lend its attorney, Arthur Garfield Hays. When William Jennings Bryan volunteered as prosecutor, Clarence Darrow and Dudley Field Malone joined Hays in the defense.

Soon Dayton was aroar with newspaper men, itinerant preachers, and thousands of the curious. Revivalists put up tents and placarded the town with signs carrying pertinent Biblical warnings. The roads swarmed with buggies, mule-drawn wagons, and mud-spattered and dust-caked Fords, as Tennessee farmers and their families came to town to watch the defense of "Genesis." They publicly and frequently affirmed their belief in the Bible from "kiver to kiver" and some said that "this Darrow feller must have horns and a tail." All of them were eager to hear Bryan, the Great Commoner, long famous on Chautauqua circuits for his "Crown of Thorns . . . Cross of Gold" oration which, when first delivered in 1896, resulted in his nomination for the Presidency.

Tradesmen did a land-office business. Hot-dog and lemonade stands were set up on every vacant lot. The crowd filled the small court room, aisles and windows, and overflowed into the court yard. During the hot summer days the trial proceeded, with smooth oratory from Malone, shrewd cross-questioning from Darrow, and violent but eloquent outbursts from Bryan.

By the time the trial ended there was a personal feud between Bryan and Darrow. Under the trees of the court yard, to which the court had moved, Bryan cried, "I want the world to know that this man who doesn't believe in God is using a Tennessee court to cast slurs on Him . . ."

Darrow's reply, "I am simply examining you on the fool ideas that no intelligent Christian in the whole world believes," brought horrified gasps from part of the audience.

Scopes was found guilty and fined $100. Bryan died here on July 26, 1925, five days after the close of the trial into which he had entered with all his nervous energy. As a memorial to him a William Jennings Bryan University was founded here.

1. Right from Dayton on State 30 to CUMBERLAND SPRINGS, 2 *m.,* an artesian spring, by which is a GEOLOGICAL FIELD STATION of Ohio State University. Practical training in field work is given here. The station was established here because of the topography of the region, which is diversified. The slopes, hills, and peaks near here represent periods in geologic history ranging from the Cambrian to the Pennsylvanian. There are more than 20 different formations, including the folds and thrust faults of a part of the great Appalachian Valley, and a part of the Cumberland Plateau. The region holds coal, clay, and iron ore.

JOHNSON'S BLUFF, 6.5 *m.,* is a summer colony on the east brow of Walden's Ridge, from which is a good view of the Great Smoky Mountains and the Tennessee River.

MORGAN SPRINGS, 7 *m.,* is at the summit of Walden's Ridge. From BUZZARD POINT (1,850 alt.), near Morgan Springs, is a beautiful view of the Tennessee Valley.

2. Left from Dayton on the Blythe Ferry Road to HIWASSEE ISLAND, 2 *m.,* formerly Jolly's Island. It was once the home of Oo-loo-te-ka, the Cherokee who adopted young Sam Houston as his son. Oo-loo-te-ka was chief of a band of about 300, and his island village was large. Oo-loo-te-ka's name in English was He-Who-

Puts-The-Drum-Away, meaning "he likes peace." Young Houston, tiring of farm life, first ran off to the Cherokee village in 1809, when he was about sixteen. Altogether he spent three years with the Cherokee, hunting with them, learning their language, playing their games. He excelled in all their vigorous sports, and proved himself worthy to be called the chief's son. The Indians named him Co-lon-nah (The Raven) and his guardian or totem animal was the eagle. Houston's three years on Hiwassee Island had a great influence on his life. He gained an insight into Indian character and life and realized that it was his own people who were to blame for much of the frontier warfare between the two races. Later he made numerous trips to Washington in behalf of the Cherokee.

The earthen mounds and village sites on the island were excavated in 1937 by WPA workers. The upper levels of village sites contained many articles of white manufacture. Beneath were the remains of a prehistoric Indian culture. Artifacts, pottery, and skeletal remains were recovered.

SALE CREEK, 45.1 *m.* (730 alt., 600 pop.), was the site of an Indian mission school established in 1806 by Gideon Blackburn, Presbyterian minister and missionary. Blackburn was unable to interest his own Presbytery in the school and took his plea to the General Assembly, which in 1803 voted $200 for the support of the work. When Blackburn started preaching "he forgot time, place, and circumstances," according to a contemporary writer. He was more than six feet tall, and "his voice was rich and silvery."

SODDY, 48.1 *m.* (788 alt., 1,173 pop.), is a coal-mining town at the foot of Walden's Ridge. Formerly, large quantities of low-grade bituminous were mined here, but only a few mines are now in operation.

DAISY, 50.9 *m.* (720 alt., 370 pop.), is a coal-shipping point. There are large tile and brick ovens here.

It was in Daisy that Dr. Charles Herty, the Georgia chemist who developed the process of making paper from yellow pine, started the manufacture of clayware turpentine cups. This was one of his earliest inventions, and although the clay cups have been displaced somewhat by aluminum cups, the former are still manufactured and used in many places.

Right from Daisy on a dirt road to MONTLAKE, 5 *m.,* on Walden's Ridge. The lake, which lies in a deep bowl on top of the ridge, is surrounded by sheer rock walls 150 feet high.

Montlake has a seasonal difference in level of more than 20 feet, probably because of the increase of water from seepage and decrease in the summer from leakage and evaporation.

At VALDEAU, 64.4 *m.,* a residential part of Chattanooga, is the junction with State 27 *(see Tour 15).* Between this place and Chattanooga are a number of tourist and trailer camps.

CHATTANOOGA, 67.5 *m.* (674 alt., 119,798 pop.) *(see CHATTANOOGA).*

Points of Interest: Lookout Mountain, Signal Mountain, Chickamauga Park, Chickamauga Dam, and TVA offices.

At Chattanooga are the junctions with US 11 *(see Tour 1),* US 64-41 *(see Tour 13),* and State 28 *(see Tour 15).* The point of intersection is at 11th and Market Sts.

US 27 crosses the Georgia Line, 70.5 *m.,* 22 miles north of La Fayette, Ga.

Tour 7

(Glasgow, Ky.)—Nashville—Columbia—Pulaski—(Athens, Ala.); US 31E and US 31.
Kentucky Line to Alabama Line, 145.4 m.

Louisville & Nashville R.R. parallels route throughout.
Roadbed paved throughout.
Hotels only in cities and county seats; some tourist accommodations elsewhere.

Section a. KENTUCKY LINE *to* NASHVILLE, *50.7 m.*

US 31E crosses the Kentucky Line, 0 *m.,* 36 miles south of Glasgow, Ky., passes over the Highland Rim, and traverses the bluegrass basin of Middle Tennessee. This area has been famous since pioneer days for the quality of stock reared in it and for its fertility. The country is particularly attractive in early spring when the hillsides are covered with the pink and white blossoms of redbud and dogwood trees. A few of the older estates remain, but most of them have been subdivided into small farms that grow diversified crops.

SUGAR GROVE, 1.2 *m.* (615 alt., 25 pop.), is named for a one-acre grove of sugar maples, a type of tree rarely found in the South. The scarred trunks are reminders of the time when the tapping of the trees and the making of maple sugar and syrup was a festive occasion in the community.

At 5.9 *m.* is the junction with State 52.

Left on State 52 is WESTMORELAND, 0.3 *m.* (612 alt., 426 pop.), most of whose inhabitants are concerned with strawberry growing, the leading cash crop. During the picking season, usually the last of May or the first of June, hundreds of people are busy in the fields surrounding the town. After the crop has been sold, annual debts are paid and merchants stock their stores for a great increase in business. Carnivals or circuses are usually on the scene to get their share of the free-flowing money.

Tobacco, much less of a seasonal crop, is second in importance to local farmers.

LAFAYETTE, 14.5 *m.* (pronounced La-fay'ette) (702 alt., 577 pop.), trade town of a farming area, was named in honor of the French general and statesman who fought with the Americans in the Revolutionary War.

The WOODMORE HOTEL, facing the public square, was the first building erected here. It was constructed in 1820 of hewn logs and hand-dressed poplar and was floored with white ash. The chimneys are the old-fashioned stack type, and the fireplaces carry four-foot logs. Near the hotel is TOWN SPRINGS, which determined settlement here. Lafayette is the home of State Senator John Butler, who introduced the anti-evolution act on which the Scopes trial at Dayton, Tenn., was conducted *(see Tour 6)*.

Right from Lafayette 10 *m.* on State 10, a graveled road, to an unusually large SUNDIAL (R) on the Payne farm. It weighs 10 tons and its shadow bar rises 25 feet.

On State 52 is RED BOILING SPRINGS, 28.6 *m.* (623 alt., 800 pop.), a summer resort, named for a bubbling spring that contains a red sediment. In 1830 Edmund Jennings, a hunter, came upon a salt lick here, found game plentiful, and settled. In 1840 another settler, Shepherd Kirby, arrived. He had an eye infection, and one day while building his log cabin he washed his eyes in the water from the "red boiling" spring. The pain was relieved, and he continued to bathe his eyes in the water until they were healed. When this story was told to other settlers, they flocked here to drink or to bathe in the waters. So many found relief that the springs were exploited commercially and this place became one of the leading health resorts of the State. It still receives large numbers of visitors.

Right from Red Boiling Springs 4.5 *m.* on a dirt road to LEONARD CAVE *(adm. 10¢)*, which is 70 feet wide and 12 feet high at the entrance. It requires four hours to walk through the cave, which is electrically lighted.

South of the junction with State 52, US 31E descends from the Highland Rim through a narrow valley, flanked by steep rock bluffs, and at 13 *m.* is in the bluegrass basin.

BETHPAGE, 13.3 *m.* (542 alt., 250 pop.), in the basin, is surrounded by fields dotted with grazing cattle. There are many prosperous and well-stocked farms.

At 16.2 *m.*, by a stone bridge, is the junction with a graveled road.

Left on this road to ROGANA *(private)*, 1.1 *m.*, Hugh Rogan, an immigrant from Ireland, came to Middle Tennessee with John Donelson's party in 1780, and was one of the signers of the Cumberland Compact. He moved to the Bledsoe Lick settlement and built this simple brick house in 1800.

At 23.5 *m.* is the junction with State 25 a hard surfaced road.

Left on State 25 5.5 *m.* to Bledsoe Creek, named for Isaac and Anthony Bledsoe, Long Hunters who came into this area in 1769. Isaac Bledsoe, on one of his hunting excursions, discovered a salt lick which was called Bledsoe Lick and to which great droves of buffaloes were wont to come. Isaac and Anthony were members of the first county court organized in Davidson County.

At 5.6 *m.* just after the road crosses the creek, is (L) UNION CHURCH.

1. Left here 0.6 *m.* on a private lane to CRAGFONT *(private)*, built in 1802 by Gen. James Winchester. It is a large solid T-shaped structure of gray limestone. Its style was inspired by the Georgian Colonial houses of Maryland, General Winchester's home State. With very little detail, the design of the exterior achieves absolute symmetry. The interior was finished by skilled artisans brought from Baltimore; their careful craft contributed a wealth of subtle detail to highly polished woodwork. Incorporated in the building was an enormous ball room, the first such luxury in the State. The General was very hospitable and often entertained men of national importance. The most noted of these were Andrew Jackson, the Marquis de Lafayette, Andre Michaux, and Aaron Burr. General Winchester was associated with Judge John Overton and Andrew Jackson in the founding of Memphis, and it was he who gave Memphis its name. This home, once the beauty spot of Sumner County, is now in great need of repair.

2. Right from the main road 0.1 *m.* on a dirt road to the EDWARD WARD CARMACK BIRTHPLACE. Carmack, who was a Representative in Congress, United States Senator, editor, author and fiery orator, was born Nov. 5, 1858. He became an ardent prohibitionist and his speeches and editorials greatly influenced the enactment of Tennessee's prohibition law. In 1908 Carmack, representing the "drys," and Malcolm Patterson, the "wets," were campaigning for the governorship. Angered by an editorial published by Carmack, at that time editor of the Nashville *Tennessean*, two political friends of Patterson's, Robin and Duncan Cooper, assassinated Carmack on the street in Nashville. Duncan Cooper was found guilty, but was soon pardoned by Patterson, who in the meantime had been elected Governor *(see NASHVILLE)*.

CASTALIAN SPRINGS, **7.9** *m.,* formerly known as Bledsoe's Lick, was one of the first settlements in Middle Tennessee. It was the home of Gen. William B. Bate, Governor of Tennessee and United States Senator.

CASTALIAN SPRINGS TAVERN *(private)* stands on a low hill overlooking the village and is surrounded by magnificent trees. The tavern, built in 1828 by four men, has 14 rooms constructed entirely of hand-hewn logs and is well preserved. The joining of logs to connect such a large number of rooms is considered an architectural feat. Col. Alfred R. Waynne, one of the four builders, bought the house in 1834, and his descendants still live in it. A hickory tree on the lawn was planted by Colonel Waynne on the day of the death of his friend, Andrew Jackson.

The THOMAS SHARP SPENCER MARKER, in the center of the village, is on the site of the tree in which Spencer, a gigantic pioneer hunter, lived during the winter of 1778. It is said he had no tools to build a cabin. The Indians, observing his tracks in the forest, nicknamed him "Big Foot." The story is told that another hunter, chancing upon Spencer's footprints, fled in terror to the nearest settlement and reported that the Cumberland country was inhabited by a race of giants.

GALLATIN, 23.8 *m.* (521 alt., 3,050 pop.), seat of Sumner County, was established in 1802 and named for Albert Gallatin, Secretary of the Treasury under Presidents John Adams and Thomas Jefferson. US 31E follows East Main Street and West Main Street directly through town. Main Street is lined with large maple trees that form a continuous arch. Houses on this street are modern and have extensive lawns. The town is the agricultural and livestock market for the county and the central Burley tobacco market of Middle Tennessee. The selling season begins December 1st and closes about March.

There are also a large tobacco manufacturing plant here, a branch factory of a large shoe corporation, and a branch factory of a large cheese manufacturing corporation.

TROUSDALE PLACE, on Main Street, one block south of the courthouse square, was the home of Gen. William Trousdale, known as the War Horse of Tennessee, who served in the Creek, Seminole, and Mexican wars, and at the Battle of New Orleans. He was also the 13th Governor of Tennessee.

Three blocks south of the courthouse on West Main Street, are the large LOOSE LEAF TOBACCO SALES FLOORS, where the county's crop of Burley tobacco is marketed.

Left from Gallatin on South Water St., known locally as Wood's Ferry Rd., to SPENCER'S CHOICE, **0.2** *m.,* which stands (R) about 150 yards from the road. While hunting in the surrounding country, Spencer selected several desirable tracts of land. When other settlers began to arrive, he discovered that under the law he was entitled to only one tract. He laid claim to 800 acres here, fertile and beautifully wooded, since known as Spencer's Choice.

After Spencer was killed by the Indians in the spring of 1794, Col. David Shelby bought the land and in 1798 built a gray stone residence. The walls are two feet thick, the doorways and windows are set deep in paneled embrasures, and the original paneling, wainscoting, and mantels are preserved. After Colonel Shelby's death, the house was bought by Gen. Joseph Miller, who brought bluegrass with him from Kentucky and introduced it into general use in the Middle Tennessee basin. The earthquake of 1812 cracked one of the walls of the house, and the outbuildings were destroyed during the War between the States.

ROSEMONT, **0.8** *m. (open),* is the home of Jo Conn Guild, author of *Old Times in Tennessee.* The structure, built in 1828 of bricks molded on the site, is well preserved. In the rear of the house are a smokehouse, a carriage house, a slave house, an ice house, and the kitchen.

At 26.2 *m.* is GRASSLANDS, an estate of about 15,000 acres, purchased and developed by a group of Northern sportsmen as a private sporting club. They planned to establish an international steeplechase here. The project was abandoned after the market collapse of 1929 and, except for Grasslands Tavern, the assembled properties reverted to the former owners. The race track is L.

The entrance to the half-mile lane of FAIRVIEW *(open by request)* is at 26.3 *m.* The house, erected in 1832 by Isaac Franklin and known at that time as "the finest country home in Tennessee," still bears evidence of its former grandeur. The house was part of the Grasslands property. The main section of the mansion is of Georgian inspiration with the typical central hall flanked by large high-ceiled rooms. The double porches of the entrance portico have white Ionic columns; they are capped with a pediment. The garden facade is a duplicate of the front one. The broad steps leading to the entrance porches have graceful, curving wrought-iron balustrades with brass finials, the front and rear doorways are surmounted with beautifully designed fanlights. On the ceilings of the attic are still visible the names with the company and regimental designations that were traced with candle smoke by Union soldiers.

The wing added to the right side of the house in 1839 is distinctly Spanish in character; it is similar to those in the Feliciana Parish of Louisiana, where Franklin owned several large plantations. Although the design of the wing is radically different from that of the central structure the effect is harmonious. There are arcades on both front and rear of the wing which houses two kitchens with huge fireplaces.

Near the house are rows of brood-mare stables and the crumbling MAUSOLEUM OF ISAAC FRANKLIN. To the left of the house is a massive, circular, brick icehouse. To the rear, at a distance, are the former slave quarters.

Isaac Franklin, first owner of this property, was born in 1789 to parents of moderate means but before his fortieth birthday he was a millionaire. Besides the home and plantation at Fairview, he owned 50,000 acres of land in Texas and had some holdings in Louisiana and Mississippi. He was still a bachelor when he built this house, but in 1839 he married Adelicia Hayes, member of a prominent Nashville family. Franklin died in 1846. In 1882 Charles Reed of New York, a rich turfman, bought the property and built an immense stone barn with a shed that covered an exercise track for his horses. He imported sheet tin from England for the roof of the barn and shed. The interior of each stall was finished in oak by expert cabinetmakers.

FOXLAND HALL *(private)*, 27 *m.*, is (L) on a hilltop near the concrete bridge over Station Camp Creek. It is reached by a driveway that runs through a grove of large maples. The two-story brick house, built by Thomas Baker in 1825, is of the Greek Revival type and has a long two-story Ionic portico across the entire front. The entrance has fanlights and sidelights. The house has been modernized and enlarged.

Winding paths, bordered with huge boxwood, lead to the garden which is known for its variety of plants and shrubs, many of them from Martinique. The kennels contain some of the outstanding fox hounds in the South, a number of them prize winners. Annually, in the late fall, a fox hunt is held here with guests from many parts of the country.

The old graveyard holds the bodies of the builder and subsequent owners.

At 27.8 *m.* is the junction with a graveled road.

Right on this road to DUNCRUZIN *(private),* 1.8 *m.,* built in 1803, and added to since that time. The main doorway came from an old house near Dover, Tennessee. In the house are a pair of bronze chandliers from the parlors of a home of Jefferson Davis, an unusual collection of china, and a large tablecloth marked with the crown, eagle, and honey bees of the Emperor Napoleon. In the drawing room is a 75-year-old Steinway piano.

At 32.7 *m.* is GRASSLANDS TAVERN, one of the old homes restored by the Grasslands Foundation.

At 34.5 *m.* is the junction with a narrow graveled road.

Left on this road 1.5 *m.* to the entrance gate, from which a lane leads 0.6 *m.* to ROCK CASTLE *(private; open on application),* one of the first stone houses erected west of the southern Alleghenies and today stands as firm as when it was built. The old house, constructed of cut stone, has seven rooms. The foundation was laid in 1784, but owing to the constant warfare with the Indians, seven years were required to complete it. Seven of the original builders were killed, and other workers had to be secured to replace them.

The house stands on land granted to Daniel Smith as a Revolutionary War bonus. George Washington appointed General Smith secretary to the Territory South of the Ohio. He later served as United States Senator and made the "best map of the State found in the *Geographical Atlas,*" said Michaux, the French botanist, who visited this country in 1802. The son of Col. Isaac Bledsoe and the son of Col. Anthony Bledsoe, staying at this house while attending school, were murdered by Indians.

Samuel Donelson, Andrew Jackson's law partner and brother-in-law, wished to marry Polly, the only daughter of General Smith. The lovers planned to elope. Jackson assisted Donelson in preparing a rope ladder, by means of which Polly escaped from a second-story window, and he also waited with horses until Polly and Donelson arrived. That night the marriage was performed at Jackson's home, Hunter's Hill.

HAZEL PATH (L), 34.7 *m.,* was constructed in 1857 by General Daniel S. Donelson on property inherited from his grandfather, General Daniel Smith. This large two-story brick structure, set back from the highway on a beautifully wooded lawn, has a central two-story, pedimented portico that shelters a second floor gallery.

General Daniel S. Donelson, the son of Samuel and Polly Smith Donelson *(see ROCK CASTLE)* was an honor graduate of West Point. He married the daughter of Governor Branch of North Carolina and became a successful planter. At the beginning of the War between the States he sided with his Confederate neighbors and was appointed one of the first officers in the Provisional Army of Tennessee, later part of the Army of the Confederacy. In July 1861, General Donelson's brigade marched into Virginia and served in the Cheat Mountain campaign under Robert E. Lee. Returning to Tennessee in 1862, he took part in the Battle of Stone's River, in which his brigade was shattered with cannon and grapeshot in their effort to break the Federal line. General Donelson died in

1863 in Knoxville, while in command of the Confederate forces in East Tennessee.

Following the fall of Fort Donelson, Hazel Path was deserted, and the enemy soldiers moved in, but by order of Governor Johnson the property was later restored to its owners.

At 41.3 *m.* is the junction with Edenwold Road.

Left on Edenwold Rd. 0.2 *m.* to EDENWOLD *(private),* an old Tennessee estate, is now a modern dairy farm. Race horses were formerly bred here.

At 42.3 *m.* is the junction with State 45.

Left on State 45 is OLD HICKORY, 3 *m.* (514 alt., 8,164 pop.), owned by E. I. du Pont de Nemours & Company. The town, situated within a loop of the Cumberland River known as Hadley's Bend, was first named Jacksonville, but because mail was constantly sent in error to other towns of the same name, it was changed to Old Hickory in 1923. Andrew Jackson lived at Hunter's Hill, in the vicinity, from 1793–1804. He later built the Hermitage nearby. In March, 1918, the land was purchased for the construction of a powder plant. On July 2 the first powder was produced. At the time of the Armistice, the plant, though unfinished, was producing 700,000 pounds of powder daily. The town was hastily built. Records show that a six-room bungalow, including plumbing and screening, was completed in nine hours. Whole blocks of houses were built in one or two days. Early in October, 1918, the school building, containing 1,200,000 feet of lumber, was destroyed by fire; it was rebuilt in ten days. Five months after construction had been started, living quarters for 35,000 people were completed. Like other war-time factory communities, this one was provided with religious and recreational facilities.

A railway from Hermitage Station to Old Hickory, a distance of 7 miles, was built in 60 days, despite a few days' delay caused by litigation over a right-of-way. The railroads transported a daily average of 18,000 employees from Nashville to the plant, and another 15,000 lived on the property. A train of 14 coaches for women employees was locally called the Powder Puff Special.

Shortly after the Armistice the tremendous activity here stopped, and in a short time the population had dropped to a few hundred. In 1920 the War Department sold the entire property to a salvage company, and in 1924 E. I. du Pont de Nemours & Company purchased the village and several hundred acres of the land and erected a plant that now manufactures 24,000,000 pounds of rayon thread annually. A cellophane factory was built later. The two plants provide employment for more than 5,000 workers.

The Old Hickory Chemical Company makes the carbon bisulphite needed by the cellophane and rayon companies, making this one of the largest self-contained rayon and cellophane producing centers in the United States.

The nine 210-foot smokestacks of the old Government powerhouse can be seen for miles in all directions; they were left standing because the material in them could not be sold for enough to pay the cost of removal.

There are two subdivisions outside of the village in which employees of the plant can own homes.

Old Hickory has two theaters, one company-owned and one privately owned, a county high school, a county grade school, a county school for Negroes, and a free vocational night school for adults. The company furnishes recreational facilities and maintains the police and fire departments. The surrounding country is slightly rolling, and many fertile farms are in the vicinity.

At 7.1 *m.* is THE HERMITAGE, home of Andrew Jackson *(see Tour 12).*

MADISON, 43.4 *m.* (432 alt., 850 pop.), is a residential village extending along Gallatin Pike (US 31E) for two miles. Most of the residents are employed at the rayon plant in Old Hickory.

At 43.4 *m.* is the junction with Neely's Bend Rd.

Left on this road **1.5** *m.* to MADISON COLLEGE, established in 1904 as the Nashville Agricultural Normal Institute; it has developed from academy status to senior college rating. The school is operated by the Seventh Day Adventist Church, and its purpose is "the teaching and training of missionaries, teachers, and farmers who are willing to devote at least a portion of their time to unselfish, unremunerative labor." Students do part-time work for three quarters of the academic year, and full-time work in the fourth. All students, regardless of financial status, are required to work for at least half of their expenses. The 40-acre undulating campus, landscaped with more than 1,000 ornamental trees, shrubs, and flower beds, occupies the center of a 700-acre farm, which is in a great bend of the Cumberland River. From a distance the six major buildings, the Administration Building, Library, Science Building, Assembly Hall, Demonstration Building, and Gotzian Hall, together with about 100 smaller ones which almost encircle them, give the impression of a village.

Twenty-seven plants and industries are operated, in part or in whole, by student labor under faculty supervision. Among these are the sanatorium and hospital, a food factory, a tailor shop, a sewing department, a broom factory, a service station, a laundry, a cafeteria, a cannery, and a press. Various other enterprises necessary to an independent community, such as a fire department, a water and sewerage system, a central heating plant, and a generating plant are maintained. Emphasis is placed upon agricultural education, and the cultivation of the farm is a major activity. Forty acres are given over to the growing of vegetables; a variety of hay crops are planted to provide feed for about 80 head of livestock; and large-scale dairying and poultry raising are carried on. In addition to the main farm, a 200-acre tract on the Highland Rim is used for fruit growing. Much of the food used by the 500 residents, of whom approximately 350 are students, is produced on the two tracts. The school and the allied industries are managed by a board of directors, an organization known as the Rural Educational Association. The buildings, chiefly of stuccoed stone, are all one-story high, except where the contour of the land permits a ground floor at two levels. The construction was done by students under supervision.

The MADISON RURAL SANATORIUM AND HOSPITAL, a unit of the Madison group, is on the farm. The plant, comprising nine buildings, connected by one-half mile of covered porches, has accommodations for 100 patients. Student labor is used in the diet kitchens and in caring for the rooms. Only persons suffering from communicable diseases or insanity are denied admittance. While the major problem at Madison Sanatorium is the healing of the sick, workers also carry on a program of preventive medicine.

MADISON FOOD FACTORY produces foods consisting mainly of vegetable proteins designed to take the place of meat, whole-grain cereals and crackers. Soy beans, of which 27 varieties are grown on the farm, form the basis for many of the health foods.

All profits derived from the varied industries are used for the support and improvement of the school; donations are used to purchase land and equipment and to erect new buildings.

At **1.8** *m.* on this road is SWEETBRIAR FARM *(private),* the former home of Maria Thompson Daviess, the novelist. After her brother had recovered his health in the neighboring sanatorium, Miss Daviess started a poultry farm nearby. In her autobiography, *Seven Times Seven,* she wrote: "Sweetbriar consists of 16 acres, entirely surrounded by a very ancient cedar rail snake fence in whose corners grow sweetbriar roses, silver mullein, goldenrod, blue asters, crimson poke, and wild cherry. An oak grove, about a hundred years old, spreads across the crest of the hill and makes a many-aisled cathedral of the tall boles and high arching branches. From the gate the road leads through a tangle of blackberries, redbud, dogwood and wild violets."

She produced her best known work, *Equal Franchise,* a novel, while living there.

South of Madison the country is more densely settled; the highway passes suburban homes of Nashville industrial and office workers.

SHERWOOD FOREST *(private),* 44.5 *m.,* is reached by a private driveway which is entered (L) between large stone pillars. The modern, rough-

RAYON THREAD, OLD HICKORY MILLS

surfaced story-and-a-half limestone building was designed by Welby Pugin of Nashville, a descendant of Augustus Welby Pugin (1812–1852), the English architect who started the Victorian Gothic revival in England. It has steep-roofed towers and a steep many-gabled roof. The living room is floored with black slate, highly waxed. All the hardware was hand wrought by Philip Kerrigan, a Nashville craftsman. The grounds and gardens are beautifully landscaped.

In the NATIONAL CEMETERY (R), 44.7 *m.,* are buried approximately 16,000 Union soldiers killed in the Battles of Nashville and of Franklin during the War between the States. This cemetery of 64 acres is on rolling land surrounded by a stone wall. The arched gateway of white marble has double iron gates.

SPRING HILL CEMETERY (L), 44.9 *m.,* is on the site of Fort Union, built in 1780. The settlement here became the town of Haysboro, where in 1785 the Reverend Thomas Craighead established the first Presbyterian Church and Craighead Academy, the first educational institution in Middle Tennessee. From this meeting-house school grew George Peabody College for Teachers *(see NASHVILLE).* The first classes were taught in the Spring Hill Meeting House. Foundation stones of the old meeting house have been stacked to form a pyramid on the church site.

GLEN ECHO, 45.1 *m.,* was built in 1811 by Thomas Craighead. The first house of hewn logs stood near the church. It was burned down by Indians. In 1794 Craighead built a brick house that was damaged by fire in 1810. The walls of the present two-story structure, built the following year, are those of the second building. The driveway to the house is bordered with cedars, some of them very old.

At 46.2 *m.* is Cahal Ave.

Left on Cahal Ave. 1.4 *m.* to the entrance into the half-mile driveway of RIVERWOOD, a house somewhat irregular in plan. There is a one-story recessed portico on the garden front between projecting one-story wings. The formal two-story portico, which shelters a second-floor gallery, is on the end.

Alexander James Porter, who built the house in 1799, came to Tennessee from Ireland in 1798.

NASHVILLE, 51.4 *m.* (546 alt., 153,866 pop.) *(see NASHVILLE).*

Points of Interest: The Parthenon, State Capitol, Fort Nashborough, Vanderbilt University, Peabody College, and others.

At Nashville are the junctions with US 31W and US 41E *(see Tour 8),* with US 41W *(see Tour 14),* with US 41-70-Alt. *(see Tour 8),* with US 70 *(see Tour 12),* with State 11 *(see Tour 7A),* with State 100 *(see Tour 12).* All junctions are at the corner of 6th Ave. N. and Deaderick St., on Memorial Square.

Section b. NASHVILLE *to* ALABAMA LINE; *94 m.*

South of Nashville US 31 follows the Franklin Pike, once a toll turnpike. In 1831 the legislature chartered the Nashville & Franklin Railroad to serve this region, with authority to use horses or steam engines for motive power. This was the first charter for a railroad granted by the

State, but rails were never laid. The later Nashville & Franklin Electric Interurban Ry. now parallels the route between the two cities.

In 1862–63 the route became the chief military highway of Middle Tennessee. This was the road over which Schofield and Thomas (Federal) and Hood (Confederate) marched their armies to Franklin. The Battle of Nashville and the Battle of Franklin were fought in gently rolling bluegrass country along the route.

South of Memorial Square in NASHVILLE, 0 *m.,* at 3.4 *m.,* is the junction with Berry Lane by a rock quarry.

Left on Berry Lane to MELROSE *(private),* 0.5 *m.,* built in 1836 by Alexander Barrow of Louisiana and sold seven years later to John W. Sanders. The new owner died soon after the purchase; his widow married Aaron V. Brown, who was Governor of Tennessee 1845–1847 and U. S. Postmaster General under President Buchanan. The simple brick Greek Revival house of the early years was remodeled and befrilled to meet the taste of the gay nineties. The view from the front terrace embraces distant blue hills.

The PEACE MONUMENT, 3.8 *m.,* the work of the Italian sculptor, G. Maretti, commemorates the Battle of Nashville. Two charging steeds, symbolizing the North and the South, are held in check by a young man dressed as a soldier of the World War.

On the grounds of (R) LONGVIEW *(private),* 4.2 *m.,* some of the hardest fighting of the Battle of Nashville took place.

GLEN LEVEN *(private),* 4.5 *m.* (L), was built in 1857 by John Thompson. The large two-and-a-half story brick structure was designed by Thompson himself in the Greek Revival style. It has a two-story Corinthian portico. The land was a North Carolina grant to Thomas Thompson, who was one of the signers of the Cumberland compact. His original dwelling was a blockhouse. Later he built a large log cabin here; it was destroyed by fire. The wide lawn is shaded by many fine trees, including a giant paulownia, several English field maples which grew from Kew Gardens cuttings, and a number of yellowwood trees. The garden contains many varieties of narcissi, daffodils, and hyacinths; some of the bulbs were imported from Holland in 1837.

On the first and second days of the Battle of Nashville, Glen Leven was between the lines. The brick walls show marks made by the bullets from both sides. After the retreat of the Confederate forces, Glen Leven was used as a Union hospital.

At 6 *m.* is the junction with a good graveled road.

Right on this road 0.2 *m.* to ROBERTSON ACADEMY, an institution now part of the public school system and named for James Robertson, founder of Nashville. The academy was one of the 27 State schools established in 1806. It received its support from the sale of public school bonds.

At 6.2 *m.* is (R) OAK HILL *(private),* designed about 1933 by Warfield and Keeble of Nashville. It is a large two-story structure with a pedimented Ionic portico and large one-story wings. As in the old plantation homes the design is straightforward, but the scale of the house far exceeds those of early days.

The beautiful grounds and gardens were designed by Robert S. Sturtevant.

At 6.7 *m.* is the junction with a private road *(open).*

Left on this road 0.7 *m.* to TRAVELERS REST and its Arabian horse farm. The simple two-story clapboarded house of the old plantation was built by Judge John Overton in 1820, just before his marriage to Mary White, daughter of the founder of Knoxville. Overton purchased the farm in 1792 and built a two-room log cabin, in which he lived until the present house was constructed. When he came here this area was in the Mero District of North Carolina, and he held an appointment as Territorial revenue collector. He was the first lawyer in Nashville. Overton boarded with John Donelson and, when Andrew Jackson arrived in Nashville, he shared a room with him. Overton became, and remained throughout his life, a close friend of Jackson's. It was always to John Overton that Jackson turned for advice. For many years Overton was a judge of the Supreme Court of Tennessee. With Jackson he founded Memphis.

This farm, frequently enlarged, became one of the most productive in the State. After Overton's death the estate went to his son, John, who added the adjoining 1,280 acres, half through purchase and half through marriage. Just prior to the War between the States John Overton was said to have been the wealthiest man in Tennessee. It was he who built the Maxwell House *(see NASHVILLE).* He contributed much of his fortune to the Confederacy. Following the war he divided his property among his children. Travelers Rest, still in the hands of Overton's descendants, was one of the leading Arabian stud farms in the United States. The first horse of Arabian breed was brought here in 1825.

At 7.8 *m.* is the junction with a surfaced road.

Left on this road 0.9 *m.* to the junction with Kelly Road; L. here 0.7 *m.* to the GORDON SITE at the end of the road. This prehistoric Indian village was surrounded by earthworks supporting a wooden palisade with watchtowers every 55 feet. There was a flat-topped mound in the center of the village. Archeologists found 87 circles of dwellings on the site. Beneath the clay floors were many stone-grave burials. The contents of the dwellings unearthed here indicate that the occupants departed without taking away any of their belongings. Household articles were found just as they had been left after use. The hard clay floors of the dwellings were still covered with a glossy black dressing. Beautiful pottery and flint implements were intact.

BRENTWOOD, 9.4 *m.* (700 alt., 150 pop.), on the Davidson-Williamson County line, is halfway between Nashville and Franklin.

MOORELAND (L), 10 *m.,* was built in 1846 by Robert Moore. The first house here, a log cabin, was built in 1800. The present house, which took three years to complete, does not contain a single piece of sawn timber; it was constructed by slaves who fired the brick and adzed all timber. The large two-story central unit has a portico across the front supported by large square columns and sheltering a second-floor gallery. On both ends are one-story wings, each with a small columned portico. The original plantation contained 1,280 acres, but this has been subdivided.

A beautiful grove of ash trees in which the house stood was cut down by Union troops during the War between the States. Mooreland was used as a hospital during the war.

MIDWAY (R), 10.8 *m.,* the McGavock-Hayes place, is reached by a half-mile private drive. The substantial two-story brick house was built in 1847 of brick made by Negroes on the place; much of the material was salvaged from the burned ruins of an earlier structure. Two columns of the four columned, two-story portico support a second-floor veranda. During the War between the States, Midway was occupied by officers and several skirmishes took place on the grounds. Under trees that still shade the grounds sharp fighting occurred and wounded men from both sides were cared for in the house.

MONTVIEW *(private)*, 11.9 *m.*, (R) is a two-story brick structure constructed in 1861. The four large columns of the high entrance portico support a cornice and parapet that is carried across the entire front of the house. A notable feature of the interior is the gracefully curving staircase that rises from the central hall. The kitchen is connected with the house by a cedar porch; a two-story brick smokehouse is nearby. The old carriage house is now a garage and the clay pit, from which came material for the bricks, is an attractive pond.

At 12.3 *m.* (L) is the junction with Callender Road.

Left on Callender Road 0.7 *m.* to the WSM, a powerful radio station with a tower 878 feet high that acts as a giant lightning rod for the immediate area; the beacon light is a landmark of airmen.

A BOXWOOD (R), 12.8 *m.*, on the lawn of the Johnson farm, is nearly fifty feet in circumference.

US 31 cuts through a narrow gap, 14.1 *m.*, known locally as HOLLY TREE GAP. The steep hills rising on both sides made this spot a favorite resort of robbers in the stagecoach days.

At 18.2 *m.* is the junction with the graveled Liberty Pike.

Left on Liberty Pike to BANKRUPT MANOR COURT *(private)*, 1.7 *m.*, the home of T. H. Alexander, Tennessee's favorite columnist, who is an advocate of agrarianism.

FRANKLIN, 18.8 *m.* (642 alt., 3,377 pop.), seat of Williamson County, is surrounded by fertile farms. On Nov. 30, 1864 one of the bloodiest battles of the war was fought in and around this town. More high staff officers were killed or wounded in this conflict than in any other major battle of the war. The Confederates alone lost six generals: Adams, Carter, Cleburne, Gist, Granbury, and Strahl; five others were wounded and one captured. About 8,500 men fell in 55 minutes.

On the hills to the east are traces of the Union breastworks thrown up before the battle. Largest of these was Fort Granger, commanded by Gen. Gordon Granger, with a force of 8,500 men and 24 pieces of artillery.

General Schofield, the Union commander, was on his way from Pulaski to Nashville where he intended to join his forces with those of General Thomas. General Hood, commander of the Confederate forces, marching rapidly from Florence, Ala., planned to intercept Schofield's army before he reached Nashville. The forces met at Columbia, which was occupied by Union troops. Hood crossed Duck River a few miles above. Aware of Hood's movements, Schofield moved his command to the north side of the river and began the march to Nashville. General Hood's army crossed the river and by 3 o'clock on Nov. 29 was within two or three miles of Spring Hill. His orders to guard the pike near Spring Hill were not carried out; the Confederates encamped near the pike; during the night the Federals passed almost within sight of the campfires. On the following day there was a desperate hand-to-hand combat here. The lines were so close together that soldiers were even dragged from one side of the breastworks to the other by their hair or collars. The battle, which began at four o'clock in the afternoon, lasted until night when Schofield withdrew.

John Bell, Constitutional Union candidate for the Presidency in 1860, began his law practice in this town. Matthew Fontaine Maury, the oceanographer, also lived here for a short time.

ST. PAUL'S EPISCOPAL CHURCH, two blocks west of the square, is a small delightful brick structure, with a square tower and hand-fashioned interior woodwork. It was built about 1830 by a parish organized in 1827 by the Reverend James Hervey Otey. He was later the first Protestant Episcopal bishop of Tennessee.

The JOHN EATON HOME *(open on application)*, Main St. (or Third Ave.) near the Interurban R.R. station, is the former residence of John H. Eaton and his wife, Peggy Eaton, who was the storm center of social and political Washington during the first administration of Andrew Jackson. The elderly Eaton, whom Jackson appointed Secretary of War, married Peggy O'Neale, the daughter of a tavern keeper of Washington. Jackson, remembering the attacks on his wife Rachel, who had recently died *(see Tour 12)*, treated Peggy with great courtesy and frowned on those who snubbed her. The social battle played a part in the next presidential election.

The delightful, little one-story CARTER HOUSE *(private)*, on US 31 (R) eight blocks south of the public square, was built by Fountain Branch Carter soon after he had come here in 1830 from Fairfax, Va. The paneled entrance has coupled columns, a fanlight and sidelights, and the two triple windows are surmounted by heavy lintels with pediments. At the beginning of the War between the States, young Tod Carter followed his two elder brothers into the Confederate Army. When Hood's army passed on the crest of a hill above Franklin, Tod Carter, then a captain, viewed his home for the first time in three years. On this wintry afternoon, with the aid of field glasses he could see the familiar red brick walls about 50 yards beyond the Federal lines. After the fierce fighting of the night had subsided, and it was safe for his family to venture from shelter, they found his body in the yard.

Edward Swanson was the first known white settler in the beautiful hills of the West Harpeth. The foundation for his home had been laid by March, 1780. It is believed that he left Fort Nashborough and settled on his homestead sometime between 1790 and 1800; when the county was organized in 1800 he was a member of the second grand jury. His grave is in a field on his land, about 6 miles southwest of this town.

Left from Franklin at the square on paved State 96 to WILLOW PLUNGE, 1 *m.*, a modern swimming pool fed by a spring at the foot of a grassy slope. *(Small fees for use of pool and suits; dining tables free.)*

At 1 *m.* on State 96 is the junction with a good graveled road; R. here 0.4 *m.* to CARNTON HOUSE *(open)*. Randall McGavock brought an architect named Swope with him from Virginia in 1824, who helped him to design and build the house on a 1,000-acre tract here. The lines of the spacious two-and-a-half story brick house, called Carnton for McGavock's family estate in Antrim, Ireland, have been somewhat obscured by a long double veranda that extends beyond the house at one end.

The floor of the long back porch held the bodies of five Confederate generals—Cleburne, Gist, Adams, Granberry, and Strahl—after the battle of Franklin, and the 25 rooms were crowded with the wounded.

A year and a half after the battle Colonel McGavock set aside two acres adjoining his family burying ground as a CONFEDERATE CEMETERY and, at his own expense, had the bodies of 1,500 Confederate dead moved to this plot. This cemetery is now maintained by the State. The large lawn, called McGavock's Grove, was often used for political debates.

At 2.5 *m.* on State 96 is the DE GRAFFENRIED WORKS, a group of Indian mounds named for the farm on which they stand. They are earthworks, spread over 32 acres along the bluffs of the Harpeth River. Within the enclosure the soil is very fertile, and a spring near the bluff furnishes a never failing supply of water. The largest of the mounds is 16 feet high, 230 feet long, and 110 feet wide. In a stone coffin removed from one of the mounds was a skeleton, evidently that of an important person, who had been buried in a sitting position with a finely chipped sword about 22 inches long beside him.

BATTLEGROUND ACADEMY (R), 19.7 *m.,* is a boys' preparatory school founded in 1889.

BREEZY HILL (L), 21.6 *m.,* is densely covered with a natural forest of cedars. It is said that 7,500 Confederate soldiers died between Franklin and Breezy Hill.

In SPRING HILL (L), 31.9 *m.* (650 alt., 417 pop.), is the SITE OF THE BRANHAM AND HUGHES PREPARATORY SCHOOL for boys, whose campus was used as headquarters at various times by Union and Confederate troops. The property is now occupied by the Church of Christ Orphanage.

The CHEAIRS HOUSE (L) *(private),* 33.9 *m.,* was built (L) in the early 1850's by Maj. Nathaniel Francis Cheairs, whose 1,500-acre farm was a part of a grant made in 1810. The large square two-story brick building has two-story recessed entrances on three sides sheltered by projecting two-story pedimented porticos. It stands in a grove of giant beech trees. The major supervised every detail of construction and had the walls torn down and rebuilt three times. The present kitchen and servants' quarters were built before the big house and the family lived in them while the long process of construction went on. The delicate plaster ornamentation of the entrance-hall ceiling is notable.

The day before the Battle of Franklin, advance guards of Hood and Schofield met in a spirited skirmish on the dusty road in front of the house. Most of Hood's army bivouacked on the estate that night. On the morning of November 30, 1864, Mrs. Cheairs had breakfast served to as many Confederate officers as could be seated in the spacious dining room.

At 34.5 *m.* is (R) HAYNES HAVEN *(open on application),* known for years as the W. M. Tolley Farm, and for its stable of pacers. The Hal mares and stallions from this stable are known wherever pacing races are held. Tolley began to assemble the Hal strain in 1909. The greatest of the pacers produced from the Hal family on this farm was Napoleon Direct, who did a mile in 1:59¾ minutes.

A one-room log cabin stands (R) in a grove of locust trees at 38.1 *m.*

HAYNES HAVEN, NEAR COLUMBIA

COLUMBIA, 43.8 *m.* (656 alt., 7,882 pop.) *(see COLUMBIA).*

Points of Interest: Polk Home, Columbia Institute, Columbia Military Academy, and others.

At Columbia is the junction with State 6. *(see Tour 7B).*

BEECHLAWN (L) is at 47.2 *m.* The plantation house is surrounded by a grove of beeches; many of these trees are four feet in diameter. In the grove are also two spruce, two hundred feet tall, and a great magnolia tree. The Beechlawn garden, planned by Cornelia Francis Warfield, wife of Maj. A. W. Warfield, is today as it was when the house was built in 1852. The brick two-story house, flanked by flat-roofed one-story wings, is a pleasing example of late Greek Revival architecture. The gabled roof is projected forward to form the pediment of the four-pillared Ionic portico that extends across the front of the somewhat narrow central unit, which is about twice as deep as it is wide. The entrance doorway was placed at one side, rather than in the center, because the limited floor space did not permit a central hall.

Beechlawn was temporary headquarters for Gen. John M. Schofield, when he retreated before Gen. John B. Hood. It was taken over in turn by the Confederate commander. In the front room Generals Hood and Nathan Bedford Forrest disagreed as to the most effective way of cutting off the Union troops on their retreat to Nashville.

While General Schofield was at Beechlawn, he promised Mrs. Warfield that, should occasion arise, he would grant Major Warfield every consideration as a prisoner of war. This promise he kept when Major Warfield was later captured in Alabama.

The entrance (R) to MILKY WAY FARMS *(open 8-4:30 daily)* is at 65.9 *m.* This estate, developed by the late Frank C. Mars, a candy manufacturer, covers 2,705 acres of rolling hills and bluegrass meadows, and has 50 miles of fence. Among the buildings on the estate are a clubhouse, a mausoleum, 50 modern houses for employees, and 25 large stock barns—some of them more than 500 feet long. The stalls for the race horses are finished in polished woods. In recent years the Milky Way horses have won many racing events of nation-wide importance. The estate has a 5/8-mile training track.

Sheep and cattle from this farm have also taken honors at various fairs.

At 74.6 *m.* is the junction with Wales Rd.

Right on this road 2 *m.* to lovely CLIFTON PLACE, whose house and gardens were designed by an architect and landscape gardener brought from England in 1812 by Tyree Rodes to build in the Tennessee wilderness an estate comparable to that of the Rodes family in England. Rodes came here from Virginia in 1809. The giant boxwoods were long cared for by a slave who had been trained especially for the job by an Irish assistant of the English gardener. On the grounds is a crape myrtle hedge 25 feet high. The large house, whose brick walls are laid in Flemish bond, shows as much skill as the garden. It is of the early Greek Revival type, simple of line but well-proportioned and finished with exquisite detail. The two-story pedimented portico with four Doric columns shelters a large second floor porch having a delicate balustrade. In the rear is a long ell. The interior trim is beautifully carved.

PULASKI, 77.6 *m.* (649 alt., 3,367 pop.), seat of Giles County, was named for Count Casimir Pulaski of Poland, who aided the Colonies during the Revolutionary War. It is the trade and shipping center of the prosperous farming area producing cattle, bluegrass, corn, cotton, wheat, and burley tobacco. A plant here sends out about 2,500,000 cans of tomatoes a year. Pulaski was the first municipality in Tennessee to buy electric current from the TVA.

The Ku Klux Klan was organized in Pulaski on Christmas Eve, 1855, by Judge T. M. Jones and his son, Calvin. The nucleus of the organization was a small group of friends who met in the Jones' law office—now bearing a commemorative marker—one-half block from the courthouse.

The Klan was conceived as a social club to revive normal fellowship after the war was over. Young Calvin and his friends wanted amusing initiation ceremonies for new members, and those weird ceremonies and whispers of mystery soon attracted wide attention to the club. The grotesque flowing sheets and tall cone-shaped hats with horns and the torchlight parades had an unexpected effect upon the Negroes and to some extent on the carpetbaggers. Members of the Klan quickly seized on the idea that the organization could be used as a means of defense against the camp followers of the military administration. A cyclone-wrecked brick house on the outskirts of Pulaski—generally reported as haunted—was selected as an appropriate ceremonial meeting place. The members began to spread mysterious hints and weird tales directed at such Negroes as were aping the white "scalawags" and to send Klan warnings to the carpetbaggers. Before long the initimidation had had its effects.

The idea spread through the South like a grass fire. Klans sprang up in every city and town. Before long there was an "Invisible Empire," under the autocratic power of a chief officer, the Grand Wizard. But a secret organization making its own judgments and carrying out punishments was hard to control. Soon the excesses of the Klan were as serious as those they had sought to remedy and many men who first sponsored the organization—including the Pulaski members and Nathan Bedford Forrest, the Grand Wizard—forced it officially to disband in 1869.

The SAM DAVIS MONUMENT on the square was erected in 1906 to the memory of the 19-year-old boy who was a hero of the Confederacy *(see Tour 8)*. On this statue are the words attributed to Davis: "If I had a thousand lives, I would give them all before I would betray the confidence of a friend, or my informer."

The SITE OF THE SAM DAVIS HANGING, on Sam Davis Ave., is marked by a small tablet. Sam Davis, taken from the basement of the courthouse in Pulaski, rode in a wagon on top of his own coffin to this spot *(see Tour 8)*.

AUSTIN HEWITT HOME *(open 9-5)*, East Washington St., is a well-endowed institution for elderly women.

COLONIAL HALL *(private)*, W. Jefferson St., is the former home of John C. Brown, Governor of Tennessee from 1871 to 1875. The house was built in the 1840's by Dr. William Batte. It is a large, square, brick building with a deep four-column central two-story portico of Greek Revival design. The cornice of the portico is carried around the flat-roofed white-painted house. The recess holding the entrance doorway is wide.

Brown was one of the leaders in the group who sought to restore the male franchise rescinded by the reconstruction administration. He was president of the Constitutional Convention held in Nashville in 1870 that did restore the franchise. A minority group fought against extending the suffrage to Negroes. "We hold that the Negro race is the lowest order of human beings," they asserted, "incapable in themselves of a virtuous, intelligent, or free government." The majority overruled them, partly out of the fear that if they failed to give the vote to Negroes the State would again be placed under military government.

Brown set the keynote for the convention by his opening address: "Let us raise ourselves above the passions and prejudices of the hour, and dare to be just and generous regardless of the temptations prompting a contrary course. We cannot, we must not, be unmindful of the great changes that have impressed themselves upon our history. Let us accept the situation, and not seek to alter circumstances which have passed beyond our control."

His election in 1870 on the Democratic ticket marked the end of Republican control of the State government.

MARTIN COLLEGE, West Jefferson St., a junior college for girls, was established in 1870 by Thomas Martin, as a memorial to his daughter, who had died, and as a token of appreciation for the patronage given his mercantile business by the people of Giles County. Martin gave $30,000 for endowment, only the income of which was to be used, and $50,000 in cash as a nucleus of a building fund. The first building was destroyed by fire. The property was later transferred to the Tennessee Annual Conference of the Methodist Episcopal Church, South.

The severity of the square two-story brick BALLENTINE HOUSE, on First St., is skillfully relieved by brick pilasters on the corners and beside the two-story recess that holds a small second-story, iron balustraded balcony and a transomed and sidelighted entrance. The lack of an entrance portico is unusual. By the house is a beautiful formal boxwood garden. This house was built in 1825 by Andrew N. Ballentine, a recent immigrant from Ireland.

The PULASKI RESERVOIR, on Reservoir Hill, is on the site of Fort Lilly, built during the War between the States. The remains of earthworks are seen about the top of the hill, from which there is an excellent view of the town and surrounding country.

At Pulaski are the junctions with US 64 *(see Tour 13)* and State 11 *(see Tour 7A)*.

As US 31 proceeds southward the bluegrass country becomes more rolling and less fertile.

US 31 crosses the Alabama Line on the southern edge of ARDMORE, 87.5 *m.* (654 alt., 700 pop.), 18 miles north of Athens, Alabama.

Tour 7A

Nashville—Lewisburg—Pulaski; 78.7 m. State 11.

Louisville & Nashville R.R. parallels route between College Grove and Cornersville.
Paved throughout.
Accommodations in larger towns.

State 11, an alternate to US 31 between Nashville and Pulaski, traverses a prosperous farming and dairying region. Before and after the Battle of Stone's River *(see Tour 8)* this road was used by the Confederate troops under General Bragg and the Federal troops under General Rosecrans. Many skirmishes were fought along the pike between Nashville and Lewisburg. The scenery is typical of the bluegrass region.

State 11 follows Fourth Avenue in NASHVILLE, 0 *m.,* and goes southward on the Nolensville Pike.

At 1.5 *m.* (R) is OLD CITY CEMETERY *(see NASHVILLE).*

TRAVIS LANDER'S STORE (R), 7.2 *m.,* is at the junction of State 11 and the Owen-Winsted Pike. Immediately opposite the store is the entrance to a private lane.

Left on this lane and over a hill to the SITE OF THE HOME OF JOHN HAYWOOD, 0.7 *m.* Haywood (1762–1826) came to Tennessee from North Carolina about 1807. He was a judge of the Tennessee Supreme Court (1810–26), and one of Tennessee's first historians. In 1820 he founded the Antiquarian Society, the forerunner of the Tennessee Historical Society. Still standing on the site is a large tree, under which Judge Haywood did most of his writing. John A. Murrell, the outlaw, said of the judge, "Old Judge Haywood up in Nashville—he lays around all day on a bull's hide under a tree, and he's so fat it takes three niggers dragging at the tail to haul him into the shade—what's he know about the law? A smart man could tie him into knots!" Haywood's most noted works were *Civil and Political History of Tennessee* and *Natural and Aboriginal History of Tennessee.*

CHAPEL HILL, 39.6 *m.,* is the birthplace of Nathan Bedford Forrest (1821–1877), brilliant Confederate cavalry officer. Forrest moved to Mississippi when he was thirteen years old. As a young man he joined an uncle in the cattle-trading business and later accumulated a fortune as a slave trader.

Although he joined the Confederate Army as a private, Governor Harris soon gave him a commission. He raised and equipped his own battalion—but not completely. Once when some recruits reported to him, Forrest told them: "There is going to be a fight with those folks over yonder, and we'll get you some guns there." He referred to Union troops and supplies. He first distinguished himself at the defense of Fort Donelson. After the Battle of Shiloh he covered Beauregard's retreat. By the end of 1862, Forrest, who was called the "Wizard of the Saddle," had written Confederate military history in letters of blood across the border States. The story is made up of accounts of daring raids, strategic retreats, brilliant cavalry actions. His "critter company" scouted along the Federal lines continuously and struck where they were least expected.

In July 1862 he circled the Union troops, captured the entire garrison at Murfreesboro, and cut Buell's line of communication. The same year he was made a brigadier general and, having recruited a new command, raided western Kentucky and Tennessee. His continuous series of thrusts kept Grant's troopers riding hard on his trail, but Forrest always defeated or outmaneuvered them. Sherman hunted him fiercely, declaring that the Federal campaign in Tennessee could not be won as long as Forrest was in the State. But Forrest could neither be driven out nor captured.

After Chickamauga, Forrest went into northern Missisippi with an independent command. Soon he was back in West Tennessee, where his successful campaign won him a commission as major general. In 1864 he was a gadfly to Sherman and in September recaptured Athens, Ga. In November he became chief commander of Confederate cavalry in Tennessee. After the Battle of Nashville, Forrest covered Hood's retreat.

At Selma, Ala., he was overwhelmed by superior numbers but, with his characteristic dash, cut his way through the enemy lines and escaped to Gainesville, Ga., where he surrendered when news of Appomattox reached him.

During Reconstruction, Forrest helped organize the Ku Klux Klan and in May, 1867, became the Grand Wizard.

The SITE OF THE FORREST BIRTHPLACE, a log cabin, is marked by a monument.

At 50.6 *m.* is the junction (L) with State 64.

Left on this highway is FARMINGTON, 1 *m.*, where there is a house that is said to be haunted by the ghost of a member of the Murrell gang. It was a rendezvous of the land pirate and his men. One of the meetings ended in a brawl and a man was killed. Many local residents believe his spirit still stalks the place.

LEWISBURG, 56.2 *m.* (736 alt., 3,112 pop.), is an important livestock-shipping point. Local farmers own many purebred Jersey cattle, and buyers from many sections of the country bid sharply for Marshall County cattle. One of the condenseries here has an annual capacity of 25 million gallons, and a co-operative creamery produces approximately 2 million pounds of cheese and 2 million pounds of butter each year. A plant here manufactures pencils from the abundant red-cedar forests nearby. The JAMES K. POLK LAW OFFICE, occupied at the time of Polk's election to the Presidency, is on the southeast corner of the public square. The national headquarters of the Walking Horse Association is here; the organization promotes national use of the "plantation horse," or "walking horse," a product of Middle Tennessee *(see SPORTS AND RECREATION)*.

South of Lewisburg State 11 runs through hilly well-watered bluegrass land that is excellent livestock range.

The UNITED STATES DAIRY EXPERIMENT FARM, 58.5 *m.*, approximately 500 acres, is maintained by the Federal Government for research in dairying and the breeding of Jersey cattle.

CORNERSVILLE, 61.2 *m.* (330 pop.), is a typical bluegrass trading crossroads.

PULASKI, 78.2 *m.* (651 alt., 3,367 pop.) *(see Tour 7)*, is at the junction with US 31 *(see Tour 7)*, and with US 64 *(see Tour 13)*.

Tour 7B

Columbia—Lawrenceburg—(Florence, Ala.); State 6.
Columbia—Alabama Line, 55.6 m.

Louisville and Nashville R.R. parallels route throughout.
Paved roadbed.
Accommodations chiefly in towns.

South of Columbia, State 6 traverses a rich farming country known widely for its livestock. This part of Tennessee at one time specialized in the breeding and training of harness horses. Now dairying is the chief business, and purebred Jersey cattle graze beside blooded horses and sturdy mules in the rolling bluegrass pastures. The country along the northern part of the route was settled by North and South Carolinians who had received land grants as bonuses for their services in the Revolutionary War. They built beautiful homes, bred fine horses, and worked their fertile acres with slaves. The smaller farms retain an atmosphere reminiscent of earlier years.

The lower part of the route crosses a phosphate-mining region and a narrow strip of ore-topped hills, called the western iron belt of Middle Tennessee, a rough terrain marked by deep valleys, rushing streams, and hills densely wooded with scrub oak. Because of the ruggedness of its soil, this region was not settled until near the middle of the nineteenth century.

COLUMBIA, 0 *m.* (656 alt., 7,882 pop.) *(see COLUMBIA).*

Points of Interest: Street mule market, Columbia Military Academy, Polk Home, Geers Memorial Park, and Columbia Institute.

Columbia is at the junction with US 31 *(see Tour 7).*

South of Columbia at 1 *m.* is (L) MERCER HALL *(private),* built in 1820 by Dr. William Heacock and at one time owned by James K. Polk. The main unit of the building is two stories high; the rather severe entrance façade is broken by the usual two-story recess and balcony, framed by a slightly projecting Corinthian portico. There are flat-roofed one-story wings. The house was purchased in 1829 by the Reverend James Hervey Otey, first bishop of the Protestant Episcopal Church in Tennessee, and named Mercer Hall in honor of Bishop Otey's friend, Dr. Mercer of Natchez. Bishop Otey was influential in the founding of several schools *(see Tour 13).*

COLUMBIA MILITARY ACADEMY (R), 1.3 *m.,* was established in a former arsenal, bought by retired military officers from the Government in 1904.

The MIDDLE TENNESSEE EXPERIMENT STATION *(open 8-6, daily),*

OX TEAM IN THE MOUNTAINS

2.2 *m.,* a 625-acre farm, is maintained and operated by the State Extension Department of the University of Tennessee.

BLYTHEWOOD *(private),* 2.4 *m.,* is an antebellum house showing the French Colonial influence. Several skirmishes of the War between the States took place near here. The stone gateposts are bullet-scarred. The Doric columns of the entrance portico are twined with rambler roses, and the southern side of the house overlooks three gardens that are noted for their beauty.

The entrance to CLIFTON PLACE *(private)* is (L) at 5.5 *m.* The house, built in 1832 by Gen. Gideon J. Pillow, is typical of the antebellum plantation headquarters of Middle Tennessee; the huge two-story brick building has the usual projecting portico, two stories high with four Ionic columns. Over the entrance is the usual gallery with a cast-iron balustrade connecting. A large central hall with a winding stairway opens into high-ceiled rooms.

Behind the big house are a two-story brick house for servants, an office, a smoke-house, a granary, and quarters for the field hands.

Gideon J. Pillow was a major general in the Mexican War and later one of the first Tennessee commanders in the War between the States.

At 6 *m.* is the junction with a graveled road.

Left on this road to PILLOW-BETHEL PLACE, 1 *m.,* built by Jerome Pillow; it is one of the Pillow homes in the neighborhood *(see Clifton Place and Pillow Haliday Place).* The three Pillow homes were built on the same general plan with only slight variations. This plan, a result of the Greek Revival, calls for a rectangular two-story brick structure having a central pedimented portico of the Ionic order that shelters a two-story recess, which holds a simple entrance and narrow second-story gallery. The high-ceiled rooms open on a central hall. Near the house is a one-story brick office building whose roof, rippled into two low gables over high-arched windows and decorated with scroll-saw drops, betrays its later construction.

For many years the estate was the home of Capt. William Bethel, son-in-law of Jerome Pillow.

Just beyond the Pillow-Bethel Place is the PILLOW-HALIDAY PLACE *(private),* built in 1845 by Granville Pillow. The most noticeable departure from the general scheme of Pillow homes is the omission of the second-story gallery. The entrance portico is topped with a low parapet instead of a pediment. A spiral stairway extends from the first floor to the roof, which once held a large reservoir for the domestic water supply.

The Pillow-Haliday Place was built on the site of the first home of Gideon Pillow, who came to Maury County as a surveyor and purchased 500 acres of land. This was later divided among the three sons.

ST. JOHN'S EPISCOPAL CHURCH (L), 6.9 *m.,* was built in 1841 by Bishop Leonidas Polk and his three brothers for the use of their neighbors and their own families and slaves. Bishop Polk, its only rector, was later a major general in the Confederate Army. They frankly copied with fine feeling the Gothic-type parish churches of England. Bricks were kilned and timbers hewn on the Polk estates by slaves. The slave balcony, the altar, and reredos were made from the wood of a huge wild cherry tree that stood near Ashwood Hall. The little church is now open for services only once each year, on Whitsunday; about 700 people attend, and dinner is served on the grounds. The GRAVE OF BISHOP

JAMES HERVEY OTEY is in the churchyard; William Polk and other members of this illustrious family are buried nearby.

The community surrounding the church is known as the ST. JOHN'S SETTLEMENT. Col. William Polk, Revolutionary War veteran and distant relative of James K. Polk, acquired 5,000 acres of land here, which was later divided among his four sons.

Opposite the church are two stone pillars at the entrance to ASHWOOD HALL, which held the second of the Polk mansions, completed in 1836; it burned in 1874. It was built by Leonidas Polk, a founder of the University of the South at Sewanee, who was later called the "fighting bishop" of the Confederacy. Polk was appointed missionary bishop of the Southwest Territory in 1837; in 1841 he was made the first bishop of Louisiana. Ashwood Hall was a large two-story brick house with one-story wings. The central portico had four huge Corinthian columns.

Antebellum life was brilliant at Ashwood Hall, centering about Antoinette, the lovely daughter of Andrew Polk, who had bought the estate from his brother Leonidas. After the beginning of hostilities, the mansion was often filled with Confederate officers until the Union forces arrived. Overhearing Federal plans to capture a body of Confederates stationed nearby, Antoinette dashed off on her horse to give warning but she was suspected and an effort was made to overtake her. All the Union pursuers caught was a plume from her riding hat.

Antoinette afterward became the Baroness de Charette, and her father, who had been seriously wounded in the early part of the war, went abroad to live with her.

At this estate is a huge old ginkgo (maidenhair) tree that was brought from Japan long before the War between the States to be tested on Tennessee soil. The trunk is five feet in diameter and 16 feet in circumference. It is 85 feet high and has a spread of 65 feet.

At 7 *m.* is the junction with an improved dirt road.

Right on this road to ASHWOOD, **0.5** *m.* (725 alt., 185 pop.) on the Polk land. At **2** *m.* on the Ashwood Rd. is the junction with another road; R. here; R. again at **2.8** *m.* to ZION CHURCH, **3.9** *m.,* on the site of a log cabin erected in 1807 by a group of South Carolina Presbyterians. The cabin was used as a school and also as a church. James K. Polk is said to have received his early education here. Under the leadership of John Dicky, the settlers from South Carolina bought 5,000 acres of the 25,000 granted to Gen. Nathanael Greene for services in the Revolutionary War. A brick church was built on the site in 1815, which was replaced in turn by the present building in 1847—a two-story brick church with a broad entrance recess under the slave gallery. The unusual but balanced composition of the front with its finely proportioned piers and stepped gable end has an unusual charm. The entrances are almost hidden on the sides of the recess. Descendants of the settlers still live in the little community and at death are buried in the church cemetery beside their pioneer ancestors.

HAMILTON PLACE (R), 7.6 *m.,* the Polk-Yeatman Home, was built by Lucius Polk. The old house, with its double front porch and its ivy-clad walls, is well preserved. The entrance hall leads through high archways to a long cross-hall, from each end of which rises a spiral stairway.

The entrance to RATTLE AND SNAP is at 8.1 *m.* (L). The lane 0.6 *m.*

long, leads to the last built and most ornate of the Polk homes. This house, completed in 1845 by George Polk, is a large Greek Revival structure with a two-story portico having ten Corinthian columns. The portico, which extends across the entire front, is projected forward in the center and pedimented. The columns arrived in sections by boat from Cincinnati, Ohio, and were hauled by oxcarts from Nashville to this place. It is said that during the War between the States, when it was necessary to find a safe hiding place for the family silver, a little son of the family lowered it into one of these columns, where it remained until the end of the war. The cornices and doorways have simple classical moldings. On the side is a one-story classical portico and on the other a delicate iron-gabled porch with an iron balcony above. There are two spiral stairways with simple but unusually graceful handrails. The interior is enriched with columns and elaborately decorated plaster cornices.

MT. PLEASANT, 11.9 *m.* (626 alt., 2,010 pop.), is the business center of an extensive phosphate mining area, in which production began in 1893. Much working of phosphate rock is carried on here, and there is one factory that makes fertilizer. The phosphate rock used for fertilizer experiments at Muscle Shoals come from this district.

In ROCKDALE, 17.2 *m.,* is the only blast furnace (inactive in 1939) in this narrow strip of ore-topped hills which, 60 years ago, was believed "capable of sustaining establishments enough to supply the world with iron for a century." The Rockdale furnace was for years a simple pigiron blast furnace, but, in later years, produced ferrophosphorus, a product made by adding phosphate to iron. For many years the Rockdale owners had a patent on this process.

At 18.9 *m.* is the junction with an improved dirt road.

Left on this road to RATTLESNAKE FALLS *(free camp sites),* 0.4 *m.* The first fall is about 60 feet high. A short distance down a deep gorge are another 65 feet high and several small ones 6 to 7 feet high. The water comes from a cold spring; 1,500 gallons pour over the high limestone ledge every minute. The falls are in heavily wooded hills covered with many kinds of wild shrubs and flowers. Bright laurel and the more delicately colored azaleas cover the hills in May. The land around the falls has been purchased for the development of a private camp and fishing ground.

At 19.4 *m.* is the junction with north fork of State 20, an improved road.

Right on State 20 to MERIWETHER LEWIS NATIONAL PARK, 11.7 *m.* Here is the GRAVE OF MERIWETHER LEWIS, leader of the first white exploratory expedition to cross what is now the United States. Lewis died here Oct. 11, 1809 in Grinder's Inn on the Natchez Trace while on his way to Washington. Although his death was called suicide, some historians believe he was murdered. Many of his papers, including those relating to the expedition that crossed the continent, disappeared here. At that time Lewis was Governor of the Louisiana Territory. A building, typical of the early inns along the trace, has been built for a museum. The park contains 300 acres, much of which is covered with azalea and dogwood. Beside the road are the two large springs. It is said that one of these, DYE STONE SPRINGS, was named by the early settlers who followed the Indian custom of crushing colored stones found in its bed to make dye. OLD SPRINGS, with a flow of about 11,000 gallons of water a day, is in a beautiful, shady spot long popular with picnic parties.

At 29.4 *m.* is the junction with a graveled road.

Left on this graveled road 4.5 *m.* to MARCELLA FALLS, twenty feet high. Below the falls is a small cascade. The area, combining rolling wooded hills and small valleys, is attractive.

LAWRENCEBURG, 35.4 *m.* (867 alt., 3,102 pop.) *(see Tour 13),* is at the junction with US 64 *(see Tour 13).*

South of Lawrenceburg State 6 passes through valleys, along streams, and over heavily wooded hills.

LORETTO, 47.4 *m.* (774 alt., 1,000 pop.), was founded in 1872 by the German Catholic Homestead Association of Cincinnati, which in 1870 purchased 15,000 acres of land in this county and divided it into 160-acre farms. The settlers converted the once barren acres into profitable truck and fruit-producing farms. Loretto has a convent, a church, and a parochial school.

ST. JOSEPH, 52.9 *m.* (754 alt., 200 pop.), was also founded by German Catholics. The town lies in a cotton-growing section.

At 55.6 *m.* State 6 crosses the Alabama Line, 17 miles northeast of Florence, Ala.

Tour 8

(Hopkinsville, Ky.) — Springfield — Nashville — Murfreesboro — Monteagle; US 41E and US 41.
Kentucky Line to Monteagle, 139.5 m.

The Louisville & Nashville R.R. parallels route between the Kentucky Line and Nashville; the Nashville, Chattanooga & St. Louis Ry. between Nashville and Murfreesboro.
Paved roadbed. Accommodations chiefly in the county seats.

Section a. KENTUCKY LINE *to* NASHVILLE, *49 m.*

South of the Kentucky Line, US 41E runs through the Black Patch, an area noted for the production of darkfired tobacco. Throughout the year tobacco dominates the scene as it dominates the economic life of the section.

In February or March smouldering fires dot the hills as the plant beds are burned to kill vegetation, seeds, and roots. After the ground is pulverized and the dust-like seed sown, the plant bed is framed and covered with white canvas to protect the plants from cold, insects and wind-blown seeds.

In May or June the plants are set out in a carefully prepared field. The richest farmers use a horse-drawn mechanical setter which makes a furrow, waters the plants as they are dropped and then packs them down with dirt. But most of the transplanting is still done by hand and must be postponed until rain has moistened the ground.

During the summer months the tobacco requires almost constant care. It must be hoed and sprayed with Paris Green or arsenate of lead. The farmer watches anxiously for rust or wildfire and the ever-present tobacco worm, a singularly unattractive pest with a long green body and a horned head that continues its cycle from moth to chrysalis to worm, defying all methods of eradication except removal by hand. The tobacco must be "topped" to give it breadth of leaf rather than height, and the suckers—small leaves that grow on the plant and sap its vitality—must be cut away.

When in late summer the leaves are dark green and crinkled, the crop is ready for harvest. It is hung on sticks four feet long and taken to barns. There for a traditional forty days and forty nights it hangs above a carefully tended fire. The finest barns have ventilators and a thermometer and hydrometer to insure the proper degree of heat and moisture during the long vigil. But the average farmer uses patience, experience, and "horse sense," knowing that his long summer's work may be ruined in an hour if too much dry heat "kills" the tobacco by destroying the oils that give it pliability and flavor. When the curing has been completed the tobacco is stripped from the stalks and tied into "hands"—convenient bundles containing five or six of the big leaves—to wait transportation to the market.

US 41E crosses the Kentucky Line at 0 *m.,* 26.5 miles southeast of Hopkinsville, Ky., and at 5.4 *m.* crosses Red River.

The BELL WITCH FARM, 5.6 *m.,* has long been so called because it is widely believed that a witch hag rode John Bell and his family here during the early part of the nineteenth century. At the turn of the century John Bell came to Tennessee from North Carolina, bought a tract of land here and settled with his large family and numerous slaves. To round out his holdings, Bell bought a section of land from Mrs. Kate Batts, a neighbor who had a reputation for meanness. Bell was noted for an almost grim piety and uprightness; yet no sooner had the land transfer been completed than Mrs. Batts began declaring that Bell had cheated her. This fancied injustice vexed the old woman for years. On her deathbed she swore that she would come back and "hant John Bell and all his kith and kin to their graves."

Sure enough, tradition says, the Bells were tormented for years by the malicious spirit of Old Kate Batts. John Bell and his favorite daughter Betsy were the principal targets. Toward the other members of the family the witch was either indifferent or, as in the case of Mrs. Bell, friendly. No one ever saw her, but every visitor to the Bell home heard her all too well. Her voice, according to one person who heard it, "spoke at a nerve-racking pitch when displeased, while at other times it sang and spoke in low musical tones."

The spirit of Old Kate led John and Betsy Bell a merry chase. She threw furniture and dishes at them. She pulled their noses, yanked their hair, poked needles into them. She yelled all night to keep them from sleeping, and snatched food from their mouths at mealtime.

The witch, so they say, did not confine her capers to the Bell farmstead. She attended every revival in Robertson County and outsang, outshouted, outmoaned the most fervent converts. The unseen Kate was also very fond of corn whisky. She constantly raided stillhouses, they say, got roaring drunk, and went home to belabor John and Betsy Bell with renewed fervor.

When Betsy fell in love with Josiah Gardener, a young man who lived on the adjoining farm, Old Kate included Josiah in her vigorous displeasure. Gardener finally gave up and fled from the State.

When Old Kate's fame at length reached Nashville, Andrew Jackson and some friends determined to face the terror and "lay" it once and for all. In very high spirits they set out for the Bell farm. Suddenly, on the boundary of Bell's property, it is related, the wagon in which Jackson and his friends were riding would move no farther. The mules strained and Jackson cursed. Out of the empty air came Kate's voice: "All right, General, the wagon can move on." And it did.

That night Kate kept the house in an uproar. She sang, she swore, she threw dishes, overturned furniture, and snatched the bedclothes from all the beds. Next morning the harried Jackson made an early start, crying out to Bell as he left, "I'd rather fight the British again than have any more dealings with that torment."

The Bell Witch disappeared when John Bell died. The original farmhouse has been torn down.

At intervals the newspapers revive the story with an account of how some descendant of Bell's is due for a visitation, which they say is the lot of one person in each generation. But Old Kate is apparently frustrated by present day publicity methods.

At CEDAR HILL, 11.4 *m.* (650 alt., 800 pop.), is the junction with an improved country road.

Right from Cedar Hill on this road to WESSYNGTON HOUSE *(private)*, 4.2 *m.*, so named by Joseph Washington, its builder, because that was the Anglo-Saxon form of his family name. He was a descendant of John Washington, great-grandfather of George, and came to Tennessee from Surry County, Virginia, in 1796. He purchased land and by marriage acquired another large adjoining tract. Both tracts were used for the growing of dark tobacco. Wessyngton House, built in 1819 of brick kilned on the place, has the simple lines of some Georgian Colonial structures. The two-story main unit has one good-sized story-and-a-half wing and several rambling one-story additions in the rear. There is a small porch on the front, and another on the side. The great charm of the well-cared-for estate lies in its gardens and trees. Towering white oaks, silver poplars, great copper beeches, tall pecans, flowering crab apple, Siberian lilac trees, figs, pink dogwoods, and others, dot the lawns. Old crapemyrtle, calycanthus, lilacs, smokebush, fringetree, and syringa border the long paths, and the peonies of old stock fill geometrically laid-out beds. Beyond the garden is the family burial ground.

SPRINGFIELD, 20.2 *m.* (595 alt., 5,577 pop.), seat of Robertson County, was named for James Robertson, founder of Nashville. It is in the fork of Carr's Creek and Sulphur Fork, a branch of the Red River. The stores face the square. Shaded streets, handsome houses, flower gardens, and broad lawns make this an attractive place.

Its busiest period is from January through June and July, during which tobacco auctions are held daily. The crop begins to come to town around Christmas time. Powerful trucks and two-horse wagons covered with bed quilts, crowd every highway and forms long lines up to the warehouse receiving platforms. Foreign buyers arrive to join the local experts who represent many foreign as well as domestic interests. The spicy smell of tobacco permeates the town. Negroes sing as they handle the leaf, the wordless, improvised music slipping from corner to corner of the big warehouses and echoing among the rafters.

Graders from the Bureau of Agricultural Economics arrive with their intricate system of classifying the leaf. Grade A is the choice wrapper leaf, B fillers and snuff tobacco, C the thin light leaf and cheap cigar wrappers, X the worm-eaten or rusted leaves known as lug. These groupings are modified by many other symbols designating color, weight and length of leaf.

When he brings in his crop the farmer receives his "advance" from the Association. This "advance" is the most important word in his vocabulary, and perhaps to set it apart from common words he pronounces it with a strong accent on the first syllable. Though it is literally an advance, it accurately predicts year after year what will be paid for each crop, and thus it represents his annual income.

About the first of the year, when the season opens, the slow tempo of life in the fields and the firing barn give way to activity that moves faster than ticker tape. It revolves about the auctioneer with his rapid sing-song that is understood by no one but the ten or twelve buyers who follow him about the warehouse floor. Even the oldest resident, whose ears have rung with this sound every year of his life, cannot tell you what the auctioneer says. The farmer who raised the tobacco, though he watches anxiously from the background, cannot understand this jargon. He only knows that his whole year's crop can be sold in the time it takes him to cut a piece of chewing tobacco from the plug in his pocket. He knows that repetition is the basis of it, and sometimes he can catch a phrase like "a quarter" or " a half."

The auctioneer is admired by small boys, and occasionally one of them displays ability to imitate him, achieving the effect perfectly long before he knows the sense of a word he is saying. If he is also quick at figures and spends most of his adolescence in the tobacco warehouse, he will probably grow up to be an auctioneer himself, a profession—like the church—to which a young man is apparently "called."

The Black Patch tobacco farmer may be slightly ill at ease with the foreign buyers, but when he goes to town on First Monday, which is County Court Day and the time to swap mules, he drives a good car. In the country he rides a Tennessee "walking horse," which he has reason to consider the noblest animal alive.

The farms here have attractive names, such as Oakhurst or Fairlawn.

Many of the children go to college, but they usually come home to stay after they are graduated.

The Black Patch farmer has learned about his own problem in a hard school. Some forty years ago the Tobacco Trust threatened to destroy him. He transferred to it all the prefixes he was just learning to discard from the word "Yankee," and he is still unable to speak of it calmly. Early attempts at organization among the farmers to combat this monster were fraught with difficulties. The farmer is not a "j'iner" by temperament, and some of the Associations were faulty in plan. Violations of contract were frequent and to punish offenders, who were locally called hill-billies, a secret organization known as Night Riders sprang up. Less violent than the activities of similar organizations in parts of Kentucky, the local "Night Rider trouble," as it is usually called, nonetheless formed a dark chapter in Robertson County history. Plant beds were scrapped, barns were burned, and farmers were called from their beds at night and conducted to quiet woods lots for conferences, the full details of which have never been recorded.

Springfield is now headquarters for the Eastern Dark Fired Tobacco Growers Association, which has gained steadily in membership since its founding in 1932. This co-operative is primarily a surplus handling agency, and members are permitted to make delivery to the organization, or to sell directly to buyers or on auction floors. The Association procures loans from Federal agencies at appraised values by grade.

The town has 34 loose leaf floors, storage warehouses, prizing and rehandling houses. In all, these buildings have nearly a million square feet of floor space. Jointly they sell about 25,000,000 pounds of tobacco a season.

The SPRINGFIELD WOOLEN MILLS, a locally owned industry, employs about 325 people and has 100 broad-looms. The plant receives wool as it comes from the sheep and performs every process in the manufacture of blankets. Some high grade blankets and a version of the Mexican serape are made. Twenty percent of the output goes to the Army, Navy, and Marine Corps.

In 1852–53 David Hughes (1831–1900), while teaching music here, experimented with the telegraph, and in 1855 he patented an improved type-printing telegraph, which he sold to the American Telephone Company. Later Hughes, who had gone abroad to live, invented a microphone and induction balance.

The Tennessee Fox Hunters' Association sponsors the annual State Meet that is held here the first week in October. The chase is conducted in the English fashion, the hunters riding after the hounds.

PERRY PARK *(small fee)*, 23.5 *m.*, has a swimming pool, dance pavilion, and picnic grounds.

GREEN BRIER, 28.1 *m.* (367 alt., 631 pop.), is the former home of the Green Brier Distillery.

RIDGETOP, 30.6 *m.* (730 alt., 196 pop.), is on the edge of the Highland Rim. The WATAUGA SANATORIUM, a 25-room hospital for tubercular patients, is on a high ridge above the village.

US 41E descends from the Highland Rim into the central basin on a winding road. In the spring dogwood and redbud bloom on the hillsides.

At 34.2 *m.* is the junction with paved US 31W.

Left on US 31W is WHITE HOUSE, 11.4 *m.* (580 alt., 209 pop.), so named because the first house here was painted white.

North of the village the route follows the contours of the thickly wooded hills and ascends the Highland Rim.

At 21.6 *m.* is the junction with State 52, a good graveled road indicated by a marker honoring Jenny Lind, who sang here in 1852. When it became known that the Swedish prima donna would pass along this stage route on her way from Nashville to Louisville, the country folk gathered at the nearby spring and, when the coach stopped, asked her to sing.

Right 4.6 *m.* on State 52 is PORTLAND (803 alt., 1,020 pop.), where about 600 carloads of strawberries are packed each season. Owing to climatic conditions the picking season sometimes varies, but it usually begins about June 1, and then this quiet country town begins to bustle. Hundreds of men and women from other counties and States join the natives in picking berries and packing them in the sheds. Pickers are paid by the quart, packers by the crate. Speed is the principal requisite, and workers attain a mechanical pace that is amazing.

At this season the streets are lined with medicine shows; salesmen hawk wares from small street stands. Crowds come miles to enjoy the carnival at night and to pick berries by day. The town gradually settles down to await the next season.

MITCHELL, 23.8 *m.* (775 alt., 200 pop.), is another strawberry-shipping point.

At 24.3 *m.* US 31W crosses the Kentucky Line, 6 miles south of Franklin, Ky.

In GOODLETTSVILLE, 36.7 *m.* (450 alt., 919 pop.), a bronze marker, facing the post office, has been erected on the site of the building in which the Goodlettsville Lamb Club was organized. This was one of the first co-operative farm marketing associations in the South and made its first sale in 1887.

Left from Goodlettsville on Long Hollow Pike; just beyond Mansker Creek is the junction with a dirt road, 0.5 *m.;* R. 0.5 *m.* on this road to the SITE OF THE HOME of KASPER MANSKER, who came into this country in 1769 with a party of Long Hunters that included Uriah Stone and Isaac Bledsoe. The party remained a year. (It was their long absences from home that caused them to be called Long Hunters.) Mansker was typical. He had his trusted rifle, just as did Crockett and the others; he called his "Nancy." He was familiar with the sights and sounds of the forests and knew the calls of birds and beasts, calls which the Indians often imitated to lure hunters out of their camps.

Mansker became known for his Indian-fighting ability and later was made a major in the State militia. That Mansker was an effective fighter is shown by a letter Andrew Jackson wrote to the Chickasaw in 1812 when he was seeking their aid. "Do you remember," Jackson asked, "when the whole Creek nation came to destroy your towns that a few hundred Chickasaws aided by a few whites chased them back to their nation, killing the best of their warriors, and covering the rest with shame?" The "few whites" Jackson referred to were led by Mansker.

Toward the end of his life Mansker became a devout Methodist, and Bishop Francis Asbury often stopped at "Mansco's Lick." The confusion about his name was the result of his German accent.

It was to Mansker's small, stoutly built house here that John Donelson brought his family after his epic water trip on the *Adventure* from the Watauga settlement to Nashville. Mansker took the whole family in. It was here, too, that Jackson decided to accompany Rachel Donelson, John's daughter—who was at that time married to Robards—on a trip down the river to Natchez. *(See The Hermitage, Tour 12.)*

The LICK, 0.5 *m.* (R), is surrounded by trees and underbrush. About 100 yards L. is MANSKER'S GRAVE, by a large hackberry tree in a strip of land covered with stones, rocks, and grass.

WESTVIEW, 46.2 *m.,* was built by Captain W. B. Walton in 1850. The house, several hundred yards from the road, was designed by Major A. Heiman, whose plans ranked next to Strickland's in the architectural contest for the State Capitol. It is a large, two-story hip roof brick structure whose façade is saved from plainness by projection of the central third. The rear ell has a long double gallery that is carried across the back of the main house. Like many of the other houses in this vicinity, the house was constructed by slaves and the building materials were obtained on the site.

The gardens, long and faithfully tended, have boxwood, lilacs, pink crapemyrtles, and most of the old fashioned flowers and shrubs.

NASHVILLE, 49.2 *m.* (546 alt., 153,866 pop.) *(see NASHVILLE).*

Points of Interest: The Capitol, Vanderbilt University, George Peabody College for Teachers, Scarritt College, Ward-Belmont, Fisk University, the Parthenon, and others.

Nashville is at the junction with US 31-31E *(see Tour 7),* State 11 *(see Tour 7A),* US 41W *(see Tour 14),* and US 70 *(see Tour 12).* The point of intersection is on Memorial Square.

Section b. NASHVILLE *to* MONTEAGLE, *90.5 m.,* US 41.

Between Nashville and Monteagle US 70 traverses three of the eight topographical sub-divisions of the State.

Between Nashville and Murfreesboro is the Central Basin, where the country is rolling and generally under cultivation. Back from the highway, on both sides, are lands covered with red cedar, the largest cedar forest in the State. South of Murfreesboro the route ascends the Highland Rim. Above the rim lie the Barrens, covering part of three counties, an area generally flat with scrub oak that attests the thinness of the soil.

Between Manchester and the point where the ascent to the top of the mountain is made, the route parallels the western escarpment of the Cumberland Plateau. This area is more fertile and under heavy cultivation. Near Monteagle are mountains and the Cumberland Plateau.

US 41 leaves NASHVILLE, 0 *m.,* on 4th Ave. S., to Peabody St.; L. on Peabody St. two blocks to 2nd Ave., the Murfreesboro Pike.

By an underpass of the Nashville, Chattanooga & St. Louis Ry., 3.5 *m.,* is (R) the camp site of the Irish Nomads. In the last week of April this roving clan of horse traders gathers in Nashville to attend the annual burial services of members who have died during the year. Between two and three thousands of them pitch their tents and park their trailers in the open field. Though they are often mistaken for Gypsies, these people are of pure Irish stock, devout Roman Catholics, and bear such names as Costello, Sherlock, and Gorman.

The clan stems from four families of horse traders who came to the United States in 1875. They have always confined their trading to the South. Today they travel about the rural sections in cars and trucks, stopping frequently to buy horses and mules. The buying is not restricted to fine work animals. Farmers know that the Nomads will take a sick mule or an overworked horse, if it is not too old. Skilled for generations in doctoring ailing horses, they are remarkably successful in salvaging such animals. At New Orleans and Atlanta the clan maintains depots on a communal basis, in which the animals are collected and sold at auction. A large part of the trade is with foreign markets. Much of the mountain artillery of the Italian Army was carried into the hills of Ethiopia on the backs of mules bought for the Italian Government by the Irish Nomads.

The burial place for those who live east of the Alleghenies is Atlanta; for those who live West, Nashville. On the first of May mass for the dead is said at St. Patrick's Church. Burial is at Mt. Calvary Cemetery, on the Lebanon Road.

COLEMERE *(private),* 6.7 *m.,* has (L) a large house with a Greek Revival pedimented portico, designed by Russell Hart and built in 1930, after the first house had been destroyed by fire. The first house was built in 1893 by E. W. Cole, retired president of the Nashville, Chattanooga & St. Louis Ry. The rose gardens are notable.

The NASHVILLE MUNICIPAL AIRPORT (L), 7.7 *m.,* has a modern hangar, an assembly hall, and a building for the use of the 105th Observation Squadron. The runways and some of the buildings on this 400-acre field were constructed by WPA labor.

The CENTRAL STATE HOSPITAL FOR THE INSANE (R), 7.8 *m.,* is on a bluegrass farm. The hospital can care for 1,800 patients. The criminal department has a capacity of 300.

Southeast of this point the highway passes through fertile fields. The grassy meadows are bordered with trees and, in late spring, starred with wild daisies. Many of the fences along the highway are covered with wild honeysuckle.

A dangerous curve at the Nashville, Chattanooga & St. Louis Ry. underpass is at 16.3 *m.*

At 17.5 *m.* is the junction with a graveled road.

Left on this road to JEFFERSON SPRINGS, 7 *m.,* a summer resort.

At 20.7 *m.* is the junction with paved State 102.

Left on State 102 is SMYRNA, 1.2 *m.* (510 alt., 531 pop.), a village in a rich farming section.

1. Left (straight ahead) 1 *m.* on an improved dirt road to the DAVIS HOME *(open Mon.-Thurs.)*; here is the SAM DAVIS GRAVE. Davis, a 19-year-old scout, was captured by Federal troops on Nov. 9, 1863, after he had been in Union territory for more than two weeks. In his boot he had plans of Federal fortifications and information about the size and positions of Federal troops.

He was taken to General Dodge, who was anxious to learn what Confederate agent in the Federal ranks had helped Davis. The general endeavored to confuse the youth by questions. Without revealing any information, Sam said, "I know the danger of my situation, and I am willing to take the consequences." Dodge persisted but found Davis adamant. He threatened court martial. Sam answered, "You are doing your duty as a soldier, and I am doing mine."

The trial was postponed to the 26th. The sentence read: ". . . the said Samuel Davis of Coleman's scouts in the service of the so-called Confederate States, to be hanged by the neck until dead." In a letter he wrote to his parents that night, he said, "I do not fear to die."

The next morning, after Davis had ridden to the scaffold on his coffin, General Dodge gave him one more chance; he sent a staff officer to ask if the boy would reveal the name of his informant. "If I had a thousand lives, I would lose them all here before I would betray my friends or the confidence of my informer," was the answer as reported in histories. The sentence was executed.

The State owns and maintains the plain, long two-story house. Hand-hewn timbers have been clapboarded. The pedimented central portico has square columns. Central halls on both floors separate the rooms. Near the house is the log cabin used before the construction of the larger house.

2. Right 3.5 *m.* from Smyrna on an improved road is OLD JEFFERSON (520 alt., 87 pop.), on Stone's River. In the days of river transportation the future of Jefferson seemed bright, for it was in a fertile region on a navigable stream. At first only flatboats and barges were cabled to its wharves, but in 1824 the keel of a steamboat was laid here. This boat carried passengers between Jefferson and Nashville. When water transportation was outmoded by railroads and good pikes, the navigability of Stone's River did not matter, and the importance of Jefferson dwindled.

3. Left from Smyrna on an improved road to JEFFERSON SPRINGS *(fishing, boating, swimming)*, a summer resort with a modern hotel. On the shady banks of Stone's River are many cottages, some of them for rent.

STONE'S RIVER NATIONAL CEMETERY (L), 29.1 *m.*, was established in 1867 for the interment of soldiers killed near Murfreesboro. Of the 6,177 graves, 2,360 hold unknown men.

East of the cemetery is a UNION MONUMENT erected in 1863 by survivors of Col. W. B. Hazen's Union brigade as a memorial to 55 of their comrades who were killed here.

STONE'S RIVER NATIONAL MILITARY PARK (R), 30.7 *m.*, was established in 1927 to preserve the relics of the Battle of Stone's River. Considered from the standpoint of the loss of life, this battle was one of the most indecisive of the War between the States. Of 37,000 men, the Confederates lost 10,000; and of 44,000 men, the Union lost 13,000. At the end of the battle the Confederate army still blocked the Union advance on Chattanooga, though the Confederates had withdrawn from the field in apparent retreat.

Bragg's withdrawal was caused largely by the over-enthusiasm and overconfidence of some of his men. On the third day of the battle they had been ordered to dislodge the Union left from high ground along the river. The order to attack was given at 4 o'clock that afternoon—just long enough before dark to take the hill—but the first rush was successful, and the men pushed on too far, coming under direct and heavy fire of the Union artillery. They were shattered and driven back. The next day councils were held in both camps, and Bragg withdrew during the night.

Rosecrans failed to follow Bragg, because many of his supplies had been taken in a cavalry raid led by Wheeler, which preceded the actual battle. With fine strategy, Wheeler had encircled the Union troops and had captured the wagon train following the army. Rosecrans held fast to what he had gained by encamping at Murfreesboro, while Bragg retreated to Tullahoma.

A pyramid of cannon balls (L), 31 *m.*, at the intersection of the

CEMETERY, STONE'S RIVER NATIONAL MILITARY PARK

Nashville, Chattanooga & St. Louis Ry. and the highway, is the site of the TEMPORARY HEADQUARTERS OF GENERAL BRAGG, commander of the Army of Tennessee.

REDOUBT BRANNAN (R), 31.3 *m.,* was built by Union troops in 1863 to protect Murfreesboro against invasion by the Confederates. The high earthworks are well preserved.

MURFREESBORO, 32.2 *m.* (616 alt, 7,993 pop.), seat of Rutherford County, is in a section noted for its purebred Jersey cattle and is an important shipping point for cotton and dairy products.

The abundant cedar forests nearby are cut on a large scale.

Murfreesboro grew from a small settlement nearby called Jefferson. Stone's River was discovered in 1766 by a party of four men and named for one of them, Uriah Stone. The county was established in 1803, and seven months later, on August 3, 1805, Jefferson (now Old Jefferson) was selected as the county seat. Thomas H. Benton, United States Senator from Missouri (1821–1851), tried his first case there.

In October 1811 a second county seat was selected and named Cannonsburg by admirers of Newton Cannon, who was later Governor of the State (1835–1839). His victory in 1835 over a candidate supported by Andrew Jackson was the first indication of Jackson's decreasing power in Tennessee politics. Cannon had been a political and personal enemy of Jackson since the time when Jackson had prosecuted a case on which Cannon sat as a juror. Jackson had fought hard for conviction, but the jury brought in a verdict acquitting the defendant. Jackson shook his finger in Cannon's face and said: "I'll mark you, young man." Later, when Cannon's popularity had waned, the name of the town was changed to honor Col. Hardy Murfree, a Revolutionary War hero.

Murfreesboro was the capital of Tennessee from 1819 to 1825. For three years after the courthouse burned in 1822, the delegates met in the Masonic Hall, but in 1825 the legislature convened in Nashville, because the hall was inadequate. Long after the legislators had left here, Murfreesboro was seeking their return and its re-establishment as the capital. It was nearer to the center of the State, its leading citizens argued, and, besides, it was "deficient in those sources of amusement which in Nashville are supposed to distract the legislators from strict attention to their duty." When the time came to select a permanent capital, feeling was so strong that the local newspaper protested, "If the members can not accede to our wishes then we go for McMinnville, for Knoxville, for any place before Nashville!" Nevertheless, Nashville was chosen.

A RED-CEDAR BUCKET FACTORY here also makes churns, filter tubs, ice pails, and wine coolers.

The CONFEDERATE MONUMENT on the square is now a meeting place for farmers who stop to exchange gossip.

The TENNESSEE COLLEGE (Baptist), the only senior college for women in the State, occupies a 20-acre campus along Main St. Its handsome brick buildings have pillared porches in the Southern tradition and are shaded by ancient oaks. The 176 students come from several States.

The $1,500,000 plant of MIDDLE TENNESSEE TEACHERS' COLLEGE includes a demonstration farm and dairy as well as an impressive group of buildings. Largest of the three State Teachers' College, it has an enrollment of 2,100 and a faculty of 45.

In a modernized antebellum home is the BRISTOL-NELSON PHYSIOLOGICAL SCHOOL where 25 sub-normal and backward children receive care and training under the direction of Mrs. Cora Bristol-Nelson, a specialist in abnormal psychology.

RUTHERFORD HOSPITAL is the home of the Rutherford County Health Department, which has lowered the infant mortality rate in this county to 26.6 per 1,000 live births. The hospital was built and the demonstration unit established by the Commonwealth Fund of New York City in 1924 as one of four child health demonstrations.

In Murfreesboro is the junction with US 70A *(see Tour 12A)* and US 241 *(see Tour 8A)*.

Left from Murfreesboro on State 96 to Rucker Lane, 5 *m.;* L. here 1.6 *m.* to MARYMONT *(private)*, built on land claimed in 1807 by Aaron Jenkins for services rendered in the Revolutionary War. The house was built by his son Nimrod. It is a large square brick Greek Revival structure with a central pedimented portico, two stories high. The portico shelters a small second floor gallery. During the War between the States, the house was a Union headquarters and later a hospital, but it received good care. Consequently, it was one of the few homes spared during the Battle of Murfreesboro.

The grounds and garden were mutilated by Federal soldiers during General Rosecrans' occupation of Murfreesboro.

1. Left from Murfreesboro on State 96, to a huge FLAT ROCK, 2.1 *m.* (R), covering three acres. This rock is in the geographical center of the State.

2. Right from Murfreesboro on State 96 to the junction with a graveled road, 8.5 *m.;* R. here 2 *m.* to SNAIL SHELL CAVE, in which 17 varieties of snail shells have been found. A small stream runs through the cave with water so deep that parts of the cave have never been explored. The mouth is about 200 feet wide by 300 feet long. It is in a hollow with perpendicular cliffs on three sides, and a gravelly slope on the fourth.

Southeast of Murfreesboro, following a former Indian trail, US 41 traverses a fertile level farming country. The land is intensively cultivated on the outskirts of the town.

At 42.1 *m.* is the junction with a graveled road.

Right on this road to the former HOME OF JOHN P. BUCHANAN, Governor of Tennessee (1891–93). Buchanan was the first president of the Farmers and Laborers Union of Tennessee (1889), a political organization known as the Farmers Alliance. The first activities of the Alliance were non-political. It undertook to eliminate the middleman by establishing co-operative rolling mills, cotton exchanges, tobacco warehouses, and stores. Later, when the organization entered national politics, its goal was the abolition of national banks and the establishment of a graduated income tax.

The Alliance was politically powerful in Tennessee by 1890; it successfully attempted to control the Democratic Party, and Buchanan was nominated for the governorship—which meant election.

The great problem of his administration arose from the practice of leasing convicts to private contractors. The United Mine Workers of East Tennessee protested. Buchanan had some conciliatory laws passed but finally called out the militia *(see Tour 5)*. Buchanan was not re-elected.

The Cumberland Mountains are in view at 61.4 *m.*

The route reaches the top of the Highland Rim, 63 *m.,* known since the days of the explorers as the Barrens because of the scarcity of timber and other growth here. Fires have often swept the area during the last forty years. They usually begin in the spring. After the timber has been killed by fire, the grass, briars, and bushes grow profusely, furnishing excellent pasturage for cattle, goats, and hogs. For this reason cattlemen from the adjoining counties have long been accused of setting these fires.

US 41 crosses Duck River on a steel bridge at 64.3 *m.* The Duck River cascades are (R) 0.3 miles downstream.

At 65 *m.* is the junction with an unmarked dirt road.

Right on this road to OLD STONE FORT, 6 *m.,* an unusually fine example of prehistoric defense works. Occupying a highly strategic position, the walls, 20 feet thick, are built of stone and earth and enclose about 32 acres. The intricate inner defenses, which surround the only gateway, were evidently the work of skilled engineers. It is not known by whom the fort was built. Some have credited De Soto with its construction during his march northward from Florida, but this theory was combatted by John Haywood, the Tennessee historian, who told of a white oak tree that had grown up over the remains. He said that it had been demonstrated by study of the rings that the tree was about 78 years old when De Soto landed on the coast of Florida. If the fort was built by a prehistoric tribe, their culture must have been much more advanced than any known to have lived north of Mexico.

TENNESSEE COLLEGE, MURFREESBORO

MANCHESTER, 65.6 *m.* (1,069 alt., 1,227 pop.), at the foot of the Cumberland Plateau, is the seat of Coffee County which was named for Gen. John Coffee (1772–1833), a surveyor and a close friend of Andrew Jackson. A garment factory here is the only remnant of Manchester's once thriving cotton factories. As early as 1791 an advertisement appeared in the Knoxville *Gazette:* "The subscriber has his machine in order for carding, spinning, and weaving and is wanting a number of good weavers—such as are acquainted with the weaving of velvets, corduroys, and calicoes. John Hague, Manchester (Mero District) Nov. 11, 1791."

Manchester has long been a shipping point for crossties; cutting them was long a source of cash income for farmers. When the farmer had gathered his crop he had little else to do except feed the stock and lay in a supply of wood. He then went to the woods to chop or saw down a tree. If the trees were tall and had few limbs, the farmer could get two "ties" from one tree, otherwise he got only one. After the tree had been felled, the length of one or two "ties" was measured off and the log notched.

When a load of crossties was finished, it was hauled into town and sold. Cash received for such a load was exchanged for shoes and heavy underwear, or for coffee, sugar, or other foods that could not be produced on the place. At Christmas time, tie money went into the purchase of nuts, apples, oranges, candy, and shotgun shells for hunting on Christmas Day.

The process of producing crossties has changed. A portable sawmill is now moved into the woods, and the logs are sawed into crossties there. This method is much faster and more economical.

At the northeast corner of the public square is a large MOUND of earth and stone, believed to have been built by prehistoric tribesmen as a signal point for the Old Stone Fort.

At 86.6 *m.* is the junction with a graveled road.

Left on this road to WONDER CAVE *(adm. $1 with guide),* 0.5 *m.* A stream runs through the mouth of the cave. The main stalactite room is about 400 yards long, 100 yards wide, and 8 feet high.

The route begins at 87.1 *m.* its 3-mile ascent to the top of the Cumberland Mountain. There are several places from which the valley below can be seen.

MONTEAGLE, 90.5 *m.* (2,006 alt., 1,000 pop.) *(see Tour 13)* is at the junctions with US 64 *(see Tour 13)* and US 68 *(see Tour 16).*

Tour 8A

Murfreesboro—Shelbyville—Fayetteville—(Huntsville, Ala.); US 241.
Murfreesboro to Alabama Line, 66.4 m.

Paved roadbed.
Accommodations limited except in county seats.

Between Murfreesboro and Shelbyville US 241 traverses country that is flat and grown sparsely with cedars. Outcrops of bedrock rising in many places above the shallow topsoil make this poor farming country. It was once said that a man living back in the cedars ". . . has got to scratch and sweat mightily if he wants to starve decent." South of Shelbyville gently rolling hills alternate with steep ridges. On the whole the countryside is bleakly forbidding, except in spring and summer, when patches of pink crowsfoot moss and white sandwort appear in the cedar barrens, bluish lichens splotch exposed rock, and the yellow of wild mustard flowers spreads across the open country.

MURFREESBORO, 0 *m.* (573 alt., 8,000 pop.) *(see Tour 8),* is at the junctions with US 41 *(see Tour 8)* and US 70A *(see Tour 12A).*

The rather prosperous farming country immediately south of Murfreesboro fades into a country of mournful cedar thickets alternating with wasteland, rocky and gouged by gullies; the people live in weathered shacks beside skimpy truck patches. A few of the old cedar snake-rail fences remain but they are rapidly being sold to manufacturers of pencils.

A marker (R) at 4.1 *m.* is in memory of Benjamin Liddon, who was awarded two tracts of land, including Liddon Springs, as a bonus for Revolutionary War services.

At 18.6 *m.* is the junction with a graveled road.

Left on this road is BELL BUCKLE, 5 *m.* (856 alt., 378 pop.) settled in 1853 and named, according to legend, for the creek that runs through the town. The creek itself was earlier so named because of a bell and a buckle carved on a large beech tree near the source of the stream. The carving is supposed to have been made by Indians or by one of the Long Hunters. Bell Buckle is surrounded by farm land that produces abundant crops and pasturage without the use of fertilizers. Freestone water is piped from springs near Wartrace. In Bell Buckle is WEBB SCHOOL, founded in 1870 by the late W. R. (Sawney) Webb, who has been called "the father of preparatory school education in the South." The school, which had been established in Culleoka, Maury County, was brought here in 1886. Now a well-known preparatory school for boys, it is non-sectarian and has accommodations for more than 200 boarding students.

SHELBYVILLE, 26.3 *m.* (771 alt., 5,010 pop.), seat of Bedford County, was named for Col. Isaac Shelby who led a force of Tennessee riflemen at King's Mountain against the British. The Duck River almost encircles the town, which is the leading business and shipping center of the Duck River Valley.

The population of this town increased by two-thirds between 1920 and 1930 with industrial development. One of the larger factories is the UNITED STATES RUBBER COMPANY PLANT, manufacturing cotton cord for tires. Another, the NATIONAL PENCIL COMPANY PLANT, ships products all over the United States and to foreign markets.

The town was laid out in 1810 by commissioners appointed by the General Assembly, and was incorporated October 7, 1819. The high point of the year in early Shelbyville was Muster Day, held in accordance with Congressional militia laws. On the day appointed by the General Assembly every man in the county subject to military service reported here to drill, "armed and equipped as the law directs." Congress had appropriated money to provide equipment for the militiamen but there was never enough to go around. At sunrise the farmers began straggling in; some carried long deer rifles and fowling pieces and a few had Government-issue muskets. The more conscientious wore homespun, home-tailored uniforms, but most came in work jeans. The light-hearted often tricked themselves out as Indians, Negroes, or tramps, and brandished willow switches, farm tools, and cornstalks. Filling the technical requirements of the law, they cavorted to the music of fife and drum, made wild whooping charges on the tavern taproom, and, in general, turned Muster Day into a roaring burlesque. When the fun had lost its edge, horse trading and serious drinking began. During the day there were shooting and wrestling matches, bouts of tall-tale telling, political speeches, private and free-for-all fights, and, usually, several shooting and cutting brawls.

1. Left from Shelbyville on State 64 to HORSE MOUNTAIN, 3 *m.,* used during the War between the States as a signal station, first by the Confederates and then by the Union forces.

2. Left from Shelbyville on State 82 is LYNCHBURG 16.4 *m.* (824 alt., 380 pop.), the seat of Moore County, where the famous Old Number 7 whisky was made by the Jack Daniel distillery. A new distillery is owned and operated by a nephew of Daniel. Lynchburg was named for a frail little man, Tom Lynch, who was always chosen to wield the lash on men sentenced to be whipped. The tree used as a WHIPPING POST still stands near the center of the town.

3. Left from Shelbyville on State 16 is TULLAHOMA, 18.6 *m.* (1,100 alt., 4,023 pop.). A Confederate force under Gen. Braxton Bragg took up winter quarters here in January 1863 after the bloody and indecisive battle at nearby Stone's River. The town fell to Union forces under General Rosecrans on July 3, 1863. Norman H. Davis (1878–), ambassador-at-large in the administration of President Franklin D. Roosevelt, was born near here. Among Tullahoma products are golf clubs, gloves, baseballs, underwear, shirts, shoes, marble, spokes, condensed milk, and cheese.

a. Right from Tullahoma on State 16, 2 *m.,* to CAMP PEAY, of the Tennessee National Guard. It covers 1,100 acres. The annual maneuvers take place here.

The TENNESSEE FEDERATION OF WOMEN'S CLUBS VOCATIONAL SCHOOL is at 3 *m.*

b. Left from Tullahoma 4 *m.* on State 55 to OVOCA by Lake Calanthe. For more than 25 years the Presbyterian Church, U.S.A., has held its summer camp for young people here. Here also is the KNIGHTS OF PYTHIAS HOME for widows and orphans. During the summer a number of churches and other organizations hold conferences and meetings by the lake.

Between Shelbyville and Fayetteville the country is again poor and stony, largely overrun with scrub cedar, but there are a few dairy farms and sheep ranches. The top layer of shale has so much bitumen and petroleum that areas near an outcrop have been known to smolder for months after a brush fire. Some of the shanty dwellers, Negro and white, mix this shale with their firewood.

FAYETTEVILLE, 53.6 *m.* (666 alt., 3,822 pop.) *(see Tour 13)* is at the junction with US 64 *(see Tour 13).*

The marked SITE OF CAMP BLOUNT is at 54.2 *m.* Here the troops of Gen. Andrew Jackson mobilized on October 4, 1813, for a punitive expedition against the Creek Indians after the massacre at Fort Mims. Jackson arrived on October 7th, his arm still in a sling from wounds received a month before in a shooting affray at Nashville. When the troops returned a few months later they were mustered out here, after they had been praised. On October 5, 1814, about 2,000 Tennessee volunteers assembled in the field before marching to Mobile to oppose the British, who were then threatening New Orleans. Camp Blount was also the mustering ground for troops used in the two Seminole Wars (1817 and 1837).

Construction of the OLD STONE BRIDGE, over Elk River, began in 1858 and was completed in 1861. Built of rock quarried nearby, it has six elliptical arches, four of them with 60 feet spans. The total length is 315 feet. It is said that Sherman led troops over this old stone bridge on his way to Georgia. A few may actually have crossed the bridge, but Sherman did not trust its strength, and had a pontoon bridge built across Elk River.

Between Fayetteville and the Alabama Line is a high plateau. The land is so level that it is not well drained and is unsuitable for cultivation, though some efforts have been made to grow cotton on it.

At 66.4 *m.* US 241 crosses the Alabama Line, 16 miles north of Huntsville, Ala.

Tour 9

(Russellville, Ky.)—Clarksville—Dover—Paris—Dresden—Martin—Union City; State 13, 76, 54, 22 (Austin Peay Highway).
Kentucky Line to Union City, 122.8 m.

Louisville & Nashville R.R. parallels route between Guthrie, Ky., and Clarksville; and Nashville, Chattanooga & St. Louis Ry. between Dresden and Union City.
Asphalt roadbed between Guthrie and Dresden, concrete between Dresden and Union City.
Accommodations chiefly in county seats.

State 13 crosses the Kentucky Line, 0 *m.,* 25 miles southwest of Russellville, Ky., just beyond a junction with US 41 *(see Tour 8),* and runs through a fertile farming area. The country between Dover and Paris, rather poor and hilly, has many men who cultivate a few acres of "sorry" soil and spend much of their time hunting with their hound-dogs. Most of these men are sharecroppers. After the spring and summer plowing, and when crops have been laid by, they spend their mornings hunting squirrel, their chief source of meat until hog-killing time. On sultry afternoons they sit in the dog runs (open hallways between the two rooms) of their log or batten cabins (weatherboarded with slatted planks). They lean back against the walls in cane or split-bottom chairs, rest their bare feet on the lower rounds, and doze, while the hound-dogs underneath the house whine drowsily as they scratch fleas. Neighbors visit, sitting in the dog run to catch the cool breeze that comes through even on the hottest days. When the womenfolk tire of community gossip, they go into the bedroom to study dress and quilt patterns, or to take naps. The menfolk go behind the house to pitch horse shoes at stakes, or dollars (iron wagon-wheel washers) at holes dug in the ground 20 feet apart.

These men like to "grabble" for fish in sloughs, or holes of the river bank, a process that calls for wading naked into the water and running the hands under logs, or driftwood, and into holes for catfish. If they are bit-

SHARECROPPER'S FAMILY

ten by snakes, they take a "slug of corn likker," but even the hardiest sometimes die. A tale is told of one man who was struck by a cottonmouth moccasin, a snake with a deep pit between eyes and nostrils, and squarish black blotches on its body. He swelled up "twicet his size at natural, and spots purple as pokeberries come out all over his hide."

In addition to these people there are moderately prosperous, hardworking farmers, owners of small farms in the creek bottoms, and "cash renters" who maintain a higher standard of living than the sharecroppers do.

In fall and winter the 'coon and 'possum are hunted, and the hound-dog comes into his own *(see Tour 12A)*.

At 7.2 *m.* is the junction with a graveled road.

Right on this road to WOODSTOCK, 5 *m.,* birthplace of Caroline Meriwether Goodlett, founder of the United Daughters of the Confederacy, and of her niece, Elizabeth Meriwether Gilmer, better known as Dorothy Dix (1870–), the newspaperwoman *(see WRITERS OF TENNESSEE)*. This house, a long, low, rambling structure, was built in 1830 by Charles N. Meriwether, father of Mrs. Goodlett. The scene of *Penhally,* a novel by Caroline Gordon (Mrs. Allen Tate), is laid at Woodstock.

At 7.6 *m.* is ST. BETHLEHEM (601 alt., 300 pop.).

Left from St. Bethlehem on an asphalt road to DUNBAR CAVE AND IDAHO

SPRINGS *(open, adm. 50¢, guide service; fishing; swimming; boating; riding; tennis; hotels; cottages),* 2 *m.,* a State game preserve. In 1932 a dam that increased the lake area to about 20 acres was constructed. The lake is heavily stocked with bass, pike, perch, bluegill, and crappie. There is a quail hatchery here also. The mineral springs have long been famous as a salt lick. The cave has 8 miles of galleries with many interesting formations studded with white and colored stalactites: Independence Hall, Counterfeiter's Room, Ballroom, Solomon's Porch, Jacob's Well, the Elephant, Peterson's Leaf, and Crystal Palace. The dance floor is in the mouth of the cave. A shaded pavilion has been built for picnics and social gatherings.

During the Mexican War saltpeter for the manufacture of gunpowder was mined in the cave. The large chamber, still called the Ballroom, was used for dances before the War between the States and a nearby chamber housed a saloon. From about 1870 to 1895 the cave was very popular for picnics and bran dances; bran was scattered on the floor to a depth of several inches and music was furnished by a 3- or 4-piece band. For years one of the favorite musicians was a colored barber, Jim Shelton, who "got religion" after a while, and would never again fiddle for a dance.

Livestock companies held fairs here until about 1923. During this period buildings were erected just north of the present Idaho Springs Hotel, for the holding of an annual camp meeting. People came for miles around, stayed in the dormitory, or lived in tents for three or four weeks at a time. In the gospel tents, or brush arbors (meeting places in which the seats are placed under the trees or have a framework covered with brush over them), were held morning, afternoon, and evening services, with fervid sermons; gospel hymn singing, led by a singing master who used a tuning fork; experience meetings, where folk publicly confessed their sins; conversions amid happy shouting; and much passing of the collection plate. Baptisms took place in the river.

The cool, even temperature at the cave mouth was a boon to sick babies in the summer. Mothers brought them here and remained all summer. Many went so far as to erect little booths with blanket partitions as bed chambers. Sometimes there would be a whole row of these little rooms along the left wall near the cave entrance.

CLARKSVILLE, 12.4 *m.* (593 alt., 9,229 pop.) *(see Tour 14),* is at the junction with US 41W *(see Tour 14),* which the route follows to NEW PROVIDENCE, 15.1 *m.* (394 alt., 904 pop.) *(see Tour 14);* here turn L. on State 76, now the main route.

West of New Providence the route winds through farm land that produces a high-grade dark-fired tobacco. In this territory, locally called Potneck and its people Potneckers, are numerous wildcat stills in the bushy hollows. Potneck is sometimes said to have received the name from a sorceress whose goiterous neck was enormous. It is extremely hard to find anyone who lives in Potneck; he either lives "just this side" or "just the other side." The favorite sport is 'possum hunting *(see Tour 12A).*

At 43.9 *m.* is a bridge over the Cumberland River.

DOVER, 44.4 *m.* (550 alt., 763 pop.), seat of Stewart County, on the south bank of the Cumberland River, was laid out in 1806, and, with the exception of four houses, was burned by Union forces in 1862 after the capture of Fort Donelson. The town was rebuilt later. For more than a half century before the War between the States, Stewart County was the center of the flourishing iron production in Middle Tennessee. There were 14 furnaces and forges in blast in the county. The furnaces closed during the war, and most of them were destroyed. Several reopened in 1873, but only two were still open by 1898. None is in operation now.

The FORT DONELSON MUSEUM *(open 8-9 daily),* Main St., on the bank of the Cumberland River, was built in 1826 and, before the War between the States, was operated as the Dover Tavern. The surrender of Fort Donelson by Gen. Simon B. Buckner to General Grant took place on the long front porch. Arms were stacked on the hillside at the rear of the house. Later the place was a hotel, called the Old Hobing House, until purchased in 1926 by the Fort Donelson Historical Society. Among the relics in the museum are a land grant signed by John Sevier (1807), a Buffalo Bill rifle, a pardon signed by Abraham Lincoln (1865), a land grant signed by Martin Van Buren (1840), a deed of trust for ten Negro slaves (1841), and a flintlock muzzle-loader rifle, loaded since 1759.

At 46.4 *m.* is the entrance to FORT DONELSON NATIONAL MILITARY PARK. In this 97-acre park are examples of defense means used in the War between the States; markers and tablets on the old fort, the earthworks, rifle pits, and water batteries enable the visitor to trace the course of the decisive battle fought here.

The capture of Fort Donelson by General Grant was one of the most critical events in the war. It brought deep discouragement to the South after the over-enthusiasm that followed Manassas; it gave the North a new start by permitting its troops to establish a firm base at Nashville from which to push further conquests into the South; and finally, it gave Lincoln the confidence in Grant that, some historians say, caused the President to place him eventually in command of the Virginia campaign that ended the war.

On Feb. 12, 1862, ten days after his capture of Fort Henry, Grant divided his forces into three divisions, giving Generals McClernand, Smith, and Wallace command, and marched along the banks of the Cumberland River to Fort Donelson. His advance was designed to hold the gains Union gunboats had already made along the Tennessee River.

That night the Union troops surrounded the fort. The next day the troops within the fort were increased by the arrival of General Floyd and General Buckner; Floyd superseded General Pillow, who had been in command of the Confederate troops.

Grant had left Wallace behind to hold Fort Henry, but after skirmishing all day and seeing his men suffer from the bitter cold of that February night, unsheltered, and afraid to light a fire, he summoned Wallace. Upon Wallace's arrival the gunboats advanced to within firing distance of the fort and began an attack, but they had moved too close and received a merciless pounding from the Confederate batteries.

They withdrew that night, and Grant led them downstream and held council with the naval commander. He expected to wait a few days before making another attack. On the night of the 14th the Confederate generals, joined by General Forrest, took council. The next morning they advanced on the Federals and, in particular, upon McClernand's flank. McClernand sought Wallace's help. Later in the afternoon when McClernand's troops were beginning to retreat, Wallace sent supplies and men, though Grant was away and had not given the command. The Federals retook the ground they had lost.

On the night of the 15th the Confederate leaders held another meeting, but this time they assembled to find ways of escape. There was some confusion about the command, but it was finally decided that Buckner should make the surrender. Pillow rowed away with his officers at the oars, and Floyd and some of his men fled up the river. Buckner turned over 13,500 men, 3,000 horses, and 20,000 muskets.

Near the line of earthworks on the west, and not far from its intersection with State 76, stands a CONFEDERATE MONUMENT, erected to honor the Southern men who fought here.

A NATIONAL CEMETERY is on a hill overlooking the old fort and both water batteries. The markers are arranged in the shape of a heart beneath evergreens.

At 57.2 *m.* is the junction with a graveled road.

Right on this road 6.7 *m.* to the SITE OF FORT HENRY, which Grant captured ten days before he took Fort Donelson.

Fort Henry, on the east bank of the Tennessee, and Fort Donelson, 12 miles away on the Cumberland, guarded these rivers. It was poorly situated, not well planned, and under-armed. Brig. Gen. Lloyd Tilghman, the Confederate officer in charge of Fort Henry, decided to send his garrison of 2,500 men overland to Fort Donelson, while he and artillerymen remained to man the guns against the advancing gunboats under Commodore Foote. General Grant's two divisions approached along the banks of the river, and Foote's flotilla steamed upstream with the four ironclads abreast in front, the wooden boats behind firing over them. It was the first use of riverboats in such close formation against land fortifications. Tilghman, with defective guns and ammunition, with not enough gunners to man what he had, and with the floodwaters of the river rising into the lower batteries, kept up his fight with the gunboats for two hours, until he felt sure that the garrison was safely away, and then surrendered.

Southeast of Fort Henry the route runs through a hilly section of scrub oak and eroded gullies. Except in the valleys bordering the streams, the region has few agricultural possibilities. Although the area is fairly well populated, the farmhouses are seldom visible from the highway, because of the thick forests and undergrowth.

At 58.9 *m.* is a toll bridge over the Tennessee River *(50¢ for car and driver; 5¢ for each additional passenger)*. Between the toll bridge and Paris the country is rolling and more productive.

PARIS, 77.8 *m.* (493 alt., 8,164 pop.), seat of Henry County, laid out in 1823, was a trading center of a large plantation area before the War between the States. Along the residential streets are several ante bellum houses. The repair shops of the Louisville & Nashville R.R. are here.

In the town are 3 large cosmetic plants, a patent-medicine, a shirt, and a cigar factory.

The HOME OF JAMES D. PORTER, on Dunlap St. three blocks west of the business section, is a red-brick, ante bellum structure with iron balconies. Porter was Governor of Tennessee (1875–79) and established the State Board of Education and the Board of Health during his administration.

The HOME OF GEN. ISHAM G. HARRIS, on N. Washington St., three blocks from the square, is a frame cottage, with high dormer windows, among beautiful magnolia trees. Harris was Governor of Tennessee from 1857–1861. In 1861, when he received Secretary of War Stanton's request for Tennessee's share of the 75,000 troops the Union sought to mobilize, he replied: "Tennessee will not furnish a single man for coercion, but

50,000, if necessary, for the defense of our rights or those of our Southern brethren." Harris was a leader in the movement for secession.

The route now passes through level countryside.

DRESDEN, 100.2 *m.* (457 alt., 1,047 pop.), seat of Weakley County, was settled by German immigrants. It is locally referred to as the "town of intensive rest" because an old settler once said that Dresden natives were born tired and needed a whole lifetime to get rested. But the town, built on thickly forested hills, is a busy trading center for lumber, staves, tobacco, and country produce.

The industrial plants are a tannery, and factories that make wooden implement handles, candy, and burial garments.

A CONFEDERATE MONUMENT, erected to Weakley County soldiers, stands at the northwest corner of the public square.

South of Dresden the route passes through a section that produces large crops of sweet potatoes. The Nancy Hall variety is the favorite because this potato is very sweet and juicy and candies well when cooked with sugar.

MARTIN, 109.5 *m.* (475 alt., 3,300 pop.) *(see Tour 10)*, is at the junction with US 45E *(see Tour 10)*.

The route continues through a prosperous section in which corn and cotton are the main crops.

UNION CITY, 122.8 *m.* (328 alt., 5,865 pop.) *(see Tour 11)*, is at the junction with US 51 *(see Tour 11)*.

Tour 10

(Mayfield, Ky.)—Martin—Jackson—(Corinth, Miss.); US 45E and 45. Kentucky Line to Mississippi Line, 114.6 m.

Illinois Central R.R. (Jackson-Grenada, Miss. branch) parallels this route between Fulton, Ky. and Jackson; the Mobile & Ohio R.R. between Jackson and the Mississippi Line.
Paved roadbed.
All accommodations.

South of Martin, US 45E passes through the southern edge of the tobacco country, which is sparsely timbered. South of Martin is the fringe of the cotton belt. Between Sharon and Three Ways Junction the route pierces the fertile truck-farming and strawberry-growing section of West Tennessee. In the spring the route is crowded with large trucks hauling sweet corn, tomatoes, snap beans, and strawberries to market.

The Obion River and tributaries of the Forked Deer River are crossed north of Jackson. Drainage canals and the levee, as well as overflow bridges, keep the route open when the bottom lands are flooded by these rivers.

US 45 crosses the Kentucky Line, 0 *m.,* 24 miles south of Mayfield, Ky. and on the southern edge of Fulton, Ky.

MARTIN, 10.8 *m.* (475 alt., 3,300 pop.), built on oak-covered slopes, is the largest town in Weakley County. It suffered severely in the yellow-fever epidemic of the summer of 1878. Hundreds died. Many people escaped to adjoining counties in early June and did not return until the first frost in late September had killed the mosquitoes that carried the disease. In South Martin is (R) the YELLOW FEVER CEMETERY, where monuments tell the story of the epidemic.

On the western edge of the town, by State 22, is the UNIVERSITY OF TENNESSEE JUNIOR COLLEGE. The larger part of the 285-acre college farm *(open daily),* is R. and the campus is L. The buildings, of varying designs, are dominated by a recently constructed one-story group of modified Georgian Colonial design by Barber and McMurray. They are constructed of brick with red tiled roofs and trim white dormers. This co-educational institution is controlled by the Extension Department of the University of Tennessee. The curriculum, planned to meet the needs of rural students, emphasizes the agricultural, domestic, and industrial sciences. The farm, which has modern equipment, is an agricultural experiment station as well as a demonstration plant.

Martin is at the junction of State 22 *(see Tour 9).*

SHARON, 18.8 *m.* (475 alt., 596 pop.), is a fruit and vegetable shipping point.

Left from Sharon on a graveled road to the fine TREECE PEACH ORCHARD, 3 *m.,* of 50 acres. One orchard is on Rock Hill, the highest point in Weakley County. The trees bloom in March; the fruit is gathered in late July and August.

GREENFIELD, 24.5 *m.* (475 alt., 1,429 pop.), is a trade town and shipping point for fruit and vegetables.

BRADFORD, 30.2 *m.* (450 alt., 570 pop.), is a typical southern village. On hot summer afternoons farmers and easy-going townsmen play checkers in front of the stores along Main Street, sometimes interrupting the games with political discussions that rival the temperature in intensity.

On the southern edge of the village is a section known as SKULL BONE, extending about six miles eastward and westward, and about five miles southward. It received its name because of the number of feuds, fights, and murders that long made it notorious. Whites have kept Negroes from settling in the area.

MILAN, 41.7 *m.* (345 alt., 3,155 pop.), is a fruit and vegetable shipping center. Almost every day the business section is crowded with traders from the rich trucking land of Gibson County. Thousands of crates and hampers of strawberries, cabbages, sweet peppers, okra, snap beans, and tomatoes are shipped from this station. The town's industrial plants include shirt, raincoat, and cigar factories.

The Negroes in this part of West Tennessee believe in the presence of "topas," animals that can be conjured into persons by those having witch powers. Negresses trace their "miseries" to the baleful activities of such "conjure men." Believers say they often see a "topa" just at nightfall, when they go to the barn to feed or milk the cows. Sometimes it is as small as the palm of a hand, at other times as large as a calf.

MEDINA, 50.3 *m.* (345 alt., 414 pop.), is also a fruit and vegetable shipping point. Here are large shipping sheds of the Illinois Central R.R.

At THREE WAYS JUNCTION, 55 *m.,* the highway meets US 45W *(see Tour 11).*

A U. S. SOIL CONSERVATION SERVICE CAMP is at 56.3 *m.*

JACKSON, 66 *m.* (412 alt., 22,172 pop.) *(see JACKSON).*

Points of Interest: Union University, Carnegie Library, Lambuth College, Lancaster Park, and others.

Jackson is at the junction with US 70 *(see Tour 12).*

BEMIS (R), 67.7 *m.* (450 alt., 675 pop.), a company town owned and controlled by the Bemis Brothers Bag Company, was founded in 1899 by Judson Bemis, a northern manufacturer. The town has 500 houses, which are rented to employees. Schools are maintained by the company but are under the jurisdiction of the county board of education.

The NURSERY OF THE TENNESSEE FORESTRY DEPARTMENT, 72.2 *m.* *(open 8-6 daily),* sends out more than 1,000,000 seedlings annually, among them black locust, yellow poplar, and pine. The young trees are transplanted for erosion control in West Tennessee.

From the top of NORTON HILL, 73.2 *m.,* US 45 is visible for approximately seven miles. The road descends into the swampy lands of the Forked River before it again ascends to the highlands. The highway runs through a thicket of willows at the northern edge of Pinson.

PINSON, 77 *m.* (450 alt., 250 pop.), a small roadside village, was almost destroyed by a tornado in 1923. Houses and churches were splintered, trees uprooted, and whole lines of freight cars on the Mobile and Ohio R.R. overturned. Several lives were lost.

Left from Pinson on a graveled country road to OZIER'S MOUND, 3 *m.* (R), the first in the mound group of CISCO INDIAN VILLAGE. The village was named for J. G. Cisco, historian and editor, who made extensive excavations here. In these thickets, swamps, and woodlands along the south fork of the Forked Deer River are the remains of an ancient fortified city, together with its outlying towns and settlements. Thirty-five mounds and other defense works, six miles long and having elaborate outer and inner citadels, are well preserved.

Ozier's Mound, 40 feet high, is the base of what was a pyramid. Because of its flat top it is believed to have been a place of assembly. This mound, a favorite spot for picnickers, is described in *Windy Hill* (1926), a novel by Jennings Perry, a former Jacksonian.

SAUL'S MOUND, 5 *m.,* can be reached by crossing Saul's woodlot. In dry weather automobiles can go within 0.8 of a mile of it.

At strategic points on every side are mounds ranging from rises of a few feet to Saul's Mound, which is 73 feet high, has a base 300 feet wide by 370 long, and a summit of 38 feet wide by 60 long.

Several other tumuli in the group are also very large, ranging from one-third to one-fourth the size of the central mound.

South of Ozier's Mound, 0.4 *m.* are the TWIN MOUNDS, believed to have been erected over the graves of a chief and his squaw. Apparently many of the smaller mounds were used for burial purposes.

On the river side Cisco was probably protected by a continuous line of wooden palisades, built along the steep bluffs. The river and a large swamp also furnished protection on one side of the city. On the land side the crumbling outer wall, made of boulders and debris from the river bed, is still standing in many places, but the wooden palisades have long since rotted away.

There is evidence that the walled city of Cisco was the central town of a large region, with a population of several thousand, and that it was suddenly deserted. William Edward Myer, an archeologist who explored the site, suggested that the city was built by some conquering king, who ruled the region in prehistoric times. Other archeologists believe that the builders were ancestors of the Chickasaw *(see FIRST AMERICANS).*

HENDERSON, 82.6 *m.* (429 alt., 1,603 pop.), seat of Chester County, was during the War between the States, the scene of a major skirmish. In 1862 the town was held by Federal troops, encamped on the bluffs overlooking the railroad. Gen. Joe Wheeler led a force of Tennessee cavalrymen into the town on a surprise raid, captured the entire Union defense, and burned the Mobile & Ohio depot, which contained Union supplies. He took his prisoners to the Tennessee River, hotly pursued by Union reinforcements. Wheeler's pickets held off the enemy while a safe crossing was made. The Union commander compelled residents of the county to pay for the supplies.

The FREED-HARDEMEN JUNIOR COLLEGE, on Main St., is an accredited co-educational school owned and operated by the Church of Christ. The buildings add much to the beauty of the town.

1. Left from Henderson on a concrete-paved road to the junction with a graveled road, 1 *m.;* R. 0.5 *m.* to SEGA-SEGA (Ind., *welcome and good cheer),* the old Garland home *(open 8-4 daily),* built in 1828 on a 1200-acre plantation. Along the outer garden walks and in the rose garden are 150 varieties of shrubs and 50 of roses. A boxwood, more than 70 years old, climbs above the northern edge of the roof. Tall cedars form a deep shade for the lawn.

2. Right from Henderson on State 105, a graveled road, into CHICKASAW STATE PARK AND FOREST, 8 *m.,* an 11,000-acre project in the heart of an area that was once the wildest back country of West Tennessee. The forest, one of the first major projects of the kind completed in Tennessee, was established to reclaim submarginal land, and to preserve trees and game. In the high plateau of western Chester and eastern Hardeman Counties, this forest is in the country that was once the home of mound builders and of the Chickasaw Nation.

In the forest are the ruins of Murrell's home *(see Tour 12).*

The country, deeply wooded and cut with precipitous ravines, has a network of roads surfaced with crushed sandstone. In a low valley on Piney Creek is LAKE PLACID *(boats; cabins, picnicking spots, trailer camps),* almost surrounded by forests of oak, hickory, elm, and pine. Nearby stood Flavius Owen's water mill. Overlooking Lake Placid from a tree-covered knoll is SAGAMORE LODGE, constructed of stone and brick. A bathhouse, a beach, and diving piers are just below the lodge.

A small pond, near the lake, is used as a fish hatchery, and was stocked with 25,000 bluegills. Fishermen can obtain supplies of live bait here. Numerous quail and turkeys are in the forest, also squirrels, rabbits, raccoons, opossums, and red fox. On May 11, 12, and 13, 1937, the Southern States' Fox Hunt was held here.

The highway goes through a cut in MURCHISON'S MOUND, 83.1 *m.* Red bluffs rise high on both sides of the road. On the top of the bluff (R) is a small frame house, whose owner long cultivated the rounded sides of the mound, growing cotton and corn. On the southern slopes was a vineyard.

South of Henderson is rolling pine country, the northern edge of the southern pine belt. The terrain gradually becomes thickly wooded; pines stand out in dark green patches among the dense scrub oak.

The western part of Chester County was long called the Hurst Nation, now the Nation, so called because numerous members of the Hurst family, staunch Unionists, lived there after the War between the States. Best known of the clan was Col. Fielding Hurst, commander of a partisan band—the Sixth Union Regiment of Tennessee Cavalry—considered a bushwhacking outfit by the Confederates. Hurst operated in West Tennessee, northern Mississippi and Arkansas, skirmishing and scouting for the Union armies. This region was a moonshine center of West Tennessee. In the ravines of Dinney Hollows, in the wooded hills around Montezuma, and in the climbing pine country near Silerton, corn "likker" was illegally distilled. Along creeks hidden by salmon-brown sedgegrass, the moonshiners regulated their fires and tamped shortdough (a mixture of bran meal and water) around the thump-kegs (kegs or barrels through which the distillation coil passes) to keep them from leaking. Under the leaves in the hollows they stashed (cached) away the fresh corn in ten-gallon kegs and let it charter (char) for months. When aged, the deep red liquor was clear of verdigris (fusel oil) and held a bead the size of number five shot. There were no "rabbit eyes on it to pop off" (big bubbles that foam and burst as soon as the bottle is shaken). Certain brands were known as "creeping likker," because they kicked "slow and powerful." The coming of legal whisky in neighboring states has decreased the market for the best corn.

SELMER, 101.6 *m.* (450 alt., 925 pop.), seat of McNairy County, is at the junction with US 64 *(see Tour 13)*. This town serves a large hill country. For many years, until modern communication changed the picture, it was little less than a frontier town of an old but isolated area. On Saturday the place resembled a boom town of the Old West, as traders, farmers, Negroes, gamblers, and moonshiners lined the muddy or dusty main street and crowded around the small courthouse. McNairy was then referred to as Snake County, because of Snake Creek, and "revenoors" ventured reluctantly into the fastnesses of the pine- and oak-covered hills.

At 104 *m.* is the junction with State 57.

Left on State 57 is STANTONVILLE, 10 *m.* At 16 *m.* is the junction with State 22; L. here 12 *m.* to SHILOH NATIONAL MILITARY PARK AND PICKWICK LANDING DAM *(see Tour 13)*.

At 114.6 *m.* US 45 crosses the Mississippi Line, 5 miles north of Corinth, Miss.

Tour 11

(Fulton, Ky.)—Union City—Dyersburg—Ripley—Memphis—(Senatobia, Miss.); US 51.

Kentucky Line to Mississippi Line, 136.4 m.

Illinois Central R.R. parallels route between Moffatt and Memphis.
Paved roadbed.
Accommodations chiefly in larger towns.

US 51 roughly parallels the Mississippi River in crossing Tennessee, running through the State's chief cotton-growing area. In the summer the workers—Negro and white—are seen "choppin" the grass and weeds from the young cotton plants. When the rows are clear of weeds, the cotton is plowed and "laid by." The croppers watch eagerly for the first blue-white flowers because several counties give prizes for the first blooms brought to town.

In the fall, when the fields are white with hanging bolls, the picksack replaces the hoe and plow, and the cropper and his family scatter along the rows, dragging their long sacks on the ground behind them as they pick the soft white sections from the bolls. *(See also Tour 11A.)*

US 51 crosses the Kentucky Line, 0 *m.*, 0.3 of a mile south of the center of Fulton, Ky., and runs through a region in which stock raising and cattle breeding are important.

UNION CITY, 10.9 *m.* (328 alt., 5,865 pop.), seat of Obion County (pronounced O-by'-on), is the principal town in a lake district; it ships cotton and fish, and is a supply station for fishermen and hunters, who live near or visit Reelfoot Lake and the Mississippi River *(see Tour 11A)*. The town is well laid out and forms a sharp contrast with the lowlands around it. The broad main street has some modern chromium-plated shop fronts, four- and five-story office buildings and two hotels. Along the shaded streets of the residential districts are large, comfortable old homes. A plaza leads from the main street to the courthouse.

The town owes its growth to the fertility of the land around it. Crops can be grown on it year after year without the use of fertilizer. The nearby landowners have large holdings and many specialize in the breeding of cattle and hogs that are fattened on corn.

Left from Union City on US 45W, which goes through one of the most fertile farming sections in the State. It produces vegetables, strawberries, and large amounts of cotton. Between Union City and Trenton is the area in which David Crockett lived. It was here that someone jokingly suggested to him that he run for Congress, and it was the residents of what is now Gibson County who elected him to the House of Representatives in 1826. By doing so they helped to begin one of the most picturesque political careers in American history. Crockett amused Washington with the eccentricities of speech and dress of the backwoodsman, which he deliberately exaggerated. He was shrewd, nevertheless, and was respected by the politicians of

WEIGHING COTTON

his day. Although he served two terms, he later opposed some of the distinctly Jacksonian policies and was denied re-election in 1835 by the people who had dared to make a reality of what had been a backwoods joke. Failing re-election, Crockett emigrated to Texas, where he participated in the defense of the Alamo. He was one of the six survivors of the battle, but was shot at the command of Santa Anna on March 6, 1836.

Between Union City and Kenton the highway crosses the OBION LEVEE and above land covered with water. Tall cypresses rise above lush vegetation. Green pastures support herds of blooded cattle and sheep.

KENTON, 16.1 *m.* (340 alt., 810 pop.), almost on the Obion-Gibson County line, is a busy trading center.

RUTHERFORD, 21.1 *m.* (345 alt., 900 pop.), is a shipping center for diversified farm products. In the SAMPLE HOME *(open by permission),* Main St., is a collection of early American relics. Among these are a flintlock pistol, made in London, supposedly for George Washington; the first razor sold in Nashville; spoons molded from the melted knee buckles of Maj. John Buchanan; an old surveying outfit; and furniture, silverware and dishes.

1. Left from Rutherford 4 *m.* on graveled road to the DAVID CROCKETT HOME SITE AND BARN. The logs of the cabin, built in 1822, were moved to Rutherford and stored in the Farmers' Gin Storehouse (1932). The logs are numbered, and the original wooden pins have been preserved so that it can be rebuilt as it was originally. The barn, also built in 1822, still stands here, as does the cedar-curbing of the well. Whole trees of yellow poplar were used in the construction of the barn, and the single logs, held together by long wooden pins three to four inches in

diameter, extend its full length. Crockett came to West Tennessee in 1821, settling in what is now Crockett County before he moved here. He hunted bear nearby with Old Betsy, his famous long rifle. One winter night, by Lick Creek, five miles east of Rutherford, he shinned up and down a tree all night to keep from freezing to death. At another time, according to his own story, when he was caught in a hollow tree by a mother bear, he held to the furious animal's tail and prodded her hams with his hunting knife until she pulled him out. He told also of how, farther north in the "Shakes Country" around Reelfoot Lake, he was trapped in a huge crack of the earth, and fought hand-to-claw with a vicious black bear until he stabbed it to death. Crockett was one of the chief participants in the shooting matches held in the Western District. Targets were set up and the riflemen fired throughout the day and by pine flares at night. Bets were paid in animal skins.

2. Right 4 *m.* from Rutherford on the Trimble Road to the GRAVES OF CROCKETT'S MOTHER AND OF ONE OF HIS CHILDREN, in the center of a field near her home, now the Quincy Dodd Farm. Two cedar trees, planted to mark the head and the foot of the graves, have been almost destroyed by lightning.

TRENTON, 34.3 *m.* (345 alt., 2,892 pop.), seat of Gibson County is known for the maples that line its streets and give it a peaceful charm. Some land deeds of Crockett's, supposedly in his own handwriting, are in the register's office in the COURTHOUSE.

In 1862 Gen. Nathan Bedford Forrest took Trenton from the Union forces that held the town. The Federal troops had been assembled at the depot and, as Forrest rode through the town, the people waved hats and handkerchiefs to indicate the Union position to him. Forrest took the Federals completely by surprise.

The TRENTON MILLS *(open daily 7 a.m. to 5 p.m.)*, established in 1885, make cloth for meat wrappings. The first plant was destroyed by fire and in 1929 was rebuilt with modern improvements.

The DAVID CROCKETT MONUMENT (R), 41.4 *m.*, was erected in 1903.

HUMBOLDT, 46 *m.* (345 alt., 4,613 pop.), named for the German naturalist, Baron Von Humboldt, is the trade center of Gibson County and the hub of the largest berry- and vegetable-growing belt in Tennessee.

At the height of the strawberry season, usually in May, the West Tennessee Strawberry Festival, a three-day celebration, is held. The "queen" of the festival ceremoniously receives visiting "princesses" from surrounding towns. The program includes vaudeville shows, circus acts, a balloon ascension, fireworks, parades, horse shows, concerts, and a beauty review. Prize-winning berries are auctioned daily.

In the southern part of the town, on US 45W, is a statue of Gen. Nathan Bedford Forrest.

THREE WAYS JUNCTION, 50.8 *m.*, is at the junction with US 45E *(see Tour 10)*, 11 miles north of Jackson.

Between Union City and Troy is one of the first stretches of concrete roadbed built in the State; some of the curves are sharp.

TROY, 21 *m.* (340 alt., 522 pop.), one of the oldest towns in West Tennessee, was laid out in 1823 with the help of David Crockett. Stores and offices are built around an open square under whose locust trees checker players spend their summer days. New concrete and brick buildings stand beside the weathered, red-brick, structures of pre-Civil War days. Clapboard and brick cottages have replaced most of the antebellum houses. The town was the seat of Obion County from 1823 to 1880, when a group of Union City citizens took the records by force to their city. After the fall of Fort Donelson and Fort Henry *(see Tour 9)*, the courthouse was used as a stable for Union horses.

At Troy is the junction with State 21.

Right from Troy on State 21 is TIPTONVILLE, 17 *m.* (295 alt., 1,359 pop.), at the foot of Reelfoot Lake *(see Tour 11A)*.

OBION, 27.4 *m.* (340 alt., 1,100 pop.), is a shipping point for products of the bottom lands, a large part of which is kept fertile by the annual overflow of the Mississippi River, which backs up into the Obion River.

South of Obion is a State-owned toll bridge spanning the Obion River and adjacent overflow lands *(25¢ for car and driver, 5¢ for each additional passenger).*

Along the levee that limits the overflow are cypresses with enlarged bases, massive trunks, and spreading limbs from which hang delicate foliage. Other swamp trees and water plants grow abundantly. When the white settlers first came here this country was filled with bear, deer, panthers, and bobcats.

NEWBERN, 38.9 *m.* (450 alt., 1,621 pop.), is a cotton trade center, whose gins handle much of the cotton from adjoining counties. The double-track main line of the Illinois Central R.R. splits the compact business section. Flour, feed, lumber, and sawmills are also operated here. *(All gins and mills are open to visitors.)*

Wagons and trucks laden with cotton stand in lines beside the gins, waiting to be unloaded. The cotton is fed through a chute into the teeth of the gins, which separate the seed from the lint. The lint is then blown into the press and compressed into bales, which are bound with jute bagging and steel ties. In this area many farmers sell their cotton by the load before it has been ginned. The seeds are made into stock feed, vegetable oils, and fertilizer *(see MEMPHIS).*

DYERSBURG, 48 *m.* (324 alt., 8,735 pop.), seat of Dyer County, is the chief town in the cotton-growing bottom lands. The DYERSBURG COTTON PRODUCTS COMPANY PLANT *(open daily 8-4),* is the largest cotton mill in the section. The town is the scene of an annual cotton carnival in May.

The HISTORICAL ROOM *(open by permission of chancery clerk 8-6 daily)* in the COURTHOUSE contains several muzzle-loading muskets, pictures of Robert E. Lee, an old sidesaddle, and a home-made bear trap supposed to have been used by David Crockett.

Fifty-one acres of woodland on the northern edge of town, adjoining the municipally-owned COUNTRY CLUB *(50¢ greens fee),* have been developed as a park, with playgrounds for children, tennis courts, and picnic grounds.

At Dyersburg is the junction with State 78 *(see Tour 11A).*

Right from Dyersburg on a well-marked graveled road to DYERSBURG AIRPORT, 1.5 *m.,* which has landing and servicing facilities except in the wet season.

At FOWLKES, 51 *m.,* is the junction with State 20.

Left on State 20 is ALAMO, 20 *m.,* seat of Crockett County, named for the Alamo at San Antonio, Texas, where David Crockett lost his life on March 6, 1836.

Local people often describe this section of the route as: "Down the Halls, through the Gates, around the Curve, and Flippin into Ripley."

At 58 *m.* is HALLS (311 alt., 1,474 pop.), a cotton-and-lumber town

GOING TO THE GIN

and a shipping point for truck products. Roark Bradford, writer of Negro folk tales, was born near here in 1896 *(see WRITERS OF TENNESSEE)*.

Right from Halls on State 88 is KEY CORNER, 11 *m.,* on the eastern bank of the Forked Deer River. A bronze tablet (R) is 60 feet from the spot where Henry Rutherford, a North Carolinian, made all of his connecting surveys of the Western District in 1785. Rutherford's party came through the territory from the east and crossed a small river called Okeena by the Indians; this they renamed the Forked Deer because of the shape of its branches at the point where it flows into the Mississippi and because at this point they killed a deer with peculiarly shaped antlers. On the first bluff, Cole Creek Bluff, Rutherford marked a leaning sycamore tree with a huge key and his initials. Many thousands of acres were entered at the land offices of North Carolina as a result of surveys by Rutherford and his colleagues. As soon as the Chickasaw Treaty had been negotiated in 1818, Rutherford returned to settle here.

Left from Key Corner on a trail to a locust thicket in the hills 2 *m.,* where the GRAVE OF HENRY RUTHERFORD and the graves of his wife and children, and his brother, John, have remained in spite of floods. The headstones have long since been worn away.

GATES is a hamlet at 60.6 *m.* and CURVE is another at 65.4 *m.*

South of Curve the route follows the old roadbed of the Illinois Central R.R. for approximately two miles. At the point where the double track of the Illinois Central is seen, is the southern end of a cut that has been so expensive to maintain that it is sometimes called the Million Dollar Cut. The soil is soft and sandy and frequently piles up between the tracks.

RIPLEY, 71 *m.* (585 alt., 3,510 pop.), seat of Lauderdale County, is on a series of wooded hills. On March 25, 1901, Ripley's first charter of Jan. 17, 1838, was repealed; when on April 3, 1901, a new charter was granted, the corporate limits were outlined: " . . . thence north 85 degrees, east to a black gum marked with a cross and with mistletoe in the top, and with a blue bird sitting on a limb, which is a short distance east of Ed Johnson's horse lot . . ."

Right from Ripley on State 19 *(paved for five miles, then graveled),* to OPEN LAKE, 9 *m.,* formed when the New Madrid earthquake of 1811–12 changed the course of the Mississippi. The lake covers approximately 8,000 acres. On the banks are private fishing and social clubhouses *(boats obtainable).*

At HENNING, 77 *m.* (375 alt., 681 pop.), is the junction with State 87.

Right from Henning on State 87 to the SITE OF FORT PILLOW, 17 *m.,* built during the War between the States at the mouth of Cole Creek near the Mississippi River bluffs. The fort was defended by a garrison of Negro soldiers, and Tennessee Unionists called "home-made Yankees" by West Tennesseans. Early on the morning of April 13, 1864, General Forrest and his Confederate cavalry surrounded the garrison. From this point on, the story of Fort Pillow is clouded with conflicting accounts. The Federals said that Forrest massacred an unnecessary number of their men, while Forrest maintained that the Federals prolonged the defense beyond any possible hope and that he was forced to kill the men in order to take the fort. It was called "an atrocity" by a Congressional committee, appointed particularly to investigate the killing of the Negro soldiers. General Sherman was also ordered to investigate, and, by the implications of the order he received, to retaliate. Since he did nothing, some historians believe that his investigations disclosed that the "Massacre of Fort Pillow" was a propaganda invention.

Somewhere near this place was the French FORT PRUDHOMME, built by the party of La Salle in 1682. The fort was named for Pierre Prudhomme, armorer of the expedition, who because he had never taken part in a hunt, left the party at this point to go hunting. Although accompanied by an Indian, Prudhomme became lost in the woods; several searching parties found no trace of him, and when his Indian guide returned, he reported large numbers of natives in the vicinity. La Salle then ordered a fort built for the party's protection and continued to seek Prudhomme and eventually found him. The armorer, with a few men, was left here while La Salle continued his exploration of the Mississippi. On his return La Salle became ill and for 40 days was unable to proceed up the river again.

COVINGTON, 86 *m.* (311 alt., 3,397 pop.), seat of Tipton County, is a typical courthouse-square town with business houses and homes of the Old South. It serves a large cotton-growing territory. In the days of big plantations it was a shipping point for cotton and many wealthy planters built homes here.

Right from Covington on State 59 is RANDOLPH, 19 *m.,* on the bank of the Mississippi, a village that in the early days was Memphis' rival. In 1830 it was the most important shipping point in West Tennessee, and it is mentioned several times in Mark Twain's *Life on the Mississippi.* The failure of Davy Crockett's scheme to cut a canal from the Hatchie River to the Tennessee, which would have brought the products of the rich Hatchie country here, and the building of a post road through Memphis to what is now Little Rock, Ark., gave Memphis the advantage.

Several minor skirmishes occurred here during the War between the States; one resulted in the destruction of the town by fire. A powder magazine, traces of old breastworks, a few old houses, and a store are all that remain. A good account of the former life of Randolph and similar river ports is in *The Outlaw Years* (1930) by Robert N. Coates, and *The Outlaws of Cave-in-Rock* (1924) by Otto A. Rothert.

South of Covington the route runs through cotton fields and swerves toward the southwest.

At MILLINGTON, 117 *m.* (272 alt., 662 pop.), is the junction with Shelby Drive.

Right on Shelby Drive to LOCKE, 12.7 *m.* SHELBY FOREST PARK lies between Locke and Island No. 39 in the Mississippi River. The park was created as part of a program of erosion control, reforestation and game preservation. Woodland covers 12,000 acres. In a developed recreational section are two lakes. *(Boating, bathing, two athletic fields, wading pools, picnic sites, bridle and foot paths, cabins, and boys' and girls' camps.)* The administration building contains an auditorium, a recreation hall, commercial amusement devices, and a cafeteria.

Between Millington and Memphis the route crosses good farm lands, thick groves, and the bottom lands of the Loosahatchie and Wolf Rivers.

MEMPHIS, 125 *m.* (280 alt., 253,143 pop.) *(see MEMPHIS).*

Points of Interest: Mississippi River waterfront, Shelby County Courthouse, Beale Street, Overton Park Zoo, and others.

Memphis is at the junction with US 70 *(see Tour 12)* and US 70-64 *(see Tour 13).*

US 51 turns southwest in Memphis on Mississippi Boulevard and at 136.4 *m.* crosses the Mississippi Line, 35 miles north of Senatobia, Miss.

Tour 11A

Dyersburg—Tiptonville—Reelfoot Lake—(Hickman, Ky.); State 78 Dyersburg to Kentucky Line, 36 m.

Illinois Central branch line parallels route.
Paved roadbed; may be closed during high water on the Mississippi.

This route runs through a part of the bottom lands made fertile by deposits of silt from the broad Mississippi Valley during the annual overflows. This is part of the normal river bed of the Mississippi in the spring and nearly all permanent improvements on it are saved from destruction by the levees built at enormous cost, largely by the Federal Government. Even without this protection people would persist in living here because of the high productivity of the land. Before the levees were built they were here, incredibly hopeful that there would be no more overflows, and refused to build houses that would survive the floods that have come at intervals since long before white men ever saw the Mississippi.

The attitude of the bottom land people toward the annual phenomenon is amazing to the radio announcers and reporters who rush in as the rivers rise; housewives resignedly take up their carpets and move their furnishings to upper rooms, but very few think of leaving their homes. Except when levees break the water arrives sluggishly, its smooth brown surface rising almost imperceptibly. The men are usually drafted for levee work, to strengthen the banks with sandbags and brush and to perform patrol duty. Even before the water arrives the highway may be closed to all but those who carry passes, because the days have not passed when men from other areas—and even from across the river—attempt to relieve flood pressure on the levees nearest them by dynamiting levees elsewhere.

State 78 branches west from US 51 *(see Tour 11)* at DYERSBURG, 0 *m.*, and traverses a badly eroded hill country covered over with second-growth timber. East of the Obion River is a stretch of swampland and then the fertile cotton-growing bottoms.

During the 1937 flood RIDGELY, 19 *m.* (300 alt., 979 pop.), near the Mississippi River, was completely covered with water.

TIPTONVILLE, 26.5 *m.* (295 alt., 1,359 pop.), seat of Lake County, is at the foot of Reelfoot Lake, three miles east of the Father of Waters. The town is the center of the Reelfoot recreational area and has sports-supply stores, a hotel, and tourist homes. There is one long street of stores and dwellings. A 21-mile Government levee protects most of the county but the Tiptonville Dome, a ridge upon which the town is built, has never been covered by flood water. In January and February 1937, Tiptonville was the headquarters of rescue work in the lake country, which was flooded after the waters of the Ohio, which had inundated Louisville, caused the Mississippi to rise and endanger the Bessie and Hickman levees.

Fearful that the Hickman levee would break, U. S. Army engineers advised the citizens to evacuate the town but most of them remained, as usual. Thousands of volunteers, highway patrolmen, and National Guardsmen fought to keep the levee intact.

The Red Cross aided those caught by the rising water. In the flooded northeastern part of the county many people had to be taken from the roofs of their houses or from trees with the aid of motorboats. Some had even built platforms in trees, or erected tents for their families on higher ground, and they obstinately refused to be moved from their inundated

SAND BAGS STRENGTHEN A MISSISSIPPI LEVEE

lands. They reasoned that the waters were sure to subside, as they always had.

Right from Tiptonville on State 21 to REELFOOT LAKE, 3 *m.* L. at 7 *m.* on a road that runs along the eastern rim of the lake—EDGEWATER BEACH is at 10 *m.*, BLUE BANK at 11 *m.*, SAMBURG, 22 *m.*, WALNUT LOG, 28.5 *m.*

Between Tiptonville and the Kentucky State Line, State 78 skirts the west side of Reelfoot Lake through level fields—land resembling the delta country of Arkansas and Mississippi. The highway is bordered (R) by the forest that surrounds the lake, and (L) by the dense willows usual along the banks of the Mississippi. At one time there were high bluffs along the river. The New Madrid earthquake, 1811–12, swept these bluffs into the stream and leveled most of the country.

PHILLIPPY, 34.6 *m.*, the northernmost village on the lake, is another outfitting point for sportsmen.

This area is the REELFOOT LAKE STATE FISH AND GAME PRESERVE.

Accommodations: Small hotels in the larger villages. Numerous tourist and trailer camps *(reasonable rates)* along lake shores. Private camps for sportsmen. Free picnic grounds and parking space. During the duck season a guide with boat costs approximately $7.50 a day. A fishing guide with boat, $3 a day. Outfitting stores are in all the lake towns.

Warning: In tramping near the lake, heavy shoes or leather boots should be worn as a protection against poisonous snakes.

Recreational Opportunities: Almost any point on the lake offers desirable places for fishing and hunting in season. Edgewater and Sunkist Beaches are favorite swimming places. The latter has an excellent natural sand beach.

The Reelfoot Lake State Fish and Game Preserve was established in 1925. The lake, 18 miles long and 2.5 miles wide, is only 2 to 9 feet deep; the 6,000 acres of State-owned land around it are almost completely covered with dense forests of cypress, oak, cottonwood, and the usual southern swamp timber, woven thick with wild grape and other vines. Many of the cypresses, dead above water, have living trunks beneath. "Seed moss," a filmy iridescent green carpet, grows in and around the twisted and grotesque cypress knees in shallow places. Rotten snags of black walnut, gum, oak, willow, and cypress lift weirdly above the clear, brownish water in some parts of the lake, whose surface is dotted with the yellow-flowered pads of yoncopin, or water lilies. Bordering the shores are dense growths of saw grass, cut grass, marsh grass, mulefoot, smart weed, and wild rice, most of them providing food for water foul; their matted roots form safe breeding places for fish.

Within the preserve are many varieties of fresh-water fishes. The alligator gar, which grows to a length of eight feet, and the spoonbill catfish are the largest and are found in great numbers. Other species abundant in the lake are crappie, bass, and bream.

The people of the area make their living by hunting and fishing. Their combined catches average 2,000 pounds a day, and during the season daily shipments reach 5,000 pounds.

More than 250 species of birds stop off here on their annual migra-

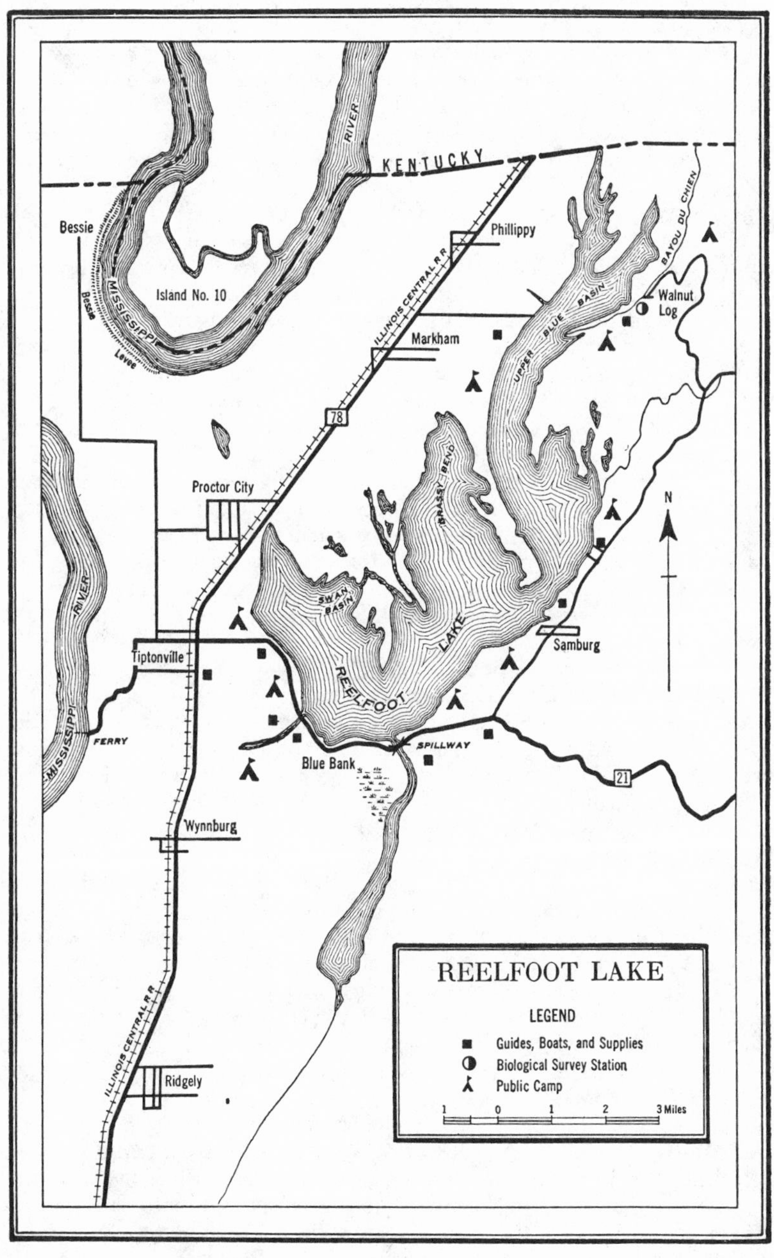

REELFOOT LAKE
LEGEND
Guides, Boats, and Supplies
Biological Survey Station
Public Camp
1 0 1 2 3 Miles
KENTUCKY
MISSISSIPPI
RIVER
Bessie
Bessie Levee
Island No. 10
Phillippy
ILLINOIS CENTRAL R R
Markham
Walnut Log
BAYOU DU CHIEN
UPPER BLUE BASIN
78
Proctor City
BRASSY BEND
SWAN BASIN
REELFOOT LAKE
Tiptonville
Samburg
FERRY
SPILLWAY
Blue Bank
21
Wynnburg
Ridgely
N

tions. Among them are ducks, geese, water turkeys or cormorants ("nigger geese"), coots, and white herons. The rail, bittern, and teal build their nests in the saw grass and lily pads. The Mississippi and swallow-tailed kites, and purple gallinule, little blue heron, chuck-will's-widow, loggerhead shrike, and Florida owl select Reelfoot as the northernmost point of their yearly migration. In late summer, following the breeding season in Louisiana, flocks of wood ibis, known locally as gourdheads, cover the lake. In the thick woods the bald eagle builds its nest and lives on fox, squirrel, swamp rabbit, and fish. The osprey, or fish hawk, is the eagle's fisherman; the eagle watches the hawk until it comes up from the water with a catch. Flying after the smaller bird, the eagle forces it to drop the fish, which it catches in midair after a bullet-like swoop. The golden swamp warbler and the Canada goose are also found here.

Of the ducks, the mallards are the most numerous, although there are about 20 varieties, including pintails, redheads, black, and teal.

The day of the elk, black bear, and Virginia deer has passed. Now raccoon, opossum, mink, and muskrat are common. The woods teem with gray and flying squirrels. Red foxes are plentiful.

Sunning itself on twisted snags or limbs along the banks is the stump-tailed moccasin, or cottonmouth, a thick-bodied, sluggish, poisonous reptile believed by the natives to possess witch power. Many aquatic reptiles of the lake are relics of prehistoric times. Found in the all but impenetrable swamp holes is the alligator terrapin, or loggerhead, thick-shelled, sharp-clawed, and possessing a head the size of a ten-year-old boy's.

Before the formation of the lake, the region was a luxuriant forest coursed by little streams of water. This area was near the center of the great New Madrid earthquake movement that occurred between December 16, 1811, and March 15, 1812, when the western section of Tennessee was still the land of the Chickasaw. The ground sank and the Mississippi, reversing its current, rushed in mountainous waves to fill the depression.

Earth waves swelled low across the surface, tilting trees and interlocking their limbs. Landslides swept down the steep bluffs of the river. Banks caved in and whole islands vanished. Leaves, dirt, and stones were thrown high. Cottonwoods, 18 to 20 inches thick, snapped off and were whirled away with thousands of other trees. The shocks were accompanied by semidarkness, deafening noise, and a sulphurous odor. People feared the Day of Judgment had come. After the formation of the lake most of the trees were still standing upright in the water, but they soon died or were set on fire by lightning.

After the upheaval Bayou de Chien (Bayou of the Dog) and Reelfoot River drained into the lake.

The torn and twisted region was not long deserted. French trappers and American hunters and settlers came in considerable numbers. David Crockett settled on the Rutherford Fork of the Obion River in 1821, and from his cabin went on frequent hunting expeditions into the "Shakes Country" around the lake.

The trappers, hunters, and fishermen of Reelfoot were in the past, as they are today, a hardy lot who considered the lake their own private preserve. The promoters, who in 1908 organized several companies to reclaim the drowned lands, ignored the "squatters' right" of these people. These promoters planned to buy the lake cheaply and by a canal to the Mississippi River, drain approximately 30,000 acres of ooze-enriched fertile land which they could sell at top prices. Reelfoot fishermen banded as nightriders, swearing to stop the venture at all costs.

Representatives of the companies, Quentin Rankin and R. S. Taylor, of Trenton, Tenn., stopped at a small lakeside hotel at Walnut Log, near the upper end of the lake in October 1908. One night the nightriders surrounded the place, broke in, and cornered the two men in their rooms. Taylor leaped from his window into the water and hid beneath a tangle of floating driftwood. Rankin was overpowered, dragged into the open, and lynched. Although the nightriders beat the brush and woods for miles around, Taylor escaped. Some of the nightriders were tried but not convicted. Several months later the State militia restored order.

The Mississippi floods of 1882–83–84 swept over the lake and formed the washout west of Blue Bank. There was a further inundation in 1912 when the great flood broke the levee just south of Hickman, Ky. Since then a spillway has been built to take care of backwaters; it is the only outlet for this body of water. When in January and February, 1937, the great Ohio-Mississippi flood threatened the Hickman levee again, thousands of workers had to toil night and day to keep the levee intact.

There is a legend that at the beginning of the nineteenth century, the chief of a band of Chickasaw living on the bluffs across the Mississippi from the old Spanish settlement of New Madrid, Missouri, was clubfooted. Because of his lumbering gait, he was called Kalopin or Reelfoot, and none of the women of the tribe would marry him. In desperation he at last gathered a few friends and went wife hunting in the territory of the Choctaw. While Reelfoot and the Chocktaw smoked the peace pipe, Reelfoot caught sight of Laughing Eyes, daughter of chief Copish, and at once told her father that he wanted the girl. The Choctaw dashed the peace pipe to the ground. Reelfoot's proposal was preposterous, he declared angrily.

The Chickasaw begged. He offered fine mussel pearls and beaver skins. Copish would not listen. Reelfoot determined to steal the girl, but in a dream Reelfoot was warned against stealing a wife. The earth would rock in anger. The waters would swallow the Chickasaw village and bury Reelfoot's people. Though Reelfoot was frightened and returned home, he could not forget Laughing Eyes. After the maize had been gathered, he and his warriors raided the Choctaw, captured the girl, and fled northward.

During the wedding festivities the earth began to roll in rhythm with tom-toms. The Father of Waters roared over Reelfoot's village. As the Indians ran to the protection of the forests, the ground gaped to receive the flood, forming this lake. On the lake floor, the Indians said, lay the bodies of Reelfoot, his bride, and his people.

At 36 *m.* State 78 crosses the Kentucky Line 11.5 miles south of Hickman, Ky.

Tour 12

(Asheville, N. C.)—Knoxville—Crossville—Cookeville—Nashville—Jackson—Memphis—(Little Rock, Ark.); US 70.
North Carolina Line to Memphis, 490.2 m.

Southern Ry. parallels route between the North Carolina Line and Newport; Tennessee Central Ry. between Rockwood and Cookeville; Nashville, Chattanooga & St. Louis Ry. between Nashville and Huntington; and Louisville & Nashville R.R. between Brownsville and Memphis.
Paved roadbed, mostly concrete. Accommodations limited outside the larger towns and the county seats.

Section a. NORTH CAROLINA LINE *to* KNOXVILLE; *66.2 m.*

Between the North Carolina Line and Newport the road descends westward through rugged mountains, winding in and out on a high shoulder, into the valley of the French Broad River. The peaks, towering above the highway, are sometimes blanketed with low-hanging clouds. Clear streams drop from the hillsides into gorges that their waters have cut in the high ridges. Great boulders, left above the ground by erosion, are covered with moss and often lie in "ripshin" thickets of laurel, or rhododendron.

Between Newport and Knoxville the low hills that rise gradually from the valley are often bare and cut with deep gullies, on which only a seared-brown subsoil remains. The rich bottom land, taking its toll from the hills, is highly productive. The major part of the crops of garden truck is sold to Newport canneries, the remainder from roadside stands at low prices.

US 70 crosses the North Carolina Line 0 *m.*, 40 miles west of Asheville, N. C., and runs through the Cherokee National Forest. At 3.2 *m.* it crosses the French Broad River, then traverses a narrow valley. For the most part the French Broad tumbles over boulders but at times subsides into natural pools. This stream is often close to the highway and, cutting a deep pass through the Bald Mountain range, provided a route for settlers from the Carolinas to the Tennessee frontier.

At 8 *m.* is the junction with a winding graveled road.

Left on this descending road to DEL RIO, 0.7 *m.* (1,139 alt., 300 pop.), the birthplace of Grace Moore. To enter it the road crosses the French Broad on a narrow steel bridge. Near the railroad station is the STOKELY MUSEUM *(open),* in the home of Frank Stokely, who for more than fifty years has collected and mounted native birds, small animals, and reptiles. The museum also contains numerous Indian relics, a stamp collection, and many hand-woven counterpanes. Before white settlers came to this valley there was a Cherokee village here. Axes, arrowheads, fragments of pottery, and other Indian relics have been excavated.

MAX PATCH MOUNTAIN (4,660 alt.), visible from Del Rio, has a fairly level summit that is bare except for moss.

Herbs, roots, the rare gopherwood, and various medicinal plants, such as butterfly root, rabbit's ear, and ginseng, grow in this section.

US 70 crosses a bridge spanning the French Broad River, 14.4 *m.;* the bluffs above are frequently wrapped in mist. West of the bridge is a wide valley containing homesteads and tourist cabins.

At 18 *m.* is the junction with a graveled road.

Left on this road is EDWINA, 4 *m.* Left from Edwina 4.6 *m.* on a graveled road, running through Deep Gap, to the summit of HALLS TOP MOUNTAIN (3,609 alt.), which became the property of William Hall in 1795. A high steel tower commands an excellent view of the surrounding country.

About 100 yards from the road, at 18.2 *m.,* is (R) RATTLING CAVE *(dangerous),* reached through a crevice believed to have been caused by an earthquake. Because of a sheer drop of 258 feet at the entrance, explorers reach the cave with the aid of a windlass. Fresh air circulates freely in the cave, and the average temperature is 50° F. One of the cave formations, known as the Symbol of Death, has the appearance of a figure with its right hand pointing downward. Most of the cave floor is covered with fish skeletons; this indicates that the water of a lake once covering the cave suddenly drained off and stranded the fish.

NEWPORT, 19.2 *m.* (1,130 alt., 2,989 pop.), seat of Cocke County, is at the foot of a series of mountain benches that rise to the crest of the Great Smoky Mountains. Side streets drop down into the long level main thoroughfare that follows the valley of Pigeon River. Across the river are high rocky bluffs.

In 1789 a colony of Pennsylvania Germans settled in this neighborhood along the northern bank of the French Broad River, on what became known as Dutch Bottoms.

Stokely Brothers, canners of vegetables, have their home office and a factory here.

Newport is the home of Ben W. Hooper, Governor of Tennessee from 1911 to 1915 and a member of the U. S. Railroad Labor Board from 1921 to 1925.

The RHEA-MIMS HOTEL, Church St., is built of stone, most of it quarried from the hillside near the hotel. Millstones used by Indians adorn the porch that extends along the front of the building. In the dining room is a large collection of rocks of various kinds.

At the western end of Church St. is the COCKE COUNTY MEMORIAL BUILDING *(open 9-5 weekdays),* erected in memory of soldiers of the county in all wars. The building has an auditorium, a gymnasium, a library, and meeting rooms.

HIGH OAK TULIP GARDENS *(open; full-flowering season during the last week in April and first week in May),* 218 North St., so named because of the tall oak in front of the house, contain almost every known variety of tulip. Thousands of new bulbs are imported each year. Interspersed among the tulips are dwarf trees, shrubs, hollyhocks, and rock plants. The 10-acre garden contains a game-fish pool, a fancy-fish pool, a wall fountain, a fly pool, and a rock garden.

Along College St. and on the Newport High School lawn are 27 maple MEMORIAL TREES, planted in memory of the 27 Cocke County men who lost their lives during the World War.

The JOHN SEVIER PRESERVE *(open)* on the southwestern side of Newport, is a tract of 125,000 acres, with a valley containing 10,000 acres of virgin timber. The waters are stocked with fish by the State. A herd of deer roams about in a large enclosure.

At Newport are junctions with US 25E *(see Tour 3)*, State 75, and State 35.

1. Left from Newport on State 75 is COSBY, 13.2 *m.*, in an area locally called the moonshine capital of the world. The moonshiners signal each other with charges of dynamite when the "revenooers" are coming. The town was named for Dr. James Cosby, one of the first physicians to practice in the county. Many rugged and picturesque peaks are visible from the village.

The VALENTINE NURSERY annually ships millions of ferns and evergreens from this place to many parts of the country. Its collection of Canadian hemlock is unusually large. The nursery extends along the northern edge of the GREAT SMOKY MOUNTAINS NATIONAL PARK. Between Indian Camp Creek and Dunns Creek —about one-fourth mile from the Pinnacle Lead Trail—on Bale's Farm is a huge wild grapevine, five feet in circumference. About 125 feet away is another vine two feet in circumference.

2. Right from Newport on State 35 is PARROTTSVILLE, 7 *m.*; L. here 3.1 *m.* on the graveled Warrenburg Road to the NATURAL BRIDGES, Big Oven and Little Oven, near Harned's Chapel. The larger of the limestone bridges, 50 feet wide and about 150 feet long, has an arch about 15 feet above the creek. Water flows under this bridge only in the rainy seasons, since Oven Creek disappears underground at a point 200 yards east of Big Oven and reappears again about the same distance west of the bridge. Between the bridges is a tunnel cave 300 yards long, with a ceiling 15 to 20 feet high. This is known as the Roaring Hole because of the noise made by the water rushing through it. About 50 feet from the entrance is a vertical shaft, called the Chimney, which penetrates the ceiling and forms an opening through the roof.

WILSON INN (L), 22.8 *m.*, was built about 1800 to accommodate travelers on stages running between Charlotte and Knoxville.

Left from Wilson Inn on the graveled Carson Springs Road to EDGEMONT ORCHARD, 1.5 *m.*, which has more than 5,000 bearing trees.

At 3.2 *m.* is CARSON SPRINGS, a spot that became a summer resort a century ago because of its mineral waters. There are croquet and tennis courts here.

At 28.1 *m.* is the junction with the White Pines Road.

Right on this graveled road to the PRITCHETT HOME *(open 8-6 daily)*, 1.2 *m.*, where are old books, relics of the War between the States, oils, and curios. In the library of 4,000 volumes are about 100 valuable books, among them Bibles bearing the dates 1644, 1654, and 1665. One of the Bibles has three dates of publication because of disturbances in the printing trades during the period in which it was being published—1650, 1669, and 1679. There is one Bible from each of the three issues made by the first printing press in America to print Bibles in a foreign tongue —1743, 1763, and 1776. This press was owned by Christopher Sauer, a member of the German Baptist Brethren, or Dunkers, who brought his press from Germany to Germantown, Pa., in 1709. There are 40 volumes of Harper's Weekly in the library. The collection contains a piece of needlepoint, a picture of Christ in Gethsemane, that was made by the Sisters of Charity in the convent at Georgetown, Ky., in 1845.

BARN

The print collection contains examples of work of the old masters. The furniture belongs to the mid-Victorian period.

At 29 *m.* (L) is Beaver Dam Garden *(open).* Stone walls support wistaria, japonica, alba, and long-erecamosa; rambling roses bloom throughout the summer. A rock walk leads to a tulip bed. In the rock garden, below the main garden, plants of many kinds are used to border hybrid irises and shaggy peonies.

US 70 crosses the French Broad River on the A. R. Swann Bridge, 29.4 *m.,* which is 1,868 feet long.

General Longstreet's Headquarters (R), 33.1 *m.,* is a two-story frame structure, occupied briefly by the Confederate general in January 1864.

DANDRIDGE, 34.1 m. (1,051 alt., 446 pop.), on the northern bank of the French Broad, was named for Martha Dandridge Custis, wife of George Washington. The first white settlement in this section was made here in 1783, and this town became the seat of Jefferson County ten years later.

On January 16, 1864, the left wing of the Confederate army under General Longstreet reached a point northwest of the town, surprising Union forces under General Granger. After a brief skirmish, the right flank of Longstreet's division drove its opponents back to Knoxville.

After the skirmish, a Dandridge woman invited the Confederate officers to her home in which General Granger, the Union Commander, had been a guest the night before. Granger had left a bottle of brandy and from it the Confederate officers drank a satirical toast to him.

In the OFFICE OF COUNTY COURT CLERK is the marriage bond of David Crockett and Polly Finley, and the record of an earlier license issued to Crockett and Miss Margaret Elder on Oct. 22, 1805, returned unused.

One-half block northwest of the courthouse is the HYNDS HOUSE, erected in 1844 on the site of an old still that had been famous for the quality of its whisky. The house was used as a hospital by the Confederates after the siege of Knoxville.

The SOLDIERS MONUMENT, northeast of the courthouse, was erected on the site of the first Hopewell Presbyterian Church in memory of ten soldiers of the Revolution who died in or near Dandridge. The Hopewell congregation, still in existence, was organized in 1785.

1. Right from Dandridge on the Oak Grove Pike to the BRANNER GRISTMILL, 2 *m.,* erected about 1850, which is on the site of the mill built by a Revolutionary soldier, Michael Branner. At 4 *m.* are the FRENCH BROAD FARMS *(open),* noted for Aberdeen Angus cattle. The farms are owned and operated by Dr. J. L. Huggins, who has an international reputation as a cattle-breeder. He owned Idol Mere, U. S. champion in 1919, and Parenthia, the 1920 international champion which he imported from Scotland. Most of the cattle now on the farms have the blood of these famous sires.

2. Right from Dandridge on State 92 to the six-foot DUMPLIN TREATY MARKER, 3.5 *m.,* commemorating the treaty with the Cherokee that threw open the country south of the French Broad to white settlers in 1785. A bronze arrow on the stone base is inscribed: "The Great Indian War Path."

3. Left from Dandridge on the graveled Shady Grove Pike to the OLD LOG HOUSE, 4 *m.,* where old-fashioned square dances are held *(first and third Saturday evenings of each month).* At 6.5 *m.* is the MCSPADDEN HOUSE, a two-story brick dwelling built in 1804 by Samuel McSpadden, a Revolutionary War veteran. The heavy doors swing on large iron hinges and have brass knobs and large locks. The interior woodwork shows fine craftsmanship. At the outbreak of the War of 1812, McSpadden made gunpowder and loaded it on two flatboats that he floated down the French Broad, Tennessee, Ohio, and Mississippi Rivers to New Orleans. He reached the town just before the Battle of New Orleans. After the battle Andrew Jackson gave McSpadden a voucher for $10,000 in gold that he had to take to Washington, D. C., for cashing.

4. Left from Dandridge on an improved road to ISLAND MOUND, 3 *m.,* in the French Broad River. At the lower end, about 300 feet from the water's edge, is the site of a ceremonial building used by Indians. The remains of the posts used in its construction indicate that it was 35 feet square. Many skeletons have been found in deep bark-lined and bark-covered pits (ossuaries). With the bodies were buried bone and shell beads, implements of stone and bone, and large shells upon which were engraved conventionalized rattlesnakes.

Between Dandridge and Knoxville, US 70 crosses a section in which many acres were so badly eroded that they were not suitable for cultivation until the CCC improved them. At several points the English Mountains are visible (L), and at one point, on clear days, the Great Smokies can be seen.

At 52.1 *m.* is the junction with US 11E *(see Tour 1),* with which US 70 is united between this point and Knoxville.

KNOXVILLE, 66.2 *m.* (933 alt., 105,802 pop.) *(see KNOXVILLE).*

Points of Interest: Headquarters of the Tennessee Valley Authority, the Courthouse, Chisholm's Tavern, the Blount Mansion, and the Church St. M. E. Church.

Knoxville is at the junction of US 11W *(see Tour 1B),* US 25W *(see Tour 5),* and State 33 *(see Tour 5B).* US 11 unites with US 70 for 19 miles southwest of Knoxville.

Section b. KNOXVILLE *to* NASHVILLE; *197.8 m.;* US 70-11, US 70

US 70-11 follows Main Ave. in KNOXVILLE, 0 *m.* to Cumberland Ave.; R. on Cumberland Ave.

In BEARDEN, 5.2 *m.* (9,225 pop.), a small residential suburb, is the GRIFFITH HOUSE, a two-story brick structure erected by Maj. Robert Reynolds in the early days of the War between the States.

At 5.4 *m.* is the junction with Weisgarber Rd., paved.

Right on this road 1.9 *m.* to Middlebrook Pike.

1. Right on Middlebrook Pike 3.5 *m.* is MIDDLEBROOK *(private),* a two-story weatherboarded structure designed and constructed about 1845 by Morgan Hazen. In 1860, small protruding one-story wings were added on each end and connected by a low one-story Doric portico with a flat roof and a baluster. The design, like many of the day, was copied from architectural publications. Ceilings in the north wing are 15 feet high, and the old kitchen and serving pantries are well preserved. Huge boxwood hedges, flower beds, and borders of fine old oak and elm trees make the grounds delightful. The trunk of one oak has a circumference of 20 feet and a limb spread of about 120. After its purchase in 1865 by Maj. Thomas Sheppard Webb, who served in Gen. N. B. Forrest's cavalry, Middlebrook was for many years the best-known dairy farm in East Tennessee.

2. Left from Weisgarber Rd. 0.2 *m.* on Middlebrook Pike to LONAS HOUSE, an old brick structure. It is now to some extent a Tennessee frontier museum; a long rifle used in the Battle of King's Mountain hangs on the wall; a grandfather's clock, bought about 1775, still keeps the time. An old sea-shell trumpet, used in calling men from the fields at mealtime and as a warning signal against Indian marauders, is another prized relic. A cedar chest with a secret drawer, that was long forgotten, contains documents dated 1791 and 1795. Among the books are a pocket-size military dictionary published in London in 1702, and several Bibles printed in Germany. One of these Bibles, which contains a picture of Martin Luther, is believed to have been printed shortly after his death.

At 8.9 *m.* on US 70-11 is the intersection with graveled Gallaher View Rd.

Right on this road 0.5 *m.* to the junction with a dirt road; R. here to the SITE OF CAVETT'S STATION, 1 *m.,* by the graves of the Cavetts killed here during an Indian attack.

At 10.1 *m.* is a junction with graveled Ebenezer Rd.

Left on Ebenezer Rd. 6 *m.* to the junction with a private road; R. here 0.3 *m.* to STATES VIEW, erected in 1809 from designs made by Thomas Hope, and rebuilt after a fire in 1823 had destroyed part of it. It is a plain two-story brick house, with one lower two-story wing that survived the fire. The windows and transomed doorway are well spaced; the rooms have fine proportions; and the paneling and molding of the doors, mantels, and chair rails are severe but excellent in workmanship. States View was the big house for the 2,000-acre plantation of Charles McClung, surveyor, lawyer, land speculator, and country gentleman. He was one of the founders of Blount College.

The THOMAS J. PAGE HOUSE, 12.6 *m.,* known locally as the old Mabry Place, was built in 1851 by George W. Mabry, son of Gen. Joseph A. Mabry, who owned much land and, with William G. Swan, gave to Knoxville the land for its municipal market. The bricks of the house were made on the plantation by slaves. Twenty yokes of oxen were used to trample the lumps of hard clay into powder suitable for mixing with straw and water. With 40 or more slaves to work his 3,500 acres, Mabry lived the life of a country gentleman of the Old South. An excellent spring of water made the estate a popular camp site for soldiers during the War between the States, and there was considerable fighting in the vicinity. A quarrel between two Union soldiers ended in the murder of one in spite of Mrs. Mabry's attempt to save the man's life by locking him in the lower front room.

FARRAGUT, 15.2 *m.* (910' alt., 75 pop.), was named in honor of David Glasgow Farragut, the first man to have the rank of admiral in the American Navy.

Left from Farragut on Lowes Ferry Pike to PLEASANT HILL CEMETERY (R), 0.5 *m.,* in the center of which is the ARCHIBALD ROANE MONUMENT. Roane was the second governor of Tennessee, succeeding John Sevier who had served three successive terms, the limit permitted by the State Constitution. Roane was elected in 1801, and served until 1803, when Sevier was again eligible to run and became a candidate. During his incumbency Sevier had been exceptionally popular, which made Roane's defeat seem certain. During the campaign it was disclosed that a large number of fraudulent land warrants were in existence, and charges were made implicating Sevier. Andrew Jackson, Superior Court judge at the time, arrayed himself against Sevier, who had appointed him to his office.

John Tipton, who was in the Legislature and who had come into conflict with Sevier in the last days of the State of Franklin, started an official investigation of the charges. John Carter had been land-entry clerk of Washington County and his son Landon an entry taker; examination of the official records resulted in this report:

"The committee are of opinion that warrants to the amount of 105,600 acres of land have been fraudulently obtained by John Sevier from Landon Carter who acted as entry taker in said office, on the file of papers purporting to be locations and grants surreptitiously obtained from the secretary of North Carolina, to wit: James Glasgow by said Sevier on said fraudulent warrants, to the amount of 46,060 acres." A motion to reject the entire report was lost, and another motion to amend the report so as to have it merely set forth the facts without attributing any design to or interpreting the motives of John Sevier was carried."

Everyone was speculating in land at the time and in spite of Jackson's growing political influence, the quiet, scholarly Roane was defeated, Sevier receiving 6,786 votes to Roane's 4,923.

The personal animosities that developed between Sevier and Jackson during this campaign continued after it was over and duels between them were twice averted.

At 1.7 *m.* is CONCORD.

Left 8.6 *m.* from Concord crossing railroad tracks on Lowes Ferry Pike to LOWE'S FERRY, on the Tennessee River. The SITE OF FARRAGUT'S BIRTHPLACE is close to the ferry landing. David G. Farragut was born here on July 5, 1801, in a log cabin. His parents later moved to New Orleans and in time he entered the U. S. Navy. Shortly after the beginning of the War between the States, Farragut was placed in command of the West Gulf Blockading Squadron and gained public acclaim by capturing New Orleans, which was not discredited by his failure to take Vicksburg.

Lowe's Ferry on the Tennessee River is believed to have been operated as early as April 1797, when according to local historians a franchise was issued to George

Farragut, father of David. It was on the route between the Quaker colony of Friendsville and Knoxville. The ferry was bought by Abraham Low (Lowe), on April 30, 1807, and the Lowe family carried on the business for nearly 100 years. During the War between the States it furnished an important communicating link for troops.

The ferry, now operated jointly by Knox and Blount Counties, is free.

A stone at 15.5 *m.* marks the SITE OF CAMPBELL'S STATION, a frontier fort erected in 1787 by Capt. David Campbell. It was a stopping place for travelers and a refuge during Indian scares.

At 19.8 *m.* is the junction (L) with US 11 *(see Tour 1).*

At 37.7 *m.* is the site of a near duel between Andrew Jackson and John Sevier. They had had an encounter near Knox County Courthouse on Oct. 1, 1803, during which Sevier made a comment that Jackson construed as a reflection on the character of Mrs. Jackson *(see THE HERMITAGE, Sec. b).* Friends prevented a fight. The next day Jackson challenged Sevier to a duel, which was declined on the grounds that dueling was prohibited by the constitution of Tennessee which the Governor had sworn to support.

Jackson replied that he was willing to fight in Georgia, Virginia, North Carolina, or on Indian Territory "if it will obviate your squeamish fears." After many days' delay and after many attempts to bring Sevier to action, Jackson threatened to denounce him in the *Gazette* as a "coward and poltroon." Sevier remained silent and Jackson had his denouncement published. Believing this measure would bring results, Jackson with one companion set out for Southwest Point, on the Cherokee boundary. After waiting five days they were ready to leave when Sevier and several armed men appeared. With pistols drawn, only twenty feet apart, the duelists began abusing each other. Then each man put aside his pistols. Jackson flourishing his cane rushed at Sevier who quickly drew his sword. The flashing sword frightened the horse and made him run away with Sevier's pistols. The governor hid behind a tree and continued to abuse Jackson for firing on an unarmed man. Finally, Sevier's men persuaded him to give up the fight. He and Jackson left the field swearing at each other. At Kingston, Governor Sevier was received with a sixteen-gun salute. This demonstration to some extent restored the Governor's pride and self-esteem.

KINGSTON, 38.7 *m.* (831 alt., 827 pop.), seat of Roane County, was a busy place by 1800 because it was at the eastern end of the Walton Road, which ran to Nashville. Nearby was the small frontier military post of Southwest Point, garrisoned to provide protection to the whites who were flocking in to expropriate the Cherokee land. The importance of the settlement as a state-route junction is evidenced by the three old taverns, or "stands," that remain.

The settlers of the area were much excited in early May of 1797 when news arrived from Knoxville that the Duke of Orleans (later Louis Philippe of France) and two brothers would pass through this place on their way to Nashville, an itinerary planned for them by President Washington. The princes enjoyed their wilderness journey though they sometimes found it difficult to adapt themselves to frontier living conditions, and particularly to the food served in overnight stands.

In the early days of Tennessee a law was passed requiring a bond of $1,250 with three signers from a would-be bridegroom before his license to wed could be granted. This law has never been repealed. A faded old document in the COURTHOUSE reads:

"Know all men by these presents that we, William Gallaher, Alexander Carmicheal and Alexander Hopkins, all of the county and state aforesaid, our heirs and assigns, are jointly and severally held and firmly bound unto his excellency, John Sevier, Governor of the state aforesaid, and his successors in office, in the penal sum of $1,250, void on condition there be no lawful objection why William Gallaher and Sally Davidson may be joined together as man and wife in the holy state of matrimony."

In 1807 Kingston was considered as the site for the State capital; the legislature met here for one day, Sept. 21, before moving back to Knoxville.

The HARVEY HOUSE, still a hotel, was built about 1830 by Edward McDuffy. Meals were formerly cooked in huge ovens in the basement. Although it has been modernized, the house still has an old-time charm.

The MORGAN HOUSE *(private),* on a corner opposite the courthouse, was constructed about 1810, by Col. Gideon Morgan. It is a brick one-and-a-half-story structure; on the front is a large dormer whose roof is extended forward to form the pediment of a two-story porch. Both entrances to the porch have graceful fanlights. The interior has a dark walnut trim.

The WARD HOUSE *(private),* corner of Third and Cumberland Sts., one block east of the Courthouse contains a large collection of old papers, books, and many Indian relics. Among the articles is a peace pipe, a tobacco pouch, arrow points, garters, leggings, pottery, old dishes, and a bone dish.

On a hill in the western part of Kingston is the SITE OF THE HOME OF COL. ROBERT KING BYRD, who in the winter of 1864 organized a Union regiment in Tennessee. From the hill is a broad view of the Tennessee and Clinch River valleys.

Left from Kingston on State 56 to SOUTH WESTPORT FORT, 1 *m.,* on the north bank of the Tennessee River. This fort was established in 1792 by John Sevier by order of William Blount, then Governor of the Territory South of the River Ohio. Troops were quartered here to prevent incursions of the Cherokee into the settlements.

US 70 here runs through an area containing many peach orchards.

At 42.7 *m.* is a junction (L) with US 27 *(see Tour 6),* with which US 70 is united for 9.8 miles.

The congregation of the POST OAK CHRISTIAN CHURCH, 45.5 *m.,* first of the sect in the State, was organized in 1813.

ROCKWOOD, 50.9 *m.* (914 alt., 3,898 pop.), was named in honor of Maj. W. O. Rockwood. Near here are Indian mounds, evidence of long habitation of the area.

The town is built on land granted to Gen. John Brown for services in the War of 1812. The front yard of the CLACK HOUSE, 7 Kingston Ave., is the site of the first house in Rockwood, a log cabin built by Brown in 1816. General Brown's son built the present structure prior to the War between the States.

In the southeast corner of the yard, adjoining the highway, is the site of what was probably the first toll gate in Tennessee. It was erected and maintained by the Cherokee, in accordance with their treaty rights, to prevent the white man's free use of the Indian trail between the Watauga Settlement and the Cumberland Settlement (Nashville). The trail passed through land reserved to the Indians by the Treaty of the Holston.

By the site of the old toll gate was the huge Rockwood Oak and a well now covered with a stone slab. Local superstition has it that the spot is "hanted" by the ghost of a Negro murderer.

When settlement was begun here in 1816 deposits of coal and iron were discovered nearby. Robert Craven and William H. Thompson, operators of the first local iron furnace, knew nothing of smelting iron with coal or coke and produced only three tons a day by the use of charcoal. In 1865 Gen. John T. Wilder, who had been here with Union troops, made an investigation that led to the building of the furnaces of the Roane Iron Company. In 1868 Pennsylvania workers trained in mining and smelting were brought here. The furnaces ran night and day for many years, and the town grew rapidly; for a time houses were so much in demand that families moved into new ones weeks before the chimneys were added.

When the mills closed in 1920, most of the employees found work in the local stove foundry, silk mill, and other small industrial plants.

At 52.6 *m.* is a junction (R) with US 27 *(see Tour 6).*

At 54.8 *m.* is the junction with a graveled road.

Right on this road 2 *m.* to the top of MOUNT ROOSEVELT (2,000 alt.), which offers a far-sweeping view. The Smokies are visible on clear days.

The highway crosses Mammy's Creek at 58.9 *m.* Tradition is that a family traveling by ox cart camped for the night by a creek some miles away. The father concluded an argument by beating his wife and to emphasize his victory, called the stream Daddy's Creek. The following night, camping by this stream, the mother and her children soundly thrashed the head of the family and named this creek for the new victor. There is no tradition concerning a further round.

By the creek is the FUR CRAFT SHOP of J. W. Hickey, who began trapping in this neighborhood about 1905. At first he, his wife, and a daughter cured the hides and made them up. After he had gained considerable business, he opened roadside stands and began purchasing hides from other trappers. He specializes in the red fox neckpiece, or "choker," and sells 300 to 400 annually. He also makes up half as many grey fox pieces, as well as those of mink, raccoon, skunk, and other furs. His stands are placed at several points along the highway between Farragut and Crossville. In Hickey's shop are a number of mounted animals and birds.

ROADSIDE FUR MARKET

At 59.8 *m.* is the junction with a graveled road.

Right on this road to WALDENSIA LAKE, 5 *m.* *(hotel, tourist cabins, store, fishing and swimming facilities),* is a popular summer resort. The lake is fed by two deep artesian wells. The surrounding hills provide opportunities for walking and hunting, and the lake is stocked with rainbow trout.

OZONE, 60.2 *m.* (2,000 alt., 200 pop.), a picturesque mountain village, was so named because of the stimulating quality of the air here. Charming OZONE FALLS (60 feet) is visible from the highway, but to approach the brink it is necessary to walk 100 yards to a point near the end of the Fall Creek bridge. The rocks by the falls are slippery, and there are no guard rails *(walk with care).*

Lovers Leap, Split Rock, and Sunset Rock are along the crest of the palisades on the east side of Fall Creek, a region particularly attractive in April, May, and June.

Between Ozone and Crab Orchard US 70 passes between Black Mountain (L) and Crab Orchard Mountain (R). During the spring this gap is notable for its gorgeous stands of mountain laurel and wild honeysuckle, and for its flowering cucumber trees.

CRAB ORCHARD (R), 64.8 *m.,* is on a grant made March 7, 1796, to William Tyrell and Stockley Donelson, brother-in-law of Andrew Jackson. The deed covered 3,000 acres on "both sides of the old wagon road from Southwest Point to Nashville, including a place known as Crab Orchard."

The SOUTHERN STATES LIME CORPORATION PLANT *(open 7 a.m.-3:30 p.m.),* manufactures high grade lime, suitable for use in the chemical and building trades, and crushes limestone to sizes suitable for roadbeds. Blocks of limestone are also quarried here and sent to Knoxville for fabrication into marble.

Beyond the railroad underpass (R) on the top of a knoll are the RUINS OF THE CRAB ORCHARD INN, built in 1802. It had brick walls 18 inches thick, hand-hewn beams, and high ceilings. Constructed by master craftsmen, the inn was built in the former Cherokee Reservation at a spot where numerous travelers of early days had felt the need of shelter. Until they were forced to compliance, the Cherokee had refused to permit any building here, though the whites had argued that women and children suffered much hardship if they had to camp in the open while waiting for the brook to subside after heavy rains. The one concession of the Indians was that travelers might hunt for sustenance in a small area near the road.

At 65.9 *m.* is the junction with a paved road.

Left on this road to a junction with State 68, 2.9 *m.;* R. here to CUMBERLAND HOMESTEADS *(see Tour 15),* 3 *m.*

DADDY'S CREEK is crossed at 67.8 *m.* The stream offers good "jack fishing."

Between this point and Crossville, the route crosses the northern part of the Cumberland Homesteads. Homes are visible from the highway.

At 72.9 *m.* is the junction with a graveled road.

1. Left on this road to the CUMBERLAND QUARRIES, where Crab Orchard sandstone is quarried. This stone, found rarely in other parts of the world, is a building material of much durability and unusual beauty. The mottled stone, which is predominantly rose in tone, accented by irregularly shaped patterns in a wide range of browns, is found in layers from one-half to twenty inches thick. It is not easily worked and is, therefore, often used as uncoursed rubble. Local people had long been using the stone for the construction of chimneys and for hearthstones before any attempt was made at commercial exploitation. The town of Crossville began to use it for curbing and sidewalks in 1887. In 1925, when the architects of Scarritt College in Nashville selected the stone to obtain pleasing color effects, it began to attract more public attention. Since that time it has been used in a number of important buildings, among them Rockefeller Center and the Church of the Heavenly Rest, in New York City, and the United States Post Office in Philadelphia.

2. Right from the highway 0.3 *m.* on the graveled road to the Crab Orchard stone finishing and shipping plant.

CROSSVILLE, 74.9 *m.* (1,881 alt., 1,125 pop.), seat of Cumberland County, was so named by Amanda Scott about 1856 because it was at the junction of the old Nashville-Knoxville Road and the Kentucky-Chattanooga Stock Road, now State 28 *(see Tour 15).* Large numbers of horses and mules from Kentucky and Alabama were driven over the Stock Road on their way to Virginia. At times as many as 1,000 head, divided into herds of 250 and 300 to facilitate handling, were moved through the town.

In PAUL LINDE'S SHOP *(open to visitors),* one block from Main St., telescopes are built with 6-, 8-, 10-, and 12-inch lenses. The glass used for the mirrors is ground and polished by hand, the polishing being done in a room that is practically dustproof.

Crossville is at the junction with US 70A *(see Tour 12A).*

Left from Crossville on State 28 to CUMBERLAND HOMESTEADS, 4.2 *m.* *(see Tour 15).*

At 83.6 *m.* is the eastern end of a mile-long GLADIOLA FIELD (L), in bloom during June and July. Blooms of the 70-odd varieties are shipped to the cities.

POMONA, 85.5 *m.* (1,900 alt., 79 pop.), was named for the Roman goddess by John W. Dodge (1807–1891), a miniature painter. Dodge painted many well-known people, including Andrew Jackson, Henry Clay, Daniel Webster, and Caleb Norvell.

The long, narrow log house (R), at the eastern end of the town, was the antebellum DODGE HOME. Dodge, a New Yorker, moved to Nashville because of ill health. He later bought 5,000 acres on this plateau and planted 82,000 apple trees. He is buried nearby in a little country cemetery.

The town has a number of frame houses built in the eighties by northern people. Opposite the church is the former HOME OF MARGARET BLOODGOOD PEAKE, the poet who became a Martinist, withdrew from the church of her family, and organized a philosophical cult. Many young people of well-to-do families joined. Here in a nearby clover field the young women took part in a morning ceremony that consisted of rolling nude in the dew-wet clover. The surrounding woods provided so much shelter for "peeping Toms" that the ceremony had to be discontinued.

HARRIMAN 37
KNOXVILLE 75
CHATTANOOGA 98
DUNLAP 52
CHATTANOOGA 87

CROSSVILLE

MAYLAND, 92.1 *m.* (1,985 alt., 250 pop.), is a plateau trade town that grew around the JOHNSON STAND, or RAINS HOUSE *(open).* This former stage stop, now near the depot, is a well-preserved, four-room structure. Among the owner's relics are looms, spinning wheels, and carding combs. On the smokehouse walls are seen the peg holes used in warping thread.

According to a local legend, when Matt Johnson and his sister, Patsy, were operating the tavern, Indians of West Tennessee passed the place on their annual trips eastward to obtain supplies of lead. On the return journey they would camp on the bluff near the spring, borrow Johnson's molds, and cast a supply of bullets. They never divulged the source of the lead, and all efforts to follow them were futile.

Right from Mayland 1.5 *m.* on a graveled road to LAKE ALOALOA, locally called Mayland Lake. The lake, created for resort purposes, covers 300 acres and is 4 to 27 feet in depth. Camp Nakanawa, a private camp for girls, is on the shore.

MONTEREY LAKE, 93.2 *m.,* in Monterey Natural Park, a wild steep-walled gorge, provides opportunities for fishing, swimming, and boating. The highway crosses an arm of the lake.

MONTEREY, 95.7 *m.* (1,800 alt., 1,731 pop.), is a trade center. A factory here produces large quantities of unfinished golf sticks. The STANDING STONE is at the eastern rim of the town. Early travelers on the Walton Road mentioned this rock, which had been used, it is believed, by the Indians for ceremonial purposes.

At 102.7 *m.* is the junction with a graveled road.

Left on this road to BEE ROCK, 0.5 *m.,* a bluff from which is a view of far valleys.

COOKEVILLE, 111.3 *m.* (1,050 alt., 3,738 pop.), seat of Putnam County, is on the Highland Rim in gently rolling hills. In 1854, lots were sold here for a town, but for more than a year there were no women among the settlers. The town is now the trade center of an agricultural region and manufactures men's shirts and shoes.

The TENNESSEE POLYTECHNIC INSTITUTE, on the northern edge of town, is a State institution with a four-year technical curriculum that leads to the bachelor of science degree. The 20-acre campus, attractively landscaped, is supplemented by two farms: one of 67 acres adjacent to the campus and another of 75 acres one-half mile north. In 1932 the school's herd of Jersey cattle set a world record; each cow produced an average of 601 pounds of butter fat. The brick buildings, which form a quadrangle, are of modified Georgian Colonial design and have stone trim.

The ANN TRIGG ROBINSON HOME *(open 8 to 4),* 1000 Spring St., contains a valuable collection of Robinson family relics. Notable among them are a pre-Revolutionary patchwork quilt, made of English prints and lined with homespun linen; a white coverlet that Mrs. Andrew Jackson helped to quilt; the Masonic apron of William Quarles (1752–1814); the Masonic apron of George Simpson (1769–1836) of County

Tyrone, Ireland; a pre-Revolutionary pewter teapot; a small old leather dressing case; hand-made spectacles; and a number of old books.

Left from Cookeville on a macadam road to the HYDROELECTRIC PLANT at BURGESS FALLS, 11 *m.* The plant, municipally owned and operated, could supply the needs of a town of 10,000 people.

At DOUBLE SPRINGS, 123.7 *m.,* are five mineral springs.

The Tennessee Central Railway, which winds along the highway between Harriman and Nashville, here loops sharply south for a few miles. This branch of the railroad, which has infrequent service, plays an important part in the lives of inhabitants of the region through which it passes. The train crews know all the regular passengers by name, share their interests, and treat them as guests. The conductors consider the trains as their personal possessions. The passenger trains do not carry diners, and some time before noon the conductor or a member of the crew goes through the two or three cars to collect orders for coffee, soft drinks, and sandwiches. These orders are wired up the line to a station where nearby housewives prepare the food and drinks that are distributed when the train arrives. A visitor who wishes to meet rural Tennesseans should ride at least once by day between Knoxville and Nashville on this road.

At 125.3 *m.* is the junction with State 56.

Left on State 56 is BAXTER, 1 *m.* (1,158 alt., 541 pop.), named for Col. Jere Baxter, builder of the Tennessee Central Ry. Here is the BAXTER SEMINARY, a preparatory school for boys and girls, founded by the Methodist Episcopal Church.

Here US 70 winds with sharp curves through rising hills and follows the tops of steep, narrow ridges.

At 135.8 *m.* is junction with State 53, a macadam road.

Right on this road to FLYNN'S LICK, 16 *m.;* L. 1.8 *m.* from Flynn's Lick on Fort Blount Road to FORT BLOUNT FERRY. On the east bank of the Cumberland River 150 yards from the landing is the SITE OF FORT BLOUNT, built in 1788 for protection during Indian attacks.

GAINESBORO, 20 *m.* (575 alt., 550 pop.), named for Edmund Pendleton Gaines, has been the seat of Jackson County since 1820. Its isolation has kept it a small trade center for farmers. Cordell Hull maintained a law office here for a short time. The surrounding countryside was explored in 1770 by Uriah Stone and his party of long-hunters. The hills and valleys were then covered with tall grass, and the area was rich in game; in 1780 a party of hunters from French Lick killed 105 bears, 75 buffalo, and 80 deer.

At 142.2 *m.* is the junction with State 25.

Right on State 25, crossing the Cumberland River on the Cordell Hull Bridge *(free),* to CARTHAGE, 1 *m.* (582 alt., 1,068 pop.), seat of Smith County. The town was founded in 1804. The first voting took place at the home of Maj. William Walton, who surveyed the old Walton Trail and gave land to cause establishment of the county seat here. In the summer of 1808 William Moore arrived from Knoxville with the press acquired when he married the widow of George Roulstone, Tennessee's first printer. Here he founded the Carthage *Gazette.* The town is one of the large burley tobacco sale centers of Middle Tennessee. William Campbell (1851–53) and Benton McMillin (1899–1903), Governors of the State, lived here.

At 6.4 *m.* on State 25 is the junction with State 85.

Right 4.4 *m.* on State 85 is DEFEATED and at 5.5 *m.* is the village of DIFFI-

CULT. Between Defeated and Difficult the road passes around Devil's Elbow and descends Angel Hill. The latter town received this name after the Post Office Department had rejected the first one selected, calling it "too difficult."

LEBANON, 164.7 *m.* (512 alt., 4,658 pop.), seat of Wilson County, was named for the Biblical Lebanon, noted for its tall cedars. Local red cedar provides material for a pencil mill, a slat mill, and several log yards. A woolen mill, producing large quantities of blankets, a spoke and handle factory, and a flour mill also provide industrial employment.

Lebanon was one of the leading Tennessee centers of culture before the War between the States. On the whole its prominent citizens were well-to-do but not wealthy, and they were interested in gracious rather than showy living. Evidence of this is found in the houses and gardens that survived the war and economic upheavals.

Lebanon life centered about little CUMBERLAND UNIVERSITY, founded in 1842 under supervision of the Cumberland Presbytery. It now has a college of liberal arts, with engineering, law, and theological schools. Judge Abraham Caruthers was the first dean of the law school. The enrollment is between 500 and 550. The university has not been able to attract the endowment funds that would have enabled it to fulfil its early promise.

Cordell Hull, Secretary of State in the Cabinet of President Franklin D. Roosevelt (1932–), and many other distinguished public men, as well as influential educators, have been graduated here.

The NATHAN GREEN HOME, S. Greenwood St., is representative of the restrained, well-designed homes of pre-war Lebanon. It is a square two-story brick structure of Greek Revival design, with one-story wings. A two-story portico with fluted, Corinthian-topped capitals and a simple cornice runs across almost the complete length of the two-story gallery unit and shelters a long shallow second-story gallery having an iron balustrade. Smaller porches of simpler design are on the fronts of the wings, fitting into the corners formed when the wings were set somewhat behind the line of the façade. The first floor windows all extend to the floor. Nathan Green, Jr., who built the house, was a graduate of Cumberland and returned to serve on the law faculty.

In 1858, while he was a teacher in Cumberland University, Green wrote a letter to the public in which he expressed the belief that Congress had the power to limit slavery in the Territories and in the District of Columbia. Proslavery feeling was strong in Middle Tennessee and soon both Green and Cumberland were being denounced; Green was called a traitor and "advised to emigrate to a free State," and the "young men of the South" were warned "not to attend Cumberland University."

The SITE OF THE SAM HOUSTON LAW OFFICE is on the north side of E. Main St.; here in 1818 Houston began the legal practice that was a stepping-stone in his public career.

On W. Main St. is the HOME OF ROBERT L. CARUTHERS, built in 1850, supposedly from designs by William Strickland. The two-story brick structure with its small one-story wings is well balanced; a two-story central recess holds two pillared and transomed entrances, one on each floor, and a shallow second-floor gallery. This recess is emphasized by a slightly projecting pedimented Doric portico with two pillars and a frieze that is also carried across the front of the house. Heavy console brackets and molded cornices, added at some later date, surmount the windows on the front of the house and the two front second-floor windows have small balconies with iron balustrades.

Robert Looney Caruthers (1800–82) was one of Tennessee's important public servants. He served as State attorney general, State Supreme Court judge, and was Representative in Congress from 1841 to 1843. With his brother, Abram Caruthers, he founded Cumberland University. Caruthers was elected Governor of Tennessee in 1862, but since the entire State was in the possession of contending armies and Andrew Johnson had been appointed Military Governor, he did not take the oath or exercise the duties of the office. Cumberland University had its beginning in one of the brick servant houses opening on the garden at the rear of the house.

CASTLE HEIGHTS MILITARY ACADEMY, at the outer edge of the town, is an elementary and college-preparatory school for boys, founded in 1902. The academy has a 225-acre campus, parade grounds, a golf course, athletic fields, a polo field. The fourteen brick and stone buildings are castellated.

In 1936 the Mitchell Mansion, adjoining the main campus, was acquired for the use of the elementary department. It is a large stone structure of Greek Revival design, with a two-story Corinthian portico and one-story porches on each side. The interior has been remodeled.

1. Left from Lebanon on the Coles Ferry Road to CAMP BELL, 1 *m.,* built about 1835 by Col. Benjamin Seawell for a daughter. It became the home of William B. Campbell (1807–67), Colonel of the First Tennessee Volunteers in the Mexican War, Governor of Tennessee (1851–53), and a Unionist who represented a southern constituency in Washington (1866–67).

The long low story-and-a-half frame house has dormers and a long recessed porch with square pillars. Its beautiful gardens were designed by Dr. J. M. Safford, at one time professor of botany at Columbia University.

2. Left from Lebanon on State 10 to the WILSON COUNTY CEDAR FOREST, 8 *m.,* a 9,000-acre tract largely of cedar, where an attempt is being made to reforest with walnut trees.

At BETHLEHEM METHODIST CHURCH (L), 167.7 *m.,* in 1838 Lavinia Kelly organized a women's missionary society. Francis Asbury, first bishop of the Methodist Episcopal Church in America, held his last conference here on September 24, 1815. Part of the old lectern and some of the original benches are still in use.

On the crest of a hill, 168.2 *m.* (L), is the HOUSE OF EDWARD FRANKLIN "POP" GEERS, a well known turfman who was born at nearby Horn Springs in 1851. His old hitching tree with an iron ring stands by the gate.

At 169 *m.* is the junction with a graveled road.

Right on this road to HORN SPRINGS *(swimming pool, dance pavilion),* 1 *m.,* in the foothills of the Highland Rim. The mineral content of the water of this spring was discovered by James Baker Horn in 1870. The Wilderness Trail runs through the grounds.

At 185 *m.* (L) is TULIP GROVE, home of Andrew Jackson Donelson, nephew of Rachel Jackson. When Jackson became President, Andrew Donelson, his political secretary, came to Washington and his wife Emily acted as Jackson's official hostess. The Donelsons took sides in the Peggy Eaton affair; Mrs. Donelson refused to receive Peggy and left Washington. The quarrel was not patched up until 1832, when Jackson was running for re-election to the Presidency; to cement the reunion, Jackson hired Joseph Rieff and William Hume to build a house for the Donelsons on this land, which the young man had inherited. Rieff was a distinguished architect of the Greek Revival period. The houses he designed include 107 Monument Street in Baltimore and the Hastings House in Cambridge, Mass. He and Hume were still at work on Tulip Grove when the nearby Hermitage was damaged by fire and they received the contract for its reconstruction. Architecturally, the Tulip Grove house is quite as interesting as the Hermitage; it is a spacious, rectangular, two-story brick structure with an ell, and has brick pilasters on the corners and a Doric frieze that is carried across the two-story four-columned and pedimented Doric portico. The façade behind the portico is recessed and holds a simple second-story gallery. The building and decoration of this house engaged the attention of the whole Jackson-Donelson clan; it was Ralph Earl who painted the walls of the hall. A beautiful mahogany spiral stairway extends upward to the third floor.

The house is reached through a curving driveway lined with the tulip trees for which the estate was named. Directly behind the house are two square gardens, one of which is devoted largely to roses.

Andrew Jackson Donelson (1799–1871) continued to play a part in public affairs after his uncle's death, becoming U. S. Minister to Prussia, then to united Germany, and in 1856 he was Fillmore's running mate in the Presidential campaign.

At 185.2 *m.* is the junction with Old Hickory Blvd.

Right on this road 0.4 *m.* to the short avenue leading to THE HERMITAGE *(open weekdays 8:30 a.m.-6 p.m., Sun. 2:30-6; adm. 25¢),* former home of Andrew Jackson; it is now owned and maintained by the Ladies' Hermitage Association. Near the house Cedar Drive is lyre shaped, sweeping in curves past the main entrance of the house. Most of the rows of tall cedars along the driveway were planted under the supervision of Jackson, who laid out the grounds with the aid of Ralph E. W. Earl (1788–1837), an artist who had married a niece of Mrs. Jackson and spent much time here.

Andrew Jackson, the son of Irish immigrants, was born in the Waxhaw district, close to the boundary between the Carolinas, on March 15, 1767, and though very young took some part in Revolutionary skirmishes of the later years in which two of his brothers were killed. His parents died before he was fourteen, but he managed to acquire some education and to read law. When he came to the infant Nashville in 1788 as solicitor for the western district of North Carolina he was only twenty-one years old. Like everyone else of the time, he speculated widely in land and acquired the Hermitage plantation early in his career. From the beginning he participated in the political life of Tennessee, helping to frame the State constitution and becoming the State's first Congressional Representative in Washington (1796). He first gained military prestige in the early part of 1814 when commanding the State militia in a successful attack on the Creeks; the hard-pressed United States Government made him a major general in the regular Army and placed him in command of the defense of New Orleans, which he managed so brilliantly, against seasoned British forces, that he gained almost hysterical national acclaim.

Since 1805 Jackson had been living here in a house that was really a collection of log cabins; part of these remain. He grew cotton and engaged in various commercial enterprises but did not have the money to build a more elegant house until 1819, when the conclusion of the War of 1812 re-established the market for American cotton in the British Isles. The two-story brick structure erected then with low one-story wings, one of which was extended in the rear to form an ell, is the shell of the present structure. In 1831 Jackson had two wings and a one-story front gallery added. Three years later the house was seriously damaged by fire. It was rebuilt under the direction of Joseph Rieff, the architect of Tulip Grove, and it has not been greatly changed since that time. After the house was rebuilt, new furnishings were ordered from Philadelphia. These were shipped by sailing vessel to New Orleans where they were transferred to a steamboat. At the Nashville wharf the cargo was destroyed by fire; everything had to be reordered.

Young Mrs. Donelson frequently acted as Jackson's hostess because his wife, Rachel, to whom he was married in 1791, died just before his inauguration as President in 1829. The Jacksons did not entertain as freely as did their neighbors because vicious animosity of political opponents kept alive an unfortunate mistake that occurred at the time of the Jackson marriage.

Before Rachel Donelson met Jackson she had left her first husband, and a divorce had been applied for. She and Jackson had misunderstood the terms of the warrant granting a hearing for the proceedings; believing it gave her the divorce, they married in good faith. The mistake was discovered sometime later; meanwhile the divorce had been granted and the couple remarried. Enemies magnified the mistake to a major scandal and frequently made remarks that the Jacksons were too sensitive to ignore. Jackson repeatedly defended his wife's reputation in public—sometimes with his fists—but the story was brought forward with increased venom, nearly forty years after the event, during his Presidential campaign; many believed that the resultant unhappiness was one of the causes of Mrs. Jackson's death.

Rachel Jackson never saw the charming house in its present condition, but its fine simplicity would have been in accordance with her taste. The central two-story structure is flanked by low one-story wings; a two-story portico running across the white-painted front of the main unit on a low foundation has a second-story gallery and six modified Corinthian columns.

The pilastered main entrance, which has a paneled door and a fanlight and side-lights, is duplicated in an entrance to the second-floor gallery. The rear of the house also has a six-columned two-story portico; it differs from that on the front in having a higher foundation, Doric columns, and a Doric pediment. The brick walls of the sides and rear of the house are of natural color, but the front walls had to be painted to hide the scars of the fire of 1834.

Some years after Jackson's death in 1845 the plantation was bought for maintenance as a memorial to Old Hickory. Great effort has been expended to preserve and restore the place to its early condition. In the hall, which has a graceful, spiral staircase suspended from the semilunar rear wall, is the wallpaper bought in 1835; it shows the search of Telemachus for Ulysses. Many of the furnishings belonged to Jackson, and those that were not his belong to his period. In an upper room are displayed miscellaneous Jackson relics.

Andrew Jackson and his wife loved their gardens, and the trees received the master's special attention. Rachel Jackson was very fond of flowers, and her husband helped her to add some exotic species to her collection, which is in a formally laid out square at the south end of the house. Here during the spring and summer, the air is fragrant with the odor of jonquils, irises, lilies-of-the-valley, lilacs, magnolias, roses, and many other blooms. The plantation graveyard is at a far corner of this formal garden; here is the TOMB OF RACHEL AND ANDREW JACKSON, a small circular Doric structure of the Temple of Love type, with a dome surmounted by an urn-shaped finial; in the temple's center is a pedestal supporting a small obelisk. Nearby are the GRAVE OF RALPH E. W. EARL and those of other relatives and of servants.

THE HERMITAGE, HOME OF ANDREW JACKSON, NEAR NASHVILLE

Behind the house are the SMOKEHOUSE, the CARRIAGE HOUSE, and the CABIN OF ALFRED, Jackson's devoted body servant. In the carriage house is the coach used by Jackson in making the long journey between Washington and the Hermitage during his days in the White House.

Opposite the entrance to the Hermitage is HERMITAGE CHURCH, erected by Jackson in 1823 at the request of his wife. He often referred to it as "Mrs. Jackson's church." It is an angular brick structure with plain entrances separated by an outside chimney.

One time when the church was in need of a new roof, the clergyman called on Andrew Jackson, whom he found watching two cocks that were about to fight. Knowing Jackson's sporting instinct the visitor said, "I'll bet a church roof that this cock wins," and indicated his choice. Jackson's eyes twinkled as he accepted the bet; he knew the cocks were well matched. When the cock chosen by the clergyman seemed to be losing, he called out, "Remember the church needs a roof! Fight, boy, fight!" The clergyman's choice won the fight, and Jackson paid the bet.

US 70 crosses Stone's River at BURR'S LANDING, 187.7 *m.,* so called because Aaron Burr embarked for New Orleans on December 27, 1806, from this place after he had failed to obtain Jackson's backing for his peculiar expedition. Burr's flatboats were built at Clover Bottom under Jackson's direction.

Where the highway crosses Stone's River is CLOVER BOTTOM. In 1780 John Donelson selected this place for his home, built a temporary shelter for his family, and planted crops; but the river overflowed the planted land, and later the Indians attacked the men who came to harvest the corn that had survived the high water. Donelson went back to Kentucky. A few years later the land was claimed under a Revolutionary War bonus grant, but in 1797 the grantee sold it to John Hoggett, who in time developed it as a large plantation. Men from nearby places, Jackson included, formed a jockey club early in the nineteenth century and laid out a racecourse here. Before long the races were drawing such large crowds that Jackson built a store and a tavern on the rise of ground on which spectators stood.

In November 1805, Jackson's Truxton was matched with Capt. Joseph Erwin's Ploughboy on this course. But on the day of the race Ploughboy was withdrawn because of lameness. Payment of the forfeit was offered by Erwin and his son-in-law, Charles Dickinson, but Jackson refused to accept notes. This misunderstanding developed into an open quarrel with much name-calling and publishing on both sides. Friends and relatives became involved and a Nashville lawyer, Thomas Swann, challenged Jackson. Instead of accepting, Jackson caned the challenger in public. This increased the bitterness of the quarrel and the situation was not helped by a second matching of the horses, which Truxton won easily. After some further publishing on both sides, Jackson challenged Dickinson, who accepted. The meeting took place in Kentucky because of a Tennessee law against dueling. Dickinson fired first, wounding Jackson, whose pistol stopped at the half-cock. Jackson recocked his pistol, took deliberate aim and shot Dickinson through the groin, fatally wounding him.

The present CLOVER BOTTOM HOUSE, 187.8 *m.,* was built in 1858. The first substantial house built on the place, OLD BLUE BRICK, so named because one of its solid walls was once painted blue, is about one-half mile behind the main house, which is separated from the road by a grove. The house was long the home of the Hoggett family; though it is known to be quite old, its exact age cannot be ascertained. It is a two-story rectangular building with a low-pitched gable roof. The main house of Clover Bottom is a large brick structure on a high foundation; its design has much interest because, while the pilastered corners show the Classic Revival influence, the very elaborate veranda, the second story porch over the central third of the veranda, with its highly stilted and bracketed arcading, have distinct Moorish effects. The design of the windows, which are double, recalls details of the Italian Renaissance. The fanlighted main entrance is within a recess with rounded top. A center hall is a flanked high-ceiled room having Italian marble mantels and large gold-framed mirrors.

DONELSON, 187.9 *m.* (515 alt., 110 pop.), was named for John Donelson, father-in-law of Andrew Jackson.

Left from Donelson on Stewarts Ferry Road 2 *m.* to the JAMES RIDLEY HOUSE, a plain two-story structure built in 1806 of stone, now stuccoed. On the side and rear the plaster has broken off, revealing the stone construction. The dog-trot, connecting the main house with the long kitchen and dining room, and the old log smokehouse with its cell-like door are typical features of old Tennessee farmhouses.

The rooms are low with paneled wainscoting, the cupboards reach to the ceiling, and the low doors are set in paneled embrasures.

It is reported that Andrew Jackson, under whom Ridley did military service, once said, "By the eternal, if I had ten thousand Jimmy Ridleys I could storm Hell and capture the devil."

At 190.8 *m.* is the junction with McGavock Lane.

Right on this road to TWO RIVERS FARM, 1.4 *m.,* so named because of its position at the junction of Stone's and Cumberland Rivers. Some time after 1800 William Harding erected the simple two-and-a-half-story frame house that faces the present main structure from the side. Harding's daughter married David McGavock, a civil engineer who came to Nashville soon after the first settlement was made. In 1786 he had made the first map of the Cumberland Settlement.

After Harding's death his daughter inherited this farm.

The present Two Rivers main house is a two-story brick-and-stone structure completed in 1859; it has an elaborately ornamented veranda whose roof is balustraded and forms a second-story veranda, the central third of which is sheltered by a portico.

A formal garden in front of the house contains about 1,400 boxwood most of them still small. In the center is a fountain. On the north side of the house is a garden containing lilacs, tulips, irises, roses, pinks, deutzia and syringa bushes, lilies-of-the-valley, and many varieties of fern.

Dr. James Priestly opened the first school for girls in Middle Tennessee in a structure that stood about one mile from the house on a bluff of the Cumberland.

At 192.8 *m.* is a junction with Pumping Station road.

Right on this road to DEMONBREUN CAVE *(guide),* 0.9 *m.,* for some years the home of Timothy Demonbreun (Jacques Timothe de Monbreun), a French-Canadian trade, who came here from Kaskaskia, north of the Ohio, about 1766 to trap and trade with the Indians. The cave entrance, which is seven or eight feet wide, is about twenty feet above the water; Demonbreun entered with the aid of a ladder which he drew up after him. When he was away during the day, he hid the ladder to prevent the Indians from stealing his supplies. An easier entrance has been carved out. When settlers began to arrive, Demonbreun moved to French Lick (Nashville) and built a store on the public square.

At 193.7 *m.* is a junction with paved Spence Lane.

Left on Spence Lane 0.7 *m.* to the Elm Hill Pike; L. here 0.6 *m.* to a bridge over Mill Creek. At the east end of the bridge is BUCHANAN STATION, (L), site of a frontier refuge built in 1786 because the settlers were on land legally claimed by the Indians. It was a log structure, two stories high with the upper story projecting about four feet and pierced by loopholes for use of guns. It was surrounded by a stockade of logs, placed upright and pointed at the top. Blockhouses at opposite corners enabled watchers to rake the walls with rifle fire and prevent attackers from setting fire to them. On Sept. 30, 1792, a band of 300 or more Creek and Cherokee attacked the place in an attempt to drive off the squatters. The women joined the men in the defense, firing rifles, molding bullets, and using various devices to create the impression that the force of the defenders was larger than it actually was. The Indians suffered heavy losses, but none of the whites was injured.

The site is on the Knapp Farm, a dairy farm owned by George Peabody College for Teachers and used by the student body for recreational purposes.

MOUNT OLIVET CEMETERY *(open sunrise to sunset),* 194.6 *m.,* was established in 1855 by a State-chartered company. A drive winds through landscaped grounds to the crest of the hill that commands a sweeping view of the many large monuments, mausoleums, and obelisks.

Among those buried in the cemetery are John Catron (1786–1865), appointed Associate Justice of the United States Supreme Court in 1837 by

Andrew Jackson; John Bell (1797–1869), State Representative, Speaker of the U. S. House of Representatives, Secretary of War in President William H. Harrison's Cabinet, member of the United States Senate, and nominee for President in 1860 on the Constitutional Party ticket; Felix Grundy (1777–1840), famous criminal lawyer of the Southwest, United States Senator, and Attorney General under President Martin Van Buren; William B. Bate (1826–1905), major general in the Confederate Army and a Governor of Tennessee; and Joseph W. Byrns (1869–1936), Speaker of the U. S. House of Representatives.

NASHVILLE, 197.8 *m.* (498 alt., 153,875 pop.) *(see NASHVILLE).*

Points of Interest: State Capitol, Vanderbilt University, reproduction of the Parthenon, and others.

In Nashville, at the corner of 6th Ave. N. and Deaderick St., on Memorial Square, is the junction with US 31 *(see Tour 7),* with 41W *(see Tour 8),* with US 41 and 70A *(see Tour 8),* with State 11 *(see Tour 7A),* and with State 100 *(see Tour 12B).*

Section c. NASHVILLE *to* MEMPHIS; *229 m.,* US 70

US 70 follows Broadway westward in NASHVILLE, 0 *m.,* to the junction with West End Ave.; R. on West End Ave.

For more than 30 miles west of Nashville US 70 ascends gradually from the Central Basin and crosses the Highland Rim; above the road are the jutting palisades of the Harpeth River, which are covered with dense second-growth timber. Between Nashville and the Tennessee River these hills form a background for short stretches of level pasture and crop lands. Between Dickson and Camden the clay-and-gravel road banks slant evenly back from the concrete as though sliced off with a knife. West of the Highland Rim the country becomes flat or gently rolling. Between Brownsville and Memphis are the dark Hatchie River bottoms and the level cotton lands of the Loosahatchie and Wolf Rivers.

At 6 *m.* is (L) Leake Ave., L. on Leake Ave. is the entrance to BELLE MEADE HOME *(private)* on the site of Dunham Station, or Fort Dunham, built in 1783. John Harding, who came to Nashville from Virginia in 1798, built the two log cabins, connected by a dog-trot, that still stand near the big house. William Giles, the son who enlarged and developed the estate, was born in the cabin on Sept. 15, 1808.

The large mansion, built in 1853, replaced one built in 1830 and destroyed by fire. It is reached through an entrance lane lined with old vine-covered cedars. The two-story structure has a long T-shaped ell. A two-story portico with square stone pillars and finely proportioned entablature extends across the front. The details are forceful but restrained in treatment.

William Harding made this one of the most prosperous farms of Middle Tennessee.

At the beginning of the War between the States, Gov. Isham G. Harris appointed Harding to the military and financial board of Confederate

Tennessee. During the Presidential campaign of 1864, Andrew Johnson, who had been military Governor of the State during the Union occupancy, made a campaign speech in which he said that "if the princely plantation of William G. Harding, who boasted that he had disbursed over $5,000,000 for the Rebel Confederacy, were parcelled out among fifty loyal, industrious farmers, it would be a blessing to the noble Commonwealth."

In 1868 Harding's daughter, Selene, was married to William H. Jackson, who had been a brigadier general of cavalry in the Confederate Army. Jackson became manager of the estate. He was a lover of thoroughbred horses, and under his direction Belle Meade became one of the most famous horse-breeding farms in America.

From 1875 to 1895 the annual colt auctions brought in large sums. Among the famous and valuable stallions of the farm were Virgil, Tremont, Inspector, Scotland, Iroquois, Bramble, Treat-tom, Proctor Knott, The Commoner, Luke Blackburn, and Enquirer. When Enquirer died, the Cincinnati *Enquirer,* for which he was named, sent 300 people to the dedication of the granite monument erected in his memory on Leake Ave.

The former deer park and part of the plantation have been broken up into building lots and developed as a residential section.

At 7.4 *m.* is the junction with State 100 *(see Tour 12B).*

The summit of NINE MILE HILL, 9.2 *m.,* offers a panorama of Nashville and the surrounding country.

At 22.3 *m.* is the junction with Dog Creek Road, unimproved.

Right on this road *(bear L. all the way)* to the NARROWS OF HARPETH, 4 *m.,* where the river makes a hairpin curve around a ridge 0.8 of a mile long and about 300 feet high. This is a good place to fish for bass, perch, and catfish. The flora on the ridge is similar to that of the East Tennessee uplands, with mountain phlox, trailing arbutus, hepatica, anemone, and ginseng. Short-needle pines are hung with a gray moss, rather like Spanish moss. A tunnel that runs through the base of the ridge was chiseled by the slaves of one of the earliest settlers, Montgomery Bell (for whom Montgomery Bell Academy was named). Water was brought through this tunnel to furnish power for an iron foundry.

Near the junction of Dog Creek and Harpeth River lies the GREAT MOUND GROUP *(private),* on both sides of US 70. These belonged to a group identified as the prehistoric stone-grave Indians because of large stone-slab coffins found here. The GREAT MOUND, 50 feet high, was topped with a ceremonial building and surrounded by a palisaded town with clay-plastered circular houses. The town was divided into an upper and lower section, each on a bend of the river about two miles apart. There are traces of the ancient roadway connecting the two settlements. The downstream section lies in what is known locally as Mound Bottom, because it is covered with mounds of various sizes. There is evidence that the heavy palisades had a tower every forty paces.

The city was probably a densely populated trading center, for it was on trails that led to ancient towns in the Cumberland and Mississippi Valleys and to others near Mobile Bay.

At 23 *m.* on US 70 is the junction with a graveled road.

Left on this road is KINGSTON SPRINGS, 2 *m.,* summer resort established before the War between the States. Much of the old furniture of the inn has been preserved. Red, black, and white sulphur waters come from the springs.

Union soldiers camped on WHITE BLUFF, 30.3 *m.* (819 alt., 464 pop.), at one time during the War between the States.

The REEDER COLLECTION of Indian relics *(open)* is in the general store by the highway. The collection contains about 2,500 Indian articles of ceremonial, domestic, and war uses, shards, and old coins and documents.

At 34.9 m. is the entrance road (L) leading into the MONTGOMERY BELL RECREATIONAL PROJECT *(swimming, boating),* a 4,500-acre tract of land under the National Park Service. The park is being developed primarily for restoration of natural resources and to afford recreation for people of low income. A large lake is surrounded by high wooden hills, on which are cabins for use of Boy Scouts and other organizations.

The Reverend Samuel McAdoo, a Presbyterian minister, came to Tennessee in 1799 and settled on land here; he was active in the Great Revival of 1800 *(see RELIGION),* and was a leader in the founding of the Cumberland Presbyterian Church, which was organized at his home on February 4, 1810. When rich iron-ore deposits were found in the vicinity of his home, McAdoo sold his land to Richard Claiborne Napier, who became one of the leading iron manufacturers of the State.

Napier, who had married a daughter of Gen. James Robertson, established Laurel Furnace here, which he operated with slave labor from 1817 until the War between the States.

In DICKSON, 42.3 *m.* (781 alt., 2,900 pop.), cigars, raincoats, and shuttles are manufactured.

Right from Dickson on State 48 is CHARLOTTE, 8 *m.* (650 alt., 291 pop.), seat of Dickson County. The town was established in 1804 and named for Charlotte Robertson, wife of Richard C. Napier. The CUMBERLAND PRESBYTERIAN CHURCH was used as a hospital during the War between the States.

At 14.2 *m.* is (L) CUMBERLAND FURNACE, built by Gen. James Robertson about 1793. Cannon balls used by Jackson's artillery at the Battle of New Orleans were molded here under the supervision of Montgomery Bell who had taken over the ironworks. About 1820 he sold it to A. W. VanLeer, who continued operation until the War between the States. After the fall of Fort Donelson, on February 15, 1862, Cumberland Furnace became a refuge for Confederate soldiers retreating before the Union advance. The furnace was idle during the last years of the war, but became active again shortly after hostilities had ended. It remained in operation until about 1924, when low price of iron made it unprofitable. In October, 1937, the furnace was reopened.

At 43.9 *m.,* just east of the railroad tracks, is the junction with a graveled road.

Right on this road 12 *m.* to the SITE OF THE RUSKIN COLONY, marked by a few frame buildings. In 1894 a group of seventeen people under the leadership of J. A. Wayland of Greensburg, Ohio, organized the Ruskin Co-operative Association; they had been inspired by the *Fors Clavigera* letters of John Ruskin. Through his paper, *The Coming Nation,* Wayland gained adherents to the movement and a stock company was formed under a mining and manufacturing charter in Tennessee. Wayland was the president. In the late summer of 1894 the members of the association arrived at nearby Tennessee City to establish themselves on a farm; the land there was so poor that it had been tax-free. In 1896 they moved to this place where the land was just as poor.

In their attempts to make the colony self-sustaining, the association set up diverse industries, and tried farming intermittently. Wayland brought his press with him and set up a print shop. Equipment was bought for a sawmill, a chewing-gum factory, a cereal-coffee shop, a blacksmith shop, a gristmill, a bakery, a laundry, a photographic shop, and a leather-suspender factory. Most of the enterprises were given a trial in competition with outside industries, but all failed. For a reason that historians of the colony fail to give, the members refused to permit non-members to patronize the laundry and the blacksmith shop though they were asked more than once to do so by people in nearby towns. One of the most profitable undertakings of the colony was the staging of picnics for outsiders in the cave on the property. Large sums were derived from the admission fees.

The members of the colony seem to have been happy in the early period of its existence. Free from economic worries, the size of the families increased rapidly. They had dormitories, a few individual houses, and a dining hall that was used for community meetings and for the sessions of the infant College of New Economy. For members of the association, food, shelter, laundry service, medical care, and education were paid for from the community fund. Scrip—the hour-check—was used instead of money with the work-hour as the credit unit.

Part of the price list of the general store reads as follows:

One pound of tea	11 hours
Three sticks of candy	½ hour
One cut of tobacco	2 hours
One pair of pants	37 hours
One lemon	½ hour
One pair of women's shoes, best	52½ hours
One pound of coffee	7 hours
One gallon coal oil	6½ hours
One quart of peanuts	6 hours
One gallon of gasoline	6 hours

(The foodstuffs in the list represent luxuries not provided from the community funds.)

Many women and all children received allowances in hour-checks. Apparently there were some among the 160 colonists who were more willing to theorize than to labor. Although the association had bought equipment for a sawmill, the task of chopping firewood was given to outside workers.

The members of the association were interested in the arts, as well as in economic and political theory. Classes in drawing and painting were taught by Isaac Broome, a cartoonist for *The Coming Nation* who was also an architect and sculptor of ability, as he proved by his bust of John Ruskin and his design for the College of New Economy, which was being conducted in the community dining hall. The foundation for this building was laid, but the structure was never completed. There was a library of about 1,500 volumes.

The members of the Ruskin Association arrived here with certain broad general theories on how the ideal co-operative society should function, though they held widely divergent theories on such matters as religion and political philosophy. Many members still gave adherence to some religious sect or the other, but there were a number of Freethinkers and several Mental Scientists. One casualty here was the result of too faithful interpretation of the Mental Science beliefs; one of the Scientists, who wished to learn to swim, went far out in a nearby stream, believing that his faith would cause him to stay above water. He drowned.

In time some of the members had modified their theories in the face of the practical problems faced by an isolated co-operative community. Some of the women had never been more than lukewarm toward the experiment, having been brought in through their husband's enthusiasm, rather than through conviction.

A widening political rift grew up among the members. Wayland was a Socialist, and the majority of his followers believed they were when they joined him in this experiment. Soon, however, one part of the membership turned to philosophical anarchism, and verbal fights demoralized the colony long before it failed financially in 1901.

One of the bitter disputes was precipitated by the question of women's suffrage within the association. The more radical theorists, chiefly the philosophical anarchists who held all the offices at the time when the matter was forced to a decision, opposed granting the vote to the women, who, they were sure, would rule against their plans. They finally proposed to grant the vote to seven whom they thought they could count as friendly to them. The socialist faction opposed this and outvoted the officers. The anarchists managed to obtain an injunction to restrain the women from voting but were voted out of office nonetheless. The ex-office-holders then set out to thwart the will of the majority, and the community property was at last forced into the hands of a receiver and eventually sold. All debts were satisfied and some money was returned to the stockholders. The undiscouraged members started a new colony in southern Georgia, which did not last long.

Dr. Walter Van Fleet, a horticulturist and physician, was the colony physician from 1897. Among the plants that he propagated the best known are roses—American Pillow, Dr. Van Fleet, Philadelphia, Silver Moon, Mary Lovett, and Heart of Gold.

McEWEN, 57 *m.* (781 alt., 620 pop.), near the site of the old stand on the stage line that ran from Nashville to Memphis, is in a dairying section and has a cheese plant that handles 30,000 pounds of milk daily.

WAVERLY, 65 *m.* (548 alt., 1,152 pop.), seat of Humphreys County, is for the most part strung along the highway, over which rows of maple trees form an archway of green in spring and summer. Peanuts grow exceptionally well in the soil of the vicinity. The town has a plant for cleaning goobers (peanuts).

Left 6.5 *m.* from Waverly on State 13 to the Homing Fork of Duck River, near HURRICANE MILLS; here is the MOUND GROUP OF HUMPHREYS COUNTY, on a village site of the stone-grave Indians.

There are two groups here, the Link site (the larger) and the Slayden site, about one mile apart. The Link site contains six mounds and several cemeteries. Although some of the largest mounds in the State are here, scientific examination of them has not yet been made. Excavation by the WPA at the Slayden site, during the early part of 1936, revealed traces of a small village. The structures were circular and from 20 feet to 40 feet in diameter. To construct one of these houses a bank of dirt about 2 feet high was first thrown up; posts were then driven into this bank to form a framework for thatched walls. The roofs were also thatched. The only openings were a small door, and a hole in the roof to let out the smoke. The floors were of hard packed clay and sloped downward toward the center. In a mound on the Slayden site were formerly two community houses, one round, the other square. As the latter contained an elevated fireplace or altar, it is believed to have been used for ceremonials. The other was probably used for governmental purposes. Though the village site showed two levels of occupancy, the temple mound showed three.

Remnants of crude furnishings have been found and in the firepit of the ceremonial house, charred corncobs. The shards unearthed indicate that some of the pottery of these people had loop handles and lip-like rings.

In the cemetery, about 100 yards from the village, were coffins made of stone slabs. Sometimes these tombs were tiered to hold six or more bodies.

No arrowheads were found among burials here. Pottery was not found in all the graves of the men, but in nearly all of the graves of women and children. The absence of the glass beads and other trinkets of the early trading days leads to the belief that this village belongs to the pre-Columbian period.

At 74 *m.* is a junction with a graveled road.

Right on this road 1 *m.* to DENVER (500 alt., 50 pop.), a little hill village. In 1879 an apparently well-to-do man, who called himself John Davis Howard, arrived here with his wife and son, bought a farm in Big Bottom and established himself as a grain and livestock dealer. He quickly became a leader in the community activities, active in church and charity work. Local people who visited Nashville often saw him in hotel lobbies and around the Democratic convention hall. His particular interest was in horse racing, and he even held races on his own farm, where he sometimes entertained visitors by showing his skill with a revolver; one of his favorite exhibitions was girdling a tree with evenly spaced bullet holes as he walked around it. After a year or so he disappeared. Only after Jesse James' death in 1882, at the hand of a treacherous member of his own band, did Denver people identify their quondam and popular prominent citizen as the reckless bandit.

Right 3 *m.* from Denver on a dirt road is JOHNSONVILLE, scene of one of Gen. Nathan Bedford Forrest's victories in the War between the States, when almost the entire town was burned. A barrack erected here for the Union soldiers is now a private home.

TROTTER'S LANDING, 79.2 *m.*, is by a toll bridge carrying US 70 across the Tennessee River *(50¢ for car and driver; 5¢ for each additional passenger).* The black soil in the low area produces fine crops of corn.

Between the river and Camden are (L) large gravel pits.

CAMDEN, 86.4 *m.* (370 alt., 955 pop.), seat of Benton County, is in a peanut- and sorghum-raising area. In September and October sorghum mills are busy along the roadsides. Smoke curls from wood clearings, and the lights from furnaces and lanterns glow far into the fall nights. The old-time horse-powered mills are still used, though steam mills are replacing them. The old mills can make from 75 to 125 gallons during a day and night cooking. After the cane has been brought to the mill, each man's crop is stacked in separate piles to await his "time to make." His team is hitched to the long pole (or tongue) of the mill and is driven in a circle to turn the wheels that crush the juice from the cane. This juice, looking like dirty green water, is caught in barrels and transferred to big flat pans over a brick or rock furnace. Some of the pans have gates; as the syrup reaches a certain stage ("thickens up"), the gate is opened to let it flow into the next pan. Foam rises as the liquid boils, and is skimmed off and thrown into a "skimming hole," dug at one side of the furnace. The "cooker" is kept very busy dipping the syrup from one pan to the other, or turning it through the gates, to keep it from scorching. The process requires great care; if the sorghum is not cooked exactly to the proper point, it will turn to sugar, become scorched, or have a raw taste.

Entire communities gather around the mills for "the cooking." From time to time the syrup is tasted with wooden paddles whittled out for that purpose. After the "making" is over, there is a big "get-together" and a candy pulling.

"They" (sorghum is never referred to as "it") are "larrupin good truck" for the table. "Lashings" or "slathers" (liberal quantities) of sorghum served with yellow butter on brown biscuits, batter cakes, or flapjacks is the "best eatin' ever intended to man." The bottom of a plate is covered with the thick "surrup," and butter mixed in thickly. The "mixtry" is eaten with a knife or sopped up with a biscuit. Sorghum seed, as well as molasses, is a source of income to the grower, and the cane itself is excellent stock feed.

An old stage road that crossed the Tennessee River at Reynoldsburg passed through Camden; US 70 follows it between Camden and Spring Creek in Madison County. This road was part of Glover's Trace, an important early route between Nashville and the Western District *(see TRANSPORTATION)*.

Right from Camden on Eva Road to NATHAN BEDFORD FORREST PARK *(picnic grounds and bridle paths)*, 9 *m.*, at Pilot Knob. The park, covering 86 acres, was established in 1929. Pilot Knob, a rocky hill commanding a view of the Tennessee River, was used by General Forrest on Nov. 4, 1864, as an observation post during the attack by cavalrymen on the Union fleet at Johnsonville, in which the Confederates destroyed large quantities of Union supplies. Large wooden cannon, seemingly camouflaged among the leaves, were successfully employed here by Forrest to give the appearance of extensive fortifications. The Federals, seeing the bristling artillery, withdrew after six boats had been sunk. A marble shaft commemorates the battle. Near the monument is a MUSEUM *(open 8-6 daily)* containing war relics. From Pilot Knob the Tennessee River is visible for many miles.

BRUCETON, 95.5 *m.* (414 alt., 1,112 pop.), is a smoky railroad-shop town established in 1922 for employees of the N. C. & St. L. R. R.

Right from Bruceton on a dirt road to the HOLLOW ROCK PRIMITIVE BAPTIST CHURCH, 15 *m.*, where an annual foot-washing and communion service is held *(first Sunday in May)*. Approximately 5,000 people witness these services. Only members are eligible to take part in the ceremonies; the men sit on one side of the church, the women on the other. Each member washes the foot of the member next to him. Hymns are sung without instrumental accompaniment, and the length of the services depends upon the number of clergymen present; each one preaches a sermon. Everyone brings his own dinner and eats it outside the church in picnic fashion.

HUNTINGDON, 106.7 *m.* (494 alt., 1,286 pop.), seat of Carroll County, is a shipping point for the Nancy Hall sweet potatoes, and for tomatoes, cotton, and small grain.

The white-marble COURTHOUSE (1936) is the third built in the county. The first was burned by Union soldiers in the War between the States and the second in 1930. One record book, saved from the fires, shows that Davy Crockett was paid a bounty here for wolf skins.

Right from Huntingdon on paved State 22 to McKENZIE, 12 *m.* (470 alt., 1,858 pop.), a railroad town at a junction point of the N. C. & St. L. and L. & N. Railroads. It also produces cheese. The town is the SITE OF BETHEL COLLEGE, a co-educational institution organized in 1842 by the Cumberland Presbyterian Church.

Among the records in the LIBRARY *(open 8-5 daily)* is a complete copy of the minutes of the Obion Presbytery since 1833.

Between Huntingdon and Jackson is one of the finest quail-hunting regions in the South. Fox, raccoon, and opossum are found in great numbers.

At 127.5 *m.* is junction (L) with State 100 *(see Tour 12B)*.

JACKSON, 142.8 *m.* (412 alt., 22,172 pop.) *(see JACKSON)*.

Points of Interest: Union University, Grave of Casey Jones, Lane College, and others.

Jackson is at the junction with US 45 *(see Tour 10)*.

At 144.5 *m.* is the junction with a dirt road.

Left on this road is DENMARK, 9 *m.;* R. here 3 *m.* on a dirt road to the JOHN A. MURRELL HOME. Murrell was reputed to be the organizer of a widespread Mystic Brotherhood of criminals. Whether there was such an organization or not,

OPOSSUM

he did lead a band of cutthroats and thieves that terrorized the lower Mississippi Valley between 1825 and 1834. "It is a mistake to compare him with such desperadoes as Jesse James," wrote Mark Twain in *Life on the Mississippi.* "Murrell was his equal in boldness, in pluck, in rapacity; in cruelty, brutality . . . and much his superior in larger aspects."

Murrell, who was born in 1804, was the son of Mom Murrell, who kept a combination tavern, brothel, and thieves' market near Columbia, Tennessee. He was a skilled thief by the time he was ten, and graduated in his early 'teens to highway robbery and murder under the guidance of Harry Cranshaw, an ex-pirate, who was one of his mother's paramours. The two roamed the Natchez Trace and nearby sections of Tennessee and Alabama for several years. They shot wayfarers from ambush, stripped the bodies to the skin, and threw them in convenient ravines or swamp holes. Mom Murrell disposed of their loot.

Murrell soon outgrew Cranshaw and cast him off. From itinerant lecturers, book peddlers, and assorted quacks, met during his wanderings, he absorbed a suave fluency and a kind of polite education. From evangelists he acquired unction and the art of preaching thunderous sermons full of the popular brand of hellfire and damnation. He was often invited to preach in churches and brush-arbor camp meetings. Since he invariably shot his victims, no one suspected the true reason for his constant shuttling back and forth along the Trace. Slight and dapper, courteous and flowery of speech, Brother Murrell was welcomed everywhere in the homes, churches, and taverns between Nashville and Natchez as a young gentleman of means and piety.

The large stone house that he built here served as his base of operations. Members of his family held down the place in his absence, and there is the usual firmly fixed legend that he buried huge treasures—estimated at a million dollars in gold—nearby. As his ambition grew and he began gathering a following of thugs, the stone house was useful as a hide-out and way station. In the deep cellar stolen Negroes were hidden until the hue-and-cry for them had died.

The so-called Mystic Brotherhood, at first simply a Negro- and horse-stealing outfit, became so powerful that Murrell determined to use it as a nucleus for a pretended insurrection of slaves to blackmail plantation owners. According to one sensational reporter the Brotherhood seems to have been in some respects strikingly like the Ku Klux Klan, for which the accounts of it may have set precedent. Its posts held shrouded midnight gatherings, and the members swore penny-dreadful oaths of fealty, sealed with their own blood. Members were said to be in every hamlet and town along the Trace and the Lower Mississippi. Presently Murrell's house at Denmark was too small for the gang's gatherings. Headquarters was shifted to an Arkansas swamp clearing about fifty miles upriver from Memphis.

In January 1834 Murrell brought a new recruit to the swamp hide-out, a young man named Virgil Stewart. Stewart, according to his own account, had set out to expose Murrell because of the gang's theft of some slaves belonging to his foster father, though some of the accounts declare that Stewart was merely a disgruntled member of the gang. At any rate, Stewart learned the secrets of the outlaws, slipped away from the hideout, and led a posse which captured Murrell and some of his ringleaders.

According to Stewart's sensational book, a plan for an insurrection had been worked out. Throughout the Mid-South slaves were to be secretly armed and trained. On Christmas Day 1835, the Brotherhood was to lead them in a general massacre of the whites. Stewart said Murrell planned to set up the independent western state and that he had prepared for simultaneous attacks on Memphis, Natchez, and New Orleans.

While Murrell was awaiting trial at Jackson, Tennessee, the gang disintegrated. An uprising that broke out at Natchez on the Fourth of July was popularly believed to be the work of Murrell's followers; its leaders were lynched. Later in the month Murrell was tried and sentenced to ten years in the State penitentiary, which he served. For a few years after his release in 1844 he lived in Pikeville, Bledsoe County, working as a blacksmith and retaining his ability to make friends in spite of his record. He died of tuberculosis contracted in prison.

HUNTERSVILLE, 152.8 *m.*, is a country village settled long ago by a group of men whose love of hunting was such that they named the place Huntersville. Fox hunting is still a favorite sport, and it is from this village that some of the chases of the National Foxhunters Association started in 1934 and 1937 *(see JACKSON)*.

BROWNSVILLE, 169.5 *m.* (344 alt., 3,204 pop.), seat of Haywood County, is one of the oldest towns in West Tennessee. It has grown because of the productivity of the cotton lands of the Hatchie River. A distinctive activity is the making of Old Virginia Brunswick Stew. For many years Brunswick stew suppers, with squirrel as a meat base, have been held in Haywood County, usually around the small lakes or in clubhouses of the river bottoms.

In the county are approximately 26,000 people, of whom 18,000 are Negroes. On an average Saturday afternoon probably a third of the county's Negroes—sharecroppers and tenant farmers—fill Wall Street, Brownsville's Negro business district, and overflow into the courthouse square. Catfish restaurants are crowded.

The brass band of the Haywood County Training School for Negroes has won honors at college demonstrations and strawberry and cotton festivals throughout the mid-South.

Before emancipation, Haywood and Fayette Counties had larger proportions of slaves than any other counties in the State. Brownsville was a plantation county seat and grew not only because it was a court center but also because of the members of commissaries and mercantile establishments.

Tabernacle Community Revivals are usually held in July or August in Haywood County. People drive in from other communities and from other States and camp together in the woods. A large tent is raised for the preaching, which continues for a week or more. Large dinners are served daily and between the services there is much visiting and gossip. The meetings had their origin long ago. In 1826 a little tabernacle, called New Hope, was built in the forest six miles northeast of Brownsville as a church and a schoolhouse. Howell Taylor, a prominent Methodist preacher of Virginia, came here with his five sons; he changed the name of New Hope to Tabernacle. For more than a century Tabernacle was the meeting place of the descendants of the prolific Taylor family, and from these meetings evolved the Tabernacle Community Revivals.

West of Brownsville the road crosses the Hatchie River bottoms, the wildest swamp country of West Tennessee. Drain Lake R., Spring Lake L., and many other lakes and sloughs abound with bigmouthed black bass which lurk among the cypress knees. Verging the river is a forest, the Big Hatchie country—extending from near the Tennessee River by the Alabama Line up to the Reelfoot Lake area *(see Tour 10)*. The Big Hatchie was set aside as a game preserve by the Chickasaw to insure their food supply. They regarded this as the best hunting and fishing ground in the South. When the white men came in the late eighteenth and early nineteenth centuries, the Indians were horrified by the wagonloads of wild turkey they carried away. In a wooded area, called Deer

Park, the whites slaughtered hundreds of deer. Bears were killed in like numbers. While many of the formerly numerous animals are now extinct here, wild turkey and deer are increasing in number again; and in the almost impenetrable growth of cypress, water oak, beech, vines, and brush there are still many bobcats, raccoons, opossums, and wild hogs. The hogs, descendants of strays from the farms, live on acorns shed by the old oaks.

Upland from this area are fields and copses where quail are found in large coveys. Weasel, otter, mink, and marten live along the creeks.

MASON, 191.5 *m.* (307 alt., 340 pop.), is a village of a few scattered stores and homes, on the edge of the Hatchie River bottoms.

Right from Mason on an unimproved county road to OLD TRINITY CHURCH, 0.7 *m.*,—Trinity in the Fields—built in 1847. A pilgrimage is made to this church each summer by former members and their descendants.

At 213 *m.* is the junction with US 64 *(see Tour 13)*, which unites with US 70 between this point and Memphis, with four-lane paving.

US 70 crosses Wolf River, 217 *m.,* not far north of the former NASHOBA, a plantation established in 1827 by Frances Wright (1795–1852). Miss Wright was a wealthy young Scottish orphan, reared in liberal and freethinking circles, who made her first visit to America in 1818 to witness the radical product of revolution and returned to the British Isles to write a glowing account of a democratic Utopia, *Views of Society and Manners in America* (1821). When she returned in 1824 she was greeted warmly as one of the very few Europeans who had spoken or written with much approval of the new United States. By this time, however, she was beginning to see some flaws in the American system, and she was particularly disturbed by the institution of slavery. Various people of importance, including Jefferson, discussed the problems and possible solutions with her. During her travels she visited several communities where cooperative living was being tried out—notably the Owen colony in Indiana. By 1827 she had brought together a group of people sympathetic with her views on slavery and had purchased the large plantation here on which "Negro slaves should be educated and upraised to a level with the whites, and thus prepared for freedom; and to set an example which if carried out, would eventually abolish slavery in the Southern States; also to make a home for good and great men and women of all countries, who might here sympathize with each other in their love and labor for humanity."

Had Frances Wright been able to stay in Tennessee and direct the experiment herself it might have had a longer life; but she had to return to Scotland shortly after she had brought several slave families to this place and had started clearance of the land. She was exceedingly unfortunate in her choice of a manager, a member of the Owen community whose enthusiasm for pure democracy was much greater than his administrative ability and his understanding of the temper of the times. The reports he sent back to the sponsoring committee in New York and New England—particularly those on his experiments with free love and interracial relations—soon alienated many whose help Frances Wright had labored to obtain. In less than three years Miss Wright abandoned the plantation and made arrangements to ship her slaves to the West Indies.

One curious product of Nashoba was *Domestic Manners of the Americans* (1832), by Mrs. Frances Trollope. Soon after she returned to Great Britain, Frances Wright met Mrs. Trollope, a widow of limited means, who was delighted and convinced by Miss Wright's descriptions of her new estate and the low cost of living there. In a short time she was on her way to Nashoba, by way of New Orleans, with her children. The voyage was difficult and she was shocked by the rudeness of frontier life and manners along the Mississippi; but she was completely unprepared for the discomforts and crudeness of Nashoba under the management of the impractical young man from the Owen colony. Her stay was brief. Raging over the waste of her small capital, she traveled up the Mississippi and Ohio Rivers and overland to the Atlantic coast, where she took passage for England. Her book on America, fairer than most Americans of the day would admit, contained caustic comments on the subject indicated by the title and was long bitterly resented on this side of the Atlantic.

MEMPHIS, 229 *m.* (280 alt., 253,143 pop.) *(see MEMPHIS).*

Points of Interest: Beale Street, Overton Park and Zoo, College of the Mississippi Valley, and others.

Memphis is at the junction with US 51 *(see Tour 11).*

Tour 12A

Crossville—Sparta—McMinnville—Murfreesboro; 98.5 m. US 70A.

Nashville, Chattanooga & St. Louis Ry. parallels route between Bon Air and McMinnville.
Paved roadbed.
Accommodations chiefly in larger towns.

For 22 miles west of Crossville US 70A crosses the tablelands of the Cumberland Plateau. The timber has been cut over and the farms are poor. Between Bon Air and Sparta the route winds down into the Highland Rim with a descent of 800 feet in 3 miles. At various points are distant views of wall-like mountains, and valleys with green pasture lands. Rough hills are covered with dense growths of trees, shrubs, and wild flowers. Dogwood and redbud blossom abundantly here in the spring. West of the plateau the route runs through a fertile region for approximately 50 miles before reaching the hill country. Between Centertown

RESTING

and Woodbury the road traverses the western edge of the Highland Rim, with its deep narrow hollows. At Woodbury the highway descends from the Highland Rim into the Central Basin, the bowl-like center of Middle Tennessee formed by the Highland Rim. Here livestock breeding is one of the leading commercial activities.

US 70A branches west from US 70 *(see Tour 12)* at CROSSVILLE, 0 *m.* (1,881 alt., 1,125 pop.) *(see Tour 12),* and descends to the flatland where the farming people earn cash by the sale of crossties, wild blackberries, huckleberries, and the furs of squirrels, raccoons, opossums, and rabbits. The meat of these animals constitutes much of their food supply.

Coon dogs are standard household equipment. The dogs are bright yellow, snuff-brown, or black-and-tan, long-eared, and sad-eyed. During the day they loll under the floor of the cabins and lazily scratch at colonies of fleas. At command they will rush into gardens or cornfields to chase out chickens or to lead pigs by their ears to the pens. These dogs, with short names like Drum, Ring, Gum, Rip, Biff, and the like, are the pride of their owners, who think the coon dog should replace the American eagle.

Raccoon and opossum hunts take place at night in the fall and winter. When the dogs are called for the hunt, they become very alert, and lead the hunters deep into the woods, calling mournfully as they pick up a trail. Having treed a 'possum or 'coon, they roar and leap around the tree trunk until the hunters arrive to "shine" the animal with a flashlight. Several methods are used in making the catch; one is to climb the tree and shake the quarry from the limb; another is to cut off the limb; a third is to cut down the tree; and the last is to shoot the animal from its perch. When the furry ball falls to the ground, the dogs pounce on it and hold it until it is retrieved by the hunters. A 'possum usually "sulls" (turns on its side and plays dead). If not watched closely, it will jump up and "high step" into the bushes, tail held over its back. An unwounded 'coon turns on its back and puts up a desperate fight; it is usually a match for two dogs. Many times the 'coon escapes and takes to water, if a stream is near; it is an expert swimmer and will rest on driftwood and logs. When a dog swims near, the 'coon reaches out one paw, or hand, and pushes the dog's head under water. These duckings will continue until the dog stays under, unless rescued by its master.

'Possums and 'coons are also found in hollow logs and are prodded, chased, or smoked out.

The captured animals are placed in tow (gunny) sacks alive, and then the hunters sit by lantern light to rest, smoke, drink corn, and tell stories.

The best way to kill a 'possum is to place a stick of stovewood on its neck, stand with one foot on each end of the stick, take the animal by the tail and give a vigorous pull. There will be a sharp crack, and the 'possum's neck is broken.

Roast or baked 'coon is a delicacy. Roasted 'possum with sweet potatoes is a prime Tennessee dish. 'Possum is even better barbecued, for it is a greasy animal that lives on persimmons and carrion. In some sections of the State 'possum and 'taters are canned.

In PLEASANT HILL, 11 *m.* (1,902 alt., 165 pop.), is PLEASANT HILL ACADEMY, established about 1875 for the education of mountain children. The large campus is along the highway. Amos Wightman and his wife, of Illinois, founded the academy and sought aid from the American Missionary Association, which did not send a teacher until 1887. Mrs. Wightman recommended that a preacher be sent also, and the Reverend Benjamin Dodge was appointed. Father Dodge, as he was called, died in 1897.

The ADMINISTRATION BUILDING has 20 large dormers on its mansard roof.

ROBERT HALL, a new dormitory for boys, and HOPKINS HALL, for classrooms, have been built recently. The old assembly hall, now WOODBURY CHAPEL, houses several elementary classes. PIONEER HALL, the oldest dormitory, is now used for administrative purposes and holds the library of 6,000 volumes.

UPLANDS CUMBERLAND MOUNTAIN SANATORIUM, 11.5 *m.* (1,000 alt.) is a 50-bed hospital that serves the scattered population in this mountain region. It is the only institution that maintains free beds for tubercular patients in rural Tennessee. Gifts and some pay-cases make free work possible. The hospital was established privately as a social-service venture.

Out-clinics are held in isolated communties. Often the dispensary is merely one room in a little cabin in an oakwood clearing. On clinic day patients straggle in over mountain trails on foot and on muleback. Since money is scarce among these people they pay in kind—wild grapes or berries, green beans, pokes of popcorn, and buckets of sorghum.

At 14.9 *m.* is the junction with an improved dirt road.

Left on this road is CLIFTY, 8 *m.* (1,826 alt., 1,582 pop.), a town about a mile square. The site was formerly in Cumberland County, but when the Tennessee Products Corporation began mining operations here, it bought the land and added it to its other White County holdings. In recent years an agreement has been reached by the two counties, and the county line now runs through the center of town.

At 20.3 *m.* is DEROSSETT (1,500 alt., 200 pop.), a coal-mining town.

Right from DeRossett on a dirt road is RAVENSCROFT (1,590 alt., 626 pop.), 7 *m.,* until 1936 the headquarters for operations of the Tennessee Products Corporation, which manufactures coal-tar products. In the distillation plant acetic acid, vinegar, and alcohol were produced. The company operated the only shaft mine in the State here. When the plant and mine were closed, many families of DeRossett, Ravenscroft, and Bon Air were thrown out of work and moved to the cities to find jobs.

At 20.5 *m.* is the junction with a dirt road.

Left on this road to CAMP BON AIR *(private),* 2 *m.* by BON AIR LAKE *(public).*

BON AIR, 21.6 *m.* was one of the Tennessee Products Corporation's coal-mining towns.

At 22.8 *m.* (R) is the BON AIR SURVEYING CAMP of the Vanderbilt University School of Engineering, a 50-acre tract on the ridge of the Cumberlands. After the freshman year all Vanderbilt engineering students are required to spend one month each summer here. Field practice in surveying is carried on.

SUNSET ROCK (L), 23.2 *m.* is a bluff 75 feet above the highway, on the western escarpment of the Cumberland Plateau. From this height on clear days the Central Basin is visible for 50 miles.

The HUGH LOWERY MEMORIAL SPRING (L), 23.5 *m.,* was named for a revenue officer who was killed in a raid in this section.

ROCK HOUSE (R), 24.8 *m.,* was built about 1812 and became a stopping place on the Knoxville-Nashville stage road, completed in 1815. This stone cabin has windows and doors only in the front.

SPARTA, 29.4 *m.* (1,000 alt., 2,211 pop.), seat of White County, was named for ancient Sparta. In the town are a handle and spoke factory, silk mills, several feed mills, hardwood lumberyards, and a lime kiln.

At Sparta are the junctions with State 42 *(see Tour 16)* and State 26.

Right on State 26 to (L) CLARK'S WATER MILL AND ANDERSON SWIMMING POOL *(admission 25¢),* 0.5 *m.,* on Town Creek. The mill wheel still runs. The pool is popular in the spring and summer.

A stone marker at 6.3 *m.* is at the junction with the Old Kentucky Road (graveled), over which cattle and hogs were driven from the Cumberland Plateau to the markets of Lexington, Louisville, and Cincinnati.

CASSVILLE, 8.3 *m.* (928 alt., 31 pop.), on State 26 is a village with two stores. The houses along the highway are of various kinds; brick and painted-frame houses stand next to log cabins of tenant farmers, where 'coon and ground-hog skins dry on walls. The cabins have one and two rooms, the latter with open hallways, or dog-trots, between them, and crude mud-plastered or mortared chimneys.

The hill country is reached at 15.2 *m.* In some places the hillsides have a grade of 40 degrees.

The highway crosses Caney Fork River, 17 *m.,* on a bridge. This river is a good stream for fishing.

SMITHVILLE AIRPORT (R), 22.4 *m.,* is an emergency landing field.

SMITHVILLE, 23.7 *m.* (1,052 alt., 700 pop.), is the seat of DeKalb County, which was named for Johann DeKalb, a Bavarian general who fought for the American Colonies during the Revolution.

The town provided the locale for Ed Bell's book, *Fish on the Steeple,* whose title was suggested by the unusual design of the weather vane on the steeple of the CHRISTIAN CHURCH, on the corner of West Main St. and Short Mountain Road, two blocks from the courthouse.

"The people of Smithville," Bell wrote, "are neither hill billies nor mountaineers. They are big men as a rule who breed in swarms. They talk unhurriedly, with much cursing and healthy laughter. They laugh at their own jokes, dread cyclones which never come over the mountains, wear neckties on Sunday, are afraid of people who doubt the Bible and God, and bathe regularly in the summer because it feels good. They work hard far into their old age.

"About the only money to be made is in fruit trees, lumber and whisky, and never a great deal. Once the plateau was too poor and lonely for the Indians: they crossed it quickly and only when they had to. But later outlaws, and still later the bushwhacking clans of the Civil War, found sanctuary there. And many of today's big men are their sons and grandsons."

Left from Smithville 0.5 *m.* on State 56 to FLATWOODS NURSERIES where fruit trees, evergreens, and shrubs especially suited to the yellowish, light soil of this section are grown. At 7 *m.* is SEVEN SPRINGS, a health resort, on the rim of the Cumberlands near the Caney Fork River. The springs produce 7 kinds of mineral water,—red, white, and black sulphur, iron, freestone, magnesia, and lithia.

On State 26 is LIBERTY, 35.4 *m.* (650 alt., 500 pop.), settled 1797. The fishing in Smith Fork Creek is good.

ALEXANDRIA, 43 *m.* (650 alt., 786 pop.), is the scene of the DeKalb County Fair, established in 1856. This fair, advertised as the "Grandpa Fair of the South" *(last days of August and first days of September),* features agricultural exhibitions and livestock. One of the chief attractions is the mule show. Although the buildings on the grounds have been badly damaged on two occasions by floods and tornadoes, the fair has never failed to open.

WATERTOWN, 49.5 *m.* (651 alt., 928 pop.), in the rich valley of Round Lick Creek, is the terminus of the old toll road to Smithville, over which a stagecoach line was operated for many years.

At 62 *m.* is LEBANON, (512 alt., 4,658 pop.) *(see Tour 12),* at the junction with US 70 *(see Tour 12).*

In the vicinity of DOYLE, 35.5 *m.* (983 alt., 400 pop.), are fishing camps of the Caney Fork River.

At 35.7 *m.* is the junction with State 111.

Left on State 111 is SPENCER, 9.2 *m.* (1,600 alt., 400 pop.), seat of Van Buren County, in the heart of the Cumberland Plateau. No railroad runs through the county, and until recent years the roads were bad. The town was named for Thomas Sharpe Spencer, a long hunter, who was killed near here.

The county was named for Martin Van Buren, who was President at the time it was organized (1840).

When the first settlers came to this region about 1830, they turned their sheep and cattle loose to range in the mountains. All were owned in common. If a person needed meat, he trailed down a cow and killed it.

Left from Spencer on State 30, 11.5 *m.,* into FALLS CREEK FALLS PARK *(see Tour 15).*

At 36.5 *m.* on US 70A is a junction with a well-marked graveled road.

Right on this road to the 20-acre SUMMER CAMP OF THE FUTURE FARMERS OF TENNESSEE (July to September), 1 *m.,* with barracks for 200 boys. The roster is changed completely every two weeks. At the end of the summer the camp is used for a one-week conference of State school superintendents.

At 40.9 *m.* on US 70A is QUEBECK, on the banks of Caney Fork River.

Right from Quebeck on a graveled road to HY-LAKE, 1 *m.,* a summer camp for boys.

At 44.5 *m.* on US 70A is the junction with a graveled road.

Right on this road to ROCK ISLAND, 0.3 *m.* (925 alt., 100 pop.), a fishing resort on the banks of Caney Fork River *(hotel, tourist camps, furnished cabins).* CAMP OVERTON and the Y.M.C.A. and Y.W.C.A. summer camps for boys and girls are here. A narrow trail follows the bank of the river beneath a high cliff to the GREAT FALLS HYDROELECTRIC PLANT AND DAM, on the Caney Fork River near its confluence with the Collins and Rocky Rivers. The large reservoir, walled by great bluffs, is popular among fishermen. Electricity generated at this plant is distributed to Nashville and other Middle Tennessee towns.

At McMINNVILLE, 57.6 *m.* (1,038 alt., 3,914 pop.) *(see Tour 16)* is the junction with State 42 *(see Tour 16).*

West of McMinnville US 70A traverses a level stretch of farming country for about 10 miles before it winds through the hills of the Highland Rim and into the Central Basin.

Because of their isolation, the early settlers of the Cumberland Plateau had to rely on handmade implements and furniture. Handicrafts have survived and approximately 500 families are now engaged in basket weaving though the returns are small. Success in the craft is dependent upon the weaver's knowledge of trees. White oak is one of the best woods. After the tree has been felled, it is sawed into logs that are cut into slats. The slats are made into splits for weaving.

CENTERTOWN, 67.3 *m.,* consists of a dozen houses along the highway. West of Centertown the country is extremely rugged, and the highway winds along the backbone of the ridges. The sides of the hills are generally under cultivation. The flat land on the tops of the hills is covered with timber. At the bottom of deep hollows, flanking the road, are occasional farmhouses.

The hill suddenly descends from the Highland Rim into the Central Basin at 78 *m.*

WOODBURY, 79.4 *m.* (714 alt., 502 pop.), seat of Cannon County, is by Stone's River. The old stores contrast with the modern courthouse in the center of the square. The steep hillsides on the north side of the square are cultivated, but the south-side hills are covered with houses. The town was named for Levi Woodbury, Secretary of the Navy under President Andrew Jackson. When Cannon County was organized in 1836, it was named for Newton Cannon, Governor of Tennessee from 1835 to 1839.

The western half of the county is in the Central Basin, and the eastern half in the Highland Rim. Between spurs of the Cumberland Mountains, which extend along the rim, are numerous small valleys. The countryside is dotted with truck farms.

This region was occupied by the Shawnee before their removal to the Ohio country. The Black Fox Trail bisected it. During the War between

RURAL SHOPPING CENTER, WOODBURY

the States, numerous skirmishes occurred near here. Gen. Nathan Bedford Forrest, ubiquitous Confederate cavalry leader, encamped here before his assault on Murfreesboro.

READYVILLE, 86 *m.* (715 alt., 125 pop.), is in a section that produces wheat, fruit, and vegetables.

West of Readyville the highway gradually passes from the foothills of the Highland Rim. The topsoil has washed away and left acres of large flat stones exposed. Where the soil is deep enough to permit cultivation, good crops are produced.

At MUFREESBORO, 98.5 *m.* (573 alt., 8,000 pop.) *(see Tour 8)*, are the junctions with US 41 *(see Tour 8)* and US 241 *(see Tour 8A)*.

Tour 12B

Junction with US 70—Centerville—Linden—Lexington—Junction with US 70; 131.9 *m.* State 100 and State 20.

Paved roadbed.
Limited accommodations.

State 100 branches southwest from US 70 *(see Tour 12)*, 0 *m.*, 7 miles west of Nashville, at what is locally known as "101," and runs through a hilly countryside. American Airlines planes follow the route, and after dark the beams of the flashing beacons are constantly visible.

CHEEKWOOD *(private)*, 0.6 *m.*, is on a wooded ridge (L); the two-story stone house, of hybrid design, is elaborate. The grounds, with terraced gardens, boxwoods, pools, and rock gardens, are among the most extensive near Nashville.

PERCY WARNER PARK, 1.7 *m.*, covers 3,500 acres of field and woods in the Harpeth Hills; it has winding roads and bridle paths, a steeplechase course, hiking trails, picnic grounds, golf course, and landscaped terraces. Much of the land was presented to the city of Nashville by Luke Lea and Edwin Warner, and the park was named in honor of Percy Warner, Lea's father-in-law. Adjoining the park on the west is a smaller tract, the Edwin Warner Park. Large areas in the parks have been set aside for the preservation of wild life and wild flowers, trees and shrubs. Twenty-five acres are planted with irises.

For the next few miles the highway parallels the park (L), and at 3.7 *m.* is another gateway.

The HARPETH RIVER, crossed at 4.8 *m.*, is not navigable now, but in the days of the flatboats it was used during high water for transporting products of the nearby plantations.

LINTON, 11.4 *m.* (325 alt., 150 pop.), is an agricultural hamlet at the junction with a graveled road.

Left on this road to CLEARWATER BEACH *(admission 25¢, swimming, cabins)*, 1 *m.*, at the base of a cliff on the South Harpeth River. Here is a large clubhouse *(open during summer)*.

Southwest of this point the route passes through a desolate region. In the spring, however, the country is picturesque, with old seesaw rail fences, rocky wooded hills, and an occasional log cabin among the ravines. Dogwood, azalea, and redbud punctuate the forest green with white and red in the spring.

At 33 *m.* is the junction with State 46.

Right on State 46 to BON AQUA, 2.2 *m.*, a summer resort with mineral springs and a rustic hotel.

At 35.2 *m.* is the junction with a dirt road.

Right on this road to WRIGLEY, 1 *m.,* in a privately owned forest of about 15,000 acres of hardwood timber, and a TENNESSEE PRODUCTS CORPORATION PLANT *(open 8 to 4 weekdays).* The furnace is on the site of the first plant, established in 1880. Co-ordinated with the furnace is a wood-distillation plant capable of carbonizing 200 cords of hardwood daily and of supplying fuel to the blast furnaces. Charcoal, wood oils, wood pitch, acetate of lime, and wood alcohol are made here.

CENTERVILLE, 46.8 *m.* (635 alt., 943 pop.), is a trade town among the farm lands of the Duck River. Phosphate mining is the leading industrial activity in the region. The valleys are fertile, but the ridges are for the most part flinty and underlaid with shale.

Left from Centerville on a graveled road to INDIAN CREEK, 3 *m.* According to a local legend, an Indian warrior was exiled from his tribe because he insisted on marrying the chief's daughter against her father's wishes.

He settled on the banks of what is now Indian Creek, built a wigwam in a secluded hollow, and made plans to return to the tribe and carry away the girl he desired. With the assistance of a friend, he was successful. Several years later a wandering band of Indians from the same tribe discovered the hidden lodge, the missing daughter of the chief, her husband, and two little boys. The chief and a band of warriors swooped down upon the members of the family, killed them, and destroyed the lodge. Not long afterward, according to the story, white hunters saw a milk-white doe and two fawns wandering in the hollow. The most skillful marksmen were unsuccessful in trying to kill them. Thereafter the pioneers, believing that this doe and her young were the spirits of the chief's daughter and her children, allowed them to roam unmolested.

At 53.9 *m.* on State 100 is the junction with State 48.

Left on State 48 to HOHENWALD (German, *high forest*), 19.9 *m.* (942 alt., 975 pop.), so named by its Swiss settlers because of its altitude in a dense wilderness. The industrious inhabitants have made it a prosperous village. Swiss embroidery, a craft of the district, has become one of the chief products. Vegetable canning is another local industry.

Left from Hohenwald 6 *m.* on State 20 to MERIWETHER LEWIS NATIONAL PARK AND MONUMENT *(see Tour 7B).*

West of this point the route passes through a dense forest.

LINDEN, 76.4 *m.* (350 alt., 530 pop.), seat of Perry County, is a trade town of farmers at the junction with State 20, which unites with State 100.

The ALVIN C. YORK MEMORIAL BRIDGE, 88 *m.,* carries the road across the Tennessee River *(50¢ for car and driver; 5¢ for each additional passenger).* Here State 100 branches L.; R. on State 20.

PARSONS, 94.1 *m.* (468 alt., 915 pop.), on State 20, has several gravel quarries and, nearby, a small silica grinding plant and phosphate mines, now inactive.

Left from Parsons on State 69 is DECATURVILLE, 3 *m.,* named for Commodore Stephen Decatur, who served in the Tripolitan War and the War of 1812.

1. Right from Decaturville on Beacon Road, graveled, to the RED CAMPGROUND, 4 *m.,* formerly a meeting place of the Cumberland Presbyterian Church. A small log church, built in 1827, still clings to the ledge of a steep hill. There is a story that John A. Murrell *(see Tour 12),* the land pirate, attended meetings here, dressed in a long-tailed frock coat, mingled with the crowd and helped with the services, shortly after he had made a daring raid on the Natchez Trace.

2. Left from Decaturville on State 69 is OLD CENTER, 10 *m.,* built about 1830

on a popular campground. The old building, now a church, is about 50 feet square and built of heavy poplar logs, mortised together into solid walls that have been weatherboarded.

3. Left from Decaturville on Fisher's Landing Road to BROWNSPORT FURNACE, 11 *m.,* where iron was mined and smelted until 1878. The property extended for 15 miles along the Tennessee River in a region known as the "Coalings" because of the charcoal used in smelting iron.

DARDEN, 99.9 *m.* (210 pop.), was named for Mills Darden, sometimes called Miles, a giant of Tennessee. Darden is said to have been 8 feet 5 inches tall but was so sensitive about his size that he would never consent to be weighed. He was born in Virginia in 1799, came to Henderson County when he was a child, and lived in the vicinity until his death in 1857. A local tailor made a suit for him that was so large that the three largest men in the county buttoned themselves into the coat at the same time. Darden, it is said, continued to grow as long as he lived. He died when rolls of fat closed his windpipe. A section of the wall of his house had to be removed when he was brought out for burial. A HOLINESS CHURCH is here, belonging to a sect strong throughout the section. Believers refuse medical care and devout adherents, to demonstrate their faith, have submitted themselves to the bites of poisonous snakes.

CHESTERFIELD, 102.7 *m.* (392 alt., 210 pop.), is a scattering of wooden and brick stopes and two churches along the highway. The BEECH BAPTIST CHURCH alternates with neighboring churches in holding what are called Fifth Sunday Meetings, survivals of the old all-day church services. Prof. S. Henry Essary, originator of the "Tennessee 76" lespedeza, is buried in the churchyard.

At 105 *m.* (L) is AIRWAY BEACON LIGHT AND EMERGENCY AIRPORT.

LEXINGTON, 110.4 *m.* (468 alt., 1,823 pop.), was named for Lexington, Mass. The Battle of Parker's Crossroads, a 12-hour engagement, was fought near here in 1863. During the skirmish Bob Ingersoll, then a colonel in the Federal Army, was captured by a troop of General Forrest's cavalry.

The Henderson County Singing Association holds all-day meetings monthly, using part-song music with shaped-notes instead of the conventional notation.

At Lexington is a junction with State 22.

Right on State 22 to NATCHEZ TRACE FOREST STATE PARK, 9 *m.,* a recreational area and wildlife sanctuary. There are picnic grounds, overnight cabins, and three artificial lakes with boathouses and beaches.

Left from Lexington on the well-marked, graveled, Lexington-Saltillo Road to the SARDIS MODEL COMMUNITY, 18 *m.,* a joint demonstration of the TVA, the University of Tennessee Extension Department, and the Sardis Farm School. A five-year crop-rotation plan has been developed for the 150 farms in the area, terracing machinery purchased, farm buildings remodeled, and lawns and orchards improved. This enterprise had its inception in the agricultural night classes conducted by Ben Douglas, a teacher in the vocational high schools created by the Smith-Hughes Act of 1917. One of the instructors employed under the act conceived the idea. The experiment was the first of its kind in the State.

At 131.9 *m.* is the junction with US 70 *(see Tour 12),* 15.3 miles from Jackson.

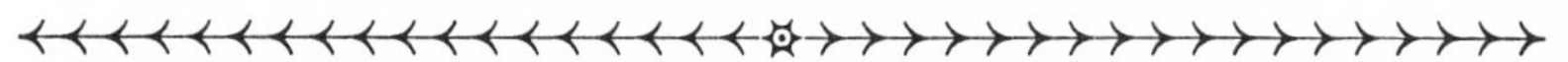

Tour 13

(Murphy, N. C.)—Cleveland—Chattanooga—Winchester—Pulaski—Selmer—Bolivar—Junction with US 70; US 64.
North Carolina Line to Junction with US 70, 383.5 m.

Southern Ry. parallels route between Cleveland and Chattanooga.
Paved roadbed.
All types of accommodations in the large towns.

US 64, traversing the entire length of Tennessee, roughly follows the southern boundary. It passes through the Appalachians and Copper Basin, through the Cherokee National Forest, over the Cumberland Mountains, and crosses the fertile farm land of Middle Tennessee, the southern plateau of West Tennessee, and the Mississippi River at Memphis.

Section a. NORTH CAROLINA LINE *to* CHATTANOOGA; *71.7 m.*

This section of US 64 runs through the Cherokee National Forest, on both sides of the North Carolina Line, 0 *m.,* which is crossed 24 miles west of Murphy, N. C.

ISABELLA, 2.2 *m.* (1,467 alt., 850 pop.), is one of three places in the large Copper Basin where copper mining and smelting are carried on.

At 4.7 *m.* is the junction with State 40, concrete paved.

Left on State 40 is COPPERHILL, 3 *m.* (1,480 alt., 1,102 pop.), whose name reveals the reason for its existence.

At 4.8 *m.* on US 64 is the junction with State 40.

Right on State 40 is DUCKTOWN, 0.5 *m.* (1,558 alt., 1,526 pop.). The huge smelter in this copper settlement stands on a hill; ramshackle houses are huddled below the smelter's giant walls. Deep gullies extend into the village from the surrounding badlands.

All through this area, and particularly around the smelting towns are barren denuded hills, a result of early smelting operations, which carried the sulphur fumes high into the air. Eventually a 400-foot chimney was built on smelters high on the mountains, but much vegetation had already been destroyed by the gases. Sulphuric acid is now an important by-product of copper smelting, and the chimneys are no longer needed. The copper deposits discovered in 1847 are in an area six miles long and four miles wide, with the richest lodes in the small intermountain plateau about 1,800 feet above sea level. The ore lies in fissure veins from a few feet to 300 feet wide; it has been mined to a vertical depth of nearly 1,600 feet. Operations have been carried on here almost continuously since the mines were opened. Small amounts of silver and gold are also taken out of the ore as a by-product of the smelting.

TENNESSEE'S LARGEST PECAN TREE—NATCHEZ TRACE FOREST

In early days the copper ore was transported in wagons to Cleveland, Tenn., and thence shipped by rail to New York.

From a high bluff at 9.7 *m.* above the beautiful Ocoee River, a wide panorama is unfolded.

US 64 crosses the eastern boundary, 10.7 *m.,* of the CHEROKEE NATIONAL FOREST, and follows the Ocoee River for 16 miles. Lakes have been formed in the river by the dams of the Tennessee Electric Power Company.

At the OCOEE PLANT NO. 2 DAM, 14.3 *m.,* the river is diverted through a wooden flume 11 feet deep and 14 feet wide. The water returns to its bed five miles downstream by the power plant, which is 240 feet lower than the upper end of the flume. The bed is dry between the dam and the power plant.

OCOEE POWER PLANT NO. 2 (L) is across the river, at 17.7 *m.;* it has a generating capacity of 25,000 horsepower.

The head of a lake in Ocoee River is at 20.3 *m.;* the route follows the lake shore for seven miles. The scenery is wild and impressive.

At PARKSVILLE, 27 *m.* (825 alt., 500 pop.), is OCOEE DAM AND HYDROELECTRIC GENERATING PLANT NO. 1, built in 1912, with a capacity of 32,400 horsepower and a 17,000 horsepower steam auxiliary plant. The dam is 130 feet high and 110 feet wide. Ocoee Inn is operated by the Tennessee Electric Power Company.

At 31.8 *m.* is the junction with State 39 *(see Tour 1A).*

East of the junction are fields of cotton; this is the only area in East Tennessee in which cotton is still an important crop. In 1803, when the Tennessee Legislature purchased rights to the use of Whitney's cotton gin in the State, cotton planting had already begun here, although the land still belonged to the Cherokee Nation.

CLEVELAND, 41.3 *m.* (873 alt., 9,125 pop.), seat of Bradley County, was named for Col. Benjamin Cleveland, who commanded a regiment at the Battle of King's Mountain *(see HISTORY).* Cleveland is on the last area evacuated by the Cherokee, who left in 1838; the town was incorporated in the same year.

Like many other towns in East Tennessee, Cleveland is an industrial community. Among the more than 30 industrial plants are hosiery mills, woodworking and lumber plants.

The PUBLIC LIBRARY has about 15,000 volumes, including the John Morgan Wooten Collection of books on history, biography, and Indian lore.

The HARDWICK WOOLEN MILLS *(visitors welcome; obtain pass at main office),* established in 1880, spin and dye raw wool, weave woolen cloth, and manufacture it into garments.

BOB JONES COLLEGE, on a landscaped campus in the residential district, is a co-educational, interdenominational institution, founded in 1933 by Bob Jones, an evangelist, who is the president of the institution. Each teacher must annually affirm his belief in a fundamentalist interpretation of the Scriptures and all classes are opened with prayer. This school occupies the buildings of Centenary Female College, which was operated from

1885 to 1928 by the Methodist Episcopal Church, South. The four central buildings, constructed for the Female College, are large brick structures of simple design. Since 1933 five new brick buildings have been added.

CENTRAL AVENUE TABERNACLE, Central Ave., a two-story stone structure between Bible and Short Sts., is the headquarters of the Tomlinson Church of God, which holds its annual assembly here. Strictly fundamentalist in their views, the members practice faith healing, foot washing, and speaking in unknown tongues. Members are not allowed to grow or to handle tobacco, and the wearing of jewelry is discouraged. The assembly, which takes place in early September, is reminiscent of the old-time camp meetings. The people shout, pray, sing, dance, and "get religion" with great fervor. Members testify to faith healings amid shouts and singing. There are parades with brass bands, floats, banners, and flags. Delegations from many states and a few foreign countries attend the assembly.

This sect is a branch of the Church of God, or the "Holiness Church," which was founded in 1886 in North Carolina. A controversy arose in 1923 during which A. J. Tomlinson, the General Overseer, was deposed. A legal battle followed, and there was a split in the organization. The courts decreed that Tomlinson could not use the original title, so his branch took the name of Tomlinson's Church of God.

At Cleveland is the junction with US 11 *(see Tour 1)*, which is united with US 64 between this point and Chattanooga.

OOLTEWAH (Cherokee, *resting place*), 54.2 *m.*, is the former seat of James County, which in 1919 was combined with Hamilton County.

1. Right from Ooltewah on Snow Hill road, paved, 6 *m.* to the YARNELL HOUSE, a simple one-story brick structure with an ell, built by James Brown about 1820. Brown was a Cherokee. When his tribesmen adopted the forms of the white men's civil government in 1825, he was elected district judge; later he became a judge of the Cherokee Supreme Court. In a few years he had one hundred acres under cultivation and owned 28 slaves. His daughter, Jane, educated at the Brainerd Mission, in 1835 married Dr. John Yarnell, who, after the removal of the Cherokee in 1838, bought the house.

2. Left from Ooltewah on a graveled road is COLLEGEDALE, 2 *m.* (870 alt., 400 pop.), the site of the SOUTHERN JUNIOR COLLEGE, a Seventh Day Adventist institution offering academic work from the elementary grades through junior college; it has special pre-medical and pre-nursing courses. The campus is landscaped and has winding drives. The main buildings are large two-story frame structures, with high central porticos. Nearly all of the 200 students pay for their tuition and living expenses by working on the campus; the institution operates a dairy, a bakery, a furniture factory, a broom factory, a book shop, a silk-hosiery mill, and a farm.

At 5 *m.* is APISON, where handiwork of the Chilhowee Mountain people is sold. Textile, wooden, metal, leather, and clay products are offered.

The SILVERDALE CONFEDERATE CEMETERY (L) is at 59.1 *m.* When Gen. Braxton Bragg was mobilizing his army during the summer of 1862, he stationed some Confederate troops near here. One hundred and fifty-five of those who died at the post were buried on this one-acre plot. Their names were placed on wooden boards that have since decayed; there is one stone, marked "L. H."

At 60 *m.* is the junction (R) with the black top East Chattanooga Road.

Right on this road to CHICKAMAUGA DAM, 7 *m.*, which rises 60 feet from the bed of the Tennessee River. In 1921 army engineers suggested a dam near Chattanooga and tentatively established the scene of operations several miles below the present site. The proposed dam was to be named for General Sherman, who threw his pontoon bridge across the river near this spot before the storming of Missionary Ridge. This offended the local United Daughters of the Confederacy and other Chattanoogans, whose grandfathers had handed down the name of Sherman as high priest in the hierarchy of demons. It was not until the election of 1932 that Chickamauga Dam promised to become a reality. Following a survey by the TVA, the chosen site, which cuts across the down river tip of Chickamauga Island, was announced December 31, 1935. Two weeks later construction was started, putting 2,000 men to work and costing ultimately $31,000,000.

Chickamauga Dam, the fifth major TVA project, is of concrete with an overall length of 5,685 feet. Earth abutments run several thousand feet on both sides of the concrete. The backwater extends 59 river miles and the shoreline of the reservoir, including that of the island, measures 502 miles. While no power units were installed at the time of construction, Chickamauga Dam will ultimately have generators for 30,000 h.p. of electricity. But the dam's primary service is to navigation; it has created a nine-foot channel to Watt's Bar.

The FRANKSTONE INN (L), 62.2 *m.;* formerly the Shepherd House, was built by Col. Lewis Shepherd, who took up a tract of several thousand acres shortly after the Cherokee Indians were removed. The two-story brick house has a two-story porch across the front that is capped with a pediment. The house was constructed about 1840 and dominated one of the few large plantations in East Tennessee. It was famous for its hospitality and still bears witness to its former splendor in its vine-covered summer houses and time-mellowed gardens. It is now an inn.

During the War between the States the house was occupied in turn by Confederate and Federal officers. Maj. James A. Garfield, afterward President of the United States, while quartered at the house, gave Mrs. Shepherd a letter of introduction to President Lincoln so that she could plead for her son's release from a Federal military prison. This boy, Lewis, had joined the Confederate army when he was 15 years old. Following the war, Lewis Shepherd practiced law. He served two terms in the State Legislature. He was special judge of Chancery and Circuit Courts (1886–88) and was a presidential elector for President Harrison in 1892.

At 64.7 *m.* is the junction with a paved road.

Right on this road to LOVELL FIELD, 1 *m.*, Chattanooga's municipal airport *(see CHATTANOOGA),* used by Eastern Air Lines planes.

A marker (L) at 64.9 *m.* shows the SITE OF BRAINERD MISSION, established in 1817 by the American Board of Commissioners for Foreign Missions and first called the Mission of Chickamauga. It was closed in 1838 after the Indians were moved west. The Reverend Cyrus Kingsbury, a Congregationalist, who was its first director, was introduced to the Indians by Gen. Andrew Jackson at the great Cherokee-Creek council.

A short distance east of two giant Spanish oaks is one of the first wells dug in this section, and nearby are the remains of the millrace built to supply power for the mission's sawmill on the banks of the Chicakamauga. Piles of stones remain to indicate the site of the mission's gristmill. South of the mill site is a cemetery in which Indians, white settlers, and members of missionary families are buried. Reverend Samuel Worcester, Secretary of the Board, died while on a visit to the mission in 1821 and was buried in the cemetery until 1844 when his body was removed to Massachusetts.

CHICKAMAUGA CREEK is crossed at 65 *m.* Mounds and village sites along this stream indicate that in prehistoric times the region was occupied by people believed to have been of Muskhogean stock. An ancient trail, later called the Chickamauga Path, connected these villages with upper East Tennessee.

In time the region became Cherokee territory. After the Cherokee outbreak of 1776, a faction led by the war chief, Dragging Canoe, refused to make peace with the white settlers. Withdrawing from the Little Tennessee Valley, they established themselves here; their town Chickamauga was near this place. Joined by warlike Indians of other tribes and by white renegades, this group became known as the Chickamauga. They remained hostile to the settlers during the Revolution, sending war parties against the frontiersmen. In 1779 Col. Evan Shelby's expedition burned Chickamauga and other towns along the creek; the Indians left, establishing the five lower towns west of Lookout Mountain.

US 64 goes through a tunnel, 68 *m.,* under Missionary Ridge, which was named for Brainerd Mission.

CHATTANOOGA, 71.7 *m.* (674 alt., 119,798 pop.) *(see CHATTANOOGA).*

Points of Interest: Lookout Mountain, Signal Mountain, and Missionary Ridge, and others.

At Chattanooga are the junctions with US 27 *(see Tour 6),* State 27 *(see Tour 15),* and US 41, which unites with US 64 for 49.6 miles.

Section b. CHATTANOOGA *to* PULASKI; *134.1 m.,* US 64-41, US 64

West of Chattanooga, Moccasin Bend of the Tennessee River is on the right, and Lookout Mountain is on the left. Crossing Raccoon Mountain US 64-41 traverses a gulch from which Walden's Ridge rises. For a few miles the route parallels the Tennessee River, then ascends the Cumberland Mountains, and traverses the Cumberland Plateau.

US 64 follows 11th St. in CHATTANOOGA, 0 *m.,* to the junction with Broad St., L. on Broad St.

At 3.2 *m.* is the junction with the Lookout Mountain road *(see CHATTANOOGA).*

At 5.1 *m.* is the junction with a paved road.

Right on this road to JOHN BROWN'S TAVERN, 3 *m.,* a two-story log house, erected in 1803 for Brown, an Indian, by Casper Vaught, who had been sent from Blount County by Col. R. J. Meigs, agent to the Cherokee.

A porch extends across the entire lower floor. This is the usual dog-trot cabin with an open passage through the center. At each end of the house is a stone chimney more than eight feet wide.

Many traders stopped here. There is an old story that Brown would carefully evaluate the contents of their wagons and, ever so often, when the stock seemed likely to bring large profits, would wait for the owner's return from his rounds, then rob and murder him in the night. To support the fiction that the man had left in the night, Brown would break up the wagons and drop the pieces into the river. The legend gained new credence when dredging operations of recent years brought up several rotting wagon hubs.

BROWN'S GRAVE is behind the house.

At 6.1 *m.* is a junction with US 11.

Left on US 11 to WAUHATCHIE VALLEY 2.5 *m.,* named for a Cherokee Indian chief who participated in the Creek War. During the War between the States this valley was the scene of the Battle of Wauhatchie, Oct. 27th and 28th, 1863. In this movement Federal forces under General Hooker drove the outnumbered Confederates under General Longstreet from the valley, opening a short line of supplies by road and river to the railroad at Bridgeport. It was from the Wauhatchie Valley that General Hooker made his attack on Lookout Mountain, Nov. 24, 1863. This battle, known as "the Battle Above the Clouds," occurred on a rainy day when fog floated low about the mountains. Concealed by the fog, the Federals marched toward the point of the mountain, completely routing the flank of General Walthall's brigade on the mountain shoulder. The misty clouds that shrouded the Point made such a perfect screen that the Confederate batteries on top of the mountain could render no effective help to their comrades below. Walthall was forced back to the Craven's House, where, receiving reinforcements, he held his position until the following afternoon when he withdrew to Missionary Ridge.

After crossing Raccoon Mountain US 64 follows the bank of the Tennessee River (R).

The hotel on Lookout Mountain is clearly visible (L) at 7.2 *m.* For several miles rock formations are prominent along the highway. Shacks dot the slopes on both sides of the road.

At 7.5 *m.* is the junction (L) with a graveled road.

Left here 0.4 *m.* to TENNESSEE CAVE *($1.50 for adults; 75¢ for children),* which contains large stalactites and stalagmites, some of them delicately colored. The cave has a year-round temperature of 54°.

WALDEN'S RIDGE, 9.3 *m.,* which rises rather abruptly from the bank of the river, was named for Elijah Walden, also known as Wallen and Walling, who explored the region in 1761 as leader of a party of long hunters who spent several months in Carter's Valley. They followed the Indian trail through Cumberland Gap and went up the Cumberland River, but after meeting a party of hostile Shawnee they turned back. Walden returned to Tennessee in 1762, and hunted along this ridge.

The rugged Cumberland Escarpment (L) is visible for several miles; landslide erosion is evident on it. The scenic beauty of this region is now marred by commercial signs, cabins, and filling stations.

At 19.3 *m.* is the junction with a graveled road.

Right on this road to HALE'S BAR DAM AND POWERHOUSE, 0.5 *m.,* recently purchased from private interests by the TVA. Completed in 1913, it was the first major hydroelectric development on the Tennessee River. The dam, 1,200 feet long and 63 feet high, forms a lake that provides good fishing. The powerhouse, which has a generating capacity of 56,723 horsepower, distributes to Chattanooga, Nashville, and many Middle Tennessee points.

RUNNING WATER CREEK, 20.8 *m.,* was named for Running Water Town, Indian village of white pioneer days. It was one of the five lower towns of the Chickamauga and the home of Dragging Canoe, chief of the Chickamauga, who died here in 1792. Running Water Town was burned by Maj. James Ore in 1794 as retaliation for the attacks of the tribesmen on the whites who were attempting to settle on Indian land.

MARION MEMORIAL TOLL BRIDGE, 21.3 *m. (50¢ for car and driver, 5¢*

TENNESSEE CAVERNS, NEAR CHATTANOOGA

for each additional passenger), dedicated to the war dead of Marion County, spans the Tennessee River in the mountainous regions of Hale's Bar. The bridge is 2,086 feet long.

From the bridge is a view (R) of Hale's Bar Dam and Powerhouse.

JASPER, 27.2 *m.* (631 alt., 1,251 pop.), seat of Marion County, lies in the fertile Sequatchie Valley. The SAM HOUSTON ACADEMY, erected in 1824, stands one block east of the town square. Alfred White, a slave and an expert carpenter, built the structure. It is said that he bought the freedom of his family and his own with the money he earned. During the War between the States he deeded himself and his family back into slavery, as records in the courthouse show. Houston taught here in the early days; since then it has been used as a church, a courthouse, a hospital during the War between the States, and is now a Masonic hall.

J. W. M. Breazele, author of *Life As It Is,* practiced law here and is buried in a little churchyard one block west of the town square. His book, published in 1842, contains pioneer sketches of Tennessee, stories of Indian wars, and frontier anecdotes.

The TENNESSEE ART POTTERY, one block west of the square, at the rear of the Phillip's Hotel, is operated by J. H. Boggs who digs clay from the banks of the Tennessee River, refines and turns it on a potter's wheel of his own construction, and bakes and glazes it. He makes flower pots, yard vases, water pitchers, and other articles. The baked ware of this, one of the few surviving old-time potteries, is widely known in the section for its durability and pleasant homely designs.

KIMBALL, 31.5 *m.*, is at the junction with US 72.

Left on US 72 is SOUTH PITTSBURG, 2.5 *m.* (620 alt., 2,500 pop.), which has hosiery and lumber mills, stove and cast-iron hollow-ware factories, and a cement plant. For several years before he became a motion picture actor Tom Mix was a night watchman at the cement plant.

According to a local tale, the ghost of a prehistoric beast visited Sequatchie Valley in June, 1936, and destroyed chickens and cattle during nocturnal prowlings. Once it ventured into the streets of South Pittsburg but vanished when attacked; machine gunners with hand grenades blasted away the river banks in search of its lair. No two observers agreed on the size, shape, or color of the beast. Later a mangy panther was shot in the nearby hills and the mystery was ended.

Left from South Pittsburg 4 *m.* on a graveled road and across the Tennessee River by ferry, is NICKAJACK CAVE. In this cave, which has an entrance 177 feet in width and 49 feet in height, is an underground lake navigated by boat for a mile from the entrance. Below the mouth of the cave was the town of Nickajack, one of the Chickamauga Lower Towns. In 1794, the town was the scene of one of the bloodiest battles between the whites and the Chickamauga. To punish the Indians for a raid on Nashville, Major James Ore led a strong party up the river. Attacking the town by surprise, the whites crushed the Chickamauga and burned Nickajack as well as the nearby town of Running Water.

West of the junction with US 72, US 41 passes through the valley of Battle Creek to DOVE, 42.6 *m.* At the head of Battle Creek a large spring flows from under a tall cliff. During the removal of the Indians from Kentucky, over the Nickajack Trail, this site was used as a camping place.

The ascent of Cumberland Mountain begins at 43.5 *m.* *(drive carefully; steep and winding road).* The route rises more than 1,200 feet within six miles.

MONTEAGLE, 50.5 *m.* (1,931 alt., 625 pop.), at the junction with US 41 *(see Tour 8)* and State 56 *(see Tour 16)*, has been a summer resort since ante-bellum days *(hotels, cottages, swimming pool; riding, tennis, dancing, concerts).*

In 1882 a group of southern churchmen organized a summer conference for Sunday school workers and bought a tract of land here. The MONTEAGLE HOTEL was built at once. This conference in time became a Chautauqua assembly lasting eight weeks, in July and August *(adm. single day, 40¢; week, $2; month, $6; entire season, $10).* A playground and a kindergarten have been provided. In the Women's Building is a library of 3,000 volumes.

Throughout its long history Monteagle has been a haven for people living in low areas. Great numbers fled to Monteagle to escape cholera and yellow-fever epidemics in New Orleans and other cities of the Deep South.

At 54.6 *m.* is the junction with an unmarked graveled road.

Right on this road to ST. ANDREW'S, 0.8 *m.*, where the Order of the Holy Cross of the Protestant Episcopal Church conducts ST. ANDREW'S SCHOOL, which cares for 100 boys from the mountains of Tennessee and neighboring States. The buildings, on a beautifully wooded campus, are of the Spanish type, most of them designed by Wilson A. Gosnell of Chattanooga. These are dominated by THE

CHAPEL, a vine-covered structure of Spanish Mission style, with a large reredos, copied from one made by Carlo Crivelli of Padua. The full liturgical service is used. The Bells of St. Andrews, chimes of three tones, are rung by the students; a boy rides the rope of each bell.

The order also maintains the monastery of St. Michael's.

SEWANEE, 56.7 *m.* (1,885 alt., 525 pop.), is the seat of the UNIVERSITY OF THE SOUTH, commonly called Sewanee, founded July 4, 1857, by the dioceses of the Protestant Episcopal Church in the southern States.

The men responsible for the founding of Sewanee were Bishop James Otey and Bishop Leonidas Polk. Many stories are told of Otey, who was as energetic as he was eloquent and long-winded. Once, when an organist ran his prelude over the allotted time, Otey stepped into the chancel and ordered him to stop. The organist jumped up and cried, "Bishop, when you are preaching one of your long sermons, I never tell you to stop." He finished the prelude.

The site was selected because of its elevation and seclusion.

The university corporation owns 10,000 acres, mostly virgin forest, of which 1,000 acres form the campus. In 1860, after the land and endowment of $500,000 had been promised, the cornerstone of University Hall was laid. Union troops, crossing the Cumberland Mountains, left the buildings in ashes; the cornerstone was broken up and pieces were carried away by the soldiers as souvenirs. One block, 18 inches square, was left and is embedded in the south wall of All Saints Chapel.

In 1865 a grammar school and an academic department were opened; a theological department was established in 1878, and a medical department was added in 1893. A number of ex-Confederate officers were teachers here, including Gen. Josiah Gorgas and Gen. Edmund Kirby-Smith.

The university operates a 500-acre farm and maintains a herd of more than 40 registered Guernsey cattle.

The first buildings were small wooden structures, one of which is still used as an office. The present buildings are of Sewanee sandstone, a beautiful pink stone quarried on the mountain. Several bishops have summer homes nearby.

The LIBRARY, designed by William Halsey Wood, with a Magdalen tower and Breslin chimes, is Gothic in type.

On the left, 100 feet from the library, is ALL SAINTS CHAPEL, with choir, presbytery, and sanctuary at the end of a long nave. The building, in use since 1910, is still unfinished. In the sanctuary are several paintings by K. A. Oertel, portraying the redemption of mankind. The chapel was designed by the firm of Cram, Goodhue and Ferguson.

OTEY MEMORIAL CHURCH is on the grounds. QUINTARD MEMORIAL HALL was designed by Richard Morris Hunt, and ST. LUKE'S MEMORIAL CHAPEL by Chester E. Haight.

Left a short distance from All Saints Chapel is the SEWANEE REVIEW PRINTING OFFICE AND UNIVERSITY PRESS, where finely printed books are produced. The Sewanee *Review* is a literary quarterly; student publications include a weekly paper, the *Sewanee Purple.*

HODGSON-EMERALD HOSPITAL serves the mountain people of the section as well as students.

REBEL'S REST, built in 1866, is a log structure with a tiled roof and with gables decorated with jigsaw frills. It was the home of a Confederate officer, Major George R. Fairbanks. The TELFAIR HODGSON HOME was built in 1872 by Gen. Josiah Gorgas, vice-chancellor of the university from 1872 to 1878, and father of William Gorgas, later Surgeon General of the U. S. Army. It has the bay windows and scrolled trimmings typical of the period in which it was built.

The BISHOP GAILOR HOME has four gables on the front, each one taller than the one before it, from left to right. The lowest gable is over a one-story section. The garden is notable for its irises.

Right from Sewanee on a dirt road between Tuckaway Inn and Sewanee Inn to the SEWANEE MILITARY ACADEMY, 0.3 *m.*, the university's preparatory school. At the end of this road is the SEWANEE MEMORIAL CROSS, 4 *m.*, a monument about 60 feet high erected in memory of Sewanee men who served in the World War.

At 57.2 *m.* on US 64 is the junction with State 56.

Left on State 56, 0.9 *m.*, to the junction with an improved road; R. here to ST. MARY'S SCHOOL, 1.5 *m.*, a boarding school for mountain girls under the direction of the Sisters of St. Mary, an order to the Protestant Episcopal Church. The students receive high school and junior college training and are taught the domestic arts. Here, as at St. Andrew's, the students sing the Anglican liturgical plain chant.

At 2.3 *m.* is the junction with a graveled road; L. here 0.6 *m.* to the NATURAL BRIDGE *(turning space for cars 100 feet above the bridge)*, an arch 20 feet high, with a span of 25 feet. A cove full of large tulip trees is visible through the arch.

LONE ROCK (R) 58.3 *m.*, is a large stone formation from which is an excellent view of the valley below.

A descent begins at 58.9 *m.* on a steep and constantly winding road, which at many points commands a broad view of the valley.

COWAN, 63 *m.* (958 alt., 1,367 pop.), lies at the foot of the western escarpment of the Cumberland Plateau. The surrounding country is flat and fertile, producing potatoes, corn, and crimson clover.

Left from Cowan on a graveled road to the CUMBERLAND MOUNTAIN TUNNEL (alt. 1,147), 2.5 *m.*, of the N. C. & St. L. Ry., bored in 1845–47 by 400 railroad-owned slaves; the tunnel is 2,220 feet long and runs through limestone.

At 63.4 *m.* on US 64 is the junction with a dirt road.

Left on this road 0.5 *m.* through a forest to KEITH CAVE *(dangerous)*, a single chamber containing hundreds of columns. The mouth is small and it is necessary to crawl 150 feet to get to the larger part. Some of the stalactites are 40 feet long. There are many rock-rimmed pools of crystal-clear water. The cave is about 1,200 feet long, 300 feet wide, and 50 feet high.

WINCHESTER, 70 *m.* (958 alt., 2,210 pop.), seat of Franklin County, has a typical courthouse square with stores facing it on all sides. The old courthouse was replaced by a new structure in 1937. Farmers sell from wagons around the square and under the trees along the nearby streets.

During the War of 1812, when many of the younger men were away fighting, the older men of the community, most of whom were veterans of the Revolutionary War, formed a group "for the purpose of defending the frontiers and property of our younger brethren when fighting our battles abroad, and to suppress and put down any combination which may manifest itself inimicable to our beloved country." They pointed out that the absence of the younger men might afford an opportunity "to the disaffected (if any such there be amongst us) to do much mischief." Their fears were unjustified.

Hopkins L. Turney, a member of the Winchester bar, who served in the United States Senate from 1845 to 1851, was a vigorous advocate of Secession. His son, Peter Turney, was Governor of Tennessee from 1893 to 1897 and during his incumbency approved the law that put an end to the leasing of Tennessee's convicts to private contractors.

In 1892 Robert Essary, State Commissioner of Agriculture, sent a peck of crimson clover seed to John Ruck, whose farm was near Winchester; Ruck planted it, and gave seeds to his neighbors, who in turn started crimson clover growing. In 1937, 5,224 acres in the county were producing crimson clover. The crop, planted in September and October, is harvested in May of the following year.

In May, during the flowering season, a festival is held on some farm near Winchester, usually the one having the outstanding clover field in the vicinity.

Winchester was for a short time the home of Francis Joseph Campbell, who was born in 1832, and lost his sight when a boy. He was educated at the State School for the Blind at Nashville, taught at Perkins Institute for the Blind in Boston, and later studied in Germany. He established the Royal Normal School for the Blind in London. Campbell was knighted for his services by King Edward VII.

On the Cowan Pike, three blocks east of the square, is the WINCHESTER CREAMERY, organized in 1910 by a group of farmers. This enterprise helped to develop Tennessee's dairying business.

Left from the courthouse to HUNDRED OAKS MONASTERY *(visitors welcome)*, 0.7 *m.*, established by the Paulist Fathers of the Roman Catholic Church in 1900. The house, Hundred Oaks, was built before the War between the States by Albert S. Marks on his 600-acre plantation. Surrounded by one hundred massive oaks, the house was supposed to be a reproduction of Sir Walter Scott's home, Abbotsford. It has castellated towers, dormers, lofty ceilings, paneled walls, elaborate staircases, and carved screens and grills.

At 80 *m.* is the junction with a graveled road where a granite marker gives directions to the burial place of Polly Finley Crockett and a well dug by David Crockett.

Left on this road is MAXWELL, 0.5 *m.* South of Maxwell the graveled road continues to DAVID CROCKETT FARM, 1 *m.*, in which is the rock-walled well, dug by Crockett *(see Tour 11)*. At 2 *m.* is the GRAVE OF POLLY FINLEY CROCKETT, Crockett's first wife.

At 89.9 *m.* on US 64 is the junction with a graveled road.

Right on this road to the FEDERAL WARREN HOLLOW FISH HATCHERY, 0.5 *m.*, which propagates rainbow trout; most of the 2 million fingerlings raised annually are sent to the mountain streams of East Tennessee.

FAYETTEVILLE, 103 *m.* (665 alt., 3,822 pop.), seat of Lincoln

County, at the junction with US 241 *(see Tour 8A)*, is a shipping center on the Elk River. In the early days the people of Fayetteville settled their quarrels by hard rough-and-tumble fights, but weapons and biting were barred. Old Lincoln County sour-mash whisky was a flourishing product and was used in some London inns.

Today it is a peaceful town, chiefly interested in the prosperity of several large condenseries and powdered-milk plants and one large hosiery mill. In the hills to the south of the town are a number of fine apple orchards.

JACKSON COURT, on Lincoln Ave., was called Fayetteville Inn when it was built in 1813. On July 8, 1826, a ball was given here for Andrew Jackson by his Creek War comrades.

Between Fayetteville and Pulaski US 64 passes through an excellent farming section in which dairying is an important activity.

At PULASKI, 134.1 *m.* (649 alt., 3,367 pop.) *(see Tour 7)*, is the junction with US 31 *(see Tour 7)*.

Section c. PULASKI *to* SELMER, *109.9 m.*, US 64

Between PULASKI, 0 *m.*, and Lawrenceburg US 64 goes westward out of the bluegrass region to the edge of the Highland Rim. White oak and hickory trees rise above an undergrowth of sumac and sassafras. The area has a thin surface soil underlaid in some sections with iron ore.

LAWRENCEBURG, 19 *m.* (867 alt., 3,108 pop.), seat of Lawrence County, was founded in 1815 and named for Capt. James Lawrence, a naval hero of the War of 1812, who issued the famous order, "Don't give up the ship."

In 1870 a group of local citizens induced the German Catholic Homestead Association to buy land nearby and lay out farms of about 160 acres each. The land had been considered worthless until the German immigrants began tilling it.

In the town are woolen mills and a large cheese factory. A municipally owned hydroelectric plant on Shoal Creek supplies the city with electricity.

The Vaughan Publishing Company brings out the *Vaughan Song Book* here. The type font for the book contains 340 characters, ranging from a clef to a dotted 32nd note; more than five million copies have been printed and distributed. James D. Vaughan conducts an evangelistic music school every winter and also sponsors the annual state singing convention at Lawrenceburg, on the fourth Sunday in September, at which the Vaughan Quartet is the major attraction.

A DAVID CROCKETT MONUMENT is on the public square, also a SOLDIERS' MONUMENT erected in honor of the Lawrenceburg soldiers who fell in the Battle of Monterey, Sept. 24, 1846.

At Lawrenceburg is the junction with State 6 *(see Tour 7B)*.

At 42.8 *m.* is the junction with improved State 48.

Right on this road 4 *m.* to the junction with a dirt road; R. here 2.5 *m.* to NATURAL BRIDGE *(25¢; children free; picnic grounds, restaurant, cottages, boats)*, formed by a powerful stream in the remote past. The Cherokee used the place for councils. Skeletons and artifacts have been found beneath the bridges. The area and the shore of a nearby lake have been developed as a resort.

SHARECROPPER'S CABIN

West of Lawrenceburg US 64 traverses cotton country. There is a large Negro population, composed of sharecroppers and day laborers. Each town has its Negro section, usually at the edge of the white section—shacks grouped near a general store, a restaurant, a lodge hall, and a church. The restaurant is a gathering place for games, dancing, general conversation, and arguments that sometimes develop into razor fights.

WAYNESBORO, 47 *m.* (752 alt., 900 pop.), seat of Wayne County, named in honor of Gen. Anthony Wayne, is at the center of a plateau surrounded by hills. Beyond these hills deep ravines radiating in every direction except eastward, are crisscrossed by other ravines. Abandoned watermills and tanneries stand along the banks of the numerous streams. Between Waynesboro and Clifton is a vein of anhydrous red oxide of iron more than 25 feet thick.

At 58.8 *m.* is the junction with State 114.

Right on State 114 is CLIFTON, 7 *m.* (384 alt., 800 pop.), the home of T. S. Stribling (1881–), a novelist, who was awarded a Pultizer prize in 1932 for *The Store.* Stribling's *Teeftallow* is the story of an attempt to build a railroad in Wayne County. Hooker's Bend on the river is the setting of his book, *Birthplace.*

SAVANNAH, 78.9 *m.* (450 alt., 1,129 pop.), seat of Hardin County, was a rather isolated town until the TVA selected a nearby site for Pickwick Landing Dam, when it became a center of construction activity. "Marble" quarries in the vicinity have been reopened; limestone and rock have been mined for cement-making.

At 79.4 *m.* is a toll bridge over the Tennessee River *(50¢ for car and driver; 5¢ for each additional passenger).*

The CHERRY HOUSE *(private),* used for several weeks by General Grant as his headquarters, is on a bluff (R) high above the toll bridge. On the morning of the Battle of Shiloh, Grant was at breakfast with Mrs. Cherry when he heard the report of a cannon. Putting down his coffee cup, the general is reported to have said to his staff officers, "Gentlemen, the ball is in motion; let us be off." The house was built long before the war by David Robinson, a cotton planter. A later owner was W. H. Cherry. The low two-story brick structure has a long double gallery across its front. The house stands at the top of terraces that were formerly landscaped.

At 83 *m.* is the junction with State 22.

Left on State 22 to the entrance of SHILOH NATIONAL MILITARY PARK *(guide service),* 4.5 *m.,* and PITTSBURG LANDING, 7 *m.* At the entrance is the ADMINISTRATION BUILDING, which contains a library, a lecture room, and a collection of prehistoric artifacts taken from the Indian mounds in the park.

The Battle of Shiloh, the second great battle of the War between the States, was fought on this land. On March 11, 1862, about a month after his victories at Fort Henry and Fort Donelson, Grant began mobilization of a large force of Union troops for an attack on Gen. Albert Sidney Johnston, who had already begun an attempt to reunite the forces split by Grant at Fort Donelson. Grant's divisions assembled around Shiloh Church, near Pittsburg Landing, while Johnston's troops were gathering at Corinth, Miss., 22 miles southeast of Shiloh.

Early Union strategy—conceived by General Halleck and President Lincoln—was designed to open the Mississippi River and to push southward the western Confederate defense line. His victories at the two forts caused the high command to place confidence in Grant, and they left to him the execution of their plan. It was to reinforce these victories and to widen the splits he had effected in Johnston's army that Grant planned an attack on Corinth to the south, on the strategically important Memphis and Charleston R.R.; if he could destroy that line, it would be a tremendous blow to the South. But Johnston was also planning an offensive, and he acted first.

Following two narrow earthen roads through dense forest, 40,000 Confederates began their 18-mile march to Shiloh on the afternoon of April 3. Johnston expected his men to be in position to attack at 7 o'clock on the morning of the 5th. There was misunderstanding and delay at the very beginning of the journey; many of the troops were raw; the maps furnished to some of the officers were inaccurate; and the Confederates did not reach the position from which they were to attack until four in the afternoon. The attack was postponed until the next morning.

There is nothing in history to prove that Grant or any of his staff were aware that the enemy was camping on his doorstep that night, although both Grant and Sherman asserted later that they knew. Grant did not entrench, nor was he properly protected by pickets, because, as he wrote to Halleck, at that time his superior, "I have scarcely the faintest idea of an attack being made upon us."

Grant's troops were arranged with regard to convenience in camping, not for fighting, in an irregular triangle with sides three or four miles long. Sherman, Prentiss, and Stuart were encamped along the base, on the south side, while McClernand, Hurlburt, and W. H. L. Wallace were behind them in the apex of the triangle, farther north. Johnston's men, coming from the south, struck Prentiss and Sherman first. The attack was a complete surprise; though strengthened by reinforcements, the Federals fell back steadily in a day of fierce fighting.

Only Prentiss held his ground. He rallied about a thousand of his retreating men on a small slope protected by trees and thick underbrush. The Confederates formed a horseshoe around him, and he was forced to surrender. Johnston was killed in one of the attacks on Prentiss' position, which has since been called the Hornet's Nest. At the end of the day, the Confederates had thrown the Union troops back to the Tennessee River, the apex of the triangle. Beauregard, who had assumed Johnston's command, ordered the attack to cease just as it was becoming dark. Nelson's division of Buell's troops arrived with the night. Beauregard had no reserves and ordered a retreat the next day. It was orderly, and Grant failed to pursue him. The Confederates reached Corinth.

Neither side could fairly claim that it had won, but whatever victory there was belonged to Grant. From Shiloh, he later pushed farther into the plantation kingdom to Corinth where he met little resistance, and from Corinth he advanced on Vicksburg. Among the estimated 25,000 men lost at Shiloh (losses on both sides were about equal) none was so gravely important to both sides as was the death of Albert Sidney Johnston. In an estimate with which historians and military experts seem to agree, Jefferson Davis wrote of Johnston: "The fortunes of a country hung by a single thread on the life that was yielded on the field of Shiloh."

The NATIONAL CEMETERY, on a high bluff overlooking the river, was established in 1866. A moss-covered stone wall encloses ten and one-half acres, in which were buried 3,649 soldiers, only about one-third of whom were identified. More than 800 tablets mark the scenes of battle events, among which are the Hornet's Nest, Bloody Pond, where the wounded crawled to drink and bathe their wounds, and the Peach Orchard, through which the Confederates attacked the Hornet's Nest and in which General Johnston was mortally wounded.

At DILL BRANCH, the farthest point reached by the Confederate advance, 0.7 *m.* from the administration building, are the remains of several prehistoric Indian mounds. Ranging from 5 to 15 feet in height, they are probably 600 to 700 years old. One is conical and the others are flat-topped. In 1899 a pipe of catlinite, in the shape of a man, was taken from the conical mound; one archeologist has described it as the "most perfect piece of prehistoric carving." The Battle of Shiloh, which one of the leaders almost lost because he failed to entrench, was fought on the most extensive fortification built by the Indians on the Tennessee River.

Left from Pittsburg Landing on Park Road 1.8 *m.* to the junction with State 57, within the park; L. here 3 *m.* to the southeastern entrance to the park; where the road became State 57 and turns L. to HAMBURG LANDING, 1.7 *m.* and to COUNCE, 6.8 *m.*, at the junction with Pickwick Landing Road.

Left on this road 5 *m.* to PICKWICK DAM. At this point the river valley is about 1.5 miles wide; the river flows westward in a channel 1,200 feet wide. Construction of the dam was begun in 1935 and completed in 1938 at an estimated cost of $31,837,000. The dam forms a lake backing up to the foot of Wilson Dam at Muscle Shoals, approximately 53 miles. The lake with an area of about 64 square miles has a maximum capacity of 1,032,000 acre-feet. The dam is partly of earth-fill construction, though in mid-channel it is built of concrete. There are a navigation lock, a spillway, and a non-overflowing section. The dam is nearly 1.5 miles long and 101 feet high. The navigation lock is 600 feet long, 110 feet wide and has a lift of 61 feet.

ADAMSVILLE, 86.8 *m.* (440 alt., 700 pop.), is a small farm-trade center with two cotton gins and two sawmills.

SELMER, 100.9 *m.* (450 alt., 925 pop.) *(see Tour 10)*, is at the junction with US 45 *(see Tour 10)*.

Section d. SELMER *to* JUNCTION WITH US 70, *76.8 m.*

Between SELMER, 0 *m.*, and Bolivar the route passes through hills covered with scrub oak. Deep ravines border the highway. Small clearings for cotton and corn are surrounded by rotting rail fences. Tin-roofed box-like houses and scarred log dog-trot cabins are scattered over the hills. The approach to Bolivar is through the dank Hatchie River bottoms. Tall dead cypresses rise from the swamp.

During the spring and summer, squirrel stews, barbecues, and ice cream suppers are held frequently in this section of West Tennessee. Stews are usually held by small groups of close friends and run smoothly, but barbecues are large affairs and seldom run their course without two or three fights. Each county has its stew maker or barbecue king, who pridefully stirs his kettle of squirrel meat and vegetables while the other picnickers drink home brew, beer, and whisky and have a roaring time. The squirrel stews are promoted principally by men, but the womenfolk are kept nearby to wait on the tables. Stews and barbecues often became political gatherings; candidates sometimes attend to show they are good fellows but most of the time because they really enjoy the delicious food and the jolly fellowship.

Strawberry and ice cream suppers are held as often as three or four times a week during the strawberry season in this section of the State.

BOLIVAR, 23.7 *m.* (446 alt., 1,217 pop.), seat of Hardeman County, was originally named Hatchie, but in 1825 the name was changed to honor Símon Bolívar, the liberator of Colombia and Venezuela. Hardeman County, in the rich Hatchie River Valley, is a cotton-growing county.

The early settlement was a trading point for the Chickasaw of northern Mississippi; it is said that there were frequently as many as 1,000 Indians on the streets at one time. Residents believed that Bolivar would become a town of importance because they expected that a canal would be built between the Hatchie and the Tennessee, thus putting the town on a great thoroughfare between East Tennessee and New Orleans. Although the canal was never built, the Hatchie was then navigable to Bolivar and furnished the merchants of West Tennessee with a water route to New Orleans.

During the War between the States, the Union Army occupied the town several times. Federal troops burned the courthouse, which was replaced in 1868 by the present building. At the close of the war a CONFEDERATE MONUMENT, one of the first to the volunteers, was erected in the yard of the courthouse.

THE PILLARS *(private)*, on the corner of Bills and Washington Sts., an excellent example of ante-bellum architecture, is a low two-story brick structure of Greek Revival design, built by Maj. John W. Bills in 1828. A few years later one-story side wings and a story-and-a-half rear wing, as well as a Doric-pillared veranda, were added. Above the entablature of the porch is a paneled parapet. The columns and railings are notable for their fine workmanship. Delicate moldings, reedings, and carvings characterize the woodwork.

At the beginning of the war $20,000 in gold was buried under a rose bush in the garden, where it remained undiscovered, protected by transplanted rosebushes. In the front yard is a boxwood 17 feet high and 55 feet in circumference, planted by Major Bills soon after the house was built.

BROOKS PLACE *(private)*, 24.3 *m.*, formerly called Mecklen, was built by Col. Ezekiel Polk, whose grandson, James K. Polk, became the 11th President of the United States. Ezekiel Polk, one of the first settlers in Hardeman County, harvested crops here in 1822 by sending hands in advance of his arrival. Three years before his death he wrote an epitaph that was to be carved on "durable wood," because "there are no rocks in this country fit for gravestones."

Here lies the dust of old E. P.
One instance of mortality,
Pennsylvania born, Car'lina bred;
In Tennessee died on his bed,
His youthful years he spent in pleasure,
His later days in gathering treasure.
From superstition liv'd quite free,
And practiced strict morality.
To holy cheats was never willing,
To give one solitary shilling;
He can foresee and foreseeing,
He equals most in being.
That church and state will join their pow'r,
And misery on this country show'r,
And Methodists with their camp bawling
Will be the cause of this down falling;
An era not destined to see,
It waits for poor posterity;
First fruits and tenths are odious things,
So are bishops, priests and kings.

The line about "Methodists with their camp bawling" was used against James K. Polk in his race for the Presidency. Feeling ran so high during the campaign that some members of the family are said to have chiseled the line from the tombstone, which has been moved from the grave in Hatchie Cemetery and is in the front yard of the house.

1. Right from Bolivar on State 18 to the junction with State 100, 12 *m.;* R. here 2 *m.* to LAC LA JOIE *(cabins; picnic grounds)* in the Chickasaw Forest *(see Tour 10)*. The 50-acre lake, on Gray's Creek, has an irregular forest-fringed shore line. Several of the ten cabins are of logs; they stand in a pine and hardwood grove at the approach to the lake; each contains a living room, bedroom, kitchenette, and bath, and is electrically lighted. A recreation building is on Honeymoon Hill, which is covered with white oak, dogwood, and redbud, and surrounded on three sides by the waters of Lac La Joie. The caretaker's home was designed to demonstrate to farmers of the area what can be done in planning a model farmhouse.

2. Left from Bolivar on State 18 to a junction with State 57, 20 *m.,* L. 2.5 *m.* on State 57 to GRAND JUNCTION (573 alt., 751 pop.), so named because it is at the junction of the Southern and Illinois Central Rys. In the fall of 1862 General Grant was delayed here on his march toward Vicksburg by thousands of Negro refugees who sought his protection; he formed camps for them and employed them in harvesting and selling the ripe cotton and corn that had been abandoned by the owners before the Union advance. Proceeds from the sale of these crops were used to furnish food, clothing, and shelter for the refugees. Col. John Eaton, chaplain under Grant, established several camps of the kind in West Tennessee. According to Grant, this experiment was the beginning of a system from which the Freedmen's Bureau evolved *(see HISTORY AND GOVERNMENT)*.

The National Field Trials for bird dogs are held annually during the first week in February on a nearby 44,000-acre plantation and game preserve. Dog and horse races are held during the two days of the trials. Registered pointers and setters are entered and tested for their ability to find coveys of quail, for "pointing" or "setting" the coveys, for retrieving the game. The judges carefully watch the form displayed by each dog—his leadership and speed, his patience in standing until the hunter arrives and is ready to shoot, and his action when the gun is fired.

Quail are hunted either afoot or on horseback. The dogs forage the sedge grass or fence rows until they sight a covey. One dog usually leads, and the others follow, running or walking at fixed intervals. When a covey is found, the dogs point or set it until the hunters arrive. On instruction from their masters, the well-trained dogs move in and cause the quail to rise. A few sportsmen shoot from horseback, but the majority dismount and tie their horses as soon as the dogs have found the birds. The dogs bring the dead and wounded birds to the hunters, and then begin hunting the ones that have escaped into thickets and brush. (This is called "going after singles.")

In the past, large 10- and 12-gage shotguns and also automatic shotguns were used, and quail had less chance to escape. Today men hunt more for sport than slaughter and like the smaller 16- and 20-gage guns.

On State 18 at 21 *m.* is LA GRANGE (573 alt., 225 pop.), which was to be the terminus of the La Grange and Memphis R.R., chartered in 1836. The hopes of the La Grange people were disappointed when the project was abandoned after the rails had been carried six miles east from Memphis *(see TRANSPORTATION)*.

The PULLIAM HOUSE, 1 *m.* E. on State 57, completed by Dr. John Junius Pulliam just before the war began, is a two-story structure of simple design with a two-story pedimented Doric portico framing the entrance. Its formal gardens are noted for their beauty. During the war Grant stayed here for a time and tents covered the lawns.

Left from La Grange on State 57, 1.3 *m.* to WOODLAWN, which stands on a wide double terrace that was handsomely landscaped in 1859. The house was built in 1828 by Maj. Charles Mitchie, who inspected every bit of wood and work with great care. The large two-story structure, of rather severe Classical Revival design, has a roof that extends forward over an Ionic portico, two-thirds of which is projected forward and capped with a pediment. There is a small balcony over the pilastered entrance.

During the War between the States the house became the West Tennessee headquarters of General Sherman and several times sheltered wounded men. In 1875 it was bought by Dr. John Junius Pulliam who restored it.

The WESTERN STATE HOSPITAL FOR THE INSANE, (L) 26.7 *m.*, occupies a tract of 640 acres and has accommodations for 1,850 patients. A unit containing X-ray laboratory, surgical ward, and hospital ward has space for 400 white patients; a building, similar in design and accommodations, was built in 1932 for Negroes, who have been admitted to the institution since the beginning of the present century. Near the main building is a formal garden. Cut flowers and potted plants are arranged in the wards and reception rooms.

SOMERVILLE, 48.4 *m.* (400 alt., 1,333 pop.), seat of Fayette County, was at one time the heart of the plantation area of West Tennessee.

At 76.8 *m.* is the junction with US 70 *(see Tour 12)*, 16 miles northeast of Memphis.

Tour 14

(Hopkinsville, Ky.)—Clarksville—Pleasant View—Nashville; US 41W and State 112.

Kentucky Line to Nashville, 55.8 m.

Paved roadbed.

Hotels in large towns; modern tourist camps along route.

US 41W crosses the Kentucky Line, 0 *m.,* about 16 miles south of Hopkinsville, and north of Clarksville traverses a fertile area with well-cultivated farms. Between Clarksville and Nashville, the route passes through a rolling country partly timbered with oak, chestnut, hickory, gum, and poplar. For several miles north of Nashville the heavily timbered hills are very high.

At 1.6 *m.* is the junction with a graveled road.

Left on this road to CLARKSVILLE AIRPORT, 0.5 *m.,* an emergency landing field.

RINGGOLD *(small entrance fee),* 3.1 *m.,* is a summer resort (R). A dam built across Ringgold Creek forms a swimming pool; modern bathhouses and campgrounds are nearby. Close to the pool on the old road is a two-lane COVERED BRIDGE, with a partition between the lanes. Heavy, rounded wooden beams form an arch.

At 6.8 *m.* is the junction with State 76 *(see Tour 9).*

At 8 *m.* is NEW PROVIDENCE (394 alt., 904 pop.).

At the south end of the town, near the end of the Red River Bridge (R) is the junction with a marked graveled road; R. 200 yds. on this road to an OLD STONE BLOCKHOUSE, built in 1788–89 by Col. Valentine Sevier. The fort has massive walls of local limestone. A large fireplace is between the two rooms. Colonel Sevier and William Snyder repulsed an Indian attack here on November 11, 1794. A letter written after the attack by Colonel Sevier to his brother, Gen. John Sevier, said:

Dear Brother: The news from this place is desperate with me. On Tuesday, 11th of November, last, about twelve o'clock, my station was attacked by about forty Indians. On so sudden a surprise they were in almost every house before they were discovered. All the men belonging to the station were out save only Snyder and myself. William Snyder, Betsy, his wife, his son, John, and my son Joseph were killed in Snyder's house. They also killed Ann King and her son James, and scalped my daughter Rebecca. I hope she will still recover. The Indians have killed whole families about here this fall. You may hear the cries of some persons for their friends daily. The engagement commenced at my house continued about an hour, as the neighbors say. Such a scene no man ever witnessed before. Nothing but screams and the roaring of guns, and no man to assist me for some time.

During the War between the States the Confederates named this Fort Defiance.

US 41W crosses the Red River.

CLARKSVILLE, 10 *m.* (444 alt., 9,242 pop.), seat of Montgomery County, in a tobacco-growing district, is on a peninsula at the confluence of the Cumberland and Red Rivers. The town is built on seven hills. Facing the courthouse square are modern red-brick business blocks side by side with gray brick and stone buildings of the 19th century. On the broad asphalted streets are the tracks of a former street-car system. Many old homes of the ante-bellum period are on the banks of the rivers and on shaded avenues.

Although Moses Renfroe and a party of explorers came here in 1780, settlement was not made until 1784, when Col. John Montgomery and Col. Martin Armstrong filed papers for 200 acres in this vicinity. In the fall of that year two men platted a town and called it Clarksville for Gen. George Rogers Clark, with whom Montgomery had fought in the Northwestern Campaign.

Clarksville grew slowly before the river bridges were built. For many years ferries were in use, the boats being propelled by a team of blind mules hitched to a heavy beam that, in turn, was attached to a wheel. Blind mules were preferred because they did not become dizzy while treading the endless circuit. Modern bridges now cross both rivers.

Cultivation of tobacco began with the first settlement, and Clarksville is now one of the leading dark-fired tobacco markets in the United States. Dark-fired tobacco is cured by fire, differing from the air-cured tobacco of other regions. First shipments of the crop went by flatboat to New Orleans for shipment to Europe, where it found quick and lasting favor.

Eleven loose-leaf tobacco sales floors and several tobacco-packing houses, a snuff factory, and a nicotine plant furnish outlets for the country's crop. Among other plants are a cannery, a creamery, a foundry and machine works, and numerous small garment factories. The *Leaf Chronicle,* a daily newspaper established in 1808, is one of the oldest periodicals in the State.

Roland Hayes, the Negro singer, worked in a local tobacco factory to earn his tuition at Fisk University and gave his first recital here. Clarence Cameron White, Negro violinist and composer, was born at First and Main Sts. in 1876.

In January, 1937, the town was isolated for several days by flood. Transmission lines fell and roads were covered with water. More than 600 persons, driven from their homes, were sheltered and fed by relief organizations.

The CLARKSVILLE FOUNDRY AND MACHINE WORKS, Commerce and Spring Sts., molded cannons and cannonballs for the Confederate Army.

The OLD CASTLE BUILDING, College St. and University Ave., originally housed the Masonic University of Tennessee. The name was changed to Stewart College in 1855 in honor of its president, William M. Stewart. In 1879 the institution was the home of the Southwestern Presbyterian University, which is now in Memphis; in 1927 it was bought by the State, and the Austin Peay Normal School was established in it.

A STATE AGRICULTURAL EXPERIMENT STATION *(open 8-6 daily),* in Madison Extension, is a farm for the study of the adaptability of new crops to Middle Tennessee soil. The care and cultivation of suitable plants are studied in the laboratories. On the farm are an administration building, a superintendent's residence, cottages for laborers, greenhouses, and barns.

The WILSON HOME, S. 2nd St. and Munford Ave., was occupied for several years by Dr. and Mrs. Joseph R. Wilson, parents of President Woodrow Wilson, while Dr. Wilson was a member of the faculty of Southwestern Presbyterian University.

The AUSTIN PEAY HOUSE, S. 2nd and Munford Ave., was the home of Austin Peay, Governor of Tennessee (1923–27).

The CONFEDERATE MONUMENT, Greenwood Cemetery on Greenwood Ave., was erected in 1922 in honor of Clarksville's three heroes of the War between the States.

Clarksville is at the junction with State 13 *(see Tour 9).*

Right 3 *m.* on State 13, at the western end of the John T. Cunningham Bridge, is the ALLEN TATE HOME, overlooking the Cumberland River. In this house Allen Tate and his wife, Caroline Gordon *(see WRITERS OF TENNESSEE),* wrote much of their poetry and prose. General Lafayette was entertained here as a guest of Mr. and Mrs. Green Rayburn in 1824.

Southwest of Clarksville, State 122, now the route, traverses a wheat-, corn-, and hay-growing section and then an area producing fine dark-fired tobacco.

At 31.2 *m.* is the junction with State 49.

Right on this highway is SYCAMORE, 4 *m.,* site of the Sycamore Powder Mills. In 1868 all the machinery of the Confederate powder works at Augusta, Ga., was bought and moved here. The industry supported about 100 families until 1904. A few of the former workers still live here, but not many houses are left. A pair of the solid iron rollers, about three feet in diameter and a foot thick, used in grinding the powder, are mounted on a granite pedestal near the west end of the Parthenon in Centennial Park, Nashville.

ASHLAND CITY, 10 *m.* (408 alt., 712 pop.), is the seat of Cheatham County. In 1859 Ashland City became an incorporated town, but through negligence of the county officials the charter was forfeited, and not until several years later was it restored.

SYDNEY BLUFF, of stratified rock, rises in a perpendicular wall on the western side of the Cumberland River opposite Ashland City. The Cheatham County housewives are noted for their "chittlin" cooking, as is commemorated in the song, "When it's Chittlin Cooking Time in Cheatham County." The word is derived from chitterlings, the small intestines of swine. After chitterlings have been cleaned, they are soaked overnight in mild brine. They are then cut into small strips, rolled in meal or flour and fried in deep fat until a golden brown.

State 49 crosses the Cumberland River on a toll bridge *(50¢ for car and driver, 5¢ for each additional person),* to an INDIAN FORTRESS, 13 *m.,* a Stone Age fort whose history is unknown. The ancient citadel, on a narrow double-faced bluff between the Harpeth and the Cumberland Rivers at their confluence, was first explored in 1920. The precipitous bluff, 150 to 200 feet high, a natural wall of defense, extends for a distance of 3,110 feet. When ascent was possible, the spot was fortified with palisades, and with breastworks that remain. At strategic points on the narrow ridgelike summit are several mounds and embankments. This cliff fortress became a place of refuge for scattered white settlers.

At 43.1 *m.* on State 112 (US 41W) is the junction with graveled Bernard Road.

Right on this road to MARROWBONE LAKE, 1.5 *m.,* an 87-acre lake constructed by WPA. It is under supervision of the State Division of Game and Fish and is being stocked with bass, crappie, bluegill, and other fishes common to streams of the State. A recreation area of 1,110 acres is being developed.

The highway descends from the Highland Rim into the Central Basin. At 50.8 *m.* is the junction with the graveled White's Creek Road.

Left on this road is the HOME OF E. B. SMITH, 0.3 *m.*, one of two or three occupied by Jesse and Frank James and their wives during their last period in hiding. The brothers always slept near windows through which they could readily escape. From the house, which stands on a knoll, the view is unobstructed in every direction for a mile or more. The two outlaws, unrecognized, were respected in the community. They attended church and often took an active part in the services. Both families left hurriedly after one of their band had visited them and returned to Nashville to boast, while drunk, of the escapades of the James brothers in Missouri. *(See Tour 12.)*

At 1.4 *m.* is the entrance to DAVIDSON COUNTY TUBERCULOSIS HOSPITAL, established in 1911 for the care and treatment of tubercular residents of Davidson County.

NASHVILLE, 55.5 *m.,* (498 alt., 153,866 pop.) *(see NASHVILLE).*

Points of Interest: Fort Nashborough, the Parthenon, the State Capitol, Fort Negley, Vanderbilt University, Ward-Belmont College, George Peabody College for Teachers, and others.

At Nashville are the junctions with US 31, 31E *(see Tour 7),* US 31W *(see Tour 8),* US 70 *(see Tour 12),* US 41-70A *(see Tour 8),* and State 11 *see Tour 7A).* The point of intersection is on Memorial Square.

Tour 15

(Albany, Ky.)—Jamestown—Crossville—Pikeville—Dunlap—Chattanooga; State 28 and 27 (Alvin C. York Highway).
Kentucky Line to Chattanooga, 144.1 m.

Graveled roadbed, hard-surfaced at intervals.
Accommodations limited. Hotels and restaurants only in larger towns.

State 28 crosses Tennessee almost directly north to south, traversing the Cumberland Plateau close to the base of the Cumberland ranges. South of Crossville it meanders through the Sequatchie Valley, crossing and recrossing the Sequatchie River. The country along the route is sparsely settled; though the three or four small county seats have movies and some other present-day attractions, for the most part the people along the route live much as they did in the 1840's. The whole region was quite isolated until the time of the World War, when the demand for lumber, coal, and other materials was so great that production was stimulated in these areas.

ONE-ROOM COUNTRY SCHOOL

Mountain and farm boys were drawn into industrial life. But after the abnormal wartime demand had ended and orders for raw materials could be filled in older and more highly developed regions operations here were sharply curtailed or carried on with low profits. The workers did not know how to return to life on the farms and in the hills and resented the end of their brief experience with "cash money." Divorced from the soil that had enabled their parents and grandparents to make meager livings, these people presented a serious social problem long before the effects of overproduction brought economic prostration in the industrial centers. Some men left to work in the large factories of the Middle West, particularly in Detroit. After 1929 some returned to the Cumberlands, but many more went on the relief rolls in the cities.

South of the Kentucky Line, 0 *m.,* which is crossed 10 miles south of Albany, Ky., the route passes through a rugged hill country, sparsely settled and with its picturesque wilderness not greatly changed since pioneer days.

PALL MALL, 10.4 *m.* (1,680 alt., 100 pop.), is the home of Alvin C. York, who was born just beyond the Wolf River bridge. In 1917, when the United States entered the World War, York was a day laborer and claimed draft exemption as a conscientious objector. This claim was overruled, and he reported for service on Nov. 14, 1917 to receive military training at Camp Gordon, Ga.; he went overseas in May 1918. On Oct. 8,

1918, in the Argonne Forest, France, he performed the "act of conspicuous gallantry" for which he was honored by the U. S. Government. "With great daring," said the citation, he charged "a machine gun nest which was pouring deadly and incessant fire upon his platoon. In this heroic feat the machine gun nest was taken, together with four officers and 128 men and several guns."

The ALVIN YORK BIRTHPLACE (L) is at 11.2 *m.,* just north of the point where State 28 crosses Wolf River on a steel bridge.

HUDDLESTON KNOB (1,708 alt.), REAGON KNOB (1,633 alt.), and DOUBLE TOP MOUNTAIN (1,800 alt.) are R.

In the spring violets, anemones, and many other wild flowers cover the valleys. In summer the mountains are green with laurel, flowering cucumber, azaleas, and rhododendrons. In the fall the golden, red, and bronze leaves of trees are vivid beneath the blue sky.

A long, high rock bluff is (L) at 15.1 *m.* The scene is wild and impressive.

At 16 *m.* is a junction with a graveled road.

Left on this road to the administration building of PICKETT STATE PARK *(fishing, picnic grounds, boating, bathing),* 15 *m.,* an 11,500-acre conservation area. Radiating from the park office are various foot trails. A 10-acre LAKE, 0.5 *m.* from the office, is stocked with bream, black bass, and rainbow trout. At the end of a marked trail leading 0.7 *m.* from the park office is HAZARD CAVE, named for James O. Hazard, State Forester. Stone artifacts found in this cave indicate that it was occupied by prehistoric Indians.

The ALVIN C. YORK AGRICULTURAL INSTITUTE (R), 20.3 *m.,* was built in 1927. The State maintains the high school, and Fentress County, the elementary department.

JAMESTOWN, 21.7 *m.* (1,700 alt., 837 pop.), named for James Fentress, a Tennessee legislator, is the seat of Fentress County. Jamestown was built upon the site of a Cherokee camp known to whites as Sand Springs; many Indian rock shelters are nearby. The first deed conveying Fentress County lands dated Sept. 22, 1800, was made to Conrad Pile, the great-great-grandfather of Alvin C. York. David Crockett was a close friend of Pile and the two often hunted together along the upper Cumberland.

For several years this was the home of John M. Clemens, father of Samuel L. (Mark Twain). He held huge land grants in this county and drew the plans for the first courthouse and the first jail, which were completed in 1827. He had a hopeful belief in the value of Fentress County land and struggled to keep its value a secret from the "natives." The efforts of his heirs to hold the land granted to Clemens resulted in much litigation. Strangers attempted to buy it up by paying the taxes, and tenants were settled on it. The final returns to the Clemens heirs on the large holdings were very meager. Jamestown is the "Obedstown" of the *Gilded Age,* and "Squire Si Hawkins" was Mark Twain's father.

In the early days of the county witchcraft trials were not unknown. In 1835 an old man named Joseph Stout was arrested and brought before Joshua Owens, a justice of the peace in Jamestown; according to the story, he was charged with bewitching a girl, who had been seized with a sudden illness that the doctor could not diagnose. The neighbors had concluded that she must have been bewitched and that the bewitcher was Stout, a solitary person who often read far into the night, made few friends, and spoke little. Neighbors, distrusting such a self-sufficient fellow, spread the story that he could go in and out of dwellings through the keyholes, and would cast strange spells even when miles away. Fearful of such a person, the posse that arrested him had carried guns loaded with silver bullets, the only kind, according to their belief, to which wizards and witches were not immune. The case was dismissed.

Stones and heading lumber, cross-ties, shafts for golf clubs, and pulpwood are shipped from Jamestown.

At 22.2 *m.* is the junction with a foot path.

Left on this path into ROCK CASTLE VALLEY or CANYON, which begins near Jamestown and is about five miles long and one mile wide. The valley is almost surrounded by perpendicular bluffs from 100 to 200 feet high. Huge rocks on the sides and bottom of the valley are visible from the top. The area is a natural game sanctuary. The FALLS OF ROCK CASTLE are at the head of the canyon, about 1.5 *m.* southwest of Jamestown. Rock Castle Creek pours over this bluff, falling about 75 feet in its first plunge and continuing over steep declivities for 500 feet, until it reaches the lower part of the valley. Just above the falls is a natural bridge.

At 24.7 *m.* on State 27 is the junction with an improved road.

Left on this road is ALLARDT, 5 *m.;* R. here 2 *m.* on a dirt road to the HOME OF MRS. WILLIAM BRADFORD STOCKTON, 7 *m.,* the first woman to run for the governorship of the State. She was the Socialist candidate in the campaign of 1936.

At 25.2 *m.* on State 27 is the junction with a dirt road.

Right on this road to POINT LOOKOUT, 0.5 *m.,* from which is a broad view of rugged slopes, deep ravines, and high bluffs. From this point can also be seen the field in which "Tinker Dave" Beatty, leader of a band of irregular Federal guerrillas, clashed with Samuel W. (Champ) Ferguson, Confederate cavalry leader. Beatty was a fierce and unrelenting partisan leader, who had recruited a large band of Union-sympathizing mountaineers and trained them as scouts and spies. His force was constantly scouting and making sudden daring raids. He made reports on the strength and position of Confederate troops in Tennessee to Dr. Jonathan P. Hale, Chief of Scouts of the Army of the Cumberland.

At 35.8 *m.* is the junction with State 85.

Right on State 85 is WILDER, 9 *m.* In November 1932 there was a violent labor dispute here. The conflict was between the United Mine Workers, who refused to accept a wage cut, and the coal operators, who contended that it was necessary. Even before the strike, production had been uneconomical and the Red Cross had been giving aid to the miners.

State 27 continues southward through a rough, thinly populated country.

The CUMBERLAND MOUNTAIN SCHOOL (R), 57 *m.,* was established in 1921 by the Methodist Episcopal Church South. Mountain boys and girls from isolated sections in which there are only grade schools, work to pay for all or part of their tuition in this high school.

At CROSSVILLE, 58.3 *m.* (1,881 alt., 1,128 pop.) *(see Tour 12),* is the junction with US 70 *(see Tour 12).*

At 63.5 *m.* is the junction with State 68.

Left on State 68 to CUMBERLAND HOMESTEADS, 0.5 *m.,* now administered by the Farm Security Administration on 22,748 acres, with 251 units of 35 acres each. This project, initiated by the Division of Subsistence Homesteads, December 10, 1933, provides for the rehabilitation of 251 "stranded families," who fall into three groups: timber workers, miners, and farmers in the poor-land areas. Many of these families had been dependent upon public or private relief funds for several years. Most of the men were miners and lumbermen who had been brought into industrial life during the World War and stranded when wartime production levels were no longer needed. These people have been given an opportunity to build new lives here under better conditions.

The homesteaders cleared the land, cut the abundant white pine and quarried the Crab Orchard stone found on the land, for building materials. Then they built their homes. The attractive stone houses of four to seven rooms stand on an average of 17 acres of land, enough for the raising of vegetables, corn, poultry, and pigs; many of the families have cows. Approximately 80,000 quarts of fruits and vegetables were canned in 1937 at a canning factory here that employs 300 workers. Some of the men work in the coal mine on the homestead land. These co-operative enterprises and others, including a store, are owned by the Cumberland Homesteaders' Co-operative Association, a non-profit association of homestead membership, operating on funds loaned by the Federal Government. Some homesteaders earn small amounts of cash by craftwork.

Community facilities include a grammar school and a high school. The women take as much part in the community life as the men. There are 12 home-demonstration club groups. The project is in charge of a manager, but the homesteaders have their own community council, which has a voice on policy.

The ADMINISTRATION BUILDING gives information and will provide guide service to visitors.

At 7.5 *m.* is GRASSY COVE, a large cove or sink in the plateau about 300 feet below the surrounding land. Entirely surrounded by mountains the place would be inundated were it not that the waters of Cove Creek have an outlet under the mountains through a limestone cave.

The soil of the cove is a rich, red clay derived from the Chickamauga limestone of the neighborhood. There are some alluvial deposits of sandy loam, however, where eroding waters have brought down soil from the surrounding hillsides. The cove produces grain, grasses, clovers, and other crops.

The first settlers came about 1787. Numerous arrowheads and crude stone implements show that prehistoric Indians were here before them.

At 64.2 *m.* is the junction with a graveled road.

Right on this road 100 feet to the entrance of CUMBERLAND HOMESTEAD PARK, an area with trails, camp sites, and a lake on the homestead property.

South of this point State 27 has a loose gravel surface and is narrow and crooked.

The Sequatchie River is crossed at 73.8 *m.*

The road here begins its descent of the Cumberland Mountains into SEQUATCHIE VALLEY, one of the loveliest in all Tennessee. The name Sequatchie is believed to have been derived from a combination of two Indian words—*sequa* (opossum) and *hatchie* (river). The valley is about 75 miles long and its width varies from three to five miles. The fertility of its soil is apparent. The floor is a mosaic of pasture, crop lands, farm woodlots, homesteads, and villages—green, red, yellow, and brown.

The Sequatchie River, again crossed at 75 *m.,* is narrow at this point.

Farms in this valley are modern, with well-kept buildings, but in some of the coves agriculture is carried on with pioneer simplicity. During the spring the women help in the fields; in summer the crops are "laid by," and the women can and dry the winter's supply of food. In the fall the

MAKING SORGHUM MOLASSES

crops are gathered and stored, and then preparation of the winter supply of firewood is started.

In the winter the men hunt and trap extensively to get the skins of skunks, raccoons, opossums, squirrels, foxes, and rabbits, which bring a small cash income.

Some families in the deeper recesses of the Cumberlands still cook around open fireplaces, but in the more populous lowlands cookstoves are in use. Fireplace cooking has its own technique. The fireplace is constructed of unhewn rocks, skillfully fitted together, and usually takes up almost all of one end of the main room of the cabin. It is wide enough to accommodate a log four feet long, or even longer. The rock body of the chimney is finished with sticks plastered over with clay or mortar.

To make a fire in this enormous fireplace a backlog, often a foot in diameter, is rolled to the rear and two oblong stones are placed in front of it to hold up the forestick, which is much smaller. Smaller sticks are thrown between the two with chips and other fragments. Eventually there is a great bed of live coals beneath the forestick.

When meal time nears, the housewife rakes out a glowing mass of embers; over them she places the covered cast-iron oven, handed down perhaps from her grandmother. When the heat is just right, she deftly removes the heavy lid, which has also been covered with coals, and deposits within pones of corn bread or biscuits, and sometimes Irish potatoes.

In the meantime an iron pot has been simmering in one corner of the fireplace; it holds a generous mess of cabbage, beans, or pumpkins, and a large piece of fresh pork or bacon. Mountain food is nearly always greasy, and dyspepsia is the most common complaint next to rheumatism. The mountain, or razorback hog, that lives in the woods upon acorns and roots, becomes comparatively fat in the late fall, when it is hunted and shot by the owner. Every mountaineer knows his hogs by his mark—the slits, crops, and underbit made with the owner's pocket knife in the ears of his pigs. These individual marks are known for miles around and are generally respected, but bitter and long-standing feuds have had their origin in the killing of some neighbor's wild hog.

The ash hopper, a lowly and useful contrivance of pioneer days, no longer used in the lowlands, is still found in the back yard of every cabin up the hollows. It is made by cutting a V-shaped trough in a log, one end of which is elevated a few inches. Four posts are set up to support a frame upon which is placed the hopper, a pyramidal box with the apex resting in the inclined trough. Wood ashes are dumped into the hopper, which is kept covered until soap-making time, when water is poured into it, and the strong lye begins to drip from the trough. When a sufficient quantity has been collected, it is boiled in a large iron kettle with scraps of fat meat. After this boiling has gone on as long as some old experienced grandmother decides it should, the fire is drawn and the contents are allowed to cool. The product is usually a semi-solid, tan substance that lathers well and is a good dirt remover; its makers prefer it to "store" soap because it has a bite that assures them of its strength. Large families often make a barrel of this soap, and at intervals the soap gourd is filled from the barrel.

Every mountain family raises gourds for a multitude of uses. The very large ones, often two gallons or more in capacity, are handy receptacles for lard, sugar, homemade soap, molasses, dried fruit, and seeds. The smaller, long-handled gourds make excellent dippers and ladles. By every spring is hung a clean, long-handled gourd, ready for any passerby to use when he wishes a drink of cool water. Soap gourds are often handed down in families for several generations. There is a belief here that gourds will not grow well if deliberately planted; the seed must be thrown around haphazardly in fence corners and other out-of-the-way places and allowed to grow without help. The long-handled variety must have a fence or something on which to climb, so that the hanging gourd will grow with a straight handle.

In the early days celebration of particular days was looked upon with religious intolerance. Only three main festivals were observed—July Fourth, Thanksgiving, and Christmas. July Fourth was quietly celebrated, as was Thanksgiving, but Christmas was and is a great day. Christmas celebrations were formerly like those of Hallowe'en, with the same tricks, costumes, pranks, and practical jokes.

The customs followed by many in this remote country have their own characteristics. Among the rules are: to cure chills, put a piece of camphor gum in a bag made of new brown domestic and wear it hanging between the shoulders next to the skin. To cure frostbite, rub the feet with molasses and soda. To keep off diseases, wear a buckeye around the neck. If a rabbit crosses your path, make a cross mark in the middle of the road and spit in it to break the evil. To cure a cold, put your head in a hollow tree where a polecat has been. Kill hogs in the dark of the moon and the meat will "swivel" away and make more lard. Plant potatoes in the dark of the moon so they won't have too many eyes.

At 90.1 *m.* is the junction with State 30.

Right on State 30 to the junction with State 101, **7.1** *m.;* R. here **7.2** *m.* to the HERBERT DOMAIN. On this 10,000-acre tract the State maintains the State Training and Agricultural School for delinquent Negro boys. Boys from the Negro department of the Tennessee Reformatory were first sent to the Herbert Domain in 1917. Since that time it has been developed into one of Tennessee's most beautiful institutions. It has 21 large buildings and a fine campus. There are 2,000 acres of cleared land, well fenced and drained, almost all of it under cultivation. Negro boys between the ages of 8 and 18, convicted of offenses punishable by penitentiary confinement, as well as delinquents, are sent here. Juveniles are also confined here. The boys receive training in farm work. For eight months of the year they are given educational instruction. The institution can care for about 400 boys.

At **11.5** *m.* on State 30 is the junction with a graveled road; L. here into the FALL CREEK FALLS RECREATIONAL DEMONSTRATION AREA, **2.5** *m.,* of 12,000 to 13,000 acres. It is being purchased and developed by funds allotted by the Farm Security Administration and is under supervision of the National Park Service, which is the planning and developing agent. The area is being developed to provide recreational tracts in which organized groups of limited means can occupy cabins for short periods at low cost. Eighty-five per cent of the land is covered with a forest growth ranging from virgin uncut timber to cut-over.

Cutting back into the area from the northwest for nearly three miles is Cane Creek Gulf, 300 feet deep. In it are five beautiful waterfalls: Walling Mill Branch Falls drops 50 feet, Piney Falls 85 feet, and Cane Creek Falls 80 feet. There is another beautiful falls, the Cascade, on Cane Creek. FALL CREEK FALLS, on one side of a basin 400 feet in diameter with overhanging walls, is a slender column of water dropping 257 feet. A smaller waterfall is near it.

Cane Creek is an attractive stream in a deep gorge. Some distance above the falls is a 40-foot cascade whose water is churned into foam.

PIKEVILLE, 96.1 *m.* (864 alt., 531 pop.), seat of Bledsoe County, is in farming country at the head of the Sequatchie Valley, but it has a lumber mill, a hosiery mill, a cheese plant, and a stove mill.

John A. Murrell, the outlaw *(see Tour 12),* died of tuberculosis here shortly after his release from the penitentiary.

On Saturday afternoons, between visits to the stores, the hill people wander over to the courthouse lawn where there are almost continuous arguments on social, political, and religious questions, usually settled by old-timers whose opinions are highly respected. There is much gossiping, too, about cooking, ailments, crops, courtships, marriages, births, and deaths. Children of all ages run in and out of the crowd, and family dogs scamper and fight. Tobacco chewing and snuff dipping are popular diversions. In the stores homemade quilts, baskets, jelly, and other canned goods, and butter, eggs, and poultry are exchanged for "store boughten goods." The Saturday wild western movie is always well attended.

The people of the Cumberland Mountains have long been isolated and have had few contacts outside of their own communities. They speak cau-

FALL CREEK FALLS

tiously, using as few words as possible, and carefully avoid all show of emotion or excitement. Though they appreciate courtesy, they meet it with an appearance of indifference. They never applaud in public meetings, no matter how interested they are; their silence dampens the ardor of the most impassioned newcomer. The mountain people speak softly, but their singing is high-pitched and sometimes harsh; the women sing in abnormally high registers. Hymns are the favorite songs, but sad ballads are very popular. A mountain group is never so happy as when wailing out endless verses about an unhappy love affair to the thrum of the easily made guitar, or a banjo.

Sunday is courting day. The young man rides up to the cabin of the girl, hitches his mule to the limb of a tree, and walks in to face the family, which, if not sympathetic toward the match, displays an uncompromising and cold front.

The old-time feuds are dying out, though some clan hatreds persist. There are still people who do not speak to neighbors because of some forgotten act of the neighbor's great-grandfather.

At 92.2 *m.* is the junction with State 30.

Left on this road to MORGAN SPRINGS, **10** *m.* and DAYTON, **18** *m.* *(see Tour 6).*

DUNLAP, 113.4 *m.* (748 alt., 1,295 pop.), is the seat of Sequatchie County, a fertile agricultural and livestock-raising section. All-day singings are popular in this part of the State. Whole families attend, bringing large baskets of food for the noon meal, which is spread on the ground in the shade of large trees. Home-cured ham, fried chicken, roast pork, light bread, pickles, pies, and cakes appear in large quantities.

During the winter, play parties and the square dance are the chief entertainments. Every neighborhood has some "caller" who is in great demand and proud of his memory. Most of the callers have their own variations of

Swing old Adam,
Swing old Eve,
S'lute your pardner
B'fore you leave.

"Turkey in the Straw," "Old Dan Tucker," "She'll Be Comin' Round the Mountain," and "Chicken in the Bread Tray" are popular tunes.

At 114.7 *m.* Sequatchie River is crossed for the last time.

At POWELL'S CROSSROAD, 127.2 m., is the southern end of State 28 and the junction with State 27; L. here on State 27, now the main route.

At 128.3 *m.* the route begins to ascend Walden's Ridge, named for Elisha Walden, a long hunter who explored the region in 1761.

At 131.7 *m.* is a clear view (L) of the Sequatchie Valley.

A marker (L) at 132.4 *m.* proudly calls attention to the highest point between Miami and Chicago.

Descending, the road follows the gulch L., where giant boulders, tall hemlocks, and dense undergrowth of laurel and rhododendron rim the road. Holly trees stand here and there. The highway touches the banks of the Tennessee River at 141.5 *m.*

Four large tunnels, made by the Signal Mountain Portland Cement Company, are (L) at 141.5 *m.*

At 142.1 *m.* is the junction with State 113.

Left on State 113, which climbs SIGNAL MOUNTAIN, which rises 1400 feet above the valley of the Tennessee. Signal Mountain forms the southern spur of Walden's Ridge. According to legend the Indians used this summit for signal fires, which could be seen for 200 miles. The mountain slopes form a popular suburb of Chattanooga.

The JAMES MARKER, 2.1 *m.,* is a metal plaque in a large boulder. This memorial was designed by Joseph Barras, of Chattanooga, in honor of C. E. James, the real estate operator who developed the area.

At 3.1 *m.* is the junction with Signal Mt. Blvd. L. here 0.2 *m.* to a fork in the road. L. again to SIGNAL MOUNTAIN HOTEL, 1.3 *m.,* long the social center of the mountain colony, and now a resort for men, operated by the Alexian Brothers, a Catholic order.

Left from hotel 0.1 *m.* to SIGNAL POINT (2,000 alt.). Signal Point gives a wide view of the river and neighboring mountains. Directly beneath and to the right, is the gorge of the Tennessee River, called locally the Grand Canyon of the Tennessee. On the opposite bank of the Tennessee is Raccoon Mountain. Clearly visible (L. of Raccoon Mountain) is Lookout Mountain. In the river below was the "Suck" of the Tennessee where the Indians waylaid flatboats; it was nearly eliminated by the building of a dam down the river.

At the 3.1 *m.* junction with Signal Mt. Blvd. State 113 becomes Palisades Dr. L. on this road, the main route, JAMES POINT, 4.4 *m.,* commands a magnificent view of the Tennessee gorge, Williams Island, Raccoon Mountain, and a more extended view of Lookout Mountain.

At 5.8 *m.* is the "W", formed by switchbacks on the cliffs, the four sections almost parallel with each other. Most of the supplies that trickled into Chattanooga during the seige of 1863 came over this road. To the east spreads the wide Tennessee Valley with the mountains of North Carolina faintly visible in clear weather.

At 10.5 *m.* is the junction with State 27.

On State 27 at 142.9 *m.* is the junction with Palisades Dr.

VALDEAU, 144.1 *m.* is the junction with US 27 *(see Tour 6)* 3 miles from the heart of Chattanooga.

Tour 16

(Albany, Ky.)—Livingston—Cookeville—Sparta—McMinnville—Monteagle; State 42, US 70-alt., and State 56.
Kentucky Line to Monteagle, 143.9 m.

Paved roadbed most of route, loose gravel at long intervals.
Accommodations chiefly in mountain towns, few tourist camps along route.

This route passes through a mountainous region, in which the Highland Rim merges with the Cumberland Plateau. On both sides of the route dark ravines open vistas of woodland and high cliffs.

The earliest white visitors here were hunters who lived on smoked venison, which they called "jerk," and which they came to consider the best food in the world. On his return to Kingston from this area, one of the hunters, "Big Jo" Copeland, asked for corn bread, a delicacy he had yearned for during long months in the woods. He found it so dry and hard that he pushed it aside and reached into his wallet for a slice of "jerk."

The region was given its name, the Knob Country, by Mark Twain, who described it in his *Gilded Age*. His father, John Clemens, had laid claim to much land in this section.

State 42, continuation of a Kentucky route, crosses the Kentucky Line, 0 *m.*, 6 miles south of Albany, Ky.

The WOLF RIVER, 2.9 *m.*, is an excellent fishing stream. There are many beautiful camp sites along its course.

BYRDSTOWN, 5.5 *m.* (1,100 alt., 300 pop.), seat of Pickett County, was established in 1879. Farming, stock raising, logging, and lumbering are the principal activities in the thinly settled country.

At STARPOINT, 7.5 *m.*, is the junction with State 53, a graveled road.

Right on State 53 2 *m.* is the BIRTHPLACE OF CORDELL HULL (1871–), Secretary of State under President Franklin D. Roosevelt. As a member of the Cabinet, he has distinguished himself by negotiating a number of international trade agreements. His father, William Hull, who owned a small farm here, moved to a place near the Obey River and began logging. There he erected a small building for a school and employed a teacher to instruct Cordell and the children of neighboring families. Young Hull became known for two accomplishments—his ability to pilot log rafts safely down the river, and his skill in debate. During his youth he was unassuming and almost shy. Legend has it that the nearest he ever came to boasting was when he talked of his ability as a log-rafter. Later, attending Mont Vale Academy at Celina, he often walked the 13 miles home to stay with his mother when his father was away. Hull was a captain in the Spanish-American War; was a delegate from the 4th Tennessee District to the United States House of Representatives from 1907 to 1931, except for the years 1921–23. He was elected to the United States Senate in 1931 but resigned on March 4, 1933, to enter the President's Cabinet. He is the author of the Federal income tax law of 1913, and of the graded inheritance tax law.

State 53 continues to DEVIL'S BACKBONE and INDIAN SHELTERS, 3 *m.*, and BUNKUM CAVE, 3.5 *m.*, where many Indian relics have been found, and passes through the Obey River Valley to LILYDALE, 13 *m.*, and then to WILLOW GROVE, 17 *m.*, where Catherine Sevier came to live in 1815 after the death of her husband, John Sevier. She was known throughout the State as "Bonny Kate." Sevier had married her in 1780, after the death of his first wife; a tradition is that their romance started four years earlier, when Sevier killed an Indian outside Fort Caswell, near Sycamore Shoals, and saved a woman supposed to have been Catherine Sherrill. Some romantics assert that Sevier was the first to apply the nickname and that he did so when pushing Catherine to safety over the palisades of the fort. Others assert that the lady merely fell into Sevier's arms after fleeing the Indians and climbing the wall unaided. Sevier held land here, and Bonny Kate built a large house and cabins to accommodate the settlers she hoped would join her. The venture was not successful, but she remained here until her death. Her body was later moved to Knoxville and placed beside that of her husband.

State 53 runs close to the OBEY RIVER where there are many places in which to fish for muskelunge, walleyed pike, bigmouthed and smallmouthed bass, non-game brook bass, cat, and red horse *(camp sites; boats can be rented).*

At 10.8 *m.* is a dangerous one-way bridge over the Obey River and at 12.1 *m.* the road begins a steep ascent *(drive carefully).*

MONROE, 20.6 *m.* (1,200 alt., 200 pop.), was the seat of Overton County from 1806 to 1835. South of it State 100 has many curves and a long gradual slope.

At 27.1 *m.* is the junction with State 85.

Left on State 85 to NETTLE CARRIER CREEK, 5.5 *m.* On the mountain above the head of this little creek was a Cherokee village. According to legend, two young Indians wanted the same girl, who lived in this village. The chief was asked to decide which of them should have her; desiring to be fair, he decided that each of the suitors should throw a twig into the creek and the man whose sprig was carried farthest should be given the girl. The young men agreed. One threw a nettle into the water, the other a thorn. The nettle floated farther, and its thrower married the girl. From that day he was called Nettle Carrier, and for him the creek, and later the community, were named.

LIVINGSTON, 28.1 *m.* (1,090 alt., 1,526 pop.), seat of Overton County, was named for Edgar Livingston, Secretary of State in President Jackson's Cabinet. People in this area raise poultry for the market.

In 1835, when the contest for county seat reached a vote, Livingston won over Monroe by a majority of four. One farmer, "Ranter" Eldridge, favoring Livingston, left his home in Nettle Carrier with 6 or 8 neighbors who intended to vote for Monroe. The party stopped overnight at an inn. The next morning "Ranter" arose before his opponents and turned their horses loose. Had the men voted, Monroe would have won.

1. Right from Livingston on State 52 to the SITE OF THE PUBLIC HOUSE OF BECKY WATSON, 4 *m.,* which was celebrated in the popular song of pioneer days, "Go to Becky Watson's to Get Some Cider." This stand was a community meeting place for the early settlers and attracted crowds particularly on Muster Day, for a military drill ground was nearby. Becky Watson had been granted the right to sell distilled spirits, on the ground that her tavern was a place of public entertainment; but cider was her specialty, as the old song indicates. Becky was a jovial character with a rugged sense of humor.

TIMOTHY, 10 *m.,* is at an entrance to the STANDING STONE STATE PARK *(bridle trails; hiking trails; camping facilities; bathing; boats),* 1.5 *m.,* where 5,500 acres of land unfit for farming have been converted into a recreational park. There is a 65-acre artificial lake. The primary purpose of this project is reforestation. Northwest of Timothy the road winds through woodland to a steep point overlooking the lake. On the point is a 12-room lodge built of hewn logs, and across a narrow ravine are several overnight cabins *(running water, shower baths, fireplaces).*

CELINA, 20 *m.* (560 alt., 756 pop.), seat of Clay County, was named for a daughter of Moses Fisk, pioneer educator. It is at the confluence of the Cumberland and Obey Rivers and was a busy place in the days when forests were being felled and logs floated down Obey River. From this point huge rafts, sometimes singly, often in fleets, were shoved off down the river to Nashville, at that time a leading hardwood center. Rafting is still carried on to some extent.

On the outskirts of Celina is FREE HILLS, a settlement of approximately 300 Negroes. The section is so named because most of the inhabitants are descendants of four slaves who were given 400 acres of land and freed here before the War between the States. They took the name of Hill, the family name of their former owner.

Betty, one of the ex-slaves, fell in love with a handsome, fleet-footed Negro whose name was Bye. She was using the money she earned from her land to buy his freedom, but the war ended shortly before the last payment became due. Bye liked to attend horse races. The spectators, as a diversion, would put Bye against one of their number. Sometimes wagers were laid that Bye could beat his opponent by running on his hands and knees. Whether on foot or on hands and knees, Bye usually won.

The arm of the law reaches this settlement only when a serious criminal offense has been committed. The inhabitants, however, are polite and friendly and have preserved many of the way of their ancestors. They like to play the guitar and to perform the square dances, and many are excellent singers. In almost every generation there is someone who is believed to have the power of voodoo.

Benton McMillin, member of Congress for 20 years, twice Governor of Tennessee (1899–1903), and Ambassador to Peru and Guatemala, practiced law at Celina early in his career.

Left from Celina 7 *m.* on State 53 to BUTLER'S LANDING, where the Clay County Court was first held. This is the point referred to by Daniel Boone as Twin Creeks, in notes he kept on his second journey into the forests of Middle Tennessee.

2. Left from Livingston on State 52 to the village of ALPINE (1,150 alt., 150 pop.), and the mountain school, ALPINE INSTITUTE, founded in 1821 by John Dillard, a young South Carolinian. Alpine Institute began life in a plain, windowless room with hewn-log benches, but with a purely classical curriculum, and was financed by subscriptions. Today (1938) classes meet in a gray stone building on a 100-acre farm. It is a self-help school, and students maintain the property. The boys farm; the girls cook and serve the meals, take care of the dormitory, and do the laundry work.

Right from Alpine, 0.8 *m.* on State 85 to a fork on Cub Creek; L. on this fork, 0.5 *m.*, to RAINBOW CAVE, where a 170-foot waterfall pours into a limestone cavern. In the middle of the afternoon, when the sun shines on the falls, a rainbow is visible.

At 29.3 *m.* on State 42 is the junction with State 85.

Right on State 85 to ZOLLICOFFER LAKE, 1.2 *m.* *(fishing, bathing, camping facilities)*. The lake was impounded at the site where Gen. Felix Zollicoffer and his Confederate troops camped before the battle of Mill Creek in 1862. A portrait of Zollicoffer hangs in the clubhouse.

At 8 *m.* is HILHAM (1,093 alt., 300 pop.), laid out in 1805 by Moses Fisk. The plans made by Fisk are believed to have been the first real attempts at town planning made in the State. Fisk was born in Grafton, Mass., in 1759, was a graduate of Dartmouth College, and for 7 years a tutor in that institution. He came to Tennessee in 1796 hoping to found a mission for the Cherokee. In seeking to establish such a mission he was cooperating with President John Wheelock of Dartmouth who, in turn, was trying to persuade the Society for Propagating Christian Knowledge, of Scotland, to finance the enterprise. Nothing came of the Indian project, but in 1806 Fisk established Fisk Female Academy here, the first institution of its kind in the South. His ability as a mathematician was employed in the marking of the Tennessee-Virginia boundary, and he aided in the preparation of Morse's *Geography*. He spent thousands of dollars on the development of this town. In 1812 he obtained a charter to open a turnpike from Hilham to the highlands of Roaring River. Five years later he received another charter for a turnpike from Hilham to Obey River. The roads were of no avail, and Hilham never became the metropolis Fisk envisioned. The HOME OF MOSES FISK, just south of Hilham, was first a one-room log hut that was enlarged and is today a two-story structure.

ALGOOD, 44.3 *m.* (1,100 alt., 643 pop.), has a brick-making plant. This section held herds of deer and buffalo. The Cherokee, the Creek, and the Chickasaw all came here to hunt.

At COOKEVILLE, 49.3 *m.* (1,050 alt., 3,750 pop.) *(see Tour 12, Sec. b)*, is the junction with US 70 *(see Tour 12)*.

South of US 70 State 42 winds through a woodland and then passes fertile farms on which tobacco, corn, hay, and livestock are grown. The buildings are neat and well kept.

State 42 crosses Falling Water River at 55.7 *m.*

SPARTA, 67.3 *m.* (1,000 alt., 2,211 pop.) *(see Tour 12A)*, is at the junction with US 70A *(see Tour 12A)*. Between Sparta and McMinnville this route and US 70A are united *(see Tour 12A)*.

McMINNVILLE, 95.1 *m.* (1,038 alt., 3,914 pop.), at the junction with US 70A *(see Tour 12A)*, is the seat of Warren County. The town-site of 41 acres was deeded to the county for $100. The town produces hosiery, silk, blankets, overalls, spokes, handles, mops, hardwood flooring, flour, and meal. McMinnville was on the old Indian war trace between southeastern Tennessee and Kentucky that later became a white man's trail.

After the establishment of circuit courts, lawyers rode the circuits like the backwoods preachers of the day. Evidently some of the jurists found court routine tiresome; Judge Joshua Haskell, who presided over the Eighth District Court, was impeached in 1829 for going out behind the courthouse here and eating a watermelon while a case was being argued.

John Lusk, one of the many Revolutionary soldiers who settled in Warren County, died near here in 1838 at the age of 104. Lusk went through the Siege of Quebec, saw Wolfe fall on the Plains of Abraham, was a member of Arnold's expedition into Canada, and fought in the Battle of Saratoga. He survived the surrender of both Burgoyne and Cornwallis and later campaigned under Wayne against the Indians.

The Southern School of Photography, operated here until 1929 by W. S. Lively, attracted students from many parts of the United States. Lively's giant camera, built at the school, used plates 60 inches long and half as wide from which contact prints were made. The school was closed after the building was destroyed by fire.

Left from McMinnville on State 56, now the main route.

The route crosses Barren Fork River at the city limits.

The office of the BOYD NURSERY is at 98 *m.;* its evergreens line the roadside for almost a mile. This is one of the 27 nurseries in the county, which together comprise more than 50 percent of the nursery industry in Tennessee and employ more than 900 people. Annual peach-tree shipments have reached 4,000,000, and apple-tree shipments 3,000,000. The largest plant ever shipped from Warren County was a holly tree more than 10 inches in diameter and nearly 24 feet high. The tree and the huge ball of earth attached to the roots weighed 7,400 pounds.

The route crosses Collins River, 110.5 *m.,* and the Collins River Valley and reaches the foot of the Cumberland Mountains. Here State 56 begins an ascent of 800 feet to the top of the plateau, from which is an excellent view of the region eastward.

BEERSHEBA SPRINGS (R), 116.7 *m.,* was a famous ante-bellum resort centered about a chalybeate spring discovered in 1833.

At 117.2 *m.* is the junction with a paved road.

Right on this road to BEERSHEBA SPRINGS HOTEL, 0.3 *m.,* a hostelry in continuous operation since its construction in 1854. It is a two-story frame structure with double galleries that extend across the 180-foot front. A long row of log cabins, built back of the hotel to house servants, now houses guests. Col. John Armfield of Louisiana purchased a home nearby; many of his friends who were wealthy plantation owners followed him to the Cumberland Mountains to escape the malaria, cholera, yellow fever, and typhoid of the lower Mississippi Valley. President Jackson was a frequent visitor. Later Charles Egbert Craddock (Mary N. Murfree) did much of her writing in a cottage near Lovers' Leap *(see WRITERS OF TENNESSEE).* A foot trail leads from the hotel to STONE DOOR, 1.4 *m.* A narrow opening in the bluff, only a few

INTERIOR OF HOUSE AT CUMBERLAND HOMESTEADS

feet wide, extends the full height of the bluff. Viewed from the top, the sides seem to converge.

At 118.2 *m.* on State 56 is the junction with an unmarked path.

Left on this path to LONG'S MILL SWIMMING POOL, 0.7 *m.,* a natural pool fed by springs. Two sides are walled in by high cliffs covered with laurel and rhododendron, and access to it is by a steep foot trail. A mile below the pool is a 100-foot waterfall.

ALTAMONT, 122.5 *m.* (1,923 alt., 600 pop.), one of the oldest towns on the Cumberland Plateau, is near a hardwood timber belt.

State 56 now passes through a section covered with scrub timber. There are few farms.

At 127.5 *m.* is the junction with State 108.

Left on this good graveled road is GRUETLI, 2.4 *m.* (1,900 alt., 306 pop.), founded in 1870 by a group of German Swiss. They had been induced to migrate by glowing real-estate development literature that described this region as having the combined charms of all Switzerland, plus greater fertility. A party of 99 reached New York, where each was given a ticket and told to proceed to Tracy City, Tennessee. As these people spoke only German, they became confused on the way south and were separated. Many of them ultimately settled only a few miles apart on their new land without being aware of one another's presence. Discouraged by their hard lot, most of the colonists sought new homes and employment in Tracy

City and Chattanooga. Those who remained worked seven days a week; to avoid criticism they tilled the part of their land farthest from the road on Sunday. Later, when their lands had been developed and paid for, the colonists gathered in brush arbors and observed the ritual of the German Reformed Church. They raised grapes, potatoes, corn, and other vegetables, and produced a high grade of Swiss cheese. The neat little white houses in gardens are reminiscent of the Swiss countryside.

At 129.9 *m.* the route passes under the TVA power lines that run from Norris Dam to Wilson Dam at Muscle Shoals, Ala.

COALMONT, 130.2 *m.* (1,923 alt., 600 pop.), is in a region of coal deposits.

TRACY CITY, 137.8 *m.* (1,923 alt., 675 pop.), was once a thriving coal-mining and lumbering town, but in recent years, both industries have slumped. Tracy City miners participated in the great Coal Creek Strike in 1891, and the town was the scene of much strife during the six months-long disturbance.

The Boy Scouts of Tracy City have one of the best privately-owned natural history collections in the State. It includes live poisonous and harmless snakes and other reptiles, mounted birds, and small mammals.

Left from Tracy City on State 27 to FOSTER FALLS, 7 *m.,* which drop 155 feet into a beautiful natural bowl, forming a lake.

South of Tracy City State 56, here well graded and graveled, crosses a flat plateau to Monteagle.

The HIGHLANDER FOLK SCHOOL, 141.3 *m.,* was established in 1930 by Myles Horton, a trade-union organizer. This is one of the few training schools for labor leaders in the South. In two small buildings, whose size helps to limit the student body to about 20, the school offers informal, discussion-type lectures on cultural and economic subjects. Union representatives meet here to discuss new contracts and organizing plans, to play ball, and to hold square dances, or to see labor plays produced by the community on an outdoor stage. Classes and recreational programs are conducted by members of the staff in industrial centers within a radius of 200 miles. The staff also assists in organizing southern workers.

Prominent educators and labor leaders come from many parts of the country to lecture. There is a permanent staff of 6 instructors. The school library, with more than 4,000 carefully selected books and numerous labor periodicals, is open to union members.

A year-around community and county program is carried on, and members of the school attempt to preserve the culture of the mountain people. They are recording mountain songs and documenting folk-dance steps.

At 143.3 *m.* is the DUBOSE MEMORIAL CHURCH TRAINING SCHOOL, a theological seminary maintained by the Protestant Episcopal Church. It occupies the plant of old Fairmount College, a school for girls established in 1873 and called "the female branch of Sewanee."

MONTEAGLE, 143.9 *m.* (1,931 alt., 625 pop.) *(see Tour 13),* is at the junctions with US 64 *(see Tour 13),* and US 41 *(see Tour 8).*

Great Smoky Mountains National Park

Location: East Tennessee and western North Carolina.
Season: Open all year. Flowering season from March through October.
Administrative Offices: Gatlinburg, Tenn.
Admission: Free. No registration for automobiles.
Transportation: State 71 *(see Tour 5)* and 73 *(see Tour 5B)*. Reached by busses from Knoxville bus terminal, 326 S. Gay St.
Highway Mileage: High grade roads 36 m.; secondary 25 m.; truck trails 160.3 m. —old wagon roads and old abandoned logging railroad grades. *(See Tours 5 and 5B for roads traversing park).*
Guides: Information about guide service, horses, and tours at park offices, hotels, and bus terminal at Gatlinburg, and the Smoky Mountains Hiking Club, Knoxville, Tenn.

Accommodations: Hotels and tourist camps in Gatlinburg, Elkmont, Kinzel Springs, Line Springs; small inns at Cade's Cove, Walland; Appalachian Trail clubhouses, open to members, at Elkmont; LeConte Lodge with bunks at Mt. LeConte; U. S. Forest Service camps at Gatlinburg and Bryson City, North Carolina; camp sites and tourist accommodations within the park are now (1939) under construction. Most small hotels and lodges closed during winter.

Climate: Winters short. Snow rarely falls in valleys before Christmas, and is gone by end of February. On the higher peaks it remains until April. Rainfall abundant but not excessive. Summers usually warm and dry with occasional showers. Nights always cool.
Clothing and Equipment: For those who spend time in hotels and motor cars usual wearing apparel is adequate. Sweaters should be carried on horseback rides. For the hiker comfortable leather shoes are necessary in sizes large enough to allow wool socks. Hiking equipment should also include raincoats, tarpaulins, flashlights, and canteens. Blankets are provided by hotels for overnight hikers, or they may be purchased with other equipment outside the park area. Mountain streams provide bathing and swimming.
Medical Service: The Pi Beta Phi Settlement School at Gatlinburg *(see Tour 5)* has hospital with resident nurse in charge and is equipped for first aid service. Resident physician at Gatlinburg. Ambulance service at Sevierville.
Fishing: Park service does not require special license for fishing in the 600 miles of park streams, but fishermen must have State license. License for Tennessee residents $1; nonresident $2.50. Except in streams closed for restocking, the open season is from May 16 to August 31 for trout; from June 16 to August 31 for rock bass and smallmouthed bass. Fishing permitted only between hours of 5 a.m. and 6:30 p.m. Only artificial bait and one hook permitted. Two artificial flies may be attached to leader. Use of spinner or plug with one hook permitted. Brook trout under 8 inches in length and smallmouthed bass under 10 inches in length must not be kept unless seriously injured. Limit: 10 fish to one person a day.
Trails: Trails, extending over 549 miles, divided into three classes. Class-A trails are for hiking and horseback riding; Class-B trails are used chiefly for horses and fire patrols; Class-C trails are foot paths for hikers of experience and for fire patrols. Inadvisable to use uncharted trails without guide service. Information on trails obtainable at park office, Gatlinburg, hotels and hiking clubs, Knoxville; checking stations at Gatlinburg, Townsend, CCC station at Middle Prong on State highway 73 near Townsend, *(see Tour 5 for trails to Chimney Tops, Alum Cave Bluffs, Indian Gap, Clingman's Dome, Mt. LeConte, Greenbrier Wilderness).*

About 60 miles of the 2,050 mile-long Appalachian Trail from Georgia to Maine passes through Smoky Mountains National Park. Here, this famous hiking path is a skyline trail following the ridge crest over some of the loftiest and most rugged mountains in the East. The trail is marked by 4-inch diamond-shaped galvanized iron markers, by square copper markers, and by painted blazes. Side paths lead to gorges, falls, and other points of interest. There are camp sites and shelters along the route. Care should be taken to avoid poison oak and poison ivy, both of which grow at low elevation.

Park Regulations: Overnight camping prohibited at present except by special permit of superintendent. Adequate camping facilities will be provided when the development of the park is completed. Smoking may be forbidden by superintendent during dry season. Hunting not permitted. Still and motion picture cameras may be freely used. Dogs and cats permitted only on leash. Customary regulations in force for preservation of property, and plant and animal life.

A part of the Appalachian escarpment, the Great Smoky Mountains form the towering eastern wall of the Great Valley which stretches southward into Tennessee from Virginia. Geologists estimate that the range, composed of sixteen peaks rising more than 6,000 feet, is the oldest mountain formation on the North American continent. Veil-like mist, called by the mountain-dwelling Cherokee the "Great Smoke," hovers over the blue peaks and shifts constantly with the wind. The Indians called the range "Great Mountains"—a name loosely applied and embracing a wider region than that of the Smokies of today.

The boundary line between North Carolina and Tennessee follows the crestline of the mountains for approximately seventy miles. The entire park —mountain, ramparts, and wooded valleys stretching northeast and southwest into both States—has a total area of 643 square miles.

Almost wholly forestland, it includes 200,000 acres of virgin hardwoods, one of the largest stands in America. In the 50,000 acres of red spruce are many trees more than 400 years old. Beech forests cover the lower slopes, and reach even to some of the higher peaks, with especially magnificent specimens at Trillium Gap. There are some fine stands of yellowwood, or "gopher tree," which the mountain people believe furnished the wood for Noah's ark.

Treeless areas or "balds"—called "slicks" by the natives because of their deceptive appearance of smoothness—are found on some of the ridgetops. Some, known as "heath balds," are covered with shrub growth and are the result of windfall, landslides, and fire. Others, with neither trees nor shrubs, are of unknown origin. The belief that these open meadows, called "grassy balds," are old Indian camp sites is strengthened by the fact that good springs are usually found nearby and that the areas show the impress of more than a century of grazing. The grassy balds were used as grazing lands until the establishment of the park. Andrew's Bald on a southern spur of Clingman's Dome is one of the largest of the grassy balds.

The great variety of both trees and flowers in the Great Smokies is due to the varied character of the terrain and to climatic conditions, which are similar to those of several floral zones. Because of good soil conditions and consistently high rainfall, maple, oak, buckeye, basswood, and chestnut trees reach their largest growth within the park area, and many shrubs attain tree dimension. The largest tree is the yellow poplar or tulip tree,

A SMOKY MOUNTAIN VIEW

which often reaches a height of nearly 200 feet and a diameter of nine feet. The mountain laurel—sometimes towering to forty feet—and the rhododendron are the commonest shrubs.

Since William Bartram, the first botanist to visit the Great Smokies, reported his findings in 1778, scientists and student groups have regarded the region as one of the richest botanical collecting grounds in America. Approximately 3,710 varieties of plant life have been listed, including mosses, liverworts, fungi, lichens, ferns, and 1,500 species of higher plant life. From the mountain bases to the high peaks grow almost every kind of wild flowers found from the deep South to Canada. Tree trunks, rocks, and seemingly every inch of soil have some kind of floral coverage.

Masses of color clothe the park from early spring to late fall. Violets, trillium, both white and yellow, trailing arbutus and phlox, open the pageant, and are followed by the azalea, which Bartram so aptly described as enveloping the hillsides in flame. In July the wild tiger lilies, some with stalks six feet high, cover the open fields with vivid orange. Laurel and rhododendron reach their fullest glory in June, their pink and white blooms giving a roseate glow to the mountainsides. Later come the white and purple asters and, less profuse, the golden. In October dogwood, witch-hazel, and sumac add a variety of tints; and the winter evergreens with festoons of icicles complete the twelve-months' cycle of color.

With the exception of waterfowl, all the birds and animals common to Tennessee are found in the Great Smokies. Wasteful hunting and lumbering have depleted the supply of game, but under the present program of conservation wild turkeys, ruffed grouse, white-tailed deer, and black bear are increasing. In a study of small mammals, made by Edward V. Komarek in 1931–33, fifty-nine species were taken and notations were made of ten others known to inhabit the area. They represented southern, eastern, and northern groups. There are no dangerous animals or reptiles in the Smokies, with the exception of rattlesnakes and copperheads.

No year-round census of bird life and of the species has yet been made. In 1926 Albert F. Ganier, editor of the *Migrant,* listed 80 species in a brief survey of elevations ranging from 1,500 to 6,642 feet within an area of approximately ten miles. Since that time the protection of bird life has resulted in an increase of both the number and kinds of birds. The golden eagle and the northern raven, at present rare species, are among those which have found sanctuary within the park.

The first white men to cross the great mountain barrier of the Smokies were traders who followed bison trails over the wooded heights to secure the Cherokee fur trade. They soon applied the term "great" to the chain of peaks. The surveyors who penetrated the high lands to trace the boundary between Washington County and North Carolina in 1777 entered the ridges on their records as "great Iron Mountain ridge." It was at this time that William Bartram, the botanist, came to the Smokies.

Two noted geologists explored the Smokies in the mid-nineteenth century: Thomas Lainer Clingman, mining expert, author, and explorer; and Arnold Guyot, mineralogist and geologist for the College of New Jersey at Princeton, and an authority on Alpine glacial markings. Guyot's table of elevations for the mountains is considered the most remarkable single-handed achievement in the history of the Great Smokies. Clingman's Dome, Mount LeConte and others were named for noted scientists. In recent years peaks have been named for Horace P. Kephart, author of *Our Southern Highlanders* (1904), and for Colonel David Chapman, whose devotion to the park project won him the title "father of the Great Smoky Mountains National Park."

During the War between the States, Colonel W. H. Thomas, an adopted member of the eastern band of Cherokee, influenced that tribe to declare for the Confederacy. The Indians built a military road across the ridgecrest at Indian Gap and served as guards for a Confederate powder mill. The Cherokee road remained the only one across the main ridge of the Smokies until after 1930.

A movement for a national park was started by Asheville, N. C. in 1899 with the organization of the Appalachian Park Association, but it was not until 1924 that the first definite move was made to create a national park along its present lines. In that year Congress appointed the Southern Appalachian Park Commission to investigate and determine a possible area

OLD WATER MILL IN THE GREAT SMOKIES

for such a project. Meanwhile several national forest associations had been formed, and W. P. Davis of Knoxville suggested the specific region for a national park. In 1925 the Asheville and Knoxville organizations joined forces. Through the cooperation of Dr. Hubert Work, then U. S. Secretary of the Interior, and on recommendation of the commission, provision was made for the Government's development of 150,000 acres of land as soon as 427,000 acres—stipulated as a minimum by law—were turned over to it.

The bill to create the Great Smoky Mountains National Park was signed by President Coolidge on May 22, 1926. In 1928 the Laura Spelman Rockefeller Memorial donated $5,000,000 to augment and complete the fund for purchasing the required amount of acreage. This gift helped smooth out legal difficulties and litigations with lumber companies. The suit to condemn a single tract of 38,288 acres owned by one company was the largest of its kind ever filed in the United States. In 1930 two land grants of 158,876 acres and 138,843 acres were transferred to the Government, and in the following year the park was officially established.

The pioneer way of life is still to be found within its boundaries. During the great westward migration of the eighteenth century, when thousands of English and Scotch-Irish home seekers poured over the Appalachians, many families halted and took up land in the mountain valleys rather than undertake the hard journey westward. Stragglers coming into the mountains after the coves and bottoms were taken up were forced to settle on the ridges where the soil was thin and stony. Even today a sharp distinction is drawn between the "Covites"—prosperous valley farmers—and the ridge-dwellers, called "Ridgemanites," a term synonymous with "poor white" or "clay-eater" in other parts of the South.

Most of the cabins of the early settlers were built at "log raisings." Notched logs, cut at the right turn of the moon to insure proper seasoning, were assembled, and a house was often erected in two or three days with the assistance of neighbors. Chimneys were sometimes constructed of logs, laid in clay, and fired hard by chimney heat. Because large families prevailed, the loft provided sleeping quarters for youngsters when they graduated from trundle beds.

The conversion of the heart of the Great Smokies into a national park ended the isolation of its people. The swift drastic changes, however, have affected chiefly the younger generation; older people still cling to traditions and customs practiced by their forefathers. In character, the highlander remains independent, unaffected and sure of himself, and never seems hurried about his work or his play. His tastes are simple, and his tradition of open-handed hospitality has the force of a religious law. Much of his social life centers about the little "church house." Congregations are predominantly Baptist, with a sprinkling of Methodist and Presbyterian.

Many of the old cabins were razed when the park land was purchased, and their owners were moved elsewhere. The homes that remained may be occupied through the lifetimes of present members of the family and will then become Government property. A few old log houses are maintained as typcial examples of pioneer homes.

PART IV
Appendices

Chronology

1541 De Soto crosses the Mississippi at or near the Fourth Chickasaw Bluff, where Memphis now stands.

1673 Needham and Arthur enter East Tennessee. Joliet and Marquette descend the Mississippi from Wisconsin River to 34° N. latitude and stop at Chickasaw Bluffs.

1682 La Salle builds Fort Prud'homme on First Chickasaw Bluff near mouth of Hatchie River.

1692 Martin Chartier, one of La Salle's men, after some years' stay with Shawnee of Cumberland Valley, travels from French Lick up Cumberland River and overland to Virginia.

1711 Eleazer Wiggan, English trader, establishes trade with Overhill Cherokee.

1714 Charleville, French trader, operates a trading post at Great French Lick, where Nashville now stands.

1730 Sir Alexander Cuming negotiates first treaty between English and Cherokee. Group of chiefs go with him to England.

1736 Christian Priber reaches Cherokee town of Great Tellico; plans to establish his "Kingdom of Paradise."
May 20. D'Artaguette defeated by Chickasaw and English traders.
May 26. Bienville's forces defeated by Chickasaw.

1748 Dr. Thomas Walker of Virginia explores vicinity of present Kingsport.

1750 Dr. Thomas Walker and party explore upper East Tennessee and pass through Cumberland Gap into Kentucky. Walker was the first explorer to record discovery of what he later named Cumberland Gap.

1756 Major Andrew Lewis builds Virginia fort near Chota, Cherokee capital.

1757 Fort Loudoun, near Virginia fort, completed; first Anglo-American fort in Tennessee to be garrisoned.

1758 Presbyterian Mission established at Fort Loudoun by Rev. John Martin.

1760 War between English and Cherokee. Indians take Fort Loudoun.
Daniel Boone commissioned by Henderson and Co. to scout East Tennessee.

1761 Peace is made between English and Cherokee.
Ensign Henry Timberlake and Sergeant Thomas Sumter travel through Overhill Cherokee country.
Elijah Walden, with party of Long Hunters, explores East Tennessee and Cumberland Valley.
Fort Robinson built by Col. Adam Stephen near Long Island of the Holston River, site of modern Kingsport.

1763 Ensign Timberlake, Sergeant Sumter, Ostenaco, and two of his warriors visit England.

1764 Henry Scaggs (Scoggins) explores Tennessee region as representative of Henderson & Co.

1766 Col. James Smith leads exploring party which discovers Stone's River, named for Uriah Stone, one of the party.

1768 Treaty of Hard Labour between English and Cherokee signed.

1769 William Bean, supposed to have been first permanent settler in Tennessee, builds cabin on Boone's Creek, near its junction with Watauga River.

1772 The Watauga Association formed; first independent government established in America by native white Americans.

1775 Washington District supersedes Watauga Association.
March 17. Richard Henderson and Co. buys Cherokee land between Kentucky and Cumberland Rivers.

1776 July 20. Battle of Island Flats between settlers and Cherokee.
July 31. Indians attack Fort Caswell.

1777 Washington District becomes Washington County, with boundaries co-extensive with present State of Tennessee.
July 20. Commissioners of Virginia and North Carolina negotiate Treaty of Long Island with Cherokee.

1779 Jonesboro, first town in Tennessee, established.
Col. Evan Shelby defeats hostile Chickamauga near present site of Chattanooga.
James Robertson, "Father of Tennessee," reaches Cumberland Settlement.
John Donelson begins voyage on flatboat *Adventure.*
Commissioners of Virginia and North Carolina run separate boundary lines called, respectively, "Walker's Line" and "Henderson's Line."

1780 Rev. Samuel Doak, pioneer evangelist, preaches at Salem.
Martin Academy (Doak's school) established at Monette, first institution of higher learning in Mississippi Valley (chartered in 1783).
April 24. John Donelson and party reach Nashborough (Nashville).
Cherokee towns are destroyed by Sevier.
May 1. The Cumberland Compact signed by Cumberland settlers.
October 7. Battle of King's Mountain. Tennessee troops participate.

1781 January 15. Battle of Freeland Station between settlers and hostile Cherokee and Creek.
April 2. Battle of the Bluffs between Cumberland settlers and Chickamauga.

1782 John Sevier defeats Chickamauga and burns their towns.

1783 June 1. McGillivray, Creek chief, forms alliance with Spanish.
Indians raid Cumberland settlements. Davidson County organized.

1784 June 2. North Carolina cedes its western lands to U. S., but repeals act in same year.
December 14. State of Franklin established; constitution adopted.
Nashville incorporated to succeed Nashborough.

1785 Davidson Academy, forerunner of University of Nashville and George Peabody College for Teachers, chartered.
March. First Franklin Legislature meets at Greeneville; John Sevier elected Governor. Four new counties established.
November. Hopewell Treaty signed by U. S. Commissioners and Cherokee chiefs. Cherokee title to Tennessee lands recognized by U. S.

1786 Treaty of Hopewell between U. S. and Chickasaw. Chickasaw title to West Tennessee recognized by U. S.
Franklin and North Carolina both claim jurisdiction in East Tennessee.
Capt. James White and James Connor settle on site of Knoxville.

1787 Franklin Legislature meets at Greeneville for last time.

Robertson conducts Coldwater Expedition against Creek Indians near Muscle Shoals.

1788 Peter Avery blazes Avery's Trace from East Tennessee across Cumberland Plateau to Nashville.
March. Government of Franklin collapses.
Spanish agents intrigue against colonists.
April. Bishop Francis Asbury holds first Methodist Conference west of Allegehenies at Half-Acres in East Tennessee.

1789 John Sevier elected first Representative to U. S. Congress from Washington District.
District of Mero established in Middle Tennessee.
December 22. North Carolina cedes its western lands to U. S.

1790 Population, Territorial U. S. Census, 35,691.
May 26. Congress passes act for government of "Territory of the United States South of the River Ohio," including Tennessee.
William Blount, appointed Territorial Governor, takes oath on September 20 and organizes Washington County on October 22.

1791 William Blount, Governor of the Territory South of the River Ohio, establishes headquarters at White's Fort (Knoxville); Knoxville platted.
July 2. Treaty of the Holston between U. S. and Cherokee signed. Indian land cession secured, new boundaries agreed upon, and Cherokee come under protection of Government.
November 5. Knoxville *Gazette,* weekly newspaper, established at Rogersville.

1792. September 10. Andrew Jackson receives his first military appointment, "Judge Advocate for Davidson Regiment."
September 30. Buchanan's Station attacked by Indians.

1793. September 25. Cavett's Station destroyed by Indians.

1794 September 10. Blount College, forerunner of University of Tennessee, chartered (opened 1795).
September 13. James Ore destroys Chickamauga towns, Nickajack and Running Water.

1795 The Walton Road completed from Knoxville to Nashville across Cumberland Plateau.

1796 February 6. First State constitution adopted.
March 29. First General Assembly meets at Knoxville.
March 30. First State Governor, John Sevier, inaugurated; serves until 1801, and again from 1803 to 1809.
March 31. William Blount and William Cocke elected first United States Senators, reelected four months later.
June 1. Tennessee admitted into Union as sixteenth state.
November 12. Jackson first Representative in Congress from Tennessee; takes seat December 5.

1797 Jackson succeeds William Cocke as U. S. Senator.
January 23. Thomas Embree, in Knoxville *Gazette,* urges organization of an abolition society.
July 8. William Blount expelled from U. S. Senate.

1798 Jackson resigns as U. S. Senator and is appointed judge of State Superior Court.

1800 Population 105,602.
Great religious revival sweeps State.

1802 Jackson elected major general of militia in contest with John Sevier and James Winchester.

1803 General Wilkinson builds Fort Pickering at Memphis.

1805 Aaron Burr visits Nashville on his way to Mississippi territory.

1806 May 30. Jackson kills Charles Dickinson in a duel in Logan, Ky.
April 18. Congress grants 1,000 acres to be sold for support of county academies; 1,000 acres more for two colleges, Blount in east and Cumberland in west.

1807 Nashville Bank, first in Tennessee, chartered.

1810 Population 261,727.
February 4. Cumberland Presbyterian Church organized in Dickson County.

1811 Bank of the State of Tennessee established.

1812 September 12. Legislature convenes in Nashville for first time.

1813 September 4. Jackson is seriously wounded by Bentons at Talbot (afterward City) Hotel, Nashville.
September 7. Jackson mobilizes troops at Fayetteville for Creek War.

1814 March 27. Jackson defeats Creeks at Battle of Tohopeka, ending Creek War.
April 20. Treaty of Fort Jackson made with Creeks.

1815 Manumission Society of Tennessee organized at Lost Creek, Jefferson County.
January 8. Jackson defeats British forces at New Orleans.
September. John Sevier dies near Fort Decatur, Ala.

1818 January–May. Jackson ordered to direct campaign against Seminoles; drives Spanish garrison from Pensacola.
October 19. Jackson and Isaac Shelby, Governor of Kentucky, as U. S. Commissioners, make a treaty with Chickasaw, who cede to U. S. all territory claimed by them east of Mississippi River and north of 35° latitude.

1819 First steamboat arrives at Nashville.
W. L. Brown and Felix Grundy appointed commissioners for Tennessee to determine with Kentucky commissioners the line between Tennessee and Kentucky.
John Overton, with collaboration of Jackson and James Winchester, lays out city of Memphis.
Manumission Intelligencer, later *Emancipator,* first anti-slavery paper in United States, published at Jonesboro.

1820 Population 422,823.
Madison County organized and Jackson settled.

1821 Jackson appointed Territorial Governor of Florida.

1823 *Pioneer,* first newspaper in West Tennessee, established at Jackson.
Jackson elected U. S. Senator to succeed Col. John Williams.

1825 Nashoba, Fanny Wright's colony for freed slaves, established.
May 4. Lafayette visits Nashville.

1826 Memphis *Advocate* established—first newspaper in Memphis.
Duel between Sam Houston and Gen. William White.
Davy Crockett elected to U. S. Congress.

1827 Davidson Academy becomes University of Nashville.
August. Sam Houston elected Governor.

1828 Jackson defeats John Quincy Adams for presidency of the United States.
First steamboat reaches Knoxville.

1829 April. Governor Houston resigns governorship; goes into voluntary exile among Cherokee in Arkansas.
March 9. John H. Eaton appointed Secretary of War by President Jackson.

1830 Population 681,904.

1831 *Railroad Advocate,* one of the first newspapers devoted to railroad promotion, published at Rogersville.

1833 Epidemic of Asiatic cholera sweeps over Tennessee. Large cities paralyzed and many small towns almost depopulated.

1834 New State constitution adopted.

1835 James K. Polk becomes Speaker of the national House of Representatives.
March 5 and 6. New constitution ratified by people.

1836 Sam Houston and other Tennesseans lead Texans in their war for independence from Mexico.
First superintendent of public instruction appointed.

1837 Uniform system of public schools in state established by law.

1838 Great Removal of Cherokee from Tennessee.
James K. Polk, Governor 1839–41.

1840 Population 829,210.

1842 First train in Tennessee makes exhibition run over LaGrange and Memphis Railroad.
Cumberland University at Lebanon chartered and opened.

1843 Nashville becomes State capital.

1844 November. James K. Polk becomes President-elect.

1845 January 1. Work begun on State capitol.
July 4. Great "Western and Southwestern Convention" held in Memphis to promote railroad connection between Tennessee and other southern States.
June 8. Andrew Jackson dies at the Hermitage, aged 78 years.

1847 New Orleans and Ohio Telegraph Company chartered—first company of kind in Tennessee.
May 26. Governor Brown calls volunteers for Mexican War.
Tennessee's quota is 2,800, but 30,000 respond and Tennessee becomes "Volunteer State."

1849 Tennessee Historical Society founded.
June 5. James K. Polk dies at Nashville, aged 54 years.
December. Memphis given city charter.

1850 Population, 1,002,717.
June 3. Southern convention opens 9-day session at Nashville to discuss slavery question.

1851 Col. John Pope wins first prize in cotton exhibit at World's Fair in London. Mark Cockrill receives same rating for sheep.
April 13. Nashville & Chattanooga Railroad, first railroad successfully operated in Tennessee, begins service.

1853 Andrew Johnson, Governor 1853–57.
State Library founded.

1854 February 28. Gov. Andrew Johnson's recommendation for tax to provide public schools becomes law.
State agricultural bureau established and county agricultural societies organized.

1855 State capitol completed.

First Biennial State Fair, forerunner of present annual State Fair, held in Nashville.
Nashville Academy of Music and Fine Arts incorporated.

1860 Population 1,109,801.

1861 May 6. Tennessee, by legislative act, secedes from the Union.
June 24. Governor Harris proclaims Tennessee's secession.
September. Gen. Albert Sidney Johnston prepares State military defense.

1862 February 6. Confederate Fort Henry surrenders.
February 16. Confederate Fort Donelson surrenders.
February 20. Seat of State government removed to Memphis.
March 3. Andrew Johnson appointed military governor of Tennessee.
April 6-7. Battle of Shiloh.
July–September. Gen. Nathan Bedford Forrest raids Federal troops in Middle Tennessee.
August 16. General Bragg begins Tennessee campaign at Chattanooga. General Forrest raids Federal troops in West Tennessee.

1863 December 31 (1862), January 1, and 2. Battle of Stone's River.
June 20–July 7. Confederate army under Bragg retires to Tullahoma, blocking way to Chattanooga.
September 19-20. Battle of Chickamauga.
November 24-25. Battle of Chattanooga (Missionary Ridge and Lookout Mountain); Bragg, outnumbered, retreats to Georgia.

1864 September 4. Gen. John H. Morgan killed at Greeneville, East Tennessee.
November 4. Gov. Andrew Johnson becomes Vice-President elect.
November 30. Battle of Franklin.
December 15-16. Battle of Nashville.

1865 Beginning of Reconstruction.
March 4. William G. (Parson) Brownlow elected Governor.
April 5. Legislature ratifies 13th amendment.
April 15. Andrew Johnson becomes President of the United States.

1866. July 19. Tennessee ratifies Fourteenth amendment to U. S. Constitution.
July 24. Tennessee restored to Union.
Fisk University (Negro) opened at Nashville (chartered 1867).

1867 Gen. John H. Eaton, Jr., former Union officer, elected State superintendent of public instruction.
Legislature passes law providing separate schools for Negroes at State's expense.

1868 Ku Klux Klan organized at Pulaski.

1869 March. Ku Klux Klan disbanded by Gen. Nathan Bedford Forrest, "Grand Cyclops."
Gen. John Eaton publishes *Report of School Conditions in Tennessee.*
DeWitt C. Senter appointed Governor.

1870 Population, 1,258,521.
Third constitution adopted.

1873 Educational law passed, establishing uniform system of free public schools.

1875 First State board of education created.
A bill abolishing the office of county superintendent of public schools is pushed through legislature but vetoed.
July 31. Andrew Johnson, former President, dies near Jonesboro.

1877 State board of health created.

1878 Worst yellow fever epidemic in history of U. S. strikes Memphis. Of the 6,000 white population 4,204 died; of the 14,000 Negroes, 946.

1880 Population, 1,542,359.
Centennial celebration of Nashville settlement.

1882 Julia Doak appointed State superintendent of education, first woman in U. S. to hold such office.

1886 "The War of the Roses." Robert L. Taylor, Democratic candidate for Governor, defeats his brother, Alfred A. Taylor, Republican candidate.

1890 Population, 1,767,518.

1891 July 21. First major strike in Tennessee history called by miners at Coal Creek.

1892 Steel cantilever bridge over Mississippi at Memphis opened.

1895 Chickamauga and Chattanooga National Military Park dedicated.

1897 May 1–November 1. Tennessee Centennial Exposition held at Nashville.

1898 Tennessee furnishes four regiments for War with Spain.

1899 County courts given power to establish county high schools and provide for their support and supervision.

1900 Population 2,020,616.

1907 Local option law extended to include all cities and towns.

1908 State militia stops activities of night riders at Reelfoot Lake.

1909 The general education bill enacted.
January. State-wide prohibition law passed; becomes effective July 1.
Francis Joseph Campbell, blind educator, knighted by King Edward VII for his services to the blind.

1910 Population, 2,184,789.
Independents elect candidates for the judiciary.

1913 One-third of the gross revenues of the State appropriated for education.
Highway improvement begun.
Workmen's compensation law passed.

1917 April 6. U. S. declares war against Germany. Many Tennesseans volunteer.
First Liberty Loan oversubscribed in Tennessee.

1918 Sergeant Alvin C. York, with small squad and armed only with pistol and rifle, takes Hill 223 in Argonne Forest.
December. Col. Luke Lea, of Nashville, leads a party of commissioned and non-commissioned officers on daring unofficial raid into Holland to capture the Kaiser. The attempt fails.

1919 State agrees to furnish $1,000,000, City of Nashville $600,000 and Davidson County $400,000 for memorial building in honor of soldiers of World War.
January 13. Eighteenth amendment (prohibition) to Federal Constitution ratified.

1920 Population, 2,337,885.
August 18. Nineteenth amendment (woman's suffrage) ratified.

1923 Gov. Austin Peay (1923–1927) puts all activities of State under eight major departments, abolishing about fifty bureaus and departments.

1925 Scopes evolution trial held at Dayton; William Jennings Bryan and Clarence Darrow are opposing counsel.

1929 By agreement with North Carolina, land for Great Smoky Mountains National

Park offered to Federal government and accepted.
March. Heavy rains cause floods with loss of life and property.

1930 Population, 2,616,556.
State has $6,000,000 in closed banks.

1931 Legislature investigating committee votes against impeachment of Governor Horton.
July 21. Tennesee votes for repeal of 18th amendment to Constitution.

1932 Coal miners strike at Wilder.

1933 August 31. Tennessee Valley Authority created by an Act of Congress to develop natural resources of territory within Tennessee River watershed.
November. Construction of Norris Dam begun.

1934 Barnard Astronomical Association founded as a memorial to Dr. Edward Emerson Barnard, Nashville astronomer.

1935 Rural Electrification Act passed by legislature regulating operation of TVA in State.

1936 January. Convict lease law repealed.
January. Construction of Chickamauga Dam begun.
March 4. Norris Dam, first Unit of TVA, completed.
December. Coal miners strike at Jamestown. State militia called out.
December. Unemployment compensation law enacted at special session of legislature.

1937 January. Floods cause much property damage.
May 18. Strike closes fabricating plant of Aluminum Company of America at Alcoa.
November 5. Governor Gordon Browning's unit bill for proportional suffrage among counties passed at special session of Legislature.

1938 County unit bill invalidated by Tennessee Supreme Court.

1939 State legislature overrides Governor's veto of act to permit, or forbid at county's option, package sales of alcoholic liquor.

Selected Bibliography

GENERAL INFORMATION

American Automobile Association. *Southeastern Tour Book.* Washington, D. C., 1938. 408 p. illus., maps. Issued annually.

Johnson, Stanley, ed. *The Tennessee Handbook.* Knoxville, Univ. of Tennessee, 1938. 140 p. maps, tables, diagr., illus.

Tennessee. State Dept. *Tennessee Blue Book and Official Directory.* Nashville, 1938. 197 p. maps, illus., ports.

DESCRIPTION AND TRAVEL

Bartram, William. *Travels through North and South Carolina, Georgia, East and West Florida, the Cherokee Country, the Extensive Territories of the Muscogulges or Creek Confederacy, and the Country of the Choctaws.* Philadelphia, James and Johnson, 1791. 520 p. front., plates, map.

Campbell, John C. *The Southern Highlander and His Homeland.* New York, Russell Sage Foundation, 1921. 405 p. front., illus. (music), plates, ports., maps.

Faris, John Thompson. *The Romance of the Rivers.* New York and London, Harper, 1927. 298 p. front., plates. Bibl. Includes accounts of the Tennessee and Cumberland Rivers.

Williams, Samuel Cole, ed. *Early Travels in the Tennessee Country, 1540–1800.* Johnson City, Watagua Press, 1928. 540 p. front., plates, ports., maps facsims.

Wilson, Samuel Tyndale. *The Southern Mountaineers.* 4th ed. New York City, Literature Dept., Presbyterian Home Missions, 1914. 202 p. front. (map), plates. 1st ed. 1906.

GEOLOGY

Cockrill, Elizabeth. *Bibliography of Tennessee. Geology, Soils, Drainage, Forestry, etc.* With subject index. Nashville, Folk-Keelin Printing Co., 1911. 119 p. (Tennessee State Geological Survey. Extract from Bulletin No. 1, "Geological Work in Tennessee.")

Safford, J. M., and J. B. Killebrew. *The Elements of the Geology of Tennessee.* Nashville, Ambrose & Bostleman, 1904. 264 p. illus.

PLANT AND ANIMAL LIFE

Ganier, Albert Franklin. *A Distributional List of the Birds of Tennessee.* Nashville, 1933, 64 p. (Tennessee Division of Game and Fish Conservation.)

Gattinger, Augustin. *The Flora of Tennessee and a Philosophy of Botany.* Pub. by authority of the State through the Bureau of Agriculture. Nashville, Press of Gospel Advocate Pub. Co., 1901. 296 p. front. (port.), illus.

———. *The Medicinal Plants of Tennessee . . .* Nashville, F. M. Paul, 1894, 128 p.

Jennison, Harry Milliken. *Preliminary Check List of the Spring Wild Flowers and Ferns of Tennessee.* Nashville, Williams Printing Co., 1929. 32 p. illus.

Webb, A. C. *Some Birds and Their Ways.* Illus. by the Author. Richmond, B. F. Johnson Pub. Co., 1900. 144 p.

ARCHEOLOGY AND INDIANS

Harrington, M. R. *Cherokee and Earlier Remains on Upper Tennessee River.* New York, Museum of the American Indian, Heye Foundation, 1922. 321 p. front., illus., plates, plans. (Indian Notes and Monographs. Miscellaneous No. 24.)

Jones, Joseph. *Explorations of the Aboriginal Remains of Tennessee.* Washington, 1876. 85 p. illus. (Smithsonian Inst. Contrib. to Knowl., v. 22, No. 259.)

Meyer, William Edward. *Recent Archaeological Discoveries in Tennessee.* Washington, D. C., Archaeological Society, 1922. 150 p.

Royce, Charles C. "The Cherokee Nation of Indians: a Narrative of their Official Relations with the Colonial and Federal Government." In U. S. Bureau of Am. Ethnology. *Fifth Annual Report, 1883–84.* Washington, 1887. p. 121-378. pl. VII-IX (maps).

Swanton, J. R. *Early History of the Creek Indians and Their Neighbors.* Washington, Govt. Print. Off., 1922. 492 p. maps. (Smithsonian Inst. Bureau of Am. Ethnology. Bulletin 73.)

Thruston, Gates Phillips. *The Antiquities of Tennessee and the Adjacent States, and the State of Aboriginal Society in the Scale of Civilization Represented by Them.* 2d ed. Cincinnati, R. Clarke Co., 1897. 369 p. front., illus., plans, plates.

Williams, Samuel Cole, ed. *Adair's History of the American Indians.* Ed. under the auspices of the National Society of the Colonial Dames of America, in Tennessee. Johnson City, Watauga Press, 1930. 508 p. map. Originally pub. 1775.

Williams, Samuel Cole. *Beginnings of West Tennessee, in the Land of the Chickasaws, 1541–1841.* Johnson City, Watauga Press, 1930. 331 p. front., maps, facsim.

HISTORY

Allen, Charles Fletcher. *David Crockett, Scout, Small Boy, Pilgrim, Mountaineer, Soldier, Bear-hunter, and Congressman, Defender of the Alamo.* Philadelphia and London, Lippincott, 1911. 308 p. col. front., plates, port.

Allen, Leslie H. *Bryan and Darrow at Dayton.* New York, A. Lee & Co., 1925. 218 p. front., ports. Describes and documents the Scopes evolution trial.

Allison, John. *Dropped Stitches in Tennessee History.* Nashville, Marshall & Bruce Co., 1897. 152 p. front., plates.

Bruce, H. Addington. *Daniel Boone and the Wilderness Road.* New York, Macmillan, 1910. 349 p. front., plates, ports., map.

Caldwell, Joshua W. *Studies in the Constitutional History of Tennessee.* 2d ed. rev. and enl. Cincinnati, Robert Clarke Co., 1907. 412 p.

Carr, John. *Early Times in Middle Tennessee.* Nashville, Pub. for E. Carr, by E. Stevenson & F. A. Owen, 1857.

Coates, Robert M. *The Outlaw Years; the History of the Land Pirates of the Natchez Trace.* New York, Macaulay, 1930. 308 p. front., plates, facsim.

Crockett, David. *An Account of Col. Crockett's Tour to the North and down East* . . . Written by himself. Philadelphia, E. L. Carey & A. Hart; Baltimore, Carey, Hart & Co., 1835. 234 p. front. (port.)

———. *Col. Crockett's Exploits and Adventures in Texas* . . . Written by himself. The narrative brought down from the death of Col. Crockett to the battle of San Jacinto, by an eye-witness. Philadelphia, T. K. & P. G. Collins, 1836. 216 p. front. (port.)

———. *A Narrative of the Life of David Crockett, of the State of Tennessee* . . . Written by himself. American ed., printed at Philadelphia, by E. L. Carey & A. Hart; London, reprinted by J. Limbird, 1834. 113 p.

Embree, Elihu. *Emancipator.* Nashville, B. H. Murphy, 1932. 112 p. illus. A reprint of the *Emancipator,* together with a biographical sketch of Elihu Embree and two hitherto unpublished antislavery memorials bearing his signature.

Fleming, Walter L. *The Sequel to Appomattox; a Chronicle of the Reunion of the States.* New Haven, Yale Univ. Press, 1921. 322 p. col. front. (The Chronicles of America Series, Allen Johnson, ed. v. 32.)

Garrett, William Robertson, and Albert Virgil Goodpasture. *History of Tennessee, Its People and Its Institutions.* Nashville, Brandon Printing Co., 1900. 351 p. front., illus., port., maps. Bibl.

Goodspeed, Weston A., and others. *History of Tennessee from the Earliest Time* . . . Nashville, Goodspeed Pub. Co., 1886. 1,402 p. front., plates, ports., maps.

Hale, Will T., and Dixon L. Merritt. *A History of Tennessee and Tennesseans; the*

Leaders and Representative Men in Commerce, Industry and Modern Activities. Chicago and New York, Lewis Pub. Co., 1913. 8 v. front., illus., plates, ports.

Hamer, Philip May, ed. *Tennessee; a History, 1673–1832.* New York, American Historical Society, 1933. 4 v. fronts., plates, ports.

Haywood, John. *The Civil and Political History of the State of Tennessee from Its Earliest Settlement up to the Year 1796, Including the Boundaries of the State.* Reprint of ed. of 1823. Nashville, Pub. House of Methodist Episcopal Church, South, 1891. 518 p.

James, Marquis. *Andrew Jackson, the Border Captain.* Indianapolis, Bobbs-Merrill, 1933. 461 p. front., plates, ports., maps, plans, facsims. Bibl.

———. *Andrew Jackson, Portrait of a President.* Indianapolis, Bobbs-Merrill, 1937. 627 p. front., plates, ports., facsims. Bibl.

———. *The Raven, a Biography of Sam Houston.* Indianapolis, Bobbs-Merrill, 1927. 489 p. front., illus., plates, ports., maps.

Luttrell, Laura, and Mary U. Rothrock, comp. *Calvin Morgan McClung Historical Collection of Books, Pamphlets, Manuscripts, Pictures and Maps Relating to Early Western Travel and the History and Genealogy of Tennessee and Other Southern States.* Presented to Lawson McGhee Library by Mrs. Calvin M. McClung. Knoxville, Knoxville Lithographing Co., 1921. 192 p. port.

Lytle, Andrew Nelson. *Bedford Forrest and His Critter Company.* New York, Minton, Balch & Co., 1931. 402 p. front., illus., plates, ports. Bibl.

Milton, George Fort, Jr. *The Age of Hate; Andrew Johnson and the Radicals.* New York, Coward-McCann, 1930. 787 p. front., plates, ports., facsims.

———. *Constitution of Tennessee, Considered with Reference to the Constitution of Other States.* Knoxville, by the Author, 1897. 35 p.

Moore, John Trotwood, and Austin P. Foster. *Tennessee, the Volunteer State, 1769–1923.* Chicago, Nashville, S. G. Clarke Pub. Co., 1923. 4 v. front., plates, ports., maps.

Owsley, Frank Lawrence. *King Cotton Diplomacy; Foreign Relations of the Confederate States of America.* Chicago, Univ. of Chicago Press, 1931. 617 p. Bibl.

Parton, James. *Life of Andrew Jackson.* Boston, Houghton Mifflin Co., 1887–88. 3 v. fronts., port. Originally pub. 1860.

Patton, James Welch. *Unionism and Reconstruction in Tennessee, 1860–1869.* Chapel Hill, Univ. of North Carolina Press, 1934. 267 p. front. (port.), plates, facsim.

Phelan, James. *History of Tennessee; the Making of a State.* Boston and New York, Houghton, Mifflin Co., 1888. 478 p. front. (map).

Ramsey, J. G. M. *The Annals of Tennessee to the End of the Eighteenth Century* . . . Kingsport, Kingsport Press, 1926. 832 p. front. (map), illus. (facsim.), plan. Originally printed in 1853. Repr. 1926 with the addition of Fain's Index. Starts with the first settlement of the Watauga Association in 1769.

Romine, Mr. and Mrs. William Bethel. *A Story of the Original Ku Klux Klan.* Pulaski Citizen, 1934. 29 p. plates, ports.

Rose, Laura (Martin). *The Ku Klux Klan, or Invisible Empire.* New Orleans, L. Graham Co., 1914. 84 p. col. front., plates, ports.

Rothrock, Mary U. *Discovering Tennessee.* Chapel Hill, Univ. of North Carolina Press, 1936. 498 p. front., illus.

Snyder, Mrs. Ann E. *The Civil War from a Southern Standpoint* . . . Nashville, Pub. House of M. E. Church, South, 1890. 308 p. front., plates.

Taylor, James B., Alfred A. Taylor, and Hugh L. Taylor. *Life and Career of Senator Robert Love Taylor (Our Bob).* By His Three Surviving Brothers . . . Nashville, Bob Taylor Pub. Co., 1913. 370 p. front., plates, ports.

Tennessee Historical Magazine. Pub. under auspices of Tennessee Historical Society in cooperation with State Dept. of Education. Nashville, 1915–37.

White, Robert Hiram. *Tennessee, Its Growth and Progress.* Nashville, R. H. White, 1936. 709 p. col. front., illus., col. plates, maps, diagrs.

Williams, Samuel Cole, ed. *Lieut. Henry Timberlake's Memoirs, 1756–1765.* Johnson City, Watauga Press, 1927. 197 p. plate, map.

Williams, Samuel Cole. *History of the Lost State of Franklin.* Rev. ed. New York, Press of the Pioneers, 1933. 378 p. front. (port.)

———. *Dawn of Tennessee Valley and Tennessee History* . . . Johnson City, Watauga Press, 1937. 495 p. ports., maps, facsim. Bibl.

TENNESSEE VALLEY AUTHORITY

Chancellor, John. *The Library in the TVA Adult Education Program.* Chicago, Am. Library Assn., 1937. 75 p. front. (map), plates.

Hart, Joseph K. *Education for an Age of Power; the TVA Poses a Problem.* New Harper, 1935. 245 p. front. Bibl.

Howard, T. Levron. *The TVA and Economic Security in the South.* Chapel Hill, Univ. of North Carolina Press, 1936. 11 p. (Southern Policy Papers, No. 7.)

Keun, Odette. *A Foreigner Looks at the TVA.* New York, Toronto, Longmans, Green & Co., 1937. 89 p. front., plates.

Tennessee Valley Authority. *The Development of the Tennessee Valley.* Washington, Govt. Print. Off., 1936. 15 p. illus., map.

Tennessee Valley Authority. *A History of Navigation on the Tennessee River System; an Interpretation of the Economic influence of This River System on the Tennessee Valley.* Message from the President of the United States transmitting a Survey. Washington, Govt. Print. Off., 1937. 192 p. illus., maps, diagrs. (U. S. 75th Cong., 1st sess. House. Doc. 254).

Tennessee Valley Authority. *An Indexed Bibliography of the Tennessee Valley Authority,* comp. by Harry C. Baur, technical librarian. Knoxville, 1936. 60 p. 8 numb. mimeographed.

Tennessee Valley Authority. *Norris Dam.* Washington, Govt. Print. Off., 1936. 39 p. illus., map.

Tennessee Valley Authority. *The Scenic Resources of the Tennessee Valley.* A Descriptive and Pictorial Inventory. Prepared by the TVA. Dept. of Regional Planning Studies, Knoxville. Washington, Govt. Print. Off., 1938. 222 p. front., illus., maps, diagrs.

Tennessee Valley Authority. *Tennessee Valley Authority, 1933–1937.* Washington, Govt. Print. Off., 1937. 83 p. front., illus.

ECONOMIC AND SOCIAL STUDIES

Allred, C. E. *Economic and Social Study of Tennessee.* Knoxville, 1924. 64 p. tables, diagrs. (Univ. of Tennessee Record. Extension Series, v. 1, No. 5.)

Couch, W. T., ed. *Culture in the South.* Chapel Hill, Univ. of North Carolina Press, 1934. 711 p. Contains 31 essays (by Broadus Mitchell, George Fort Milton, Jr., Donald Davidson, Bruce Crawford, B. A. Botkin, Charles W. Pitkin, etc.).

Eaton, John, Jr. *First Report of the Superintendent of Public Instruction of the State of Tennessee.* Nashville, Printer to the State, at the Press & Times Office, 1869.

Holt, Albert C. *The Economic and Social Beginnings of Tennessee.* Nashville, 1923. 170 p. illus. (maps, facsim.) (Ph.D. Thesis George Peabody College.) Bibl.

Odum, Howard W. *Southern Regions of the United States.* Prepared for the Southern Regional Committee of the Social Science Research Council. Chapel Hill, Univ. of North Carolina Press, 1936. 664 p. maps, charts, tables.

Patterson, Caleb Perry. *The Negro in Tennessee, 1790–1865.* Austin, The University, 1922. 213 p. (Univ. of Texas Bulletin, No. 2205.) Bibl.

Twelve Southerners. *I'll Take My Stand.* New York and London, Harper, 1930. 359 p. A series of essays on the Southern agrarian movement by John Crowe Ransom, Donald Davidson, Allen Tate, Andrew Nelson Lytle, Frank Owsley, John Gould Fletcher, and others.

U. S. Bureau of Education. *A Survey of Higher Education in Tennessee, 1924.* Maryville, Tennessee College Assn., 1926. 114 p.

Vance, Rupert B. *Human Geography of the South; a Study in Regional Resources and Human Adequacy.* Chapel Hill, Univ. of North Carolina Press, 1932. 596 p. illus. (maps) (Univ. of North Carolina Social Study Series.) Bibl.

AGRICULTURAL AND MINERAL RESOURCES

Bayley, William Shirley. *The Magnetic Iron Ores of East Tennessee and Western North Carolina.* Nashville, McQuiddy Printing Co., 1923. 252 p. (Tennessee Dept. of Education. Division of Geology. Bulletin 29.)

Boyd, Willis Baxter, ed. *Tennessee.* Nashville, 1934. 111 p. ports., illus., indexes. (Tennessee Dept. of Agriculture. O. E. Van Cleve, Commissioner.)

Glenn, L. C. *The Northern Tennessee Coal Field* . . . Nashville, 1925. 478 p. illus., maps, tables. (Tennessee Geological Survey. Bulletin 33-B.)

Gray, Lewis Cecil. *History of Agriculture in the Southern United States to 1860.* By Lewis Cecil Gray, assisted by Esther Katherine Thompson, with an int. note by Henry Charles Taylor. Washington, Carnegie Institution, 1933. 2 v. illus. (maps), diagrs. (Carnegie Inst. of Washington. Pub. No. 430.)

Killebrew, Joseph Buckner. *Tennessee: Its Agricultural and Mineral Wealth, Showing the Extent, Value and Accessibility of Its Ores, with Analyses of the Same.* By J. B. Killebrew, Commissioner of Agriculture, Statistics and Mines. Nashville, Travel, Eastman & Howell, printers, 1876. 196 p. illus., map.

Payne, Henry Mace. *The Undeveloped Mineral Resources of the South.* Washington, D. C., American Mining Congress, 1928. 368 p. Bibl.

Tennessee Dept. of Agriculture. *Biennial Reports.* Knoxville, 1856–1911. 10 v.

RELIGION

Asbury, Francis. *The Journal of the Rev. Francis Asbury, Bishop of the Methodist Episcopal Church, from Aug. 7, 1781, to Dec. 7, 1815.* New York, N. Bangs & T. Mason, 1821. 3 v.

Cartright, Peter. *Autobiography of Peter Cartright, the Backwoods Preacher.* Ed. by W. P. Strickland. New York, Carlton & Porter, 1857. 525 p.

Cleveland, Catherine C. *The Great Revival in the West, 1797–1805.* Chicago, Univ. of Chicago Press, 1916. 215 p. maps. Bibl.

Dow, Lorenzo. *The Dealings of God, Man, and the Devil, as Exemplified in the Life, Experience, and Travels of Lorenzo Dow, in a Period of More Than Half a Century* . . . 4th ed. Norwich, Printed and sold by W. Faulkner, 1833. 704 p.

McDonald, B. W. *History of Cumberland Presbyterian Church.* Nashville, Cumberland Presbyterian Pub. House, 1888. 679 p.

McFerrin, John B. *History of Methodism in Tennessee.* Nashville, Southern Methodist Pub. House, 1869–73. 3 v. V. 1 from 1773 to 1804; v. 2 from 1804 to 1818; v. 3 from 1818 to 1840.

Tyler, B. R. "History of the Disciples of Christ." (In *American Church History* series. New York, 1893–97. v. 12 (1894) p. 1-162.) Bibl.

Williams, Samuel Cole. "Tennessee's First Pastor." (In *The Baptists of Tennessee.* Kingsport, Southern Publishers, 1930. 2 v.)

LITERATURE AND JOURNALISM

Baskervill, William Malone. *Southern Writers: Biographical and Critical Studies.* Nashville, Pub. House, M. E. Church, South. 2 v. Vol. 1 (1897) contains essays on Irwin Russell, Joel Chandler Harris, Maurice Thompson, Sidney Lanier, George W. Cable, and Charles Egbert Craddock. Vol II (1903) is a supplementary volume containing 11 essays by Baskervill's pupils.

Link, Samuel Albert. *Pioneers of Southern Literature.* Nashville, Pub. House, M. E. Church, South, 1903. 2 v. Deals with Paul Hamilton Hayne, William Gillmore Simms, John Pendleton Kennedy, Edgar Allan Poe, David Crockett, and others.

McMurtrie, Douglas C. *Early Printing in Tennessee.* With a bibliography of the Printing House Craftsmen, 1933. 141 p. facsims.

Parks, Edd Winfield, ed. *Southern Poets.* Representative Selections, with introduction, bibliography, and notes. New York, Cincinnati, etc., Am. Book Co., 1936. 419 p. (American Writers series; H. H. Clark, general ed.)

ARCHITECTURE

Brandau, Roberta Seawell, ed. *History of Homes and Gardens of Tennessee.* Comp. by Garden Study Club of Nashville, Mrs. John Trotwood Moore collaborating. Nashville, Parthenon Press, 1936. 503 p. front., illus.

Caldwell, Mrs. Mary French. *Andrew Jackson's Hermitage.* Nashville, Ladies' Hermitage Assn., 1933. 106 p. front., plates, ports.

Wilson, Benjamin Franklin, III. *The Parthenon of Pericles and Its Reproduction in America.* Nashville, Parthenon Press, 1937. 140 p. col. front., plates.

FOLKLORE AND MUSIC

Bell, Charles Bailey, *The Bell Witch, a Mysterious Spirit.* Nashville, Lark Bindery, 1934. 228 p. port.

Cox, John Harrington, ed. *Folk-songs of the South.* Collected under the auspices of the West Virginia Folk-lore Society. Cambridge, Harvard Univ. Press, 1925. 545 p. plates, ports., map.

Handy, W. C., ed. *Blues, an Anthology.* With int. by Abbe Niles; illus. by Miguel Covarrubias. New York, A. & C. Boni, 1926. 180 p. front., illus., plates.

Ingram, M. V. *An Authenticated History of the Famous Bell Witch . . . The Mysterious Talking Goblin That Terrorized the West End of Robertson County, Tennessee . . .* Clarksville, W. P. Titus, 1894. 316 p.

Jackson, George Pullen. *White Spirituals in the Southern Uplands.* The Story of the Fasola Folk, Their Songs, Singings, and "Buckwheat" Notes. Chapel Hill, Univ. of North Carolina Press, 1933. 444 p. front., illus. (incl. music), plates, ports., facsims. Bibl.

Lee, George W. *Beale Street, Where the Blues Began.* With foreword by W. C. Handy. New York, R. O. Ballou, 1934. 296 p. front., ports.

Marsh, J. B. T. *The Story of the Jubilee Singers.* London, Hodder & Stoughton, 1903. 7th ed. 311 p.

Richardson, Mrs. Ethel Park, comp. *American Mountain Songs.* Ed. and arranged by Sigmund Spaeth. New York, Greenberg, 1927. 120 p. illus. With music.

Work, John Wesley. *Folk Song of the American Negro.* Nashville, Press of Fisk Univ., 1915. 131 p. illus. (incl. ports.).

CITIES AND TOWNS

Allen, Penelope Johnson. *Guide Book of Chattanooga and Vicinity,* Chattanooga, 1935. 27 p. Pub. under auspices of Volunteer Chapter, U. S. Daughters of 1812.

Beard, William Ewing. *Nashville, the Home of History Makers.* Nashville, Civitan Club, 1929. 93 p.

Keating, John McLeod, and O. F. Vedder. *History of the City of Memphis and Shelby County, Tennessee.* With illus. and biographical sketches. Syracuse, N. Y., D. Mason & Co., 1889. 2 v. Vol. I by Keating, Vol. II by Vedder, front., ports., maps.

Long, Howard. *Kingsport; a Romance of Industry.* Kingsport, Sevier Press, 1928. 304 p. front., plates, ports.

Rule, William, ed. *Standard History of Knoxville . . .* Ed. by William Rule; George F. Mellen, Ph. D., and J. Wooldridge, collaborators. Chicago, Lewis Pub. Co., 1900. 590 p. ports.

COUNTIES

Clayton, W. W. *History of Davidson County, Tennessee.* With illus. and biographical sketches. Philadelphia, J. W. Lewis & Co., 1880. 499 p. front., illus., plates, ports, maps.

Foster, Austin P. *Counties of Tennessee.* Nashville, 1923. 124 p. (Tennessee Dept. of Education. Division of History.)

Taylor, Oliver. *Historic Sullivan; a History of Sullivan County, Tennessee.* Bristol, Tenn., King Printing Co., 1909. 330 p. front., plates, ports., maps, facsims.

GREAT SMOKY MOUNTAINS NATIONAL PARK

Great Smoky Mountains Pub. Co. *The Great Smoky Mountains National Park, Tennessee.* Knoxville, 1930. 32 p. front., illus.

Hunnicutt, Samuel J. *Twenty Years of Hunting and Fishing in the Great Smoky Mountains.* Knoxville, S. B. Newman & Co., 1926. 216 p. illus., (incl. port.)

McCoy, George William. *A Bibliography for the Great Smoky Mountains.* Asheville, N. C., 1932. 31 p. Mimeographed.

McCoy, George William, and George Maas. *Guide to the Great Smoky Mountains National Park.* Asheville, N. C., Inland Press, 1935. 2d ed. 161 p. illus.

Mason, Robert Lindsay. *The Lure of the Great Smokies.* Boston and New York, Houghton, Mifflin Co., 1927, 320 p. front., plates, ports., map.

Smoky Mountains Hiking Club. *Annual Handbook . . . Smoky Mountains Hiking Club* . . . Knoxville, 1932 to date. illus., plates, map.

Thornburgh, Laura. *The Great Smoky Mountains.* By Laura Thornborough (pseud.), with drawings by Vivian Moir and full-page illus. from photographs. New York, Crowell, 1937. 147 p.

REELFOOT LAKE

Fuller, Myron L. "Our Greatest Earthquake." *Popular Science Monthly,* July 1906, v. 69:76-86.

Glenn, L. C. "The Geography and Geology of Reelfoot Lake." *Journal of Tennessee Academy of Science,* Jan. 1933, v. 8:3-12.

Nelson, Wilbur A. "Reelfoot an Earthquake Lake." *National Geographic Magazine,* Jan. 1924, v. 45:104-107.

Index

A and I Concert Singers, 204
Abell, Father, 115
Abraham of Chilhowee, 296
Acklen, Col. J. A. S., 200
Adair, James, 34
Adair, John, 347
Adair's Station, 347
Adams, Gen. John, 377, 379
Adams, John Quincy, 52
Adams, President John, 210, 368
Adventure, 181, 396
Aebli, Casper, 239
Agar, Herbert, 152
Agrarian Group *(see Writers)*
Agricultural Adjustment Administration, 24, 25, 100
Agriculture, 74-80
Agencies and organizations, 26, 76, 80, 102, 164, 248, 300, 361, 386-388, 394, 402, 414, 494, 495, 503; cooperatives, 79, 80, 300, 301, 385, 396, 402, 500; cotton, 72, 75-77, 104, 133, 208-210, 417, 420, 422, 449, 476, 487, 490; dairying, 75, 78-80, 301, 363, 381, 385, 485, 512; forage crops, 76, 77, 473, 485, 495; fruit growing, 78, 413, 438; future outlook, 90; grain production, 72, 75-78, 276, 308, 458, 495; livestock, 75, 78, 79, 274, 275, 363, 375, 376, 379, 381, 385, 386, 400, 402, 417, 434, 442, 444, 505; poultry, 79, 301, 508; schools, 413, 498, 503; submarginal lands, 20-25, 100, 102, 329, 402, 404, 407, 424, 430, 489, 500-503; tenancy, 76, 82-84, 89, 90, 107, 407, 408; tobacco, 72, 75, 78, 296, 297, 300, 301, 308, 367, 368, 391, 392, 394, 395, 409, 445, 494; truck farming, 78, 308, 329, 366, 396, 412, 413, 417, 420, 459, 500, 512. *See also* Conservation, Education, Labor, Schools, Tennessee Valley Authority
Airlines *(see Transportation)*
Airports, 96
Clarksville, 493; Dyersburg, 420; Emergency Airport (Chesterfield), 473; Lovell Field (Chattanooga), 478; McGhee Tyson (Knoxville), 348, 349; McKellar (Bristol-Kingsport-Johnson City), 321; Nashville Municipal, 398; Smithville, 468
Alden, A. E., 184
"Alden Ring," 184
Alexander, T. H. 153, 377
Alleghany, 220
American Baptist Home Mission Society, 108
American Civil Liberties Union, 364
American Federation of Labor *(see Labor)*
American Missionary Association, 58, 108, 203, 227, 466
Amis, Thomas, 310
Anderson, Joseph, 336
Anderson, Joseph R., 290
Anderson, Rev. Isaac, 121, 350
Andrew's Bald, 514
"Andrews Raiders," 263
Animal Life, 15-18, 354, 426-428, 445, 462, 463, 473, 514, 516
Aphrodite, 229
Appalachian Basin, 475
Appalachian Club, 357
Appalachian Park Association, 516
Appalachian Trail Conference, 131, 315, 342
Appalachian Valley, 364
Archeology *(see Indians)*
Architecture, 155-166
Corinthian, 159, 160, 375, 389, 390, 446, 447, 449; Classical Revival, 162; "dogtrot" houses, 155, 156; Doric, 160, 381, 388, 446-449, 492; Egyptian influence, 161; Georgian Colonial, 157, 159, 162, 166, 367, 393; Greek Revival, 159-161, 369, 375, 380-382, 390, 398, 401, 446-448, 490; Gothic Revival, 160, 161, 164, 360, 388, 483; industrial, 166; Jeffersonian Classicism, 159, 162, 451, 492; neo-Classic, 162; neo-Gothic, 162; Pioneer, 155, 156; Queen Anne style, 162; Spanish influence, 158, 159, 482, 483; Victorian, 162. *See also* Churches, Hotels, Houses, Schools, Museums, Public Buildings, and office buildings under their own names
Armfield, Col. John, 510
Armstrong, Col. Martin, 494
Armstrong, Drury P., 248, 357
Art, 167-171
Cartooning, 171; handicrafts, 82, 126, 167, 170, 339, 340, 345, 355, 469, 472, 477, 481; landscape painting, 167, 168; mural painting, 169, 442, 448, 483; organizations, 169-171; portraiture, 167, 194, 230, 361; sculpture, 170; woodcarving, 168 *(see Museums)*
Arthur, Col. A. A., 328
Arthur, Gabriel, 43, 330
Asbury, Bishop Francis, 111, 316, 323, 351, 396, 447
Ashford, Mrs. E. L., 174

Association South of the Holston and French Broad Rivers, 338
Atkins, C. Brown, 245
Atlas, 94
Attakullakulla, Chief, 37, 285, 311, 352
Avent, Mayna Treanor, 171
Avery, Peter, 91
Avery's Trace, 48, 91 *(see Transportation)*

Bachman, Rev. John Lynn, 305
Baisden, Frank M., 171
Baker, Thomas, 159, 369
Balch, Rev. Hezekiah, 121
Baldridge, Cyrus LeRoy, 169
Ballads *(see Folklore, Music)*
Ballentine, Andrew N., 383
Balloon *Buffalo,* 96
Banking *(see Commerce)*
Bank of Nashville, 70
Bank of the United States, 52
Baptists *(see Religion)*
Barber and McMurray, 245, 247, 413
Barnard, E. E., 190
Barras, Joseph, 506
Barrow, Alexander, 375
Barton, Bruce, 360
Barton, Rev. William E., 360
Bartram, William, 515, 516
Bate, Gen. William B., 368, 453
Batte, Dr. William, 382
Bauman and Bauman, 292
Baxter, Col. Jere, 445
Bayou de Chien, 428
Beale Street, 221, 222
Bean, George, 312
Bean, Jesse, 312
Bean, Robert, 312
Bean, Russell, 292, 293
Bean, William, 45, 312, 321, 355
Bearden, C. B., 263
Bear Pen Gap, 342
Beatty, "Tinker Dave," 499
Beauregard, Gen. P. G. T., 271, 384
Beaux, Cecilia, 225
Beaver, Leon, 245
Bell, Betsy, 392, 393
Bell, Ed, 150, 468
Bell, John, 392, 393
Bell, Sen. John, 55, 56, 192, 193, 378, 453
Bell, Montgomery, 82, 454, 455
Bell Witch, 392, 393 *(see Folklore)*
Bemis, Judson, 414
Beneike, Frederic, 361
Benn, Samuel, 330
Bennett, Belle H., 200
Benton, Mrs. Jesse, 202
Benton, Thomas H., 202, 400
Bethel, Capt. William, 388
Bienville, Jean Baptiste le Moyne de, 219
Big Creek Gap, 334
Biglow, Elijah, 271
Bijou Theater, 176
Bills, Maj. John W., 490
Birds *(see Animal Life)*
"Black Bob," 106
Blackburn, Rev. Gideon, 39, 365
"Black Friday," 185
Blacklock, Rev. Joseph, 360
Blashfield, E. H., 261
Bledsoe, Anthony, 367, 370
Bledsoe, Isaac, 45, 367, 370, 396
Bledsoe Lick, 367
Blount, Barbara, 238
Blount, Gov. William, 39, 47, 50, 156, 234, 238, 291, 308, 350, 438
Blount, Mary Grainger, 314, 350
Boar Hunting, 128, 354, 355 *(see Animal Life, Sports and Recreation)*
Boggs, J. H. 481
Bon Air Surveying Camp (Vanderbilt University School of Engineering), 467
Boone, Daniel, 15, 45, 181, 280, 309, 315, 321, 326, 509
Boone Trail, 280, 312 *(see Transportation, Wilderness Road)*
Booth, John Wilkes, 176
Bowman, John, 236
Boyd, Dr. John Mason, 242
Boyd, Dr. Robert Felton, 109
Boyd Nursery, 510
Boyle, Virginia Frazer, 148
Bradford, Roark, 151, 421
Bragg, Gen. Braxton, 255, 268, 384, 399, 400, 406, 477
Bragg Reservation, 268
Brainerd Mission, 40, 253, 478, 479
Branner Gristmill, 434
Breazele, J. W. M., 481
Breckinridge, John C., 56
Bridges
  A. R. Swann (Dandridge) 433; Alvin C. York Memorial (nr. Linden), 472; Cordell Hull (Carthage), 445; Frisco (Memphis), 207, 229; Harahan (Memphis), 207, 212, 228, 229; Henley (Knoxville), 245; John T. Cunningham (Clarksville), 495; Loudon, 305; Marion Memorial, 480, 481; Old Stone (nr. Fayetteville), 406; Ringgold Covered, 493; Sink's (nr. Elkmont), 358
Bristol-Nelson, Cora, 401
Brooks, Mrs. Samuel, 225
Broome, Isaac, 456
Brown, Aaron V., 375
Brown, Gen. John, 438
Brown, Gov. John C., 382, 439, 479
Brown, James, 477
Brown, Jane, 477
Browning, Gov. Gordon, 62
Brownlow, Gov. W. C. ("Parson"), 55, 56, 58, 59, 146, 249, 292
Brush, George De Forest, 168
Bryan, William Jennings, 364
Buchanan, Gov. John P., 336, 402, 418
Buchanan, President James, 375
Buchanan Station, 452
Buckner, Gen. Simon B., 410, 411
Buell, Gen. Don Carlos, 184, 254, 384
Bull, Ole, 174
Burnett, Frances Hodgson, 303
Burnside, Maj.-Gen. A. E., 236, 328, 351
Burr, Aaron, 285, 336, 367, 450
Burr's Landing, 450
Butler, John Washington, 126, 366

Butler, Roderick R., 316
Byrd, Col. R. K., 362, 438
Byrns, Rep. Joseph W., Sr., 453

Cade's Cove, 358
Cagle, Charles, 171
Caldwell, James H., 175
Calhoun, John C., 52, 115, 307
Cameron, James, 167
Cameron Hill, 167
Camp Overton, 469
Camp Peay, 406
Campbell, Alexander, 114
Campbell, Capt. David, 437
Campbell, Francis Joseph, 485
Campbell, Gov. William B., 46, 445, 447
Campbell, John R., 273
Campbell, Judge George W., 189
Campbell's Station, 437
Cannon, Gov. Newton, 400, 401, 469
Carey, Matthew, 329
Carmack, Sen. Edward W., 60, 153, 190, 367
Carmicheal, Alexander, 438
Carpetbaggers, 184, 201 *(see History)*
Carrick, Dr. Samuel, 121, 238, 349
Carroll, Gov. William, 52, 201
Carter, Fountain Branch, 378
Carter, Garnette, 266
Carter, Gen. John, 319, 377, 436
Carter, James, 291
Carter, Landon, 317, 436
Carter, Tod, 378
Carter's Valley, 38, 45, 480
Cartwright, Peter, 113
Caruthers, Judge Abraham, 446, 447
Caruthers, Robert Looney, 447
Cash, Harold, 170
Castle Building, 160
Catron, John, 452
Caves
  Alum, 342; Bishop's, 315; Bunkum, 507; Craighead, 306; Demonbreun, 452; Dunbar, 408, 409; Hazard, 498; Indian, 314; Keith, 484; Leonard, 367; Lookout Mountain, 265; Mansker's, 396; Nickajak, 39, 482; Rainbow, 509; Rattling, 431; Saltpeter, 335; Snail Shell, 402; Tennessee, 480; Wonder, 404
Cavett's Station, 235, 435
Cedar Knob, 189 *(see State Capitol)*
Cemeteries
  Andrew Jackson Family (Hermitage), 449; Confederate (Chattanooga), 263; Confederate (nr. Franklin), 379; Crockett Family, 419, 485; Elmwood, 227; Greenwood (Clarksville), 495; Greenwood (Columbia), 278; Jarnagin, 301; Lebanon Presbyterian, 349; Mount Calvary Roman Catholic, 398; Mount Olivet, 452, 453; Nashville City, 201; National and Old Gray, 249; National (Chattanooga), 263; National (nr. Dover), 411; National (nr. Madison), 374; National (Shiloh), 489; Pleasant Hill, 436; Riverside, 272; Roman Catholic (Jackson), 273; Silverdale Confederate, 477; Springhill, 374; Stone's River National, 399; Tazewell Baptist, 329; Yellow Fever, 413
Chapman, Col. David, 516
Chapman, Maristan (Mrs. John S. Higham), 151
Charette, Baroness de, 389
Charles Daggett, 202
Charleville, Charles, 44, 65
Chartier, Martin, 44
Chase, William, 169
Cheairs, Maj. Nathaniel Francis, 379
Cherokee *(see Indians)*
Chickamauga *(see Indians)*
Chickamauga Battlefield, 256
Chickamauga Island, 478
Chickasaw *(see Indians)*
Chickasaw Bluffs, 43, 44, 65 *(see Memphis)*
Chickasaw Purchase, 50, 51, 420
Chisholm, Capt. John, 91, 242
Choctaw *(see Indians)*
Choctaw Purchase, 285
Cholera Epidemics, 185, 256
Christian, Gilbert, 280
Church, R. R. (Bob), 108, 222, 224
Church, R. R., Jr., 222
Churches (by denomination)
  Baptist
    Beale Street, Negro (Memphis), 224; Beech (Chesterfield), 473; Hollow Rock Primitive, 459; Old Springdale (nr. Tazewell), 329; Union (nr. Bethpage), 367
  Christian Science
    First Church (Nashville), 194
  Church of Christ
    Christian (Smithville), 468; Post Oak (nr. Rockwood), 438
  Hebrew Reformed
    Vine Street Temple (Nashville), 194
  Holiness
    Holiness Church (Darden), 473; Tomlinson Church of God (Cleveland), 477
  Lutheran
    First Lutheran (Nashville), 190
  Methodist Episcopal
    Barton Chapel (Robbins), 360; Bethlehem (Lebanon), 447; Church Street (Knoxville), 162, 245; First (Memphis), 218; Jonesboro, 294; McKendree (Nashville), 182, 194; Methodist Episcopal (Jonesboro), 294; New Hope Tabernacle (nr. Brownsville), 462
  Presbyterian
    Chelsea Ave. (Memphis), 161, 229; Cumberland (nr. Decaturville), 472; First (Bristol), 293, 294; First (Chattanooga), 261; First (Greeneville), 298; First (Jonesboro), 293, 294; First (Knoxville), 238; First (Nashville), 161, 193, 194; Hermitage (nr. Nashville), 450; Idlewild (Memphis), 162,

Churches (*Continued*)
225; Lebanon (nr. Knoxville), 349; Zion Church (nr. Columbia), 389
Protestant Episcopal
All Saints Chapel (Sewanee), 483; Calvary (Memphis), 161, 218; Christ (Nashville), 195, 202; Holy Trinity, Negro (Nashville), 161, 202; Otey Memorial (Sewanee), 483; Rugby Parish, 360; St. Andrews Chapel (nr. Sewanee), 482; St. John's (nr. Columbia), 388; St. Paul's (Franklin), 378; Sisters of St. Mary (nr. Sewanee), 484
Quakers
Friends Meeting House (New Market), 303
Roman Catholic
Cathedral of the Incarnation (Nashville), 195; Hundred Oaks Monastery (nr. Winchester), 485; St. Mary's (Nashville), 190; St. Mary's (Memphis), 161, 219, 230; St. Patrick's (Nashville), 398; St. Peter's (Memphis), 217
Cisco, J. G., 271, 414
City Island, 229
Civilian Conservation Corps, 24, 25, 100, 434
Civil Works Administration, 88, 89, 96
Clark, Gen. George Rogers, 494
Clark, Lardner, 65
Clarkston, Father J. H., 217
Clay, Henry, 55
Clay Compromise, 55
Cleage, Samuel, 158, 306
Cleburne, Gen. Patrick R., 377, 379
Clemens, John, 498, 507
Clemens Family, 498
Cleveland, Col. Benjamin, 476
Climate, 10, 11
Clinch Valley, 45, 329
Clingman, Thomas Lainer, 516
Clouston, Joe, 106
Clover Bottom, 450, 451
Coates, Robert N., 423
Cobb, William, 291
Cocke, William, 48, 49
Cockrill, Mark, 76
Coffee, Gen. John, 403
Cohen, Mrs. George Etta, 200
Colbert, Chief James, 209
Cold Water Knob, 358
Cole, E. W., 398
Colored Christian Singers, 204
Columbia Earthquake, 275, 276
Columbian Mutual Tower Building, 207
Colyar, A. S., 185
Commerce, 65-73
Early, 35, 36, 44, 65, 91-94, 210, 252-254, 280, 311, 330, 422, 490, 516; insurance and banking, 61, 70-72, 221; present development, 67, 68, 71-73
Committee for Industrial Organization (*see Labor*)
Committee of Guardians, 182
Commonwealth Fund, 401
Confederacy (*see History*)
Conley, Sara Ward, 168, 171
Conservation, 7-26
Flood control, 99, 214, 229, 424; reforestation, 19-22, 25, 26, 100, 130, 131, 345, 355, 414, 415, 423, 498, 508, 514, 515; soil conservation, 22-26, 414, 423, 434; wild life, 15-18, 128-132, 301, 314, 324, 409, 423, 426-429, 432, 485, 495, 496, 498, 516. *See also* Fish and Game Reserves, Parks and Forests
Constitutional Convention of 1834, 53, 382
Constitutional Union Party, 56
Contemporary Tennessee, 3-6
Cook, Anna ("Madame Annie"), 212
Cook, James B., 161, 215
Cooper, Col. Duncan, 60, 190, 367
Cooper, Gov. Prentice, 62
Cooper, Robin, 60, 367
Cooper, Washington, 167
Cooper, William, 230
Cooperatives (*see Agriculture*)
Copeland, "Big Jo," 506, 507
Copper Basin, 9, 475
Cornwell, Dean, 191
Cosby, Dr. James, 432
Cossitt, Frederick H., 221
Cotton Exchange Building, 221
Counties
Anderson, 78, 336, 362; Bedford, 405; Benton, 13, 458; Bledsoe, 461, 503; Blount, 350; Bradley, 78, 476; Campbell, 335; Cannon, 469; Carroll, 459; Carter, 11, 317; Cheatham, 445; Chester, 14, 415, 431; Claiborne, 328; Clay, 508; Cocke, 11, 431; Coffee, 403; Crockett, 419, 420; Cumberland, 442, 467; Davidson, 86, 367, 376; Decatur, 13; DeKalb, 468; Dickson, 107, 455; Dyer, 420; Fayette, 106, 462, 492; Fentress, 61, 498; Franklin, 80, 484; Gibson, 78, 413, 419; Giles, 58, 381, 383; Grainger, 314; Greene, 47, 296; Hamblen, 301; Hamilton, 78, 477; Hardeman, 415, 416, 490; Hardin, 13, 14, 487, 488; Hawkins, 290, 310; Haywood, 462; Henderson, 14, 473; Henry, 78, 411; Humphreys, 457; Jackson, 445; James, 477; Jefferson, 433; Johnson, 316; Knox, 78, 234, 350; Lake, 424; Lauderdale, 422; Lawrence, 486; Lincoln, 485, 486; Loudon, 305; Madison, 270, 271, 459; Marion, 481; Marshall, 385; Maury, 274-276, 278, 388, 405; McMinn, 306; McNairy, 14, 416; Monroe, 353, 354; Moore, 406; Montgomery, 494; Morgan, 361, 362; Obion, 417, 419; Overton, 507, 508; Perry, 13, 472; Pickett, 507; Putnam, 444; Rhea, 363; Roane, 78, 437, 438; Robertson, 393-395; Rutherford, 400, 401; Scott, 360, 362; Sequatchie, 505; Sevier, 234, 338; Shelby, 14, 206-231; Smith, 445;

Counties (*Continued*)
Stewart, 12, 409; Sullivan, 47, 308; Sumner, 367, 368; Tipton, 422; Unicoi, 324; Union, 106, 346; Van Buren, 468; Warren, 510; Washington, 46-48, 291, 320, 436, 516; Wayne, 487; Weakley, 78, 412, 413; White, 467; Williamson, 376, 377; Wilson, 446
Court Square (Memphis), 207, 215
Craddock, Charles Egbert (Mary N. Murfree), 147, 148, 358, 359, 510
Craig, John J., 248, 350
Craighead, Rev. Thomas, 120, 374
Cram, Goodhue and Ferguson, 162, 483
Cranshaw, Harry, 461
Crass, John T., 264
Cravens, Robert, 266, 439
Creek *(see Indians)*
Creeks
Abram's, 358; Alum, 342; Battle, 482; Beaver, 235; Big, 290; Boone, 321; Buffalo, 66; Carroll, 321; Carr's, 394; Chickamauga, 38, 252, 255, 479; Clear, 345; Coal, 335, 344; Coon, 14; Cove, 500; Crooked Fork, 362; Cub, 509; Daddy's, 439, 441; Dill Branch, 489; Dog, 454; Drake's, 112; Dunn's, 432; Fall's, 309; Gray's, 491; Indian, 472; Indian Camp, 432; Knob, 323; Lick, 419; Little Limestone, 66; Lost, 54; Mammy's, 439; Mansker's, 396; Mill, 66, 452; Mill Brook, 296; Mossy, 302; Nettle Carrier, 508; Nonconnah, 207; Norton, 339; Oven, 432; Porters, 14; Reedy, 280, 321; Ringgold, 493; Roan, 316; Roaring, 341; Rock Castle, 499; Round Lick, 468; Running Water, 480; Sale, 39; Shoal, 486; Smith Fork, 468; Snake, 416; Spring, 459; Station Camp, 369; White's, 66; Yellow, 66
Creswell, R. T., 249
Crivelli, Carlo, 483
Crockett, David, 134, 141, 142, 147, 219, 296, 396, 417-420, 423, 428, 434, 459, 485, 498
Crockett, Polly Finley, 485
Cross, John, 171
Crump, Edward Hull, 174, 213
Crutchfield, Robert, 306
Crutchfield, Thomas, 158
Crutchfield, William, 257, 263
Cumberland, Duke of, 44
Cumberland Compact, 181
Cumberland Furnace, 455
Cumberland Gap, 45, 91, 327
Cumberland Mountain Tunnel, 484
Cumberland Settlement, 209, 234, 439, 452 *(see History, Nashville)*
Cumberland Valley, 44
Cuming (Cumin), Alexander, 35
Cummings, Rev. Charles, 111
Curry, Dr. Walter Clyde, 152
Custis, Martha Dandridge, 433
Dams
Calderwood, 331, 350; Chickamauga, 100, 477, 478; Coulter Shoals, 100; Gilbertsville, 100; Great Falls, 469; Guntersville, 100; Hale's Bar, 100, 480, 481; Hiwassee, 100; Muscle Shoals, 214; Norris, 100, 344; Ocoee, 476; Pickwick, 100, 214, 487-489; Tapaco, 331; Watt's Bar, 100; Wheeler, 100; Wilson, 94, 100, 489
Dan Patch, 230, 278
Darden, Mills, 473
Darrow, Clarence, 364
D'Artaguette, Pierre, 35, 36
Daugherty, Edward, 188
David, Bishop, 115
Davidson, Donald, 151, 152
Davidson, Sally, 438
Davidson County Tuberculosis Hospital, 496
Daviess, Maria Thompson, 148, 372
Davis, Commodore C. H., 211
Davis, Jefferson, 56, 215, 218, 224, 230, 257, 268, 370, 489
Davis, Norman H., 406
Davis, Sam, 382, 398, 399
Davis, W. P., 517
Deaderick, Judge Charles, 301
DeBrahm, James William Gerald, 352, 353
Decatur, Stephen, 472
DeKalb, Johann, 468
Demere, Capt. Paul, 37, 45, 352, 353
Democrat Party, 55, 60, 62
DeMonbreun, Timothe, 45, 452
Denny, Mrs. Daniel, 363
DeSoto, Hernando, 30, 43, 44, 104, 207, 209, 228, 252, 402 *(see History, Indians)*
DeSoto's Ship Yard, 220
Dickinson, Charles, 451
Dickinson, Perez, 245
Dicky, John, 389
Dillard, John, 509
Dinney Hollows, 416
Dix, Dorothy *(see Elizabeth M. Gilmer)*
Doak, Rev. Samuel, 120, 294, 295, 297
Dod, Charles, Jr., 24
Dodd, Quincy, 419
Dodge, Gen. G. M., 189, 398
Dodge, John W., 168, 442
Dodge, Rev. Benjamin, 466
Doe River Gorge, 317
Dogtrot Cabins *(see Architecture)*
Donelson, Andrew Jackson, 448
Donelson, Col. John, 181, 234, 367, 376, 396, 450
Donelson, Emily, 448
Donelson, Gen. Daniel S., 369, 370
Donelson, Polly Smith, 370
Donelson, Rachel, 396, 449
Donelson, Samuel, 369, 370
Donelson, Stockley, 441
Douglas, Ben, 473
Douglas, Stephen A., 55, 56
Douglass, Aaron K., 169, 204
Dow, Lorenzo, 111, 112
Downing, H. B., 261
Dragging Canoe, 289, 479, 480

Drake, Samuel, 175
Drake's Creek Meeting, 112
Draper, Earl S., 279
Driver, Capt. William, 201, 202
Dromgoole, Will Allen, 148
Dudley, William L., 198
Dudley Stadium (Nashville), 198
Dunham Station, 453
Dunmore's War, 38
Dunn, Capt. Cynthia, 351
Dury, George, 361

Earl, Ralph E. W., 448, 449
Eastern Dark-Fired Tobacco Growers' Association, 395
East Tennessee Land Company, 362
Eaton, Col. John, 58, 378, 491
Eaton, Peggy *(see Peggy O'Neal)*
Echota (Chota), 33
Edmunson, William, 170
Education, 120-127
  Academies, 120-122, 374, 452; adult education, 127; anti-evolution law, 125, 126; colleges, 120-125, 509; Negro schools, 58, 108, 125; public schools, 121-124, 316, 375; school lands, 54, 121; state aid, 62, 125, 316, 372, 411, 473; vocational training, 90, 126, 127, 282, 372. *See also* Negroes, Religion, Schools
Elder, Margaret, 434
Eldridge, "Ranter," 508
Elgin Marbles Reproductions, 196
Elliott, Dr. Collin, 122
Embree, Elihu, 54, 294, 295
Embree, Thomas, 295
Emory Gap, 91
Enquirer, 454
Episcopalians *(see Religion)*
Ervin, Dr. J. N., 324
Erwin, Capt. Joseph, 451
Essary, Henry, 473
Essary, Robert, 485
Evolution Trial *(see Education)*
Exchange Building (Memphis), 207

Fairbanks, Maj. George R., 484
Fairs and Festivals
  Cotton Carnival (Memphis), 133, 208, 209; DeKalb County Fair, 468; Dogwood Festival (Knoxville), 133; Dyersburg Cotton Carnival, 420; First Monday and Mule Day (Columbia), 133, 274; Iris Festival (Nashville), 133; National Foxhunters' Meet (Huntersville), 462; Negro Cotton Fiesta (Memphis), 221; Rhododendron Festival (Gatlinburg), 133; Strawberry Festival (Humboldt), 133, 419; Tennessee Foxhunters' Meet (Springfield), 395; Tennessee State Fair (Nashville), 54; West Tennessee District Fair (Jackson), 272
Fairyland, 266
Falls
  Abram's, 359; Dome Cascade, 341; Fall Creek, 503; Laurel Creek, 356; Marcella, 391; Ozone, 441; Piney, 503; Potter's, 362; Rainbow, 341, 509; Rattlesnake, 390; Rock Castle, 499; Twin, 341; Twisting, 316; Walling Mill Branch, 503
Farmers and Laborers Union of Tennessee (Farmers Alliance), 402
Farm Security Administration, 80, 300, 500, 503
Farragut, Admiral David Glasgow, 436
Farragut, George, 437
Fauna *(see Animal Life)*
Fay, Calvin, 161
Federal Art Project, 169, 170
Federal Relief in Tennessee, 61
Fentress, James, 498
Ferguson, Major Patrick, 46
Ferguson, Samuel W. (Champ), 499
Fighting Creek Gap, 356
Finley, Polly, 434
First Airmail *(see Balloon Buffalo)*
Fish and Game Reserves
  Big Hatchie State Game Preserve, 462; Buffalo Springs State Game Farm, 129, 314; Idaho Springs State Game Preserve, 409; Jeffrey's Hell Federal Game Preserve, 354; John Sevier State Preserve, 432; Pickwick Dam Reservation (TVA), 132; Reelfoot Lake State Game Preserve, 129; Shelby State Forest Recreational Demonstration Area, 130, 131; Tellico Game and Fish Management Area, 355; TVA Doak Rearing Pools, 328; Warren Hollow Federal Fish Hatchery, 485. *See also* Conservation, Parks and Forests
Fishing *(see Sports and Recreation)*
Fisk, Gen. Clinton B., 203, 362
Fisk, Moses, 508, 509
Fisk Jubilee Singers, 173 *(see Music, Negroes)*
Flatwoods Nurseries, 468
Fleming, Walter L., 153
Fletcher and Winter, 161
Flick, C. Roland, 174
Flisher, Edith E., 171
Floods, 62, 212, 214, 424, 429, 494
Flora *(see Forest and Plant Life)*
Floyd, General John B., 184, 410
Folklore, 134-144
  Balladry, 142-144, 273, 304; dancing, 409, 505, 512; folkways, 138, 192, 274, 300, 303, 306, 340, 341, 362, 392, 394, 407, 408, 416, 439, 472, 490, 498, 500-505, 518; Indian legends, 141, 317, 429, 508; Negro beliefs and practices, 139-141, 144, 222, 413, 414, 421, 508, 509; speech, 134, 135; superstitions, 135-138; witchcraft, 392, 393, 498, 499. *See also* Music
Foote, Commodore Andrew Hull, 411
Foreign Groups *(see Racial Elements)*
Forest and Plant Life, 19-22, 354, 366, 390, 426, 498, 514, 515, 518
Forest, Col. Jeff, 271
Forrest, Capt. William H., 221

Forrest, Gen. Nathan Bedford, 59, 193, 201, 211, 221, 224, 228, 271, 380, 384, 385, 410, 419, 422, 458, 470, 473
Fort, John Porter, 151
Fort Donelson Historical Society, 410
Forts
Adams, 210, 220; Assumption, 36, 104, 219; Blount, 445; Craig, 350; Donelson, 132, 184, 371, 384, 409-411, 419, 455, 488; Dunham, 453; Gillespie's, 349; Granger, 377; Henry, 410, 411, 419, 488; Ish's, 352; Johnson, 189; Loudon, 36, 37, 45, 253, 331, 352, 353; Mims (Ala.), 50, 406; Nashborough, 155, 181, 191, 192, 378; Negley, 200, 201; Oglethorpe (Ga.), 267; Old Stone Blockhouse, 493; Old Stone Fort, 402; Patrick Henry, 280, 309; Pickering, 220; Pillow, 422; Prince George, 37; Prudhomme, 44, 209, 422; Redoubt Brannan, 400; Robinson, 280, 309; San Fernando de las Barrancas, 219; South Westport, 438; St. Stephens (Ala.), 285; Toulouse (Ala.), 36, 330; Virginia, 44, 45, 331; Union, 374; Watauga, 319, 355; White's, 39, 234, 348
Foster, Austin P., 153
Foy, Benjamin, 219
Franklin, Isaac, 159, 369
Frazee, John, 217, 218
Freedmen's Aid Society, 108
Freedmen's Bureau, 58, 203, 228, 491
Free-for-all Preachings, 192 *(see Folklore)*
Free Hills Settlement, 508, 509
"Free Joe", 106
French Lick, 44, 181, 445, 452 *(see Nashville)*
Fugitive Group *(see Writers)*
Fuller, Thomas O., 151

Gainer, Albert F., 18, 516
Gaines, Gen. Edmund Pendleton, 285, 445
Gaines' Trace, 285
Gallaher, William, 438
Gallatin, Albert, 368
Gallatin Loose Leaf Tobacco Sales Floor, 368
Gardener, Josiah, 393
Gardens
Beaver Dam (nr. Dandridge), 433; Beechlawn (nr. Columbia), 380; Chickasaw (Memphis), 207; Clifton Place (nr. Columbia), 381; Ginseng Garden (nr. Lenoir City), 305; Gladiola Garden (nr. Pomona), 442; High Oak Tulip (Newport), 431; Savage Rock Garden (nr. Briceville), 336; Wessyngton House (nr. Springfield), 393
Garfield, Maj. James A., 478
Garland, Landon C., 198
Garret, William Robertson, 148
Garrison, William Lloyd, 55, 105
Gattinger, August, 361
Gaul, Gilbert, 169, 188
Gayoso de Lemos, Don Manuel, 210, 219, 221
Geers, Edward Franklin ("Pop"), 230, 278, 447
General Arbitrators, 181
General Assembly, 56, 63, 335, 365
General Jackson, 93
Geographical Divisions
Cedar Barrens, 397, 402; Central Basin, 8, 12, 13, 23, 397, 467, 469; Cumberland Plateau, 8, 9, 12, 16, 17, 19, 22 ,80, 91, 361, 364, 403, 467-469, 479, 484, 496, 506; East Tennessee, 7, 8, 75, 81, 92, 104-106; Highland Rim, 8, 12, 19, 22, 366, 397, 402, 469, 470; Middle Tennessee, 8, 104, 106, 366; Mississippi Bottoms, 420, 423, 424; Tennessee Valley, 8, 12, 13, 22, 25, 43, 98, 305, 359, 363; West Tennessee, 8, 104, 106, 271, 416-421, 462
Geology, 7-9, 11-14, 364, 390
German Catholic Homestead Association, 391
Giles, William, 453
Gillespie, George, 296
Gilmer, Elizabeth Meriwether (Dorothy Dix), 408
Gilpin, Mrs. Kenneth, 247
Gist, Christopher, 286
Gist, Col. Nathaniel, 286
Gist, George *(see Sequoyah)*
Glover's Trace, 458, 459
Goodlett, Caroline Meriwether, 408
Goodpasture, Albert Virgil, 148
Goodrich, J. H., 171
Goodwyn, William A., 215
Gordon, Caroline, 150, 408, 495
Gordon and Keelber, 204
Gorgas, Gen. Josiah, 483, 484
Gorgas, William, 484
Gosnell, Wilson A., 482
Government, 62-64
Government South of the Holston and French Broad Rivers, 47
Graham, William, 329
Granbury, Gen. Hiram Bronson, 377, 379
Granger, Gen. Gordon, 377, 433, 434
Grant, Gen. U. S., 56-58, 184, 224, 229, 230, 263, 268, 271, 384, 410, 488, 491
Grant, Ludovick, 36
Grasslands, 369
"Grassy Balds," 514
Grassy Cove, 500
Greasy Cove, 292
Greasy Cove Race Track, 325
Great New Market Wreck, 304
Great Removal, 307 *(see Indians)*
Great Revival *(see History, Religion)*
Great Seal of the State of Tennessee, 292
Great Tellico, 35, 36
Great Trading Path, 35
Greenbriar Cove, 341
Greene, Gen. Nathanael, 389
Greene, Nathan, Jr., 446
Greeneville, 47, 54, 291, 297, 300
Grundy, Felix, 175, 188, 453
Guess, George *(see Sequoyah)*
Guild, Jo Conn, Sr., 264, 368

Guion, Capt. Isaac, 210, 219, 220
Guyot, Arnold, 516

Hadley, Dr. W. A., 109
Hague, John, 66, 403
Hahn, Mrs. Nancy Coosman, 225
Haight, Chester E., 483
Hale, Dr. Jonathan P., 499
Hale, Will T., 148, 149
Hale's Bar, 481
Hall, H. A. Morgan, 248
Halleck, Gen. Fitzgreene, 488, 489
Halliburton, Richard, 153
Hamburg Landing, 489
Hamer, Philip, 153
Hammarskold, P. H., 161, 224
Handicrafts *(see Art)*
Handy, W. C., 154, 173, 209, 222
Happy Valley, 317
Hardie, Col., 215
Harding, J. A., 203
Harding, John, 453
Harding, Selene, 454
Harding, William G., 452-454
Harpe Brothers ("Terrible Harpes"), 235, 236
Harper, William, 350
Harpeth Hills, 471
Harpeth Narrows, 454
Harriman, Gen. Walter, 362
Harris, George Washington, 147
Harris, Gov. Isham G., 56, 384, 411, 453, 454
Harris, Nathaniel E., 316
Harrison, Henry Sydnor, 148
Harrison, Wm. Henry, 453
Hart, Freeland and Roberts, 162
Hart, Joseph J., 191
Hart, Joseph W., 155
Hart, Russell, 398
Haskell, Judge Joshua, 510
Hatch, Gen. John P., 271
Hatchie River Valley, 490
Hawkins, Sen. Benjamin, 310
Hayes, Adelicia, 369
Hayes, Roland, 494
Haynes, Landon Carter, 292, 322
Hays, Arthur Garfield, 364
Haywood, Judge John, 145, 384, 402
Hazard, James O., 498
Hazen, Morgan, 435
Hazens, Col. W. B., 399
Heacock, Dr. William, 386
"Heath Balds," 514
Hedrick, Wyatt C., 215
Heiman, Maj. A. 160, 190, 397
Heiskell, F. W., 145
Heiskell, Judge Samuel G., 153
Henderson, Col. Richard, 45, 46, 181, 326
Hendrick, Wyatt C., 164
Henneman, John Bell, 149
Henry, Howard, 171
Henry, Patrick, 227
Henry, Robert Selph, 153
Herbert Domain, 503
Hergesheimer, Ella Sophonisba, 171
Hermitage *(see Houses)*
Heron, Susan L., 200
Herty, Dr. Charles, 365
Hertz, Henry B., 263
Hibbs, Henry C., 162, 191, 198, 200, 204, 227
Hickey, J. W., 439
Higham, Mrs. John Stanton *(see Maristan Chapman)*
Hill, Col. D. B., 259
Historic Inns and Taverns
  Beersheba Springs Hotel, 510; Bell Tavern (Memphis), 219, 220; Castalian Springs Tavern, 368; Chester Inn (Jonesboro), 292; Chisholm's Tavern (Knoxville), 91, 242; Crab Orchard Inn (nr. Ozone), 441; DeVault Tavern (Telford), 295; Dover Tavern, 410; Fayetteville Inn, 486; Frankstone Inn (nr. Chattanooga), 478; Greystone Inn (Tazewell), 329; Grinder's Inn (nr. Lawrenceburg), 390; Harvey House (nr. Kingston), 438; John Brown's Tavern (nr. Chattanooga), 479; Maxwell House (Nashville), 193, 376; Nashville Inn, 193; Netherland Inn (Kingsport), 283; Public House of Becky Watson (nr. Livingston), 508; Rains' Stand (Mayland), 444; Red House (nr. Knoxville), 314; Rock House (nr. Sparta), 467; Rogersville Inn, 311; Sam Stodgens' Place (Memphis), 219; Sewanee Inn, 484; Tuckaway Inn (nr. Sewanee), 484; Tucker Tavern (nr. Jefferson City), 303, 304; Whiteside Inn (nr. Rutledge), 312; Wilson Inn (nr. Newport), 432; Woodmore Hotel (Lafayette), 366
History, 43-62
  Antebellum period, 50-55, 182, 204, 210, 211, 235-237, 256; development since 1870, 58-62, 124, 162, 184, 185, 200, 201, 211, 212, 237, 256; early statehood, 46-48, 401, 436; exploration and conflicting claims, 43-45, 181, 209, 228, 234, 252, 253, 330, 331, 360; period of settlement, 45-49, 181, 182, 191, 196, 197, 210, 219, 220, 233-235, 252-254, 263, 264, 289, 290, 310, 360, 361, 375, 376, 403, 450-452, 469, 516; Reconstruction, 58, 59, 66, 67, 71, 185, 201, 203, 211, 212, 228, 237, 256, 491; Secession, 56-58, 297; State of Franklin, 46-48, 234-247, 291, 292, 296-298, 319, 323, 324, 338, 436; Washington District, 46, 91, 291, 320; Watauga Association, 38, 45-47, 111, 181, 291, 317, 320, 322, 396. *See also* Commerce, Education, Indians, Industry, Labor, Negroes, Religion, Revolutionary War, Seminole War, Tennessee Valley Authority, War between the States, War of 1812

Hiwassee Island, 364
Hodgson-Emerald Hospital, 484
Hoggett, John, 451
Holabird and Root, 257
Holly Tree Gap, 377
Holt, Judge Advocate General J., 215
Holy Butt, 356
"Home-Made Yankees", 422
Homer, Winslow, 169
Hood, General John B., 184, 276, 375, 377-380
Hood, Ida E., 200
Hood, Raymond, 198
Hooker, General Joe, 255, 480
Hooker's Bend, 487
Hooper, Gov. Ben W., 60, 61, 431
Hope, Thomas, 348, 435
Hopkins, Alexander, 438
Hopwood, Joseph, 320
Horn, James Baker, 447
Horton, Gov. Henry, 61, 86
Horton, Myles, 512
Hotels
  Beersheba Springs, 510; Cumberland (Knoxville), 244; Farragut (Knoxville), 234; Gayoso (Memphis), 161, 169, 221; Harvey House (Kingston), 438; Hermitage (Nashville), 169, 188; Idaho Springs, 409; Maxwell House (Nashville), 193; Monteagle, 482; Phillip's, 481; Read House (Chattanooga), 257; Rhea-Mims (Newport), 431; Signal Mountain, 506; Wonderland (Elkmont), 357; Woodmore (Lafayette), 366
Houses
  Allen Tate Home, 495; Alvin York Birthplace, 498; Amis Stone House, 310; Andrew Johnson, 298; *Ashwood,* 389; Austin Hewitt, 382; Austin Peay, 495; Ballentine, 383; *Bankrupt Manor,* 377; Barclay McGhee, 350; *Beechlawn,* 380; *Belle Meade,* 453, 454; *Belmont,* 200; Bishop Gailor, 484; *Bleak House,* 248; Blount Mansion, 156, 239; Blythewood, 388; *Boxwood Manor,* 300; Brazelton, 303; Brooks, 490, 491; Brotherton, 268; *Camp Bell,* 447; Carmack, 367; Carnton, 378, 379; Carter, 317, 378; Caruthers, 446, 447; Casper Cable's Cabin, 316; Cassell, 362, 363; Cheairs, 379; *Cheekwood,* 471; Cherry, 488; Christopher Taylor, 294; Clack, 439; Cleage Home, 306; Clifton, 159, 381, 388; *Clinchdale,* 312; *Clover Bottom,* 451; *Colemere,* 398; *Colonial Hall,* 302, 382; Cragfont, 82, 158, 367; Crutchfield, 257; Daniel Stover, 319; David Crockett, 418, 419; Davis, 398; Deaderick, 301; Dickinson-Atkins, 245; Diocesan, 230; Dodge, 442; Duncruzin, 370; E. B. Smith, 496; Edgewood, 273; Edward Franklin ("Pop") Geers, 447; *Fairlawn,* 394; *Fairview,* 302, 369; *Foxland Hall,* 159, 369; Gillespie, 156; Gillespie *Armored,* 352; *Glen Echo,* 374; Glen Leven, 375; *Grasslands,* 370; Greek, 161; Griffith, 435; Guilford Cannon, 354; Hamilton, 389; Harris, 316; Haynes, 323, 324; Haynes Haven, 379, 380; *Hayslope,* 300; *Hazel Path,* 370; 371; *Hermitage,* 158, 182, 371, 448; Hodgson-Burnett, 303; *Hundred Oaks,* 485; Hunt-Phelan, 161, 224; Hunter-Kennedy, 238; *Hunters Hill,* 370; Hynds, 434; Isham Harris, 346, 411; Jackson, 239; James K. Polk, 159, 276; James D. Porter, 411; James Ridley, 451, 452; John Bell, 192; John Blair, 305; John Chandler, 337, 338; John Eaton, 378; John Haywood, 384; John A. Murrell, 415, 459, 461; John Ross, 267; Kasper Mansker, 396; Kelly, 267; Kennedy-Rathburn-Nottingham, 259; *Limestone,* 295; Lonas, 435; *Longueval,* 248; Longview, 375; *Mabry,* 436; Magevney, 217; *Mansion,* 212, 319, 354; Maples, 302; Margrove, 362; *Marymont,* 401; Mayes-Hutton, 276; *Melrose,* 248, 375; Mercer Hall, 386; *Middlebrook,* 435; *Midway,* 376, 377; *Milky Way,* 381; Mitchell, 447; *Montview,* 377; Mooreland, 376; Morgan, 438; Moses Fisk Home, 509; McGavock-Hayes, 376; McSpadden, 434; Nathan Green, 446; *Oak Hill,* 375; *Old Blue Brick,* 451; Old Center, 472, 473; Old Garland Home *(Sega-Sega),* 415; Park House, 244; Pearson, 309; Pettite, 161; *Pillars,* 490; Pillow-Bethel, 159, 388; Pillow-Haliday, 159, 388; Polk-Yeatman, 389; Pritchett, 432; Pulliam, 492; Rains, 444; Ramsey, 348; Rattle and Snap, 159, 389; *Rebel's Rest,* 484; *Riverwood,* 374; Col. Robert King Byrd, 438; Robertson Topp, 161, 224; Robinson, 444; *Rock Castle,* 156, 370; *Rock House,* 467; *Rocky Mount,* 291; Rogan, 367; *Rosemont,* 368; *Rotherwood,* 309; Sample, 418; Samuel K. Polk, 276; Scott, 347; Sevier-O'Keefe, 300; *Sherwood Forest,* 372; *Spencer's Choice,* 368; *States View,* 435; Stickley, 354; Stockton, 499; *Stoneleigh,* 312; Sunnyside, 202; *Sweetbriar,* 372; Telfair Hodgson, 484; Thomas J. Page, 436; Tipton, 323, 324; *Travelers Rest,* 376; Trousdale, 368; *Tulip Grove,* 448; *Two Rivers,* 452; Ward, 438; *Wessyngton,* 393; *Westview,* 397; Westwood, 202; Wilson, 495; *Woodlawn,* 492; Yarnell, 477
Housing, 164-166
  Andrew Jackson Place, *Negro* (Nashville), 203; Cheatham Place (Nash-

Housing (*Continued*)
ville), 203; Cumberland Homesteads (Crossville), 126, 164, 300, 441, 500; Dixie Homes, *Negro* (Memphis), 230; Lauderdale Courts (Memphis), 219; Norris Village, 166; Sardis Model Community (nr. Lexington), 473
Houston, Sam, 40, 52, 53, 350, 351, 364, 365, 446, 481
Howard, Len, 230
Howard Association, 212
Hubbard Hospital, 109
Huggins, Dr. J. L., 434
Hughes, David, 395
Hughes, Thomas, 360
Hughetta (Snowden), Sister, 230
Hull, Cordell, 445, 446, 507
Hull, William, 507
Humboldt, Baron Von, 419
Hume, William C., 158, 448
Hundred Oaks Monastery, 485
Hunt, Reuben Harrison, 259
Hunt, Richard Morris, 483
Hurlburt, Gen. Stephen A., 221, 488, 489
Hurst, Col. Fielding, 416
Hurst Nation ("the Nation"), 416

Immigration, 22, 46, 91, 182, 289, 437, 517
Indian Gap, 342
Indians, 27-42
Prehistoric, 27-30
Mound Builders, 197, 198, 209, 228, 314, 360, 363, 365, 376, 379, 402, 404, 414-416, 434, 438, 454, 457, 479, 488, 489, 494, 495, 498, 507
Historic, 30-42
Trails: Black Fox, 469; Chickamauga, 479; Chickasaw Path of Peace, 91; Chickasaw War, 36; Great War, 31, 252, 312, 434; Nickajack, 482; Shawnee, 252
Treaties: Cherokee, 38, 40, 42, 47, 91, 92, 197, 234, 253, 280, 285, 286, 289, 307, 319, 338, 434, 439; Chickasaw, 33, 40, 91, 196, 197, 421; Choctaw, 91, 92, 196, 197; Creek, 92
Tribes: Cherokee, 30, 33, 35-40, 42-45, 53, 65, 91, 182, 234, 252, 253, 286, 289, 307, 308, 330, 331, 337, 350-353, 364, 365, 430, 438, 441, 475-480, 482, 498, 509, 514; Chickamauga, 39, 46, 182, 191, 192, 253, 290, 296, 324, 479, 480, 482; Chickasaw, 27, 30, 31-33, 36, 40, 43, 50, 65, 75, 207, 209, 210, 219, 220, 396, 415, 422, 428, 429, 462, 463; Choctaw, 27, 35, 285; Creek, 27, 30, 39, 50, 469, 480
Wars: 35-37, 39, 45, 50, 191, 192, 234, 235, 253, 280, 285, 289, 330, 348, 352, 353, 406, 448, 452
Industrial Plants
Aluminum Company of America, 87, 331; American Bemberg Corporation Plant, 317; American Glanzstoff Corporation, 86; American Snuff Plant, 229; American Zinc Company, 304; Appalachian Marble Company Quarry, 349; Ashby Veneer and Lumber Plant, 272; Bemis Bag Company, 414; Borden Mills, 283; Brookside Mills, 249; Brownsport Furnace, 473; Chalfant Dock Steel Plant, 230; Clarksville Foundry and Machine Works, 494; Cumberland Furnace, 455; Cumberland Quarries, 442; Du Pont de Nemours and Company Cellophane and Rayon Plants, 67, 371; Dyersburg Cotton Products Plant, 420; Embreeville Iron Works, 294; Fall Branch Mine, 334; Federal Compress and Warehouse Plant, 230, 231; Fentress Coal and Coke Company, 86; General Shale Products Company, 283; Hardwick Woolen Mills, 476; Jack Daniel Distillery, 406; Jones and Laughlin Steel Plant, 220; Kingsport Foundry and Manufacturing Plant, 283; Kingsport Press, 282, 283; Lenoir Car Works, 305; Linde Telescope Plant, 442; Madison Food Factory, 372; Mead Corporation, 283; Morgan-Hitchcock Plant, 272; Murfreesboro Red Cedar Bucket Factory, 401; National Pencil Company, 405; Old Hickory Chemical Company, 371; Pennsylvania-Dixie Cement Plant, 283; Rockdale Furnaces, 390; Rust Cotton Picker Plant, 231; Signal Mountain Portland Cement Company, 505; Southern Potteries Plant, 325; Southern States Lime Corporation Plant, 441; Springfield Woolen Mills, 395; Stokely Brothers Cannery, 431; Tennessee Art Pottery, 481; Tennessee Eastman Corporation, 283; Tennessee Products Corporation Plant, 467, 472; Trenton Sack Mills, 419; Union Compress Plant, 219; United States Rubber Plant, 405; Universal Exploration Company Mines and Mills, 303; Vaughan Publishing Company, 486; Zenith Coal Mine, 87
Industry, 65-73
Clay products, 10, 282, 360; copper and zinc, 9, 10, 68, 304, 475; coal, iron, and steel, 9, 67, 82, 95, 220, 230, 252, 256, 257, 280-283, 294, 303, 334, 335, 390, 409, 439, 455, 467, 473, 495; early products, 49, 67, 82-85, 280, 290, 294; flour and corn milling, 66, 70, 180, 286, 434; lumber, 68, 70, 257, 272, 283, 329, 360, 385, 401, 403, 420, 446, 449, 510; other industries, 182, 219, 229, 230, 257, 272, 283, 368, 371, 381, 441, 442; phosphates, 68, 72, 102, 386, 472; printing, 68, 107, 282, 283, 301, 329, 445, 486; quarrying, 10, 67,

Industry (*Continued*)
68, 237, 314, 349, 442, 483; textiles, 66, 67, 182, 237, 249, 276, 283, 305, 371, 395, 403, 419, 446, 476, 510. *See also* Agriculture, Commerce, Labor
Ingersoll, Bob, 473
Inness, George, 169
Institutions
Austin Hewitt Home for the Aged, 382; Brushy Mountain State Prison, 85, 86, 362; Central State Hospital for the Insane, 398; Church of Christ Orphanage, 379; Knights of Pythias Home, 406; Pressmen's Home, 90, 310; State Agricultural School for Delinquent Negroes, 503; U. S. Soldiers' Home, 323; Western State Hospital for the Insane, 492
Insull, Samuel, 169
Invisible Empire *(see Ku Klux Klan)*
Iris, State Flower, 21
Irish Nomads, 397, 398
Irving Block site (Memphis), 215
Island No. 39, 423

Jack, Capt. James W., 335
Jackson, Andrew, 41, 49, 106, 158, 175, 182, 191, 194, 210, 220, 228, 270-273, 276, 283, 292, 294, 325, 326, 348, 367, 368, 370, 371, 376, 378, 393, 396, 400, 401, 403, 406, 418, 434, 436, 437, 444, 448-454, 469, 478, 486, 508, 510
Jackson, Dr. George Pullen, 173, 239
Jackson, Granberry, 198
Jackson, Rachel Donelson, 378, 396, 437, 444, 448, 449
Jackson, Wm. H., 454
Jacobs, Old Ned, 171
Jake's Gap, 357, 358
James, C. E., 506
James, Frank, 496
James, Jesse, 458, 496
James Hobby Farm, 302
James Point, 506
Jarnagin, Jeremiah, 314
Jefferson, Thomas, 48, 248, 368, 463
Jeffrey's Hell, 354
Jenkins, Aaron, 401
Jenkins, Flemming, 220
Jenkins, Nimrod, 401
Jennings, Edmund, 367
Jobe, David, 322
John Gaston Memorial Hospital, 224
Johnson, Andrew, 54-56, 58, 59, 76, 122, 184, 224, 346, 347, 371, 454
Johnson, Dr. Mordecai, 109
Johnson, Elijah, 354
Johnson, Henry, 322
Johnson, Irene Charlesworth, 171
Johnson, James Weldon, 154
Johnson, Matt, 444
Johnson, Patsy, 444
Johnson, Postmaster-General Cave, 316
Johnston, Gen. Albert Sidney, 56, 57, 184, 488, 489
Johnston, Gen. Joseph E., 184
Joliet, Louis, 43, 209
Jones, Bob, 476
Jones, Calvin, 381
Jones, John Luther ("Casey"), 273, 459
Jones, Judge T. M., 381
Jones, Sam, 118
Jones, William, 175
Jones, Willie, 291
Jones and Furbinger, 224
Jonesboro Courthouse, 292
Jordan, C. N., 282
Jordan, J. B., 171
Jubilee Hall (Fisk University), 203, 204

Kane, John, 202
Kate Adams, 220
Kearfott, C. B., 290
Keating, Col. J. M., 59
Kelly, Father J. A., 212, 217
Kelly, Lavinia, 447
Kennedy, James, 238
Kephart, Horace P., 516
Kerrigan, Philip, 374
Kimball, 482
King, Ann, 493
King, Col. James, 280, 290
King, William, 280
King's Boatyard, 280
Kingsbury, Rev. Cyrus, 40, 253, 478
King's Meadows, 290
King's Mill Station, 286
Kinney, Belle, 162, 188, 196
Kirby, Shepherd, 367
Kirby-Smith, Gen. Edmund, 327, 483
Kitchen Cabinet, 52
Kleibacker, Frederick, 176
Knapp Farm, 452
Knickerbocker, William S., 149
Knoblauch, Henry, 363
Knox, Jack, 171
Knox, Maj. Gen. Henry, 234
Koasati (Cusatee), 30
Komarek Mammal Studies, 341
Kroll, Harry Harrison, 150
Krutch, Charles Christopher, 247
Krutch, Lou, 247
Ku Klux Klan, 58, 59, 193, 201, 381, 382, 385, 461 *(see History, Nashville)*

Labor, 81-90
Early conditions, 70, 75, 81, 82, 90, 189, 376, 455; federal assistance, 89, 102, 398; laws, 62, 87-89, 335; prison, 59, 60, 62, 85, 336, 362; strikes, 59, 61, 62, 85-87, 335, 402, 499; trade schools, 310; unions, 84-87, 90, 310, 335, 402, 499, 512. *See also* Agriculture, Negroes
Ladies Hermitage Association, 448
Lafayette, Marquis de, 182, 367, 495
Lakes
Aloaloa, 444; Bon Air, 467; Calanthe, 406; Drain, 462; La Joie, 491; Marrowbone, 495, 496; Monterey, 444; Montlake, 365; Norris, 131, 132, 335, 344, 345; Open, 422; Placid, 415; Reelfoot, 8, 14-16, 18, 129, 130, 417, 419, 424, 426-429,

Lakes (*Continued*)
462; Spring, 462; Waldensia, 441; Zollicoffer, 509
Lambert, Jeremiah, 111
Land Grants, 44
Lane, Bishop Issac, 271
Lane, Tidence, 111
Lanier, Lyle, 152
La Salle, Robert, Sieur de, 43, 44, 209, 422
Lattner, Thomas J., 259
Laura Spelman Rockefeller Memorial Fund, 517
Lawrence, Capt. James, 486
Lea, Luke, 471
Ledgerwood, Col., 348
Lee, George, 151, 222
Lee, W. A., 310
Le Moyne, Dr. Julius, 227
Lenoir, William Ballard, 305
Levees, 424, 429
Lewis, Lalla Walker, 171
Lewis, Maj. Andrew, 44
Lewis, Meriwether, 132, 390, 472
Lewisburg Walking Horse Association, 385
Libraries
Bayard Cairns Architecture (Memphis), 221; Carnegie (Jackson), 271, 272; Carnegie (Knoxville), 249; Cleveland Public, 476; Cossitt (Memphis), 207, 221; Fisk University (Nashville), 169, 204; Harper (Maryville), 350; Hughes Public, 360; Lamar (Maryville), 351; Lawson McGhee (University of Tennessee, Knoxville), 244; Peabody College (Nashville), 198; Nashville Public, 188; Rugby Free Public, 360; Tennessee State, 54, 189, 271; University of the South (Sewanee), 483; Vanderbilt University (Nashville), 197; WPA Art (Memphis), 169
Liddon, Benjamin, 405
Lincoln, President Abraham, 56, 215, 276, 346, 410, 478, 488, 489
Lind, Jenny, 396
Lindsey, Judge Ben B., 271
Literature *(see Writers of Tennessee)*
Little, Thomas, 171
Little Carpenter *(see Attakullakulla)*
Little Tennessee Valley, 479
Lively, W. S., 510
Livingston, Edgar, 508
"Long Hunters," 44, 45, 104, 181, 367, 396, 405, 445, 506, 507
Long Island of the Holston, 38, 280, 285
Longmire Ridge, 335
Longstreet, Gen. James A., 237, 248, 268, 312, 433, 480
Look-Off Rock, 334
Lookout Mountain Incline Railway, 264
Looney, Moses, 308
Lotz, Matilda, 168
Loudoun, Earl of, 45, 352
Louis Philippe of France, 242, 354, 437, 438
Love, Col. Robert, 234, 325
Lowe, Abraham, 437
Lowe's Ferry, 436
Loyalists, 297, 346
Loyal Land Company of Virginia, 44
Ludlow, Noah M., 175
Ludlow and Peabody, 198
Lundy, Benjamin, 54, 105, 295, 297
Lusk, John, 510
Lynch, Tom, 406
Lynn, Joseph, 271
Lyric Theater (Memphis), 176, 242
Lytle, Andrew Nelson, 153

Mabry, Gen. Joseph A., 244, 436
Mabry, George W., 436
Madison, James, 353
"Madison Greys," 271
Madison Rural Sanitarium, 372
Maffi, Vigelio, 222
Malone, Dudley Field, 364
Malone, Walter, 148, 215, 227
Mansker, Kasper, 45, 181, 396
Mansker's Lick, 396
Manumission Society of Tennessee, 295
Maretti, G., 375
Markers
Barnard, 190; Bloody Pond, 489; Boone Trail, 292; Chief Jack Walker, 307; Dumplin Treaty, 434; Hornet's Nest, 489; Isaac Franklin, 369; James, 506; James White, 348; Meriwether Lewis, 472; Natchez Trace, 196, 197
Market Street Theater, 175
Marks, Albert S., 485
Marquette, Pere Jacques, 43, 209
Mars, Frank C., 381
Marsh, Lieut.-Col. John F., 215
Martin, Thomas, 383
Mason, Samuel, 236
Massacre of Fort Pillow, 422
Maury, Commodore Matthew Fontaine, 24, 378
Maynard, Horace, 249, 346, 347
McAdoo, Rev. Samuel, 455
McAdoo, William Gibbs, 249
McAlister, Gov. Hill, 61, 62
McCardle, Eliza, 297
McClellan, Gen. 346
McClellan, George, 151
McClernand, Gen., 410, 488, 489
McClung, Charles, 435
McCormack, John, 234
McCormack, Nancy Cox, 190
McDonald, John, 267
McDuffy, Edward, 438
McElwee, Samuel A., 108
McEwen, Hetty, 194, 195
McFarlane, John, 93
McGavock, Bessie Dawson, 171
McGavock, Col. Randall, 378, 379
McGavock, David, 452
McGee, Hubert, 227
McGee, John, 307
McGee, William, 112
McGhee, Charles M., 244
McGhee, May Lawson, 244
McGready, James, 112

McKim, Mead and White, 162, 188, 198, 261
McKinley, President William, 185
McLean Rock, 328
McLemore, John C., 210
McLemore, John S., 227
MacMillan, Rev. W. E., 249
McMillin, Benton, 445, 509
McMinn, Joseph, 311
McPherson, Col. J. B., 259
McSpadden, Samuel, 434
McTyeire, Bishop Holland M., 113, 197
Meagher, Paddy, 219, 220, 228
Meharry, Alexander, 204
Meharry, Jane, 204
Meigs, Col. R. J., 54, 479
Meininger, Julius C., 174
Melton, James, 175
Melungeons *(see Racial Elements)*
Memorials, Monuments, and Statues
Andrew Jackson equestrian, 190; Archibald Roane, 436; Benjamin Liddon, 405; Boyd's Creek, 337; Boy Scout, 363; Commodore Vanderbilt Statue, 198; Confederate monuments, 325, 401, 411, 412, 490, 495; David Crockett, 419, 486; Doughboy, 225; Dumplin Treaty, 434; Edward Ward Carmack statue, 190; First Wisconsin Cavalry, 268; Henry Rutherford, 421; Illinois, 268; Iowa, 267; Isaac Thomas, 339; James Robertson, 196; Jefferson Davis, 215; John Overton, 225; John W. Thomas, 196; Maynard, 347; Meriwether Lewis, 472; Morgan, 298; Nathan Bedford Forrest, 224, 419; Ochs Memorial Temple, 266, 267; Peace, 375; Pioneer, 291; Sam Davis, 189, 382; Samuel Wear, 339; Soldiers', 317, 434, 486; Sycamore Shoals, 319; Treaty of the Holston, 242; Thomas Sharpe Spencer, 368; Union, 399; United Daughters of the Confederacy, 198
Memphis Art Association, 169
Memphis Little Theater, 176, 227
Memphis Navy Yard, 220
Meriwether, Charles N., 408
Mero District, 91, 396
Mexican War, 53, 55, 61, 285, 388, 402, 407-409
Michaux, Andre, 367, 370
Middle Tennessee Experiment Station, 386-388
Mid's Gap, 356
Mid-South Fairgrounds, 213
Miles, Bishop Pius, 115, 190
Miller, E. E., 84
Miller, Gen. Joseph, 368
Miller, Grant B., 244, 247
Miller, Harvey E., 227
Milligan, Robert, 320
Mills, Clark, 190
Milton, George Fort, Jr., 153
Mims, Dr. Edwin, 152
Mims, Thomas Puryear, 170
Missionary Ridge, 251, 479
Mitchell, Maggie, 176
Mitchie, Maj. Charles, 492
Moccasin Bend, 252, 265
Modjeska, Ralph, 229
Mondelli, Signor, 176
"Monkey Trial," 363, 364 *(see Education)*
Montgomery, Col. John, 494
Mooney, C. P. J., 149
"Moonshine," 409, 416, 432
Moore, Grace, 175, 334, 430
Moore, John Trotwood, 147, 148, 153
Moore, Merrill, 151, 152
Moore, Robert, 376
Moore, William, 445
Morgan, Col. Gideon, 438
Morgan, Gen. Daniel, 361
Morgan, Gen. George, 327
Morgan, Gen. John H., 334
Morgan and Baldwin, 161
Mound Builders *(see Indians)*
Mountain Gap, 362
Mountains
Bald, 430; Bays, 309; Black, 441; Blanket, 342, 357; Brown's, 337; Brushy, 362; Buffalo, 309; Bullhead, 341, 342; Byrd, 361; Chapman, 338; Cheat, 370; Chestnut Ridge, 309; Chilhowee, 305, 331, 338; Chimney Top, 279, 309, 342; Chinquapin Ridge, 356; Clinch, 91, 279, 301, 329; Clingman's Dome, 342, 514; Cold Water Knob, 358; Cove, 356; Crab Orchard, 441; Cross, 335; Cumberland, 8, 91, 94, 279, 300, 332-334, 402-404, 469, 475, 483, 503-505, 510; Curry He, 358; Curry She, 358; Double Top, 498; English, 329; Fodderstack, 358; Great Smokies, 7, 8, 11, 15, 16, 22, 78, 431, 434, 513-518; Greenbriar Knob, 358; Guyot, 338; Hall's Top, 431; Harrison, 356, 357; Holston, 315; Horse, 406; Hudleston Knob, 498; Iron, 315; Le Conte, 78, 338, 341, 342, 516; Lookout, 39, 252, 479, 480, 506; Max Patch, 431; Pilot, 361; Pinnacle, 324, 327; Raccoon, 264, 479, 480, 506; Reagon Knob, 498; Rich, 358; Roan, 317; Rocky Spur, 341; Roosevelt, 439; Signal, 264, 505, 506; Siler's Bald, 358; Sugarland, 356; Thunderhead, 358, 359; Unaka, 7, 78, 80, 320, 324, 329; Walden's Ridge, 480; Ward, 361
Moytoy, Chief, 37
Murfree, Col. Hardy, 401
Murfree, Mary N. (Charles Egbert Craddock), 147, 148, 358, 359, 510
Murrell, John A., 219, 384, 385, 415, 459, 461, 472, 503
Murrell, "Mom," 461
Muscle Shoals, 26, 93, 98, 214, 236, 254, 489 *(see Tennessee Valley Authority)*
Museums
Adolph S. Ochs, 264; Anderson County Federal Art Center, 170; Andrew

Museums (*Continued*)
Johnson Tailor Shop, 298; Ann Trigg-Robinson Home, 444, 445; Audigier Art, 247; Baldridge, 169; Barnes Cherokee Indian, 340; Brooks Memorial, 169, 225; C. M. McClung, 244; Cohen Memorial, 200; Dyer County, 420; Federal Art, 170; Fort Donelson, 409, 410; Geologic, 198; Great Smoky Mountain, 340; Stokely, 430; Holbrook, 328; Indian Relic, 328; James Lee Memorial, 169; LeMoyne Federal Art, 170; Lonas House, 435; Memphis Art, 176; Nashville Art, 194; Natural History and Industrial Arts, 227; Parthenon, 162, 169, 185, 196; Pritchett House, 432, 433; Reeder, 455; Robinson House, 444; Sam Davis, 398, 399; Sample Home, 418; Tennessee State Historical, 188; Thruston, 197, 198; Ward House, 438; World War, 188
Music, 171-175
Big Singings, 172, 173, 340, 473, 486; Negro Spirituals, 109, 139, 143, 144, 173, 202, 204, 209. *See also* Folklore
Muster Day, 405, 508
Myer, William Edward, 415
"Mystic Brotherhood" *(see John A. Murrell)*

Nancy Hall Sweet Potato, 78, 412
Napier, J. C., 107, 108
Napier, Richard Claiborne, 455
Napoleon Direct, 379
Nash, Gen. Francis, 181
Nashborough *(see Towns: Nashville)*
Nashoba Experiment, 463, 464
Nashville Allied Architects, 203
Nashville Centennial Exposition, 162, 185
Nashville City Wharf, 192
Nashville Community Playhouse, 176
Nashville Thespian Society, 175
Natchez Trace, 31, 50, 91, 196, 197, 285, 390, 461 *(see History, Indians: Trails, Transportation)*
National Field Trials Association, 129, 492
National Foxhunters Association, 462
National Park Service, 130, 131
Natural Bridge, 432, 486
Natural Setting, 7-11
Neal, W. H., 76
Needham, James, 43, 44, 330
Negley, Gen. James S., 184, 200
Negroes, 104-110
Abolition, 54-58, 61, 83, 105, 106, 108, 228, 295, 303, 306, 351, 422, 491; since Reconstruction, 62, 107, 108, 118, 124, 125, 127, 139-144, 151, 154, 220-223, 227, 462, 491, 503; slavery, 53-56, 58, 59, 62, 63, 75, 81, 82, 89, 104-107, 295, 330, 461-464, 508. *See also* Folklore, Labor, Religion
Netherland, Richard, 283
Nevin, Arthur, 174
Newfound Gap, 342
New Madrid Earthquake, 422, 426
Newman, Willie Bettie, 168
New Market Valley, 329
New Orleans, 210
Newspapers, 145-146
Athens Post-Athenian, 154; *Burley Bulletin*, 297; *Chattanooga Gazette*, 253; *Chattanooga News*, 153; *Chattanooga Times*, 256; *Clarkesville Leaf-Chronicle*, 154, 494; *Cleveland Banner*, 154; *Columbia Herald*, 154; *Columbia Observer*, 276; *The Coming Nation*, 455, 456; *Emancipator*, 54, 295; *Franklin Review-Appeal*, 154; *Gallatin Examiner-Tennessean*, 154; *Genius of Universal Emancipation*, 54, 105, 297; *Greenville Sun*, 297; *Hamilton Gazette*, 253; *Hamilton Observer*, 254; *Independent Journal*, 146; *Jackson Christian Index*, 271; *Jackson Forked Deer Blade*, 271; *Jackson Gazette*, 271; *Jackson Truthteller*, 271; *Jackson Pioneer*, 271; *Jackson Sun*, 271; *Jackson Watchman of the West*, 271; *Jackson Western Index*, 271; *Jackson Western Tennessee Republican*, 271; *Knoxville Daily Chronicle*, 146; *Knoxville Gazette*, 47, 54, 66, 68, 146, 234-235, 311, 403; *Knoxville Journal*, 153; *Knoxville Sentinel*, 148; *Manumission Intelligencer*, 54, 295; *Memphis Advocate and Western District Intelligencer*, 210; *Memphis Commercial Appeal*, 59, 148, 149, 153, 154, 171, 210; *Memphis Press-Scimitar*, 153; *Memphis Western Times and Memphis Commercial Advertiser*, 210; *Nashville American*, 148; *Nashville Banner*, 148, 153; *Nashville Impartial Review*, 93; *Nashville Tennessean*, 60, 153, 154, 190, 367; *Nashville Union and American*, 185; *Pulaski Citizen*, 154; *Railroad Advocate*, 94, 311; *Rights of Man*, or *Nashville Intelligencer*, 182; *Southern Statesman*, 271; *Tennessee Gazette and Mero District Advertizer*, 182; *Weekly Whig and Chronicle*, 146; *Whig and Rebel Ventilator*, 146
Niehaus, Charles Henry, 224
Night Riders, 395
Nolan, Dr. John, 279
Nolichucky Gorge, 326
Norris, Sen. George W., 344
Norris Basin, 11
Norris Freeway, 344
Norrison, Peter, 65
North Carolina, 44, 45, 291

Oberteuffer, Karl, 171
Obion Levee, 418
Ochs, Adolph S., 256, 264
Oconaluftee Gorge, 342
Oconostota, Chief, 37, 285, 311, 353
Oertel, K. A., 483

Ogden, John, 203
Old Castle Building, 494
"Old Glory," 201, 202
Old Hickory Division, 61
Old Hop, Chief, 37, 352, 353
Old Smoky Rifle Grounds, 341
O'Neal, Peggy, 52, 378
Oolooteka, Chief, 40, 364, 365
Orchard Knob, 255, 263
Ore, Major James, 39, 182, 253, 480, 482
Orr, Carey, 171
Osborn, Charles, 54
Ostenaco, Chief, 37
O'Sullivan, Patrick, 174
Otey, Bishop James H., 115, 378, 386, 388, 389, 483
Overton, Col. John, 52, 65, 193, 210, 367, 376
Overton Hills, 184
Owen Colony, 463
Owens, Flavius, 415
Owens, John E., 176
Owens, Joshua, 498
Owsley, Frank, 152, 153

Palmer, Col. J. M., 259
Panic of 1893, 256
Parham, F. A., 253
Park, James, 245
Parkinson, Capt. Peter, 324
Parks and Forests
  Municipal: Centennial, 185, 195; Confederate, 207, 220; DeSoto, 228; Edwin Warner, 471; Geers Memorial, 278; Handy, 221; Jefferson Davis, 207, 220, 221; Lancaster, 272; Memphis Zoological and Botanical Gardens, 225; Overton, 225, 464; Percy Warner, 471; Point, 265; Victory, 185
  National: Cherokee National Forest, 290, 330, 430, 475, 476; Chickamauga and Chattanooga National Military, 60, 132, 257, 264, 267, 268; Falls Creek Falls National Recreation and Demonstration Area, 468, 503; Fort Donelson National Military, 410; *Great Smoky Mountains National Park,* 61, 330, 331, 341, 342, 356, 432, 513-518; Meriwether Lewis National, 390, 472; Shanghai Branch TVA Recreation Area, 335; Shiloh National Military, 132, 488; Stones River National Military, 132, 399
  State: Big Ridge Park and Forest, 132, 335, 346; Bledsoe Forest, 130; Chickasaw Forest and Park, 130, 415, 491; Lebanon Cedar Forest and Park, 130, 147; Marion-Franklin Forest, 130; Natchez Trace Park and Forest, 130, 473; Nathan Bedford Forrest Park, 224, 459; Norris Park and Forest, 131, 132; Pickett State Park and Forest, 130, 498; Reelfoot Lake Park and Game Preserve, 426-428; Shelby Forest, 423; Standing Stone Park and Forest, 508, 509
Park Theater, 175
Parrish, Joe, 171
Partee, McCullough, 169
Parthenon, 162
Parton, James, 153
Patterson, Caleb, 104
Patterson, Gov. Malcolm R., 60, 190, 367
Patton, Col. James, 290
Peake, Margaret Bloodgood, 442
Peay, Gov. Austin, 61, 495
Perry, Jennings, 150, 414
Pfiel and Awsumb, 225
Phiel, Charles Oscar, 217
Philbin, Harry, 175
Pickup, Ernest A., 171
Pike, Capt. Zebulon M., 220
Pile, Conrad, 498
Pillow, Gideon J., 159, 388, 410, 411
Pillow, Granville, 388
Pillow, Jerome, 388
"Pinch," 219
Ploughboy, 451
Poe, Hugh, 170
Point Lookout, 499
Polk, Andrew, 389
Polk, Antoinette, 389
Polk, Bishop Leonidas, 56, 211, 224, 388, 389, 483
Polk, Col. Ezekiel, 491
Polk, George, 390
Polk, James K., 53, 188, 190, 194, 272, 276, 283, 386, 389, 491
Polk, Lucius, 389
Polk, Samuel K., 276
Polk, William, 159, 389
Polk Memorial Association, 276
Pope, Colonel John, 76
Pope, Lewis S., 61
Porter, Alexander James, 374
Porter, Edward, 230
Porter, Gov. James D., 411
Postel, Capt. John, 352
"Potneck" Community, 409
Potter, Bertha, 171
Powell's Valley, 45, 326, 334
Prentiss, Gen., 488, 489
Priber, Christian, 36
Priestly, Dr. James, 452
Prohibition, 60, 367
Prudhomme, Pierre, 422
Prudhomme Bluff, 36 *(see Towns: Memphis)*
Publications
  Calvinistic Magazine, 311; *Fugitive,* 151; *Migrant,* 18, 516; *Philanthropist,* 54; *Progressive Teacher,* 301; *Sewanee Review,* 149; *Taylor Trotwood Magazine,* 149
Public Buildings
  Carroll County Courthouse, 459; Chattanooga U. S. Post Office and Courthouse, 259; Church Park Auditorium, 224; Cocke County Memorial Building, 431; Davidson County Public Building and Courthouse, 191; Ellis Municipal Auditorium,

Public Buildings (*Continued*)
213, 218; Harriman City Hall, 362; Hawkins County Courthouse, 311; Kingsport U. S. Post Office, 280; Knox County Courthouse, 242; Monroe County Courthouse, 353; Nashville U. S. Custom House, 195; Nashville War Memorial Building, 188; Rhea County Courthouse, 363; Roane County Courthouse, 438; Shelby County Courthouse, 217; State Capitol, 160, 161, 189, 397; State Supreme Court Building, 188; Washington County Courthouse, 292
Public Works Administration, 89, 203, 230
Pugh, John, 323, 324
Pugin, Augustus Welby, 374
Pulaski, Count Casimir, of Poland, 381
Pulliam, Dr. John Junius, 492

Quarles, William, 444

Racial Elements
English, 180, 212, 237, 253, 280, 517; Germans, 361, 412, 431; Irish, 180; Melungeons, 362; Negroes, 104, 106; Scotch, 180, 210, 280; Scotch-Irish, 111, 289, 517; Swiss, 361, 472, 511, 512
Raffaellino, Del Garbo, 225
Ragsdale, W. F., 259
Railroads (*see Transportation*)
Rainey, Paul, 227
Ramsey, Dr. J. G. M., 145, 348, 349
Ramsey, F. A., 234, 348
Ramsey, John, 210
Rankin, Quentin, 429
Ransom, John Crowe, 151, 152
Rappelyea, George, 363
Rayburn, Green, 495
Raynor, Seth, 266
Read, Opie, 147
Reagon Knob, 498
Rebel, 270
Red Cross, 212, 213, 424, 499
Reed, Charles, 369
Reelfoot Nightriders, 429
Religion, 111-119
Denominations: Baptist, 55, 112, 114, 459; Church of Christ, 114, 118, 415; Cumberland Presbyterian, 114, 118; Hebrew, 118; Holiness, 473, 477; Lutheran, 114; Methodist, 55, 111, 118, 294, 477, 491, 499, 518; Negro, 107, 115, 118; Presbyterian (Southern, U. S. A.), 39, 55, 111, 114, 116, 225, 294, 374, 406; Protestant Episcopal, 115, 116, 378, 386, 482-484, 512; Quakers, 351; Roman Catholic, 115, 212, 397, 485; Seventh Day Adventist, 371, 372; developments since 1870, 118, 119; Great Revival, 49, 112-114; "Monkey Trial," 363, 364; mountain religion, 518; Negro, 107, 115, 118; pioneer period, 49, 111-113, 300, 409, 472, 478; war and Reconstruction, 116-118. *See also* Churches, Colleges, Education, Folklore, Schools
Renfroe, Moses, 494
Republican Party, 56, 59, 60
Reservoir Hill, 346
Resorts
Avondale Springs, 314; Beersheba Springs, 510; Bon Aqua, 471; Cade's Cove, 358; Carson Springs, 432; Castalian Springs, 368; Chilhowee Springs, 355; Cumberland Springs, 364; Dye Stone Springs, 390; Galbraith Springs, 311, 312; Horn Springs, 447; Idaho Springs, 408, 409; Jefferson Springs, 398, 399; Kingston Springs, 454; Kinzel Springs, 358; Lea Springs, 314; Liddon Springs, 405; Line Springs, 339; Mineral Springs, 329; Monteagle, 397, 482; Montvale Springs, 352; Mooresburg Springs, 312; Morgan Springs, 364; Rhea Springs, 363; Red Boiling Springs, 367; Ringgold, 493; Rock Island, 469; Seven Springs, 468; Tate Springs, 312; Unaka Springs, 326; Williams Springs, 331
Revolutionary War, 38, 39, 46, 48, 253, 289, 290, 295, 366, 370, 401, 484; Battles: Boyd's Creek, 337; Island Flats, 280; King's Mountain, 46, 50, 295, 337, 405, 476
Reynolds, Maj. Robert, 435
Rhind, J. Massey, 217
Rice, John, 210
Rich Gap, 359
Ridge, John, 42
"Ridgemanites", 518
Ridley, James, 452
Rieff, Joseph, 158, 448, 449
Rivers
Barren Fork, 510; Caney Fork, 468, 469; Citico, 15; Clinch, 10, 44, 100, 344; Collins, 469, 510; Cumberland, 10, 18, 45, 46, 56, 66, 91, 93, 180, 184, 185, 371, 372, 409-411, 480, 495, 508; Dee, 317; Doe, 317; Duck, 10, 18, 274, 275, 377, 402, 405, 457, 472; Elk, 10, 316, 407, 486; Emory, 362; Falling Water, 509; Forked Deer, 270, 412, 414, 420, 421; French Broad, 10, 11, 329, 338, 430, 433, 434; Harpeth, 82, 379, 453, 454, 471, 495; Hatchie, 43, 52, 209, 423, 453, 462, 463, 490; Hiwassee, 307; Holston, 10, 94, 279, 280, 285, 286, 291, 309, 321; Little, 358; Little Pigeon, 331, 341-342; Little Tennessee, 29, 43, 253, 330; Loosahatchie, 423, 453; Mississippi, 7-10, 18, 50, 93, 94, 207, 209, 210, 212, 227-229, 417, 420-422, 424, 429; Nolichucky, 38, 45, 93, 296, 309; Obed, 27; Obey, 507, 508; Obion, 412, 420, 424, 428; Ocoee, 476; Pigeon, 431; Powell, 328, 344;

Rivers (*Continued*)
Red, 394, 493, 494; Rocky, 469; Sequatchie, 496, 500; South Harpeth, 471; Stone's, 383, 399, 400, 450, 452; Tellico, 15, 43; Tennessee, 8, 10, 18, 23, 92-94, 98-103, 236, 254, 280, 305, 364, 410, 415, 423, 438, 453, 458, 473, 479, 480-482, 489; Watauga, 45, 291, 317; West Harpeth, 378; Wolf, 207, 210, 220, 229, 423, 463, 497, 507
Roan, Thomas, 295
Roane, Gov. Archibald, 49, 50, 436
Roan High Bluff, 21
Roan Iron Company, 439
Robert E. Lee, 220
Robertson, Charles, 46
Robertson, Charlotte Reeves, 196, 201
Robertson, Gen. Felix, 201
Robertson, Gen. James, 104, 181, 191, 192, 201, 204, 209, 316, 375, 393
Rock Castle Valley, 499
Rockefeller Foundation, 197, 282
Rockwell, Kiffen, 301
Rockwood, Maj. W. O., 438
Roddey, Col. James, 300
Rodeheaver, Homer A., 334
Rodes, Tyree, 381
Rogan, Hugh, 367
Rogers, James Gamble, 217, 225
Rogers, Joseph, 310
Rogers, Nancy, 339
Rogers, Will, 275
Roller, William, 282
Roosevelt, President Franklin D., 406, 507
Rose, Mrs. S. E. F., 201
Rosecrans, Gen. William Starke, 184, 254, 255, 268, 399, 406
Ross, Albert Randolph, 188
Ross, Dr. Frederick A., 66, 309
Ross, John, 41, 42
Rossville Gap, 255
Rothert, Otto A., 423
Rotherwood Elm, 309
Roulstone, George, 146, 235, 311, 445
Round Top, 358
Rousseau, Gen. Theodore, 184
Ruby Falls, 265
Ruck, John, 485
Rugby Settlement, 360
Rule, Fay S., 171
Ruskin Colony, 455-457
Rust, Dr. R. S. 204
Rust, John D., 231
Rust, Mack, 231
Rust Cotton Picker, 231
Rust Foundation, 231
Rutherford, Henry, 421
Rutherford Hospital, 401
Rutledge, Gen. George, 314
Ryan, Father Abram J., 148, 190
Ryder, Albert, 169

Safford, Dr. S. M., 447
Said, C. M., 171
St. Clair, Brig.-Gen. James, 201
St. Michael's Monastery, 483
Sanders, John W., 375
Sanders, Newell, 256
Sandheimer, Rosalie, 171
Sanford, A. F., 249
Saunders, Clarence, 227
Saunders, L. Pearl, 171
Saunders, Wallace, 273
Scaggs, Henry, 45
Scalawags, 201
Scarritt, Dr. Nathan, 200
Schofield, Gen. John, 184, 375, 377-381
Scholz, Belle Kinney, 169
Scholz, Leopold F., 162, 169, 188, 196
Schools
Extinct: American Temperance University, 362; Belmont College, 122, 200; Bethel College, 459; Blount College, 121, 238, 349; Branham-Hughes Preparatory, 379; Buffalo Institute, 320; Centenary Female College, 476; Central Tennessee College, 108; Central University, 124, 197; College of New Economy, 456; Craighead Academy, 374; Cumberland College, 122; Davidson Academy, 120; Fairmount College, 512; Fisk Female Academy, 509; Greeneville College, 121; Harrogate University, 328 *(see Lincoln Memorial University);* Jefferson Academy, 308; Martha and Fanny O'Bryan School, 122; Martin Academy, 294; Masonic University of Tennessee, 494; McKee School, 108; Mississippi Valley College, 464; Montvale Academy, 507; Mooney School, 362, 363; Nancy Academy, 339; Nashville Academy of Music, 174; Nashville Agricultural Normal Institute, 372; Nashville Bible School, 202, 203; Nashville Female Academy, 122, 174; Robertson Academy, 375; Roger Williams University, 108; Sam Houston School, 351, 481; Southern School of Photography, 510; Southwestern Baptist College, 272; Stewart College, 494; Tate School, 362, 363; University of Nashville, 122, 197, 198; Walden University, 108; Ward Seminary, 122, 200; Washington College, 121, 295, 296; West Tennessee Baptist College, 272
Negro: Agriculture and Industrial State Teachers' College, 127, 180, 204; Fisk University, 58, 108, 124, 180, 203, 204; Haywood County Training School, 462; Knoxville College, 108; Lane College, 272, 273, 459; Le Moyne College, 227; Meharry Medical College, 108, 109, 124, 204; Morristown Normal and Industrial College, 301; State Training and Agricultural School for Delinquent Negroes, 503
White: Alpine Institute, 509; Alvin C. York Agricultural Institute, 126, 498; Austin Peay Normal, 127; Battleground Academy, 379; Baxter

Schools, White (*Continued*)
Seminary, 445; Bob Jones College, 476, 477; Bristol-Nelson Physiological, 401; Carson-Newman, 302; Castle Heights Military Academy, 446, 447; Columbia Military Academy, 386; Cumberland Mountain School, 499; Cumberland University, 446, 447; David Lipscomb College, 202-203; Dubose Memorial Church Training School, 512; Freed-Hardeman Junior College, 415; George Peabody College, 122, 124, 125, 198, 200, 361, 374; Goodwyn Institute, 215; Harrison-Chilhowee Institute, 338; Highlander Folk School, 335, 512; Hiwassee Junior College, 354; Hume-Fogg High School, 195; King College, 290; Lambuth College, 272; Lincoln Memorial University, 126, 328; Madison College, 372; Martin College, 382, 383; Maryville College, 121, 350, 351; McCallie School, 268; Middle Tennessee Teachers College, 127, 401; Milligan College, 320; Montgomery Bell Academy, 124; Morgan School, 124; Pi Beta Phi Settlement, 126, 340, 341; Pleasant Hill Academy, 466; Pressmen's Trade School, 310; St. Andrews School, 482; St. Cecilia Academy, 124; St. Mary's School, 484; Sardis Farm School, 473; Scarritt College, 123, 162, 200, 442; Sewanee Military Academy, 125, 484; Southern Junior College, 477; Southwestern University, 162, 225, 227, 494; Technical Trade School, 310; Tennessee College, 401; Tennessee Federation of Women's Clubs Vocational School, 406; Tennessee Military Institute, 305; Tennessee Polytechnic Institute, 127, 444; Tennessee School for the Blind, 127; Tennessee School for the Deaf, 127, 348; Tennessee Wesleyan College, 306, 307; Tusculum College, 297; Union University, 272, 459; University of Chattanooga, 261; University of the South, 115, 122, 125, 162, 483; University of Tennessee, 24, 121, 125, 126, 224, 238, 246, 247, 386, 388, 413, 473, 494, 495; University of Tennessee College of Agriculture, 80; University of Tennessee Junior College, 126, 413; University of Tennessee Medical and Dental School, 126; Vanderbilt Medical College, 197, 198; Vanderbilt University, 124, 197, 198; Ward-Belmont College, 124, 200; Watkins Institute, 194; Webb Preparatory School, 124, 405; West Tennessee State Teachers College, 227; William Jennings Bryan University, 364
Scopes, John T., 363, 364
Scopes Trial, 125, 126, 366
Scott, Amanda, 442
Scott, Charles, 227
Scott, Cyril Kay, 150
Scott, Evelyn, 150, 151
Scott, Gen. Winfield, 307
Scott, James, 347
Searcy, Elisabeth, 171
Seawell, Col. Benjamin, 447
Seminole War, 50, 271, 285
Senter, Gov. DeWitt Clinton, 59, 201
Sequatchie Valley, 8, 496, 500-503
Sequoyah, 40, 53, 286
Sevier, Catherine ("Bonny Kate"), 507
Sevier, Col. Granville, 202
Sevier, Col. Valentine, 493
Sevier, Dr. William, 109
Sevier, John, 46-49, 245, 312, 319, 323, 336, 338, 339, 347, 352, 363, 410, 436, 437, 493
Shackelford, Chancellor James O., 184
Shaffran, Jascha, 171
Shakes Country *(see Reelfoot Lake)*
Shanty-hyphenate boatmen, 229
Sharp, Cecil J., 171
Shawnee *(see Indians)*
Shelby, Col. David 368
Shelby, Col. Evan, 39, 46, 234, 285, 479
Shelby, Col. Isaac, 290, 308, 347, 405
Shelton, Jim, 409
Shepherd, Col. Lewis, 478
Sherman, Gen. William Tecumseh, 230, 237, 255, 268, 351, 384, 406, 407, 422, 478, 488, 489, 492
Shields, Alice Watkins, 247
Shields, Sen. John K., 312
Shook's Gap, 337
Simerly, Elijah, 316
Simpson, George, 444
Skull Bone Community, 413
Skyline Trail, 131
"Slicks," 514
Smith, Bessie, 175
Smith, Col. James, 45, 104, 146
Smith, Gen. Daniel, 156, 369, 370
Smith, Gen. John E., 211
Smith, Myrtis, 171
Smith, Polly, 369, 370
Smith, Roy Lamont, 174
Smith, Seth, 156
Smith, W. H., 363
Snodgrass Hill, 268
Snyder, William, 493
Socialist Party, 499
Society for Propagating Christian Knowledge, 509
Soldiers and Sailors Memorial Auditorium, 261
Sol Smith's Thespians, 175
Southern Appalachian Park Commission, 516, 517
Southern Convention, 55, 182
Southern States Fox Hunt, 415
Spanish-American War, 256
Spencer, Thomas Sharp, 368, 468
Sports and Recreation, 128-133
Fishing, 495, 496, 507; horseback riding, 133, 385; hunting, 128, 129,

Sports and Recreation (*Continued*) 355, 459, 462, 481, 492. *See also* Animal Life, Conservation, Game Reserves, Parks and Forests, Tennessee Valley Authority
Squires, Mrs. Mary, 175
Stacker Lee, 220
Stagg, Clarence A., 171
Standing Turkey, Chief, 37
State of Tennessee
  Archives, 184, 188; Bureau of Agriculture, 23, 26, 76, 79, 80, 300, 394, 494, 495; Commission of Labor, 86; Department of Conservation, 64; Department of Health, 88, 89, 411; Department of Insurance and Banking, 71; Division of Forestry, 20, 414; Division of Game and Fish, 355, 495; Employment Service, 88; Planning Commission, 24, 63, 64; Relief measures, 61; Supreme Court, 62, 229
Staub, Peter, 244
Staub's Theater, 176, 244
Sterling, Ross, 215
Sterrick Building, 164, 207, 215
Stewart, Capt. John, 352, 353
Stewart, Dr. F. A., 108, 109
Stewart, Gen. A. P., 263, 268
Stewart, Virgil, 461
Stewart, William M., 494
Stickley, Vastine, 354
Stockton, Mrs. Wm. Bradford, 499
Stodgen, Sam, 219
Stokes, Frank Wilbert, 168
Stone, Barton, 114
Stone, Uriah, 396, 400, 445
Stout, Joseph, 498, 499
Strahl, Gen. Oscar, 377, 379
Stribling, T. S., 149, 487
Strickland, Francis W., 193
Strickland, William, 160, 189, 190, 193, 202, 446
Stuart, Capt. John, 37, 353
Stuart, Gen. J. E. B., 488, 489
Sturtevant, Robert S., 376
Suck of the Tennessee, 506
Sullivan, Gen. John, 308
Sully, Thomas, 225
Sulphur Dell, 181
Sulphur Fork, 394
Summit Hill, 244
Sumter, Sergt. Thomas, 37, 234
Sunset Rock, 467
Swag Gap, 335
Swan, William G., 244, 436
Swann, Thomas, 451
Swanson, Edward, 378
Sweetbriar Farm, 372
Sycamore Shoals, 46, 507
Sydney Bluff, 495

Taft, President William Howard, 108
Talequah, 354 *(see Indians)*
Talley, Thomas W., 151
Tassel, Chief, 319
Tate, Allen, 152, 495
Taylor, Alfred A. ("Alf"), 59, 318
Taylor, Howell, 462
Taylor, Kit, 292
Taylor, Marie Barton, 188
Taylor, Robert Love ("Bob"), 59, 60, 149, 318, 319
Taylor, R. S., 429
Tazewell, Senator Henry, 328
Tecumseh, 285
Temple, O. P., 248
Tennessee Antiquarian Society, 384
Tennessee Coal, Iron and Railway Company, 85, 336
Tennessee Court of Law and Equity, 49
Tennessee Electric Power Company, 476
Tennessee Federation of Music Clubs, 174
Tennessee Fox Hunters Association, 395
Tennessee Historical Society, 384
Tennessee National Guard, 85, 86, 267, 336, 398, 406, 424, 448
Tennessee Ornithological Society, 18
Tennessee Playmakers, 176
Tennessee State Constitution, 58, 59, 62
Tennessee State Legislature, 63, 95, 182, 184, 204, 212, 291, 297
Tennessee Valley Authority, 89, 103
  Beginnings, 61, 62, 98, 99; conservation, 24-25, 100-103, 329, 345; education, 102; future outlook, 90, 102, 103; hydroelectric development, 68, 73, 80, 99, 100, 166, 214, 381, 476, 478, 489; reforestation, 20, 131, 132, 335, 478; planning, 98, 164, 166, 233, 279, 345, 346, 473; river control, 26, 94, 99, 100, 489
Terrell, Mary Church, 108
Territorial Assembly, 91, 350 *(see* Tennessee State Legislature)
Territory South of the River Ohio, 47, 234, 291, 326, 336, 350, 438 *(see History)*
Theater, 175, 176, 227
Thespian Society of Nashville, 175
Thomas, Col. W. H., 516
Thomas, Gen. George H., 58, 184, 263, 268, 375, 377
Thomas, Theodore, 174
Thompson, John, 375
Thompson, Thomas, 375
Thompson, William H., 439
Thoni, Melchior, 168
Tilghman, Gen. Lloyd, 411
Timberlake, Ensign Henry, 34, 37, 234, 331
Tipton, John, 323, 324, 436
Tiptonville Dome, 424
Todd, Charles, 145, 352
Tolley, W. M., 379
Tomerlin, Lyle, 175
Tomes, Rev. Charles, 202
Tomlinson, A. J., 477
Towns
  Adamsville, 489; Alamo, 420; Alcoa, 62, 71, 87, 350; Alexandria, 468; Algood, 509; Alpine, 509; Allardt, 499; Altamont, 511; Apison, 477; Ardmore, 383; Ashland City, 495; Ashwood, 389; Athens, 306; Baxter, 445; Bean Station, 312, 329; Bearden, 435; Bell Buckle, 405;

Towns (*Continued*)
Bemis, 414; Benton, 355; Bethpage, 367; Blountville, 308; Blue Bank, 426, 429; Bolivar, 490, 491; Bon Air, 464, 467; Bon Aqua, 471; Bradford, 413; Brentwood, 376; Briceville, 336; Brick Mill, 352; Bristol, 289, 290; Brownsville, 462; Bruceton, 72, 459; Bulls Gap, 300; Butler, 316; Butler's Landing, 509; Byrdstown, 507; Calderwood, 331; Calhoun, 307; Camden, 458; Cannonburg, 400; Carthage, 445; Caryville, 335; Cassville, 467; Castalian Springs, 368; Cedar Hill, 393; Celina, 508; Centertown, 464, 469, 472; Centerville, 472; Chapel Hill, 384; Charlotte, 455; Chattanooga, 60, 71, 86, 251-269, 365, 475, 479, 480, 506; Chesterfield, 473; Chickamauga, 58, 60; Chilhowee, 331; Christiansville, 280; Clarksville, 72, 78, 409, 494, 495; Cleveland, 71, 476; Clifton, 487; Clifty, 467; Clinton, 336; Coal Creek, 335; Coalings, 473; Coalmont, 512; Collegedale, 477; Columbia, 72, 375-378, 380, 386; Concord, 436; Cookeville, 79, 444; Copperhill, 475; Cornersville, 385; Cosby, 432; Covington, 422; Cowan, 484; Crossville, 442, 464, 465; Culleoka, 405; Cumberland Gap, 44, 45, 285, 286, 327; Curve, 420, 422; Daisy, 365; Dandridge, 433; Darden, 473; Dayton, 125, 126, 363, 364; Deer Lodge, 361; Decaturville, 472, 473; Defeated, 445; Del Rio, 430; Denmark, 459; Denver, 457, 458; De Rossett, 467; Dickson, 72, 455; Difficult, 445, 446; Donelson, 451; Dove, 482; Dover, 370, 407, 409; Doyle, 468; Dresden, 412; Ducktown, 475; Dunlap, 505; Dyersburg, 73, 420, 424; Edwina, 431; Elizabethton, 67, 71, 86, 317; Elkmont, 357; Embreeville, 294; Englewood, 355; Erwin, 71, 324-326; Etowah, 355; Falls Branch, 309; Farmington, 385; Farragut, 436; Fayetteville, 406, 485; Flippin, 420; Flynn's Lick, 445; Fowlkes, 420; Franklin, 184, 375, 377; Friendsville, 351; Fulton, 8; Gainesboro, 445; Gallatin, 368; Gates, 420, 422; Gatlinburg, 339, 340; Goodlettsville, 396; Grand Junction, 491; Green Brier, 395; Greenfield, 413; Greeneville, 47, 54, 71, 77, 78, 291, 297, 300; Gruetli, 511, 512; Half Acres, 111; Halls, 420, 421; Hampton, 316; Harriman, 71, 86, 91, 362; Harrogate, 328; Haysboro, 374; Henderson, 415, 416; Henning, 422; Hilham, 509; Hohenwald, 472; Humboldt, 73, 419; Huntersville, 462; Huntington, 459; Huntsville, 360; Hurricane Mills, 457; Isabella, 475; Jacksboro, 335; Jackson, 66, 72, 270-273, 459, 461; Jacksonville, 371; Jamestown, 498; Jasper, 481; Jefferson City, 302; Jellico, 332-334; Johnson City, 321, 323; Johnsonville, 458; Jonesboro, 47, 291-294; Kenton, 418; Key Corner, 421; Kimball, 482; Kinzel Springs, 358; Kingsport, 44, 66, 71, 91, 279-286, 309; Kingston, 91, 254, 437, 438; Knoxville, 18, 39, 56, 61, 62, 66, 68, 71, 86, 93, 232-249, 290, 348, 371, 401, 434, 435; La Fayette 366; La Follette, 60, 334, 335; La Grange, 492; Lawrenceburg, 72, 391, 486; Lebanon, 96, 446, 468; Leesburg, 295; Lenoir City, 71, 305; Lewisburg, 385; Lexington, 471, 473; Liberty, 468; Lilydale, 507; Limestone, 296; Linden, 471, 472; Linton, 471; Livingston, 508; Locks, 423; Loretto, 391; Loudon, 305; Lynchburg, 406; Madison, 371, 372; Madisonville, 353, 354; Manchester, 66, 397, 403; Marbledale, 349; Martin, 412, 413; Maryville, 11, 71, 350, 351; Mascot, 304; Mason, 463; Maxwell, 485; Mayland, 444; Maynardville, 346, 347; McEwen, 457; McKenzie, 459; McMinnville, 401, 464, 469, 510; Medina, 414; Memphis, 8, 18, 19, 43, 52, 59, 60, 71, 72, 105, 108, 184, 206-231, 376, 423, 463, 464; Mentor, 351, 352; Milan, 413; Millington, 423; Mitchell, 396; Monroe, 507; Monteagle, 397, 482; Monterey, 444; Morley, 334; Morristown, 71, 237, 301, 329; Mountain City, 316; Mt. Pleasant, 390; Murfreesboro, 93, 397, 399-401, 404, 405, 464, 470, 471; Nashville, 18, 52, 56, 60, 66, 68, 71, 72, 81, 82, 91, 93, 96, 105, 106, 176, 179-205, 235, 377, 393, 397, 398, 401, 406, 410, 418, 448, 449, 452, 453, 469, 471; Newbern, 420; New Market, 303; Newport, 431, 432; New Providence, 409, 493; New River, 360; Norris, 166, 345, 346; Oakdale, 362; Obion, 420; Old Hickory, 67, 70, 371; Old Jefferson, 399, 400; Oneida, 360; Ooltewah, 477; Ovoca, 406; Ozone, 441; Palmyra, 66; Pall Mall, 61, 497; Paris, 73, 407, 411; Parksville, 476; Parrotsville, 432; Parsons, 472; Petros, 362; Phillippy, 426; Pigeon Forge, 339; Pikeville, 503; Pinson, 414; Pleasant Hill, 466; Pomona, 442; Portland, 396; Pulaski, 58, 377, 381, 383, 385, 475, 486; Puryear, 14; Quebeck, 469; Rafter, 354; Randolph, 8, 423; Ravensport, 467; Readyville, 470; Red Boiling Springs, 367; Reynoldsbury, 458; Ridgely, 424; Ridgetop, 395; Ripley, 420, 422; Robbins, 360; Rock

Towns (*Continued*)
City, 266; Rockdale, 390; Rockwood, 67, 86, 436, 438; Rogersville, 67, 68, 235, 310, 311; Rugby, 360; Russellville, 300; Rutherford, 418, 419; Rutledge, 314; St. Andrews, 482; St. Bethlehem, 408; St. Joseph, 391; Sale Creek, 365; Samburg, 426; Sapling Grove, 290; Sardis, 473; Savannah, 487; Selmer, 416, 475; Sevierville, 338; Sewanee, 483; Sharon, 413; Shelbyville, 404-406; Silerton, 416; Smithville, 468; Smyrna, 398; Soddy, 365; Somerville, 492; South Pittsburg, 482; Sparta, 464, 467, 509; Spencer, 468; Spring City, 363; Spring Creek, 459; Springfield, 72, 393, 394; Spring Hill, 377, 379; Springtown, 355; Strawberry Plains, 304; Sugar Grove, 366; Sunbright, 361; Sweetwater, 305, 306; Tallassee, 331; Tazewell, 328, 329; Tellico Plains, 354; Tennga, 355; Three Ways Junction, 414, 419; Timothy, 508; Tiptonville, 419, 420, 424; Townsend, 358; Tracy City, 85, 512; Tremont, 358; Trenton, 417, 419, 429; Trotter's Landing, 458; Troy, 419; Tullahoma, 66, 399, 406; Unicoi, 324; Union City, 56, 412, 417, 419; Vasper, 335; Walland, 359; Walnut Log, 426, 429; Wartburg, 361, 362; Wartrace, 405; Watertown, 468; Waverly, 457; Waynesboro, 487; Westmoreland, 366; White Bluff, 455; White House, 396; Wilder, 86, 499; Willow Grove, 507; Winchester, 80, 475, 484, 485; Woodbury, 465, 469; Woodstock, 408; Wrigley, 472; Valdeau, 365
Townsend, W. B., 358
Trade *(see Commerce, Transportation)*
"Trail of Tears" *(see Indians)*
Transportation, 91-97
Airlines, 96, 97, 232, 251; early roads, 28, 31, 35, 44, 65, 91, 92, 210, 211, 280, 312, 319, 330, 419, 445, 454, 458; motorways, 92, 214, 232; railroads, 94, 96, 211, 236, 254, 256, 257, 264, 270, 271, 273, 282, 285, 290, 314, 322, 324, 332, 371, 374, 386, 391, 397, 398, 407, 411, 412, 414, 417, 420, 445, 459, 464, 488, 492; waterways, 92, 94, 98, 99, 220, 236, 490, 508
Transylvania Land Company, 38, 46, 181, 319, 326 *(see History)*
Treaty Oak, 204
Trent, William Peterfield, 149
Trillium Gap, 514
Trollope, Frances, 464
Trousdale, Gen. William, 368

Umbrella Rock, 266
Unionists, 236
United Daughters of the Confederacy, 408, 478
United States Bureau of Dairy Industry, 79, 385
United States Bureau of Fisheries and Hatcheries, 130
United States Commission of Education, 58
United States Department of Agriculture, 79, 100, 300
United States Forestry Service, 20, 355
United States Mine Rescue Station, 334
United States Soil Conservation Service, 24, 414
United States Soldiers' Home, 323
Uplands Cumberland Mountain Sanitarium, 466
Utopia, 36

Valentine Nursery, 432
Van Buren, Martin, 276, 410, 453, 468
Vance, Dr. Patrick, 286
Vanderbilt, Commodore Cornelius, 197
Van Fleet, Dr. Walter, 457
Van Leer, A. W. 455
Vaudreuil, Marquis de, 36
Vaughan, James D., 486
Vaught, Casper, 479
Vendome Theatre, 176
Veterans Reserve Corps, 215
Viniard Field, 268

Walden, Elisha, 45, 480, 505
Walden's Ridge, 9, 254, 359, 360, 363-365, 479, 480, 505
Walker, Chief Jack, 307
Walker, Dr. Thomas, 44, 280, 309
Walker, James, 275
Walker, Sarah Gray, 202
Walker, William, 193
Walker's Valley, 358
Wallace, Gen., 410, 488, 489
Walthall, Gen., 480
Walton, Capt. W. B., 397
Walton, Maj. William, 445
Walton Road, 437, 445
War between the States, 55-60, 66, 67, 71, 92, 116, 122-124, 148-150, 161, 182-184, 189, 193-195, 200-202, 211, 215, 221, 224, 228, 229, 236, 237, 244, 248, 254, 256, 257, 259, 261, 263, 264, 276, 282, 298, 327, 328, 334, 346, 351, 368-370, 374-379, 383-385, 388, 389, 398, 399, 401, 406, 408, 409, 410, 411, 415, 416, 419, 422, 423, 433, 434, 436, 437, 453-455, 458, 469, 470, 478, 480, 481, 488, 489, 499, 509, 516
Battles
Chattanooga, 57, 58, 255; Franklin, 57, 58, 377, 379; Horseshoe, 268; Lookout Mountain, 57, 255; Memphis, 210, 220; Mill Creek, 509; Missionary Ridge, 57, 255, 256, 268; Murfreesboro, 57-58, 402; Nashville, 57, 58, 201, 202, 375, 384; Parker's Crossroad, 473; Pilot Knob, 459; Shiloh, 57, 254, 384, 488, 489; Stone's River, 57, 58, 399; Wauhatchie, 480

Ward, Nancy ("Beloved Woman"), 355
Ward, Rev. William E., 200
Warfield, Maj. A. W., 380, 381
Warfield, Cornelia Francis, 380, 381
Warfield and Keeble, 375
War Memorial Building (Nashville), 188
Warner, Edwin, 471
Warner, Percy, 471
War of 1812, 50, 285, 406, 439, 449, 484, 486
  Battle of New Orleans, 50, 434, 449, 455
"War of the Roses," 59
War with Spain, 60
Washington, George, 46, 49, 291, 370, 393, 417, 433
Washington, John, 393
Washington, Joseph, 393
Washington District *(see History)*
Watauga *(see History)*
Watauga Sanatorium, 395
Water Cress Farm, 304
Watkins, Samuel, 194
Watts Bar, 478
Wauhatchie Valley, 480
Wayland, J. A., 455, 456
Wayne, General Anthony, 487
Waynne, Col. Alfred R., 368
Wear, Col. Samuel, 339
Wear Cove Gap, 358
Webb, W. R. ("Sawney"), 405
Webber, Henri Christian, 174
Weber, Mrs. Ann E., 194
Webster, Major W. J., 79
Weir, James, 235
Wells, Newton Alonzo, 169, 221
Wells, Rhea, 168, 169
Wells Creek Basin, 12
Wesley, John, 33
West, Benjamin, 169
West, Edward, 202
West, William Edward, 167, 201
Western, Helen, 176
Western District, 271
Western Freedmen's Aid Commission, 58, 203
Western State Hospital for the Insane, 492
Wharton, Alene Gray, 170
Whatcoat, Bishop, 112
Wheeler, Gen. Joseph, 399, 415
Whig Party, 55
White, Alfred, 481
White, Clarence Cameron, 494
White, Capt. James, 234, 238
White, Dr. Robert, 153
White, George L., 173
White, James, 348
White, Lynn, 264
White, Mary, 376
White Caps, 338
Whiteside, Thomas, 312
Wiggan, Eleazer ("Old Rabbit"), 330
Wiggers, Alvin S., 174
Wightman, Amos, 466
Wilder, Gen. John T., 439
Wilderness Road, 48, 91, 182, 196, 280, 282, 326, 332, 447
Wilder Tower, 268
Williams, John, 348
Williams, Samuel Cole, 152
Williams Island, 252, 506
Wills, Ridley, 150, 151
Wills and Dudley, Inc., 161, 202
Wilmot Proviso, 55
Wilson, Rev. Joseph R., 227, 495
Winchester, Gen. James, 52, 82, 158, 210, 367
Winchester Creamery, 485
Winston, Dorothea S., 227
Women's Christian Temperance Union, 362
Women's Missionary Council, 200
Women's Suffrage, 457
Wood, Abraham, 43
Wood, William Halsey, 483
Woodbury, Levi, 469
Woods, Robert, 202
Woolwine and Herons, 191
Worcester, Rev. Samuel, 478
Work, Dr. Hubert, 517
Work, John, Jr., 154
Work, John Wesley, Sr., 154, 173
Works Progress Administration, 89, 96, 127, 170, 201, 321, 349, 353, 365, 398, 457, 495, 496
World War, 61, 188, 237, 247, 257, 375, 484, 497, 498
Writers, 145-154
  Agrarian-Fugitive group, 151, 152; early, 145, 146, 352; first humorists, 147; novelists of 19th century, 148; contemporary, 149-153, 487, 510; present-day newspapers, 153, 154
Wright, Frances (Fanny), 219, 463 *(see Nashoba)*

Yellow Fever Epidemics, 59, 211
York, Sergt. Alvin C., 61, 497, 498

Zollicoffer, Gen. Felix, 56, 509
Zolnay, Julian, 189